Society: Problems and Methods of Study

CONTRIBUTORS

MICHAEL ARGYLE

NORMAN T. J. BAILEY

B. BENJAMIN

M. G. BENNETT

C. A. BOUCHER

ASA BRIGGS

TOM BURNS

N. H. CARRIER

PETER CAVANAGH

A. B. CHERNS

VALERIE A. COWIE

D. RUSSELL DAVIS

J. W. B. DOUGLAS

JEAN FLOUD

F. GARWOOD

RUTH GLASS

E. GREBENIK

D. LOCKWOOD

O. R. McGREGOR

T. F. MAIN

HERMANN MANNHEIM

JAMES MAXWELL

C. A. MOSER

RICHARD H. PEAR

V. G. PONS

R. N. RAPOPORT

ALEC RODGER

GRISELDA ROWNTREE

NANCY SEEAR

M. W. SUSSER

P. E. VERNON

CHRISTOPHER J. WARDLE

A. T. WELFORD

LESLIE T. WILKINS

BRYAN R. WILSON

SOCIETY

Problems and Methods
of Study

Edited by

A. T. Welford, Michael Argyle
D. V. Glass, J. N. Morris

ROUTLEDGE & KEGAN PAUL LTD
LONDON

First published 1962
by Routledge & Kegan Paul Limited
Broadway House, 68–74 Carter Lane
London, E.C.4

Made and printed in Great Britain
by Cox & Wyman Limited
London, Fakenham and Reading

CONTENTS

Contents

INTRODUCTION

THIS book arose out of the need of those interested in social studies and social problems for an authoritative introduction and outline which would indicate the main areas in which knowledge about social behaviour exists and act as a guide to further reading. The present volume is thus intended both for those setting out upon a systematic study of social processes, and also for those whose main interests lie elsewhere but who wish to orient themselves in particular parts of the field. Because of these aims, efforts have been made to present material which, while representative of leading work and thought, is as free as possible from technical language beyond that which becomes familiar in the normal course of almost any university or college education.

A few years ago such a book could have been fairly brief and yet inclusive. Social studies have, however, expanded greatly since the Second World War and, because of this, the present editors have necessarily been selective. In particular, they have concentrated upon the study of contemporary Western society, and more particularly upon recent British thought and research. Within this framework they have attempted to include not only problems and methods commonly associated with social study but also some others such as 'operational research', social medicine, and social psychiatry, which seem likely to prove of importance and to make an increasing contribution to the understanding of society during the next few years. Inevitably the reader will find gaps: some of these have been deliberate, and result from the necessity of producing a book of reasonable size; others are more regrettable and are due to the fact that there are still relatively few people working in the social sciences and these few carry heavy commitments.

Part One of the book describes some of the principal methods and lines of approach to social study which are applicable to a wide range of problems. Part Two points to leading issues and findings in some of the main areas in which studies have been made. In the sections of Part Two

1

Introduction

chapters have, as far as possible, been grouped together in such a way that the reader concerned with a particular area can find the material he wants collected in one place. Where such grouping is not possible, cognate chapters in other sections have been indicated.

With a large number of contributors it is difficult to avoid some overlapping of statement, although in the event this has proved to be small. No attempt has been made to reconcile conflicting views; the editorial hand has been kept light in an attempt to preserve the individuality of the contributions in an area of study which presents in full measure the variety, controversy and enthusiasm associated with rapid development and progress.

A. T. WELFORD
MICHAEL ARGYLE
D. V. GLASS
J. N. MORRIS

PART ONE

Approaches and Methods of Study

Chapters 1–9

Pages 5–168

PART ONE

Approaches and Methods of Study

Chapter 1

I

STATISTICAL SURVEYS

E. Grebenik and C. A. Moser

ANY attempt to study society must begin with observation—the collection and gathering of facts and their interpretation. When these facts concern social groups, and sometimes even when they concern individuals, this process inevitably entails the use of the statistical method. Indeed, the beginning of sociology as an empirical discipline is closely linked with the development of statistics; the political arithmeticians of the seventeenth century used statistical methods to obtain the simple elementary facts about the society in which they lived, such as the number of individuals of each sex, the number of houses, and the density of crowding, a knowledge of which is today taken for granted in civilized society. Graunt and Petty, the earliest writers of this school, were closely associated with the 'invisible college', the forerunner of the Royal Society, and it seemed natural to them that the method of observation which had yielded such valuable results in the natural sciences could be applied to the study of society. Indeed, it was only when some of the elementary social facts became available that it was possible for even a theoretical sociology to become more than a branch of speculative social philosophy.

The period between 1662, when Graunt's *Natural and Political Observations on the Bills of Mortality*[25] were first published, and the end of the nineteenth century, when Charles Booth conducted the first modern social survey on the *Life and Labour of the People of London*[9], saw a gradual but slow extension of the empirical investigation of social problems. In Britain Gregory King, John Howard, Patrick Colquhoun, C. T. Thackrah, and Bisset Hawkins—to name but a few—used the numerical method in their descriptions of the problems with which

5

they were concerned, though not all their work was primarily statistical in character.* But the power of the method for the elucidation of information was sufficiently recognized in the nineteenth century to lead to the foundation of statistical societies in many countries; in England, Manchester led the way in 1833, and London followed in the succeeding year, on the motion of the Rev. T. R. Malthus that ". . . it is advisable to take immediate steps to establish a Statistical Society in London, the object of which shall be the collection and classi-fication of all facts illustrative of the present condition and prospects of Society . . ."[2] In the early years of its existence the Society set up com-mittees which were to carry out investigations themselves, such as a survey of the condition of the poor in St. George's in the East, which was carried out in the 1840s.[3] But, on the whole, private surveys were few in number, and most of the statistical information we have about nineteenth-century England derives from the labours of official statis-ticians, or Royal Commissions and similar inquiries.

It has already been mentioned that the first social survey which is considered modern was Booth's monumental work on London. It was the problem of poverty in the midst of an increasingly affluent middle class which led Booth to undertake his inquiry. The lack of information about the problem, and an unwillingness to accept theories which attributed poverty to personal inadequacies or fecklessness, stimulated him to undertake a factual investigation, using the method which Beatrice Webb has called 'wholesale interviewing'. As Professor and Mrs Simey have shown in their recent appreciation of his work,[53] he took considerable trouble to eliminate any personal bias on the part of his colleagues and collaborators and was at pains to devise methods which could be repeated in other circumstances so that a cumulative body of knowledge could be built up. His invention of the poverty line, later to be refined by Seebohm Rowntree,[49, 50] was one of the first operational definitions used in social investigation, and Rowntree's and Bowley's successive investigations were sufficient to end argument about the extent of poverty. When Bowley added the sampling method in his Five Towns Surveys,[10, 11] thus bringing social investigation within the reach of the researcher with limited funds, the local social survey, that distinctive British contribution to the study of society, had arrived.

Although poverty surveys—the main subject matter of the chapter on *Social Surveys* in the previous edition of this book[61]—are now the exception rather than the rule, the technique and rationale of the methods used by social scientists, government departments, and market and opinion researchers, owes a heavy debt to the early pion-

* For Gregory King's work see [23]; see also [31, 14] (Colquhoun used statistics collected by others to illustrate his points, rather than collect data himself); [56, 28].

Statistical Surveys

eers.* Their aim was to fill gaps in our information about society and social conditions, and this information had to be accurate and reliable (in the sense that it was to be independent of the individual investigator collecting it). Whenever possible, the facts were to be given in quantitative form, and one does not have to go all the way with Lord Kelvin's view of measurement,† to prefer such facts to personal impressions. To say this is not to belittle the non-statistical form of investigation: the Lynds' books on Middletown,[40, 41] or F. Zweig's investigations in Britain[65, 66, 67] for example, have been very fruitful in suggesting hypotheses and providing an insight into social phenomena. But statistical surveys are essential for the testing and validation of these hypotheses. The 'sociological imagination' may be a necessary, but is not a sufficient, condition for social investigation; it needs to be supplemented by the disciplined testing of its products, and it is in this testing that surveys are vital.

It is rare nowadays for a survey to be purely descriptive. Occasionally in market research, commercial organizations may be satisfied with simply ascertaining the consumption pattern for their products; newspapers and advertising agencies may wish to estimate numbers of readers, viewers, or listeners, but even here the numbers are generally subdivided in a way which implies the existence of certain presuppositions. Indeed, when a survey is completely descriptive, it is generally of limited value. The limitation of purely factual reports can be seen in Kinsey's surveys of sexual behaviour:[37] Kinsey and his colleagues were so concerned with providing estimates of the frequency of 'outlets' of different kinds that anyone unfamiliar with the facts of life might remain ignorant of the connexion between sexual 'outlets' and reproduction (though it must be stated in fairness that Kinsey and his associates were studying aspects of human behaviour about which there was little systematic knowledge). Such single-minded devotion to factual description is mercifully rare; much of more recent survey work has been more sophisticated, and attempts have been made to use surveys to test previously formulated hypotheses about certain areas of social life. Thus, the Indianapolis survey on social and psychological factors affecting fertility[62] was designed to test a number of hypotheses on reproductive behaviour, and to link fertility with other socio-psychological variables. Mrs Floud and her associates in their work on social class and educational opportunity[21] attempted amongst other problems to elucidate the extent to which equality of opportunity followed

* For an idea of applications in varied fields see [1, 19, 45, 63].

† 'When you can measure what you are speaking about and express it in numbers you know something about it; but when you cannot measure it, when you cannot express it in numbers, your knowledge is of a meagre and unsatisfactory kind.'

7

E. Grebenik and C. A. Moser

changes in educational legislation. Douglas and his colleagues investigated factors showing the importance of the social environment on child growth and development.[17] Doll and Hill attempted to study the link between carcinoma of the lung and smoking.* Himmelweit and her colleagues studied the effect of exposure to television on the subsequent behaviour of children.[30]

These surveys differ from the early poverty surveys in many respects, but most fundamentally in that they were designed to test theories which were explicitly formulated. In fact, it is broadly true to say that, whereas the earlier surveys provided data to inform discussion of social problems or for people to theorize upon, to-day social scientists more often use surveys to test theories already formulated, almost to serve as a substitute for social experimentation.

An experiment is normally used to test the consequences of a theoretical prediction. If the consequences are not in accord with the theory, the theory is discarded; if there is no difference, then, provisionally at any rate, the theory stands. The formulation of the theory or hypothesis to be tested is thus of prime importance, and the survey will have to be designed with this in mind. Thus, in the Indianapolis survey on social and psychological factors affecting fertility, some twenty-three hypotheses were set up, suggesting associations between different variables to be tested, and the results added considerably to our understanding of behaviour in this field.

The demonstration of associations between different variables is, of course, important, and in a properly designed survey may contribute to the understanding of the phenomenon studied. But it is a big step from this to the assertion of causal connexions. The surveys on the relation between cigarette smoking and lung cancer may be taken as an example: although it seems clear that heavy smokers are considerably more likely to contract cancer of the lung than others, little is known as yet about the mechanism by which this association works, and it is at least logically possible that the association is due to a third variable, itself associated both with proneness to cancer and the liability to smoke heavily. In a survey one can never be certain that some relevant variable has not been missed from the analysis, and may be confounding the picture. This is the fundamental difficulty in trying to unravel relationships between variables through surveys. By a judicious use of matching, control groups, and ingenious analysis the surveyor can often minimize the problems, but he can never achieve the security of causal interpretation that a randomized experiment can provide.†

* See [16] for a discussion of these investigations, and for a list of references.

† For discussions of the problems of explanatory surveys see [32], [36], [38].

8

Statistical Surveys

SAMPLING

Principles of Design

What is the particular merit of statistical surveys as a way of contributing to our knowledge? The most important aspect is that the design of surveys can be based on statistical theory, and that from a properly designed sample survey it is possible to draw valid generalizations with a known margin of sampling error. This possibility depends upon the use of probability theory in survey design, for nowadays most surveys are taken by sample. Occasionally, the population studied may be so small that it is feasible and desirable to study every member, but such situations are exceptional. Normally, we are interested in large populations, and the additional expense and trouble of a full inquiry are rarely repaid in terms of increased accuracy; indeed the reverse may be the case, for the study of a selected sample may be easier to control, and more money may be available to obtain and process the information for each unit studied, whilst yielding considerable economies in total expenditure.

But if inferences about a population (which must be precisely defined) are to be drawn, it is essential that some form of random sampling should be used. Only this method leads to results that are statistically unbiased, and enables us to calculate sampling errors. To say this, is not to deny the value of case studies. A research worker may, for practical reasons, confine his work to a particular district, or to a particular section of the population. The studies of Young and Willmott in East London are a case in point.[64] Such studies yield valuable information about the areas studied, provide an insight into problems, and suggest hypotheses for testing; but they apply only to the areas investigated, and cannot be generalized to a wider population. Thus, we cannot know whether Young and Willmott's results relating to the relationship between mothers and daughters are specific to London, or whether they apply throughout English urban society. In order to establish their general applicability a national sampling scheme of some kind would have to be used.

The essential point is that the researcher must be clear about the kind of generalization he wants. If he is content not to generalize beyond the cases actually studied, no selection problem need arise. But as soon as he aims at drawing inferences from these cases to a wider population, he needs to avail himself of the apparatus of random sample design.

The basic principles of sampling design are not hard to grasp.* The first essential is randomness, i.e. every member of the population to be

---

* For textbooks on sampling, see [13], [63]. For a more elementary presentation see [45], and for an illustration of sample designs used by the government Social Survey see [26].

E. Grebenik and C. A. Moser

surveyed must have a calculable, non-zero chance of being selected. There is no need for this chance actually to be calculated, but it must be calculable. Nor is it essential that the chances of selection should be the same for every member of the population; sampling with varying probabilities is more common than sampling with equal probabilities, and often carries distinct advantages.

A simple type of random sample might involve taking some complete record of the population—say, a list, map, card-index or hat full of numbers corresponding to the population members—and picking out the number required for the sample. The actual mechanism depends on the type of record or, to use the technical term, 'sampling frame'. But whatever the frame, randomness requires a rigorous and impersonal method of selection.*

Randomness in fact characterizes the method of selection rather than the sample selected. One cannot recognize a sample as random by looking at it; a perfectly random method of selection may produce a sample which looks markedly 'untypical or unrepresentative'. This is not particularly important; what matters is that the method of choosing the sample has not been biased for or against any section of the population, and has given each population member a calculable (and non-zero) chance of selection. The results of such a method—and of no other—can be investigated mathematically in ways which notably include the calculation of sampling errors attending the survey results.

So far only the simplest kind of random sample has been mentioned. In practice, designs tend to be complex. One almost universal refinement is to divide the population into strata according to factors relevant to the survey topic (and convenient with the sampling frame used), and then to take a random sample from each stratum. The gain, apart from practical convenience, is to make the sample more safely representative of the population, by ensuring that, in certain important respects, it is not left to chance whether the sample is right or not; this rightness is built into the sample by the stratification itself, and the results are almost invariably made more precise.

There are many other refinements. Samples are often designed in stages; thus a sample of the population of a town may be confined to certain parts of the town, perhaps to one or two polling districts. With this in mind, one might first select a sample of wards, then a sample of polling districts in the wards selected at the first stage, and finally a

---

* A method much favoured in market and opinion research is quota sampling. Here interviewers are given interview quotas (e.g. according to age, sex, social class) to fill, and are, broadly speaking, left to choose individuals to fit these quotas. This human element in the selection cuts across the basic requirement of random sampling and is the reason why quota sampling—in spite of its ease and cheapness—is not favoured by most statisticians.[46]

10

sample of households in the selected polling districts. Such multi-stage designs clearly reduce costs and labour, but they also, less obviously, increase sampling errors; they are almost invariably used when a widely dispersed population needs to be covered.

We may also mention multi-phase sampling, where some of the information in a questionnaire is asked of all sample units, while additional questions are confined to sub-samples. This procedure is appropriate, for example, when different accuracy is needed for different items of information, so that smaller samples are adequate for some parts of the survey than for others. The 1961 Population Census in Great Britain is an example.[7]

The sample designer's task may be summarized as follows. First, he must know the precise nature of the information to be obtained, and the way it is to be analysed. Secondly, he must know what precision is required for the overall and the sub-group results; in other words, what margins of sampling error can be tolerated. With this information, and with knowledge of the resources available, he can decide the sample size needed, and design a sample to provide optimum precision for given resources, or given precision at minimum cost. The central feature of this design will be randomness, with such use of stratification, distribution between stages and phases, and other refinements, as may be appropriate.

Non-response

It is sometimes argued that much of the now customary sophistication in sample design is misplaced, first because the remaining phases of a survey tend to be far less rigorous, and secondly because the beauty of a sample design may in any case be marred by non-response. The first argument hardly needs discussion, since it is an unsound principle not to use reliable methods at one stage just because this is not yet possible in others. As regards non-response, improvements in survey techniques have in fact considerably improved levels of response. Response rates of 70–90 per cent are customary in well-administered surveys, and rates over 90 per cent are not uncommon. Even in mail surveys, non-response is often reduced to small proportions.[51] Certainly one cannot dismiss the problem of non-response, in the sense that the respondents *may* be sufficiently numerous and different from the rest of the population to cause bias. But enough is known about ways of increasing response and follow-up methods for the problem not to dominate survey design.* On no account is the likelihood of non-response to be regarded as an argument against rigorous sample design.

* See discussion in [13]: and [15, 18].

E. Grebenik and C. A. Moser

Inferences from Samples

It now becomes necessary to deal in general terms with the kind of inference that may be drawn from a sample. Fundamentally, there are two problems which are dealt with: the testing of significance, and the problem of estimation. In the former case, we wish to establish whether certain populations or sections of a population differ from one another in particular characteristics; in the second we attempt to estimate the value of a hitherto unknown quantity from our information on the sample. The two procedures use essentially different analytical techniques.

Take the question of significance testing first. A typical problem in this field is that investigated by Bowley in his two surveys in the Five Towns: *Livelihood and Poverty* and *Has Poverty Diminished*? He surveyed the towns by sample twice; once before and once after the First World War, and obtained in each case the proportion falling below a well-defined poverty line. The problem he had to investigate was, whether the differences shown by these proportions indicated real differences between the two populations, or whether they could be accounted for by sampling fluctuations.

The procedure is as follows:* A hypothesis—the so-called null hypothesis—is formulated which postulates that there is no difference in poverty between the two populations. It should be noted that this hypothesis asserts nothing about the actual level of poverty, either before or after the First World War. It is possible by mathematical argument to deduce from this hypothesis the probability that if there were no difference in the level of poverty in the populations, two samples taken from that population would show proportions in poverty differing from one another by more than a given amount. Obviously, the larger the difference between the sample proportions, the smaller this probability would be. If it is sufficiently small (in practice the values taken are usually 5 per cent, 1 per cent or even 0·1 per cent), this difference is said to be *statistically significant*, and the null hypothesis is rejected at that level of significance. Thus, if a difference between two proportions or averages is said to be significant at the 5 per cent level, this means that the probability of a difference of this magnitude, or larger, arising by chance would be 5 per cent or less, and we could conclude that there is a *prima facie* case for believing that the two populations really do differ.

A number of points need to be made in this connexion. First, certainty can never be achieved. Improbable events do happen. A difference may be found to be statistically significant, when there is no real difference between the populations. But we know that if we use a

* See, e.g., [22], [42], [60].

12

Statistical Surveys

5 per cent level of significance, this will happen in the long run only on one occasion out of twenty, and the probability can be made lower still, by using a different significance level. Secondly, significance depends on sample size, and a difference which turns out to be not significant may well prove to be significant when a larger sample is taken. Often the magnitude and direction of a difference are of greater intrinsic interest than the mere determination of statistical significance. Yet the sociological literature is full of the results of significance tests, and there is a tendency to confuse statistical significance with substantive importance. The establishment of significant differences is not the end of survey research, but the beginning (cf. [8, 38]).

Estimation is a different process altogether. Whereas in significance testing the argument is deductive, proceeding from a hypothesis about the population to the behaviour of samples, in estimation we attempt to infer something about the population as a whole from our knowledge of the sample. Thus, we might wish to estimate the extent of poverty in the population of one of the five towns from the poverty level found in the sample. Now at the time that the survey was taken there must have been a determinate proportion of persons living below the poverty line in that town. It is not, therefore, possible to make a statement about the probability of such and such a proportion of people living in poverty. The statistician overcomes this difficulty by computing a so-called 'confidence interval'. This procedure designates an interval within which the true population value will lie in a determinate proportion of cases. This proportion is often 95 per cent but may be as high as 99 per cent, or even 99·9 per cent. If it were stated, for instance, with 95 per cent confidence that poverty in one of the five towns lay between 12 and 15 per cent of the population, this would imply that a procedure had been used for estimating the interval which was known to contain the correct population value 95 per cent of the time.

The two procedures which have been described in general terms depend upon the use of the random sampling method, and the application of rigorous sample design. It is this design which makes possible generalizations about large populations, on the basis of the study of smaller groups, and the estimation of the margin of uncertainty associated with these generalizations. This process plays a vital role in the study of contemporary society; without sampling, accurate knowledge of social processes could take place only by aggregating successive case studies, a much less satisfactory procedure.

OBTAINING THE DATA

The most striking aspect of the survey phases discussed so far is their mathematical basis. Sampling is a branch of theoretical statistics, so that in this part of a survey more than in any other the researcher can be on safe scientific ground. When we turn to the task of data collection we find no such security. Psychology offers some help, but it must be admitted that many of the decisions on question wording, choice of approach, and the like are heavily determined by past experience, trial and error, and hunches. Clearly this is a serious weakness, since the compilation of correct data is after all the purpose of the whole operation; everything else, including the sampling, is merely a means towards this end.

The difficulties start at the beginning, in deciding what topics to include in the survey. It is necessary to confine investigations to items which are, in principle at least, measurable or orderable. The questions or definitions used are therefore often only operational approximations to the matters it is desired to investigate. An example is the use of occupational groups as an indication of social class differentials. These are used, not because it is believed that occupation is identical with social class, but merely in order to make the latter concept 'countable' or 'measurable' for survey purposes. It is up to the sociologist to decide which indicator or combination of indicators approximates most closely to what he means by 'social class'. It is sometimes objected that reliance on such indicators leads to the loss of something essential in the study of these phenomena. On the other hand, the gain in the comparability of the results of different investigators is undeniable, and it is an accepted procedure of science to study phenomena which are not directly observable through indices which can be used in experimental testing.

Documentary Sources

This is not the place to discuss in detail the different ways of data collection open to the research worker,* since so much must depend on the resources available, the subject matter, the accuracy demanded, and the depth and degree of quantification required in the individual survey. But a few general remarks are in order.

First of all there are the many documentary and statistical sources which can give background data about the populations, institutions, or groups covered by a survey. But our interest here is with ways of getting information about individual units, and in this documentary sources are of limited use. Perhaps the most interesting possibilities are personal documents, such as diaries, essays, and the like. If unsolicited, personal documents often provide a fuller, less self-conscious picture than can be reached by formal methods, but then unsolicited documents are of little help as a systematic form of

* See, e.g.[20, 32, 52]. For a useful reference source see [5].

inquiry. If solicited, personal records at once lose some of their advantages. Even so, they can provide illuminating data, as was demonstrated, to take only two examples, in the study of evacuation by Isaacs[34] and the survey of the effects of television by Himmelweit and others.[30] In both cases the essay-writers were children, and this form of approach is of particular attraction in such cases. But by and large personal documents are of only marginal importance as a source of survey data.

The same must, one supposes, apply to case records collected by social workers, such as almoners, probation officers, and psychiatric social workers. There is no doubt that such records often throw searching light on the persons concerned, but they are difficult to harness to a systematic social survey. Such difficulties may, however, be overcome by systematic attempts to make the information collected comparable and to eliminate personal bias on the part of the compiler. If this were done such records could be more widely used in throwing light on the particular populations they cover.

Mail Questionnaires

The attraction of using a postal questionnaire in collecting survey data is that it is cheap, quick, and suitable for reaching widely dispersed populations, and that it avoids interviewer bias. What is more, when the questions are few and simple, there seems little need to have recourse to personal interviews. When, on the other hand, one is dealing with a complicated survey topic, with unavoidably lengthy questionnaires, with issues where prior consideration or consultation is undesirable, or with questions which might require probing, the postal approach is ruled out.

For many years mail questionnaires were considered a very inferior mode of approach even when the subject matter seemed suitable. The reason was the problem of getting an adequate response. The literature was full of response rates of 20–30 per cent or even lower in which case it was difficult to take the results seriously. Mail questionnaires were regarded as suitable for surveys of special populations—e.g. members of a profession—but not for general populations. A trend in the opposite direction is now discernible. Research by the Social Survey has aimed at discovering ways of designing schedules and covering letters so as to improve response rates to mail questionnaires, and rates of 90 per cent or more have been achieved even for general population surveys, though always on simple questionnaires. A particularly useful application is in surveys of special populations for which no convenient sampling frame exists. An example might be a survey of all those in the population with university degrees. A form could be sent to a large sample of the entire working population, with enough questions to identify the graduates; these would then be used for the main survey, probably by interview. This is a form of multi-phase sampling where the first phase, by mail, is used to produce a sampling frame for the second.

There naturally remain many types of inquiries for which a personal approach is essential, but the recent work of the Social Survey, which seems to be supported in other organizations, suggests that the mail questionnaire deserves more sympathetic consideration than it has been receiving. A comprehensive discussion on this subject has been given by Scott.[51]

Interviewing

The most prominent and obviously the most valuable method of survey inquiry is personal interviewing. For the overwhelming majority of survey topics, the information can be obtained only by direct inquiry, rather than from documents or by observation, and this nearly always means a personal interview. Once this is decided, however, there is a wide range of interviewing techniques to choose from. The type that comes most readily to mind pictures the interviewer on the doorstep, asking a housewife a number of pre-set questions in a supposedly uniform manner, both the order and the wording of the questions corresponding to precise instructions. And in fact this is probably the predominant approach in official inquiries, in commercial surveys and perhaps even in social research. But it is by no means the only one. Often the interviewer is given scope to choose the precise form and order of the questions, though within a well-defined framework of points to be covered. In some surveys, the interviewer may be allowed even more latitude. Interviewing of the 'depth' type, often used to discover people's attitudes and motivations, demands that the interviewer has a clear idea of the level of information to be reached, and is given great latitude in achieving it (cf. [29]).

This is not the place to discuss the technical features of interviewing,* but it must be stressed that the choice between alternative approaches to interviewing involves important issues of methodology. Though any classification is bound to over-simplify, one can conceive of these approaches as ranged along a continuum of formality. At one extreme is the completely formalized interview: the interviewer behaves as much like a machine as is humanly possible. The more closely she is able to keep to the question form and order laid down, the more alike different interviewers are in their approach, in their accents and so forth, the more exactly comparable will be the final answers obtained from different respondents to the same interviewer, and by different inter-

* On interviewing see [20, 83, 35, 52].

16

viewers. In other words, the aim underlying formal interviewing is to maximize the *reliability** of the results. But reliability is not everything. The correct answers may lie at different levels with different respondents, and it may require quite differently orientated and worded questions to elicit them. From this viewpoint, it might be better for the interviewers not to behave like machines, but to adjust their approach to the individual respondent, in an effort to penetrate to the valid (i.e. correct) reply. This sort of approach aims at maximizing the *validity* of the responses. The more straightforward and simple the subject matter, the more one inclines to the formal approach; the more complex, the more desirable does it seem to use a flexible, informal mode of attack. Survey practitioners differ in their preferences. Some believe that even the most complex problem—say a survey seeking views on homosexuality—is best handled formally, so that at least comparable pieces of information are obtained from all respondents. Certainly the results are then easy to aggregate and to quantify. But there remains the doubt whether pre-set questions, and an inflexible approach, are right for a delicate situation, with the respondent perhaps hesitant to disclose his true inclinations, or unsure where he stands. In such a case, an informal approach has much to commend it, giving full rein to the respondent's own way of thinking about and answering the questions. But then the real problem comes in the analysis; the very comparability of the answers given by different respondents must be open to question, and there is the severe difficulty of coding and aggregating the qualitative kind of material which such an approach produces.

Questionnaire design

This discussion may suffice to show that it is necessary to decide whether to go mainly for comparability, reliability, and easy quantification, or for depth, detail, and validity. We will not take the sub ect further here, nor embark on the matter of questionnaire design.† It has to be recognized that question framing is one of the hardest tasks in a survey, especially when—as is increasingly the case—the questions relate to attitudes and opinions. Sometimes these relate to future behaviour, such as in investigating voting intentions in pre-election surveys, and here the record of the pollsters has in recent elections been

* The term 'reliability' is here used in a technical sense, to denote the extent to which repeated interviews on the same respondents by the same interviewers get the same results; by a slight extension, the word may be taken to cover *different* interviewers working under comparable conditions.

† On questionnaire design see [20], [32], [45], [52] for a summary of problems and for references; and also [48].

creditable.[12, 47] On the other hand, it is not always easy to know how much importance to attach to expressions of opinions, which can vary so radically in 'informedness' and intensity. Furthermore, it has been shown that interaction between interviewer and respondent, the exact framing of the question, the order in which questions appear, and other factors may affect the response elicited from the questionnaire. A great deal of research on the measurement of attitudes is proceeding, but it is doubtful whether the problems have yet been satisfactorily resolved. (See [20, 39, 57]). In any case, the subject of question design is hard to deal with in general terms, and will not be further pursued here.

Response errors

Whatever method of obtaining the survey data is adopted, we can be sure that some errors will enter the results at the various stages of the survey.* Those due to sampling, mentioned earlier, are the least worrying, since they are subject to scientific treatment. Errors of a non-sampling type—many of which are as likely to occur in complete as in sample surveys—are much more elusive. Respondents may give inaccurate answers because they are disinclined to tell the truth—perhaps actuated by prestige feelings or by the personality of the interviewer, or perhaps because they do not recall the correct answer, or have misunderstood the question. Interviewers, though provided with the right answer, may misunderstand it, misinterpret and therefore wrongly classify it, and may make purely clerical errors. Numerous other types of error may occur in the interview situation. Postal questionnaires are subject to some of these errors and to others, and so are observational techniques. And to all these must be added errors occurring in the editing, coding, and analysis of the results.

This is a list of some *potential* sources of error. Not every survey is beset by errors of every kind, for the quality of performance may be so high as to reduce some of them to negligible proportions. And even when a particular type of error is met with, different types of error may partially cancel out. There is in fact an essential distinction between gross errors and net errors.

Some of the possibilities of detection and measurement can be mentioned briefly. *External checks* of the survey results against known facts are of less value than the layman might suppose. For one thing, the check data have to be of high comparability if they are to serve as a yardstick for assessing the survey aggregates, and such situations are rare. Secondly, the check data are themselves probably subject to error, and one may well have less faith in them than in the survey results. Thirdly, even where the survey results can be checked in certain

* See the references in chap. 13 of [45].

particulars, these will not include the main topic of the survey, for otherwise why was the survey necessary? Fourthly, external checks on survey aggregates only disclose net errors, yet it is the gross errors that have to be tackled if survey procedures are to be improved. Sometimes individual records, e.g. birth certificates, can be used for checking individual responses and therefore for assessing gross errors, but these situations are rare indeed. In sum, though external checks should be used wherever possible, they rarely take one much of the way towards measuring response errors.

Certain *internal checks* are worth considering. Kinsey and his colleagues in some cases checked accuracy by collecting information from both husband and wife.[37] Sometimes the same piece of information can be sought in more than one way in the same interview, such as by asking a respondent not only how old he is but what his date of birth was. But consistency checks are one-sided: if both results agree one gains in confidence, though it is possible that both are wrong. When the two results do not agree, one does not—without additional information—know which is correct.

What is wanted is a check measurement which is known to be at a higher level of accuracy than the original one. In this lies the attraction of quality checks or *post-enumeration surveys*, which are now customary in census work in the United States and elsewhere.[6, 7, 59] This involves re-surveying a sub-sample of the original sample, but with procedures at an assumedly higher level than used on the first occasion. Various steps are taken to ensure this. Only the very best interviewers (usually supervisors) are employed; several questions are asked, in place of one on the original occasion, in order to ensure that the question intent has been correctly understood and the answer properly interpreted; efforts are made to get the information from the person most likely to give it accurately (and not just from anyone in the household); and so forth. In these ways, it is hoped that the second measurement is more accurate than the first, and information is obtained not only on the accuracy achieved in the main survey but on the ways in which errors entered. For it is an essential part of quality checks to track down how a particular error came to be made. So far, quality checks have been used mainly as a way of detecting sources of error and thus of improving future procedures. Whether they can be used for adjusting the survey estimates is another matter; there remain problems in the conduct of these check surveys that need to be settled, and the number of recalls would have to be larger than has been customary.

In any event, quality checks are the most hopeful method yet developed for dealing with response errors, but it remains to be seen whether they can be as useful for *ad hoc* surveys of modest scale as they have proved to be for large-scale censuses on the one hand, and for regular inquiries (like the labour force surveys in Canada and the United States) on the other.

There are many other ways of tracking down errors, and given sufficiently careful survey design, some components of total response error can even be treated in a theoretically precise manner (see e.g. [27]). The subject of response errors has been discussed at relative length because the improvement in the accuracy achieved in surveys constitutes the main challenge in this field. Inaccurate measurements remain inaccurate, however sound the sample design or sophisticated the statistical analysis. Research workers in the social sciences should be much more demanding in the standards of accuracy they ask of their evidence.

ANALYSIS

This is not the place to discuss the practical survey operations, such as editing, coding, and tabulating, which intervene between the return of the raw survey material and the presentation of the data, or the specific statistical techniques which may be used in their analysis.* What is necessary is a general comment on the argument often advanced by critics of quantitative sociology, namely that elaborate statistical techniques are out of place in dealing with the approximate, vague, and highly involved data the sociologist often produces.

While it is unfortunately true that some of the concepts used in sociology are vague and approximate, this is no argument against the use of statistical methods, but should rather be a challenge to the sociologist to revise his concepts so that their vagueness disappears. It is usually considered to be an essential part of a scientific discipline that its result should be capable of being empirically tested; and it is surely essential that sociological information should be capable of objective classification. The methods that are used are often exceedingly simple, little more than counting and categorization is involved, and this is hardly likely to 'stretch' the data. The computation of ratios, percentages, averages, and measures of dispersion, where applicable, is standard descriptive technique in statistics and is normally well understood.

Objection is frequently taken to the application of more elaborate mathematical techniques. It has already been shown that the use of probability methods follows logically, if sampling procedures are used. Their employment is a function of the method of conducting the survey, rather than of the kind of data studied. In the attempt to unravel relationships between variables, however, it is often necessary to combine series of measurements into indices, or to assess the influence of one or more variables upon others. Statistical methods have been

* See [22, 42, 60, 63].

devised in the field of multivariate analysis, which have proved very powerful in social research.* The complexity of the relationships studied makes it more rather than less necessary for the appropriate statistical methods to be used. At the same time, however, it is necessary for the research worker to understand the rationale of the methods which he employs. Multivariate analysis is based upon models which are subject to certain assumptions, and it is essential that these assumptions should be clearly understood. This is particularly important, as a number of the techniques that are commonly used in statistics have been devised with the needs of the agricultural or biological sciences in mind, and may have to be modified before they can be applied in social research.

This is not to say that statistical techniques should replace all other kinds of survey analysis. No one familiar with the writings of Mayhew and Charles Booth or, in our own day, with some of the work of the Institute of Community Studies (cf. [58, 64]) can deny that verbal descriptions of individual cases, institutions, and the like can often give a more vivid, richer and, in a sense, deeper picture of life than the statistical tables to be found in conventional survey reports. The two ways of presenting data are complementary; the statistical tables are essential for conveying the characteristics of aggregates, for testing relationships and the like, whilst the qualitative description can be brought in to give a fuller account of parts of the picture. But, as regards the latter, infinite care needs to be taken not to present the case-studies with a greater implication of 'typicality' than they merit.[4]

In recent years more use has been made of the so-called 'longitudinal' surveys. This rather unfortunate term is used to describe surveys in which a specific group of individuals is observed and surveyed over a relatively lengthy period of time. Thus, in the National Survey of the Health and Development of Children, a group of children born in 1946 has now been kept under observation for fifteen years,[17] and a group of children tested in the Scottish Mental Survey of 1947 has been kept under observation in order to relate their test performance to subsequent development. Such surveys present difficulties of their own, particularly in connexion with the wastage of respondents due to removals etc., and also tend to be expensive. Nevertheless it is possible to obtain from them information which it would be very difficult to obtain in any other way.

Our discussion of statistical surveys has necessarily been somewhat selective and limited. It will, however, have shown the importance of the survey as an instrument of sociological research, and a perusal of sociological journals will demonstrate its increasing frequency. Some will welcome this trend as a confirmation of their belief that sociology is at last becoming 'scientific'; others will see in it a substitution of

* See e.g. [24, 43, 44, 54, 55]. For discussion of relevant problems see also [32, 36, 38].

E. Grebenik and C. A. Moser

facile techniques for hard thinking. There is some truth in both views. A well-conducted survey can produce data of better quality and greater significance (in the non-statistical sense) than most other research methods. But it is also true that it is not very difficult to collect facts or compile tables, though it must be added that even this is not quite as easy as would appear at first sight. Some surveys, as a result, are more distinguished for technical virtuosity than for the contribution they make to sociological knowledge. This is often due to the fact that there exists a gulf between the sociologist, who is frequently trained on the Arts side, and who will know little about statistical techniques, and the statistician, whose knowledge of the subject-matter of the survey is often limited. The design and execution of a survey is thus left to the specialist statistician, who is an expert in techniques. It is to be hoped that in the future there will be more sociologists whose training will include the necessary mathematics and statistics useful in survey analysis.

The main fields in which research is necessary in surveys, however, lies outside statistics proper. It is in the control of response errors, and in the improvement of the quality of data collection, that one hopes for advances in the future.

REFERENCES

1. ABRAMS, M. *Social Surveys and Social Action* (London, 1951).
2. *Annals of the Royal Statistical Society*, 1834–1934, p. 10.
3. *ibid.*, p. 49.
4. BARTON, A. H., & LAZARSFELD, P. F. 'Some Functions of Qualitative Analysis in Social Research'. In: *Sociologica*, Frankfurter Beiträge zur Soziologie, Vol. I, 1955.
5. BELSON, W., & BELL, C. R., *A Bibliography of Papers Bearing on the Adequacy of Techniques Used in Survey Research* (London, 1960).
6. BENJAMIN, B. 'Quality of Response in Census Taking', *Popul. Stud.*, 1955.
7. BENJAMIN, B,. 'Statistical Problems Connected with the 1961 Population Census', *J. R. statist. Soc.*, A, 1960.
8. BLALOCK, H. M., *Social Statistics* (New York, 1960), chap. 10.
9. BOOTH, CHARLES. *Labour and Life of the People of London* (London, 1889–91), 2 vols. *Life and Labour of the People in London*, 2nd ed. 9 Vols. (London 1892–7). 3rd edn., 17 Vols. (London, 1902–3).
10. BOWLEY, A. L., & BURNETT-HURST, A. R. *Livelihood and Poverty* (London, 1915).
11. BOWLEY, A. L. & HOGG, M. H. *Has Poverty Diminished?* (London, 1925).
12. BUTLER, D. E., & ROSE, R. *The British General Election of 1959* (London, 1960), chap. 8.
13. COCHRAN, W. G. *Sampling Techniques* (New York, 1953).

Statistical Surveys

14. COLQUHOUN, P. *A Treatise on the Police of the Metropolis*, etc. 2nd edn. (London, 1800).
15. DEMING, W. E. 'On a Probability Mechanism to Attain an Economic Balance Between the Resultant Error of Response and the Bias of Non-response', *J. Amer. Statist. Assoc.* (1953).
16. DOLL, R., 'Retrospective and Prospective Studies', chap. 4, in Witts, L. J. (ed.) *Medical Surveys and Clinical Trials* (London, 1959).
17. DOUGLAS, J. W. B., & BLOMFIELD, M. *Children Under Five* (London, 1958).
18. DURBIN, J., & STUART, A. 'Callbacks and Clustering in Sample Surveys: An Experimental Study', *J. R. statist. Soc.*, A, 1954.
19. EDWARDS, F. (ed.). *Readings in Market Research* (London, 1956).
20. FESTINGER, L., & KATZ, D. (eds.). *Research Methods in the Behavioral Sciences* (London, 1954).
21. FLOUD, J. E., HALSEY, A. H., & MARTIN, F. M. *Social Class and Educational Opportunity* (London, 1957).
22. FREUND, J. E., & WILLIAMS, F. J. *Modern Business Statistics* (London, 1959).
23. GLASS, D. V. 'Gregory King and the Population of England and Wales at the End of the Seventeenth Century', *Eugen. Rev.*, 1946.
24. GLASS, D. V. (ed.). *Social Mobility in Britain* (London, 1953).
25. GRAUNT, JOHN. *Natural and Political Observations Mentioned in a Following Index and Made upon the Bills of Mortality* (London, 1662).
26. GRAY, P. G., & CORLETT, T. 'Sampling for the Social Survey'. *J. R. statist. Soc.*, A, 1950.
27. HANSEN, M. H., HURWITZ, W. N., & MADOW, W. G. *Sample Survey Methods and Theory* (New York, 1953). 2 vols.
28. HAWKINS, F. BISSET. *Elements of Medical Statistics* (London, 1829).
29. HENRY, H. *Motivation Analysis* (London, 1958).
30. HIMMELWEIT, H., et al. *Television and the Child* (London, 1958).
31. HOWARD, JOHN. *The State of the Prisons in England and Wales, with Preliminary Observations and an Account of Some Foreign Prisons and Hospitals.* 2nd edn. (Warrington, 1780).
32. HYMAN, H. H. *Survey Design and Analysis: Principles, Cases, and Procedures* (Urbana, Ill., 1955).
33. HYMAN, H. H., et al. *Interviewing in Social Research* (Chicago, 1955).
34. ISAACS, S., et al. *The Cambridge Evacuation Survey: A Wartime Study in Social Welfare and Education* (London, 1941).
35. KAHN, R. L., & CARNELL, C. F. *The Dynamics of Interviewing: Theory, Techniques and Cases* (New York, 1957).
36. KENDALL, P. L., & LAZARSFELD, P. F. 'Problems of Survey Analysis', in Merton, R. K., and Lazarsfeld, P. F. (eds.), *Continuities in Social Research* (Urbana, Ill., 1950).
37. KINSEY, A. C., POMEROY, W. B., & MARTIN, C. E. *Sexual Behaviour in the Human Female* (Philadelphia, 1953).
38. KISH, L. 'Some Statistical Problems in Research Design'. *Amer. Sociol. Rev.*, 1959.

E. Grebenik and C. A. Moser

39. LINDZEY, G. *Handbook of Social Psychology* (chapters on attitude measurement).
40. LYND, R. S., & H. *Middletown* (New York and London, 1929).
41. LYND, R. S., & H. *Middletown in Transition* (New York, 1937).
42. MCCARTHY, P. J. *Introduction to Statistical Reasoning* (New York, 1957).
43. MANNHEIM, H., & WILKINS, L. T. *Prediction Methods in Relation to Borstal Training* (London, 1955).
44. MARTIN, J. P. *Social Aspects of Prescribing* (London, 1957).
45. MOSER, C. A. *Survey Methods in Social Investigation* (London, 1958), Chap. 2.
46. MOSER, C. A., & STUART, A. 'An Experimental Study of Quota Sampling'. *J. R. statist. Soc.*, A, 1953.
47. MOSTELLER, F., *et al. The Pre-Election Polls of 1948* (New York, 1949).
48. PAYNE, S. L. *The Art of Asking Questions* (Princeton, 1951).
49. ROWNTREE, B. SEEBOHM. *Poverty: A Study of Town Life.* (London, 1899).
50. ROWNTREE, B. SEEBOHM. *Poverty and Progress: A Second Social Survey of York* (London, 1941).
51. SCOTT, C. 'Research on Mail Surveys'. *J. R. statist. Soc.*, A, 1961.
52. SELLTIZ, C. *et al.* (eds.) *Research Methods in Social Relations* (London, 1954).
53. SIMEY, T. S. & M. B. *Charles Booth: Social Scientist* (London, 1961).
54. STOUFFER, S. A., *et al. The American Soldier* (Princeton, 1949), 2 vols.
55. STOUFFER, S. A., *et al. Measurement and Prediction* (Princeton, 1950).
56. THACKRAH, C. T. *The Effects of Arts, Trades and Professions . . . on Health and Longevity* (London, 1832).
57. TORGERSON, W. *Theory and Methods of Scaling* (London, 1958).
58. TOWNSEND, P. *The Family Life of Old People* (London, 1957).
59. United States Bureau of the Census. *The Post-Enumeration Survey*, 1950. Technical Papers, No. 4 (Washington, 1960).
60. WALLIS, W. A., & ROBERTS, H. V. *Statistics: A New Approach* (Urbana, Ill., 1956).
61. WELLS, A. F., 'Social Surveys', chap. 18 in Bartlett, F. C., *et al.* (ed.), *The Study of Society: Methods and Problems* (London, 1939).
62. WHELPTON, P. K., & KISER, C. V. *Social and Psychological Factors Affecting Fertility.* 5 vols. (New York, 1946–58). Cf. also the resumé of the study by these authors in *Popul. Stud.*, 1954.
63. YATES, F. *Sampling Methods for Censuses and Surveys* (3rd edn. London, 1960).
64. YOUNG, M., & WILLMOTT, P. *Family and Kinship in East London* (London, 1957).
65. ZWEIG, F. *Labour, Life, and Poverty* (London, 1948).
66. ZWEIG, F. *Women's Life and Labour* (London, 1952).
67. ZWEIG, F. *The British Worker* (Harmondsworth, 1952).

2

THE POPULATION CENSUS
AS A SOURCE OF SOCIAL
STATISTICS

B. Benjamin

INTRODUCTION

AN essential and irreplaceable approach to the study of society is provided by the population census which is taken in Britain and in most other developed countries of the world at regular intervals, usually of ten years. Although the population census considered as a field operation has much in common with other kinds of field survey, it is nevertheless sharply distinguished by its traditional background, legal sanctions, coverage, and by the whole scale of the operation and the resources normally devoted to it, which permit a far greater content and depth of analysis than can normally be encompassed in other types of field study.

Definition of a Census

The words used internationally to describe a population census are as follows: 'A census of population may be defined as the total process of collecting, compiling, and publishing demographic, economic, and social data pertaining, at a specified time or times, to *all* persons in a country or delimited territory.'[11]

Certain essential features follow from this definition. An official census is sponsored by the government of the area or of some larger region within which the area falls. The area covered is precisely defined. The principle of universality applies. The enumeration should either include every member of the community to which the census relates without omission or duplication or, if sampling is used, must give every member of a stratum equal likelihood of inclusion. For reasons which will be discussed later, it is desirable to include every member of the community in the basic enumeration and to reserve the use of sampling for the economical collection of data on supplementary topics.

Legal Basis for the Census

Population censuses carried out in Great Britain are at present covered by the Census Act of 1920, the main provisions of which are :

(i) power is given to the Registrars General of England and Wales, and Scotland, respectively, under the control and direction of the Minister of Health, to hold enumerations at intervals of not less than five years (the actual interval has never yet been less than ten years).

(ii) the direction to take a census is to be by Order in Council, and may be for Great Britain or any part of Great Britain (the minimum time interval is specific to a particular part; i.e. a census cannot be 'taken in any part of Great Britain in any year unless at the commencement of that year at least five years have elapsed since the commencement of the year in which a census was last taken in that part . . .').

(iii) the questions to be asked at any census are to be prescribed by the Order in Council, but must fall within the following general scope of topics as listed in the Schedule to the 1920 Act.

(a) Names, sex, age.
(b) Occupation, profession, trade or employment.
(c) Nationality, birthplace, race, language.
(d) Place of abode, character of dwelling.
(e) Condition as to marriage, relation to head of family, issue born in marriage.
(f) Any other matters with respect to which it is desirable to obtain statistical information with a view to ascertaining the social or civil condition of the population. (Any questions specified under this heading come under the close scrutiny of Parliament, since these must be the subject of an affirmative resolution of both Houses.)

(iv) The Registrar General may at the cost of any local authority or private person satisfy a 'reasonable' request for statistical information derived from the census but not contained in the published reports. (The use of this provision has increased and

The Population Census

is likely to increase as a result of an increased demand for data specific to a local or sectional population but not of sufficient general interest to warrant incorporation in the main tabulations of the census.)

Restraints upon the Scope of Census Inquiries

The scope of paragraph (*f*) of the Schedule to the 1920 Act is very wide, but it has to be borne in mind that two important restrictions may operate to limit the amount of information which can be made available to research workers. First, the requirement that these topics shall be the subject of affirmative resolution by both Houses of Parliament means that any topic which may offend public opinion (e.g. a question about personal incomes) or which appears to be too remotely connected with the main objective of the census as an instrument of social administration (e.g. possession of pet animals) is likely to be ruled out. Secondly, since the Government pays the piper it expects to call the tune. Census questions which supply information essential to the business of government or directly useful to the community at large (which pays taxes to meet the bill), are likely to come before other topics, especially those related to a specialized demand and not commanding wide interest. Further, a ceiling is bound to be placed upon the total cost of the census, and since processing cost is roughly proportional to the number of questions, this number is bound to be effectively limited.

Apart from these considerations, there is a practical restriction on the extent of the census inquiries. Merely to ask an additional question in the census schedule does not ensure a correct answer. Any progressive elaboration of the schedule is likely to reach a stage at which indifference, if not resentment, will introduce inaccuracy, and this may cause doubt to be cast on the validity of the whole enumeration. This is a very important consideration where the householder is required to complete the schedule, but even where canvassers are employed, steps have to be taken to reduce the burden of questions to be directed to any one household. If the number of aspects on which population statistics are sought (additional to the basic details of age, sex, marital condition, size of household and dwelling, etc.) are too numerous to be covered at one census without excessive complexity in the schedule, it is better to cover them some at a time by a set of supplemental questions at successive censuses, especially if these by virtue of their simplicity can be held more frequently than at ten-year intervals. Another possibility is for the supplemental or more complicated questions to be shared over the whole population by reserving them to schedules addressed to samples of the population, a different battery of such questions to each sample. In this way it would be possible to cover many more topics than the average number with which any one person may be concerned.

The basic approach would be that if there are thirty-two questions to be asked and no one person can be expected to answer more than sixteen, then a particular question can only be applied to half of the population. Normally, the situation is more complicated in the sense that (i) there are some questions which it is thought desirable to apply to every person, e.g. sex, age, marital status; (ii) it is not always essential that every person should have exactly the same number of questions to answer as another (much depends on the attitude of the population and whether they appreciate the implication of sampling in selecting some but not others); (iii) the minimum size of a sample consistent with a specified level of reliability may vary with the topic and the intended mode of exploitation of the information. Thus, in the U.S.A. in 1950, a 20 per cent sample was used for migration, birthplace, education, income and service in the Armed Forces, while a $3\frac{1}{3}$-per cent sample was used for last occupation and industry (for persons who had left the labour force) and fertility.

Certain technical problems arise. If, as is more convenient, systematic rather than random sampling is adopted, steps have to be taken to avoid the bias which is often associated with the former method. In the United States census of 1950, for example, the conditions under which new enumeration sheets were completed gave rise to some degree of association between population characteristics and the order of line on the sheet. This did not seriously affect the 20-per cent sample, but it was found that for the $3\frac{1}{3}$-per cent sample, which consisted of the persons listed on the last sample line of each schedule, persons in small households were under-represented (by about 4 per cent) as a result of the instruction given to enumerators to start a new sheet whenever the set of twelve housing lines on the back of a schedule had been completed, thus leaving some lines blank on the front of the schedules where population questions were recorded. In the self-enumeration type of census (as in the United Kingdom) with a household schedule there is a choice between (i) a systematic selection of serially listed households using complementary numbers to avoid bias (as in the selection of the 1951 1-per cent sample); (ii) some system of shuffling schedules of different types before distribution. The scale of the operation militates against refined methods and some degree of departure from high standards of randomization has to be accepted.

Steps must also be taken to reduce sampling errors, e.g. by regression methods based on relationship of sample values to values recorded in complete enumeration and by intelligent choice of sampling fraction.

A further problem is presented by the need for cross-tabulation of several factors; this can only be effected for those members of the population who have been asked *all* of the relevant questions. This need does in fact operate as a serious restraint upon the possible sharing out of questions to ease the burden of response; for most of the answers asked for in British censuses, such as those on occupation, industry, education, require correlation one with another in tabulation and so the questions must all appear on the *same* schedule. In practice therefore sampling would be used not to increase the total questions asked but to reduce the total number of persons required to answer any questions at all other than those which are involved in the simplest exact count of heads. For such a count is required as a sure starting-point for the intercensal estimates of local populations that form the basis of Exchequer Grants, and here not only must justice be done but it must be seen to be done. The idea would be to have two schedules, one containing only questions on age, sex, marital condition, and addressed to $(100-x)$ per cent of the population, and another containing the full battery of questions but addressed to only x per cent of the population (where x is determined by reference to the likely sampling errors in the smallest cells of the tabulation).

In passing it should be stressed that sampling in enumeration may ease the burden on the respondent and also that on the census authority in terms of volume of units of information to be coded and tabulated, but, because of the problems already mentioned and the additional control measures to ensure that rules are properly adhered to, there is some addition to administrative costs. In the final outcome the advantages may not be as great as might appear from superficial examination. The advantages are diminished if there are alternative means of easing the burden of response, e.g. use of check lists and self-coding devices to reduce the manuscript content of the response.

Earlier Censuses in Great Britain

In England and Wales and Scotland the first census was held in 1801, and others took place at decennial intervals to 1931. World war rendered it inexpedient to have a census in 1941, and the fifteenth took place in 1951. The census of 1801 counted the number of males and females of each house and family and the number of persons engaged in agriculture, trade, manufacture, or handicraft, and other occupations not specially classified. That of 1821 was the first at which information was sought as to age, but it was left optional whether this should be furnished or not. Just prior to the 1841 census the civil registration of births, deaths, and marriages had been instituted in England and Wales and the newly appointed local Registrars replaced the parish overseers as the officers responsible for conducting the census. In addition the duty of completing the enumeration form for each family was delegated to the head of the household instead of to an official, thus enabling simultaneous entry of every person to be made. In Scotland civil registration was not established until 1855 and the census of 1841 was entrusted to the official schoolmaster or other fit person. (The Scottish census of 1861 was the first to be conducted by the Registrar-General for Scotland.) The census of 1851 was carried out under Dr William Farr's supervision and was more detailed than earlier enumerations. The questions concerned occupation, birthplace, relationship (husband, wife, etc.), marital condition (married, widowed, bachelor, etc.), education, and the number of persons deaf and dumb or blind; and, for the first time, the precise age at last birthday of each person had to be furnished.

In the census report of 1881, the age and sex distribution of the population of each urban and rural sanitary authority as then constituted was given for the first time.

At the census of 1891 the schedule contained new questions as to number of rooms and of their occupants in all tenements with less than five rooms; and an important economic distinction was made between employers, employees, and those working on their own account. In 1901 no further additions were made to the subjects of inquiry.

In 1911 a number of important changes were made. The difficulty of defining a 'house' was avoided by the enumeration for each urban and rural district of the number of various classes of buildings used as dwellings—ordinary dwelling houses, blocks of flats and the separate flats or dwellings composing them, shops, institutions, etc., with the corresponding populations. The limited accommodation inquiry of the 1891 census was extended to tenements of all sizes. The industry as well as the occupation of each worker was recorded. The tabulations gave ages in single years of life instead of groupings.

The most important development of 1911 was a detailed inquiry into fertility. The following questions were asked in respect of every married woman.

   (i) Duration of marriage in completed years.
   (ii) The number of children born alive to the present marriage who:
      (a) were still alive at the census
      (b) had died before the census.

This information was related to other census data as to age, marital status, occupation, etc., and enabled a study of area and social class differences in marriage and childbearing experience to be attempted.

In preparing for the census of 1921 it was thought that a point had been reached in progressive enlargement of census inquiries at which any further addition to the total quantity of information might lead to indifference or resistance and consequent inaccuracy. Most of the changes were therefore in the nature of substitutions. The fertility inquiry of 1911 was not repeated, on the ground that in 1921 such an inquiry would have reflected not normal experience but the disturbance of the 1914–18 war, but instead the schedule was designed to seek dependency information, i.e. details of all living children and step-children under the age of sixteen for each married man, widower, or widow on the schedule (whether these children were enumerated on the same schedule or not). Such information as to the numbers and ages of existing children according to age and marital status of parent was essential to the development of national widows' and orphans' pensions provision then contemplated. The questions as to infirmities (blind, deaf, dumb, and lunatics) of earlier censuses were dropped, since it was generally recognized that there was a natural reluctance to disclose these which militated against completeness in response; but a new question was added as to place of work. New industrial and occupational classifications were introduced.

Although as at previous censuses the 1931 enumeration was on a *de facto* basis, i.e. each person was enumerated where found at the time the census was taken instead of at the usual place of residence (referred to as the *de jure* basis), for the first time a question was inserted in the schedule asking for a statement of the address of usual residence of each person enumerated in the household. The 1931 schedule omitted any inquiry into education, workplace, and either dependency or fertility, and was thus simpler than in 1921. This reduction in scope was made partly for economy and also because it was anticipated that in future more frequent enumerations would be made and that emphasis would be placed at different times on different additions to this minimum in order to spread the complete survey over several censuses. (It was intended to hold a census in 1936, but it was later decided not to fulfil this intention.) As a reflection of the economic depression of the time the 1931 schedule was extended to include particular mention of those 'out of work'.

The 1951 Census

The enumeration was carried out as at midnight of 8/9 April 1951 in England, Wales, and Scotland. In addition to the customary questions as to age, sex, marital condition, occupation, etc., certain special questions were included.
These were:

Fertility:

Married women under the age of fifty were asked to state:
  (i) The date of present marriage (and if married more than once the date of the first marriage).

31

(ii) The total children born alive to her (all marriages).

(iii) Whether she had given birth to a live-born child during the last twelve months.

Education:

All persons were asked whether they were attending an educational establishment for the purpose of instruction at the date of the census and if so whether full-time or part-time. Persons not then receiving full-time instruction were asked to state the age at which such full-time education ceased.

Household arrangements:

Heads of households were asked to indicate the availability to the household of the following facilities:

(i) A piped water supply within the dwelling (as distinct from a tap in the yard or public standpipe).

(ii) Cooking stove with an oven.

(iii) Kitchen sink with drainpipe leading outside (not a wash-basin).

(iv) Water closet (not an earth or chemical closet).

(v) Fixed bath with waste-pipe leading outside.

The question on place of work, last asked at the 1921 census, was re-introduced.

As in earlier census enumerations the schedule was completed by the head of the household and was collected by a paid enumerator who gave such assistance as was necessary on matters of interpretation regarding the completion of the form.

The 1961 Census

Since this chapter was drafted the 1961 enumeration has taken place. Innovations include questions on tenure of dwelling, movement of usual address, and scientific qualifications; and the use of sampling in enumeration (90 per cent of the population were asked only questions on sex, age, marital conditions, birthplace, citizenship, and fertility).

International Recommendations

The Statistical Office of the United Nations[11] have published a report on 'Principles and Recommendations for National Population Censuses' in which they submit a list of topics to be covered. The list (given below) is prefaced by the reservation 'Because of the many factors which determine the topics to be covered by any national census, no inflexible recommended list is desirable. The topics of general national and international value given below are those in most universal use which have emerged after decades of census experience as of greatest value for both national and international purposes. Nevertheless countries may find that it is not necessary or practicable to include certain of the recommended topics. Their decisions would depend upon their evaluations of how urgently the data were needed, upon resources available, and upon whether information from other sources could be used. . . . The numbers or the order of the topics do not indicate priority or relative importance. . . .

'A. *Topics directly based on questionnaire items*:

Geographic items.

    1. Location at time of census and/or place of usual residence.

Household or family information.

    2. Relation to head of household or family.

Personal characteristics.

    3. Sex.
    4. Age.
    5. Marital status.
    6. Place of birth.
    7. Citizenship.

Economic characteristics.

    8. Type of activity.
    9. Occupation.
    10. Industry.
    11. Status (as employer, employee, etc.).

Cultural characteristics.

    12. Language.
    13. Ethnic or nationality characteristics.

Education characteristics.

    14. Literacy.
    15. Level of education.
    16. School attendance.

Fertility data.

    17. Children—total live-born.

'B. *Derived topics.*

    18. Total population.
    19. Population by size of locality.
    20. Urban-rural classification.
    21. Household or family composition.

B. Benjamin

'Each country may wish to consider the inclusion of other topics of national value but of lesser universal interest.

'Topics for additional consideration include: prior place of residence, farm or non-farm residence, farm tenure status, number of dependents, type of marriage ceremony, income, secondary occupation, time worked, length of employment or unemployment, household enterprises, professional or vocational education, total number of children born, total number of children living, number of times married, duration of married life, religion and mental and physical disabilities. . . .'

For particular application to Europe these recommendations have been adapted by a Working Party on Population Censuses set up by the Conference of European Statisticians, a representative body of official statisticians which meets under the auspices of the Economic Commission for Europe. Topic 2 has been replaced by:

'*Household and family information.*
Relation to main economic supporter (or head) of household.
Relation to main economic supporter (or head) of family nucleus.'

Topics 14 and 16 have been omitted from the main list as superfluous (there is little illiteracy in Europe and statistics of school attendance are in many countries derived from the educational system itself), but they have been included in the 'additional topics'. To the group of derived topics the following have been added:

Socio-economic categories.
Dependency relationship.

Recent Developments in Analysis of Census Results

There have been many developments in demographic analyses of census results in recent years and most of them fall within the same broad direction of orientation, namely, the provision of more information about the social and economic characteristics of populations and about the pattern of social and economic organization of communities. This is partly a product of the increasing need of governments for economic statistics of various kinds and partly a reflection of the growing realization, very evident in international discussions, that social and demographic changes are indissolubly linked with economic changes, constant reaction taking place between them. The increasing emphasis upon economic aspects of population changes has been an outstanding feature of demography in recent years. In addition there have been new pressures at work. Growing interest in the social stresses of modern industrial development and concomitant urbanization and the relationship between economic and social changes has led to intensified studies into these aspects of sociology, which in turn have brought

34

demands for relevant statistical data. The tremendous growth of market research has placed heavy demands on census material both as supplying basic information about the household as a purchasing unit, with all the social and areal differentials involved, and as providing controls for local sample surveys.

Fertility Analyses

Interest in fertility as the most important element in population growth is general. In countries where fertility is high there is a need to assess the rate at which population growth will both permit, by providing the necessary man-power, and require, by increasing consumer demand, the expansion of industrial productivity. There may be a need to adjust the pace of one to the pace of the other. Where fertility is low there is equally a need to measure it in order to consider whether a restraint upon the expansion of the economy is being influenced; and, if inducements to greater fertility are provided (e.g. by family allowances) as part of national policy, to discover whether these inducements appear to be successful.

The complexity of the census fertility analyses ranges from the very crude indication given by the ratio of the number of children in the population to the number of women of fertile age, to detailed distributions of family size by marriage age and marriage duration.

In order to assess the pace and direction of changes in family building it is necessary to possess serial sets of fertility rates by age at marriage, calendar year of marriage, and duration of marriage, and, if possible, by birth order. From this information one may see in respect of succeeding marriage cohorts the ultimate size of family likely to be produced and the way in which their fertility is spread over the duration of married life. It is also possible to observe secular changes in the likelihood that a woman who has had, say, two children, will have a third child.[9] Finally the age-duration fertility rates, if stable or moving in a predictable manner, may be used in connexion with a nuptiality table, to calculate generation replacement rates.[7] The fertility rates are derived from birth registrations and are not themselves census analyses. The role of the census analysis is to provide:

(a) Controls on the intercensal estimation of population at risk.
(b) Controls on the year to year estimation of family sizes of which the specific fertility rates form increments.

Some rates may be more accurately derived from the census itself. In respect of age, marriage duration, and parity, there is no reason to suppose that at the census the mothers will be differently classified from

B. Benjamin

the way in which, in relation to their offspring, they are classified at birth registration. With regard to socio-economic characteristics (occupations, branch of economic activity, etc.) it is not so; for it is well known that, for example, occupational description may vary significantly not only as between one informant and another but also for the same informant at two different times. This is because a slight change of wording may seriously affect the classification of the occupation. Further, occupation coding is complex and laborious, and if it can be done in respect of the mother and births at the same time the work is much reduced. For this reason an additional question was asked at the 1951 census of England and Wales; married women were asked to indicate whether they had borne a child in the preceding year. In this way fertility rates, specific for occupation, etc., were derived from the census, for which the population at risk (the denominators of the rates) were automatically provided by a single process of classification; the occupation, socio-economic group, etc., *and* the fact of bearing a child within the year of observation (or not doing so) being punched on the same machine card. In consequence it was possible to carry out an investigation of a number of fertility differentials of a social and economic character[7] which could not otherwise be studied except with considerably greater strain on resources.

Household and Family Composition

The population census is concerned not only with 'counting heads' but with identifying the family and household groupings, i.e. the way in which individual people combine together to satisfy their living needs. This is clearly an essential requirement for understanding the social and economic conditions of the people; it is a part of those conditions, it is a part of the mechanism by which the total national product is created, distributed, and consumed. A knowledge of the life cycle of the growth and disruption of families is necessary for the proper assessment of consumer demand for almost all commodities and especially for estimating housing needs.

The concept of the family is easy to grasp because of its primary biological significance; that of the household, with its economic rather than biological content, is more difficult to define. Because there has been some confusion about both concepts, the Working Group on Censuses of Population and Housing of the E.C.E. Conference of European Statisticians has recommended the following definitions:

A private household* may be:

* An institutional household is separately defined as comprising persons 'living in hotels, boarding houses, colleges, schools, hospitals, military installations, penal establishments, who are subject to a common authority or are bound by a common objective and/or personal interests and characteristics.'

36

The Population Census

(a) a one-person household, viz. a person who lives alone in a separate housing unit (defined as a structurally separate and independent place of abode) or who occupies, as a lodger, a part or the whole of a separate room or rooms in a part of a housing unit but does not join together with any of the other occupants of the housing unit to form part of a multi-person household as defined below; or

(b) a multi-person household, defined as a group of two or more persons who combine together jointly to occupy the whole or part of a housing unit, and to provide themselves with food or other essentials for living. The group may pool their incomes and have a common budget to a greater or lesser extent in different circumstances. The group may be composed of related persons or unrelated persons or a combination of both, including boarders but excluding lodgers.

The basic criteria under this concept of household, which for the sake of convenience may be referred to as the housekeeping unit concept, are that the persons constituting the household jointly occupy a common dwelling space, that they share principal meals (unless prevented for example by working conditions), and that they make a common provision for basic living needs (such as lighting, heating, laundry, etc.). Thus, a multi-person household may be comprised of the members of a family and relatives, resident domestic servants, employees and other persons living with the family as a single housekeeping unit whether or not this group occupies the whole or only a part of a structurally separate dwelling. (It is implicit for this concept that members of the household temporarily absent on census night should be brought within its scope, i.e. we are concerned here with the *de jure* household.)

In the population census it is possible within households to identify families defined as persons who are related by blood, marriage, or adoption. In this definition the marriage relationship includes stable *de facto* unions. The broad concept is of a group or groups of related persons found to be living together within a household. In many cases the family and the household will be identical. There may be different specific concepts according to the object of the statistical analysis. For example, it may be desirable for some purposes to consider:

(a) The family in the narrow sense, limited to a married couple with one or more unmarried children, a married couple without children, or one parent with one or more unmarried children, each of which may be called a 'family nucleus'.

(b) The family comprising all the related members of a household.

37

B. Benjamin

(c) Family relationships extending beyond the household are sometimes considered for sociological or genetic purposes, but this
concept of the entire biological family is not suitable for census
purposes.

For census purposes the primary unit is the family nucleus because it is
the unit which most facilitates analysis of family and household
structure.

It is important to bear in mind that there is a clear methodological
distinction between the household and the family (as defined above).
The household is identified by the census enumerator; the family, as
such, is not identified by the enumerator but is fixed mechanically during
the data processing on the basis of information written into the census schedule in respect of all members of the household. It is therefore
more natural to proceed from households to families. It will also be
important to bear in mind that a classification of households will
to some extent involve a classification of family components of households.

The head of the household is usually considered in the conduct of the
census to be that person who is acknowledged as such by the other
household members. It is more important for purposes of household
composition and dependency statistics, however, to identify the person
on whom falls the chief responsibility for the economic maintenance of
the household, i.e. the main breadwinner or the principal contributor
to the household budget, who may be called the 'main economic
supporter'. The identification requires either a direct question in the
census schedule or the establishment of criteria, e.g. economic activity,
socio-economic category, sex, seniority of age, etc., by means of which
a choice is made during the data-processing.

The same approach can also be made in relation to the family nucleus.
This gives rise to the concepts of the head of the family nucleus and the
supporter of such a family. Often these persons are identical; and when
the household comprises only one family nucleus, the analysis of the
household coincides with that of the family.

Households may be classified first according to whether they constitute private or institutional households. Private households can then
be classified into non-family, one-family, and multi-family households
(the latter may be further subdivided according to the number of family
nuclei they contain). *Non-family households* may be classified into one-
person and multi-person households; the multi-person households may
be further subdivided into those consisting of related persons only, of
related and unrelated persons, and of unrelated persons only. Distinction could also be made between direct descent and other relationship
(e.g. between a grandfather and a grandchild on the one hand and two

The Population Census

sisters on the other). *One-family* households may be classified into the following types:

    (*a*) A married couple with one or more unmarried children.
    (*b*) A married couple without children.
    (*c*) One parent with one or more unmarried children.

Each of these types of family nucleus may be combined with other persons either related, unrelated, or both within the household. *Multi-family households* are classified according to whether or not any of the family nuclei are related and whether or not this relationship is in direct descent; in addition, the family nuclei themselves may be classified by type as already indicated for those in one-family households. The number of possible combinations of axes of classification is therefore large, and it has been suggested that, though full analysis may have to be undertaken on occasions, for most practical purposes the analysis of households (as distinct from families) would be facilitated if each multi-family household could be typified by a *primary family* within it. This primary family could be selected on the basis of criteria related to the object of the analysis. For example, it could be the family nucleus with the oldest head, or the family nucleus containing the main economic supporter of the household, etc. The breakdown of a large household in accordance with the principles outlined above is shown in Table 1.

The great difficulty in this kind of analysis is that whereas there are certain well-defined simple structures which occur frequently and present no problem, there is also a large range of structures each of which, though occurring infrequently, is of considerable interest. These latter cases represent an important part of the analysis that contributes inordinately to the total workload. The use of the 'primary family' is suggested mainly as a means of reducing to a minimum an analysis that is inherently complicated. It is particularly necessary where, for purposes of economy or otherwise, the analysis is carried by using a single punch-card to represent a structure of a whole household. The analysis can be more flexible though much more voluminous where it is conducted on the basis of a card for each individual person containing complete information concerning his household and family attachments.

The analysis of families is best undertaken in terms of family nuclei. Just as in household analysis the development is from households to the family nuclei of which they are composed and which serve to differentiate the households, so it is necessary in family analysis to proceed from different types of family nuclei to their disposition within the households into which they are integrated. For completeness, it should be borne in mind that family nuclei living as members of institutional households

B. Benjamin

TABLE 1

A THREE-FAMILY HOUSEHOLD

No.	Name	Relation-ship to Head	Sex Age	Marital condition	Occupa-tion	Chief economic supporter House-hold	Family
1.	Henry Brown	Head*	M. 65	Married	Retired Farmer		
2.	Emily Brown	Spouse	F. 60	,,	Housewife.		
3.	George ,,	Son	M. 42	Single	Farm Mgr.	X	X
4.	Helen ,,	Daughter	F. 39	,,	House duties		
5.	John ,,	Brother-in-law	M. 62	,,	Carpenter (non-agric.)		
6.	James Robinson	Employee	M. 60	,,	Farm worker	———	
7.	Eric Brown	Son	M. 40	Married	Welder (non-agric.)		X
8.	Joan Brown	Daughter-in-law	F. 38	,,	Housewife		
9.	David ,,	Grandson	M. 10	—	—		
10.	Jane Jones	Sister-in-law	F. 50	Widow	Family worker (farm)		X
11.	Mary ,,	Niece-in-law	F. 30	Single	Teacher		

Primary family nucleus: [1 + 2 + 3 + 4]
(Note that 5 and 6 though related and unrelated respectively are *not* part of the family)
Secondary family nuclei: [7 + 8 + 9] in direct descent and [10 + 11] not in direct descent

Dependent on agriculture: economically inactive [1 + 2 + 4]; economically active [3 + 6 + 10]
Dependent on other industry: economically inactive [8 + 9 + 11]; economically active [5 + 7]

* Head in the conventional sense of accepting responsibility for the census schedule.

40

have to be included. Thus, in the first place, it is necessary to identify the three types of family nuclei, living in both private and institutional households. Secondly, the family nuclei living in private households are classified according to whether they are in one-family, two-family, three-family, etc., households. Where for the purpose of household analysis certain family nuclei have been designated as primary families and the others as secondary families, this designation provides a further axis of classification.

These household classifications are relatively simple and capable of further development, as indeed has been the case in some countries, notably in the Federal Republic of Germany, where they have introduced the interesting concept of the 'functional scope of households', i.e. for each individual the extent to which he participates in the basic functions of the household, for example, by:

(a) Sharing meals which are prepared for the household in common.
(b) Having laundry washed together with that of the total household.
(c) Contributing to a common budget from which the requirements of daily life are financed.

This clearly provides a further measure of the cohesion of households and an additional axis of classification.

In the census of England and Wales of 1951 the structure of the household was based on affinity to the 'head of household' and did not show clearly the separation of one-, two-, or three-generation households; on the other hand there was a more deliberate distinction of the 'family nucleus' (e.g. a married son or daughter with spouse or with children of their own) within a composite household. These family nuclei were important as representing an accumulated demand for new housing which when available would lead to the creation of new households from the nuclei. In the United States of America the reference point in 1950 was also the head of the household, but a new definition of family was introduced, and the useful concept of the subfamily (somewhat similar to the U.K. family nucleus). An excellent exploitation of the tabulations has been published as a special monograph.[8]

Cross-tabulations from the basic distribution of household or family types would show for each type the number of persons in the household, the number and ages of children, and the number of earners and income recipients.

Another type of analysis that has been developed involves classifying households by the social and economic characteristics of a principal member, e.g. the chief economic supporter of the household. The characteristics cover a wide range and include occupancy of dwelling (as owner or tenants), level of education, type of activity, occupation, branch of economic activity, employment status, socio-economic group, as well as sex, age, and marital status. Examples may be found in the 5 per cent Sample Tables of the French census of 1954 (1958).

Housing

To the census authority, dwellings and people are inseparable in the sense that it is difficult and very largely meaningless to measure housing resources without relating those resources to their present as well as their potential use. It is therefore customary in most countries to conduct the housing census simultaneously with, and as an integral part of, the population census. On the one hand, this enables housing data to be classified in relation to the characteristics of the population accommodated in the dwelling units (as a means of assessing the adequacy of housing), and on the other hand, it makes it possible to classify the population in relation to their housing (as a means of measuring both current levels of living and potential housing demand).

Analytical developments have taken the form of more detailed cross-tabulations between household structural groups and classifications of types of housing accommodation. It is now regarded as inadequate to classify housing units merely according to the number of rooms they contain. A number of new axes of classification have been introduced.

In the first place there has been some standardization, as a result of United Nations guidance, in the classification of housing units,* viz.:

1. Private housing units:
   (i) Conventional (permanent) dwellings (house, apartment, flat, etc.).
   (ii) Rustic (semi-permanent) units, e.g. huts, cabins, etc., and improved units, e.g. shacks.
   (iii) Mobile housing units, e.g. trailers, caravans, boats, etc.

2. Collective housing units (designed for occupancy by two or more households or by an institutional household):
   (i) Hotels and boarding houses.
   (ii) Institutions, e.g. hospitals, boarding schools, barracks.
   (iii) Camps, e.g. lumber camps or military camps without fixed location.

There is also a need to classify the type of building structure in which the housing units are situated. There is the question whether it is a residential building or a non-residential building (commercial, indus-

---

* 'An independent room, group of rooms, apartment, flat or house *designed* for habitation by a private or institutional household *or* a boat, wagon, hut, cave or any other structure *occupied* as living quarters.'

trial, etc.). In many countries owing to a general shortage of housing there has been a rapid increase in the provision of flats, both by new building and by the conversion of existing large houses. The period of construction may also be recorded as an indicator of obsolescence.

A further axis for cross-tabulation is the tenure as owner-occupier, tenant, or sub-tenant. (This may also be regarded as an economic characteristic of the household.)

The main characteristics of the housing unit to be tabulated within the type-groups discussed above are:

  (i) Size, i.e. number of rooms.
 (ii) Number of occupying households, and persons.
(iii) Facilities (water supply, toilet, bath, ventilation, etc.).
(iv) Social and economic characteristics of head of household.

Commonly (i) and (ii) are crossed (to give density of housing for each household size) within each housing unit type.

Recent developments in housing analyses have been attempts to examine the housing of special sections of the population (for example, old people living alone or certain specified household structures); estimates of the adequacy or inadequacy of the existing stock of housing on various hypotheses as to the space needs of different household (and family) structures; studies of the sharing of dwellings in terms of the structural types of household which combine to share: studies of obsolescence (as indicated by lack of facilities or evidence of conversion from original design).[5]

Dependency

In keeping with the new economic emphasis in demography much attention has been given to the classification of the population according to their mode of participation in the economy. A simple classification by type of economic activity has been drawn up as follows:

A. *Economically active population*
  1. Employed.
  2. Unemployed.

B. *Inactive population*
  1. With income
    (i) Former members of active population (i.e. pensioners deriving their subsistence from former activity).
    (ii) Living on income from capital, State aid, etc.

B. Benjamin

2. Without income, i.e. dependents
   (i) Students.
   (ii) Home houseworkers.
   (iii) Persons in institutions.
   (iv) Other adults in the home.

Since it is the active population who provide the goods and services which are consumed by all, it is an important part of long-term economic planning to assess, from a total population point of view, the likely trend in the numerical relationship between the inactive and active populations (see, for example 1).

The same kind of study is of importance at the household and more particularly at the family level for the purpose of measuring the economic strength of different structures. The problem is to attach the dependent members of the family to the member or members upon whom they are dependent. The supporters may be further classified to show not only the numbers of their dependents but also the sector of economy or branch of economic activity on which they, the supporters, are in turn dependent. Much important work in this field has been carried out in the Federal Republic of Germany,[10] in Czechoslovakia, Yugoslavia, and some other European countries.

It is important to note that the analyses of household and family structure, and of dependency, are problems of arrangement of data already on the census schedule; they do not involve specific questions except that, in the case of dependency, a question is needed to identify income recipients.

Income

As distinct from analyses of dependency which are concerned with the presence or absence of incomes, there has been little development in the direction of analysing incomes by size. As a result it has been necessary in the study of levels of living to turn to a battery of indicators such as food consumption, infant mortality, education facilities. Some countries have carried out household income and expenditure surveys on an *ad hoc* basis but not as part of the population census, so that it is only possible to cross-tabulate with a limited number of other social and economic characteristics. Nevertheless, with the exception of the United States of America among the larger countries, there is a general inclination to regard a question on amount of income as objectionable in a population census. It has to be borne in mind that household budget inquiries of the *continuous* sample survey type provide constantly up-to-date information in circumstances of prices and wages which are always changing, and this is a strong balance of advantage in favour of the survey method.

In the United States of America income distributions have been tabulated for sex and age groups, for different branches of economic activity, in families, for different statuses (head, relative of head, unrelated individual), and according to weeks worked in 1949. Separate distributions have also been given for different classes of worker (private, government, self-employed, etc.).

Occupation and Branch of Economic Activity

Tabulations indicating the distribution of skills in the labour force and the apportionment of the labour force among the different branches of economic activity are of fundamental importance to labour recruitment and mobility, to measurement of the development of branches of economic activity, and to an appreciation of the economic characteristics of population groups. The general interest in the provision of comparable statistics for international comparative studies of economic development is evident from the establishment of international standard classifications of other occupation (I.S.C.O.) and branch of economic activity (I.S.I.C.). There are also international recommendations on the subsidiary classification of the active population by employment status, *viz.*:

Employers.
Workers on own account.
Employees.
Family workers.
Members of producer's co-operatives.

New developments in analyses have been less in the direction of elaborating the basic distributions of occupation and industrial groups by sex, age, and employment status, than in cross-tabulation with other characteristics such as housing, education, or fertility, or household structure. There is nevertheless a growing recognition of the scope for meaningful subdivision of skill and function within the framework of minimal standard classifications. Most broad occupational groupings are concerned with separating managers, non-manual workers, skilled, semi-skilled, and unskilled workmen. Not only are the assignments to these groups somewhat arbitrary but the groups themselves are large, unwieldy, and heterogeneous. It seems likely that either by utilizing non-census data on types of training required (especially distinguishing re-employment from in-service training) or by cross-tabulation with census data on education, duration of employment, and employment status, it might be possible to break up these groups into an approximation to levels of skill, or responsibility.

There is considerable interest in the separation of the managerial element in industry; in the distinction between the makers of policy and those who, albeit with some elbow-room of discretion, merely carry out a prescribed policy. The relationship of the managerial to the non-managerial labour force in different industries throws light upon the development of the organizational structure. Here again a single group of managers is too large and heterogeneous, and splits are made according to branch of economic activity (agriculture, extractive industry, productive industry, distribution, government, etc.) and also by size of establishment (total number of workers). With regard to this latter factor of size it would, of course, be more meaningful to classify managers by the number of workers they manage, but this would require a specific question, and it would be naïve to expect reliable answers. If 'manager' is incorporated into the employment status classification as well as in the classification of occupations, then a single tabulation of the economically active by branch of economic activity and status is sufficient for all these purposes. Such a tabulation shows, for example, from one census to another, the trend in the proportion of 'own account' workers (a downward trend indicating the organization of industry in larger units) and in the incidence of the 'family worker' status as a general indicator of economic development.

In order to provide information relating to the inter-industry or inter-occupation (as distinct from geographical) mobility of labour, as a background to the assessment of economic stability or flexibility, tabulations may usefully be made of 'duration of present employment' (in relation to age). Such a distribution shows to what extent labour is mobile and to what extent the occupation and industries recorded may be regarded as 'usual'. Another kind of tabulation which is partly related to labour mobility is that of secondary occupations. This is only relevant to countries where there are significant numbers of workers with more than one occupation, either simultaneously, or consecutively within a short time interval; to every secondary occupation there would also be a secondary industry and a secondary employment status. To be useful the tabulation must be presented as a cross-tabulation of primary and secondary occupations (and industries), and this is a formidable undertaking.

Another aspect of labour statistics, in respect of which in some countries there is a tendency to regard the population census as the source, is that of hours of employment per week. A tabulation showing a distribution of hours of work for each occupation and industry provides an indication of relative working conditions in different avenues of employment; furnishes information on under-employment where it exists; and serves to provide standards for regulating social security schemes. For this latter purpose it is useful also to have tabulations of frequency and method of payment.

Socio-economic Grouping

One of the most interesting of modern developments in demographic analyses, and one which illustrates forcefully the increased emphasis upon economic aspects of population statistics, has been the production of socio-economic groupings. In order to observe the inter-relationship of population trends (in the wider sense which embraces cultural and behavioural changes) and economic factors, it is necessary to divide the population into groups which are homogeneous in respect of the level of living (in material terms), educational background, and social attitude.

Two alternative approaches have been made. The first method is to attribute to each of the occupations distinguished in the classification a ranking based either on social values, for example that of standing within the community (such as in the United Kingdom from the 1911 census onward*), or on a score derived from a battery of such values. This has two disadvantages:

    (i) There is a likelihood that the ranking will be influenced by preconceived notions of just those differentials of health or behaviour which the groupings are to be used to discover.

  (ii) It is difficult to provide an economic interpretation of the ultimate inter-relationships of the groups and other social characteristics because of the abstract and subjective character of the ranking.

A second method has therefore been developed which is of a much more objective character in that it is derived automatically from a cross-tabulation of the four economic classifications already referred to, viz:

    (i) Type of activity in the economy.
   (ii) Occupation.
  (iii) Employment status.
  (iv) Branch of economic activity (industry).

* Under this system which is still in use, especially for occupational mortality purposes, every occupation (and therefore every person who follows it) is assigned to one of five social classes (really occupational classes), viz., (I) Professional, etc., (II) Intermediate, (III) Skilled workers, (IV) Partly skilled workers, (V) Unskilled workers.

B. Benjamin

The individual cells of such a cross-tabulation represent groups with substantial homogeneity of social and economic characteristics, and these can be gathered into broader groups to the extent of contraction in numbers of groups that may be desired. An important feature of these groups is the fact that they are not necessarily ranked in any preconceived order; it is claimed only that they are economically *different*, not that one group has higher social standing than another. Clearly in material terms the level of living is higher for one group than another, so that some degree of economic ordering is inevitable.

The European Working Group on Population Census of E.C.E. has subjected this system to close study and has recommended the following combinations:

SOCIO-ECONOMIC CLASSIFICATION

A. *Economically active population*
1. Farm-employers
2. Farmers on own account without employees
3. Members of agricultural producers' co-operatives
4. Agricultural workers
5. Employers in industry and commerce; large enterprises
6. Employers in industry and commerce; small enterprises
7. Employers in industry and commerce; own account workers without employees
8. Liberal and related professions
9. Members of non-agricultural producers' co-operatives
10. Directors (managers) of enterprises and companies
11. Senior non-manual workers
12. Intermediate and junior non-manual workers and sales workers
13. Supervisors and skilled, semi-skilled and specialized manual workers
14. Labourers
15. Service staff (domestic servants, cleaners, caretakers) and related workers
16. Members of armed forces on compulsory military service
17. Economically active persons not classifiable in the above groups

B. *Economically inactive population*
18. Former farm-employers
19. Former non-agricultural employers
20. Former employees
21. Other independent inactive persons

22. Children below minimum school-leaving age
23. Students and school-children above minimum school-leaving age

The Population Census

24. Housewives
25. Other adults in the home
26. Inmates of institutions

(Further subdivisions were suggested, and also summary groups, but these have been omitted in the interests of brevity.)

These socio-economic groups may then be used to classify the whole population (attributing to dependents the groups of those on whom they are dependent) or the active population only, or whole households (by the group of the chief economic supporter). The method has been developed to a high level of refinement in France, and an excellent account of the use of the socio-economic groups has been given by a member of the French Census Office.[2]

As in the case of the analysis of household structure, this socio-economic grouping is essentially a matter of exploiting information already provided on the census schedule; it does not involve additional specific questions.

Sector of the Economy

As has already been demonstrated, the economic information provided on the census schedule may be organized in a number of different ways. One additional way is to divide the active population between the public and private sectors of the economy by reference to branch of economic activity, occupation, and employment status. This is particularly of interest in countries where it is desired to observe the extent and pace of socialization of industry. Such an analysis is also of importance in any planned economy where it is desired, for example, to maintain a balanced programme of expansion as between the different sectors and it is necessary to observe the related man-power problems. An example of this kind of census tabulation may be found in the 2 per cent sample tables of the census of Yugoslavia of 1953.

Workplace

Where many people live in one locality and work in another, as in the United Kingdom, the geographical distribution of numbers of workers in different branches of economic activity has to be carried out on the basis of the area in which the workplace is situated as distinct from the area of residence of the worker. Since, in these circumstances, the address of residence and the address of the workplace are both recorded on the one schedule it is possible to attach area codes to these addresses and to carry out two types of analysis:

B. Benjamin

(i) Measurement of the difference between the day and night populations of urban localities and an examination of the character of the net inward movement each day and its distribution by sex, age, occupation, etc.

(ii) A cross-tabulation of area of residence and area of workplace to indicate the broad lines of journey (since the tabulation has to be in terms of persons crossing administrative area boundaries, movements *within* an administrative area are excluded and long and short movements across the boundary are given equal weight).

These analyses are of value to transport authorities who want to know the number of people to be moved and the social and economic characteristics of those who journey to work; and to town planning authorities who have to consider whether such movement is tolerable or could be avoided by re-siting industry or residential centres, or both. An increasing volume of movement to work is also of interest as indicating the later stage of town development in which the mixed market, residential, and cultural core is displaced by the growing commercial centre; and when both the diminishing residential accommodation and the noise and atmospheric pollution of expanding factory and office areas compel workers to seek dwellings in more open spaces on the periphery of the town.

Internal Migration

Of more general importance is the urbanization which accompanies industrialization in all countries and which, in many, results in large internal migratory movements of population. In turn this migration may have extensive demographic effects in changing population structure in different parts of the country and in producing mortality and fertility differentials. Even where economic development is already advanced, there are streams of movement the direction and pace of which are of interest to administrative bodies. Internal migration has become, again as part of the economic orientation in population studies, an important topic of demographic analysis. In many countries questions of the type 'Were you living at this address a year ago? If so, how long have you lived here? If not, what was the address of your usual residence a year ago?' have been introduced into the population census.

Movements may be classified by the type—for example, rural to rural, rural to urban, urban to rural; within the same region and outside the region of former residence. These movement types may then be cross-tabulated with sex, age, occupation, branch of economic activity, socio-economic group, and household and family structure. There can also be a cross-tabulation of area of present residence and area of former residence, so as to show up the main streams of movement taking place within the country. Further, the movers themselves may be treated as a selected population and a special study can be made of their social and economic characteristics.

Urban and Rural Population

The present stage of development of the continual urbanization which has been taking place may be gauged by separating the population into urban and rural elements and examining the size and disposition of the clusters of population.

This involves establishing conventions for the identification of population clusters. The most practical method is to work with large-scale maps which reveal street formation and the disposition of scattered buildings. The population of such street formations or scattered buildings which are not separated by more than a specified distance may be regarded as comprising one cluster. For this purpose administrative boundaries are ignored,* as the concept of the cluster is quite distinct from that of the local authority area. The clusters and any residual scattered buildings are then grouped into *localities*, i.e. population groups forming a unity indicated by social and economic interdependence in their daily lives. Localities may then be classified as urban or rural on the basis of population size and the distribution of the active population by industry. The criterion of size of population can be used to distinguish three categories consisting of small, medium-sized, and large localities. Some countries use 2000 as the dividing line between the first two categories and 10,000 as the dividing line between the second and third.

A second criterion of industrial activity can be used to distinguish within the smallest size-group between agricultural and non-agricultural localities. These localities in which the proportion of the active population engaged in agriculture exceeds say 20 per cent would be classed as rural agricultural localities and the others as rural non-agricultural localities.

This would mean that four basic categories would be distinguished, namely, rural agricultural, rural non-agricultural, intermediate, and urban localities.

The next stage in classification would be to break down the heterogeneous intermediate category, either by the application of the simple

---

* 'It should be borne in mind that we are dealing here with a special purpose, and not a complete alternative to administrative areas which must still form the basis of the main census tabulations.'

B. Benjamin

criterion of the proportion of the active population engaged in agriculture, or by the separation of the proportions engaged in agriculture, industry, and service activities or, if the necessary data be available, by reference to such criteria as the presence of an administration centre, the type of building (one-storey or multi-storey), availability of hospitals, etc. Localities can also be classified according to their functional type (industrial centre, university centre, holiday resort, etc.).

Education

An important development in the population census has been the progress from a mere assessment of literacy to a study of standards of instruction attained and even to a survey of the acquirement of university degrees and especially of technological diplomas and qualifications. The extent to which education and employment are correctly matched is of immense importance to the attainment of high levels of productivity. Definition of standards of instruction must inevitably be in terms of the administration of the educational system of the country concerned, and they will probably only have meaning within the context of that system. The analyses then take the form of cross-tabulations of standards of instruction with occupation, branch of economic activity, status, socio-economic group, and with other characteristics such as housing, family structure, and fertility.

Structure of Census Analyses

The main structure of census analyses can be set out systematically as follows:

Units	Axes
Person.	Sex, age, marital condition, fertility, birthplace, nationality, education, economic activity, occupation, industry, workplace, migration.
Family	Structural type, situation in household, economic strength (ratio of economically active to dependent members).
Household . . .	Structural type, family content, economic strength, characteristics of chief economic supporter, housing.
Locality (cluster) .	Size, industrial character, urban/rural division, function.
Administrative area .	Principal aggregate of tabulation.

The Population Census

Timing of the Census

The census is taken on a particular day, at intervals of several years, of a population which is not only continually changing in total size, but is also changing in constitution (age, sex, occupation, etc.) and in its geographical disposition within the national boundary. In times of industrial crisis or of mobilization of military forces, violent changes may be taking place; on a minor level, sharp changes in regional distribution occur in the usual holiday seasons. It would be ideal therefore to fix a time at which such changes are minimal, so that on the one hand the actual enumeration may be facilitated by stable conditions, and on the other the results may be more likely to reflect the average condition of the population about the time of the census, i.e. the census will be representative of that era and intercensal changes will typify broad trends rather than sharp and often transient fluctuations. Choice of census year is largely determined, however, by considerations of continuity and regularity, such as the desirability of maintaining equal decennial intervals from the first census in Britain in 1801 and in America from 1790.

In any particular year the day chosen should be such as to find most people at their usual occupation and in their usual residence, so as to narrow the gap between *de facto* and *de jure* enumerations. While it is desirable to choose a week-end out of the holiday season so as to minimize absences from home for holiday, social, or business reasons, it is also desirable to carry out the enumeration at a time of the year when the weather is not inclement and the evenings are light so as to facilitate the task of the enumerators. There are statistical advantages in choosing a date near the middle of the year so that little adjustment is needed to produce a mid-year estimate. In Britain the choice of a Sunday in April is a compromise which attempts to take account of all these considerations. In 1951 the census was held on 8 April (midnight).

If as in some countries the enumeration is spread over a period of weeks rather than made on a single day, certain problems are created. Some persons who move during the enumeration period may be missed altogether, since the area in which they originally lived may not be canvassed before they move and enumeration may be completed in the area of their new home by the time they arrive; there is equally the possibility of double enumeration. Furthermore, enumerators tend to ignore the nominal date of enumeration and to record information as at the date of the visit; in spite of instructions it is found that some infants are included in the census though born after the census date, and some persons who died after the census date are excluded. The fact that in Britain a householder completes the schedule, instead of giving answers to an interviewer, enables a simultaneous count to be taken in all parts of the country on a single day and thus avoids these difficulties.

De facto *and* de jure *populations*

A person may for purposes of local enumeration be recorded according to usual residence (*de jure*) as in America, or according to where he is at the time of the census (*de facto*) as in Great Britain. For many purposes it is desirable to have *de jure* tabulations; for example, if the local populations are to be used for the calculation of birth and death rates and birth and death registration is on a *de jure* basis as in Great Britain. On the other hand, where the schedule is to be completed by the head of the household, it is clearly simpler to request the enumeration of all persons in the household at the time of the census; it avoids awkward distinctions between permanent and temporary residence, and the special treatment of instances where, for example, a family live in one house in the summer and another in the winter. The *de facto* enumeration is least satisfactory in health resorts and other districts where transient waves of migration periodically occur. In most areas of Britain, since the census takes place everywhere in a single night (so that no person can be enumerated in two places) and at a time of year when holiday movement is minimal, the two populations do not differ greatly.

De facto *and* de jure *Comparison in England and Wales*

The inclusion of the 'usual residence' question at the 1931 and 1951 censuses of England and Wales did provide considerable information about the difference between *de jure* and *de facto* populations. Of the total population enumerated in England and Wales in 1951, 1,013,567 persons (2·3 per cent of the whole population) stated that their 'usual residence' was elsewhere than in the borough, urban or rural district in which they were enumerated. Of this figure 107,600 were foreign or other visitors to England and Wales with their homes outside, while the balance of 905,967 represents the amount of the displacements within the national boundary on census night.

On the basis of the sample investigation of schedules the following very rough distribution was obtained:

Census of England and Wales 1951
(*thousands*)

Total persons enumerated other than at their usual place of residence	1014
Visitors from abroad	108
Home population allegedly displaced	906

The Population Census

Estimated distribution:

Armed Forces on leave from Stations ⎫
Students on leave from residential ⎬ 160
   schools and colleges ⎭
Hospital patients 210
Visitors 416

Probably incorrectly recorded as having a usual residence elsewhere:
Boarders and lodgers 120
                                        906

It should be borne in mind that these figures are not much more than guesses and do no more than indicate the possible order of size of the elements involved. Moreover, these figures relate only to cases where the usual residence is in a different local authority area from that of enumeration. Transfers within the same locality are probably not important except for hospital patients of which there were probably a further 100,000. But it appears likely that, as compared with a *de jure* enumeration, a *de facto* enumeration took *from* households some 300,000 hospital patients and about 400,000 visitors; it virtually restored to their homes 160,000 of Forces personnel and students, though on a *de jure*, i.e. a true *local* population basis, they do not belong there. Only a little more than 100,000 of the 900,000 'visitors' were found to be boarders, including those not stated to be boarders but nevertheless having a workplace local to the place of enumeration and therefore presumed to be boarders.

Areas with relatively large percentage deficiencies in the resident as compared with the enumerated populations, were the administrative counties of the Isle of Wight (2·3), Merionethshire (2·3), Cornwall (1·6), Norfolk (1·6), and Devon (1·5), which include holiday resorts favoured in the springtime as well as institutions and hospitals with patients resident elsewhere and coastal ports with visiting seamen. Within these counties the towns concerned included holiday resorts such as Dawlish (5·7), Lynton (12·7), Sidmouth (5·7), Salcombe (5·4), and Torquay (4·5) in Devon; Ryde (2·6), Sandown–Shanklin (2·4), and Ventnor (6·6) in the Isle of Wight; Looe (5·3), Padstow (6·1), and St. Ives (4·9) in Cornwall; Barmouth (5·3) in Merionethshire; and Sheringham (3·3) and New Hunstanton (2·6) in Norfolk. Other resorts with relatively large proportions of visitors were Bournemouth (4·2), Hastings (1·2), Blackpool (1·0), Southport (0·8), and Eastbourne (0·8).

Areas whose resident population exceeded the enumerated population by relatively large numbers included those with residential schools, and colleges from which large numbers of students were absent on vacation at census day (e.g. Oxford with 8·1 per cent excess and Eton 42·6). There were many areas with Defence Establishments from which personnel were absent at sea, or on leave at census date (e.g. Portsmouth 5·3, Plymouth 5·1).

Errors in Census Data

In spite of publicity about the nature of the questions to be answered on the schedule, and of care taken in the framing of the questions, there may be persons who do not understand the questions, who do not trouble to ascertain the precise answer, or find the official concepts unacceptable. Inaccuracy in a population census cannot be entirely eliminated.

Error in the total number of persons enumerated is probably small. After the 1921 census it was stated (in the Preliminary Report) that a population estimate at census date, built up from the 1911 census population but based only on provisional migration statistics, exceeded the provisional 1921 count, of nearly 38 million, by 33,000, or less than 1 per 1000, though later examination suggested that the difference was a little greater. At the 1931 census the estimate carried through the inter-censal period to 1931 was less than the enumerated population by barely $\frac{1}{2}$ per 1000, though this agreement was admitted to be fortuitously close. After the 1951 census it was stated[4] that an estimate at census date exceeded the final count of nearly 44 million, by 134,000, a difference of less than 3 per 1000, These comparisons are not a true test of census coverage. The estimates involved are built up from the base population with recorded births and deaths and estimated migrants, the latter being much less accurately assessed than the other elements. The comparisons are thus primarily a test of migration estimates, but, since errors in the latter could account for the whole of the differences revealed, they do at least suggest that any error in census coverage is quite trivial, and certainly too slight to be measured by the available standards.

A particular feature of any short fall, and one which commonly occurs and is easy to recognize, is a deficiency of very young infants as compared with those expected from recent birth registrations after allowing for mortality. In 1921, 795,000 infants aged 0 and 826,000 infants aged 1 were enumerated, compared with 819,000 and 848,000 expected from registration records, a total error for the two ages of 46,000. It was thought that the error arose from difficulty in entering on the census schedule newly born children who were unchristened or unnamed. In 1931 therefore a note was inserted to the effect that such infants should be described as 'baby'. As a result the error was reduced to 13,000—11,000 at age 0 and 2,000 at age 1. In 1951 the corresponding deficiencies were 14,000 and 12,000.

The Population Census

When the age distribution of an enumerated population is examined a distinctive type of irregularity often becomes obvious; there are inordinately large numbers returned at ages with certain digital endings, especially 0 and 8, but sometimes at 5. It may be that where there is uncertainty as to age there is a tendency to approximate to the nearest ten or to an even number close to a multiple of ten. In addition there is an error arising from the fact that those within a short period of a birthday tend to return the higher age instead of the attained age. These errors have decreased at successive censuses. At earlier censuses there was some evidence (based on a comparison of the enumerated population with that derived from past births, allowing for mortality and migration) that females tended to understate their ages when approaching middle age. There has been much less evidence of this in recent censuses.

The recording of occupations is subject to errors or defects of three kinds: (i) there is a tendency to elevate the status, e.g. an unskilled labourer may describe himself in terms suggesting special skill, and some persons describe themselves as working in a supervisory capacity when they have no such responsibility: (ii) a man who has been out of work for some time or who has been forced to change his occupation temporarily may quote his former occupation if he is likely to return to it, or his temporary occupation if he thinks it is likely to become his permanent means of livelihood; at a time of widespread unemployment as in 1931 this could seriously misrepresent the true industrial pattern: (iii) some of the older unoccupied or retired persons, especially those who have preferred, and still hope, to continue work, return themselves as engaged in their old occupations. There are many other kinds of possible error, and a full account of them will be found in the General Report of the 1951 census.[7]

The incidence of these errors is not precisely known, and in past censuses could only be surmised from anomalies in the tabulations and from various consistency tests. The general impression is that self-enumeration can be combined with a high standard of accuracy. In many countries it is considered prudent to carry out, in advance of the full enumeration, a small-scale sample test census combined with interviewer call-back to establish not only the nature and incidence of errors but also the reasons for their occurrence. From information thus gathered it is possible, by improvements in schedule design or variations in the form of the questions, to minimize the incidence of errors in the full enumeration. Further, the residual incidence of errors is measured by a sample post-enumeration survey, again conducted by call-back interview. In this way a 'quality label' can be attached to the census tabulations.

B. Benjamin

Programme of Census Reports for England and Wales

The Census 1951, England and Wales, Preliminary Report, published in July 1951 contained a general note on the taking of the census, a brief preliminary statistical commentary, and provisional populations for all local authority areas (counties, boroughs, urban and rural districts).

The Census 1951, Great Britain, One per cent Sample Tables published in two parts in July and November 1952, presented an advance picture of the pattern of the main results. The tables related to Great Britain and, with correspondingly less detail, to various smaller areas according to the size of their populations. The subjects covered were Ages and Marital Condition; Occupations; Industries; Housing, Characteristics and Composition of Private Households; Non-Private Households; Education; Birthplace and Nationality; Fertility; Welsh and Gaelic Languages; together with a Conurbation Supplement.

The 1951 series of *County Reports* comprised most of the statistics of predominantly local interest, namely, populations and acreages of local government, parliamentary and petty sessional areas; private households, the rooms and dwellings in which they lived and the household arrangements possessed by them, together with the complementary record of institutions, etc., housing various categories of non-private population; birthplace and nationality; education; social class; distribution of the local populations according to sex, age and marital condition.

The *Report on Greater London and Five Other Conurbations* published in 1956 gave statistics for the six major conurbations in England and Wales (Greater London, South-East Lancashire, West Midlands, West Yorkshire, Merseyside, Tyneside) and for certain main divisions and subdivisions, as already identified in the *Sample Tables*, generally on the lines of the *County Reports*.

The *Report on Usual Residence and Workplace* published in 1956 contained tables showing the population resident in one specified area and working in another, the units of area being boroughs, urban and rural districts; tables comparing the enumerated census population in local areas, using the same units of area already mentioned, with an alternative allocation based on the statement of usual residence returned on the census schedules, together with the numbers enumerated there who were usually resident outside England and Wales, and tables classifying the latter by country of usual residence and by age.

The volume of *Occupation Tables* (1956) gave statistics of the occupied population based on their personal occupation (classified according to the unit group of the Classification of Occupations, 1950), including statistics of local populations according to the area in which

The Population Census

they were enumerated, and with reference to age, marital condition, industrial status in employment (manager, employer,etc.), social classes, and socio-economic groups.

The volume of *Industry Tables* (1957) gave statistics of the occupied population based on the industrial activity to which their occupations contributed with identification of industrial status categories, age groups, and married women, the industry units being those of the Standard Industrial Classification. Statistics of local populations were based on the area (borough, urban and rural district) containing the place of work. The volume also contained an analysis of each important industry or group of industries showing the principal occupations contributing to the industry.

The *Housing Report* published in 1956 summarized the housing information given in the *County Reports* relating to private households, with a commentary on the figures.

The *General Tables* (1956) mainly comprised summaries of the information given in the *County Reports* on local populations with figures for county court districts in addition, the various categories of non-private population, birthplace and nationality, ages and marital condition, and education.

The *Fertility Report* (1959) gave statistics derived from the questions, put to married women under the age of fifty, on the date of marriage and number of children, with a commentary.

The *General Report* (1958) contained a report on the census operation as a whole, together with a commentary on those fields of census statistics not covered elsewhere, such as the occupation and industry, education, birthplace, and population tables.

REFERENCES

1. BACON, F. W., BENJAMIN, B. and ELPHINSTONE, M. W. D. (1954) *J. Inst. Actu.*, **80**, 141.
2. BRICHLER, M. (1958) *J. R. statist. Soc.*, **A 121**, 160.
3. FRANCE: INSTITUT NATIONAL DE LA STATISTIQUE ET DES ÉTUDES ÉCONOMIQUES (1958). Census 1954. Results of 1/20 Sample, Paris.
4. GENERAL REGISTER OFFICE (1954) *Annual Statistical Review*, 1951 Test. London: H.M.S.O.
5. GENERAL REGISTER OFFICE (1956) *Census of England and Wales, 1951. Housing Report*. London: H.M.S.O.
6. GENERAL REGISTER OFFICE (1958) *Census of England and Wales, 1951. General Report*. London: H.M.S.O.
7. GENERAL REGISTER OFFICE (1959) *Census of England and Wales, 1951. Fertility Report*. London: H.M.S.O.
8. GLICK, P. C. (1957) *American Families*. Census Monograph Series. New York: Wiley.

B. Benjamin

9. HENRY, L. (1953) *Fécondité des mariages*. Paris: Institut National d'Études demographiques, *Travaux*, no. 16.
10. HORSTMANN, K. (1958) Bulletin of the International Statistical Institute, No. 36, Part 2, pp. 289–95. Stockholm.
11. UNITED NATIONS (1958) *Principles and Recommendations for National Population Censuses*. New York: Statistical Office of the U.N., Statistical Papers M 27.
12. FEDERAL STATISTICAL INSTITUTE OF YUGOSLAVIA (1958) *1953 Census. 2 per cent sample Tables*. Federal Statistical Institute, Belgrade.

3

MEASUREMENT OF ABILITIES, ATTITUDES, AND PERSONALITY TRAITS

P. E. Vernon

IT is doubtful whether human psychological attributes can ever be measured, like height or weight, on *ratio scales*, but this does not mean that other types of measurement are not entirely legitimate[2,16], indeed essential, in the scientific description of individuals and of groups. These types include:

1. *Classification* into discreet groups, and frequency counts. For example, much valuable work on the causation of delinquency and the prediction of recidivism has been carried out by observing the numbers of delinquents and controls who come from broken homes, or who truant from school, etc. Most Gallup polls, B.B.C. Audience Research and Government Social Survey and other questionnaire studies likewise provide quantitative information on group differences in terms of percentages of samples which give specific answers.
2. *Ordinal Scales*. Teachers' rankings of their pupils in order of suitability are often used in selecting those most suitable for grammar school education. Ranking of colours or pictures, of school subjects, or of nationalities in order of preference, or of crimes in order of seriousness, have provided useful material for surveys of group attitudes; and these can be statistically analysed by the techniques of Thurstone and Kendall.

3. *Interval Scales.* Here the psychologist sets out to measure some variable—an ability, attitude or trait—by means of a series of questions or items which have been chosen, by item-analysis techniques, as representative of that variable. The number of items which a person can answer correctly (often, though not necessarily, within a given time limit), or the number to which he responds in a specified direction, gives his 'raw score'. A frequency distribution of raw scores in a population sample (e.g. an age group of children, American college students, Army officer candidates, etc.) provides the test 'norms'. The person's standing on the variable is then expressed as a percentile rank, or some derivative 'standard score' such as the Intelligence Quotient with a fixed mean and standard deviation.

This is the type of test with which this chapter is mainly concerned. However, a variety of other measurements are commonly employed in psychology, e.g.:

speed of simple reaction time, speed and accuracy in motor performances, output measures in industry;

just noticeable differences in pitch, weight, etc., as tested by the well-established psychophysical techniques;

electrical conductance of the skin (psycho-galvanic reflex), respiratory rhythms, eye-blink rate;

subjective judgements or ratings, of self or others, on complex variables which are less susceptible to objective testing, including examination marks or grades, merit ratings in industry, etc.

The raw-score distributions for most of the tests so far mentioned approximate more or less closely to the normal curve of error. Psychometrists—that is, psychologists concerned with mental measurement—tend too readily, perhaps, to assume that all psychological attributes are normally distributed, and thus to select their test items in such a way as to enhance normality. But the assumption is a useful one in that it makes it possible to add or average test scores as though they were physical units, and to apply techniques of correlational or variance analysis.

A psychological test is not a miraculous technique for finding out something that could not be detected in any other way. Just as in everyday life we judge a child's intelligence from his conversation, or a man's sociability from his behaviour in social situations, so the tester takes samples of the person's behaviour or thinking, but in a more scientific or controlled manner. In particular, three characteristics are important:

Measurement of Abilities

Objectivity: the questions or materials used, the conditions of application and timing are uniform, and the recording and scoring of responses are designed to eliminate any personal influence of the tester.

Reliability or Error Variance[4, 6]: parallel forms of the test (or subsections or separate items) should inter-correlate highly, showing that they measure the same variable (coefficient of equivalence); and the results should be consistent on two or more occasions (coefficient of stability).

Validity: the extent to which the test measures the variable or construct it is supposed to measure it distinguished from reliability. Sometimes validity is self-evident from the content, as in a test of arithmetical attainment (logical or content validity). More often evidence is sought by correlations with external criteria, as when mechanical aptitude test results are compared with later proficiency in a mechanical occupation (predictive validity). Or the test is compared with a large battery or series of overlapping tests, and from the clustering of the correlations the underlying variables or factors are deduced (factorial and construct validity). Thus a test may be shown by factor analysis to embody so much '*g*' or general intelligence, so much verbal, spatial, numerical, or other types of ability, an ability specific to that test alone, and an error component. The technique of factor analysis, first developed by Spearman and greatly extended by Burt in Britain and Thurstone and others in America, plays a vital function in psychometrics by helping to classify variables and to show which are consistent and distinguishable dimensions of intellect and personality.[11, 18]

Types of Test

The table below lists the main varieties of psychological tests, with well-known examples of each. * The best descriptive textbooks available to date are all by American psychometrists—Anastasi,[1] Cronbach,[4] and Freeman.[5] In British psychology, tests are regarded as relatively coarse research tools, and are generally used as supplementary rather than as main sources of information.

1. *Intelligence tests:*	individual, mainly verbal—Binet-Simon, Terman
	individual, mixed—Wechsler-Bellevue Merrill
	group tests, verbal—Moray House, Otis, Simplex
	group tests, non-verbal—Progressive Matrices
2. *Tests of other mental factors, diagnostic cognitive tests:*	Thurstone's Primary Mental Abilities
	Vigotsky Blocks
	Ishihara card test of colour-blindness

* A complete list of tests published in Britain in 1956 is given by Vernon[12]. Critical reviews and fuller details of most current American and British tests may be found in Buros's series of *Mental Measurement Yearbooks*[3].

P. E. Vernon

3.	*Attainments tests:*	Burt's and Schonell's tests for educational guidance
		Moray House English and Arithmetic tests
		Stanford Achievement tests
		Co-operative and E.T.S. tests at college level
4.	*Aptitude tests:*	Bennett—Mechanical Comprehension
		Seashore—Tests of musical talent
5.	*Interest tests:*	Strong's Vocational Interest Blank
		Kuder Preference Record
6.	*Attitude tests:*	Thurstone's scales
		Eysenck—radicalism-conservatism test
7.	*Personality inventories:*	Minnesota Multiphasic Personality Inventory
		Maudsley Medical Questionnaire
8.	*Temperament, personality and character tests:*	Sheldon's somatotypes
		Cattell—personality factor tests
		Hartshorne and May—honesty tests
		Personality ratings
9.	*Projective techniques:*	Rorschach inkblot test
		Murray—Thematic Apperception

Individual Intelligence Tests

The first scale of mental assessment was developed by Binet and Simon in 1905, for the purpose of segregating virtually ineducable children in Paris for special schooling. It consisted of a series of short, simple oral tasks, each chosen to be typical of the mental development of average children of a specified chronological age, for example:

How old are you?
Name these colours.
Describe this picture.

An 8-year-old child, say, who could only accomplish the tasks typical of 5-year-olds is said to have a Mental Age of 5, and is 3 years retarded.

The scale has been widely translated, revised, and extended, for example by Burt in England and Terman in America. The best-known versions are the Stanford-Binet scale (1916) and the Terman-Merrill scale (1937).[9] The latter covers Mental Ages from 2 to superior adult by two parallel series of 122 graded tasks, including vocabulary, reasoning problems, short-term memory, recognition of absurdities, and—for younger children—problems based on play materials. Terman also introduced the Intelligence Quotient, that is the ratio of Mental to Chronological Age (multiplied by 100), as giving an approximately constant index of relative advancement or retardation. Since there seemed to be no further improvement in performance with age beyond 14 to 16 years, adult I.Qs were obtained by dividing Mental Age by some constant figure, e.g. 15. However this 'classical I.Q.' was unsatisfactory in many respects: large variations occurred in dispersion of

Measurement of Abilities

I.Qs at different ages, and M.As above 15 were quite arbitrary. Hence it has been abandoned in more modern tests in favour of standard-score or 'deviation I.Qs'.[13]

Levels of intelligence are conventionally designated as follows (when the dispersion or standard deviation is 15):

I.Q.	Proportion of population	Designation
140 & over	$\frac{1}{2}$%	Very superior, 'genius'
130–139	2%	Superior
110–129	22$\frac{1}{2}$%	Above average
90–109	50%	Average
70–89	22$\frac{1}{2}$%	Dull and backward
60–69	2%	'Defective'
Below 60	$\frac{1}{2}$%	'Imbecile and Idiot'

It is recognized, however, that these are not distinct classes, and that such terms as 'genius' and 'defective' imply certain personality qualities, not merely high or low I.Q. Moreover the distribution is seldom as accurately symmetrical as this; in particular the pathological or 'exogenous' defectives (resulting from brain injury or endocrine abnormality) produce an excess at the bottom end of the curve with I.Q.s in the 0–50 range.

Technically superior instruments are the Wechsler Adult Intelligence Scale (WAIS) and Wechsler Intelligence Scale for Children (WISC), with separate norms for age groups from 5 years up to 70+ years.[13] Each consists of a series of verbal and non-verbal or performance sub-tests, thus yielding distinct Verbal and Performance I.Qs. Other tests based on pictures, form-boards, block patterns, etc., which are often used in an attempt to offset the considerable verbal bias of the Terman-Merrill scale, include the Drever-Collins or the Arthur scales, the Porteus Maze test, Goodenough's Draw-a-Man test, and Kohs' Block Designs.[1, 5] Some of these have been shown to measure a spatial ability or 'k-factor' which is relevant to aptitude for technical jobs. But for the most part they are merely rather unreliable tests of general intelligence, which certainly cannot justify the claim to be 'culture-free'. Several scales are available for pre-school children, even down to the first few weeks of life, though in so far as these rely on sensori-motor functions, and early play and speech, they have little predictive value for later intelligence as evidenced in tests of concept development and thinking skills. Many of the best-known intelligence tests are of American origin, and though adapted to English usage, they have seldom been adequately restandardized with British norms.

65

P. E. Vernon

Group Intelligence Tests.[6, 13, 47]

All the above tests must be given individually by a trainer or examiner if their results are to be trustworthy, and they may occupy an hour or more per person. With the entry of America into World War I in 1917, printed booklets of questions, the answers to which could be written by large groups at a time, were introduced; and the recruits' scores were shown to give useful predictions of their trainability for skilled jobs. Most group test items are couched in 'new-type' or 'multiple-choice' form, in order to reduce the amount of writing and to render the scoring wholly objective. Thus the Army Alpha (verbal) test contained Analogies, Synonyms, Comprehension and other sub-tests, each given with its own time limit, of which the following are specimen items. The right answer to each question is to be underlined.

GUN is to SHOOT as KNIFE is to: run cut hat bird
BOOK is to WRITER as STATUE is to: sculptor liberty picture state
allow permit (mean the) SAME OPPOSITE
effeminate virile (mean the) SAME OPPOSITE

The Army Beta test, for non-English-speaking recruits, was constructed from pictorial and diagrammatic materials. The modern group verbal test, of which hundreds are available, typically contains some fifty to one hundred varied items, mixed together and given with an overall time-limit of twenty to sixty minutes. Well-known examples include Cattell's Scale III and Heim's AH5 (partly non-verbal) for superior adults, and the Moray House and National Foundation for Educational Research tests which are issued annually for testing 11-year children for grammar school entrance. Such tests depend too largely on capacity to read the items and instructions to be suitable much below the age of 9–10 years; but some pictorial or non-verbal group tests can be applied as far down as 6–7 years, and others can be administered to groups of children orally. Raven's Progressive Matrices test, consisting of non-verbal reasoning problems, is one of the most widely used among Army recruits, mental hospital patients, and children. Thorndike has shown that a 20-item vocabulary test, which gives a quick estimate of verbal intelligence, can not only be given to an adult group in five to ten minutes, but can also be applied in doorstep interviews by Gallup poll interviewers to representative samples of the total population.

Most of these tests show a high short-term reliability (stability) coefficient of around 0·93, though the correlations between similar tests over five-year periods of primary or secondary schooling drop to approximately 0·70. This means that the majority of children, on repeated retesting, tend to stay in the same zone ($\pm$ 10 I.Q. points);

Measurement of Abilities

but some 17 per cent may fluctuate 15 points or more, and about 1 in 100 by as much as 30 to 40 points. Nevertheless many researches have shown that the I.Q. gives valuable predictions of general educability, and of the level of vocation for which a person is suited, though correlations with success in secondary school or university courses or with occupational proficiency are moderate to low. Thus the chief uses of intelligence tests are for educational and occupational guidance, and for surveys of classroom, school, or other groups. No consistent sex differences are observed, though girls generally have slight superiority in linguistic and memory tests, boys in inductive reasoning and in any tests involving non-verbal or numerical materials. Scores seem to begin to decline with age soon after cessation of schooling, though this applies mainly to speeded and to non-verbal tests, and increases are observed, particularly on tests of verbal comprehension, well into the 30s and 40s among persons in higher-grade occupations.

Correlations between parent and child I.Qs average close to 0·50, and between child I.Q. and parental socio-economic class 0·35. Thus the mean I.Q. of professional adults is about 130, and of their children 115; that of unskilled labourers about 90 and their children 95. At the same time there is such a wide dispersion within classes that the largest number (not the largest proportion) of very high I.Q. children are drawn from clerical and skilled working-class families. Such findings are sometimes alleged to show that intelligence tests merely reflect a child's absorption of middle-class culture. Thus Davis, Eells, and their co-workers at Chicago have tried to devise a test from pictorial materials which will be free from class-bias, though with little success. On the other hand there is ample evidence from studies of identical twins reared apart and of foster children, and from comparisons of groups who have received different amounts and kinds of schooling, that the I.Q. is to some extent affected by upbringing and environment.* The importance of genetic determinants is demonstrated both by the small but significant correlations between the intelligence of orphans and the social class of parents who have not reared them, and by the wide differences (rather than the resemblances) often observed between siblings, and between children and their parents. Thus we can best interpret intelligence as ultimately dependent on a multifactorial genetic potentiality for the building-up of complex mental processes; but its actual expression in daily life or in test performances also depends on

* The further finding that scores can be appreciably raised by coaching and practice on similar test materials is irrelevant, though it does mean that test results can only be interpreted in the light of the previous experience the individual may have had with that kind of test. Such gains are limited in amount, and are achieved quite rapidly, suggesting that they represent familiarization with the 'mechanics' of the particular test, not an improvement in all-round intellectual ability.

67

P. E. Vernon

the extent to which this potentiality is stimulated by appropriate experience and upbringing. It is illegitimate, therefore, to attempt to use intelligence tests—even non-verbal ones—for genetic comparisons between racial, social-class, or other groups which differ widely in environmental stimulation.[12]

Differential and Diagnostic Tests

Intelligence cannot readily be identified with any single mental faculty, but rather comprises efficient mental functioning in general; it represents a group of overlapping capacities, chief of which—as Spearman showed—are abstraction and the grasping of relationships. Many American psychologists, however, prefer to break down this vague global entity into a series of separate factors; and Thurstone, Guilford, and others have published sets of tests designed to provide, not a single I.Q., but a profile of scores for V (verbal comprehension), R (reasoning) or I (indication), W (word fluency), S (spatial ability), N (number facility), M (rote memory), etc.[1] In practice, however, the scores tend to inter-correlate rather highly, and it is the $V + R$, or general verbal intelligence component, which is of most value for educational and vocational purposes.

From a very different starting-point, clinical psychologists also, particularly those working with adult mental hospital patients, try to obtain fuller insight into abnormalities of cognitive functioning by applying more varied diagnostic tests and observing qualitative differences of performance, than may be obtained from a Wechsler or group test I.Q.[8] In the Wechsler scale itself, some sub-tests are notably more affected by ageing, by brain injury, and possibly by certain psychotic conditions, than others.[13] The Babcock scale for mental deterioration likewise contrasts functions which are liable to impairment with vocabulary which is supposed to show the 'crystallized' or maximum level of intelligence achieved. Eysenck and his co-workers have shown that speed of performance at simple intellectual tasks, together with a number of other sensory and perceptual functions, may be differentially affected by psychosis and neurosis. The Bender Visuo-motor Gestalt test, the Hanfman-Kasanin or Vigotsky tests of concept formation, are others which are claimed to give useful diagnostic indications, though there is a serious dearth of scientific evidence regarding the validity of these and other clinical instruments.

Educational Attainment Tests

In 1921 Burt published a series of tests, standardized for children from 5 to 15, for measuring various aspects of reading, spelling, arithmetic, handwriting, composition, and drawing—the latter consisting of standard specimens by comparison with which a child's product could be assigned a composition or drawing age (quality scales). Schonell's more recent series includes tests for diagnosing types of backwardness in reading and arithmetic.[7] American publishers provide a number of batteries of 'new-type' tests in all the main school subjects for evaluating individual or class progress at each grade level from primary to college (e.g. the Stanford Achievement tests).[3] Frequently these have separate answer sheets which can be scored by I.B.M. machines. In this country the Moray House English and arithmetic tests are widely used at 11 years because of their ease and objectivity of scoring; and the National Foundation for Educational Research has begun to issue standardized tests for this and other age levels.

Objective attainment tests are excellent for survey purposes (cf. for example the Ministry of Education's surveys of illiteracy among school-leavers). However most examining bodies in Britain, unlike America, do not allow that new-type questions can cover the broader, non-factual aspects of attainment, despite the evidence as to the unreliability of essays or other more conventional forms of examination.[12] Perhaps the most serious weakness of objective attainment tests arises whenever they are used competitively, namely the tendency among the schools to coach, and the pupils or students to study, for the particular kinds of questions contained in the tests and to neglect topics, or aspects of attainment, which are not included.

Aptitude Tests

In the early days of industrial psychology, much work was done in developing batteries of tests to measure the sensory, motor, and temperamental qualities shown, by job analysis, to be required for particular jobs.[10] During World War II, also, an elaborate series of psychomotor tests was shown by the United States Army Air Force to contribute to the selection of recruits suitable for training as pilots. Relatively little use is made of such tests nowadays, partly because of full employment and Trade Union restrictions on recruitment and promotion in industry, partly because greater importance is attached to good training, work methods, and social relations within the working group; but also because such tests seldom show consistently higher validities than do written or oral tests of trade knowledge and paper-and-pencil tests of intelligence, mechanical comprehension and information, clerical ability, etc. These tests of more general aptitudes are more useful, also, for vocational guidance of school-leavers, and for allocating recruits in the Services to suitable types of work or 'job-families'. Published batteries include the General Aptitude Test Battery (United

P. E. Vernon

States Employment Service) and the Differential Aptitude Tests (Psychological Corporation).[1, 3] Spatial judgement tests are sometimes applied in selection for technical education or engineering apprenticeships. Other tests of specialized abilities include the Seashore and the Wing tests for musical talent, and code-learning tests of aptitude for Morse receiving.

Personality Testing

Here there are much greater difficulties since, as Cronbach[4] points out, we wish to sample habitual responses rather than maximal performances, and such responses are greatly affected by the attitudes of the subject and the kind of impression he wants to convey. Moreover emotional and conative characteristics—traits, attitudes, interests, etc. —are less consistent and distinctive than abilities, more variable in different situations, and often influenced by unconscious and irrational motivational forces.[20]

The most practically useful tests are questionnaires dealing with interests in different vocations, or with attitudes towards social issues (e.g. the Church, anti-Semitism, educational policies, etc.).

Interest Tests. Strong's Vocational Interest Blank consists of long lists of occupations, school subjects, leisure activities, etc., which the subject checks according as he likes, dislikes, or feels indifferent. Scoring is based on comparing the pattern of his responses with those of groups engaged in some forty different occupations; and these scores have been shown (in America) to be highly stable over many years, and predictive of the likelihood of entering these occupations. More general types of interest may be assessed by asking for preferences in a series of concrete situations, as in the Allport-Vernon-Lindzey Study of Values, and the Kuder Preference Record. For example:

To what extent do the following famous persons interest or **attract** you? (Rank them in order).

(a) Florence Nightingale   The answers have been shown to
(b) Napoleon   indicate humanitarian, power-
(c) Henry Ford   seeking, economic, and intellectual
(d) Charles Darwin   interests or values, respectively.

Tests of information or general knowledge about scientific, artistic or other matters are sometimes used to give more objective indices of interest, and Cattell has experimented with a variety of other tests designed to reflect the influence of interests and attitudes.[15]

Measurement of Abilities

Attitude Scales.[17] It has been found that the proportion of people who state that they favour a given political or other policy varies markedly with the way in which the question is formulated, and the stereotypes it arouses. More accurate measurements of attitudes, at least towards well-crystallized issues, may be obtained by scales containing twenty to thirty questions dealing with different manifestations of the attitude, and either ranging from strongly 'pro-' to strongly 'anti-' (so-called Thurston-type), or else providing multiple-choice responses covering 'pro-' and 'anti-' reactions (Likert-type). Guttman has demonstrated that short tests of a few items, carefully chosen by his scaling technique, will give reliable results.[16] Much use has been made of these various scales in research into the morale and other attitudes of industrial employees, Army recruits, teachers, and pupils, and even in cross-cultural studies of different nationalities. They can also be applied in assessing the effectiveness of various types of propaganda or indoctrination.

Personality Tests and Ratings

Questionnaires. In answering attitude scales, most people will naturally express their 'public' rather than their 'private' views, and their responses will not necessarily tell much about their actual behaviour. Even more subject to intentional or unconscious distortion are the many questionnaires which claim to measure emotional instability, neuroticism, extraversion, rigidity, and other personal traits.[20] Among the most widely used in America are the Bernreuter Personality Inventory, the Guilford-Martin scales, and the Minnesota Multiphasic Personality Inventory. Only the last of these is accepted as a useful instrument among British clinical psychologists. The typical responses of a number of psychopathological groups—schizophrenics, hysterics, depressives, etc.—to the 532 MMPI items have been established. Thus a mental hospital patient's responses are scored by comparison with these group norms, and the pattern of his schizophrenic, hysteric, and other scores, though certainly not providing a mechanical diagnosis, can be of value to the experienced clinician. Under good motivational conditions, other questionnaires have proved useful, e.g. in guidance work with college students and in screening potential neurotics in the Army, but more often their results seem to be quite untrustworthy and misleading.

Personality Ratings. In the absence of valid and objective tests of temperamental or personality qualities, gradings or ratings on specially constructed scales are often used in assessing the traits of school pupils (for Record Card purposes), in industry (merit ratings), and in the Armed Services. Here too there are difficulties. Different raters adopt varying standards, e.g. in rating on an A to E scale, though this is partly met by defining each step on the scale in concrete terms ('graphic' scales). When several apparently different traits are to be rated, little distinction is made among them, showing that all ratings largely reflect the rater's good or bad overall impression: this tendency is known as the 'halo effect'. Differences in interpretation and unwitting bias are shown, too, by the generally low agreement between different raters of the same individuals, particularly when their relations to these individuals differ. Thus there may be virtually no correlation between ratings of officer candidates for leadership by their peers and by superior officers. Nevertheless, provided this subjective bias is borne in mind, the combined assessments of several raters can be of great value in research on personality as well as for practical purposes. Peer ratings or nominations are used, for example, in Moreno's sociometric technique, where the social structure of a group of workers or pupils can be mapped out by asking which of their fellows they would prefer to work alongside.

Objective Tests. That physical characteristics such as hair colour and shape of the skull or features are quite valueless as signs of temperament or personality qualities has been fully demonstrated. However, the type of bodily physique, particularly when assessed by Sheldon's morphological indices, has shown interesting relationships to personality characteristics, for example in researches at the Warneford Hospital, Oxford, though they are less marked than is claimed by Sheldon himself. The psychological significance is also obscure of electroencephalographic patterns, of measures derived from the psychogalvanic reflex, and of other physiological variables. A variety of simple sensori-motor tests of perseveration, rigidity, oscillation (instability), extraversion-introversion, and other traits have been proposed, but have usually failed to yield consistent results in extended researches. Nevertheless two of the most prominent workers in the field of personality, Cattell[15] in America and Eysenck[18] at the Maudsley Hospital, London, are strong advocates of objective tests. The latter claims that they can measure degrees of neuroticism, extraversion-introversion, and psychoticism, and thus be used for psychiatric diagnosis; while the former has developed batteries of tests for assessing a dozen or more principal dimensions of personality.

If we regard a test simply as a sample of the behaviour that can be classified under a certain ability or trait, then more realistic samples would be expected to yield more valid tests. Thus Hartshorne and May[19] and others have successfully measured such traits as honesty and persistence by putting children into real-life situations which elicit honest or dishonest, or persistent, behaviour. Nevertheless it is still found that reactions tend to be highly specific, that people may be honest in one situation, dishonest in another, depending presumably on the way they interpret these situations. Many psychologists, therefore, have given up the search for direct tests of personality traits, and favour the following, more indirect, approaches.

Qualitative Observations and Situational Tests of Personality.[20] When a subject is doing a difficult formboard or other performance test of intelligence, he may display his caution or impulsiveness, persistence, sociability, and other traits in a more natural manner than in situations designed to yield direct samples. Observations made in such situations are, of course, subjective. The Porteus Maze test, however, yields a quality or Q-score which has been found to differentiate quite well between delinquent and normal children. Gestures, style of speech and handwriting, and other 'expressive movements' likewise show some promise of providing useful information about underlying personality trends, though attempts to validate graphological diagnoses of character have usually proved disappointing.

More elaborate are the situational or group observation techniques developed by the War Office and Civil Service Selection Board in the 1940s, where a small group of candidates is put in a situation similar to that which they may meet in the job, e.g. moving a heavy object over a wall, or running a committee discussion. Judgements are made by observers, not so much of their skill, as of their social reactions and leadership qualities. Similar methods have been adapted in the selection of industrial executives. While these are highly dependent on the experience of the observer, and the tendency among subjects to 'play a part', they at least yield richer samples of personal behaviour than does the highly artificial and unreliable employment interview.

Projective Techniques.[14] These constitute another approach which, under the influence of Gestalt psychology and psychoanalysis, tries to throw light on dynamic trends in the subject's personality without resort to tests of isolated traits. In a free or unstructured situation (unlike the ability test or personality questionnaire where a restricted range of responses is allowed), he will unwittingly express or project his personality characteristics. For example, in Murray's Thematic Apperception test he is shown a set of somewhat indefinite pictures, and makes up a story as to what is happening in each. Most widely used of all is the Rorschach ink-blot test: the subject states what he sees in each of ten rather complex blots, and his responses, after classification by type of detail chosen, by the relative influence of shape, colour, shading, or apparent movement, and by content, are claimed to reveal both his qualities of intellect and his emotional make-up. Jung's Word Association test, and its derivatives such as Sentence Completion, free drawings and painting and—among children—play activities also belong under this heading. There is fairly strong evidence of the usefulness of such instruments in clinical work with neurotic patients, but their value in diagnosing personality characteristics among normal children or adults is much more dubious. Though relatively non-fakeable, they seem to depend greatly on the subject's temporary mood and his attitude to the testing situation; and the interpretation of responses, particularly in terms of unconscious personality dynamics, is highly subjective.

REFERENCES

A. *Abilities.*

1. ANASTASI, A., *Psychological Testing*, New York: Macmillan, (1954).
2. BANKS, C. & BURT, C. (1953) 'Statistical analysis in educational psychology'. *Current Trends in British Psychology* (edit. C. A. Mace & P. E. Vernon), 152–71, London: Methuen.
3. BUROS, O. K. *The Mental Measurement Year-books.* Highland Park, N.J., 1941; Rutgers University Press, 1949; Gryphon Press, 1953.
4. CRONBACH, L. J., *Essentials of Psychological Testing*, New York: Harper.
5. FREEMAN, F. S. (1955) *Theory and Practice of Psychological Testing.* Revised edn. New York; Holt.
6. GULLIKSEN, H. (1950) *Theory of Mental Tests.* New York: Wiley.
7. SCHONELL, F. J., and SCHONELL, F. E. (1951) *Diagnostic and Attainment Testing*, Edinburgh: Oliver & Boyd.
8. SEMEONOFF, B., & TRIST, E. L. (1958) *Diagnostic Performance Tests*: *A Manual for use with Adults.* London: Tavistock Publications.
9. TERMAN, L. M., & MERRILL, M. A., (1937) *Measuring Intelligence*, Cambridge, Mass. Houghton Mifflin; London: Harrap.
10. TIFFIN, J., (1952) *Industrial Psychology*, 3rd edn., Englewood Cliffs, N.J.: Prentice Hall.
11. VERNON, P. E., (1950) *The Structure of Human Abilities*, London: Methuen; New York: Wiley.
12. VERNON, P. E., (1956) *The Measurement of Abilities*, 2nd ed. London: University of London Press.
13. WECHSLER, D., (1941) *The Measurement of Adult Intelligence.* Baltimore: William & Wilkins.

B. *Personality.*

14. BELL, J. E., (1948) *Projective Techniques*, New York & London: Longmans.
15. CATTELL, R. B., (1958) *Personality and Motivation Structure and Measurement*, New York & London: McGraw-Hill.
16. COOMBS, C. H., (1953) 'Theory and methods of social measurement'. *Research Methods in the Behavioural Sciences* (ed. L. Festinger & D. Katz), pp. 471–535. New York: Dryden Press; London: Staples (1954).
17. EYSENCK, H. J., (1953) 'Social Attitude Research'. *Current Trends in British Psychology* (ed. C. A. Mace & P. E. Vernon), pp. 205–22. London: Methuen.

Measurement of Abilities

18. EYSENCK, H. J., (1953) *The Structure of Human Personality*, London: Methuen; New York: Wiley.
19. HARTSHORNE, H., MAY, M. A., & SHUTTLEWORTH, F. K. (1928–30) *Studies in Deceit. Studies in Service and Self-Control. Studies in the Organization of Character.* New York: Macmillan.
20. VERNON, P. E., (1953) *Personality Tests and Assessments.* London: Methuen.

4

EXPERIMENTAL STUDIES
OF SMALL SOCIAL GROUPS

Michael Argyle

INTRODUCTION

DURING the last twenty years the experimental study of small social groups has developed very rapidly with the force of a minor social movement. New research techniques have been invented and a very large number of carefully planned experiments performed. It is the aim of this chapter to describe the main research designs, methods of experimental manipulation, and measuring instruments which have been found most successful in this area.

Although a number of the examples of small group experiments cited here are British, this is in a way misleading, since the main impetus of research has undoubtedly been in the U.S.A., particularly in the laboratories of Michigan[9] and Harvard.[6] The British work has largely been carried out in the American tradition. On the other hand there is something of an independent British tradition in some of the applied aspects of small group research, such as the study of industrial work groups and of therapy groups.

This chapter attempts to instruct the reader in how to carry out various kinds of small group experiments. Reference is made to more detailed discussions of particular points as well as to examples of all the techniques described. Much of the published work is to be found in the periodicals *Human Relations* and the *Journal of Abnormal and Social Psychology*; reviews of the literature can be found in the two books cited above, and in Kelley and Thibaut[24] and Argyle.[1]

Michael Argyle

By a small social group is meant a number of people, generally less than fifteen or twenty, who talk, work, or do something together. Such groups have been studied in all kinds of real-life settings, as has been indicated, and there has been an assumption that the same laws of behaviour should hold true for all. To some extent this hope has been justified, and a number of generalizations have been confirmed in a wide variety of groups, though other studies have shown that the content of the group task influences the pattern of interaction. Many studies have been conducted in a laboratory setting, often without trying to simulate any particular real-life situation, in the attempt to discover the empirical laws governing small group behaviour in general.

Part of the excitement about small group experiments is due to the fact that relatively precise and rigorous scientific procedures are here being applied to an order of events hitherto studied only by vaguer and less satisfactory methods. There is, however, a serious difficulty: the more rigorous and controlled the experimental conditions, the more artificial and remote from real life is the behaviour studied, while the nearer to real life it is, the less rigorous tends to be the research. Different investigators adopt different attitudes to this dilemma; some carry out rigorous, artificial research and claim that they are interested in 'laboratory behaviour'; others study real life and use designs and measurements which give the greatest rigour possible under the conditions available. We shall return to this problem when discussing different experimental designs.

Much experimental work here, as in other parts of the social sciences, is planned to test predictions from theories. The experimenter has to exercise his originality and ingenuity to devise a situation and task where the predictions can be tested satisfactorily.[16] The dimensions of behaviour to be measured are generally built in to theories following previous exploratory or methodological research. For instance it was found by Jennings[23] that sociometric preferences* for leisure activities were quite different from those for work. These two aspects of sociometric choice may become embodied in subsequent theoretical statements, such as that of Homans.[21]

The Design of Small Group Experiments

In this section the relative merits of different types of small group experiment will be considered, and examples of each cited. The majority conducted so far have been *laboratory experiments*, using artifiical groups engaged on tasks simulating real life activities. Some laboratory experiments are more realistic than others, and it is possible by means of skilful deception to disguise the aims of the experiment, or even the

* See page 85.

78

Experimental Studies

fact that it is an experiment. Lippitt,[27] for example, invited the boys who were his subjects to join a club for making masks, and so far as they were concerned that is what they did. The observers can be concealed behind one-way screens, and a plausible but untrue account can be given of why the group is meeting. The ethics of all this will be considered later. On the other hand, the less realistic the experimental arrangements are, the less does one feel able to extrapolate the results to real-life situations, and furthermore one is less able to bring strong social forces to bear, so that there is a danger that the experimental manipulation will be ineffective.

Most laboratory experiments compare the behaviour of groups in different experimental conditions; the way these manipulations are produced will be discussed in the next section. In each condition there must be enough groups for the inter-condition differences to be statistically significant; this depends of course on the size of the differences and the intra-condition variation, but usually between ten and thirty are used in each condition. In many of these experiments no attempt is made at matching the groups that are being compared; subjects are simply allocated alternately to groups in different conditions, and randomization replaces matching. In a few experiments groups have been matched in pairs, either on structural aspects such as cohesiveness, or on the characteristics of the individual members. When matching is used, it is possible to obtain significant results with a smaller number of groups.

As an example of a laboratory experiment we shall give Deutsch's[12] study which was set up to test an elaborate set of predictions following from Deutsch's theory of co-operation and competition. Ten groups of students were set up as part of their work for a psychology course at the Massachusetts Institute of Technology, and their grades for the course depended on performance in the groups, thus providing a real-life incentive for the experiment. The groups met five times for three hours each, and were divided into two sets of five, matched in pairs. Five of the groups were placed in the competitive condition, being told that their grades would depend on individual performance; five were placed in the co-operative condition, and were told that all members of each group would receive the same grade, depending on the group's performance as a whole. There were two kinds of activity at each meeting: solving logical puzzles and discussing human relations problems. Observers recorded the behaviour of each group and made overall ratings; questionnaires were filled in by subjects after each meeting.

In other experiments the emphasis has been on individual differences rather than on experimental conditions. Recent research has seen an increased interest in personality mechanisms and processes in group behaviour. It is clearly best if the social situation is standardized for every subject, so that individual differences are the only source of variance. Crutchfield[11] has designed an experimental situation which does this admirably. Groups of five subjects are screened off from one another and make a series of perceptual judgements from the same display. Each subject presses a button to indicate his choice, and this is believed to be shown on a panel in front of the other group members. In fact every subject receives the same signals and his choices are simply recorded for later analysis. On certain crucial trials the signals suggest to the subjects that they are the last in order to make their judgements, and that the four other subjects have apparently come unanimously to an incorrect decision. The point of the experiment is to compare those who yield in these crucial trials with the non-yielders, on various personality measures.

In another kind of experiment the structure of the group as a whole may be the variable which is manipulated. Mohanna and Argyle[28], following earlier work by Leavitt, compared groups where the member in the central position of the communication system was popular or unpopular. Sixteen groups of five boys were selected in which one of the five had been chosen by at least three of the others in a previous sociometric survey; sixteen further groups were selected in which one boy was not chosen by any of the others. Screens were arranged so that a 'central' member was in touch with all the other four but these were unable to communicate with each other: it was the central member who was popular or unpopular. Communication about the problem took place by means of message slips, which were analysed later. The principal measures were the number of messages and the time taken to come to a solution in the different conditions.

The difficulties of artificiality encountered with laboratory experimentation are avoided in the field experiment. Here different experimental treatments are given to existing groups apparently as part of routine administration; the subjects should not realize that an experiment is taking place. The difficulties with field experiments are practical ones: it is necessary to establish a sufficiently good relationship with administrators to be able to persuade them to carry out the desired manipulations, and these must be kept secret from most of the people concerned. It is essential, furthermore, to find control groups sufficiently well matched to eliminate the effects of other changes during the experiment, yet which will not be contaminated by the manipulations of the experimental groups. An example of a field experiment is Bavelas's study of group decisions by industrial workers.[17] Twenty-four groups of size 4–12 participated in decisions about levels of output and set new production goals. Their output was compared with that of a number of similar groups who received no experimental manipulation, over a period of four months. It was found that the output of the experimental groups rose by 18 per cent, that of the control groups not at all. However, since the experimental groups were also provided with knowledge of results, it is not clear how much of the increase was due to the variable of group decision.

There is another danger in this kind of experiment, sometimes known as the 'Hawthorne effect'. If the experimental groups get the idea that they are receiving special attention, it is found that industrial output tends to increase for this reason alone. This can be avoided in field experiments by performing some manipulation in all experimental conditions or by not letting people know about the investigation.

Better still, it is sometimes possible to make use of administrative decisions which were being made in any case, and will not have aroused the suspicions of the subjects. This is called a *natural experiment*. It is unfortunately extremely rare for such routine changes to meet scientific requirements, but it does sometimes happen. Feldman[13] reports on what took place when twenty-two industrial foremen were changed round so that the foremen of high-output sections went to low-output ones, and vice versa. It was found that the rank-order of output depended on the foremen, not on the sections, and that changes of from 6 to 18 per cent followed the change.

Another type of research design often used in field studies of small groups is that of statistical comparisons of existing groups. Although this is strictly not an 'experimental' design, it can conveniently be included here. A number of existing groups are selected, and the statistical relations between two or more measures of the groups are studied. A simple example is the relation between size and satisfaction with membership. It is desirable to hold constant those variables which are not under investigation, and might otherwise confuse the results. For example, Argyle, Gardner and Cioffi,[3] following up previous work by Katz at Michigan, studied the efficiency of ninety work groups in relation to the behaviour of the foremen. The ninety groups were divided into sets of two to five groups equated for the section of the factory they worked in, the foreman's supervisor, the kind of work, and the incentive system. Statistical relations between style of supervision and various efficiency measures were then examined.

One of the difficulties about these statistical comparisons is that it is often not clear which is the direction of causation. In an experiment, it is obvious that the manipulated experimental variable must be the cause of any changes which occur; in a statistical design, either of two correlated variables could be the cause of the other, or both might be independent effects of a third. In some cases one of the variables is known not to have varied, in which case it must be causal. For instance, in the study by Festinger, Schachter and Back[16] of a housing estate, a

Michael Argyle

connexion was found between sociometric choice and physical proximity of apartments. Given that no choice or changing of housing was allowed it follows that proximity was cause, not effect.

Manipulation of the Experimental Variables

The most usual way to manipulate small groups experimentally is to vary *the pre-experimental instructions, and the layout of the group task.* Four examples may be briefly mentioned:

(a) Information may be given about the other group members as was done in the study of Back[4], who manipulated the attraction of subjects for each other in groups of two. He told one set of groups that they had been matched on personal characteristics so that they would be congenial and like one another; other subjects were told that it had been impossible to match them in this way. Such instructions made a considerable difference in the behaviour of the subjects to each other.

(b) The content of the task can be an experimental variable, as in the study of Schutz,[31] who used three different group tasks, which varied in the degree of co-operation and reliance on one another required of members.

(c) The kinds of communication allowed between members can be varied: for example, Mohanna and Argyle[28] compared groups of five where communication could only take place along a circular route with groups where four members could only communicate with the fifth.

(d) The pre-experimental instructions can change the motivation of the subjects, as in Deutsch's experiment on co-operation and competition.[12] In a cross-cultural study by Schachter, de Monchaux and others,[30] groups of boys were set up as aviation clubs. Different motivational conditions were created, corresponding to rewards of differing desirability, and differences of probability in getting the reward.

As the experiment proceeds there are further possibilities of manipulation, by means of *false reporting* of the behaviour or opinions of other members. One example has already been mentioned in Crutchfield's experiment.[11] Another is provided by a paper-and-pencil test given by Israel[22] to members of six-person groups; regardless of the actual scores, he told each subject that he had obtained a score of 7, while the others had scored 12, 9, 7, 5, and 2. The experimenter then studied the effect of this knowledge on sociometric choices under co-operative and competitive conditions.

Another technique for manipulating the experimental conditions is by means of *accomplices*, who play carefully defined roles. A well-known example of this is Lippitt's experiment[27] where leaders of boys' clubs behaved in a 'democratic', 'autocratic', or 'laissez-faire' way with

Experimental Studies

different groups. These styles of leadership were rehearsed and inter-action recording* of the sessions showed the precise ways in which the roles were different. A less elaborate example is provided by Argyle's study[2] of social pressure in public and private situations. Groups of two were formed in which one subject was an accomplice. The latter adopted an opposite opinion to that of the real subject on the topic being discussed, and sent one of a prearranged series of messages which were either accepting or rejecting in tone, though otherwise identical in context.

Finally, *selection of subjects* can be used as an experimental variable. This can be done on the basis of such characteristics as age, sex, social class, religious affiliation, or according to personality dimensions. For example, Hardy[19] compared the behaviour under social pressure with and without social support of subjects high and low in 'need for affiliation' and in 'need for achievement', as measured by the usual projection test method.

Measurement of the Dependent Variables

Although part of the interest attached to small group research is due to the application of scientific procedures in a hitherto inexact field, the measurements made are usually quite unlike those made in the physical sciences. Observations of behaviour are made by human observers, who make subjective judgements and categorization of what is going on; relations between group members are found by questioning the members. However, the use of the 'human instrument' as a measuring device in social research can be defended by assessing its accuracy in the same way as that of any other instrument. Imagine that an observer is concealed in a box; the box is placed in front of a group, and a moving strip of paper emerges from the box giving information about interaction in the group. If other similarly placed boxes provide much the same information as the first, this device will be regarded as at least *reliable*.

Before going into interaction recording proper, there are two useful related devices which should be mentioned. In the first place, com-munication between group members may be artificially restricted to the use of message slips. This has the advantage of leaving a permanent record which can be analysed at leisure, while experimental interference with the messages can be easily arranged, as was done by Argyle.[2] The second procedure is that of self-recording. Burns[8] has used Carlson's method whereby industrial managers fill in a form each time they meet or contact someone else, with details of what happened. This is a valuable way of exploring the informal life of an organization.

* See p. 84.

Michael Argyle

Interaction recording proper is done by trained observers, who watch the group through a one-way vision screen, and categorize the behaviour taking place in every minute or half-minute, leaving a record of who said what, to whom, and how. This is laborious, both in the initial observing and in the subsequent analysis of the records, so that there has been some move towards the use of overall ratings of longer periods of interaction. This means that more dimensions of behaviour can be covered by a single observer, though of course the detailed sequences of behaviour are lost.[20]

The most familiar method of intereaction recording is that of Bales,[5] who devised twelve categories for use with discussion groups. Half of these categories are in the 'social-emotional' area (divided into positive and negative), half are in the 'task' area (divided into asking for and giving opinions, etc.). This system is linked to an interesting conceptualization of group behaviour, it has been widely used, and is described clearly enough for others to use it with confidence that they are making the same divisions of behaviour.

A quite different method was devised by Chapple,[10] which records the timing of verbal interaction regardless of the content. An observer presses one of two keys while one member of a two-person group is speaking. The keys mark a moving paper, and leave a record of length of speeches, pauses, interruptions, etc. It was found by Goldman-Eisler[18] that individuals have characteristic styles of interaction in this sense.

Many other sets of categories and ratings have been devised for particular purposes. While there are obvious advantages in the general use of the same categories for different studies, it is often convenient to devise a rather small number of categories, easy to use and with high face validity, which bear directly on the problem at hand. Schachter, de Monchaux et al.,[30] for example, used six categories dealing with persuasion and aggression towards deviates.

The method is widely used; we must now consider its scientific acceptability. *Reliability* can be calculated by finding the percentage of acts which are similarly categorized by two observers, or the correlation between ratings on the same dimension of behaviour. A very high level of agreement (75 per cent to 95 per cent) can be obtained by observers who have been trained together. It may be objected that the observers may have been trained to make the same mistakes, i.e. that their observations may not be *valid*. In one sense this is a meaningless objection, since there is no further criterion against which their scoring can be checked. On the other hand it can certainly be argued that the scoring has validity in the sense that theoretical predictions are confirmed, and that stable empirical relationships can be found against other measurements.

Experimental Studies

We turn from observations of behaviour to the measurement of relations between group members. The best-known method of doing this is *sociometry*, originally devised by Moreno.[29] Each subject is asked which of the members of a given group he chooses as a companion for a specific activity. He may be given a limited or unlimited number of choices, and he may also be asked whom he rejects. It is important that a definite activity ('criterion') is specified, that the subjects should believe that their choices will lead to actually getting the companion, and that the choices be made in private. This is the basic technique, though there are variations on it.[26] For example, the group member receiving most choices is popular but not necessarily a *leader*; other questions asking who each subject would like to lead the group in a given activity would indicate the informal leaders. Kraupl Taylor[25] working with therapy groups has developed measures of love-hate, and the love-hate feelings subjects guess that other members have for them.

When a sociometric survey has been carried out in a group, various analyses may be made. To begin with, a *sociogram* can be drawn, with arrows to show attractions and repulsions between members. The total number of choices indicates popularity; this is a simple practical procedure for use in classrooms or elsewhere, for locating the unpopular people. Cliques and cleavages in the group can be detected on the sociogram; the *cohesiveness* of a sub-group can be measured as the percentage of total choices made to members of the sub-groups. Many other and more elaborate mathematical procedures have been used,[26] but one suspects that the basic data are too crude for such subtle manipulations.

With these techniques there is no problem about inter-observer reliability, as there is with interaction recording. On the other hand it may be wondered how stable sociometric choices are with time. This is not a question of the accuracy of the instrument, but rather of the stability of what is being measured. It seems that choices are fairly consistent with adults, for groups which have been in existence for some time, particularly for first choices. On the question of validity, we are faced as before with the fact that there is probably no better measure of whom a person likes, so that further validation is impossible. There is, however, considerable evidence that sociometric choices are related to such overt behaviour as spending time with people, as well as having stable relationships with many other empirical variables.

Before leaving sociometry, some constructive comments can be made. The relations even between two people are immensely complex, and sociometric choice extracts only a small part of the conscious element in this. What is needed is a dimensional analysis of the subjective and behavioural aspects of their relations. As a start two other aspects might be added to sociometric choice. One is the extent to which A identifies with B, i.e. takes him as a model to be imitated in certain respects; the other is the extent to which A accepts B as an authority to be obeyed.

Interaction recording and sociometry have been given special attention since they are almost unique to small group research, and are of particular importance for it. There are, however, various measures developed in other areas of social science which are frequently used in small group studies. Perceptual judgements, as in psychophysics, are used in influence experiments on norm-formation, as are opinions and attitudes. Experiments on group problem-solving use measures of time and errors, as in studies of individual thinking. Research on small groups in industry makes use of the usual efficiency measures of output, absenteeism, labour turnover, accidents, and job satisfaction.[1]

Ethical Problems Created by these Experiments

Many small group experiments involve deceptions of some kind—'stooges' who pretend to be subjects, messages which are supposed to come from other group members, instructions about whether the rest of the group will be compatible or not. Some of the experiments use the one-way mirror for making observations without disturbing the group—since a group of two plus an observer tends to become a group of three. In evaluating the moral acceptability of these things, it may be suggested that the consequences of the act be given more weight than the nature of the act itself. Furthermore the immediate consequences—to the subjects—should be very carefully considered, and not discounted in favour of remote scientific results—the end does *not* justify the means. When subjects have volunteered for a psychological experiment, it may be argued that there is nothing wrong with a certain amount of deception; this happens in many other kinds of experiment and is to some extent expected by the subjects. On the other hand the experimenter has a duty to look after the subjects in his charge, and to be careful that they neither suffer at the time, nor are affected by the experiment afterwards. From this point of view all experiments which study variables such as frustration and stress are less desirable than any small group experiment. If moral attention is directed towards the consequences, there is no reason why a lengthy denouement should be given at the end of the experiment, as is often done by experimenters with guilty feelings. As long as the subjects go home happy, there is no need to apologize for deceptions which were not seen through; this may annoy the subjects unnecessarily, and the news of the deception may get around. The general conclusion is that mild deceptions are probably justified in these experiments, provided that the subjects are spared annoyance, embarrassment, or other damage.

Experimental Studies

Evaluation of the Results of Small Group Research

The results of the investigations which have been carried out so far may be evaluated from three points of view: as a body of empirical findings, for their contribution to theory and explanation, and for their practical applications.

As a body of empirical findings, the results of the several hundred carefully controlled studies on small social groups are extremely impressive. A very extensive quantity of empirical information about functional relationships has been established, and in several areas the effects of variables have been repeatedly studied and in a variety of situations. A good example of this is the study of social influence by group norms: it is known how this is a function of various personality traits, various aspects of the group, the relation of the member to the group, and the issue in question. It is not yet possible to incorporate all these variables in a single equation, as in some types of animal learning, but that step is not far off.

The theory and explanation of small group behaviour is in a much less satisfactory condition. There are several isolated theoretical models —such as Festinger's[13] theory of social comparison processes, which is concerned with the tendency to compete with others of similar ability and to check opinions against those of other group members. Another example is Bales' theory[5] of equilibrium processes in groups, which is concerned with social status and differential frequencies of interaction. None of these, however, is very satisfactory, and they make no contact with one another. Many of the theories which have been put foward consist of loosely connected generalizations about groups. Since all are at the group level, it is not clear which are the axioms and which the theorems. The present author favours a reductive axiomatic approach, in which established conclusions at the lower level of motivation, learning, and personality research are used as the axioms for explaining the more molar generalizations about groups.

The two best known applications of group methods do not really derive from the experimental research at all; these are group therapy and the 'group dynamics' method of leadership training. However, research into small groups in industry, the Services, education, and crime is taking its place in the textbooks on those subjects, and it may be assumed that the practitioners are making use of the results in understanding and handling their various kinds of groups. Some of these applications are reviewed by Bonner.[7]

Michael Argyle

REFERENCES

1. ARGYLE, MICHAEL (1957) *The Scientific Study of Social Behaviour.* London: Methuen.
2. ARGYLE, MICHAEL (1957) 'Social Pressures in Public and Private Situations.' *J. abnorm. soc. Psychol.*, **54**, 289–94.
3. ARGYLE, M.; GARDNER, G.; and CIOFFI, F. (1958) 'Supervisory Methods Related to Productivity'. *Hum. Relat.* **11**, 23–40.
4. BACK, K. W. (1951) 'Influence through Social Communication.' *J. abnorm. soc. Psychol.*, **46**, 9–23.
5. BALES, R. F. (1951) *Interaction Process-Analysis.* Cambridge, Mass.: Addison-Wesley.
6. BALES, R. F.; BORGATTA, E. F.; & HARE, A. P. (1955). *Small Groups.* New York: Knopf.
7. BONNER, H. (1959) *Group Dynamics.* New York: Ronald.
8. BURNS, T. (1954) 'The Directions of Activity and Communication in a Departmental Executive Group: A Quantitative Study in a British Engineering Factory with a Self-Recording Technique'. *Hum. Relat.*, **7**, 73–97.
9. CARTWRIGHT, D., & ZENDER, A. G. (1953) *Group Dynamics.* Evanston, Ill.: How, Peterson.
10. CHAPPLE, E. D., & ARENSBERG, C. M. (1940) 'Measuring Human Relations. An Introduction to the Study of the Interaction of Individuals'. *Genet. Psychol. Monogr.*, **22**, 3–147.
11. CRUTCHFIELD, R. S. (1955) 'Conformity and Character'. *Amer. Psychol.* **10**, 191–8.
12. DEUTSCH, M. (1949) 'An Experimental Study of the Effects of Co-operation and Competition upon Group Process'. *Hum. Relat.* **2**, 199–232.
13. FELDMAN, H. (1937) *Problems in Labor Relations.* New York: Macmillan.
14. FESTINGER, L. (1953) 'Laboratory Experiments'. Chap. 4 in Festinger, L. and Katz, D., *Research Methods in the Behavioural Sciences.* New York: Dryden.
15. FESTINGER, L. (1954) 'A Theory of Social Comparison Processes'. *Hum. Relat.* **7**, 117–40.
16. FESTINGER, L., SCHACHTER, S., & BACK, K. (1950) *Social Pressures in Informal Groups.* New York: Harper.
17. FRENCH, J. R. P. (1950) 'Experiments on Changing Group Productivity', in *Experiments in Social Process*, ed. J. G. Miller. New York: McGraw-Hill.
18. GOLDMAN-EISLER (1957) 'The Measurement of Time Sequences in Conversational Behaviour'. *Brit. J. Psychol.*, **42**, 355–62.
19. HARDY, K. R. (1957) 'Determinants of Conformity and Attitude Change'. *J. abnorm. soc. Psychol.*, **54**, 289–94.
20. HEYNS, R. W., & LIPPITT, R. (1954) 'Systematic Observational Techniques'. Chap. 10 in G. Lindzey, *Handbook of Social Psychology.* Cambridge, Mass.: Addison-Wesley.

Experimental Studies

21. HOMANS, G. (1961) *Elementary Social Behaviour*. New York, Harcourt Brace.
22. ISRAEL, J. (1956) *Self-evaluation and Rejection in Groups*. Stockholm: Almqvist and Wiksell.
23. JENNINGS, H. H. (1943) *Leadership and Isolation*. New York: Longmans.
24. KELLEY, H. H., & THIBAUT, J. W. (1954) 'Experimental Studies of Group Problem Solving and Process'. Chap. 21 of *Handbook of Social Psychology* (see 20 above).
25. KRAUPL TAYLOR, F. (1954) 'The Three-Dimensional Basis of Emotional Interactions in Small Groups'. *Hum. Relat.* **7**, 441–72.
26. LINDZEY, G., & BORGATTA, E. F. (1954) 'Sociometric Measurement', Chap. 11 of *Handbook of Social Psychology* (see 20 above).
27. LIPPITT, R. (1940) 'An Experimental Study of the Effect of Democratic and Authoritarian Group Atmosphere'. *Univ, Ia. Stud. Child. Welf.*, **16**, 43–195. Shorter version: Lippitt, R., and White, R. K. (1952). 'An Experimental Study of Leadership and Group Life'. In *Readings in Social Psychology*, ed. G. E. Swanson, T. M. Newcomb and E. L. Hartley. New York: Holt.
28. MOHANNA, A. I., & ARGYLE, M. (1960) 'A Cross-Cultural Study of Structured Groups with Unpopular Central Members'. *J. abnorm. soc. Psychol.* **60**, 139–40.
29. MORENO, J. L. (1934) *Who Shall Survive?* Washington: Nervous and Mental Disease Pub. Co.
30. SCHACHTER, S., DE MONCHAUX, C., *et al.* (1954) 'Cross-Cultural Experiments on Threat and Rejection'. *Hum. Relat.* **7**, 403–40.
31. SCHUTZ, W. C. (1958) *FIRO, A Three-Dimensional Theory of Interpersonal Behavior*. New York: Rinehart.

5

SOCIOLOGY AND HISTORY

Asa Briggs

HISTORY and sociology are sometimes considered as rivals. The sense of rivalry, however, is based largely on misunderstanding. Both historians and sociologists are concerned with the same set of problems which stretch back from the present into the past. The present is always moving ineluctably into the past, and since all data are historical in one sense the data of both history and sociology are the same.

The sense of rivalry along with the contrasting behaviour and postures of historians and sociologists are best explained in terms of the different and distinct histories of the two disciplines. The place of both history and sociology in university curricula and in the bigger pattern of intellectual activity varies considerably in different countries, as does their status as subjects. Where history has highest status, it is not necessarily, of course, most highly developed as a discipline, least of all as a 'social study'. Its public status derives from the role of the historian not so much as a collector and interpreter of facts as an expositor and guardian —often privileged and established—of the values of that society. Even in societies where the subject is 'open' to critical discussion, social history may well be neglected in favour of other sub-histories, among which political and diplomatic history have traditionally stood out. In most countries it is only a minority of historians who have seriously concerned themselves with the history of societies or have viewed their discipline in some sense as a 'social study'. Often the minority has been a creative one and has produced works of scholarship of a high order, but there has seldom been any close link between social historians and sociologists. Paradoxically the increasingly close link between economic historians and theoretical economists has induced many historians, who

Asa Briggs

previously thought of themselves as economic historians, to seek greater freedom by proclaiming themselves to be social historians. They have reacted, as have some economists themselves, against what they consider to be too narrowly economic interpretations of basic social changes. Their examination of economic growth, for instance, has sometimes led them from economics into economic history, from economic history into social and other kinds of history, and from social history into sociology. Their speed of movement and ease of assimilation serve to demonstrate how artificial are most of the boundary lines between the different social studies.

Sociology has often had highest status as a subject precisely in those countries where the status of history is low—where the past is thought to be not particularly relevant to action in the present, where sociology can establish its 'usefulness' (history being treated at best as auxiliary, at worst as an escapist 'humanity'), and where there are no firmly established 'schools' of academic historians. In such countries it has been easy to condemn historians not only as 'escapist', but as either pedantic grubbers of uninterpreted facts or wild prophets of doom or glory. There has been a marked revulsion in sociology itself away from nineteenth- and early twentieth-century sociological writing which suggested that the main task of the sociologist was to discover 'the laws of evolution' of society. Only recently has a minority of sociologists reacted against exclusive concern for empirical fact-finding or pyramidal theory-building and either produced applied historical studies, using theoretical models, or more drastically demanded a genuine 'historical sociology'. By genuine historical sociology they mean a sociology which makes use of historical materials and recognizes that all contemporary social structures have historical foundations. 'History,' Professor C. Wright Mills has written, 'is and must be the very shank of social science.' The arguments which may be advanced to support this proposition form the content of this chapter: it is important to note, however, that they have been aired only recently after more than one generation of neglect.

Between the two subjects there are vast areas of suspicion. The historian is proud not only of his tradition of scholarship but of his considerable ability to appeal directly to his most powerful neighbour, the general public. He detests jargon and likes plain speaking. The sociologist is proud of his analytical as distinct from his descriptive powers, of his skill in inventing and handling concepts, and his capacity to talk to scientists. On each side of the jurisdictional fence there are many people who would argue that, given the same data, historians and sociologists would make very different use of them.

Attempts have been made to define jurisdictions and boundaries.

92

Sociology and History

Some are simple but unsatisfactory, like the popular view that sociologists are concerned with the present and historians with the past. Others are more sophisticated. From the time of Windelband and Rickert it has been argued, for example, that sociology is 'nomothetic', generalizing, a *Natur-wissenschaft*, while history is 'idiographic', particularizing or individualizing, a *Geistes-wissenschaft*, dealing with the unique rather than the repetitive. More recently, following Collingwood, it has been claimed that history is 'practical', pivoted on the desire for 'human self-knowledge', significant primarily as a 'personal discipline' not so much on account of what the historian makes of history as on account of what history makes of him, while sociology by contrast is 'theoretical', prompting hypotheses, providing conceptual frameworks, analysing factors and relations.

Neither of these sophisticated distinctions describes the actual conduct of sociologists and historians: they are rather attempts to direct attention to where distinctions ought to be made. In practice, historians often generalize (about 'feudalism', for instance) and sociologists often particularize (about the behaviour of selected groups or the problems of chosen areas). It is clear that the distinction between 'nomothetic' and 'idiographic' refers not to isolated and mutually exclusive jurisdiction but to two poles of a continuum. At one pole are relatively dated and relatively localized phenomena, at the other relatively undated and unlocalized phenomena. Many sociologists and historians prefer to dwell not at the poles but in the middle regions. Moreover, the second distinction is equally difficult to draw in practice. Many historians, perhaps most, either implicitly or explicitly dispute many of Collingwood's arguments and conclusions, while on the other side it can be argued convincingly, as Gunnar Myrdal and others have done, that sociology as a subject, like history, derived from practical concern and commitment at least as much as from the yearning to theorize. To draw too sharp a distinction between 'practical' and 'theoretical' makes little sense in relation to what is sometimes called 'the classical tradition' in the history of sociology, the tradition which has illuminated the 'big' problems of changing society. It inhibits the creation of an effective partnership between historians and sociologists to diagnose the problems of our own time—'where we stand' or move—to study what Paul Sweezy has called 'the present as history'. It narrows the scope of both sociology and history, robbing the former of much of its inspiration and driving force and forcing the latter into one kind of approach.

Before setting out the terms and potentialities of a closer partnership between historians and sociologists, it is useful to summarize the arguments which support the view that 'history is and must be the very shank of social science'. Some of these arguments already have a long history; changes in the contemporary world as much as changes of theory have pushed them once more into the foreground.

First, history provides a greater variety of social forms and of social problems than does the contemporary world. Generalizations about contemporary forms (e.g. bureaucracy) or even initial questions asked about contemporary forms and problems may be misleading unless historical evidence—the kind collected by writers like Max Weber—is also taken into account. In an obvious way the study of history extends the scope of the comparative method.

Second, contemporary forms are themselves historical products, and they can be understood neither singly nor comparatively without attention being paid to their historical dimension. The same is true of so-called 'contemporary problems' and the language (e.g. 'class', 'mass', 'culture') in which they are formulated. Of course, an attempt to understand contemporary forms may well begin—as is sometimes the case in 'personality' studies—with contemporary functions and contemporary setting before 'the past' (in the case of personality studies genetic factors) is taken into the reckoning at all. To put the present first and the past second may give the sociologist the healthy feeling that he is avoiding the conservatism of many distinguished historians. The important point, however, is not the order of priorities but the willingness (and ability) to take the past into the reckoning. The necessity to do this has become far more obvious in recent years as sociology has moved (literally) into new territories, some of them previously occupied by anthropologists. In dealing with the sociology of their own immediate environments (e.g. industrial society) sociologists often smuggle in their history (in the same way that historians often smuggle 'general' conclusions into their detailed monographic studies). In dealing with societies very different from their own, particularly those of Asia, history must be deliberately learned, not simply assumed. The terms in which problems are formulated and social argument conducted must also be surveyed historically; such a survey often provides, *via* semantics, valuable insights. In his *Culture and Society* Raymond Williams has related social trends since the industrial revolution to the development of a new social vocabulary. One of the most interesting tasks of historical sociology is to move further into this kind of field.

Third, as soon as the sociologist wishes to consider 'long-term' factors, he must turn to history. Eighteenth- and nineteenth-century sociologists were particularly concerned with this aspect of sociology. Their prophetic propensities, their dogmatism and the values which underlay both their prophecies and their dogmas led to an inevitable reaction, even revulsion. It became fashionable for most sociological studies to be a-historical, concerned with short-term changes in limited milieux within the context of contemporary society. A group of philosopher-historians, of whom Professor A. J. Toynbee has been the most influential, took over the prophetic role. Fashions are changing, however. Some recent anthropological studies have been so concerned with history that they have provided invaluable historical material for African historians who have genuinely wished to study the history of Africans as well as of Europeans in Africa. Even in a book about contemporary American society, David Riesman's *The Lonely Crowd*, an attempt is made to relate the emergence of character types—tradition-centred, inner-directed and outer-directed—to the long-term movements of population curves. In *The Organization Man* W. H. Whyte began by contrasting nineteenth-century individualism in American business and education with twentieth-century conformity. He did not trace the pattern of change in detail, but the main conclusion of his book rested on a historical contrast. This change in fashion should in time produce better social history. The historical premises of sociologists will inevitably be scrutinized and criticized by historians. Frequently, however, it will only be possible to revise them authoritatively after further research has been carried out.

Fourth, and in the view of some sociologists most important, any given society can only be understood in terms of the 'specific period' in which it exists. All social phenomena are 'placed' in time and must be located in a time scale. Sociologists who emphasize this point, notably Professor C. Wright Mills, refer back to Marx's 'principle of historic specificity'. The image of any society, they argue, is a historically specific conception. However 'period' may be defined—and historians have had great difficulty in defining it once they have tried to treat it as something more than a unit of convenience—the institutions, the ideologies, and the 'types' of men and women to be found in any society constitute something of a unique pattern.

Contemporary society is particularly interesting in that it involves the confrontation at the same moment of time of societies at different 'levels'—again a difficult word—of development. The confrontation becomes more meaningful if the historian and the sociologist (including the anthropologist) joins hands in seeking to understand it. Many contemporary phenomena, although contemporary, 'belong' in some sense to earlier periods of history. It is for this reason that Professor Geoffrey Barraclough has urged the need to study 'remote' as well as 'recent' history in order to understand the present. The general point was made with great force by Marc Bloch in his fascinating little book *The Historian's Craft*—'a society that could be completely moulded by its immediately preceding period would have to have a structure so malleable as to be virtually invertebrate'.

These four arguments, if implemented in practice, mark a significant shift within sociology itself. How would they affect history, and would they make it possible to produce a fuller and richer partnership between practitioners of the two subjects?

Essentially history is a subject which lends itself to specialization. As Sir Lewis Namier has written, 'there are hardly any limits to its auxiliary disciplines, except those set by the capacities of the individual historians'. The past may be a 'seamless robe', but this has not prevented historians from doing a great deal of cutting and stitching. It may be reasonably argued that a more 'historically-minded' sociology would lead to a more 'sociologically-minded' social history: its effects on other sub-histories would be more complicated. In some cases there might be a chain reaction, in others a stubborn resistance.

Social historians and historically-minded sociologists would usually deal with the same material, and the distinction between them, never a real one in practice, would wither away. The more disciplined social historians are already dissatisfied with views of social history which limit it to 'the history of everyday things'—this limitation can be explained historically—or to 'history with the politics left out'. They dislike also the tendency of the subject to move with fashion rather than to discover a continuously sustaining discipline. In France, in particular the group of historians associated with the periodical *Annales* have refashioned their subject both in terms of content and method. Georges Lefèbvre revolutionized the study of the French Revolution, and authors of recent detailed monographs, notably Albert Soboul in his *Les Sans-culottes Parisiens de l'an II* (George Rudé has written on similar subjects in England) have brought social and political history into a new alignment with each other. The numbers of social historians who are genuinely concerned to refresh their study by drawing on outside disciplines (notably demography) or turning to neglected topics (such as riots, epidemics, changing value systems, technical innovations and disturbances, and so on) is always increasing. So too is the number of economic historians who are concerned with something more than the application of contemporary economic theory to the data of the past and who are discontented with what they consider to be narrowness of emphasis in 'quantitative economic history'. In Britain, at least, it is already almost impossible to distinguish between the work of accomplished social historians and historical sociologists, and in certain spheres, notably demography, their work already converges. Mr J. A. Banks's study of one aspect of nineteenth-century population change— his technique is as interesting as his conclusions—may, for example, be set alongside Mr D. E. C. Eversley's *Social Theories of Fertility and the Malthusian Debate*. In relation to urban sociology Mrs Ruth Glass has written more generally that 'the outstanding sociological writers on urbanism have not usually outlined an urban sociology as such, that is, a specific, clearly limited field. Max Weber, Pirenne, Sombart and

Sociology and History

others have dealt with the history of urbanism in its varied aspects, with comparative urban institutions and their interactions, in the endeavour to outline a successive typology of cities.' In this field, social historians and sociologists cannot, indeed, be separated out at all.

In other sub-histories there would be differing reactions to a more 'historically-minded sociology'. There have already been attempts, most of them inspired in Britain by Professor C. W. Manning, to change the foundations of the study of international relations from diplomatic history to sociology. In political history there are many entrenched interests, but subjects like the changing role of kinship in politics, the relationship between social and political authority, and the extent of political involvement, demand far fuller co-operation between political historians and sociologists. Short-term election studies are no substitute for analysis of this kind. Administrative history also tends to be studied in comparative isolation: it has even proved possible to write about the government of cities without paying attention to any of the problems raised by urban sociologists.

A closer partnership between historians and sociologists would involve not only a pooling of themes but an open discussion of concepts and techniques. Historians would have to abandon or at least re-assess the claim which many of them make that the best history is that which deals with events in the order in which they happened. They would bring to the debate, however, valuable assets of their own, notably an increasingly sophisticated approach to the problems of historiography, a relatively highly-developed sub-history. In recent years historians have shown clearly how each generation rewrites its past. The understanding of the past is in perpetual flux, not only because of the discovery of new knowledge or the emergence of new schools of historians, prepared to use new kinds of evidence, but because of new perspectives. Among the changes which distinguish a 'later' from an 'earlier' age is a change in the understanding of preceding ages. The relationship between changing views of past, present, and future is one on which historians and sociologists might ponder together. Historians have also shown the importance through historical study of freeing the present from the past. 'Despite our inevitable subordination to the past', Marc Bloch has observed, 'we have freed ourselves at least to the extent that, eternally condemned to know only by means of its "tracks", we are nevertheless successful in knowing far more of the past than the past itself had thought good to tell us.' It is through the study of history, not through evading history, that we get rid of what Mircea Eliade has called 'the terror of history'. In the process of learning history we unlearn and disentangle. There is a link here between historiography and the sociology of knowledge, just as there is a useful, but little appreciated, link between sociological writing on value judgements and historiography. The therapeutic role of history as a serious study has been emphasized by many recent historical writers. In a limited context it is referred to, for example by Mr Eversley. 'The analysis of past bodies of theory,' he says, 'is of great help to the present student in almost every field. Every age produced its own ideological distortions, its prejudices, and its superstitions. By tracing the influences which gave rise to particular ideas we are helped in our attempt to rid our own thinking of much of its inevitable bias.'

It is unlikely that there will be general agreement among all historians about the nature and scope of the study of history. Debate will doubtless continue, but so too will partnership between historians and sociologists. There are already many signs that the sense of rivalry is not only redundant but is believed to be so.

6

ANALYTICAL STUDIES OF SOCIAL INSTITUTIONS

Bryan R. Wilson

ALTHOUGH statistical techniques have advanced and improved in their application to sociological data in recent years, it is still true to say, as Durkheim somewhere said over half a century ago, that because of the complexity of variables distinguishable in sociological analysis, acute observation and rigorous analysis remain the core of sociological method. Durkheim, who examined his perhaps not very adequate data with a high degree of sophistication[10], was in a strong position to say this, and indeed ethical neutrality, empirical procedures of observation, and comparative method, such as that of concomitant variations, remain the basic methodological precepts of sociology. Sociology is more than just a descriptive discipline; it seeks to provide an explanatory analysis of social phenomena, and it is this search for a set of explanatory hypotheses, as well as the comparative method it employs, which most clearly distinguishes it from history and political theory. In this sense a sociological study of institutions seeks to be scientific rather than literary, to use comparisons systematically rather than illustratively and at random, and to avoid the value assumptions which usually characterize the work of the political theorist or the political philosopher. For the historian, facts are often the central concern, but for the sociologist, important as facts are, they are always only a step to hypotheses of explanatory value. The methods of sociology are scientific methods, but the specific techniques which can be employed are often necessarily different from those of the natural scientist. The obvious illustration is that of the controlled experiment, which is rarely possible in the study of society: the sociologist must necessarily examine the phenomena which exist and attempt to explain the differences between them in the light of the differing factors operative in each case. This is essentially the method of science, but the data are uncontrolled, and usually the variables are far more numerous and far more complicated. Sociology has, however, built up a body of sensitizing concepts, which in themselves indicate relationships and associations and draw the investigator's attention to particular aspects of data, and suggest hypotheses which may then be tested and refined.

Social institutions and organizations are a particularly valuable set of social phenomena for the development of methods of sociological inquiry. While they do not offer all that designed experiments provide for the natural scientist, they are phenomena which are at least fairly clearly circumscribed, which are individually distinctive, but which exist in various forms which allow for relatively easy categorization and classification. Social institutions comprise such phenomena as industrial concerns, government departments, trades unions, military organizations, agencies of mass communication, political parties, hospitals, universities, schools, churches, sects, clubs, and voluntary organizations of all kinds.

Although these institutions comprise 'a field', it would be mistaken to suppose that *all* studies of such organizations are specifically sociological studies in the strict sense. The needs of public administrators themselves sometimes lead to research into, for example, hospital organization; but the focus of attention here, geared usually to a pragmatic end, is too formally defined, too much concerned with the constitutional framework and administrative structure, to be counted as sociological research. Likewise, the political theorist might be interested in the power structure of Trades Unions, but such studies, important and valuable as they often are, do not use—do not pretend to use—rigorous techniques of sociological analysis. Clearly, they are frequently invaluable aids to the sociological investigator, as stepping-stones to the type of theoretical insight he wishes to obtain. Thus there is, from a strictly sociological point of view, what might be termed 'peripheral literature' and 'core literature' about particular institutions, and it is unfortunate that popular, and sometimes academic, usage of the word 'sociological' allows for so much confusion between the two. Thus Allen's stimulating and insightful study of trades unions,[1] Mayfield's thorough description of the workings of the established Church,[7] Bruce Truscott's justly celebrated commentaries on Redbrick universities,[16, 17] are the peripheral literature of sociology. Philip Selznick's study of the Communist Party,[13] the work of Robert Merton and his associates on medical schools,[9] Rose Laub Coser's studies of hospitals,[3]

Analytical Studies of Social Institutions

Marshall Sklare's work on Conservative Judaism,[15] and the work of S. M. Lipset and his colleagues on the American Typographers Union[5] are core literature of social institutions. It must be emphasized again that the distinction here is descriptive and not evaluative: obviously peripheral literature may, in some respects and for some purposes, be more useful, more competently written, display greater scholarship, and so on; our concern is simply to distinguish the focus of sociology from that of social history, political theory, and other kindred disciplines.

A sociological study of a social institution attempts to view it as a social system of relationships, some formally prescribed, some conventionally accepted, and others informal (sometimes even unapproved) procedures and arrangements which maintain the institution in its on-going operations. The purely formal or constitutional arrangements are obviously important for an understanding of a given system, but it is the informal relationships, the latent motivations, the areas of tensions and strain, which sociologists regard as crucial. Formal rules are sometimes almost like myths, functional in that the system needs these points of reference as a basis for common understanding between people with disparate interests, statuses, functional roles, and images of what the institution is really trying to do, and yet, as we know, for instance when the railways 'work to rule', the formal regulations are often more honoured in the breach than in the acceptance.

The sociological analysis is essentially a functional analysis, in terms of understanding how particular action serves the system of relationships and actions which we term an 'institution'. If institutional analysis ended there it would, of course, tend to be somewhat static, concerned with system-maintenance and little else. But institutions change, and exist in a changing context, and consequently it is necessary to take the analysis further and to see how systems are affected by outside changes, how the particular responses which they make to external or internal pressures affect them as systems; how the relationships of the groups within the institutions are regulated; and just what patterns of motivations and interests these various groups maintain.* Such an approach uses the dimension of history, but, particularly when comparative material is available, it is possible also that it might lead to conclusions of predictive value. Prediction as such is perhaps not the fundamental aim: what is sought, as in other sciences, is generalizations which will be true in the future as they are true in the present. The data of sociology are so complex, and the variables so numerous, that testable hypotheses for the future are difficult to formulate: in the field of social institutions, however, there are some beginnings.

* See [19], which attempts to bring sharply into focus those aspects of sect organization important to the understanding of the changing nature of the sect as an institution.

Bryan R. Wilson

The study of a social institution begins with the description of the formal organization, for at some level—in a constitution, on an executive's charts, in the regulations and decrees of a government office, or at the behest of a leader—there is a formal structure of inter-related roles, hierarchy of command and rules of operation. This formal structure must be the point of departure for further analysis. The investigator must undertake a thorough study of the provisions of original consitutional formulations and determine the implicit and explicit value-assumptions of these, so that he can subsequently examine in these terms the actual operation of the institution itself. This he can do only by a survey of its functioning—its current production or activity and its means of operation—and by what he can discover by participating with the different segments of the structure, and by learning what he can of their more specific goal-orientations.

The sociologist is interested in the nature of authority, the instruments of command, the character of leadership, and the criteria for promotion. To Max Weber we owe the basic concepts in terms of which the nature of authority is to be analysed,[18] and these concepts have been widely used in many different studies. But sociology is concerned also with the way in which the motivations and interests of different groups are embraced within one institutional structure; the way in which different sections of those involved in an institution endow the institution with diverse meaning, and seek to make institutions vehicles for their own satisfactions. The institution itself has certain manifest purposes, which may indeed be formally defined in a charter, constitution, or creed, but invariably there will be, among divergent groups within the organization, a variety of other manifest, or latent, purposes, some of which may closely relate to the position of such groups within the structure, and be contradictory of the purposes sought by others. Thus all institutions are interpreted dominantly by their personnel, their principal officials, but institutions are also affected by the demands of their clientele, whose conception of the organization is usually a very different one, and this notwithstanding the proclaimed ideology of the personnel, which may be 'Our sole aim is to serve the public', or 'We exist to express the political wishes of the people', or 'Our job as a civil service is to implement the policy of the party in power'. In fact, of course, the personnel's disclaimers of a dominant role ignore the innumerable ways in which the personnel can affect policy and determine the character of an institution and the ends it seeks to promote. They ignore, too, the subsidiary motivations of the personnel; their search for status; the satisfaction of monopoly of access to power; the conservatism of administrative agents. Thus the sociologist is concerned with the various conceptions of the mission of an institution as found among different participants: personnel, clientele, general public,

Analytical Studies of Social Institutions

directors or leaders, rivals, colleagues in other institutions, opponents, and so on.* They ascribe different values to a given organization and may have different views about the way in which these values should find expression, and may also wish to make the institution a vehicle for different values of their own.

The core issue of institutional analysis, therefore, is the value commitments of institutions and of the various segments who participate in their operation. This mission of a particular company, or work organization, will be differently understood by those with differing investment in it: the owners; the managers; the workers; the trades union officials; the shop stewards; the agents within the organization, for instance, Communist Party agitators; the works chaplain; the general public; and the consumers of the product or service.† Any one group may have somewhat ambiguous or ambivalent ideas about their aims, and it is just such points of tension which the sociologist seeks to understand. Especially in new organizations, and particularly those with a strong charismatic element in their leadership, highly contradictory and inconsistent ends may be espoused. This is often strikingly so in religious and political organizations, which tend to have a highly articulate response to external circumstances, and in the operation of which ideological defence is a specially important phenomenon. In such organizations too—and sometimes in others though for less sustained action—the clientele may itself be mobilized on the basis of deep-seated discontents and unconscious needs. This mobilization may often be disruptive of an institution's operation, as, for example, in the case of strikes. In such cases institutional action is prompted more by inner needs than by any objective appraisal of the external situation, or by any clear value conception of the role of the organization within the wider society. Cogent examples of a whole set of basically similar institutions—albeit ephemeral—is to be found in Peter Worsley's work on

---

* See, for example, [8] and [20], two analyses which are not concerned with institutions as such, but relate to institutional contexts.

† Likewise the sense of mission of a Youth Club may vary radically among the various elements: official leadership may see it as educational, religious, and moral; the clientele may regard its mission as social; the general public and the city authorities which grant subsidies may see it as custodial. Where new functions are grafted on to an existing institution, analysis brings to light the latent consequences of such developments for the system as a whole and for the various social groups participating in it. Thus a Youth Club which developed a new custodial function as a consequence of liaison by its leaders with the police might experience radical reactions from its clientele—'rough lads' might, on being brought in at police behest, drive out 'nicer types', or, if the co-operation with the police became known to an existing clientele, marginal delinquent types might grow suspicious of the leadership and withdraw. For an analytical framework for such problems see [2, 11, 12].

103

Bryan R. Wilson

Melanesian cargo cults.* The other polar type is where hidden value commitments exist but are consciously understood and concealed by the leadership, as in the case of institutions used as front organizations, which can occur in the field of financial speculation as fully as in the case of political parties.[13]

One important aspect of the study of social institutions is a close attention to policy declarations and public statements put forth by an organization. Such statements may be reviewed over time, and a content analysis will often reveal the latent tensions and stresses which an organization has undergone, as well as providing more overt evidence of policy changes. Selznick's study of the Tennessee Valley Authority provides a particularly cogent analysis of this type, and throws into relief the divergent aims fathered on to an institution by diverse sections of those who had interest in it.[14] Political and religious organizations, for whom expressive functions have high significance and which have consequently developed important organs of articulation, cannot be understood without close investigation of these public statements. But to look at these alone is not enough: they must be seen in relation to the entire social system of the institution itself, for it is this which distinguishes the sociological from what might be termed the theological type of inquiry. A history of doctrine, or a history of policy, is only a starting-point; a sociological study of an institution seeks to show the causes of doctrinal and policy changes and to locate their origins in terms of the groups, the events, and the position within the institution from which pressure for change arose. There are always groups who for certain reasons support pristine values, groups which, perhaps in the struggle for status, take change as an ally, groups whose real values undergo compromise as their own position in the structure becomes precarious. The search is for latent motivations; policy statements and pronouncements contain defence statements, and defence mechanisms are brought into play when an institution feels itself vulnerable. Thus the study of institutional ideology, which is in the best stream of sociological tradition, and which draws on Marx and Pareto as well as on Freud and Karl Mannheim, is crucial for sociological inquiry, if the latent structure of motivation within an organization is to be properly understood.

There is one aspect of statements on public policy which in a democratic society cannot be ignored by the study of institutions: the need which most organizations feel for maintaining good 'public relations'.

* See [22]. In a sense the cargo cults movements which Worsley examines are too ephemeral to qualify as social institutions, but they are an institutionalized expression, often of a complex type, of conflicting needs, problems, and tensions within given societies, and have much in common with established institutions such as some sects, union movements, and political parties.

Analytical Studies of Social Institutions

The attempt is essentially to induce the public at large to accept an image of the institution which is especially favourable to it. The public as such may not, of course, ever see the 'good face' which the organization puts forward, but with the agencies of mass media of communication undertaking, as they tend to do in democratic societies, a gratuitous role of protectors of the public good, institutions become highly sensitive to their vulnerability to bad publicity. Some organizations—government agencies, economic organizations, professional associations (particularly those of groups in direct public service)—are more vulnerable than others, because every member of the society is potentially a member of their clientele, and because their work operations involve them in some form of support for the democratic welfare ideology of the age. The issue with which the sociologist is concerned is not simply to discount as 'public relations propaganda' some of the policy statements of institutions, but to see how far public relations considerations do in fact have implications for institutions in their structure and functioning. The relative power of the public relations official of companies or agencies is one crucial aspect, since he, for this particular interest, may bring pressure to bear which vitally affects the operation of the organization, and may even modify its basic value-commitment and its particular mission.

Sociology, as we have seen, provides particular types of focus for the study of institutions, but there are more general sociological considerations which are important for such investigations. The status struggles within an organization are usually affected by status considerations which participants bring to their institutional role from other status positions which they occupy elsewhere. Thus it is highly significant for the character of an institution from which classes it draws its personnel and its clientele. The status of the personnel is itself susceptible to that of the clientele; thus the status of teachers is partially determined by the groups they teach and the localities in which they teach. Grammar school teachers are highly conscious of status distinctions which mark them off from elementary school teachers, and tend to support more prestige-giving professional organizations and to dissociate themselves more radically from workers and trades unions. Yet as the clientele of the grammar school changes, the status of the teacher there is likely to change, and particularly so as the catchment area for this profession is likewise extended. Such changes will necessarily affect the implicit, and even the explicit, values to which grammar schools as social institutions are committed.

The second point made in this example is clearly of wider significance for many institutions. As people of more limited background have wider opportunity to enter jobs once closed to them, so the institutions in which these positions are available are affected by the different value

105

Bryan R. Wilson

commitments of their new personnel. Some of the entrenched values concerned may, in fact, be marginal to the institution's mission, but may not be so regarded by the established personnel, whose conception of the institution may be heavily suffused with just these ideals. Thus struggles may arise within an institution about issues which are not fully articulated and are not even central to the institution's functioning. There have, for example, been expressions of concern about the less cultured persons now entering the ministry of the Church of England, but obviously opinions about the extent to which cultural awareness is really vital to the Church's functions may differ widely. The converse case is that of a sect or nonconformist group which originally recruits its ministry from people of little education, but gradually comes to accept schemes of training and academic excellence as appropriate for its ministry. In this case too, the differing class assumptions of the key personnel are likely to have a radical impact on some of the values of the organizations in which these key personnel are employed.

Techniques of recruitment, both of personnel and clientele, are a dimension of institutional analysis which the sociologist will not neglect. Particular attention to the methods of training of key personnel is especially rewarding, since it is often in the training institution (itself worthy of institutional analysis in some cases) that the self-image of the professional is evolved in the mind of the trainee.[9] Methods of recruitment or means of selection are obviously significant processes in the sociology of professions, but they are also of significance in the study of institutions as such. The data and techniques are often the same, but the focus of attention is different in these two types of sociological inquiry; hence it is that much can be learned for institutional analysis from such admirable studies as Lockwood's work on the clerical profession.[6] Different generations within an institution often display wide disparities in interpretation of both their own role and their institutional image. Old-style trades union leaders usually have a different conception of the union's mission from that held by younger men who have grown up with the union as an established part of the industrial scene. This divergence is enhanced when training methods have also changed, when, for instance, professional and specialist leadership has replaced the man who has come up through the ranks of the workers themselves. Obviously other examples exist—between the owner-manager of a business who is a self-made man, and newer business executives who have taken degrees in economics and business administration.

It will be observed that greater emphasis is given here to the sensitizing concepts which should inform institutional analysis than to the specific techniques of inquiry. This appears to be necessary at a time when basic techniques are little differentiated in this type of study from

106

those in more general use in sociology. What is often lacking is an adequate statement of the problems of a piece of research—of the hypotheses being tested, their inter-relation with each other, and the significance they have for a particular theoretical formulation. The empirical procedures are often given closer scrutiny and are subject to much more specific expertise and thus to more objective and expert criticism. This fact, however, should not allow anyone to suppose that specific techniques of inquiry can be any sort of substitute for philosophical and methodological sophistication at a more theoretical level. There is even a prospect in sociology that with the advancement of more perfected techniques of research—particularly with the development of computers—we shall have research impeccable at a technical level and puerile in terms of the philosophical assumptions upon which it rests. This is especially likely when research itself becomes vulnerable to the suggestion that inquiry should only be undertaken in the form most suited to the computers.

Our persisting orientation in sociological analysis must be to ask the significant questions and test the important hypotheses towards the establishment of firmly-grounded theory. Institutional analysis employs the research techniques of historical study, but with a perhaps more rigorous content analysis of documents in terms of the existing body of theory about the character of institutions. Content analysis of charters, manifestos, reports, conference discussions, defence-statements by 'the platform', re-orientations of policy, and the like, may be followed by interviews. The unstructured interview is likely to be of more value, particularly in the early stages, than the rigorous questionnaire. A great deal of what is being sought is more easily said than written. The use of informants is an extension of the same technique.

The data gained by this method are to be treated for what they are: asking questions alone is not an adequate basis for sociological inquiry; much less adequate is the acceptance at their face value of the answers. This type of data is to be used in the study of institutions to point up the information gained by participant observation within an institution, and by examination of its formal and informal operational structure and content analysis of its ideological pronouncements and its formal self-interpretation. The interview information should provide evidence of the value-assumptions—often latent rather than manifest—of the different groups within the institution. The process is not to be confused with 'attitude-testing'; the responses in institutional analysis will be more specifically focused and more structurally induced. What is being sought is not the range of random attitude in a selection of individuals, or even within a collectivity, but the differential value-commitment among those differently placed within an integrated structure of highly complex social relationships which are, nominally, embraced within

Bryan R. Wilson

one context of activity and one set of common purposes. The tensions inherent within the structure are what are being discovered, and the giving of a substantial number of interviews should ensure that idiosyncratic and chance elements do not distort the information obtained. *

It should be already apparent that the sociological orientation to institutions relies essentially on empirical inquiry and observation. It does not disregard the formal data of constitutions, charters, trust deeds, and creeds, and indeed the study of the values embodied in such documents and in statements of policy is a vital focus of attention. Such a content analysis may itself suggest the most significant hypotheses for understanding the whole structure of expressed and latent motivation of the various groups and sections which make up the institution. To know from whom in an institution certain policies and pronouncements orginated, in what circumstances they were put forward, to what public directed, and what contradictions, retractations, or deviations from previous policy they involved, is the beginning of a living understanding of an organization. From this beginning analysis can lead to an understanding of the significance for other parts of the institution of changes in policy, leadership, personnel, clientele, competitors, or in other external circumstances, such, for instance, as changes in the law which affect the operation of the institution in some way or other. Thus, for instance, pacifism is a relatively unimportant aspect of the principles of a sect or a radical political movement except in circumstances of war, when the maintenance of such a principle may have highly significant consequences, both manifest and latent for the structure of a movement and for its functioning in other directions.

To put forward hypotheses of this kind the investigator must, obviously, be thoroughly immersed in the institution and its operation. He must, by careful annotation of all its pronouncements, decisions, and policies, know exactly what action is consistent with its past history. He must be able to recognize rationalizations; the dilution of commitment; the attenuation of pristine values; the consequences of pressure exerted by particular strata; the defence-mechanisms of an institution which finds itself exposed and vulnerable to external forces. He is in this position only if the documentary evidence has been rigorously examined and if he has participated in the institution as totally as possible, where this method can be adopted. Documents must be critically assessed; compared; related to the documentary and the action context of the occasion of their creation; examined for intrinsic inconsistencies, compromise, and defence statements; and understood in terms of the position of those responsible for them.

Content analysis of policy statements will demand augmentation by other techniques, such as the use of informants who have participated

* For examples of variations within institutional analysis compare [4, 20, 21].

Analytical Studies of Social Institutions

in the organization, concealed or revealed participation by the investigator, and perhaps even interview methods of eliciting information from personnel, leaders, clientele, and others involved in the institution. Different techniques are obviously appropriate to different institutions; the study of a sect, a secret society, or a prison could probably be successfully undertaken only by use of concealed participation and observational methods and the use of informants; such procedures are, however, neither appropriate nor useful to the study of trades unions or government agencies. But if method must be appropriate to subject, at least the overall canons of the sociological approach remain constant. Essentially the sociological approach is not a polemic, an apologetic, or a therapeutic orientation, but rather a search for explanations of just how an institution functions, its focal points of tension and conflict, and its adaptability to change.

REFERENCES

1. ALLEN, V. L. (1954) *Power in Trade Unions.* London: Longmans.
2. CLARK, BURTON R. (1956) 'Organizational Adaption and Precarious Values: A Case Study'. *Amer. Sociol. Rev.*, **21**, 56–63.
3. COSER, ROSE LAUB. (1958) 'Authority and Decision Making in a Hospital: A Comparative Analysis'. *Amer. Sociol. Rev.*, **23**, 56–63.
4. HARRISON, PAUL M. (1959) *Authority and Power in the Free Church Tradition.* Princeton, N.J.: Princeton Univ. Press.
5. LIPSET, S. M., COLEMAN, J, S., & TROW, M. A. (1956) *Union Democracy.* Glencoe, Ill.: Free Press.
6. LOCKWOOD, DAVID (1958) *The Black Coated Worker.* London: Allen and Unwin.
7. MAYFIELD, GUY (1958) *The Church of England.* London: Oxford Univ. Press.
8. MERTON, R. K. (1957) 'The Role Set: Problems in Sociological Theory'. *Brit. J. Sociol.*, **8**, pp. 106–20.
9. MERTON, R. K., *et al.* (1957) *The Student Physician.* Cambridge, Mass.: Harvard Univ. Press.
10. SELVIN, HANAN C. (1958) 'Durkheim's *Suicide* and Problems of Empirical Research'. *Amer. J. Sociol.*, **63**.
11. SELZNICK, PHILIP (1948) 'Foundations of the Theory of Organization'. *Amer. Sociol. Rev.*, **53**, 25–35.
12. SELZNICK, PHILIP (1951) 'Institutional Vulnerability in Mass Society'. *Amer. J. Sociol.*, **56**, 320–32.
13. SELZNICK, PHILIP (1952) *The Organizational Weapon.* New York: McGraw-Hill.
14. SELZNICK, PHILIP (1949) *TVA and the Grass Roots.* Berkeley and Los Angeles: Univ. of California Press.
15. SKLARE, MARSHALL (1955) *Conservative Judaism.* Glencoe, Ill.: Free Press.
16. TRUSCOTT, BRUCE (1943) *Redbrick University.* London: Faber.

Bryan R. Wilson

17. TRUSCOTT, BRUCE (1945) *Redbrick and These Vital Days*. London: Faber.
18. WEBER, MAX (1947) *Theory of Social and Economic Organization*. Edinburgh: Hodge.
19. WILSON, BRYAN R. (1959) 'An Analysis of Sect Development'. *Amer. Sociol. Rev.*, **24**, 3–15.
20. WILSON, BRYAN R. (1959) 'The Pentecostal Minister: Role Conflicts and Status Contradictions'. *Amer. J. Sociol.*, **64**, 494–504.
21. WILSON, BRYAN R. (1961) *Sects and Society*. London: Heinemann.
22. WORSLEY, PETER (1958) *The Trumpet Shall Sound*. London: MacGibbon and Kee.

7

OPERATIONAL RESEARCH

Norman T. J. Bailey

INTRODUCTION

OPERATIONAL RESEARCH is most conveniently and simply defined as 'the application of scientific methods of investigation to the kind of problems that face executive and administrative authorities'. The sociological content is thus of central importance. In the more 'exact' sciences a distinction is often made between pure and applied research. A mathematician working on atomic structure is pursuing knowledge for its own sake. On the other hand, an engineer engaged on the design of an atomic power station is doing applied research. There is also a social aspect here, since the sort of application involved is determined primarily by the aims and objects of the community in which the engineer lives. At the same time, most of his efforts will probably be directed towards solving the technical problems raised by the requirement of building the power station to the specification laid down. In operational research, however, we are concerned all the time with the activities of a group of individuals. Moreover, we not only study these activities as such, but have to gain the co-operation of the group, first to allow itself to be investigated, and secondly possibly to allow itself to be reorganized in accordance with the results of the investigation. Further, operational research teams usually involve several workers with very different types of training and background. Solution of the problems of communication and understanding between the research workers themselves is of vital importance to the success of the work.

Operational research is thus a markedly sociological science, although so far it has seldom been consciously and deliberately pursued as such by sociologists. Before looking at a number of specific examples of operational research we shall first consider the roles of mathematics, probability, and statistics in the conduct of scientific work. This will enable the special functions and methods of operational research to be seen more clearly.

Of course, it should be realized that in most human activities practice comes before theory. Men were using speech long before books on grammar were compiled, and elementary science was practised before its philosophical analysis was undertaken. Similarly, operational research began in practical common-sense attempts to improve organization before self-conscious reflection tried to codify the actual processes involved. Nevertheless, classification of the latter should lead to greater understanding and control.

The Scientific Approach

It is generally accepted that the underlying unity of the sciences lies not so much in their subject matter as in their adoption of a common method of approach and investigation. Theories should be based on facts, and arguments should be followed whithersoever they may lead. Although hypotheses may be inspired by imagination, they should be tested by appeals to evidence. Scientific progress results from a continually repeated cycle of events: study of relevant facts; construction of abstract 'explanations' of the data; deduction from these theoretical ideas of various consequences or predictions; tests of the predictions by collecting new data or by specially designed experiments; further development of the theory if the predictions are verified, or modification if they are not. The cycle then begins again.

Scientific method is thus a more highbrow version of ordinary 'trial and error'. It can be applied to any subject having a factual basis, though this is much more easily done in the case of 'exact' sciences like physics and chemistry than it is in, say, psychology or sociology. The facts of operational research are often very complicated patterns of social activity, whether this is the conduct of a military campaign or the functioning of a hospital. Nevertheless, they are still facts, and as such are capable of scientific investigation when the appropriate methods of inquiry have been found.

Mathematical Methods

Although the scientific method *can* be applied to any subject having a factual basis, the greatest success is achieved when the basic observations are capable of some form of measurement. This is because

Operational Research

measurement automatically permits the application of standard mathematics. Vague statements can be replaced by more precise ones, and this helps one to determine more easily whether or not predictions are verified or falsified by the relevant data.

Another important use of mathematical methods is the technique of constructing mathematical pictures or 'models' of the situations and processes being studied. These may be relatively simple, as with the Newtonian picture of the solar system, or extremely complicated and abstract, as in quantum theory. In dealing with social phenomena, on the other hand, such as population growth or the provision of medical care, for example, realistic models may be fairly complicated though usually not highly abstract.

In any case, whatever the type of mathematical model depicting the phenomena under investigation, and however recondite the mathematical reasoning employed, it should always be possible to interpret theoretical conclusions in terms of events in the real world. This is essential if crucial tests of the theory are to be made by an appeal to fresh facts.

The use of mathematical methods greatly facilitates scientific advance in general and operational research studies in particular. Although most people with a scientific training can handle a certain amount of mathematics, beyond a certain point it may be necessary to enlist the services of an expert. This naturally leads to difficulties in communication and co-operation between research workers with very different modes of thought. But the difficulties can be overcome with a little effort, and the results are usually well worth while.

Probability Theory

Now most of the mathematical work in the exact sciences is in a sense fairly straightforward in so far as it is ultimately based on relatively exact observations. (The so-called errors of observation are usually easily eliminated by averaging over a few repeated measurements.) In some cases, however, e.g. statistical mechanics and quantum theory, it has been found essential to use probability ideas in the basic description of the phenomena investigated, because an appreciable degree of inherent irreducible variability seems to be involved.

Though uncommon in physics and chemistry, large basic variability is commonplace in all biological, medical, and sociological work. Physiological functions, anatomical measurements, susceptibility to disease, genetic characteristics, intelligence, patterns of behaviour, learning processes, social organization, etc., all show such immense ranges of variation that even the average of several repeated measurements may still be a rather imprecise quantity. Operational research is nearly always concerned with some complex situation in which the human element is prominent, and therefore frequently has to make use of mathematical descriptions in which probability ideas form an integral part.

Statistical Methods

When, in the classical sciences, mathematical development leads to certain predictions, about, for example, the advance of the perihelion of Mercury, it is usually a comparatively straightforward matter to decide whether or not the theory fits the facts. But the large variability present in the material of the biological and social sciences presents a new difficulty. Not only do the basic mathematical pictures involve probability ideas, but predictions as well may be encumbered with a marked degree of variation and uncertainty. It is then not easy to decide whether a discrepancy between observation and hypothesis is indicative of some real effect, or whether it is due merely to chance variations. It is one of the tasks of statistics to provide reasonable rules for settling such questions.

Modern statistics has several functions to perform and is one of the key disciplines in operational research. There is, first, the problem of reducing a large body of data to manageable proportions, and using methods of describing the salient features concisely yet realistically. Secondly, there is the problem of finding efficient estimates of various indices, coefficients, and parameters, together with indications of their reliability. Again, the question of testing hypotheses and using significance tests is of central importance. In some investigations surveys have to be planned. We want these to do their job as economically as possible, and at the same time to be reasonably free from various forms of bias and error. On other occasions we may have to consider the design of specially patterned experiments, again with the object of providing as much information as possible for a given outlay.

Operational Research Methods

All the topics briefly mentioned above are basic to most operational research work. It should, however, be remarked that in general highly abstruse methods are not required, although they may on occasion be extremely valuable. The main thing to remember is that we are dealing with executive and administrative problems. Though these are very far from being abstract, it is usually of great help to have a simple mathematical picture, and more often than not the variability involved necessitates the use of probability. This in turn is liable to entail the subsequent application of statistical methods.

Operational Research

A number of examples of operational research investigations will be outlined below. These are intended to show the variety of possible applications, and also to illustrate the principles discussed above.

Operational Research in Wartime

Operational research as a conscious and deliberate activity arose during World War II in connexion with organizational problems in the Armed Forces.[9] Much of the research on producing better weapons was of a scientific or technological nature. At the same time there were many problems arising from the actual tactical use of men and equipment. For example, given a limited number of efficient heavy bombers and highly trained aircrews, what is the best way of using them to cripple the enemy's heavy industry? What size bombs should be used? How should they be distributed over the target? What flying formations are best, both offensively and defensively? What are the best resting periods for crews? How should they be accommodated in an aircraft so as to strike a balance between safety, comfort, and operational efficiency? Often one is forced by circumstances merely to make the best of a bad job. But when choices are available, one should try to settle the issues in a scientific and objective manner.

Let us consider in more detail a problem with which the writer was personally concerned. This was, in essence, to estimate the most probable position of a radio transmitter, given a set of direction-finding bearings taken on its signals. Accurate bearings plotted on a gnomonic map projection would all pass through the transmitter's position. But in practice, even with the best available equipment and the best operators, bearings may be highly erratic and inaccurate, especially at high frequencies. This is due, amongst other things, to unpredictable deformations of the ionosphere.

When large numbers of bearings are available, the inherent information is also extensive; but, paradoxically, often unusable because of the visually confusing configuration of lines that is produced on the chart.

The method of attacking the problem followed the principles suggested above. First, a mathematical model of the whole process was constructed, using, in particular, probability representations to describe the variation that occurred in the accuracy of bearings. Secondly, the model was employed to develop a statistical technique for utilizing all the information supplied by any set of bearings. This provided the most likely position of the transmitter, together with a rectangle within which there was a given chance, say 95 per cent, of the transmitter's lying.

In order to apply the mathematical theory in practice, a streamlined

115

Norman T. J. Bailey

computing procedure had to be developed. This meant finding a fairly rapid method that could be used by ordinary computing staff, aided only by charts, tables, and a desk calculating machine.

There are several advantages in such a semi-mechanized technique. Not only is one enabled to be more precise, objective, and scientific in dealing with a specific technical difficulty, but one extracts more information from the data, and does so moreover in such a way that Service personnel can use it with greater ease. Further, the judgement of direction-finding 'plotters' is improved and refined by contact with an objective routine, and they can then, when necessary, make better intuitive decisions on their own. Although one cannot discuss details here, it is clear that all such technical improvements are liable to have considerable repercussions on the handling of intelligence material over quite a wide field.

The Design of Scientific Laboratories

In recent years operational research methods have been applied quite widely in industry with a view to improving the efficiency of laboratories, plant, and organization. As usual the successful outcome of such work depends not only on the improvement of purely technological aspects, but also on securing the active co-operation of staff, whose organization may be subject to scrutiny and require subsequent modification. As an illustration of current work in this field, let us consider a particular, relatively unexplored aspect, namely the *designing* of a laboratory.

Davies *et al.*[5] have given a preliminary account of work in progress, and a fuller report will be published in due course. In planning a laboratory, decisions have to be made about the general size needed and the extent of the various service facilities to be supplied. In practice, senior staff likely to work in the new buildings may be consulted, or decisions may be made even without consultation by administrative officials on the basis of general knowledge and experience. Expert opinions often differ markedly from each other, and it is clear that more objective criteria are required. A further complication is that many laboratories have to be used over several years for a variety of purposes. It may then be desirable to try to develop general purpose buildings which are reasonably adequate over a range of activities, even if not of maximum efficiency for any single one of them.

The investigation in question began with a survey to collect data on the use actually made of existing space and services in a large number of fairly well-equipped laboratories. The staff whose activities were to be surveyed were all 'put in the picture', and there were no difficulties in collecting the material required. Distinctions had, of course, to be

116

Operational Research

made between different grades of scientific workers and their assistants, and also between the different scientific disciplines pursued.

By examining the statistical distributions of what actually happened one could predict the consequences of various degrees of provision which might be made in a new laboratory. In the matter of bench length, for example, it was found in the first pilot survey that a scientific or experimental officer was using about ten feet or less of bench run for 95 per cent of the time. Thus to provide ten feet would, in a sense, produce 95 per cent satisfaction. If twelve feet were available, 98 per cent satisfaction would result. Further, the probabilities observed could be compounded to calculate what provision should be made for groups of workers. Thus it was found that two scientists and two assistants working in a team would need only thirty-three feet for 98 per cent satisfaction.

These figures are to be regarded as only illustrative. The main survey, of which the results are not yet published, goes into greater detail, distinguishing between different disciplines. Moreover, considerable care has to be taken in examining the assumptions on which such calculations are based, in order to ensure that the simplifications used are not likely seriously to invalidate the conclusions.

Similar considerations apply to sinks, draining-boards, gas, electricity, water, etc. Considerable progress was also made in predicting the quality of illumination obtained in a room of given size, shape, glazing, and furnishing.

The main point is that data of this type can be used to assess the suitability of alternative architectural designs. In the first instance the latter are produced by a somewhat intuitive process, but they can then be submitted to objective criteria, on the basis of which a rational choice can be made.

It is true that this work has not yet advanced very far. Nevertheless it is eminently worth pursuing. Inevitably, administrators will take decisions about the design of laboratories that will affect the work, organization, and efficiency of large numbers of scientists, so there is considerable advantage in trying to provide factual data on the basis of which more objective and rational decisions could be reached. Much more needs to be learned about measuring what happens in laboratories, about discovering what degree of 'satisfaction' should be achieved in carrying out certain tasks, about the effect of scientists co-operating in teams, etc. Only when appreciable advances have been made in such studies will it be possible to strike an optimum balance between theoretical requirements on the one hand and practical possibilities on the other.

Norman T. J. Bailey

The Design of Hospitals

Another extremely important field of application for operational research methods is the provision of medical care.[3, 10] One major problem is to decide how big a hospital should be in order to serve a particular community. So far only the surface of the problem has been scratched. Some idea of what is required can be obtained by studying the records of several hospitals over a wide area. We can estimate the total demand in each specialty, as well as discovering the effective population served. Such calculations tell us how many beds are required for the supply and demand exactly to balance. It can be shown theoretically that in general an exact balance of supply and demand entails an infinite average waiting time to gain admission. However, the 'critical' number of beds calculated in this way usually needs to be increased by only a few units for reasonably short waiting times to result. Queueing theory can be used to derive the precise adjustments that should be made.

We can thus predict what is required to meet the needs of a new town, or can use the theory to make regular checks on the performance of an existing hospital. For example, we can calculate whether waiting lists are longer than would be expected, given the current accommodation and demand. If they are, then further investigation is worth while. We can also predict the effect on the waiting list of changes in clinical practice, such as the adoption of early ambulation policies resulting in shorter lengths of stay.

Apart from the general size or bed complement of a hospital, there are also many problems relating to the more detailed design of particular internal aspects. In ward design, for example, one requirement is to reduce the walking distances of the nursing staff as much as possible. Existing wards can be surveyed in order to obtain a standard average pattern of movement between the main elements of a ward unit, e.g. beds, duty-room, sluice-room, etc. The standard pattern specifies, in fact, the average number of journeys per shift between any two of these elements. Given a number of alternative ward designs, the standard pattern can be applied to estimate in each case the average distance walked per shift. This method therefore supplies one important criterion of design. Other things being equal, we should select the design that entailed the shortest walking distance. But in practice a balance between conflicting requirements may have to be struck.

Another aspect, the provision of lavatories and day spaces, can be met by surveying existing wards to find out how many patients are bedfast, partially ambulant or fully ambulant.[6] Moreover, this can be done, not only recording what actually happens, but also estimating the effect of a different ambulation policy, i.e. what would have

118

happened if this had been more conservative or, alternatively, more in favour of early ambulation. For a ward with a given number of beds, one can calculate how many patients on average are likely to use the facilities in question, and hence how large the latter ought to be. Although still not a precise yardstick, this method does enable the architect to avoid purely subjective judgements.

Again, there is the question of how many beds should be installed in single rooms or cubicles.[1, 7] Starting with a survey of suitably chosen existing wards, one can estimate the chance of any given patient requiring separate accommodation on any one day. In one study of surgical wards this was found to be about 10 per cent. With a sixteen-bed unit we should expect two single rooms to be roughly adequate (since 10% of 16 = 1·6). But this simple calculation is liable to be misleading, and more exact analysis is needed to gauge the probable consequences in practice of any particular degree of provision. It can be shown mathematically that, on average, two single rooms would allow 84 per cent of the demand to be satisfied, while the single rooms would be used for their intended purpose for 73 per cent of the time. If we provided three such rooms, the corresponding figures (which may be regarded as measurements of efficiency) would be 92 and 59. It is clear that one type of efficiency can be raised only at the expense of the other. The practical value of such calculations is to allow the architect, as well as medical and administrative authorities, to see the consequences of making a particular decision, and hence to discriminate more surely between alternative choices.

Out-Patient Appointment Systems

A somewhat different kind of problem worth considering is the largely organizational one of designing an optimum kind of appointment system for an out-patient department. This has architectural repercussions on the size and layout of consulting rooms as well as on the dimensions of the waiting space provided. However, the main impact seems to lie in trying to resolve the tricky question of whose time is most valuable, and in attempting to find a method of striking a balance between the interests of patients and consultants.[2]

Current practice varies enormously. Some departments have fairly streamlined appointment systems, while others have arrangements which are rather rough and ready. In some clinics the patients have very little waiting, and in others considerable periods may elapse between the booked appointment time and actual consultation. Again, views differ widely about what, if anything, can be done. Clearly, however, there are important problems worth investigating, though it may turn out in the event that they are too complex for any easy solutions to be forthcoming.

119

Norman T. J. Bailey

When a large number of clinics were critically investigated it seemed that very large average waiting times were usually due to the consultant's heavily over-insuring himself against the risk of wasting a few minutes. Naturally the consultant's time is valuable, but so is that of office workers, industrial employees, and housewives. The basic problem is not to ensure that nobody waits, which is in general impossible, but to strike a balance between conflicting claims.

In order to exhibit more clearly some of the essential features of the problem it was found convenient to construct a theoretical model which, though simplified, still retained many of the salient characteristics of the real situation. It is obvious that excessive waiting time for the patients can be avoided by staggering their appointment times and by starting the clinic with only a few present. But if this idea is over-done, we may find the consultant wasting much of his time waiting for patients. We want to know how these disadvantages are related, and a good deal of light is shed on the subject by the studies described below.

The fundamental aspect of the succession of patients in a clinic is determined by the patients' consultation periods. These may vary from a few seconds to perhaps half an hour or more. We must therefore use a statistical frequency distribution (χ^2 with five degrees of freedom seems fairly typical) to describe this source of variation. Random numbers can then be employed to produce an artificial series of typical consultation periods (which we shall assume covers all the activities in which the consultant's time is occupied with a given patient).

The investigation referred to took fifty such series, each of which contained twenty-five patients' consultation periods. Each series could be taken as a typical succession of arrivals at a clinic, and so a number of different appointment systems could be experimented with, all the consequences being calculated arithmetically. On the whole it seemed best to give the patients individual appointments at intervals equal to the average consultation period. The number of patients present at the beginning of the clinic was highly critical. Thus, if we assume an average consultation time of five minutes, the relationship between the patients' average waiting time and the consultant's average idle period *per session* is as shown in the Table.

A fairly reasonable arrangement would be to start the clinic with only two patients present before the consultant arrives. The patients as a whole then wait on average only nine minutes each, and the consultant wastes on average only six minutes per clinic. Most if not all of the latter would normally be covered by unavoidable clerical work. It can be seen from the Table that if the consultant arrives only when there are as many as six patients present his theoretical wastage is only $\frac{1}{2}$ minute per clinic. The patients on the other hand wait on average

No. of patients present at beginning of clinic	Patients' average waiting time (min.)	Consultant's average idle period per clinic (min.)
1	7	9
2	9	6
3	12	3
4	16	2
5	20	1
6	24	$\frac{1}{2}$

twenty-four minutes each, i.e. a total of 600 (= 25 × 24) minutes per clinic. With a larger initial reserve the situation is even worse.

Naturally it may be difficult to make an appointment system quite so simple as this in practice. Patients are often, for good reasons, not dealt with by a single doctor in strict rotation. There may in fact be a rather complicated pattern of multiple consultations. Emergency cases may arrive. Doctors may be detained on ward rounds. Patients may be late or fail to turn up. Nevertheless, it is often possible to use a model such as that above as a first approximation, and then to modify some of the results in accordance with any special features of a particular clinic.

The point is that this kind of investigation can be used to develop new ways of organizing the working pattern of a clinic. Increased efficiency is of benefit to patients and doctors alike. Architectural design is also affected, since shorter queues mean that less accommodation is required in waiting spaces.

The National Health Service

Another fertile field of investigation into the provision of medical care is the operation of the National Health Service. So far comparatively little has been done, but the importance of an operational research approach has been fully recognized for some time. The Guillebaud Committee's *Report*[11] on costs recommended that 'the Ministry of Health and the Department of Health for Scotland should set up a Research and Statistics Department which would devote the whole of its time to statistical investigation and operational research in general'. It was pointed out that such a department would not be very costly and one could 'regard the additional expenditure as a sound investment which would yield its return in the form of a wiser use of the community's resources in the future'.

For example, Regional Hospital Boards are always concerned to reduce costs and to utilize existing resources to the maximum. Because of the great variation between hospitals and the patients they serve, it is often very difficult to elicit the causes of high costs. But it is important to discover in any particular case whether they are really due to some form of extravagance or to inefficiency, or whether they are an inevitable result of the hospital having some highly specialized function to perform, such as neurosurgery.

The rising cost of the national drug bill is also a matter for concern. Some of the mechanisms at work have been studied by Martin.[8] Doctors should of course be free to prescribe whatever they think is best, but the freedom is difficult to exercise. Individual practitioners may have little direct acquaintance with the clinical properties and relative costs of each of a wide and complex range of alternative drugs. Some kind of administrative control such as the educative and coercive measures exercised by the Ministry of Health seems inevitable if regrettable.

Martin found that the frequency of prescribing depended on geographical position, morbidity, climate, and local custom, while the average total cost per prescription was related to social conditions. Authoritative recommendations about effecting economies without interfering with standards of treatment are not yet available. But such recommendations are what we really require, and they are likely to be sound only when formed on the basis of several careful investigations of the type mentioned.

There are obviously many other aspects of the provision of medical care that could be discussed, such as maternity services, diagnostic centres, home care schemes, etc. Most, if not all, of the topics referred to in this section can be regarded as coming under the heading of 'Social Medicine'. Whenever Social Medicine passes from the natural history stage of mere observation and classification to that of discovering and recommending appropriate action, it is involved in operational research.

Organizing Operational Research

It is easier to define the kind of problems with which operational research is concerned than to specify precisely how investigations should be planned and organized. The use of a multidisciplinary approach means that one of the basic difficulties is that of getting several people with very different types of background and training to work together in a constructive way. Members of research teams must, therefore, not only be experts in their own special subjects but also be capable of a considerable degree of co-operation with others. They must be able to appreciate sympathetically views which are radically different from their own, and at the same time be able to press their own arguments with tact if the data appear to demand it. A great deal of time may be taken up with long-drawn-out discussions, but this is unavoidable if essential differences are to be resolved, and if the team is to advance in a united and integrated manner.

The actual composition of an operational research team varies with the type of project. Thus in medical applications one may require doctor, nurse, architect, engineer, sociologist, accountant, statistician, etc. The co-operation of other organizations, such as local Medical Officers of Health or Regional Hospital Boards, may also have to be enlisted. It is usually best in practice to have a fairly small basic team of no more than about half a dozen research workers. At least half of these should have had some previous experience of operational research, and all should have a rational objective approach to their work. Ancillary workers such as clerical staff, computers, field workers, etc., may of course be required in much larger numbers.

The basic research team should be led by a director who, though personally responsible for the whole project, is able to allow the individual members a good deal of freedom in using their own particular skills. He should be able to inspire and control the general progress of the research with a light touch, as well as being capable of taking part in detailed discussion and argument if necessary.

The director will usually be responsible to some higher level organization or controlling committee. The latter should, so far as possible, allow him a fairly free hand, while keeping a close check on progress every three or six months. Apart from this overall control, it is often useful to have a standing panel of experts who can be consulted from time to time. Since the panel is mainly advisory, it can be made fairly large if necessary. The advantages of a broad reference can then be gained without the difficulties inherent in trying to reach working decisions with a large committee.

Books, Journals, and Societies

Since operational research is still a fairly new subject, it is perhaps worth making one or two remarks about books, journals and societies primarily concerned with the subject. Apart from the book by Morse and Kimball[9] already mentioned, that by Churchman *et al.*[4] may be recommended.

Papers having some contact with operational research may appear almost anywhere. However, the British *Operational Research Quarterly* and the American *Operations Research* are two key publications. The former is relatively non-technical, while the latter is rather more highly specialized. Quite a number of papers appearing in *Applied Statistics* are also, at least by implication, concerned with operational research.

Operational research societies are gradually increasing in number, and there is now an International Federation of Operational Research Societies, the individual societies of Britain and America being associated respectively with the journals mentioned above.

Conclusion

It has been possible in the limited space available in this chapter to discuss only some general principles and a few specific applications. Further examples of operational research methods are almost numberless. In the medical field, to take only a single case, we might consider the control of outbreaks of epidemic disease. Much more remains to be done in developing adequate mathematical models; in attempting to provide statistical predictions, perhaps using electronic computers; and in trying to devise more efficient methods of using medical knowledge that are at present socially and administratively acceptable.

Again, there are problems such as rehousing and the development of new communities. How best does one measure the degree of health, happiness, and efficiency in any social group, or indeed in the individual? How can one devise appropriate experiments or collect relevant data so as to promote social policies likely to augment these desirable qualities?

Road research is also a subject where the operational approach is vital. This has, of course, a marked technological aspect, as well as many economic, social, and psychological factors. There is also the difficulty of collecting relevant data and analysing them in time for useful applications to be made.

Education is another vast field in which a deliberately operational research approach would certainly repay the effort expended.

Without multiplying such examples further, it can be seen that the methods of operational research have almost unlimited scope in the social field. They are relevant by definition whenever questions arise of developing and implementing new policies. Moreover, the increased conscious use of objective and scientific methods in this field is bound to have a beneficial effect in generally sharpening concepts and in improving the precision with which they are handled.

REFERENCES

1. BAILEY, N. T. J. (1951) 'On Assessing the Efficiency of Single-room Provision in Hospital Wards', *J. Hyg. Camb.*, **49**, 452–57.

Operational Research

2. BAILEY, N. T. J. (1952) 'A Study of Queues and Appointment Systems in Hospital Outpatient Departments, with Special Reference to Waiting Times', *J.R. statist. Soc.*, **B. 14,** 185–99.
3. BAILEY, N. T. J. (1957) 'Operational Research in Hospital Planning and Design', *Operat. Res. Quart.*, **8,** 149–57.
4. CHURCHMAN, C. W., ACKOFF, R. L., & ARNOFF, E. L. (1957) *Introduction to Operations Research.* New York: Wiley.
5. DAVIES, R. LLEWELYN, NIGHTINGALE, J. W., & BAILEY, N. T. J. (1955) 'Laboratory Design: Survey of Space and Services Required in two Agricultural Research Laboratories', *Nature*, **176,** 999–1001.
6. GOODALL, J. W. D. (1951) 'Early Ambulation: A Survey of Hospital Practice', *Lancet*, **1,** 43.
7. GOODALL, J. W. D. (1951) 'Single Rooms in Hospital: Estimate of the Medical Need', *Lancet*, **1,** 1063.
8. MARTIN, J. P. (1957) *Social Aspects of Prescribing*, London: Heinemann.
9. MORSE, P. M., & KIMBALL, G. E. (1951) *Methods of Operational Research.* New York: Massachusetts Institute of Technology & Wiley.
10. NUFFIELD PROVINCIAL HOSPITALS TRUST (1955) *Studies in the Functions and Design of Hospitals*, London: Oxford Univ. Press.
11. *Report of the Committee of Enquiry [Guillebaud Committee] into the Cost of the National Health Service* (1956) London: H.M.S.O.

8

SOCIAL MEDICINE IN BRITAIN: STUDIES OF SOCIAL CLASS*

M. W. Susser

SOCIAL medicine has been variously defined. First, it has been regarded as a preserve of traditional Public Health, which for many has come to mean that branch of medicine practised by Medical Officers of Health. As prescribed in the National Health Service Act, this now includes the provision of services through social workers and health visitors, and the prevention of illness as an end in itself, unrelated to cure. Prevention is practised through the personal and educational methods of the maternity and child welfare clinics developed early in this century, and through the community measures initiated in the nineteenth century for the control of the physical environment. By the nature of the task, Public Health is obliged to take account of the social relations of disease.

Second, social medicine has been regarded as the proper exercise by the doctor of his responsibility for the social well-being of his individual patients, an extension of the social aspects of medical practice from the curative field. This position also leads to the recognition and study of society as a factor in disease and cure.

A third school in social medicine would develop the investigation of disease in populations as an academic discipline. This discipline had its

* Many of the ideas used in this paper were worked out with Dr William Watson during our collaboration on the book *Sociology in Medicine*.

127

origin in the needs of Public Health; essentially it undertakes large-scale studies by numerical methods, as distinct from the old-established 'case' method of clinical medicine, or from the newer techniques of the laboratory. Together with this method of large-scale research, a fourth school would include the application of its results through the various agencies for medical care.

It seems wise therefore to define terms. For the purpose of this paper we are concerned with social medicine as an academic discipline, and this we may take to be the study of the social relations of health and disease and medical practice. The application of the results of these studies, the practice of social medicine, is a matter for each agency of medical care, whether hospital, general practitioner, local authority, or administrative unit. The principal techniques for the study of social medicine are taken from epidemiology and sociology. These are its basic sciences, for social medicine is applied science, like all medicine, in so far as it is scientific.

In its present-day form, epidemiology closely resembles the branch of sociology known as ecology. It requires the use of numerical methods, and may be defined as the study in populations of the distribution of health and disease, and of factors that cause these distributions. Knowledge of these distributions can be put to a variety of uses.[72] 'Unexpected' distributions point up circumstances which occur in association with them as possible causes of disease, and at the same time distinguish vulnerable groups who can be afforded special protection. Regularities can also be identified, for instance in the concurrences of symptoms and signs which form the syndromes of clinical medicine. The identification of syndromes has always been a necessary first step in the progress of medicine. Moreover, the epidemiological method can bring into view the full range of the manifestations of a disorder and not only that aspect selected for care by a particular agency. Hence it allows of a proper evaluation of the importance of the disorder in the population, and of the precise need for prevention, control, and cure. Changes in diseases over time and in different circumstances can be recognized; services can be adapted accordingly and their efficiency continuously measured.

The interpretation of the distributions revealed by epidemiology requires sociological as well as medical insights, and so too may the choice of the factors and correlations to be sought by the method. The study of disease and health in populations is a study of processes of survival and selection, and in many respects these are social processes. Ageing and longevity are to a large extent determined by such processes, as are also the thresholds for complaint, the recognition of illness, the allocation of special types of sick role, and the selection of the chronic sick and handicapped for particular social positions. In many, social selection and cultural transmission contribute more to change and variation than do natural selection and genetic transmission, although both social and genetic processes are linked and interact.

The developing contribution of sociological concepts to studies of social medicine in Britain can perhaps best be seen in studies of social class and disease.

The Registrar General's Social Class Scale

Social factors in disease have long been recognized. In the early nineteenth century they began to be enumerated by men like William Farr, who in 1839 was the first statistical medical officer to be appointed to the General Registry Office. Shortly afterwards John Simon, who had been the first Medical Officer of Health to the City of London, began a series of classic socio-medical investigations.[8] As medical officer to the Privy Council from 1858 he directed a distinguished team in the study of such factors as nutrition, food, industrial hazards, housing, and venereal disease. The means of defining and differentiating social environments, however, were imprecise except in so far as they were separated in space. One early attempt to study disease in the different strata of society is reported to have been made in France by Villerme, who was a mentor of Farr. Villerme collected the deaths in Mulhouse over a decade, and in 1840 published an analysis of these by class and occupation.

In Britain T. H. C. Stevenson, a successor to Farr, made a major advance by devising an objective index for defining the social class position of individuals for the census of 1911. Beginning with the census of 1851, the enumeration had included occupations, and for that of 1911 Stevenson graded the occupations of heads of households into five separate classes. The census thus provided an estimate for the populations at risk in five social classes, and in some special groups such as unoccupied persons. Deaths were also registered by occupation, and therefore overall death rates, and death rates for specific diseases, could be stated for each class aggregate of occupations. Despite many limitations, this social class scale of the Registrar General has provided a convenient summary of the socio-economic environment and experience of large populations. The Registrar General now considers the basis of the classification to be the social prestige of occupations, although its original basis is more obscure, and was probably intended to be socio-economic.

Social Class Gradients in Disease

The most obvious disparities between classes were found in the ills associated with poverty. Social class gradients increasing towards the lower classes were found in deaths from many conditions. High infant mortality was already known to reflect poor social conditions, and malnutrition, gastro-enteritis, and pneumonia caused many deaths in the first five years of life among children of the lower social classes. Infectious diseases in adults, bronchitis, pneumonia, and tuberculosis, ulcers and cancers of the stomach, and rheumatic heart disease, were all commoner among the poor. The enumeration of this 'heap of ills' among the lower classes provided ammunition for arguments among reformers, some of whom even contemplated the radical cure of social ills through the elimination of the unfit, an idea derived from the misapplied fusion of the theories of Darwin and Mendel. But equally the revelation of social gradients acted as a stimulus to the social reform that had begun during the industrial revolution.

The planners of the Welfare State intended to eliminate poverty, and with this, the different incidence of disease between rich and poor. Taking stock now, in 1961, we can say that this has not yet come about. The infant mortality rate, for instance, has fallen in almost parallel fashion in each social class, and among the newborn in the first month of life the disparity is perhaps greater than before.[72, 73]

Many reasons have been suggested for this failure to abolish differences between the social classes. The disparity has been ascribed to 'culture-lag', in the sense of an imbalance arising from an uneven rate of change in interrelated cultural elements. The alleviation of poverty is thought to have proceeded more rapidly than the alleviation of ignorance, and than changes in the customary behaviour and values which affect health. Thus there is a social class gradient in the efficient use of health services as well as in diseases, and the lower social classes make less use of some of the services which are provided by the National Health Service, for example, general hospitals, and maternity and child welfare services.[5, 25, 52, 70] In marked contrast with the wives in the professional and salaried classes, the wives of manual workers get less antenatal care, use fewer vitamins and supplementary foods, and their children are less often immunized.

These disadvantages may be reinforced through unwitting discrimination made between the classes by the services themselves, and examples of this have been documented in the United States in the treatment of psychiatric illness.[49] Although these differences have not yet been shown to operate in psychiatric illness in Britain,[43] criteria with a cultural content, for instance the 'co-operation' of parents, are widely used for selecting patients suitable for treatment in child guidance clinics. Similar social criteria enter, in other fields of practice, into relations with 'uncooperative' patients: for example, health visitors have been found to call more often on clinic attenders than on others.[62]

This cultural explanation of persisting class differences in disease is not in itself sufficient, for cultural factors cannot be dissociated from physical, economic, and demographic factors. Although stark poverty is much rarer, extreme differences in physical environment still exist. One consequence is seen in the social pattern of road accidents, which affect many more lower-class children, a pattern correlated with their lack of playing space.[2] Other consequences follow from the facility of spread in overcrowded houses of respiratory infections, including pneumonia and tuberculosis.[92]

The influence of such demographic factors as the age and sex structure of the population and age at marriage appears in the different courses of individual and family life cycles in different social classes. Women of the lower social classes bear more illegitimate babies, have more pre-nuptial conceptions, marry younger, have larger families, and in sum are more fertile. Although their youth gives them some advantage in childbearing, all these other factors concentrated in the lower social classes act against efficient reproduction. High fertility with close spacing is not only wearing to maternal health, but also leads to high foetal and child death rates, for irrespective of social class, mothers with many births have high stillbirth rates, and in infancy their children have high mortality rates.[21, 35, 45, 47, 76] Moreover, after the neo-natal period young mothers lose more infants than older mothers, and the incidence of infections is greater among their children.[60, 80] Illegitimacy too is associated with high infant mortality.[46]

Physical, social, and economic factors combine to produce disease gradients between the social classes, such as those that appeared in a follow-up study of a national sample of children.[25] The impact of illness in the lower classes seemed to depend less on the more frequent occurrence of illness than on its greater severity. Thus colds were evenly distributed, bronchitis showed a moderate social class trend, and other serious respiratory diseases such as pneumonia showed a marked trend, that is, the lower classes suffered the more severe and fatal forms of a given disease. Some of the reasons for this may be sought in the pattern of family life. In large families, pre-school children are often exposed to the infection commonly brought home by school-going siblings.[3] Resistance to infection is low in very young children, and may be further reduced by poor nutrition, so that they suffer more severely. In these families parents may also be less alert to danger signs, or less ready to seek medical attention, or their children may be admitted to hospital less readily. Taking all infant deaths, distinctly more infants from Social Class I die in hospital than do infants from lower social classes.[80]

From the point of view of health the very young and the very old are both especially vulnerable groups in society. In the lower social classes there are fewer survivors into old age. Those who do survive retire from work sooner, and have more and worse disabilities,[27, 28] and find

M. W. Susser

less alleviation for their infirmities. Their housing is less suitable, they tend to have fewer domestic amenities, and they lack prepared meals, domestic and nursing care, and company.[57]

The interconnexion between way of life and the form of disease is well displayed by studies of schizophrenia. This psychosis is most commonly found in young men in unskilled occupations, and hospital patients come particularly from deteriorated city areas.[9, 42, 93] The apparently high incidence among the lowest social classes is attributed by some to the pressure of adverse social conditions, by others to the downward social drift of individuals predisposed to schizophrenia or suffering from it. The consistently poor prognosis of patients from the lower classes, however, must be ascribed largely to unfavourable social circumstances. Lower-class patients spend longer in mental hospitals, run a greater risk of becoming chronic cases, and more often fail to remain in the community after discharge.[20] In part these poor results can be related to the attitudes to mental illness current in the lower classes: lower-class patients co-operate less well in treatment, and the general impression is that they are often reluctant to seek the aid of psychiatric agencies.

Recognition and acceptance of mental illness and tolerance of its effects may therefore play a part in prognosis, but the ability to benefit from such favourable attitudes is much restricted by social conditions. The social roles which the discharged patient is obliged to play as a member of a household have been shown to be of great importance in resettlement,[11] and perhaps the most important of these is his role as a worker. Patients in the higher social classes tend to return to their former occupations, while those of the lower classes more often move into a series of new jobs, or new trades, or into a state of chronic unemployment.[20] The opportunity for a gradual return to work and for adjusting the job to the person, and tolerance of such things as poor time-keeping or erratic behaviour, are possibly greater in middle-class than in lower-class occupations. Also, as reflected in studies of prognosis, the community provides more satisfactory roles for the resettlement of middle-class than of lower-class patients. This is probably related to the difference in family, social, and economic resources between the classes, and to personal training and skills.

Variations in health between the social classes thus hinge on the whole pattern of living. Since these patterns are changing, so is the incidence of disease. Mortality from rheumatic heart disease has fallen most steeply in the lower classes, causing the social class gradient to level out. In addition the gaps in overall mortality are narrowing within certain age-groups. The mortality rate in Social Class V, for children aged one to two years, was 400 per cent higher than that in Social Class I twenty years ago: it is now only 63 per cent higher.[73] These changes may be attributed to new modes of life, including the more even use and distribution of medical care.

Duodenal Ulcer

This dynamic quality of the social environment can be illustrated by an analysis of the social class distribution of duodenal ulcers. There has been a steep rise in mortality from the disease since the beginning of the century, particularly in men,[4, 51] and because of this rise it has earned a place as one of the 'diseases of civilization'. In the 1950s, however, a plateau was reached, and a fall in mortality has now begun (see Fig. 1). Although this change in death rates has been attributed to better medical care,[53] further study indicates that it is probably connected with a real fall in incidence. The explanation with the best fit, it may be suggested, is that the generations born in the last quarter of the

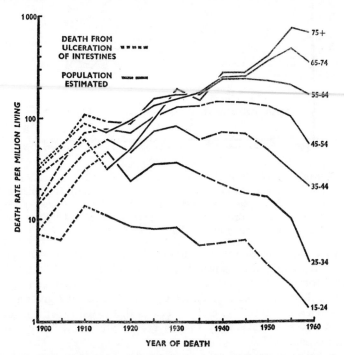

FIG. 1. Male deaths from Duodenal Ulcer 1900–1959 by age groups. Log Graphs constructed from Annual Reviews of the Registrar General. (From 1900 to 1911 deaths were not certified to duodenal ulcer, and the figures for ulceration of the intestine have been used. The populations at risk have been estimated for the period of World War II.)

nineteenth century were exposed to particular environmental hazards which produced a risk of bearing duodenal ulcers, and this risk they have carried throughout life.[96]

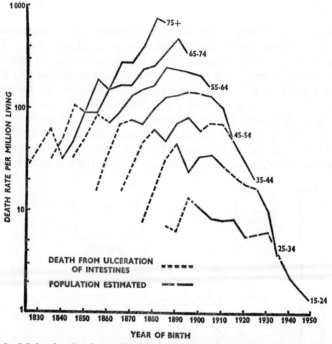

FIG. 2. Male deaths from Duodenal Ulcer 1900–1959 by cohorts. Log Graph constructed from Annual Reviews of the Registrar General. The points along each age curve represent the death rates of successive generations. The death rates of a particular generation are read by passing vertically from curve to curve above the year of birth.

An examination of the experience of each age-group through the years reveals that the chance of death from duodenal ulcer first increased for each successive cohort born from 1850 to about 1890, and declined thereafter (see Fig. 2). Analysis by age-cohorts gives a longitudinal view of mortality, and segregates the actual experience of the generations more effectively than a cross-sectional view at a single point in time.[34, 64]

Social class death rates support this result. They show that each class as well as each age-group carried forward its own specific risk of death from duodenal ulcer. The first statistics available are those for the period of the 1921 census (Table I). Although there was then no social class gradient below the age of forty-five, a gradient emerged above this age, with the highest rates occurring in the higher social classes.[78] A decade later, at the period of the 1931 census, the social class gradient first appeared in the age-group now ten years older, that is, at age fifty-five. Finally at the time of the 1951 census, this gradient only appeared in the age group over seventy (at these high ages, however, statistics on specific causes of death may not be very reliable).

TABLE I

MORTALITY IN MALES FROM DUODENAL ULCERS BY AGE AND SOCIAL CLASS

(Deaths per 100,000 Living to the nearest whole number)

Year	Social class	20–24	25–34	35–44	45–54	55–64	65–69	70+
1921–23	I & II	1	3	5	10	12	18	15
	III	1	2	5	7	9	11	7
	IV	2	2	6	8	8	10	7
	V	2	3	8	8	9	6	6
1930–32	I & II	1	3	6	13	19	24	35
	III	1	3	7	13	15	18	18
	IV	2	4	8	11	13	14	13
	V	1	4	9	14	14	13	15
1949–53	I & II	1	1	3	11	20	40	62
	III	1	2	5	13	26	44	48
	IV	1	1	6	12	21	37	46
	V	1	3	6	16	29	40	46

In the absence of statistics relating to earlier cohorts it can only be inferred that the higher social classes were the first to be exposed to some noxious environmental factor of limited duration, so that death rates among them are now the first to recede. Thus the fall in mortality in the younger age-groups at the period of the 1951 census was most evident in the higher social classes; a social class gradient with the lowest death rates in these classes appeared among younger men, the reverse of the gradient in previous censuses.

M. W. Susser

The falling trend of incidence is shown in some but not all of the available sickness statistics. In a disease with a low case-fatality rate such as duodenal ulcer, morbidity and mortality statistics may diverge and render interpretation difficult, for the few individuals who die of the disease may be unrepresentative of those who suffer from it. The lack of correspondence between diverse measures of incidence is only one problem among many which complicate the interpretation of the current pattern of duodenal ulcer mortality, and explanations other than the cohort hypothesis need to be considered, such as unequal and selective survival in each social class, or uneven distribution of treatment in different age and class groups. None of these, however, appears to be consistent with all the facts. For instance, the high mortality rate among the oldest age-groups in the higher social classes is contrary to what would be expected if better treatment accounted for the decline in the overall death rate from ulcers, for all available studies show that among the higher classes the use of services is more effective.

On this analysis duodenal ulcer is on the decline, and cannot be regarded simply as a disease of civilization in the sense that it is caused mainly by stresses common to industrial societies, for these might be expected to increase or at least to continue as the society becomes more elaborate, and to affect a greater proportion of the population as more individuals are caught up in urban modes of life. Upheavals which had an uneven impact on successive generations, such as World War I and the unemployment of the 1930s, may provide a better explanation; but the nature of the hazards in the environment to which the most affected generations might have been exposed remains obscure. An alternative explanation is possible, because disease is a consequence of interaction between environment and host, and the altered incidence could arise as well from changes in the host as from changes in the environment. Large sections of the population may be learning to adapt to the demands of industrial society, so that these have become less stressful than before.

Duodenal ulcer seems to have moved through the classes in the wake of economic and cultural movements, with their accompanying changes in health and medical care. In an open society diseases, like persons, objects, and ideas, may also exhibit social mobility. In some cases the diagnosis rather than the disease may be mobile, for fashion in diagnosis can show the same mobility as fashion in women's clothes, and this enjoins a certain caution in interpretation of the data on duodenal ulcer. Thus social movement from the higher to the lower classes has been traced for such operations as tonsillectomy and circumcision,[25] and for many other forms of medical treatment which have fluctuated with the fashion of medical opinion. This, however, does not seem to be sufficient to explain the cohort phenomenon in duodenal ulcer, because

136

medical opinion has tended to lag behind the actual changes. For instance, duodenal ulcer was thought especially to affect young men, until a survey after World War II showed it to be a disease of middle-aged and elderly men; presumably earlier in the century physicians had observed the increasing incidence in these same cohorts, who were then young men.

Many attempts have been made to identify factors which might influence the changing incidence of duodenal ulcer, such as those connected with particular occupations, and thereby with social class.[23] Farm-workers have been found to have a low ulcer morbidity, managers and foremen a modest excess. These findings may indicate a relationship between duodenal ulcer and work fraught with conflict situations, for they seem to be particular to the occupation.

Readily expressed anxiety about work was much more common among managers and foremen than among others, and among patients with duodenal ulcers than among controls. This could have arisen from external sources of anxiety, or from a process of selection. Anxious, conscientious men might have the greatest chance both of becoming managers and foremen, and of falling sick with duodenal ulcer. On the other hand miners, a very different category of men, are also beset with special anxieties, and they too have a high rate of sickness from duodenal ulcer.[22, 40] Selection can hardly account for high rates of sickness in both occupational groups, for the social and personal factors which determine the selection of miners for their jobs are entirely different from those which determine the selection of managers and foremen in industry. Hence these associations seem to support the clinical impression that external sources of anxiety may be conducive to duodenal ulcer.

Coronary Disease

Studies of *coronary heart disease* provide a further example in which study of a disease in contrasting social environments has proved illuminating in the search for causes. This form of heart disease results from occlusion of the coronary arteries of the heart, and it may be fatal or seriously crippling to those who suffer from it. Middle-aged men of Social Classes I and II are the chief victims, and mortality from the disease declines through Social Classes I to IV. Affluent societies suffer more coronary heart disease than poor societies, and in accord with this, the mortality from the disease in Great Britain has shown a definite and sharp increase since 1925, when it first began to appear in mortality statistics.[71] A further example is provided by Yemenites in Israel in so far as a change from poor to relatively affluent circumstances can be equated with migration from the Arab Yemen to Israel. A recent study in Israel showed that the group of Yemenites who immigrated in the 1920s, and whose way of life since then had become relatively westernized, had a death rate nearly ten times as high as a second group of the same age who entered the country following World War II. This finding is important because racial factors, variation in diagnosis, and medical care are held constant, thus providing a well-controlled study.[97]

There are obvious contrasts in the life of rich and poor in such matters as the type and amount of food eaten, and the type and amount of physical exercise taken. Both gluttony and sloth have been pursued as causes of coronary heart disease, although not finally incriminated.

Most dietary studies have focused on the fat content of the diet. Certain types of fat raise blood cholesterol levels, and high cholesterol levels tend to precede the occurrence of coronary heart disease; at the same time cholesterol appears to play a part in the pathological processes underlying the occlusion of coronary arteries. Correlations have been made between mortality from coronary heart disease and fat consumption in populations. [36, 55] But this is by no means confirmed in all studies, and the dietary hypothesis has been challenged. The total calorie intake and other components of diet, for instance proteins, minerals, fibre, and starch, also affect cholesterol levels and vary as much as fat in different environments.[82, 83, 100] Indeed, the precise elements and balance of diets that lead to raised cholesterol levels are not agreed upon. Furthermore, in Britain diets have tended to be fairly uniform between the social classes since 1940, nor do diets appear to have changed at the rate that mortality from coronary heart disease has increased.

Exercise has been found to keep cholesterol levels down, and with sufficient exercise high fat diets do not increase cholesterol levels.[66] In a national post-mortem survey, occupations were graded according to the amount of activity they involved. By this grading, the less active at work had the most disease.[75] Within each grade of occupation, 'light', 'active', and 'heavy', the evidence of coronary heart disease showed no social class trend. However, the overall distribution of lesions is consistent with the established social class gradient, for 'light' occupations predominate in the higher social classes, and 'heavy' ones in the lower.

Further study by occupations suggests that the particular effect of exercise may be to protect the younger members of the affected age-groups against acute episodes. The conductors of double-decker buses are both less sedentary than the drivers and less subject to acute deaths from coronary heart disease; postmen are much less sedentary at work than most post-office clerks and switchboard operators, and they too are less subject to acute coronary deaths.[74, 77]

Emotional factors connected with certain occupations and thereby

Social Medicine in Britain

with social class have also been considered, although not established, as a factor in coronary heart disease. One American study showed a rise in cholesterol levels in men at defined stress periods. Two groups of accountants, each with a different time of maximum pressure in their jobs, had peak cholesterol levels which coincided with these periods. Other studies have attempted to show that coronary heart disease is related to a type of personality in men which is encouraged by conditions in large American organizations. These are men committed to deadlines and competition and a continuing sense of urgency.[31, 32]

Thus there are several specific factors which may contribute to the social class gradient in coronary heart disease. The higher classes may eat more of some types of food and less of others, they drive more often than walk, sit at desks rather than bend over work-benches, and perhaps they commit themselves more readily to a particular kind of emotional stress.

Social Mobility

Analysis of disease by social class is not enough to describe its relation to stratification in a class society. Social mobility complicates the distribution of populations within a class system, and epidemiological studies are beginning to take account of this. Allowance must be made for it in framing genetic and environmental hypotheses, both of which have often treated the social classes as stable populations with fixed characteristics. Individuals may be selected for mobility by genetic and social traits through education and occupation, or through marriage, and so alter the distribution of the traits between the classes. Moreover, vertical social mobility may bring with it special stresses, similar in kind to those ascribed to the lateral movement of migration.[33, 65, 81]

Durkheim recognized that the transitions accompanying social mobility, whether upward or downward, could lead to stress in individuals, and in some cases to suicide. He related suicide in populations to a number of social factors, including the state of *anomie* that accompanies the breakdown of cultural values in certain groups subjected to the pressure of urban societies.[26] An excessive pressure towards anomie in the lowest social strata of the United States has been attributed to the conflict between the cultural goal of success and the impossibility of its fulfilment for these social groups. Corresponding subjective and individual responses have been described in which the fulfilment of impulse tends to replace social norms, and these have a bearing on psychopathology.[63, 67, 84, 86] In Britain this phenomenon has been little explored, except in the case of suicide and schizophrenia. Thus an ecological study of London boroughs showed a positive correlation between high rates of suicide and single-room households.[87] While such ecological studies can discover associations between phenomena, they cannot identify causal relationships without relating the suspected factor to particular cases. Well-designed studies made to identify vertical social mobility as a cause of stress in particular cases are very few. Moreover, the possible compensatory effect of successful mobility, in societies where this is an approved social goal, has been little considered.

In Britain the effects of social mobility on patterns of disease have been studied especially in childbearing, in mental subnormality, and in schizophrenia, but in each case these studies relate to the distribution of certain traits between the classes, and not to the stresses of mobility. [38, 50, 79, 94, 95]

In a population of women attending hospital during their first pregnancy in Aberdeen, those who were well-favoured in height tended not only to have favourable obstetric rates, but also to have moved upwards in the occupational scale at marriage, in the sense that their husbands were of higher occupational class than their fathers.[50] In contrast, stunted women with poor obstetric rates tended to have moved occupationally downward at marriage. From this it appears that women who reproduce efficiently are recruited from the lower occupations to the higher, while those who are inefficient remain in the lower occupational categories, or join them. This suggests that in the selection of spouses there is also a selection of traits related to fitness for reproduction, whether these are genetic or social or both. The association of upward movement with favourable reproductive rates, and downward movement with poor rates, will tend to make the gradient in obstetric rates steeper between the social classes.

Some of this social movement may be an artefact produced by the inadequacy of the Registrar General's scale as a model of society, in that the allocation of occupations to the various social classes is largely arbitrary, and may not be in accord with the social esteem in which they are held among the people. The Registrar General's scale may sometimes indicate a disparity in social class between husband and father which would not appear if social class were determined by local criteria. A greater problem is that the scale cannot allow for the effect of age on occupational status. Fathers may belong to the same social milieu as sons-in-law and yet have occupations of higher standing because of their seniority. On the other hand the trend of social mobility has been upward in any recent interval between the entry into occupations of fathers and sons-in-law, and would have tended to counter this effect. Despite such difficulties, the Aberdeen figures show a consistency which suggests that obstetric death rates in the various social classes are affected by social selection and movement between the classes.

This very tidiness of the Aberdeen results has been criticized, because

Social Medicine in Britain

irregularities in occupational mortality rates militate against such consistency. Some occupations in Class III have mortality rates for infants, and for the 'social' diseases, which are in excess of those for occupations in Classes IV and V. For instance, among colliery faceworkers and other skilled occupations of coalminers in Class III these rates are distinctly higher than among textile workers of Class IV.[44]

Disparities of this kind between the social class grading and expected biological results may be caused either by the nature of the biological phenomenon, or by arbitrary classification in the social class scale. In the case of textile workers and coalminers, the irregular results do appear to be artefacts caused by the construction of the scale. An examination of a number of occupations reveals a pattern of disease which cuts across the social class grading of the Registrar General. On the whole high infant mortality rates, and high mortality from bronchitis, pneumonia, and tuberculosis, are found in the occupations which involve rough manual labour; in contrast lighter sedentary occupations are associated with lower rates.

In trying to devise a unilineal scale of social class which is valid for the nation, the Registrar General faces an impossible task. Each occupational group has a very wide span, so that pedagogues can include vice-chancellors of universities as well as kindergarten teachers. Specific occupations may embrace an equally wide range of social classes; a farmer may be a duke or a tenant, and a company director may direct anything from a small local business to the Bank of England.

Individuals have multiple social roles which cannot be described by a single index such as occupation. Over a period of time they may have multiple occupations as well, and their mobility between occupations will tend to be in different directions at different ages, upward before retirement and downward after. This effect of age on occupational mobility varies with occupational category; for instance, downward mobility after retirement occurs less often among entrepreneurs and the self-employed. Difficulties are increased by the technical problems of recording. In one national survey 12 per cent of the information recorded by health visitors had later to be re-classified, and similar errors contribute at least some part of the high death rates among faceworkers in the coalmines.[24, 48, 68]

More fundamental problems of classification are caused by the inescapable subjective elements that enter into the ranking of occupations. A blurring of the social gradations recognized by an observer tends to accompany increased geographical or social distance, and the Registrar General is not immune to this. Thus his scale discriminates fairly well at the upper end of the social spectrum, for instance between the learned and the other professions, but poorly at the lower end. Half the population falls into Social Class III, which includes such large and

141

divergent occupations as colliers and clerks. The pitfalls of subjective judgements are multiplied by the relative rigidity of any scale which has to be applied to the constant flux over time of an expanding industrial economy. The content and structure of occupations change, and so does their social prestige, and the elements of skill and training necessary to them as new methods of production are introduced.

These difficulties cannot be avoided in any usable social class scale, although ingenuity may diminish them. Watson's 'spiralist' theory postulates a plurality of cultures and of social gradations, each with its own set of reference groups.[98] Spiralists are persons engaged in professional and managerial work in large-scale organizations; they are socially and spatially mobile, and they share a generic culture and dispersed social networks. They form a social class distinct from the many local cultures of British society. Broadly, each of these communities has at the top its own group of burgesses, for instance local businessmen, lawyers, and general practitioners, with below a working-class differentiated into groups by their varying potential for social mobility. The definitive feature of the local cultural groups is their stability, for they have a large proportion of geographically circumscribed marriages and a low rate of emigration.

Mental Subnormality

Social mobility must be considered as a factor in the distribution of mental subnormality, and models of the class distribution of intelligence generally try to allow for it. In the 1920s Lewis made a national survey of the prevalence of mental deficiency which was published in the findings of the Wood Report. This study led him to conclude that a large proportion of the mentally subnormal were of a type he termed 'subcultural'. By this he meant that they were unable to meet the demands of the local culture and thus fell below its standards, and not that they were a subgroup of the culture in the sociological sense. He considered that this category of cases was medically normal, and that biologically it represented the lower end of a continuum on which intelligence is distributed in the population.[58, 99] Such cases comprise perhaps three-quarters of all those classified as subnormal, and they are concentrated among the lower social classes. Although some workers have regarded this distribution as largely genetic in origin, other evidence has accumulated to suggest that levels of intelligence in populations are related to the cultural milieu.[12, 19, 41, 88]

On the basis of these facts, the type of subnormality described by Lewis as 'subcultural' might indeed be specific to a subculture in the sociological sense. A study was therefore made in Lancashire of a number of young adults in their early twenties who had been 'ascertained' at school as 'educationally subnormal'.[94, 95] This means that teachers had recognized them as backward, and referred them to the school doctor, who in turn had recommended special schooling for them. The educationally subnormal form a marginal group between dull children and the severely subnormal who have been excluded from school.

An attempt was made to devise an objective means, based on the 'spiralist' hypothesis, of identifying the subcultural groups to which the subjects belonged. All their parents had belonged to a local working-class culture. By criteria of occupation and education, the families were allocated either to an 'aspirant' and potentially socially mobile category or to a 'demotic' and socially stationary category. (*Aspirant* families were defined as those with fathers belonging to a non-manual occupation or with at least one child who had attended grammar school: *demotic* families were defined as those with fathers belonging to manual occupations and with no child who had attended grammar school.) Families differentiated in this way shared a number of other characteristics, such as amount of migration between generations, use of services, acceptance of the research, and family size, which would seem to support the assumption that they belonged to distinct subcultures.

Independent clinical examinations showed that the distribution of clinical types between the two subcultural categories was quite different. The nine children from the aspirant subculture formed a heterogeneous class, all of whom had presumptive evidence of brain damage or, in one case, severe deafness. Some of the ninety-seven subjects from the demotic subculture had similar lesions, but the majority were medically normal. In this sample, such medically normal cases were confined to the demotic subculture. They were further distinguished from those with presumptive brain damage by a tendency to have gained in intelligence in the years since their childhood tests. This suggests that they suffered from intellectual retardation and not from a permanent intellectual deficit—a result in keeping with a previous study among the subnormal in hospital.[16, 17]

This distribution of cases might not have represented the true incidence, but could have come about because of biased selection and ascertainment depending on social factors. The selection process was therefore examined against the actual distribution of low intelligence in the appropriate Lancashire city of 160,000 people.

The schools were graded according to social standing, taking into account occupation of parents, residential rating, and educational levels in the area served by each school. In the schools of low social standing the proportion of children with intelligence quotients under eighty was ten times as high as in the schools of high social standing. The proportion of children selected as subnormal reflected this distribution. (See

143

M. W. Susser

Table II.) A search of local private schools showed that dull children were not hidden from the survey in such schools.

TABLE II

Distribution of I.Q.s and referrals for backwardness by social standing of schools.

	SOCIAL STANDING OF SCHOOLS			
	Low	Low Average	High Average	High
Children at risk.	11,000	22,500	4,000	1,500
I.Q. at 11 years: % under 80	9·7	8·0	5·4	0·65
% referred as backward	2·5	2·4	1·8	0·9
% referred as backward I.Q. less than 80	1·1	0·8	0·7	0·1
% referred as backward I.Q. less than 80 'clinically normal'	1·0	0·7	0·6	0·06

This epidemiological evidence on the distribution of low intelligence can be supported by material from other surveys which have shown a class distribution for all levels of intelligence,[13, 29, 89] and it indicates that there are very few children of 'subnormal' intelligence in the higher social classes. Moreover, taken together with the preceding clinical and sociological study it suggests that these few children are likely to be brain-damaged or to suffer from a physical or psychological handicap to learning which can be discovered on thorough investigation. If this is confirmed, the 'subnormal' range of intelligence in clinically normal subjects can be regarded as a specific attribute of the demotic subculture.

The segregation of this attribute in a single subculture might be caused either by a process of social selection which confined genes for intelligence to that subculture, or by the adverse effects of the cultural milieu. The genetic hypothesis alone does not appear adequate to explain such a distribution. Despite the relative social and spatial

144

immobility of demotic families, there is sufficient intermarriage and social movement to discount the possibility that genes for low intelligence might be confined to a single group, which by implication would constitute a separate race. Alternatively, the distribution would require an almost perfect correspondence between social mobility and genes for intelligence, which nowhere occurs.[59]

Nevertheless, selection for social mobility by *measured intelligence* has been demonstrated. A Stockholm study of young men related their intelligence scores and their occupations to paternal occupations,[7] and the study of Aberdeen mothers bearing their first child related intelligence scores to social mobility through marriage. In both studies those of higher measured intelligence tended to ascend the social scale, and those of low intelligence to descend. An American attempt has been made to quantify the contribution of measured intelligence to the disparity in social prestige between paternal and filial occupations, and an estimated 40 per cent of actual mobility was ascribed to intelligence.[1] All the evidence shows that the correspondence of intelligence and mobility is a partial one.

Whatever the degree of this correspondence, social mobility in one generation could not produce the social class gradient of intelligence in children, because the social class position of a child depends on the attributes of his family at a time before genetic endowment or other factors could act to displace him into the class appropriate to his degree of intelligence. According to the theoretical models of genetic transmission, in these circumstances subnormal intelligence should occur in some clinically normal subjects in all social classes, and this seems not to be the case.

This discussion cannot be conclusive, however, until a clinical study has been made of *all* children of low intelligence within a defined population, for social selection has not so far been entirely excluded as a cause for the apparent segregation of low intelligence in the clinically normal. Children selected for ascertainment are recognized by their educational backwardness, and clinically normal children of low intelligence from the higher social classes might not be backward—as is perhaps suggested by the greater educational attainments of higher-class children for a given level of intelligence.[30]

Nevertheless, on the basis of a wide range of evidence, cultural and family influences may be considered as of major importance in social class differences in measured intelligence. Comparative surveys suggest that an impoverished cultural environment depresses measured intelligence, and experimental work shows that a stimulating intellectual environment produces improved intellectual performances.[6, 16, 17, 18, 56, 61] Thus the cultural milieu of each class is likely to be a main determinant of the distribution of the measured intelligence within it, and where social conditions and the climate of values are hostile to intellectual achievement, a downward shift can be expected. The range of individual variation for innate intelligence within each class is not known, but it seems probable that susceptible individuals, presumably those with a limited innate endowment, will suffer from intellectual retardation only in an unfavourable environment.

Social Medicine and the Social Sciences

The preceding discussion illustrates that social medicine shares fields of study with other disciplines in the social sciences, and that the results from various fields may be needed to reinforce one another. A main task of the doctor, including the specialist in social medicine, is to synthesize the contributions from a large range of basic sciences, and to apply them to the study and care of the patient. Sociological concepts have been used in this way in the study of the problems of social class in medicine, and as always, applied research interacts with pure research, and each feeds the other.

Socio-medical investigations in Britain cover more areas relevant to sociology than can be encompassed in a short paper. Each school of social medicine has its special interest. The topic of social class has been used here as the basis for an account of the research in social medicine which may be of sociological interest, but even an account with this restrictive aim has had to be incomplete. There are signs besides the few studies quoted that the concepts of sociology and social anthropology are finding a place in medical research in Britain, although they are few in comparison with American developments, where it is reported that some two hundred medical sociologists are registered.[85] Ideas from sociology have been used to study aspects of medicine other than social class phenomena. Examples can be found in researches into the ecology of schizophrenia and of suicide, the stay in hospital and the resettlement of chronic schizophrenics, the life of old people and of working women in the community, family influences in duodenal ulcer, and the evaluation of the effect of health education campaigns on popular beliefs. Some of the work on the development and functioning of medical care has also had a sociological bias.[9, 10, 11, 14, 20, 37, 42, 90, 93]

A large but undeveloped area still awaits exploration. Medical sociology may provide rewards for the doctor in the elucidation of disease processes, and it may reward the sociologist no less as a well-defined social field, in which indices of health and disease provide objective parameters. So far, British work has been limited to the relevance of social factors in two main aspects of medicine: first, in the configuration of disease and the precipitation of illness, and second, in the restoration of function to sick persons and the efficient delivery of

Social Medicine in Britain

medical care. In the United States analysis of the functions of medicine in industrial society has gone further, and has yielded insights into the nature of the social system.[84] A model for the process of acquiring professional values has been found in medical education, and the study of medical institutions has illuminated the interplay of bureaucratic and professional organizations.[15, 39, 54, 69, 91] In Britain these major aspects of medical sociology are largely untouched.

REFERENCES

1. ANDERSON, C. A., *et al.* (1942) 'Intelligence and Occupational Mobility'. *J. Pol. Econ.*, **40**, 218–39.
2. BACKETT, E. M., & JOHNSTON, A. M. (1959) 'Social Patterns of Road Accidents to Children'. *Brit. med. J.*, **i**, 409.
3. BADGER, G. F., *et. al.* (1953) 'A Study of Illness in a Group of Cleveland Families. II: Incidence of Common Respiratory Diseases. III: Introduction of Respiratory Infections into Families'. *Amer. J. Hyg.*, **58**, 31 and 41.
4. BAGER, B. (1929) *Acta chir, scand.*, **64**, Suppl. 11.
5. BARR, A. (1929) 'Hospital Admissions and Social Environment'. *Med. Offr.*, **100**, 351.
6. BERNSTEIN, B. (1958) 'Some Sociological Determinants of Perception'. *Brit. J. Sociol.*, **9**, 159.
7. BOALT, G. Quoted by Lipset and Bendix (59).
8. BROCKINGTON, C. F. (1959) 'Public Health at the Privy Council'. *Med. Offr.*, **101**, 185.
9. BROOKE, E. M. (1959) 'National Statistics in the Epidemiology of Mental Illness'. *J. ment. Sci.*, **105**, 893.
10. BROWN, G. W. (1959) 'Social Factors Influencing Length of Hospital Stay in Schizophrenic Patients'. *Brit. med. J.*, **ii**, 100.
11. BROWN, G. W., CARSTAIRS, G. M., & TOPPING, G. (1958) 'Post-Hospital Adjustment of Chronic Mental Patients'. *Lancet*, **ii**, 685.
12. BURT, C. (1943) 'Ability and Income'. *Brit. J. educ. Psychol.*, **13**, 88–92.
13. BURT, C. (1950) *The Backward Child*, 3rd edn. London: Univ. of London Press.
14. CARTWRIGHT, A., *et al.* (1960) 'Efficiency of an Anti-Smoking Campaign'. *Lancet*, **i**, 327.
15. CAUDILL, W. *The Psychiatric Hospital as a Small Society.* Cambridge, Mass.: Harvard Univ. Press, 1958.
16. CLARKE, A. D. B., & CLARKE, A. M. (1953) 'How Constant is the I.Q.?' *Lancet*, **ii**, 877.
17. CLARKE, A. D. B., CLARKE, A. M., & REIMAN, S. (1958) 'Cognitive and Social Changes in the Feeble-minded—Three Further Studies'. *Brit. J. Psychol.*, **49**, 144.
18. CLARKE, A. M., & CLARKE, A. D. B. *Mental Deficiency: The Changing Outlook.* London: Methuen, 1958.

147

19. CONWAY, J. (1958) 'The Inheritance of Intelligence and its Social Implications'. *Brit. J. stat. Psychol.*, **11**, 171-90.
20. COOPER, B. (1961) 'Social Class and Prognosis in Schizophrenia'. *Brit. J. prev. soc. Med.*, **15**, 17 and 31.
21. DALY, C., HEADY, J. A., & MORRIS, J. N. (1955) 'Social and Biological Factors in Infant Mortality: III. The Effect of Mother's Age and Parity on Social Class Differences in Infant Mortality'. *Lancet*, **i**, 445-8.
22. DEPARTMENT OF HEALTH FOR SCOTLAND. *Fourth Report on Incapacitating Sickness, 1933-4.* London: H.M.S.O., 1935.
23. DOLL, R., JONES, F. A., & BUCKATZSCH, M. M. (1951) 'Occupational FACTORS in the Aetiology of Gastric and Duodenal Ulcers' Special Report Series, Medical Research Council, No. 276.
24. DOUGLAS, J. W. B. (1958) Communication to the Society for Social Medicine.
25. DOUGLAS, J. W. B., & BLOMFIELD, J. M. *Children Under Five.* London: Allen and Unwin, 1958.
26. DURKHEIM, E. *Suicide: A Study in Sociology.* Trans. by J. A. Spaulding and G. Simpson. Glencoe, Ill: Free Press, 1951.
27. EDWARDS, F., McKEOWN, T., & WHITFIELD, A. G. W. (1959) 'Incidence of Disease and Disability in Elderly Men'. *Brit. J. prev. soc. Med.*, **13**, 51.
28. EDWARDS, F., McKEOWN, T., & WHITFIELD, A. G. W. (1959) 'Contributions and Demands of Elderly Men'. *Brit. J. prev. soc. Med.*, **13**, 59.
29. EELS, K., *et al. Intelligence and Cultural Differences.* Chicago: Univ. of Chicago Press, 1951.
30. FRASER, E. *Home Environment and the School.* London: Univ. of London Press, 1950.
31. FRIEDMAN, M., ROSENMAN, R. H., & CARROLL, V. (1958) 'Changes in the Serum Cholesterol and Blood Clotting Time in Men subjected to Cyclic Variation of Occupational Stress'. *Circulation*, **17**, 852.
32. FRIEDMAN, M., ROSENMAN, R. H., & CARROLL, V. (1959) 'Association of Specific Overt Behaviour Pattern with Blood and Cardiovascular Findings'. *J. Amer. med. Ass.*, **169**, 1286.
33. FROST, I. (1938) 'Home-Sickness and Immigrant Psychosis'. *J. ment. Sci.*, **84**, 801-47.
34. FROST, W. H. (1939) 'The Age Selection of Mortality from Tuberculosis in Successive Decades'. *Amer. J. Hyg.*, **30**, 91.
35. GLASS, D. V., & GREBENIK, E. (1954) *The Trend and Pattern of Fertility in Great Britain.* A Report of the Family Census of 1946. Papers of the Royal Commission on Population, vol. VI, Parts I and II. London: H.M.S.O.
36. GOFMAN, J. W. *et al.* (1956) 'Evaluation of Serum Lipoprotein and Cholesterol Measurements as Predictors of Clinical Complication of Atherosclerosis'. *Circulation*, **14**, 691.
37. GOLDBERG, E. M. (1958) *Family Influences and Psychosomatic Medicine* London: Tavistock.

Social Medicine in Britain

38. GOLDBERG, E. M. (1960) Reported by J. N. Morris, 'Health and Social Class.' *Lancet*, **i**, 303.
39. GREENBLATT, M., YORK, R. H., & BROWN, E. L. *From Custodial to Therapeutic Patient Care in Mental Hospitals.* New York: Russell Sage Foundation, 1955.
40. HALLIDAY, J. M. *Psychosocial Medicine.* London: Heinemann, 1948.
41. HALSEY, A. H. (1958) 'Genetics, Social Structure, and Intelligence'. *Brit. J. Sociol.*, **9**, 15–28.
42. HARE, E. H. (1955) 'Mental Illness and Social Class in Bristol'. *Brit. J. prev. soc. Med.*, **9**, 191.
43. HARE, E. H. (ed.). Triennial Statistical Report, Years 1955–57, of the Bethlem Royal Hospital and the Maudsley Hospital London, 1959.
44. HEADY, J. A. (1959) 'Occupation and Mortality: Filial Mortality'. *Brit. J. industr. Med.*, **16**, 68.
45. HEADY, J. A., DALY, C., & MORRIS, J. N. (1955) 'Social and Biological Factors in Infant Mortality: II. Variation of Mortality'. *Lancet*, **i**, 395–7.
46. HEADY, J. A., & HEASMAN, M. A. (1959) Social and Biological Factors in Infant Mortality. General Register Office, Studies on Medical and Population Subjects No. 15. London: H.M.S.O.
47. HEADY, J. A., et al. (1955) 'Social and Biological Factors in Infant Mortality: IV. The Independent Effects of Social Class, Region, the Mother's Age, and Parity'. *Lancet*, **i**, 499–502.
48. HEASMAN, M. A., et al. (1958) 'The Accuracy of Occupational Vital Statistics'. *Brit. J. industr. Med.*, **15**, 141.
49. HOLLINGSHEAD, A. B., & REDLICH, F. C. *Social Class and Mental Illness.* London: Chapman and Hall, 1958.
50. ILLSEY, R. (1955) 'Social Class Selection and Class Differences in Relation to Stillbirths and Infant Deaths', *Brit. med. J.* **ii**, 1520.
51. JENNINGS, D. (1940) 'Perforated Peptic Ulcer'. *Lancet*, **i**, 395, 444.
52. Joint Committee of the Royal College of Obstetricians and Gynaecologists and the Population Investigation Committee. *Maternity in Great Britain.* London: Oxford Univ. Press, 1948.
53. JONES, F. A. (1955) 'Social Aspects of Peptic Ulcer'. *J. R. Inst. Publ. Hlth*, **18**, 64.
54. JONES, M. *Social Psychiatry: A Study of Therapeutic Communities.* London: Tavistock, 1952.
55. KEYS, A., & GRANDE, F. (1957) 'Role of Dietary Fat in Human Nutrition. III: Diet and the Epidemiology of Coronary Heart Disease'. *Amer. J. publ. Hlth*, **47**, 1520.
56. KIRK, S. A. *Early Education of the Mentally Retarded.* Urbana: Univ. of Illinois Press, 1958.
57. LEMPERT, S. M. (1960) 'The Stockport Survey of the Aged'. *Publ. Hlth, Lond.*, **74**, 382.
58. LEWIS, E. O. (1933) 'Types of Mental Deficiency and their Social Significance'. *J. ment. Sci.*, **79**, 298.
59. LIPSET, S. M., & BENDIX, R. *Social Mobility in Industrial Society.* London: Heinemann, 1959.

60. LOWE, C. R., & McKEOWN, T. (1954) 'Incidence of Infectious Disease in the First Three Years of Life, Related to Social Circumstances'. *Brit. J. prev. soc. Med.*, **8**, 24.
61. LYLE, J. C. (1960) 'The Effect of an Institution Environment upon the Verbal Development of Imbecile Children'. *J. Ment. Defic. Res.*, **4**, 1.
62. McDONALD, A. D. (1957) 'Child Health Services in a New Housing Estate'. *Public Health* (London), **70**, 122.
63. MacIVER, R. M. *The Ramparts We Guard.* New York: Macmillan, 1950.
64. MacMAHON, B., *et al. Epidemiologic Methods.* London: Churchill. 1960.
65. MALZBERG, B., & LEE, E. S. *Migration and Mental Disease.* New York: Social Science Research Council, 1956.
66. MANN, G. V., *et al.* (1955) 'Exercise in the Disposition of Dietary Calories'. *New Engl. J. Med.*, **253**, 349.
67. MERTON, R. K. 'Social Structure and Anomie', in *Social Theory and Social Structure.* Glencoe, Ill.: Free Press, 1949.
68. MERTON, R. K. *Social Theory and Social Structure.* Glencoe, Ill.: Free Press, 1949.
69. MERTON, R. K., READER, G. G., & KENDALL, P. L. *The Student Physician.* Cambridge, Mass.: Harvard Univ. Press, 1957.
70. MILLER, F. J. W., *et. al. Growing Up in Newcastle on Tyne.* London: Oxford Univ. Press, 1960.
71. MORRIS, J. N. (1951) 'Recent History of Coronary Disease'. *Lancet*, **i**, 1 and 69.
72. MORRIS, J. N. *Uses of Epidemiology.* Edinburgh: Livingstone, 1957.
73. MORRIS, J. N. (1959) 'Health and Social Class'. *Lancet*, **i**, 303.
74. MORRIS, J. N. (1959) 'Occupation and Coronary Heart Disease'. *Arch. intern. Méd. exp.*, **104**, 903.
75. MORRIS, J. N., & CRAWFORD, M. D. (1958) 'Coronary Heart Disease and Physical Activity at Work'. *Brit. med. J.*, **ii**, 1485.
76. MORRIS, J. N., & HEADY, J. A. (1955) 'Social and Biological Factors in Infant Mortality: I. Objects and Methods'. *Lancet*, **i**, 343–9.
76a.MORRIS, J. N., & HEADY, J. A. (1955) 'Social and Biological Factors in Infant Mortality: V. Mortality in Relation to the Father's Occupation, 1911—1950'. *Lancet*, **i**, 554–9.
77. MORRIS, J. N., HEADY, J. A., & RAFFLE, P. A. B. (1956) 'Sickness Absence before the First Clinical Episode of Coronary Heart Disease'. *Lancet*, **ii**, 569.
78. MORRIS, J. N., & TITMUSS, R. M. (1944) 'Epidemiology of Peptic Ulcer: Vital Statistics'. *Lancet*, **ii**, 841.
79. MORRISON, S. L. (1959) 'Principles and Methods of Epidemiological Research and their Application to Psychiatric Illness'. *J. ment. Sci.*, **105**, 999.
80. MORRISON, S. L., *et al.* (1959) 'Social and Biological Factors in Infant Mortality: VIII. Mortality in the Post-Neonatal Period'. *Arch. Dis. Childh.*, **34**, 100.

81. ØDEGARD, Ø. (1932) 'Emigration and Insanity'. *Acta psychiat. Kbh. Neurol.* Suppl. 4.
82. OLSEN, R. E. (1957) 'Dietary Fat in Human Nutrition'. *Amer. J. publ. Hlth.* **47,** 1537.
83. PAGE, I. H., *et al.* (1957). 'Atherosclerosis and the Fat Content of the Diet'. *Circulation,* **26,** 163.
84. PARSONS, T. *The Social System.* Glencoe, Ill.: Free Press, 1951.
85. READER, G. H., & GOSS, M .E. W. (1959) 'Medical Sociology with Particular Reference to the Study of Hospitals'. *Transactions of the Fourth World Congress of Sociology,* **II,** 139.
86. RIESMAN, D. *The Lonely Crowd.* New Haven: Yale Univ. Press, 1951.
87. SAINSBURY, P. *Suicide in London: An Ecological Study.* Maudsley Monograph No. 1. London: Institute of Psychiatry, 1955.
88. SARASON, B., & GLADWIN, T. (1958) 'Psychological and Cultural Problems in Mental Subnormality—A Review of Research'. *Amer. J. ment. Defic.,* **62,** 1115.
89. *Social Implications of the Scottish Mental Survey.* Scottish Council for Research in Education, XXXV, 1953.
90. SOFER, C. (1955) 'Reactions to Administrative Change'. *Hum. Relat.* **8,** 291.
91. STANTON, A. H., & SCHWARTZ, M. H. *The Mental Hospital.* New York: Basic Books, 1954.
92. STEIN, L. (1950) 'A Study of Respiratory Tuberculosis in Relation to Housing Conditions in Edinburgh'. *Brit. J. soc. Med.* **4,** 143.
93. STEIN, L. (1957) 'Social Class and Gradient in Schizophrenia'. *Brit. J. prev. soc. Med.,* **11,** 181.
94. STEIN, Z. A., & SUSSER, M. W. (1960) 'The Families of Dull Children'. *Brit. J. prev. soc. Med.,* **14,** 83.
95. STEIN, Z. A., & SUSSER, M. W. (1960) 'The Families of Dull Children: II. Identifying Family Types and Subcultures; III. Social Selection of Family Type; iv. Increments in Intelligence'. *J. ment. Sci.,* **106,** 1296, 1304, and 1311.
96. SUSSER, M. W. (1961) 'Environmental Factors and Peptic Ulcer'. *The Practitioner,* **186,** 302.
97. TOOR, M., *et al.* (1957) 'Serum-Lipids and Atherosclerosis among Yemenite Immigrants'. *Lancet,* **i,** 1270.
98. WATSON, W. Paper read at the Scientific Conference of the Association of Social Anthropologists, Edinburgh, 1957 (in the press).
99. *Wood Report. Report of the Mental Deficiency Committee.* London: H.M.S.O., 1929.
100. YUDKIN, J. (1957). 'Diet and Coronary Thrombosis'. *Lancet,* **ii,** 155.

9

EXPERIMENTAL

PSYCHOLOGY AND THE

STUDY OF SOCIAL BEHAVIOUR

A. T. Welford

EXPERIMENTAL psychology occupies a position intermediate between the social sciences on the one hand and the older human biological disciplines on the other. In his studies of individual human behaviour the psychologist has been forced from time to time to recognize that certain social factors may exert important effects. On the other hand, he knows that he is studying a biological organism whose behaviour is based on a nervous system reacting via sense organs and muscles with the environment, so that he must sooner or later look to physiology for his explanations. Both physiologist and psychologist recognize that these explanations cannot at present be supplied, and indeed that the goal is not fully attainable because the detailed breakdown of behaviour into physiological terms would be impossibly complex.

The need to maintain contact nevertheless remains. The division between the two disciplines is in a sense an arbitrary one in terms of the size of unit studied—between, for psychology, the whole organism and, for physiology, individual cells and structures. In many ways this division is both convenient and necessary. Nevertheless there are occasions upon which consideration by the psychologist of the detailed mechanism of the human brain and body can tie together many facts at first sight disconnected or even discordant. At the same time, the physiologist considering the action of large masses of nerve cells has often to resort to the study of behaviour at the level normally within the realm of psychology. There is thus a two-way traffic between the disciplines in which psychology seeks theory and explanation downwards, and physiology seeks the testing of hypotheses upwards in the scale of functional units.

It is reasonable to suggest that psychology can and should play the same role in relation to social studies as physiology does in relation to psychology, providing the means of conceptualizing the detailed 'mechanisms' of the behaviour of groups and organized social units. For it to do so, however, certain principles must be recognized by both sides:

(a) It must be acknowledged that social units are composed of individuals, and that it is their interaction with their environment and each other that produces social phenomena.

(b) Such recognition implies that accounts of social phenomena need to be broken down from steady states or slow changes into *processes* in which, ideally, chains of detailed individual actions can be described.

(c) It is often impossible to make this kind of breakdown, just as it is impossible to analyse individual behaviour into detailed physiological processes. The difficulty may, however, be largely overcome by considering the ways in which organisms with certain defined individual characteristics are likely to interact with each other in given circumstances. Significant attempts have, for example, been made to formulate mathematical models for simple cases of group problem-solving behaviour based on known individual capacities.

(d) Just as psychological studies have sometimes drawn attention to matters requiring physiological study, so social studies are likely to direct the attention of psychologists to problems within their own field that might otherwise pass unrecognized.

The psychologist would ask the sociologist to remember especially the first two of these points, to ensure that his theorizing does not fly in the face of what is known of individual behaviour, and to bear in mind that psychology may be in a position to give him a more fundamental analysis and terminology than he is using at present. The psychologist must, in return, attempt to consider social phenomena in terms of what he knows, and to see what suggestions he can make regarding individual processes which are likely to be of especial importance in relation to social studies.

The work of psychologists in relation to personality, mental testing, and the measurement of attitudes is described by others in this volume and nothing more will be said about it here in detail. This work is now at the stage of genuine give and take between sociology and psychology without, however, the true integration which is beginning to be seen between psychology and physiology. Most of the studies attempt to relate a psychological variable to the incidence of a social phenomenon or of socially interesting behaviour such as delinquency. The attempt to discover the detailed process of interaction between individual behaviour, environmental conditions, and social results is less frequent. Were this done on a more substantial scale, we should be in a much better position to understand some of the surprisingly low correlations at present found between many psychological and social variables.

Our discussion here will be concerned with four topics which have emerged in recent experimental psychological studies and which seem to be germane to thought about social behaviour.

Capacity for Resolving Uncertainty

It has been well known since the early days of experimental psychology that if a subject has to identify which of a number of possible signals has occurred, or to choose one of a number of possible actions, the time he takes rises as the number of alternatives increases. To put it another way, the amount of uncertainty about which signal will occur or action be required is a function of the number 'at risk', and time is taken to resolve uncertainty. Recent work has shown that in many cases the time can be calculated on the assumption that information in the 'information theory' sense is gained at a constant rate (for a review see [17]).* The results are consistent with the view that in making an identification or a choice the subject first selects a large class to which the object or action belongs and then progressively smaller classes within the large class until one sufficiently specific has been found.

The subject's capacity to process information is conceived as limited. It varies between different individuals and according to the nature of the task and the way it is organized, but the rates at which information is processed show some striking consistencies within given types of task. Precise work in this area has so far been in the form of laboratory experiments, but attempts to extend its principles to shop floor work in industry have been promising.[4, 10]

These concepts have not yet been applied systematically to decision-making in managerial work or in everyday life, but it seems reasonable

* When all possible signals occur with equal frequency we can write:
$$T_D = K \log N$$
where T_D = mean decision time, N = the number of alternatives the subject has to consider, and K is a constant. When the possible signals occur with unequal frequencies we write instead:
$$T_D = K \sum_{i=1}^{N} p_i \log \frac{1}{p_i}$$
where p_i is the probability of the ith signal in the ensemble of N.[7]

to assume tentatively that they could be in principle. If so, they open an important new line of approach to the quantitative treatment of many tasks and environmental situations which have hitherto been defined only in somewhat vague terms. For example, the task of an administrator will depend not only on the number of decisions required in a given time, but also on the range of their possible variation. If he is given too great a '*load*', decisions will be hurried and lead to errors, since the process of selection will not be carried far enough and the final resolution among two or three alternative courses may be virtually at random.

Some of the social consequences of this type of human limitation seem fairly obvious. For example, the lowering of capacity with advancing age, leading to slowing of performance, causes a great many changes of job in middle age. The tempo of most industrial jobs seems to be pitched for people in their thirties. Those older than this manage to keep up the required speed until the late forties or early fifties, often with some signs of strain, but after this a great many of them move. Their change of work is frequently attributed to causes other than age. Many moves, for example, are made 'on medical grounds' following a minor illness. Often, however, the illness is obviously too trivial to account for the magnitude of the change.[12] The drift is, understandably, very great from jobs in which the speed is inflexible, as on some conveyor-lines. Belbin[1] found a marked fall in numbers between the ages of forty-five and fifty-five on jobs of this kind, and the fall seems to come five to ten years earlier in them than it does in jobs making very severe physical demands.

It should be remarked in passing that these findings have three implications for the study of statistics concerning older people. Firstly, little can be inferred from the study of the *performances* of those on a job at different ages, since the older tend to be a selected group in which the 'fittest' have survived. If possible, we need to study the pattern of moves made from one job to another. If this cannot be done, it is best merely to study the age distributions of workers on different jobs: if due allowance is made for the tendency for newer jobs to have a younger working group than those which are old-established, the proportions of young and old on a job probably gives the fairest indication available of its suitability for older people.[16] Secondly, statistics about numbers employed at different ages are of little use if they are calculated for whole industries or factories: it is essential to deal with individual jobs and types of job. It is not unfair to say that, owing to failure to recognize this point, no valid inferences of any consequence can be drawn from the great majority of statistics dealing with age in relation to industrial work. Thirdly, those attempting to deal with industrial problems of ageing must recognize that existing terminology is sometimes misleading; for example, much so-called 'light' work is fast, and thus less suitable for older people than many jobs in which the physical effort is moderately heavy: there is, indeed, occasional evidence of a change with age from light to heavier work of these kinds.[2]

Two other consequences of this concept of capacity may be briefly mentioned, although systematic data on them have yet to be collected.

(*a*) Mr. R. A. F. Harcourt in a personal communication has urged that the concept is important in relation to problems of leadership and size of group. The individual members of a group will generate for a leader an amount of information depending upon the nature of their job, the conditions under which it is done, and their personal characteristics. The size of group that one person can lead will depend upon the amount of information generated by its members. If they are doing a routine job under stable conditions and are of even temperament, one leader can deal with a large number, but variability of job or of the conditions under which it is done, or unstable personalities among the team, will reduce the maximum size of group which can be led effectively.

(*b*) Quite apart from questions of leadership, the effects of the size of working group on the morale and job-satisfaction of members are often discussed. It has been urged that a small group is more 'democratic', while a large group tends to generate a 'dictatorial' leadership, which is resented. The terms 'democratic' and 'dictatorial', apart from being emotionally toned, are hard to pin down to precise meanings in such a context, and in any case the evidence upon which type of organization leads to better results and is preferred by workpeople is conflicting.

Consideration of the capacities of both leader and led suggests possible reasons for such a conflict of evidence. The morale of a group is likely to depend very greatly upon whether the leader has the capacity to carry the load his group imposes. As we have seen, he can in certain circumstances deal with a fairly large group without being overloaded. In these circumstances a large group may well be content. If, however, the information load upon him becomes too great, his decisions will be ill-considered so that the effectiveness of the group will be diminished. When this is liable to happen two courses are possible: either the group can be split into smaller sub-groups, each with a leader who is responsible in turn to a leader higher in a hierarchy, or a large group can be preserved but members required to refer different problems to different specialists added to the group as deputy-leaders. The disadvantage of the second system is that the individual members of the group have to decide which specialist to go to in any given circumstances and are thus exposed to all the difficulties that may ensue from possible mis-diagnosis of their problems leading them to a tedious round from one specialist to another. Reference of all problems to a single leader obviates this difficulty for the individual members, although, of course, it may merely transfer it to him. From the standpoint of one looking at the morale and effectiveness of the group as a whole, however, the small group is likely to appear preferable in cases where technical and management functions are complex.

The limitation upon individual capacity for decision not only sets maximum speeds of performance, but also may have a number of indirect effects.

(i) Perhaps the simplest reaction to an excessive demand is to shed part of the load by ignoring some of the signals that should be considered or of the actions that ought to be performed. Experimental tasks have shown such reactions in the ignoring of signals from peripheral parts of a display.[5] It is reasonable to suggest that the same kind of process is seen in the busy manager who ignores departments which do not continually impinge upon his notice, or in the administrator who deals only with problems which have become pressing. By such 'load-shedding' the range of decisions is reduced and, therefore, the speed of each decision made is increased. Obviously there is some loss of effectiveness because of omissions, but if, as tends to happen, the less important parts of the task are dropped first, the result may not be unduly serious. Looking at the matter the other way round, the tendency clearly indicates a principle for effective delegation: when authority has to be shared with others, it is better to surrender certain parts completely and thus reduce the range of decisions to be made, than to share responsibility for all aspects of an administrative job with an assistant.

(ii) An effective method of shortening average decision time is to learn the relative probabilities of the several types of event which may demand action, and to 'try' the more likely possibilities first when identifying any event which has occurred. By this means the more frequently demanded decisions are made quickly and the saving of time on them outweighs the slowing of decision that is implied for rare events.*

(iii) The most important economies of decision are achieved by recognizing the ways in which groups or series of objects, signals, or actions cohere together, and by treating the coherent series or groups as single 'units'. When this is done separate decisions are no longer required about each individual member of the

---

* The quickening of frequent choices and slowing of infrequent are predicted by the second of the equations in the footnote to page 155, since $p \log 1/p$ varies with p. $\Sigma p \log 1/p$ is maximized when all the ps are equal, so that any deviation from equality in the frequencies of different events will tend to reduce average decision time.

group or series: instead a single decision can initiate the whole, which will then 'run off' more or less 'automatically'. The price paid for this economy is that some flexibility is lost: the set routines may not be optimally suited to the precise requirements of the situation, so that the subject may show some 'rigidity' in the face of changing circumstances, or lack of subtlety in his appreciation of fine distinctions between one situation and another. There is no doubt, however, that for most situations the advantages conferred by such 'coding' in extending the range and quantity of data that can be handled quickly far outweigh the disadvantages.

The coding of data at the individual level seems to be analagous in both manner and results to social customs and socially determined attitudes, and one can think of the two as acting and reacting upon each other. The learning of social customs and attitudes is an important part of the structuring of individual perception and behaviour; at the same time it is reasonable to suppose that social customs represent the codifying of insights, attitudes, and techniques of dealing with the environment which survive because of their value, if viewed in a broad enough perspective, as structuring for individuals.

The building up of such codes in both individuals and groups is likely to increase with experience, and to make for greater efficiency in stable conditions but greater rigidity in the face of change. Just as these tendencies almost certainly contribute to the characteristics of old age in individuals, so they are likely to be an important factor in the 'ageing' of societies, making older societies more stable and easier to live in since fewer decisions of policy are open to question, but less capable of absorbing new ideas quickly than societies in which rules of conduct are less developed and entrenched.

Complexity

Analysis in terms of probability does not explain the whole of the load imposed by decision requirements. A number of other capacities are involved in dealing with what may be broadly termed 'complexity'. It is clear that complexity cannot be regarded as a unitary variable in the psychological sense, and that it may involve any one or more of several seemingly distinct demands, such as:

Piecing together different data either present all at once or, more difficult, arriving at different points in time.

Recognizing the general implications or principles lying behind a number of particular instances.

A. T. Welford

Distinguishing significant differences between examples which are closely alike.

Manipulating data 'in the abstract' or in one's head.

Separating sets of data having different characteristics and thus avoiding confusion due to failure to distinguish relevant from irrelevant.

The effects of demands exceeding capacity for dealing with these types of difficulty will vary. In some cases the result will be that no action is taken, but in others attempts to produce some response may lead to the substitution of emotionally determined for rational judgements, or of 'flat', 'concrete' responses for abstract ones. An example of this last effect is seen in mental patients who, when given a proverb, can clearly understand its literal meaning but cannot see any general significance.

Although there seem to be several 'dimensions' of complexity, it is not clear how many should be distinguished. There is a tendency for difficulties in coping with one type and another to go together: for example in old age or in clinical mental disease the handling of several types of complexity may be impaired. It is uncertain, however, whether this is due to a single mechanism which underlies all the changes observed, or whether age or disease tend to cause changes in several different mechanisms simultaneously. The question could be settled by examining in detail the correlations between abilities to handle different types of complexity, but this has not yet been done to any great extent.

There is some evidence to suggest, however, that a factor common to several types of complexity is *short term memory*. This is obviously involved in temporal integration, and perhaps also in spatial, since the amount that can be seen at one glance is so limited that much of the integration of apparently simultaneous data must in fact be temporal. Certainly short-term memory is involved in a number of problem solving and abstraction processes in which the subject is required to gather one set of data, hold it while searching for another set, and then combine both sets. It has been found that subjects tend to forget the first set while searching for the second, and that this limits the complexity of problem they can solve.[3, 16]

Short term memory seems also to be involved when the required data have been gathered but completion of the decision is delayed, either through procrastination or for lack of opportunity to put the decision into effect. Some details have to be held in memory during the period of the delay and, while they are so held, they may distract attention from immediate matters and thus interfere with other decisions. It seems fair to suggest that a heavy load of incomplete decisions can act as a major factor in producing strain among those in administrative positions, whether the load is imposed by frailty of personality or force of circum-

160

stances, and that it is important to ensure that the contents of the 'mental pending tray' are kept to a minimum.

Whatever the cause of limitations in the level of complexity that an individual can handle, two points follow which have implications for social behaviour:

(a) Since the level varies in different individuals, any decision or statement which is to be understood by a group must be at a level below the maximum attainable by many of the individuals in the group, being 'flatter' and less subtle, or perhaps more emotional and less rational, than they would individually attain. This fact is well known empirically for the design of mass entertainment, but seems likely to apply also to small groups such as committees.

(b) The capacities for handling complexity and for decision-making generally, have important implications for the study of communications in an organization such as an office or factory. The customary charts plotting the course of communications, either in intention or in fact, give only the barest beginning of the data necessary for a meaningful analysis. What is needed is an assessment of the load imposed by the communication system upon the particular individuals who make it up. For this, at least tentative assessments are necessary not only of the sources of information converging on any one person, but also of the nature, complexity, range, and timing of the decisions required, together with any inevitable delays between the receipt and use of information. The collection of the necessary data for the study of a large system in this way would be a formidable task, and it would seem better, wherever possible, to use more restricted studies examining the communications involved in dealing with particular types of problem, or the load handled by selected individuals suspected of occupying key or limiting positions.

The Predominance of Initial Experience

If the results of an experiment in which a series of actions has to be learnt are plotted for a group of subjects against the number of repetitions of the series, a smoothly rising curve of performance is obtained, and from this it has often been inferred that the course of learning is one of gradual mastery of the task. Detailed studies of rote learning make it clear, however, that this is not so. What appears to happen is that a subject learns *something* in the first few trials which is partly correct and partly in error, and that this initial impression tends to persist.[9, 14, 15, 18] Subsequent mastery is due largely to a gradual process of eliminating the initial errors. A number of studies with other types of task have obtained similar results, tending to show the predominant effect of initial experiences with new material. The principle has been recognized empirically in the teaching of skills such as games and typewriting, where emphasis is laid on the acquisition of correct habits at the beginning: if incorrect methods are allowed, they are difficult to eradicate later.

Such predominance of initial experience is understandable. The way in which a subject approaches a new task when he has no detailed knowledge about it can only be in terms of expectations, perhaps coloured by hopes or fears, from the general background of his past experience. Once something has been learnt, it provides a positive means of dealing with the task, which tends to be used on subsequent occasions. Conditions, whether in experiments or in everyday life, are usually such that definite action, even if not wholly correct, is preferable to none at all.

The general picture of learning as the modification of initial impressions is in line with the now well recognized principle that experience is cumulative: each new event or environmental demand is met in terms of what the subject can bring to it from the abilities and experience he has built up in the past, and it, in turn, modifies the individual so that he approaches the next situation different from what he was before.

If, as seems likely, this observation is of general application, it carries the clear suggestion that in giving information of a controversial nature, such as in political propaganda, it is important to 'get one's view stated first'. The initially stated attitude is likely to be accepted relatively uncritically and to be disproportionately difficult to modify with subsequent counter-propaganda. Conversely, if the initiative has been lost, it seems likely that a greater impact will be secured by a campaign designed to build an entirely new viewpoint than by an attempt to negate an impression already made. Attempts to check the validity of this principle by studying the extent to which social attitudes are changed by statements designed to persuade and by subsequent counter-statements, have yielded conflicting results. The laboratory experiments on learning which have been mentioned here suggest that the effects of statements and counter-statements are likely to depend upon whether or not the first enables a situation to be *comprehended* or *mastered*, either by providing a satisfying explanation of what has not previously been understood or by making possible a confident decision between alternative courses of action.

Motivation

It is obvious that for any action to take place, the organism must have the necessary capacity and that there must be an occasion provided

Experimental Psychology

by environmental circumstances. It is commonly argued, however, that these are not enough, and that there must, in addition, be some *drive* or *motive*. Thus, for example, the mere capacity to eat, coupled with the presence of food, is not sufficient to ensure that eating will take place: there must also be hunger or some social pressure to eat.

The problem of what forces motivate human beings and how they operate is one of the oldest common concerns of psychology and the social sciences, and discussions of motivation have been prominent in almost all works on social psychology from McDougall's famous book[11] onwards. It cannot be claimed that our understanding is yet anywhere near satisfactory, although it can be said confidently that any simple view such as that 'the only incentive that counts is money' is quite inadequate: many other factors such as desire for achievement, prestige, and social intercourse are clearly important.

Several theories of motivation have attempted to trace all incentives back to certain primary biological necessities without which the life of the individual or of the race would be in jeopardy. Such necessities obviously exist, for example for food, water, and air so far as the individual is concerned, and for sexual intercourse and care of the young if the race is to continue, but how many should be distinguished and what is their relative importance, are matters of controversy. It is clear also that the individual commonly does not eat in order to preserve his life or engage in sexual intercourse with a view to preserving the race. Such motives may occasionally exist at a highly sophisticated level, but usually motivation is of a more sensual nature. Normally, for example, a person eats because of sensations of hunger, and enjoys food for the sensations it produces of taste and smell, and perhaps for its appearance. The biological necessity of eating is not in mind, and the sensory satisfactions precede any satisfaction of bodily need: for example, hunger is satisfied long before the food is digested and made available to the tissues of the body.

Any attempt to base motives on primary biological needs also runs into difficulty when trying to account for play activities and for interests such as hobbies. The proposed ways out of this difficulty, such as the suggestion that activities which once served a biological purpose may become 'functionally autonomous' so that they are continued for their own sake, or that the achievement of sub-goals on the way to more remote primary satisfactions may itself be satisfying, have an *ad hoc* quality which destroys their explanatory value. More significant is, perhaps, the fact that the motives behind any one action are usually mixed, and the ways of satisfying any one motive are many, so that an activity which starts for one reason may be continued for quite others: for example, a man may join a sports club because he enjoys exercise and may continue as a member for the sake of the friendships he has formed.

A. T. Welford

Woodworth[19] has made trenchant criticisms of the whole idea that primary motives are derived from biological needs, criticizing particularly the views of Freud and Hull. He proposes instead that motivation is essentially based on an inherent and fundamental tendency for the organism to 'deal with its environment' and to develop its capacity for doing so. He suggests that biological appetites such as those for food, water, and sex 'use' this tendency, and are thus essentially subsidiary motives.

Now it is well known that the central nervous system is spontaneously active, and activated still further by sensory input. It is also clear that the direction of activity depends upon the structure of the central nervous system both inherited and acquired by learning in the course of experience. The broad lines are laid down by heredity to an extent not commonly realized, as studies of twins living apart (e.g.[8]) have shown, although the development of inherent potentialities and of the fine detail of behaviour is clearly due to learning. Woodworth recognizes that for certain very simple acts such as 'jumping' when startled, the structure of the central nervous system is a sufficient 'explanation' of behaviour, and that no further motive need be postulated. At a more complex level, however, some factor deriving from the results of action in terms of 'good', 'bad', and 'indifferent', or 'pleasant', 'unpleasant', and 'neutral' seems to be required: the first is sought, the second avoided, and the third ignored. The distinction between these types of result can again be regarded as built into the structure of the central nervous system. For example, Woodworth points out that almost all species of mammal show a liking for sweet substances and a dislike for bitter, and will explore what is novel and avoid what is painful. Such basic likes and dislikes are, however, subject to modification by learning: most adults, for instance, dislike sweet substances early in a main meal, but have acquired a liking for some bitter substances such as coffee or beer.

We may perhaps sharpen Woodworth's treatment and press it a step further by taking account of six points:

(i) The question of *what* motives actuate human behaviour should probably be separated from the question of *how* they operate. Traditionally, discussion of motivation has tended to deal only with the first question. Such discussion is likely, however, to be unfruitful because we cannot state *a priori* what situation or sensory stimuli, signals or actions will be regarded as 'good' or 'bad' or 'indifferent': this is a question which can be settled only by painstaking empirical study. Some preliminary guide can be obtained from a consideration of biological necessities: if the organism had no mechanisms for satisfying these, it, or its species, would die; but there is no reason to suppose that these are the only, or even the main, sources of motivation. We know, in fact, that curiosity, achievement, companionship, and prestige can be powerful motives which are not directly connected with biological needs, although it is arguable that they are so indirectly. Whether this is so or not, any compelling importance of the means of satisfying biological needs is likely to be overlaid in civilized life where, for example, eating and drinking have many functions having little or nothing to do with bodily requirements.

(ii) Researches over the last few years have shown that the organism is activated by sensory stimulation and that, although it may adapt to steady stimuli, it continues to be aroused by novelty, change, and input of 'information' in the information theory sense. If conditions are monotonously certain, boredom, loss of vigilance, and eventually sleep are likely to ensue.

(iii) Several studies have shown that knowledge of the results of action has an incentive effect, although it is probable that this applies only if the success or failure of the action is not certain; in other words so long as the knowledge of results conveys information about the performance which can act as a guide to future efforts.

(iv) One might expect on grounds of cybernetic theory that motivation would be strongest when the discrepancy between the present state of the organism and the state aimed at was greatest, and would diminish as the task neared accomplishment. The reverse, however, seems to be the case: motivation seems to rise with achievement and thus to increase as the task approaches completion. In cybernetic terms, the feedback from achievement is positive rather than negative.

(v) Incentive effects tend to increase with the strength or amount of the feedback that results from an action, so that vigour of approach rises with increased reward, and of avoidance with increased punishment. The incentive effect of a result also seems to be related to the effort involved in obtaining it. It is not certain whether this is due to some kind of ratio of effort to result being reacted to directly, or to result and effort each being reacted to absolutely with the latter acting as a *dis*incentive, partially cancelling the former. This kind of relationship can give at least a partial explanation of the rise of motivation following deprivation, say of food. The change of state following satisfaction of an appetite or other desire will increase with its strength, and thus raise the ratio of result to effort for any action producing satisfaction.

A. T. Welford

(vi) All performance, except very simple reflexes, seems to be organized on a hierarchical principle with larger 'units' formed of smaller. One example will suffice: if we saw a student in a library looking at a book open in front of him and we were to ask him what he was doing, he might correctly reply, 'reading this book'. He might, however, equally well reply 'This is one of several things I must read to prepare for a seminar'. If we were further to ask him why he should want to prepare for the seminar he might admit that it was in order to obtain a good result in an examination, that this in turn was sought in order to secure a particular job, and that the job was desirable because it would lead on, in due course, to a position of respect and influence. The reading of the book, the preparation for the seminar, the obtaining of a good examination result, job, and career can all be thought of as *tasks*, each on a larger scale or 'higher level' than the last, and each containing a number of smaller or 'lower' units. We may note, for the sake of completeness, that the process can also be carried downwards from our starting-point to the fundamental activities of the very simplest human behaviour: for example, the reading of a book involves co-ordinating the perception of words, phrases, and paragraphs with eye movements scanning the print and with hand actions in turning the pages: even the turn of a page involves a highly complex co-ordinated and phased set of muscular movements.

There is evidence that in sensori-motor tasks the 'unit of performance' at each level controls and shapes the units below it in the hierarchy and affects their characteristics (e.g. [6, 13]). The speed at which the book will be read thus depends in part on the urgency with which preparation for the seminar is being made. The larger units can be said to motivate the smaller in the sense that the results of the smaller have their main significance as means to a larger end.

It would be premature to try to base a 'grand theory' of human motivation on facts such as these, but it can be tentatively suggested that they indicate the organism as having a primary motivation to maintain a *throughput of information*, and to try to maintain this throughput as efficiently as possible. What actual level is sought we do not know. It probably varies with circumstances, and there is some indication that it is related to individual capacity, tending to be higher amongst those who are more able. To initiate behaviour in the first place the information required must, presumably, come from outside or from sensory states arising as a result of conditions in the body which arouse appetites. Continued behaviour would seem to depend upon the information sent back from the results of previous action, bringing about either changes of environmental stimulation, as in the case of exploration or achievement, or the cancellation of the sensory states associated with appetites.

If the view outlined here, or something like it, is accepted, the study of motives and incentives becomes different from what it would be following more traditional views. The primary question is no longer 'What are the basic springs of action', but 'By what *mechanism* is the human being activated and directed'. Instead of proceeding from a hypothetical list of basic needs downwards to their manifestations in detailed behaviour, we are free to give our main attention to the more immediate objects of action and to tracing these in the service of larger units of performance. The 'goodness' or 'badness' of the results of action is still, like basic needs, largely unknown *a priori*, but the tracing of reasons for action forward to larger tasks provides a promising method of getting at them. Such a procedure might reveal that the simple reflexes which are 'ends in themselves' have their analogues in more highly organized behaviour: although the tracing forward might often carry us a very long way, it might sometimes stop short at actions which seem to have no real motive beyond themselves.

What appear to be examples of such behaviour have formed the subject of many recent studies of animals. Patterns of activity can often be observed which have biological utility under natural conditions but are continued under domestication, although they are then useless. For instance, a dog may try to bury a bone in the floor of a room, making the appropriate movements of the nose to pile earth over the bone, even though the action is patently unsuitable to the conditions and produces no result. Such activities can be shown not to have been learned from other animals, and so must be assumed to be carried in the inherited structure of the animal's nervous system, presumably in the same way as are reflexes. It seems probable that many human activities which are evidently deep-seated and tenaciously pursued although they are not 'useful', are similarly the by-products of a nervous system which is not constructed only to cope with the demands of modern civilized life, but carries vestiges of a more fundamentally biological existence.

It must be emphasized that the points discussed in this chapter are a few examples only of fields in which co-operation between experimental psychologists and those studying social behaviour seems likely to be fruitful. The opportunities for such co-operation appear to be very substantial. A sustained attempt to exploit them in a two-way traffic between the disciplines concerned would seem to be very much to their mutual advantage, lending to social studies an often needed precision and to psychology a very desirable perspective.

A. T. Welford

REFERENCES

1. BELBIN, R. M. (1953) 'Difficulties of Older People in Industry'. *Occup. Psychol.* **27**, 177–90.
2. BELBIN, R. M. (1955) 'Older People and Heavy Work'. *Brit. J. industr. Med.* **12**, 309–19.
3. CLAY, HILARY M. (1957) 'Age Changes in Problem-Solving Tasks'. *Proceedings of the 4th Congress of the International Association of Gerontology*, **1**, 309–13.
4. CROSSMAN, E. R. F. W. (1956) 'Perception study—a complement to motion study'. *The Manager*, **24** (2), 141–5.
5. DAVIS, D. R. (1948) *Pilot Error*. Air Ministry Publication A.P. 3139A. London: H.M.S.O.
6. DENTON, G. (1953) 'Times Spent Handling and Transporting Shoes'. *British Boot, Shoe and Allied Trades Research Association Report*, T.M. 1123.
7. HICK, W. E. (1952) 'On the Rate of Gain of Information'. *Quart. J. exp. Psychol.* **4**, 11–26.
8. KALLMANN, F. J. (1957) 'Twin Data on the Genetics of Ageing'. In *Ciba Foundation Colloquia on Ageing*, Vol. 3 (Edited by G. E. W. Wolstenholme and Cecilia M. O'Connor). London: Churchill.
9. KAY, H. (1951) 'Learning of a Serial Task by Different Age Groups'. *Quart. J. exp. Psychol.* **3**, 166–83.
10. KITCHEN, J. B., & GRAHAM, A. (1961) Mental Loading of Process Operators: an attempt to devise a Method of Analysis and Assessment. *Ergonomics*, **4**, 1–15.
11. McDOUGALL, W. (1908) *Social Psychology*. London: Methuen.
12. RICHARDSON, I. M. (1953) 'Age and Work: a Study of 489 Men in Heavy Industry'. *Brit. J. industr. Med.* **10**, 269–84.
13. SIMON, J. R., & SIMON, BETTY F. (1959) 'Duration of Movements in a Dial Setting Task as a Function of the Precision of Manipulation'. *J. appl. Psychol.*, **43**, 389–94.
14. VON WRIGHT, J. M. (1957) 'A Note on the Role of "Guidance" in Learning'. *Brit. J. Psychol.*, **48**, 133–7.
15. VON WRIGHT, J. M. (1957) *An Experimental Study of Human Serial Learning*. Societas Scientiarum Fennica: Commentationes Humanarum Litterarum 23, 1. Copenhagen: Munksgaad.
16. WELFORD, A. T. (1958) *Ageing and Human Skill*. London: Oxford Univ. Press, for the Nuffield Foundation.
17. WELFORD, A. T. (1960) 'The Measurement of Sensory-Motor Performance: Survey and Reappraisal of Twelve Years' Progress'. *Ergonomics*, **3**, 189–200.
18. WELFORD, A. T., BROWN, RUTH A., & GABB, J. E. (1950), 'Two Experiments on Fatigue as affecting Skilled Performance in Civilian Aircrew', *Brit. J. Psychol.*, **40**, 195–211.
19. WOODWORTH, R. S. (1958) *Dynamics of Behavior*. London: Methuen.

PART TWO

Problems and Applications

A. INDUSTRY

Chapters 10–13

Pages 171–243

Industrial problems are also discussed in Chapters 9 and 14.

10

INDUSTRIAL RESEARCH
IN BRITAIN

Nancy Seear

THE development of industrial research by human scientists in Great Britain has been strongly influenced by the nature of British industry, by relations between industry and the universities, and by the position of the human sciences within the universities.

When some degree of specialization in management in industrial firms gradually evolved, the earliest specialists were engineers and accountants. The training of both these groups was for generations mainly of a practical kind, with a strong emphasis on apprenticeship, and with no link with the established disciplines in the universities. Until well into the twentieth century the leaders in industry and in the academic world were separated by barriers of social class and intellectual training, and communication between them was slight.

If this gulf had not existed, it is unlikely, however, that the impact of human sciences in industry would have taken place much sooner or would have been more profound. The tradition of British universities was not favourable to the development of the human sciences, which until World War II did not begin to compete with the older academic disciplines in status, in financial resources, or in the career opportunities available to their students. Psychology departments were established in most universities during the interwar period, but were mainly small in scale; while sociology, as understood today, was not studied at all in the majority of British universities.

In these circumstances it is not surprising that it took an event as

M 171

abnormal and disturbing as World War I to rouse interest in the human problems of industry and to establish the case for research in this field. The urgent need for the production of munitions and the fear of serious industrial unrest gave Government a keen and unprecedented interest in industrial efficiency and industrial peace, and led to direct Government action of a kind which would not at that time have been tolerated except during war. Government took powers to improve working conditions, but any serious attempt to raise standards required knowledge of what constituted optimum working conditions; knowledge which was inevitably lacking since the research that alone could provide it had not been undertaken. To begin to build up this body of knowledge the Government in 1915 set up the Health of Munition Workers Committee to investigate the problem of the influence of hours and conditions of work both on output and on the health of the workers. This Committee in its final report pressed for a national scheme for research in this field. Though the Committee was disbanded in 1917, the Medical Research Committee (later the Medical Research Council) and the Department of Scientific and Industrial Research shortly afterwards set up the Industrial Fatigue Research Board, which subsequently became the Industrial Health Research Board, and ultimately the Industrial Psychology Research Group operating at University College, London.

The original inquiry of the Health of Munition Workers Committee into problems of fatigue set the pattern and illustrated some of the difficulties and limitations of research in this field. The dual purpose of the study, focusing both on efficiency and on the health of the worker, pointed the way in which subsequent work was to develop, concerned as it has been both with the utilization of labour in productive processes and with the effect of these processes on people in industry and on the society in which they live. The problem initially chosen was one that could be recognized by both managements and trade unions as a question of urgent industrial importance. From the point of view of the research worker interested only in the pursuit of knowledge for its own sake, the practical problem-solving approach of this type of research could not but be suspect. Yet since industry was itself the laboratory in which the work had to be undertaken, it is difficult to see how the essential collaboration between researchers and industry could have been effectively established unless the inquiries were seen by sufficient people in industry as an answer to a felt need. But if this was to be the approach, then the subject for research had to be decided to some extent by industrial requirements and not exclusively by the interests of the researchers. Criticism has also been levelled at these early investigations on the grounds that they were too exclusively concerned with limited problems, often mainly of a physical nature,

Industrial Research in Britain

such as inquiries into standards of ventilation and seating. But this concentration on the immediate questions thrown up by industry was not the result of unawareness on the part of the research workers of more fundamental issues to be tackled, but was the inevitable consequence of the need for understanding to be established between industrialists and researchers.

If progress was to be made after the war it was essential for this need for collaboration to be recognized, and in 1920 the National Institute of Industrial Psychology was established as a result of the combined efforts of a group of psychologists, including Dr Myers, then Director of the Experimental Psychology Laboratory at Cambridge University, and of industrialists, among whom was Mr B. Seebohm Rowntree. In wartime, Government-sponsored research into industrial problems was practicable, particularly in industries directly or indirectly dependent on Government for their existence: but if the human scientists were to be able to study industrial problems in the free enterprise industry of the 1920s, they needed to convince industrialists that their work was of positive value in the development of business. The form of the Institute, independent both of universities and of Government, gave the psychologists working for it a considerable degree of independence, with both the advantages and the disadvantages of having to earn their living by solving problems put to them by industry and commerce and by providing services for which business men were prepared to pay. Some additional funds were also forthcoming from independent trusts.

Both the state of psychological study in Great Britain and industry's limited perception of its human problems led to considerable emphasis on the importance of knowledge of individual differences, particularly in relation to the selection and training of workers, and on the study of their physical environment. In the course of devising improved methods the psychologists at the Institute were, however, able to build up a substantial body of knowledge on industrial practices and problems— the essential raw material for work in this field—and gradually to accustom an increasing number of people in industry to understand that psychology had some relevance to their daily work.

From 1939 to 1945 war again focused attention on questions of productivity and morale. Both in the services and in industry it was urgently necessary to make the most effective use of the men and women available. The Services especially turned to psychologists for advice and help, particularly with regard to selection and training. While research in the academic sense was not appropriate or possible in this situation, the scope and scale of the psychologists' activities and their need to develop means of assessing the reliability and validity of their methods led them to undertake investigations which made an invaluable contribution to occupational psychology. One indication of the increasing part played by psychology was the establishment by the Medical Research Council of the Applied Psychology Research Unit at Cambridge in 1944.

If the use of psychologists in dealing with occupational problems was on a restricted scale until World War II, the influence of sociologists, and opportunities for sociological research, had been non-existent. Though the possible contribution of the sociologist to the solution of wartime problems was scarcely recognized in comparison with the extent to which the contribution of the psychologist was appreciated, interesting beginnings were also made in the use of sociological methods of investigation. In particular Dr T. T. Paterson's study of the causes of accidents on an airfield[10] demonstrated the value of sociological studies in the occupational field. Finally, the greatly increased use of psychiatrists to deal with mental and emotional casualties among both servicemen and civilians extended both the psychiatrists' knowledge of occupational problems and the public's knowledge of the psychiatrist's role. As a result of these wartime developments, by the end of the war large numbers of people had first-hand experience of some aspects of the work of human scientists, and the time was ripe to attempt to expand knowledge in this field by systematic research. But for any such programme to be undertaken there were three prerequisites: money was necessary to support the research; competent research workers had to be found to undertake it; and industry had to be willing to provide research facilities.

The post-war need to improve productivity and expand exports was recognized as calling for leadership from Government as well as from industry, and in 1947 a Committee on Industrial Productivity was set up under the Lord President of the Council, with four panels including a Human Factors Panel, of which the Chairman was Sir George Schuster. This Panel sponsored research in this sphere by making grants to bodies able to undertake research programmes. By this means the National Institute of Industrial Psychology was able to embark on research into aspects of foremanship and to undertake an inquiry into joint consultation in British industry. The long-established relationship between the Institute and industry made collaboration easy, while the grant from public funds relieved the Institute of the need to raise so large a proportion of its finances by services immediately valuable to particular firms. The subject of joint consultation was also studied with the aid of a grant from the Schuster Panel, by the Liverpool University Social Science Department—the approach in this case being primarily scoiological. The problems of the older worker, a question to which increasing attention was being paid as a result of the rising proportion of older people in the population, was already being investigated by the Nuffield Unit for Research into Problems of Ageing at the Cambridge University

Industrial Research in Britain

Psychological Laboratory, and further support was given by the Panel to this work. A Medical Research Council research team was assisted in a study into social and psychological problems in the East Fife coalmining industry, while a new independent institute, the Tavistock Institute of Human Relations, also received a grant to examine the human aspects of certain technical changes in the mining industry.

This Institute had been established in 1946 as the industrial and social division of the Tavistock Clinic, a leading London Centre for outpatient psychological medicine. It was incorporated separately after the Clinic entered the National Health Service in 1947. The Institute was assisted by the Rockefeller Foundation, and its objects included the study of the psychology of relations between human beings, and of the influence of environment in all its aspects; research and the training of students. In conjunction with the Research Center for Group Dynamics at Michigan University it had launched a quarterly journal, *Human Relations*. It was undertaking research and consultancy in industry and elsewhere in attempting to solve specific occupational problems, particularly in the field of group relations and communication. This was an important source both of finance and of research material. A proportion of the staff had a clinical, often a psycho-analytic background, while others were trained in psychology, anthropology, and sociology.

In 1948 the Schuster Panel was able to extend the scope of this Institute by a grant for industrial research purposes, and a research team under Dr Elliott Jaques began a study in the Glacier Metal Company of the psychological and social forces affecting the group life, morale, and productivity of the enterprise, attempting to develop ways of dealing with stress and of bringing about desired changes. This investigation was subsequently described in a book by Dr Jaques.[5]

The nature of the programmes sponsored by the Schuster Panel, when compared with the work undertaken during and after World War I, is evidence of a relative lessening of interest in the purely physical problems of men at work and a growing appreciation of psychological and sociological factors. From the point of view of the researchers this was accompanied by a realization of the vast, unexplored territory opened up by this change of approach and of the need to devise increasingly effective research methods.

The study in the Glacier Metal Company is an interesting illustration of these points. It was the first time that a large-scale research programme in an industrial company had been led by a psychiatrist, thus bringing new insights, knowledge, and techniques to bear on human problems in industry. The method adopted in this study was also new. The research workers were only prepared to examine problems which were identified for study by the organization and were only willing to proceed with the study when they had the support of all concerned at

Nancy Seear

every level within the company. To enable this to be done the research team reported not to the Board of Directors but to the Works Council. Thus, although the research workers maintained an attitude of the strictest academic detachment, unlike traditional academic researchers they studied problems which were not of their own choosing, but which had been selected by people in industry as requiring detailed examination. Not only did this method help to build a bridge between researchers and industry, it also enabled essential information to be made available which might not have been forthcoming if any other approach had been adopted.

Of interest, too, was the inter-disciplinary nature of this investigating team, which, though led by a psychiatrist, included sociologists and economists. This highlighted one of the problems of research of this type, which it has been increasingly found often calls for team work between researchers of varying background and training if the problems under examination are to be seen as a whole. While this in some ways greatly increases the interest of the studies, it can undoubtedly present research workers with difficulties in methods of working.

The investigation was also breaking new ground in Britain in examining problems of organization and in stressing the importance for the establishment and maintenance of effective working relationships of realistic and acceptable definitions of roles and responsibilities. In this way the study reflected the influence of research in group relationships, which had developed considerably in the United States but of which little had been heard in the United Kingdom when the Glacier Metal study was undertaken.

In addition to research assisted by grants from the Schuster Panel, another body, the Acton Society Trust, was set up in 1948 by the Joseph Rowntree Social Service Trust to undertake economic, political, and social research. The establishment of the nationalized industries at that time was leading to experiments in industrial organization of exceptional interest, and the Acton Society quickly embarked on investigation into various aspects of the operation of these industries, publishing a series of reports on such topics as 'The Framework of Joint Consultation' and 'The Future of the Unions'.[1, 2] This interest in large-scale organization has been developed in the Society's subsequent work, which has included studies in hospitals and in large private firms. The problems of the impact on the individual of organizational developments have been one of the Society's continuing concerns.

At the same time, small-scale but important changes were beginning to take place in the universities. In London University studies in industrial psychology which had begun soon after World War I were extended. An Occupational Division of the Department of Psychology was developed, with a growing number of students working for higher

176

degrees and undertaking research in industry as part of their programme. Universities which established departments of psychology and new departments of management studies, as at Edinburgh and Leeds, began to strengthen their links with industry, and in Edinburgh a Social Sciences Research Centre was set up. In Birmingham inter-disciplinary work under the leadership of Dr Sargent Florence extended the relationship already established with industry in the Birmingham area, while at Liverpool University work of a predominatly sociological character was already under way in industry in and near Liverpool as a result of the initiative of Professor Simey.

Some work of this type could, of course, be supported as part of the normal research activities of university staffs. Social research in industry is, however, frequently team work, and is apt to involve considerable travelling. Equipment, though slight in comparison with the requirements of the physical sciences, is not negligible if this work is to be efficiently undertaken. Moreover, whatever changes may have taken place in the fifties, in the immediate post-war years studies of this kind were still struggling for recognition in the university world and research workers had often to fight hard to obtain the resources necessary to carry out even quite humble schemes. In such a situation human scientists were caught in a vicious circle. Money from university sources would not be forthcoming until work of an outstanding quality was produced, but without adequate funds the chance of producing such work was seriously limited. This position within the universities was undoubtedly one reason for the establishment and growth of the independent institutes which have characterized the work in Great Britain.

In 1951 the Human Factors Panel under Sir George Schuster was disbanded, and with it went a main source of Government assistance. For two years research workers were forced back on such support as was available in the universities, from industry and from independent research funds. But in 1953 the Medical Research Council and the Department of Scientific and Industrial Research, in consultation with the Lord President of the Council, set up two Committees for the further development of research: one on Human Relations in Industry, and the other on Individual Efficiency in Industry. These Committees consisted of men and women drawn from industrial management, from trade unions, and from University departments concerned with the human sciences. It was thought that tripartite committees of this kind, brought together and supported by Government Departments one of which was already concerned with industrial research in the physical sciences, would be well placed to tackle the problems of allocating resources, of developing research personnel, and of creating effective relationships between industry and research workers in the human sciences.

The immediate pattern of the Committees' work was to some extent established for them by American Conditional Aid Funds being placed at their disposal soon after their formation. Under the Conditional Aid programme research projects, to justify support, had to be related directly to increasing productivity and industrial efficiency, and researches had to be planned to show promise of producing applicable results within three years. Partly for this reason, the main areas in which the Human Relations Committee concentrated were management organization, technical change, incentives, training and promotion, and problems of special groups in industry. The Individual Efficiency Committee supported researches on the influence of equipment design and working conditions on operator efficiency; on the acquisition of skill; and on aspects of work study.

Where a proposed project did not fulfil the requirements of the Conditional Aid Programme, the Committees were sometimes able to assist with funds from other sources. This was done when emphasis was laid by the research workers on the wider social implications of industrial development, for example in studies in the employment of married women. Research in industry, it was considered, should be influenced by one of its most important findings: the interaction between activities and attitudes in industry and in the community outside the factory gates.

The work of the Committees enabled a number of investigations to be launched and to be carried to conclusion in due course, with varying degrees of success. Research is inevitably a gamble and not every risk investment can be expected to pay dividends. Work which aroused considerable interest included studies in industrial relations and technical change undertaken by Liverpool University in a steel mill in North-West England,[11] and investigations by Dr Burns at the Social Science Research Centre in Edinburgh into problems of acceptance of change at management level, where new scientific ideas were being introduced into established firms.[4] Work on incentive schemes made more knowledge available to illuminate the continuing argument on the advantages and disadvantages of financial incentive payment systems, and with a grant from the Committee, Mr R. Marriott of the Medical Research Council Industrial Psychology Research Group was able to summarize and review the evidence in this controversy.[8] The subject of management succession investigated by the Acton Trust Society[3] was widely discussed, while assumptions on management organization were challenged by Miss Joan Woodward's study[12] on the relation between management structure and technology.

While the immediate task of the Committees was to allocate funds for projects fulfilling Conditional Aid requirements, the long-term problems of the future development of research in industry were continuously under review. The Committees, recognizing the need for

Industrial Research in Britain

industrial collaboration, regarded it as a vital part of their work to stimulate the interest of industrial managers and workers. It was felt that this could be done only if steps were taken to enable representatives from industry to discuss research projects while they were still in progress, and meetings were arranged so that research workers and industrialists could learn from each other as projects developed. It was recognized, too, that industry expected results, and that much greater efforts than had formerly been made were necessary to feed research findings back into industry. Encouragement was given to research workers to write for journals read by managements and workers, and to talk at meetings and discussion groups on research projects. The very considerable interest created by these meetings was evidence of the wide audience for research material presented in a relevant manner. In addition, the D.S.I.R. arranged for the publication of 'industrial versions' of research studies, summarizing the conclusions and significance of researches. The demand for these publications has testified to industry's growing willingness to recognize the value of work of this kind.

For the most effective development, the Committees believed that research centres should be widely dispersed throughout the country. It was thought that not only should a number of both old and new universities be encouraged to establish work in the industrial field, but that possibilities of research based on technical colleges should be explored. From some points of view the long-established contacts between technical colleges and local industry make them peculiarly suitable for work of this type, and with the extension of scope and rising academic standards in the major technical colleges it appeared especially important that research activities should be fostered. It was hoped that Miss Woodward's study in industry in Essex, based on the South-East Essex Technical College, would be a pioneer development in technical college work.

Apart from the universities, technical colleges, and the established independent research units, it is of interest that two studies supported by the Industrial Efficiency Committee were undertaken by an Industrial Research Association, the British Boot, Shoe, and Allied Trades Research Association. The Industrial Research Association is obviously a medium for research likely to be particularly productive of results that will be used by industry. The D.S.I.R. was also itself directly responsible for a study into the human aspects of work study.

But it would be of little use to rouse national interest unless the supply of competent research workers could be increased and maintained. So long as grants were made on a short-term basis there were almost no career prospects for researchers, who were continually moving to jobs in industry. The need for a more dependable source of finance was plain, and when the two Committees were wound up and were replaced in 1957 by a combined Human Sciences Committee of the D.S.I.R., the Council of the Department agreed to a continuing grant to this Committee which enabled it to give somewhat greater security to research workers than had previously been possible. Whether this is in fact the best way for the work to be developed remains an open question. An article in *Nature* (December 1958), commenting on the final report of the two Committees, questions whether the D.S.I.R. is in fact the appropriate body to be the main sponsors of such work. It is arguable that human sciences research in industry can hardly develop on an adequate scale if its claim to public funds is handled by a Department primarily equipped by personnel and tradition to deal with the physical and natural sciences. A separate Social and Industrial Research Council able to focus exclusively on these problems may ultimately be required. Support from public funds may, however, in the future be considerably supplemented by other sources of finance. There are encouraging signs that in important sections of industry hostility and apathy are being replaced by an interest that is leading, not merely to collaboration, but to positive initiative by industrialists. A petroleum company, for example, is contributing to the cost of human sciences research at a university, and certain steel companies are themselves employing human scientists as research workers in their own organizations. In certain cases the human scientists employed by industry are collaborating with operational research teams in what may well be one of the most fruitful partnerships. The growing support from the trade unions is seen in the City and Guilds Survey of the Educational Needs of the Clothing Industry, which was sponsored by the National Union of Tailors and Garment workers.

An unknown factor which will greatly influence the development of this work is the attitude of the universities. The traditional suspicion in British universities of applied studies useful in the solution of practical industrial problems has not eased the path of researchers in the past. It can only be said that many science and engineering departments have gone much further in collaboration with industry than have the human scientists. The future support of the universities is likely to depend on the extent to which work undertaken in industry is seen to lead to a real contribution to the knowledge of the subject. In the final report of the two M.R.C. and D.S.I.R. Committees[6,7] it is claimed that:

> Some of the best projects we have sponsored have combined an attack on practical problems with penetration of underlaying theoretical issues. We might go as far as to say that it is a peculiar condition of social science that the best results come from those persons who are able to operate on both the practical and theoretical levels.

Industrial Research in Britain

To the extent that this is true the anxieties of the universities may be set at rest and the study of men at work will take its place as a proper field of academic inquiry.

In reviewing the progress that has so far been made it could be claimed that by the end of the 1950s a useful extension of human sciences research in industry had taken place, and that there was much greater awareness in industry both of the importance of the social and human aspects of industrial activity and of the assistance research workers could give. But it is probably true that the improvement appears considerable mainly because so little had been done until the end of World War II. In a subject of such recent growth and in an area so ill-defined, assessments of achievement and forecasts for the future are possible only in very general terms.

In dealing with the physical working environment, the work of the Industrial Health Research Board and of the National Institute of Industrial Psychology has done a great deal to provide scientifically based standards for good working conditions where previously much had to be left to the judgement of the individual employer and the local factory inspector. The continuing change from general to specific requirements in the regulations issued under the Factories Acts is evidence of ground gained in this area. This is not, however, to say that there is nothing left to be done. Scientists, employers, and trade unions have all in recent years been awakened to the need to adjust the job to the worker to a far greater extent than has been done in the past, and the study of *ergonomics* is now being pursued with increased vigour.

In problems associated with individual differences, improved selection methods have certainly enabled gross misfits to be avoided and can be shown to have reduced labour turnover, though attempts to provide reliable personality tests have so far not produced results of much practical value in industry. Studies of the acquisition of skill have led to improvements in training schemes with quicker learning, better quality of work, and reduced labour turnover. The vitally important questions of motivation and morale have been examined, and growing understanding of the complexity of these matters has at least shattered some of the simpler assumptions of common sense, even if it has not put any clear-cut alternative explanations in their place and is unlikely to do so. In this area, as in so many aspects of this work, what has been gained is much greater insight into problems rather than established principles of universal application. In the same way the more recent studies of group relations have given a new understanding of the social aspects of organization and of the dangers that arise from a refusal to take them into account.

That tremendous gaps in knowledge remain is beyond doubt. In none of the problems explored have final answers been reached, and in many

Nancy Seear

spheres the soil is still virgin. If studies of the individual and the small group have received a growing amount of attention over the last twenty years, broader problems of the relations of industry to the community and of the relations between the unions and employers and between unions and unions have been studied only descriptively or by statistical analysis.

In methodology research workers will be the first to agree that, in the living and untidy field in which they work, the acquisition of sound methods is continuously pursued, but rarely finally achieved. Indeed, as the growing complexity of these problems is more fully appreciated, methodological difficulties increase in proportion. Reference has been made to the need for inter-disciplinary work among human scientists. Sir George Schuster, summarizing his experience as Chairman of the Human Factors Panel, remarked in 1952: 'In any real life situation in industry, human and technological factors tend to be so intimately intermingled and to react so decisively on each other, as to call for a joint consideration of the two aspects.'[9] There are signs that human scientists are increasingly aware that inter-disciplinary studies may need to be extended, not only among human scientists but also through collaboration with those trained in operational research and in the natural and physical sciences. The problems of method that this must raise form an exciting area still largely unexplored.

Much remains to be done, but it is the triumph of the last fifteen years that this area of study is no longer barred in the face of the human scientist. Today it is the workers and the tools for the job that are in short supply, not the opportunities for discovery.

REFERENCES

1. Acton Society Trust. (1952) *The Framework of Joint Consultation.* Studies in Nationalized Industries, 10.
2. Acton Society Trust (1951) *The Future of the Unions.* Studies in Nationalized Industries, 10.
3. Acton Society Trust. (1956). *Management Succession.* London: 1956.
4. CROOME, HONOR (1960) *Human Problems of Innovation.* London: Department of Scientific and Industrial Research.
5. JAQUES, ELLIOTT (1951) *The Changing Culture of a Factory.* London: Tavistock Publications.
6. Joint Committee on Human Relations in Industry, 1954–57. Final Report. Medical Research Council and Dept. of Scientific and Industrial Research. 1958.
7. Joint Committee on Individual Efficiency in Industry, 1953–57. London: H.M.S.O. 1958
8. MARRIOTT, REGINALD (1957) *Incentive Payment Systems.* London: Staples.

Industrial Research in Britain

9. Ministry of Labour (1952) Report of the Human Relations in Industry Conference, 1952. London: H.M.S.O.
10. PATERSON, T. T. (1955). *Morale in War and Work*, London: Parrish.
11. SCOTT, W. H., BANKS, J. A., HALSEY, A. H., & LUPTON, T. (1956) *Technical Change and Industrial Relations*. Liverpool: Liverpool Univ. Press.
12. WOODWARD, JOAN (1958) *Management and Technology*. London: Department of Scientific and Industrial Research.

II

THE SOCIOLOGY OF INDUSTRY

Tom Burns

THE sociologist's interest in industry reflects that of society at large. He shares a pervasive, rather anxious, concern with industrialism as the characteristic institution of modern advanced societies and as the prime mover of social change in them; or he may participate in efforts to diagnose those failings of the industrial system or of single undertakings which impoverish or disrupt the lives of individuals, families, groups of people, or whole sections of society.

Such interests bear on the *external* references of the industrial system; the issues and questions lie not so much in industrial organizations themselves as in changes in social structure, in improvement or deterioration in welfare, and in alienating or pathological conditions attributable to industrialism.

On the other hand, he may desire to elucidate the irrational forces which operate in social systems brought into being and maintained by self-interest. Frequently, again, he may accept more or less uncritically the aim of making industrial and business undertakings more efficient as instruments of the material progress of society, or more efficient or less troublesome as instruments of private profit-making. Studies of these latter kinds are directed towards the *internal* order of industry and the situation arising within it; with very few exceptions they tend to accept the existence, values, and purposes of industry and individual undertakings at their face value.

In this chapter we shall follow this general division by considering first the study of the institutional nature of modern industrialism, and thereafter inquiries into the internal structure of industrial concerns and the roles and situations prevailing in industrial milieux.

Tom Burns

THE EXTERNAL RELATIONSHIPS OF INDUSTRY
WITH THE SOCIAL ORDER: THE SOCIOLOGY OF INDUSTRIALISM

Inquiries into the external relationships of industry extend far beyond the commonly accepted boundaries of industrial sociology and, indeed, make up most of the matter of social and economic history over the past two centuries. The demands of capitalist industry for human effort and material resources, and the increased flow of goods and services which it produces, have since its formative years occasioned the most profound disturbances in individual lives, extinguished and created social institutions, and substantially altered the structure of society. Because it has continued to demand new as well as more materials, and new kinds of human effort and skills, and because it has produced entirely new kinds of goods and services as well as more of those already in familiar use, the disturbances, social innovations, and structural changes have gone on.

But there is an area central to the history of the social consequences of industrialism which received the chief attention of Marx and Weber and which, after a period of neglect, is being discussed afresh. This has to do with the institutional nature of industrialism itself. The industrial system imposes its own structure of relationships on managers and workpeople. To maintain and expand the system requires the widespread acceptance of an ordered array of values by which persons in different positions in the system set their aims in life and guide their day-to-day actions, and these values have to be inculcated by a variety of means. For industrial concerns to operate at all there has to be specified a range of roles, each with a set of constraints; there have to be also disciplinary codes or social controls in order to confine admissible conduct within these constraints. In all these senses, the industrial system marks the host society with its own special imprint. The members of such a society are, so to speak, 'processed' by industry into human resources and, as now appears, into conformity with its needs as users of its products.[34]

The kind of 'processing' effected by the industrial system has changed with its own institutional character. For this has changed as well as the inputs of effort and materials and the outputs of goods and services. It is still changing. The general theme of this first kind of study is the nature of these changes.

Material and Social Technologies in the Three Phases of Industrialism

Industrialism itself is the product of techniques of social organization linked with techniques of manufacture. It has developed in spasmodic fashion from the rudimentary forms of the eighteenth century by alternate advances in first one technology and then the other.

The Sociology of Industry

The elementary form of industrialism lies in Adam Smith's conjunction of the division of labour traditional in advanced society with the extension of its advantages by 'those machines by which labour is so much facilitated and enlarged'.[78] The modern industrial system was founded when the perception by early mechanical scientists that natural events 'obeyed' certain laws became widely diffused in the eighteenth century. The legend that Arkwright was first struck by the feasibility of mechanical spinning 'by accidentally observing a hot piece of iron become elongated by passing between iron rollers' ([77], p. 41) may be fiction, but it reflects truly the commonplace terms in which the new habits of scientific thought could be used by craftsmen-inventors, who saw not just an interesting analogy but one process obeying a law which might also apply to a different and entirely new process.

Simultaneously with Adam Smith's observation of the archetypal form of the two technologies, a third step was being taken with the creation of the first successful factory, by Strutt and Arkwright.[29] By 1835 Ure[88] could discount the basic principles of division of labour as outdated and misleading (p. 19); the industrial system was simply the factory system as developed by Arkwright, the term 'factory' meaning 'the combined operation of many workpeople, adult and young, in tending with assiduous skill a system of productive machines continuously impelled by a central power' (p. 13). 'It is,' he adds, moreover 'the constant aim and tendency of every improvement in machinery to supersede human labour altogether.' (p. 23).

At the time Ure was writing (1832) only a small fraction of the working population of the United Kingdom was employed in factories, and some of these were central workshops rather than organized factories. Bendix, in his study of industrial management in England during this period ([6], chap. 2) points out that the usual form adopted for comparatively large-scale industrial undertakings was a system of subcontracting—very little different from what Zimmern describes as obtaining in classical Greece ([100], p. 261). Bendix cites evidence that this system prevailed not only in building and engineering, but in clothing, cutlery, iron-founding, and even in textiles. 'It was obviously up to these subcontractors to deal with their underhands whom they recruited, employed, trained, supervised, disciplined, paid and fired' ([6], p. 53).

Factory organization stayed for three generations at the point at which Arkwright had left it, a collection of machines in a building, all driven by one prime mover, and, preferably, of the same type and engaged on the same process. Attending the machines were men and women who themselves were attended by 'feeders', most of them children, who fetched and carried away materials. There was also a 'superior, but numerically unimportant' class of maintenance and repair workers ([55], Bk. I, ch. XV, sect. 4, 'The Factory'). All of these worked under a master, and a few chief workmen or foremen. Where the factory system had gained ground, the subcontractor had been incorporated, along with his 'underhands', into it, first as agent and then as foreman. But he was shorn of many of his functions. Those that were removed from him passed to the master. The primitive social technology of the factory system still confined it, even by the 1850s, largely to the mass production of textiles. Outside this there remained 'domestic' industry and small tradesmen.

Technical developments in transport and communications, the impact of the international exhibitions of London and Paris, freer trade, and the armaments revolution supported by the development of machine tools and of steel and chemical technology, all combined during the fifties and sixties to form the springboard, in material technology, of the next advance in the social techniques of industrial organisation.

As yet, there is no account of how that advance took place. All that can be said is that with the extension of the factory system into engineering and chemicals, iron and steel processing, food manufacture and clothing, an organizational development took place which provided for the conduct and control of complex series of production processes within the same plant. The overt sign of this development is the increase in the number of salaried officials employed in industry. According to Bendix ([6], p. 214), quoting unpublished sources, the proportion of 'administrative employees' to 'productive employees' in Britain had risen to 8·6 per cent by 1907, and thereafter to 20 per cent by 1948. Similar increases took place in Western Europe and the United States.

The growth in the numbers of industrial administrators and functionaries or managers reflects the growth of organizational structures. Production department managers, sales managers, accountants, planning engineers, inspectors, training officers, publicity managers, research managers, and the rest emerged as specialized parts of the general management function as industrial concerns increased in size. Their jobs were created, in fact, out of the master's either directly, or at one or two removes. This gives them and the whole social structure which contains their newly created roles its hierarchic character. It is indeed— what one would expect to emerge from the spontaneous sub-contracting phase of management if history followed set patterns—a quasi-feudal structure. All rights and powers at every level derive from the immediate superior; fealty, or 'responsibility', is owed to him; all benefits are 'as if' dispensed by him. The feudal bond is more easily and more often broken than in feudal polities, but loyalty to the concern, to employers, is regarded not only as proper, but as essential to the preservation of the system.

Chester Barnard makes this point with unusual emphasis: 'The most important single contribution required of the executive, certainly the

The Sociology of Industry

most universal qualification, is loyalty, domination by the organization personality. ([4] p. 220). More recently, Gouldner has pointed out that 'Much of W. H. Whyte's recent study of "organization man" is a discussion of the efforts by industry to attach managerial loyalty to the corporation' ([37] p. 216).

The growth of a bureaucratic system of control which made possible the increase in scale of undertakings had other aspects. The divorce of ownership and management,[7] although by no means absolute, has gone far enough to render survival of the enterprise (and the survival of the existing management) at least as important a consideration as the maximization of profit, which, indeed, wears a different aspect for the large-scale corporation ([44] p. 254). More important, the growth of bureaucracy as the social technology which made possible the second stage of industrialism was only feasible because the development of material technology was held steady. The early years of industry based on major technological advances show a high death-rate among enterprises; growth occurs when the rate of technical advance slows down. Thereafter, consumer demand tends to be standardized, through publicity and price reductions, and the consequent restraint of technical progress enables undertakings to maintain relatively stable conditions, in which large-scale production can be built up through the conversion of manufacturing processes into routine cycles of activity for machines or semi-skilled assembly hands.

Under such conditions not only did concerns grow in size, not only could manufacturing processes be routinized, mechanized, and quickened, but the task of co-ordination, of ensuring co-operation and of planning and monitoring could also be broken down into routines and inculcated as specialized management tasks.

It is this second phase of industrialism which is now generally accepted as dominating the institutional life of Western societies. Between 1870 and 1930 the formal organization of industrial undertakings along bureaucratic lines, coupled with the concurrent growth of national armies and governmental administrations, suggested to sociologists that 'bureaucratization' was as intrinsic to the character of modern society as was scientific and technological progress. For Weber, the founder of the study of bureaucracy, it seems to have exhibited the same feature of rational thought applied to the social environment as does technology in the case of the physical environment. Tönnies, earlier, had provided a key to the development of a technology of social organization by indicating the transformation of the relationships involving the individual which were characteristic of earlier small-scale society ('Gemeinschaft') into 'Gesellschaft' systems.[84]

Bureaucracy, then, stands as the 'formal organization' of industrial concerns. The formulation given by Weber is a generalized description

189

Tom Burns

of the 'ideal type' of bureaucracy—i.e., a synthetic model composed of what are understood in society at large to be the distinguishing features of actual bureaucratic organizations, military, ecclesiastical, governmental, industrial, etc. These distinctive characteristics are:

    (i) The organization operates according to a body of laws or rules, which are consistent and have normally been intentionally established.

    (ii) Every official is subject to an impersonal order by which he guides his actions. In turn his instructions have authority only in so far as they conform with this generally understood body of rules; obedience is due to his office, not to him as an individual.

    (iii) Each incumbent of an office has a specified sphere of competence, with obligations, authority, and powers to compel obedience strictly defined.

    (iv) The organization of offices follows the principle of hierarchy; that is, each lower office is under the control and supervision of a higher one.

    (v) The supreme head of the organization, and only he, occupies his position by appropriation, by election, or by being designated as successor. Other offices are filled, in principle, by free selection, and candidates are selected on the basis of 'technical' qualifications. They are appointed, not elected.

    (vi) The system also serves as a career ladder. There is promotion according to seniority or achievement. Promotion is dependent on the judgement of superiors.

    (vii) The official, who in principle is excluded from any ownership rights in the concern, or in his position, is subject to discipline and control in the conduct of his office.*

It is 'bureaucratized' industry and business which has given advanced industrial societies their distinctive social character. Managers, clerical workers, functionaries, and the professional workers employed by large companies and industrial concerns are regarded as forming a new middle-class, larger in size than, and different in interests and values from, the earlier middle-class of small entrepreneurs, shopkeepers, and professional men.[15, 16, 50, 54, 60] Less attention has been given to the social effects of the ordering of these new men in hierarchies. Most positions in a bureaucratic structure involve these incumbents in the role of both subordinate and superior. The structure also serves as a career ladder, in which co-operation for the success of the organization goes

    * For Weber's formal statement of bureaucracy as an ideal type see [92] (pp. 329–34).

The Sociology of Industry

alongside, or masks, or even expresses, competition for career success. * More easily dramatized are the alienating effects (in Freudian terms) of immersion in the occupational roles provided by bureaucratic systems† and the alienating effects (in Marxist terms) of the ideologies and institutions created in response to the need to adapt conduct and beliefs to the requirements of effective co-operation and competition.‡

While the greater part of the industrial system is in the second, bureaucratic phase of the historical development of industrialism (and some older and smaller establishments remain in the first), it is now becoming clear that a third phase has been initiated during the past two or three decades. A new, more insecure, relationship with the consumer has appeared as production has caught up and overtaken spontaneous domestic demand¶ and the propensity to consume has to be stimulated by advertising, by styling, and by marketing promotions guided by consumer research, motivation research, market research. Also, partly as one of the endeavours to maintain expansion, partly because of the stimulus of government spending on the development of new weapons and military equipment, industry has admitted a sizeable influx of new technical developments,§ and agreed to accept industrial development as a major commitment of its own. So far, the implications of this new phase in the evolution of industrialism have been studied only in so far as they have presented themselves as overt, public, social problems: the shortage of scientific manpower, the new forms of human effort called for by machinery automatically operated and controlled, and the effects of automation on employment.

There are signs that industry organized according to the now traditional principles of bureaucracy is no longer able to accommodate the new elements introduced by large-scale industrial development and by the new relationship with the markets industry serves. Both demand a much greater degree of flexibility in internal organization, much higher

---

* Some aspects of the ambiguity of the demands of rationalized functional roles and pursuit of promotion are discussed in Bendix[6] Chap. 5. See also. [11, 48, 89]

† These form the theme of D. Riesman's *The Lonely Crowd*[68] and W. H. Whyte Jr's *The Organization Man*.[95] For a general statement of the Freudian thesis see H. Marcuse.[53]

‡ See, *e.g.*, W. H. Whyte,[94] and Bendix.[6]

¶ See the discussion of this relationship in J. K. Galbraith's three studies. [32, 33, 34]

§ The best available indications of the rate of growth of industrial research and development are provided by the U.S. National Research Council Bulletins, *Industrial Research Laboratories in the United States*, issued from 1921 onwards. [87] For Britain, no comparable figures exist for the period before 1955, the year of the survey carried out by E. Rudd,[24] for the Department of Scientific and Industrial Research. G. L. Payne[66] gives an exhaustive review of published information.

levels of commitment to the commercial aims of the concern from all its members, and an even higher proportion of administrators, controllers and monitors to operatives.*

Industrial Relations

Some of the firms most exposed to the new situation are, in sporadic and tentative fashion, developing organizational techniques which will equip them for living with rapid technological development and unstable markets. But these moves are masked by the much more widespread—though by no means universal—change in the norms governing the relationships between persons and categories of persons within industry. In particular, there is a distinct shift in the relationship, between management and labour, reflecting but also generating a concurrent shift in the distribution of income, power, and social standing between the two.

There are, as Dr Lutz[51] has pointed out, two elements of the relationship. 'As it is part of a class society, an industrial undertaking is an instrument of domination. The power exercised over the workers also derives, however, from the element of constraint which seems essential to any system for the division of work.' It is the *responses* to these two elements which have for the most part been the object of study. Trade unionism and cognate forms of organization outside the workshop, and restrictive practices of an institutionalized kind within it, have been extensively examined and reported on as responses to the power exercised over the lives of workers by employers and managers as a class. Absenteeism, labour turnover, and sickness and accident rates have been studied as indicators of pathological response to the adverse psychological as well as physical conditions attaching to industrial labour.

It is the first of these subdivisions to which the title 'industrial relations' has been appropriated for text-books, and indeed, official government publications. Normally, it is reserved for all aspects of collective bargaining between employers and labour, whether the issues are national or local, apply to single concerns or many, and whether they involve trade unions and employers' associations or *ad hoc* organizations (such as unofficial strike committees). Description of the historical development of labour organization, of the kinds of procedure employed in bargaining, and of types of trade union represents the bulk of the literature on the subject. During the past decade studies at the level of wages, and of the criteria which are

* For some material differences in the internal situation of firms in stable and changing circumstances, see Burns.[12] For a more general discussion of the current organizational dilemma, see Burns and Stalker.[13]

used when wage-claims are discussed (e.g.,[99]), case-studies and statistical analyses of strikes,[45] and descriptions of the vicissitudes encountered during the post-war years by the joint management-labour production committees forced on industrial concerns during the Second World War[71] have reflected to some extent the shift in the fundamental relationship of management and labour, without attempting to explain it.

Of particular interest and relevance in this context is the new direction taken by the study of Trade Unionism. The increased standing and power of workers has been demonstrated quite explicitly in the increased political and industrial influence exerted by trade union leaders. At the same time, trade union consensus about objectives and about attitudes to the often divergent, sometimes opposed, objectives of both industrialists and government has broken down. Thirdly, trade unions, which grew up during the phase of bureaucratic expansion, have, like industrial undertakings themselves, carried into the new situation structural forms shaped according to the needs and circumstances which prevailed then. So far British studies have not advanced beyond the stage of posing questions or debating the democratic or undemocratic nature of trade union organization. In America, a series of studies by Tannenbaum[80, 81, 82] of the nature and the distribution within unions of control over policy and decisions introduces a reconsideration of the distribution of power between the different levels within a hierarchy—hitherto treated as a single invariant form—similar to that which has occurred in the case of management structures.

Both the obsolescence of bureaucratic forms and the changed nature of industrial relations are arguably the outcome of the same features of industrialism's third phase, which we have already sketched.* Unfortunately, no aspect of industrialism is so little explored in Britain and America as the link between its internal evolution and the sequence of roles, commitments, and changes in power open to working members of society. The dramatic change in management-worker relations which has occurred in every Western country during the past twenty years has still no more profound interpretation in English than the road-to-Damascus revelation of the business virtues of good relationships† and the premise of a Social Ethic replacing the Protestant Ethic.[95] In Britain, attempts at interpretation of the change have stopped short at any convenient point at which the task could be handed over to the economists—where one could invoke, for example, the change from mass

---

* See also Chap. 8, 'Economic Security', in Galbraith.[34]

† Ideally (in the sense of almost too good to be true) presented in the Buchsbaum Case, an autobiographical narrative of the way one American employer changed over from the inflexibly tough-with-labour policy of the thirties to the 'playing-along-with-the Unions' and 'human relations' strategy of the forties.[93].

unemployment to full employment, or inflationary pressures catching wage-levels up in a rising spiral of claims, or the increased importance of export markets, or the replacement of a surplus-dominated international situation by one of chronic shortages.

The Sociology of Work

Developments in the study of the second aspect of the worker's situation—his experience, as 'an appendage to the machine', of an extreme form of the constraints of the factory system—have taken a rather different path. What began, in the first post-war flush of enthusiasm for raising productivity, as a series of investigations into local managerial problems of labour turnover, low productivity, and absenteeism has turned into interpretations of these and similar kinds of behaviour as 'alternative methods of withdrawal' from the work situation, and as symptomatic of a malaise engendered by the alienating pressures of industrialism. Such analytical studies reveal a growing interest in the interaction between work and the rest of life, which is also apparent in some recent and current observational studies of dock workers,[49] steel workers,[72] fishing communities,* and labour groups in large civil engineering schemes.[79] This interest is still tentative as far as Britain is concerned, but may lead in the direction of the sociology of industrial work which is the necessary complement to a sociology of industrialism.

The most relevant work in this connexion is largely French, beginning with Naville's 'occupational demography'—studies of the duration and age-structure of different occupations and the distribution through the working population of different skills and vocations.[63]† Intimations of a new kind of interaction between work and the rest of life are contained in the work of Dumazedier[25] on the influence of leisure-time pursuits, interests, and obligations on the structure of occupational careers and choices.

Finally, the development of a new work situation for the industrial worker has been a major theme of French industrial sociologists. The growing complexity of industrial processes, especially in engineering, is seen not only as constantly destroying or reducing or modifying the skills and knowledge on which both the comparative standards of living and the self-regard of the worker depend, but also as changing the social

---

* Studies now in progress in Hull and Aberdeen.

† As early as 1945, Naville produced a general critique of vocational guidance as claiming to be a straightforward technique capable of pointing the child in the direction best indicated by his aptitudes. The objectives of vocational guidance, according to Naville, are impossible to achieve outside the context of a vast apparatus of organized information about the structure of employment, the economic system, and technical industrial and economic trends.[62]

The Sociology of Industry

context of work. The autonomy that used to invest work, once orders were received from superiors is now replaced by enclosure in a network of requirements and expectations from an increasing number of specialist functionaries.[31,85] For Touraine, this new work situation involves a new working-class situation, and underlies the estrangement of the worker from traditional working-class movements and ideologies which were rooted in values derived from the former proletarian situation of subjection and poverty.[86]

THE INTERNAL RELATIONSHIP OF INDUSTRY: INDUSTRIAL SOCIOLOGY

As in the case of educational institutions, central and local government departments, prisons, military units, trade unions, hospitals, and other closed establishments, access to industrial undertakings for research purposes is only granted by the controlling authorities when they are assured that the research will further the interests the establishment exists to serve; and most controlling authorities reserve the right to make their own appraisal of these interests and of the pertinence to them of the research proposed. The great majority of industrial studies, therefore, have had as their ostensible purpose the improvement of work methods, the control of industrial delinquency, the extension of understanding and control of workers' conduct, the development of a technical understanding of organization and of management roles, the elimination of frictional waste caused by inadequate co-operation and communication.

It is as well to recognize the consequent 'ideological bias against business' and against 'internal' studies of industrial undertakings that Lazarsfeld has recently discussed.[46] 'Aiding the doctor, promoting justice, or supporting the agencies of the law—all these are in accordance with accepted norms; helping the businessman make money is not.' While this last aim may not be present in the researcher's mind, he is unlikely to obtain licence to enter and study industrial or other closed establishments unless the possibility of his realizing such an aim is entertained by the head of the undertaking. The moral issue may not be different in essence from that present in any study which may result in increasing the power of controllers and manipulators and the subjugation of the controlled and manipulated; Lazarsfeld implies as much. But it presents itself more blatantly and unavoidably. It is certainly not avoided by rotating the axis of moral values and applying terms like pathology and therapy to business concerns; the one still finds its only effective expression in less earning capacity and the other in more. It cannot be glossed over by professing sympathy with the underdog or squaring Trade Union officials.

195

Tom Burns

There are considerations which blunt the dilemma somewhat; one may also regard money-making by businessmen as proper or necessary. Eventually, however, one has to decide whether the existence of the moral issue puts an embargo on one's studying the internal affairs of industrial undertakings (other than in disguise) or whether other considerations override it. These other considerations are, first, that industrial undertakings, industrial work, and industrial milieux are of central importance in our society, and it is becoming rather more difficult to equate ignorance with objectivity in studying the nature and more immediate consequences of industrialism. Secondly, the institutional forms which work has assumed, the organization of individual and co-operative work, the beliefs about its nature and about related motives and aims, and the systems of values associated with different kinds of work together represent a sizeable section of the fields of study appropriated by the social sciences. Thirdly, business and industrial undertakings exist as communities, or sub-communities, in which a wide variety of forms of behaviour are far more accessible to study than in any other milieu. They exist as enclosed, separate, social establishments, in which people are obliged to deal with each other, and to do so observably. Lastly, such communities have many other aspects than those directly related to work; they are social structures with their own systems of stratification, with different rights and duties, privileges and obligations attached to positions in each level, their own criteria of esteem and marks of prestige, and with their own internal politics. And in both these last respects, because there is a constant pressure towards rationalization, towards making the whole structure of roles and relationships more explicit and understandable to the members of the community, the detailed study of social structures and of institutionalized conduct is in many ways more easily and more fruitfully pursued in such milieux than in most others.*

Such inducements, and some rather more mundane, have been enough to maintain growth in industrial studies, especially in the last decade. Yet it remains true that for every twenty studies of the lowest ranks of manual operatives there is perhaps one of managing directors, whose work and occupational situation are of possibly equal interest and significance; that demarcation disputes and absenteeism among workers attract attention, and identical conduct equally prevalent among managers never does; that there are scores of diagnostic studies of such delinquencies as shirking, or of 'lightning' and unofficial strikes, and none of such offences as pilfering and expense-account swindling, which are possibly more prevalent, more costly, and more damaging to industrial efficiency, but are either condoned or are cloaked under a

---

* For example, most of the illustrations of 'expressive' behaviour in Goffman [35] are drawn from studies of occupational milieux.

conspiracy of silence which involves the highest and lowest ranks in industry.

Human Engineering

The earliest studies reveal their alignment with managerial interests very clearly. The tradition of industrial studies as now established begins in America, at the beginning of the century, with Frederick Taylor.[83] 'Taylorism' was based on the principle, which its founder constantly reaffirmed, that there is ordinarily a large margin between the potential and the actual amount of work done by workers. The task of management was to reduce this margin.

The Health of Munition Workers Committee,[40, 41, 42] with whose investigations the continuous tradition of industrial studies begins in Britain, was created in 1915 out of a similar though less evangelistic enthusiasm for making better use, in the engineering sense, of human resources. Disappointed in the expectation that women could fill twice as many shells in sixteen hours as they did in eight, doubting whether —as so many members had asserted in the House of Commons— shipyard men working a seventy-hour week absented themselves for one or two days at a time entirely because of incorrigible drunkenness, the Ministry of Munitions set afoot a series of inquiries into the nature of industrial fatigue and the causes of absenteeism.

The experimental and observational studies carried out in Britain during the First World War added the merits and prestige of scientific study to the more dramatic attractions of Taylorism, which had made themselves felt in Europe before 1914. These circumstances seem to have determined the line of development in Britain between the wars. The study of human problems internal to industry was conducted almost exclusively under the auspices of the National Institute of Industrial Psychology and the Industrial Health Research Board, the lineal descendant of the Health of Munition Workers Committee. Their studies were usually directly to do with operatives and the efficiency (in engineering terms) of their labour. Methods were developed for guiding them into, or selecting them for, jobs which matched the resources, fixed, limited, and measurable, of intelligence or manual dexterity or physical capacity they brought into industry. Other sequences of studies dealt with the effect of conditions of work and environment on their efficiency, and with methods of economizing their work movements, time, and effort. *

The assumption of the role not only of human resources engineer but of management consultant and aide, which was implicit in Taylorism,

* The topics covered during the inter-war period by the research reports of the I.H.R.B. have been classified by F. E. Emery.[27]

Tom Burns

was reinforced by the psychologist's bent for—in Friedmann's words—individualizing the task and always considering the workers as separate individuals.[30] This set of conditions still applies to a large part of the contribution now being made by psychology; but since 1939 the growth of interest and activity among other social scientists has set rather better defined limits to the aspects of work behaviour to which their assumptions and methods apply. The scope of studies now comprehended by workers in this tradition are, briefly, vocational selection and guidance, techniques of training, and ergonomics, i.e., the design of working conditions, machinery and other equipment in the light of what is known about human capacities and limitations. Since 1939 also, in response partly to the development of methods of selecting officers for the armed forces, and partly to the development of other interests by social scientists, studies related to vocational selection and guidance have reached upwards in the industrial hierarchy to include foremen and managers.

Hawthorne and After

The general movement away from exclusive preoccupation with the individual—as resource, machine, or response system—has taken place since 1939. While the Second World War, like the first, provided the operating cause of this development, it would be a mistake to ascribe its theoretical origins to wartime activities in industry and the armed forces of teams of psychologists, psychiatrists, and other social scientists—although undoubtedly it was their work which changed the whole scope of industrial social studies during the 1940s. So far as one can discern now, it is the successive impact of ideas imported from Freudian psychology and social anthropology before the war, social psychology and the classical sociology of Weber and Durkheim during the 40s, and, after 1950, communication engineering and biology*

* It might be useful to set down here the points at which these fertilizing ideas have penetrated industrial studies.

    (a) The interviewing techniques developed as a result of the first Hawthorne experiment were admitted to 'owe something to the methods developed by psychopathology' (Mayo, [56] p. 86). Mayo himself had practised as a psychiatrist.

        For the much fuller development of the connexion, see A. T. M. Wilson[96] and other papers contributed by members of the staff of Tavistock Institute of Human Relations to *Social Therapy, Journal of Social Issues*, Vol. III, no. 2.

    (b) The second major study at Hawthorne, begun in 1931, was of restriction of output among a team of men employed in wiring and soldering connexions in telephone exchange equipment. 'The general methodological concepts employed throughout this study were chiefly derived from Mr. Lloyd Warner . . . at that time Assistant Professor of Social Anthropology at Harvard University [70] p. 389, footnote).

The Sociology of Industry

that has widened the scope of the social study of industrial undertakings. Without using too procrustean a method of simplifying, one can arrange the kinds of studies now current under three heads, each of them corresponding to one of these three successive expansions of the theoretical horizon.

Observational Studies of Working Groups

The psychological holism of the psychoanalytic school bears a distinct resemblance to the sociological holism of social anthropology, as developed by Malinowski and Radcliffe-Brown. The concurrence of these two during the 1930s in one or two American academic milieux bore issue: the theories of the culture-personality school, with which we are not here concerned, and the painstaking exploration of the forms of interaction between social roles and social norms in the behaviour observable among small groups of people.

(c) The origins of attempts to study the nature of the social norms governing behaviour with *ad hoc* groups, especially with the aim of re-setting the norms (Group Dynamics), lie in Kurt Lewin's wartime projects [47].

(d) Weber has been the reference point in American sociological studies of the formal organization of undertakings, which have developed with great speed and vitality since the publication of Barnard's *Functions of the Executive* in 1938. See [38, 58, 75]

(e) Studies of labour turnover and absenteeism by Rice and Trist and by Baldamus most clearly show Durkheimian influence in the treatment of withdrawal from work as a 'social fact', but the method of the comparative study of institutions, which may be traced to the same source, is central to an increasing body of later work.

(f) Apart from the appropriation and misappropriation of a number of the more familiar terms, the exploitation of the concepts of communication engineering in the social sciences has come largely through the recent experimental studies of Alex Bavelas and the school founded by him at the Massachusetts Institute of Technology and the observations of Colin Cherry and D. M. Mackay. Much of the experimental work inspired by Bavelas has to do with the comparative efficiency and economy of different organization patterns considered as communication networks, and with the kind of decisions made by individuals when confronted with calls for action and when in possession of varying amounts of information [5]. The contributions of Cherry and Mackay have less empirical reference to industrial contexts, but are of obvious importance to the study of interaction in formal organizations. See [17].

(g) Many of the statements made some years ago in 'cybernetics' terms may be —and some have been—rendered into equivalent terms taken from biology; this fashion trend follows upon the popularizing work of J. Z. Young, Konrad Lorenz, and L. von Bertalanffy. Again, apart from this kind of conceptual infection, the notions developed by some biologists about the interaction between an organism, considered as a system, and its environment, have been of considerable influence on the work of members of the Tavistock Institute of Human Relations.

Tom Burns

Not surprisingly, the groups of people most easily accessible for such study have been either employed in industrial activity, or have been convened for some semblance of the same purpose; they are given a task to perform or a problem to solve.

In the first kind of study, the usual procedure has been that of the direct observation of behaviour and the wide-ranging interviews with amenable informants practised by social anthropologists. From the accumulated records of such experiences the observer compiles a detailed description of the relationships prevailing between members of the group, predicates a system of beliefs which might be expected to uphold such relationships, or which have in fact been expressed about them, and goes on to suggest the function, or implicit purpose, which the structure of relationships and the system of beliefs serves for the group and its members. There are variants of the role of observer. He may, as in the Bank-Wiring Observation Room at Hawthorne ([70] Pt. iv), be present without disguise as an observer of the group, a procedure which has obvious disadvantages even when, as we are assured was the case in this classic instance, he gained acceptance as an observer, and enough time was allowed for the group to learn to ignore his presence. These disadvantages are avoided, albeit at some risk of injury or embarrassment, by assuming the guise of a *bona fide* member of the group, and thus becoming a participant observer. The liveliest account of the procedures and hazards involved here is Dalton's.[22] Thirdly, a student may assume some role for which society already provides—of the interested outsider, offering for information some return in receptive listening and informed discussion. The expectation attached to this role may be raised to the point at which the student becomes a consultant and technical assistance is looked for in specific instances, or still further to the assumption of a therapeutic relationship which may require diagnostic exploration of the whole system, psychological, social, technical, or economic, of the undertaking or of any of its parts.

If one compares the work undertaken from each point in this range of strategies, the underlying theoretical and methodological unity becomes discernible. Anthropological studies of mining communities in Yorkshire[23] and Fife,[65] carried out with no heavier disguise than—presumably—an ingratiating demeanour, are directed towards the unveiling of the autonomous systems of beliefs and of social relationships existing in them; the reflections of larger systems which bespeak their membership of a total British society are only very lightly suggested, and then mainly to stress the incompatibilities between the larger society's norms and expectations and those obtaining in the communities studied. That there are losses as well as gains from the blinkered intensiveness of these methods when practised in complex

200

societies has been well known since their first application in the Hawthorne studies of workpeople, in which very little mention of unemployment, and none of Trade Unions, occurs, although the period covered was that of the Great Depression and was also one of the most disturbed in the history of management-labour relations in America. Participant observer studies such as those of J. Sykes in Glasgow and T. Lupton in Manchester tend to avoid this kind of oversight in that the workingman role they assume for lengthy periods brings a more comprehensive appreciation of their associates' ideas, the constraints on their conduct, their interests, and the means adopted to pursue them; on the other hand, they are, like their workfellows, locked into one compartment of the social system they are studying. Dalton appears to have avoided at least the awareness of this effect by moving out from firm to firm during his study.[22] Nevertheless, the research aim is very similar: to characterize the systems of relationships and beliefs existing among the groups of which they are temporary members, and to indicate their incompatibility with the overt aims and beliefs of management as well as their compatibility with the covert aims of the managed.

The clear advantages in the amount of information open to access and the insights gained by close and continuous association with the group to be studied, or by actually playing an assumed part in it, are lost to the observer who stays inside his role of academic observer; the compensatory gains lie in his freedom to move between all groups in the total system of the undertaking, a freedom which is entirely dependent on his remaining, and appearing to remain, detached from the interests of one group which are in conflict with those of other groups. This can most easily be ensured by withholding responses other than non-committal ones to the information asked for in interviews, and this detachment is won most effectively by formalizing the situations in which information is obtained by using questionnaires or other standardized interview procedures. However, the point of studying groups of people is at least to collect information, and while standardized procedures and carefully prepared questionnaires may give the wished-for appearance of detachment, it would be presuming too much to reckon on the information collected in this way being equally standardized. Whatever the merits of survey techniques in collecting information from a population when the members of it are fully aware of both their anonymity and their own disengagement, and when the purpose of the inquiry is remote from their interests or generally approved, they are not to be looked for in closed social systems, where beliefs, commitments, attitudes, facts, and observations of fact may all bear closely on the perceived self-interest of each member. Discrepancies between the accounts of the self-same incidents, between facts and between views, unfailingly appear in interviews with different people in the system. It is these

Tom Burns

discrepancies, indeed, which provide the starting-point for inquiry proper in observational studies of the kind* in which the student declares, accepts, and enacts his role of social scientist, and is prepared to interpret as he goes the information he collects and to discuss his interpretations with his informants.

Such procedures require the exercise of restraint and care in avoiding breaches of confidence. This need arises in all studies of industrial situations. It becomes peculiarly awkward, however, when the student is also confessedly active as a management consultant. While senior managers themselves may feel more disposed to facilitate inquiries, they are also possibly less ready to regard the student differently from all the other resources at their disposal, and so less willing to see themselves as equally under observation (except for form's sake, to encourage the others); the student exposes himself to any resistance or hostility to management from those who feel their interests opposed to management's, and although he may circumvent this, the dilemma of breaking either confidence or the terms of his contract with management is sharpened. Lastly, and perhaps most seriously, his inquiries must be pursued with the primary aim of improving efficiency. These are the terms on which he must necessarily be engaged, and they govern not only the criteria by which the outcome of the study will be judged but also the terms in which it must be planned and carried out. All these limitations are visible even in work which has nevertheless produced findings of the greatest interest.†

The Sociology of Organizations

In reciting the methods and approaches which have developed since the intrusion of ideas from Freudian psychology and social anthropology, we have included some which are applicable to the second kind of studies, those which can be said to have originated in a specifically sociological interest in organizational forms and processes. What we have termed the methods of detached observation and of consultancy have been those most widely used in studies of the operation of bureaucratic hierarchies, of differences in the structure of business and industrial organizations, and of the working relationships of their members. In the first half of this chapter, it was suggested that the second phase of industrialism was giving place to a third, characterized by a new unstable relationship between manufacturing industry and the consumer and the importation on a large scale of scientific

* See [13] pp. 12–14, for an account of this observational and interviewing procedure.

† A demonstration of the possibilities and limitations of the consultant role may be seen in A. K. Rice's book.[67]

202

The Sociology of Industry

techniques as a major, and continuing, industrial resource. Changes in the social technology of industrial organization which would adapt the undertaking to this new situation were also, it was said, visibly in progress, or at least were being attempted or resisted. This general disturbance in the industrial system underlies the recrudescence of interest in organization, some two generations after the accounts of the bureaucratic organization developed in industrialism's second phase had been sketched by Weber, Veblen, and others. During the 1930s, when industrial sociology became an established branch of the study of society, the bureaucratic structure of business enterprises seems to have been accepted as given, and attention focused on the deviant and pathological aspects of human conduct and relationships which prevented the bureaucratic system from achieving the full effectiveness properly belonging to it. The hierarchy of management as illustrated by an organization chart and the description in an organization manual of the specialist functional roles attached to each position on the chart were together regarded as the 'formal organization': an ideal system of control, information, and authority aimed at the most efficient use of physical and human resources. Over against the 'formal organization' was set the 'informal organization'—the behaviour, the relationships, the sentiments and beliefs, the commitments and self-identifications of workers which are irrelevant to the 'formal organization', or even incompatible with it and its purposes.*

By the early 1950s this dualism had become an accepted dogma of industrial sociology. 'Although formal organization is designed to subject production to logical planning, things never seem to go "according to plan". This is evidenced by the many "problems" managers encounter. They find that no matter how carefully they organize, despite the concern in anticipating problems, unanticipated ones always arise. For these eventualities formal organization offers little guidance because it is created as a guidepost for the routine, the typical, and the unforeseeable' ([59], p. 160).† For an explanation of these unanticipated consequences, the authors prescribe a study of the 'informal organization', and this, indeed, is what represents the object of study in the observation of work groups discussed in the previous section.

There are three fairly distinct stages in the subsequent attempt to resolve this dualism. The first accepted the 'pathological view' and attempted a 'cure' by treating the informal organization as if it were the Freudian unconscious of the system, using observation, attitude surveys, and open interview programmes to explore it, bringing its

* [70]Pt. IV, 'Social Organization of Employees', esp. ch. 23, 'Formal *versus* Informal Organization'.

† See also [69], ch. V, 'A Disinterested Observer Looks at Industry', and [61], Ch. VI, 'Blueprint Organization', and Ch. XV, 'Informal Organization of Workers'.

hidden activities and commitments and conflicts into the open (i.e. to the knowledge of management) and enabling its misdirected efforts to be checked or harnessed to ends consonant with those of the enterprise. The complement to this pragmatic exercise (seriously and expensively undertaken by many companies in America and, latterly, in the U.K.) was the widening of the conception of management beyond the limits of the functions defined by formal organization to comprise a range of training activities, of welfare provisions, and of attempts, tagged generically 'human relations', to remove hostilities and improve working relationships.

The second phase is one in which the formal organization is treated simply as part of the institutional environment of a community at work.[73] This line of interest has led directly into studies of the third type, dealt with in the next section, in which the industrial undertaking is examined as a sub-community, i.e. with its commercial purposes treated as only one of its many institutional aspects, all of which form an interconnected social system.

Thirdly, there has been a dawning realization that the 'formal organization' itself is not a management machine which social scientists may safely ignore as they do other technical apparatus like accounts and production technology, but an institutional system which can re-pay study in the same way as the informal organization. Gouldner[38] has described how managers and workers can devise a variety of systems by which they mutually sustain each other's beliefs, expectations, status, and self-regard in face of an imposed organizational structure. 'Organization theory' is the name given to a new preoccupation with the way in which co-operative systems work, whether in business, manufacturing, government, service industries, or the armed forces. While the subject of study is the structure of organizations and their efficiency, attention is focused on what had previously been assumed as axiomatic —the rationality of formal organization. It is, as Eisenstadt ([26] p. 106) says, 'concerned with the conditions which make for maximum rational behaviour, calculations, and performance within a given structural organizational setting, or, conversely, the extent to which various structures and organizational factors limit rational calculations and efficiency.'

Turning the picture face upwards in this way has been as revelatory as the oddly similar discovery that educational performance might be related to the organization and institutional character of schools, as well as to the structure and the material and social circumstances of families.

There are three fairly distinct levels of research, each with its own methodology. Studies of whole structures are normally pursued by observation and open interviews. They are aimed at eliciting the rationale of the distribution of functions throughout an organization and the way in which the total task is thereafter discharged by the co-operation of functionaries through the means provided for them, and the means devised by them. Such studies as Gouldner's,[38] Woodward's,[98] Crozier's [18, 19], and Burns and Stalker's [13] are more or less taxonomic in intention: it is now fairly well established that there is no one system of 'bureaucracy' rationally appropriate to any of the kinds of tasks which confront working organizations. The central problem of this kind of study, therefore, has shifted away from exploration of the nature and progress of 'bureaucratization', founded on the notion of the perpetually denser ramification of bureaucratic order in every aspect of social organization, as well as of the increase in scale and in complexity of existing bureaucratic structure. There is now more concern with the types of organizational structure which exist, and the reasons for their existence.

It is below this level of the total organizational structure that the focus of study becomes the scrutiny and comparative analysis of the institutionalized procedures of which an organization is made up. It is here also that one or two significant extensions of empirical methods of study have occurred. Simon and others have painstakingly recorded the discussions, transactions by correspondence, journeys, and meetings involved in the course of a management decision to instal new kinds of business machinery.[21] Sune Carlson obtained the co-operation of several managing directors in recording, on standard diary schedules, the way in which their working time was distributed among activities, places, and people.[14] The present writer extended the self-recording method to comprehend the simultaneous activities of top management groups in some ten manufacturing concerns over periods of three to five weeks.[12] Guest trained observers to accompany foremen and record their conversations verbatim and their actions from minute to minute during a single working day.[39] Mechanical devices have also been used for recording the frequency and direction of the traffic of oral information as well as written information and signals.

The effect of a good deal of this work has been to destroy the image of the formal management structure as a rational system applying known techniques to the mastery of known problems. Even the most complicated, or the most successful, or the largest organizations reveal themselves as meaningful largely in terms of ritual and traditional beliefs, of unconscious adaptations to the requirements of the situation, of codes of management practice thought to be strictly standardized, and of the use of such codes of practice to justify or to advance interests divorced from, and even opposed to, those of the undertaking. What we have called the social technology of industrialism, in fact, is a primitive and rather heterogeneous collection of skills and crafts practised for the

Tom Burns

most part without much regard to the ends they are supposed to serve, and without much knowledge of the extent to which they serve them.* The first apprehensions of this situation have prompted the exploitation of operational research methods in fields other than the accepted one of the better control of manufacturing processes. In particular, it is thought possible, or at least worth the attempt, to improve control and understanding of working organizations, especially business enterprises, by treating them as response systems, with material technology, the market, and the sources of supply of financial, material, and human resources as the external conditions to which they respond. It is in this connexion that some of the elementary concepts and analytical procedures of cybernetics and communication engineering in general have been brought into use.

Doubts about the assumption of rationality in working organizations have also helped to generate, and later been generated by, the study of artificially constituted work groups. There is by now a large body of experimental studies of the kind discussed in Chapter 4. Some are designed to test out hypotheses about the effectiveness of different organizational structures in different situations. Others enable close observations to be made under controlled conditions of the way in which simple co-operative systems work. A third group is concerned with how decisions are made in competitive or co-operative situations.

The Study of Working Communities

During the 1930s students of the roles and conduct of industrial operatives had to forego the simple engineering conceptions of the economic or wasteful use of a fixed flow of human effort, and of workers' time being spent either in working or in shirking. Similarly, the distinction between the rational formal organization, uniformly bureaucratic in structure, and the largely irrational informal organization partly or wholly at odds with it has been discarded. The relics of the distinction remain in that still drawn between the studies described in the previous section, which start from a critical analysis of the overt tasks of the organization and the means believed to be used in carrying them out, and those others which start from a consideration of the community at work as a social system, with a large number of inter-related institutions and a generalized, organic, function of keeping itself in being on the best possible terms.

* Not so much the writing and publication as the striking popularity of C. Northcote Parkinson's *Parkinson's Law* [64] has provided one indication of how widespread are the doubts about the rationality of bureaucratic structure and of traditional features of bureaucratization.

The Sociology of Industry

Theoretically, and empirically, in the kind of problems attacked and the methods employed, these two approaches seem to be merging. During the years immediately after the war, Selznick, in the United States, could write: 'All formal organizations are moulded by forces tangential to their rationally ordered structure and stated goals. Every formal organization—trade union, political party, army, corporation, etc.—attempts to mobilize human and technical resources as means for the achievement of its ends. However, the individuals within the system tend to resist being treated as means. They interact as wholes, bringing to bear their own special problems and purposes. . . . It follows that there will develop an informal structure within the organization which will reflect the spontaneous efforts of individuals and sub-groups to control the conditions of their existence. . . . It is to these informal relations and structures that the attention of the sociologist will be primarily directed. He will look upon the formal structure, e.g. the official chain of command, as the special environment within and in relation to which the informal structure is built' ([73] pp. 250–1).

Such a statement would be fairly applicable to the general theoretical orientation of the research team of the Tavistock Institute of Human Relations at the beginning of its work in Glacier Metals.[43] Both Selznick[74] and the Tavistock researchers have moved substantially towards treating the social techniques of management—the formal structure itself—as an intrinsic part of the total system of institutions by which the members of a working community achieve their own ends. The Tavistock Institute, indeed, has been evolving a unitary conception of the 'socio-technical system' existing in any industrial milieu; this envisages the total material circumstances (including machinery and technical processes) and working behaviour observable in any workplace as a complex organic system by which individuals achieve, through various combinations and tensions, some balance between the explicit and implicit psychological, cultural, and physical demands of the work situation and their own goals. A parallel development appears in the work of Argyris over the past decade.*

Working from the other end, so to speak, Simon has expanded his earlier concern with such formal elements of management structure and technique as composite decision-making and planning to an examination of the total institutional setting to which individuals' actions have to be referred, and a wide-ranging critique of the 'rationality' of management systems and even the aims of business enterprise.† This particular course has been followed empirically by the writer's own

* Compare C. Argyris' early study, reported in *What Budgeting does to People*[3], with his recent papers.[1, 2]

† Cf. Simon *Administrative Behaviour*[75] with *Models of Man*[76] and *Organizations.*[52]

207

Tom Burns

research. The study which began as an attempt to observe the organizational adjustments made by established firms which were entering the field of electronics development and production, and moving from a stable market and technical situation into one of rapid change, had to develop into an inquiry into the reasons why no such organizational adjustments were in fact made. As a consequence, the internal politics of firms, the manoeuvres of groups and individuals in order to advance or defend their status, the different limits put to commitment to the interests of the firm, the significance for the whole organization of the social isolation of the managing director at the top of a hierarchy, all had to be considered in the light of their bearing on the capacity of the working organization to adapt itself to its actual tasks and circumstances.[13] The development of such interests, and their conjunction with those emerging from the tradition of studies of informal organization and 'human relations', gives added significance to inquiries into the internal politics of organizations on such lines as Crozier's analysis of the power structure of a large office,[20] and Tannenbaum's comparative study of the distribution of control over decisions in Trade Unions.[81, 82]

The present situation in the very wide field of research subsumed here under the title of 'Studies of Working Communities', is one in which there is a growing connexion, in empirical as well as theoretical terms, between studies of the internal structure and institutions of industrial undertakings, those of the way in which the industrial system is evolving, and those, again, of the way in which industrialism processes society and its members. There is, in fact, an explicit seeking after a synthetic view of the institutional patterns in modern society which derive from and contribute to its essentially industrial character.

Method

Some remarks have already been made on the 'techniques' of field inquiries carried on inside industrial undertakings. Little need be added here; apart from the specialized techniques of psychometric tests, and the traditional procedures of attitude surveys, both developed within the established discipline of industrial psychology on the one hand, and experimental closed-room studies of small groups on the other, there are very few technical methods specific to industrial studies beyond those of Guest and Carlson, mentioned above. What do apply to industrial studies with particular force, however, are certain general methodological considerations which may do something to explain the procedure normally followed by researchers.

This review of studies has to some extent, and inevitably, given a false coherence to the paths of development they have followed. Like any other kind of inquiry which has a history and an establishment, industrial studies seem at the time to be pursuing not so much the right kind of knowledge, as the right kind of questions, not definitive information, but fresh hypotheses; not exploring and mapping new territory, but staking claims and prospecting.

R. K. Merton has recently ([57], p. x) quoted Aubrey, Darwin, and Agnes Arber to remind us, that, as the last of these has said, 'the difficulty in most scientific work lies in framing the questions rather than in finding the answers'. What is not so often insisted upon is that questions do not suggest themselves. They arise from doubt.* Doubt, in turn, arises from the existence of an alternative where none was previously suspected; it arises from a discrepancy between facts, or between accepted interpretations, or between facts and interpretations. A stricter system of management raised doubts about the inevitability of 'bureaucratization' and suggested to A. W. Gouldner the possibility of alternative sub-types of bureaucratic system.[38] More prosaically, the present writer started a lengthy and elaborate study in nine firms of the structure and functions of senior management because individual managers in one firm were unable, when asked, to describe their present jobs. They recited instead the main episodes of their careers in the firm and explained, equally lucidly, what they would be doing when the 'current panic' was over or an overdue reorganization completed, and they could settle down to the work their department was now planned to do. After a succession of interviews, it became impossible not to suspect that all such descriptions, including those given by other managers in more stable firms, were interpretations of history or of an ideal working programme, rather than reports of actuality.†

Incompatibilities in the information given by members of the same milieu about facts, situations, and purposes are, in the writer's experience, always present. The student's own misconstructions, and the errors of chance or the casualness or sheer ignorance of informants have to be distinguished from incompatibilities inherent in the fact that

---

* It should also be said that an important purpose of social studies has been to raise doubts about current assumptions or traditional wisdom in the minds of administrators and the public. The earliest 'participant observer' studies were directed towards collecting facts about wages and conditions in the 'sweated industries' in order to challenge contemporary apathy (see [8] esp. Chap. III by Beatrice Potter, 'The Tailoring Trade'. See also [90] and [91] pp. 311–339.) The astonishing feature of the 'Our Towns' report on the conditions of children evacuated from city slums in 1940 was not the squalor and unseemliness of the children but the blank ignorance of all other sections of society about them. [97]

† In fact, the subsequent study, carried out in nine firms, revealed a sizeable discrepancy between the way in which senior managers spent their time and their ideas, or recollections, of the way in which they had spent it ([12] pp. 45–60).

people speak from different situations and roles; this can be done in the interview itself, but is an essential part of 'reporting back'.

This last is an intrinsic part of social research in industrial milieux, and constitutes a peculiar advantage (or perhaps disadvantage, in certain circumstances) of industrial sociology. Research reports are usually, and properly, read and criticized in the first instance by the people to whom they most directly refer and who supplied the information on which they are based. When information has been winnowed in ensuing discussion, the question presented by internal inconsistencies is not 'Which version is right?' but 'How do these differences arise? How is it that these different versions of the same set of circumstances have arisen in the minds of people who have to co-operate in the very circumstances they view so differently?' The need to account for these differences marks the first stage beyond description. Many studies are wholly concerned with the definition and explanation of different accounts by managers and factory operatives of the same circumstances. Latterly, for example, R. M. McKenzie has examined the incompatible beliefs and statements of fact expressed by production workers and managers and inspection staff about each other's work. This study has provided evidence of the manner in which the social situation of individuals prescribes their appraisal of measure and quantity and has some connexion with the more general hypotheses of Friedmann and of Touraine (see p. 195) concerning the development of functionally specialized management systems as a way of substituting impersonal authority for personal command, a relationship increasingly rejected by both sides, and perhaps increasingly irrelevant.

The significance for the social scientist of these differences and incompatibilities of viewpoint and fact lies in the help they provide in ascertaining what for him are the essential elements in the structure of the institution: viz., those elements which vary with variations in the external or internal situation of the concern, and those elements which, by contrast, appear to remain unaffected. Thus, Woodward,[98] from a study of the organization of a hundred firms in Essex, found that the number of ranks in the management hierarchy was less in process industries than among large-lot engineering manufacturers. In the writer's study of a hundred managers in nine firms previously cited, it was found that the amount of time they spent in conversation with each other grew, and subordination to seniors was increasingly rejected, the greater the rate of technical development in which the firm was involved.

There is also a method, perhaps resembling that of comparative anatomy, in which the social character of an institution is matched with that of some other socially remote institution. Engelhardt[28] has presented the latest of a series of reconstructions of organizational in-

The Sociology of Industry

efficiency in terms of the adjustment of a patient to sickness or disability. Bradney[9, 10] and Sykes (in an unpublished paper) have explored the social significance of 'joking' and 'quasi-familial' relationships, both part of the familiar currency of concepts used in investigating primitive societies, in attempts to elucidate the status system of employees in a department store and a large office. The danger when studies are directed to the establishment of such parallels is that they may be regarded as complete when a description has been translated into the technical language of psychiatry, social anthropology—or sociology for that matter—or that the heightening of descriptive writing by an elaborate simile may be taken for explanatory analysis of new information.

Nevertheless, the purpose of comparative social studies is to achieve an understanding of social institutions which is different from that current among the people through whose conduct the institutions exist: different, new, and better. The practice of sociology is criticism: to criticize or to raise questions about claims and assumptions concerning the value or meaning of conduct and achievement. It is the business of sociologists to conduct a critical debate, in this sense, with the public about its equipment of social institutions. This purpose is as important in the social study of industry as in any other field.

REFERENCES

1. ARGYRIS, CHRIS (1957) 'The Individual and Organization'. *Admin. Sci. Quart.*, **2.**
2. ARGYRIS, CHRIS (1959) 'Individual-Organization Actualization'. *Admin. Sci. Quart.*, **4.**
3. ARGYRIS, CHRIS. *What Budgeting Does to People.*
4. BARNARD, CHESTER I. (1938) *The Functions of the Executive.* Cambridge, Mass: Harvard Univ. Press.
5. BAVELAS, A. (1951) 'Communication Patterns in Problem-Solving Groups'. In von Foerster, H., (ed.), *Cybernetics: Transactions of the Eighth Conference, March 1951.* New York: Josiah Macy, Jr., Foundation, 1952.
6. BENDIX, R. (1956) *Work and Authority in Industry.* London: Chapman and Hall.
7. BERLE, A. A., JNR., & MEANS, G. C. (1932) *The Modern Corporation and Private Property.* New York: Macmillan.
8. BOOTH, CHARLES (1893) *Life and Labour of the People in London,* vol. 4. London: Macmillan.
9. BRADNEY, P. (1957) 'The Joking Relationship in Industry'. *Hum. Relat.*, **10,** 179-87.
10. BRADNEY, P. (1957) 'Quasi-Familial Relationships in Industry'. *Hum. Relat.*, **10,** 271-278.

11. BURNS, TOM (1956) 'The Reference of Conduct in Small Groups; Cliques and Cabals in Occupational Milieux'. *Hum. Relat.*, **8**, 467–86.
12. BURNS, TOM (1957) 'Management in Action'. *Operat. Res. Quart.*, **8** (2).
13. BURNS, TOM, & STALKER, G. M. (1960) *The Management of Innovation.* London: Tavistock.
14. CARLSON, S. (1951) *Executive Behaviour.* Stockholm: Stroenberg.
15. CARR-SAUNDERS, A. M., JONES, D. CARADOG, & MOSER, C. A. (1958) *A Survey of Social Conditions in England and Wales.* London: Oxford Univ. Press. Chap. 9.
16. CARR-SAUNDERS, A. M., & WILSON, P. A. (1933) *The Professions.* London: Oxford Univ. Press.
17. CHERRY, C. (1958) On Human Communication. New York: Wiley.
18. CROZIER, M. (1955) *Petits Fonctionaires au Travail—Compte rendu d'une enquête sociologique effectivée dans une grande administration publique Parisienne.* Paris. Centre National de la Recherche Scientifique.
19. CROZIER, M., & GUETTA, P. (1956) *Une Organization Administrative au Travail. Résultat d'une enquête sociologique sur le personnel d'une compagnie d'assurances.* Paris. Univ. de Paris, Inst. des Sciences Sociales de Travail.
20. CROZIER, M. (1960) 'Les Relations de pouvoir dans un système d'organisation bureaucratique'. *Sociologie du Travail*, **1**, 61–70.
21. CYEST, R. M., SIMON, H. A., AND TROW, D. B. (1956) 'Observation of a Business Decision'. *Journal of Business of the Univ. of Chicago*, **29**, 237–248.
22. DALTON, M. (1959) *Men Who Manage.* London: Chapman and Hall.
23. DENNIS, N., HENRIQUES, F. M. *et al.* (1956) *Coal is Our Life.* London: Eyre and Spottiswoode.
24. Department of Scientific and Industrial Research. (1958) *Estimates of Resources devoted to Scientific and Engineering Research and Development in British Manufacturing Industry. 1955.* London: H.M.S.O.
25. DUMAZEDIER, J. (1957) 'Loisirs et dynamique socioculturélle'. *Cahiers Int. de Sociologie*, **22**, 75–96.
26. EISENSTADT, S. N. (1958) 'Bureaucracy and Bureaucratization'. *Curr. Sociol.*, **6** (2).
27. EMERY, F. E. (1960) 'Applied Social Science in British Industry', O.E.E.C., *Social Research and Industry in Europe*, pp. 81–82.
28. ENGELHARDT, H. N. (1958) 'Medical Comments on the Use of the Word "Disease" in Sociology (Social Pathology)'. Paper presented to Cégos International Conference, Brussels, 1958.
29. FITTON, R. S., & WADSWORTH, A. P. (1958) *The Strutts and the Arkwrights.* Manchester: Manchester Univ. Press.
30. FRIEDMANN, GEORGES (1955) *Industrial Society.* Glencoe, Ill.: Free Press.

The Sociology of Industry

31. FRIEDMANN, G. and REYNAUD, J. D. (1958) 'Sociologies: Techniques de Production et du Travail' in Gurvitch, G. (ed.). *Traité de Sociologie*. Paris: Presses Univ. de France.
32. GALBRAITH, J. K. (1952) *American Capitalism*. London: Hamilton.
33. GALBRAITH, J. K. (1955) *The Great Crash, 1929*. London: Hamilton.
34. GALBRAITH, J. K. (1959) *The Affluent Society*. London: Hamilton.
35. GOFFMAN, ERVING (1956) *The Presentation of Self in Everyday Life*. Edinburgh: Social Sciences Research Centre, Univ. of Edinburgh, Monograph no. 2.
36. GOULDNER, A. W. (1959) 'Organization Analysis'. In: Merton, R. K., Brown, Leonard, and Cottrell, L. S. (eds.), *Sociology To-day*. New York: Basic Books.
37. GOULDNER, A. W. (1954) *Patterns of Bureaucracy*. Glencoe, Ill.: Free Press.
38. GOULDNER, A. W. (1956) *Patterns of Industrial Bureaucracy*. London: Routledge.
39. GUEST, R. H. (1956) 'Of Time and the Foreman'. *Personnel*, pp. 478-86.
40. Health of Munitions Workers Committee (1915-17) *Memoranda 1-20*.
41. Health of Munitions Workers Committee (1917) *Interim Report on Industrial Efficiency and Fatigue* (Cd. 8511). London: H.M.S.O.
42. Health of Munitions Workers Committee (1918) *An Investigation of the Factors concerned in the Causation of Industrial Accidents: Memorandum no. 21*. (By H. M. Vernon). (Cd. 9046). London: H.M.S.O.
43. JAQUES, ELLIOTT (1951) *The Changing Culture of a Factory*. London: Tavistock.
44. KEIRSTEAD, B. S. (1948) *The Theory of Economic Change*. London: Macmillan.
45. KNOWLES, K. C. J. C. (1952) *Strikes*. Oxford: Blackwell.
46. LAZARSFELD, PAUL F. (1959) 'Reflections on Business'. *Amer. J. Sociol.*, **65**, 1-31.
47. LEWIN, K. (1947) 'Group Decision and Social Change'. In: Newcome, T. M. and Hartley, E. L., *Readings in Social Psychology*, pp. 330-44. New York: Holt.
48. LEWIS, R., & STEWART, R. (1958) *The Boss*. London: Phoenix House.
49. Liverpool University Department of Social Science (1954) *The Dock Worker*. Liverpool: Liverpool Univ. Press.
50. LOCKWOOD, D. (1951) *The Black-Coated Worker*. London: Allen and Unwin.
51. LUTZ, B. (1960) 'Notes on Industrial Sociology in Germany'. In *Social Research and Industry in Europe*. (Organization for European Economic Co-operation.)
52. MARCH, J. G. & SIMON, H. A. (1958) *Organizations*. London: Chapman & Hall.
53. MARCUSE, H. (1956) *Eros and Civilization*. London: Routledge.
54. MARSHALL, T. H. (1939) 'The Recent History of Professionalism in

Tom Burns

Relation to Social Structure and Social Policy'. *Canad. J. Econ. Polit. Sci.*, **5**, 325–34.
55. MARX, KARL. *Capital.*
56. MAYO, ELTON (1933) *The Human Problems of an Industrial Civilization.* New York: Macmillan.
57. MERTON, R. K. (1959) 'Problem-Finding in Sociology'. In *Sociology To-day* (see 36 above).
58. MERTON, R. K., GRAY, A. P., HOCKEY, B., & SELVIN, H. C. *Reader in Bureaucracy.* Glencoe, Ill.: Free Press. 1952.
59. MILLER, D. C., & FORM, W. H. (1951) *Industrial Sociology.* New York: Harper.
60. MILLS, C WRIGHT (1951) *White Collar.* New York: Oxford Univ. Press.
61. MOORE, W. G. (1947) *Industrial Relations and the Social Order.* New York: Macmillan.
62. NAVILLE, PIERRE (1945) *Théorie de l'orientation professionnelle.* Paris: Gallimard.
63. NAVILLE, PIERRE (1954) *La Vie de travail et ses problèmes.* Paris: Armand Colin.
64. PARKINSON, C. NORTHCOTE (1958) *Parkinson's Law.* London: Murray.
65. PATTERSON, T. T., & WILLETT, F. J. (1951) 'Unofficial Strike'. *Sociolog. Rev.*, **43**, (4).
66. PAYNE, G. L. (1960) *Britain's Scientific and Technological Manpower.* London: Oxford Univ. Press.
67. RICE, A. K. (1958) *Productivity and Social Organization: The Ahmedabad Experiment.* London: Tavistock.
68. RIESMAN, DAVID (1953) *The Lonely Crowd.* New York: Doubleday.
69. ROETHLISBERGER, F. J. (1941) *Management and Morale.* Harvard Univ. Press.
70. ROETHLISBERGER, F. J., & DICKSON, W. J. (1939) *Management and the Worker.* Harvard Univ. Press.
71. SCOTT, W. H. (1952) *Industrial Leadership and Joint Consultation.* Liverpool: Liverpool Univ. Press.
72. SCOTT, W. H., BANKS, J. A., HALSEY, A. H., & LUPTON, T. (1956) *Technical Change and Industrial Relations.* Liverpool: Liverpool Univ. Press.
73. SELZNICK, PHILIP (1948) *TVA and the Grass Roots.* Berkeley: University of California Press.
74. SELZNICK, PHILIP (1957) *Leadership in Administration.* Evanston, Ill.: Row Peterson.
75. SIMON, H. A. (1945) *Administrative Behavior.* New York: Macmillan.
76. SIMON, H. A. (1957) *Models of Man.* New York: Wiley.
77. SMILES, SAMUEL (1859) *Self-Help.* 58th edn. London: Murray, 1910.
78. SMITH, ADAM (1776) *The Wealth of Nations.* Book I, chap. 1.
79. SYKES, J. Unpublished papers.
80. TANNENBAUM, A. S. (1956) 'The Concept of Organisational Control'. *J. soc. Issues*, **12**.

The Sociology of Industry

81. TANNENBAUM, A. S. (1956) 'Control Structures and Union Functions'. *Amer. J. Sociol.*, **61**, 536–45.
82. TANNENBAUM, A. S., & KAHN, R. L. 'Organizational Control Structure. A General Description Technique as applied to Four Local Unions'. *Hum. Relat.*, **10**, 127–139.
83. TAYLOR, F. W. *Scientific Management*. New York: Harper. (Includes *Shop Management* [1903], *Principles of Scientific Management* [1911], and Taylor's testimony before the Special House of Representatives Committee to Investigate the Taylor and other Systems of Management [1912].)
84. TÖNNIES, E. *Gemeinschaft und Gesellschaft*. Leipzig, 1887. Trans. C. P. Loomis, *Community and Association*. London, Routledge.
85. TOURAINE, A. (1955) *L'Évolution du travail ouvrier aux Usines Renault*. Paris, Centre National de la Recherche Scientifique.
86. TOURAINE, A. (n.d.) 'Situation du mouvement ouvrier' in *La Classe ouvrière: Mythe et Réalités*. Paris (collection publ. from *Argument* 12–13. Editions de Minuit.
87. U.S. National Research Council (1921ff.). Bulletins on 'Industrial Research Laboratories in the United States'.
88. URE, ANDREW (1835) *The Philosophy of Manufactures*. London.
89. WARNER, W. L., & ABEGGLEN, J. G. (1955). *Big Business Leaders in America*. New York.
90. WEBB, BEATRICE (1898). 'Diary of an Investigator', in S. and B. Webb, *Problems of Modern Industry*, London, Longmans, chap. 1.
91. WEBB, BEATRICE (1929) *My Apprenticeship*. London: Longmans.
92. WEBER, MAX (1947) *The Theory of Social and Economic Organization*. Edinburgh: Hodge.
93. WHYTE, WILLIAM F. (1949) 'Patterns of Interaction in Union-Management Relations', *Hum. Organiz.*, **8**, 13–19.
94. WHYTE, WILLIAM H., JNR. (1952) *Is Anybody Listening?* New York: Simon and Schuster.
95. WHYTE, WILLIAM H., JNR. (1956) *The Organization Man*. New York: Simon and Schuster, Harmondsworth: Penguin Books.
96. WILSON, A. T. M. (1947) 'Some Implications of Medical Practice and Social Casework for Action Research', *Social Therapy, J. soc. Issues*, **3** (2).
97. Women's Group on Public Welfare (1943) *Our Towns: A Close-Up*. London: Oxford Univ. Press.
98. WOODWARD, J. (1958) *Management and Technology*. London: H.M.S.O.
99. WOOTTON, BARBARA (1955) *The Social Foundations of Wage Policy*. London: Allen and Unwin.
100. ZIMMERN, ALFRED (1936) *The Greek Commonwealth*. London: Oxford Univ. Press.

12

PERSONNEL SELECTION
AND VOCATIONAL GUIDANCE

Alec Rodger and Peter Cavanagh

The Interviewer's Search for General and Persisting Traits.

WHAT is going on in the mind of an interviewer who is selecting someone for a vacancy or giving him advice about his career? In most cases,
whether he realizes it or not, he is making an assumption about the
existence and importance of certain 'traits' (he may call them 'qualities'); and he is looking for signs of them in his applicant for employment or advice. By listening to what he has to say, by observing him,
by scrutinizing again his letter or form of application and maybe his
testimonials or school report, he is picking up clues which lead him to
judge what the applicant is 'usually' like.

Many interviewers do all this in a rather sketchy and haphazard
fashion. The sophisticated interviewer, clearer in his aims and tidier in
his procedure, goes about it differently. He is methodically making
inferences, from the information he is assembling, about traits (or
'behaviour tendencies') in the applicant which he can perhaps regard
as general (that is, as likely to be displayed in a variety of situations) and
as persisting (that is, as likely to be enduring and resistant to change).
For example, he may at one stage be thinking, 'That was a good reply.
He saw the point of my question immediately. I wonder whether he
would be as intelligent as that always, and in everything, if we gave him
a job here?' At another stage he may be saying to himself, 'That was a
tactless remark. I wonder whether he might prove tactless in many other
situations and on many other occasions?'

Alec Rodger and Peter Cavanagh

Traits of marked generality and persistence are, for selectors and advisers, characteristics of the utmost importance. They provide the main foundations for attempts to explain and forecast human behaviour. Indeed, the purposeful interviewer is, all the time, seeking evidence which will support or refute the initial impressions about traits that he gains from talking to his applicant and from considering any other information he has about him. He is, in effect, repeatedly asking himself, 'Is that sample of his behaviour indicative of some trait which is broad in its ramifications and enduring in its influence?'

In the applications of psychology—not only in the employment field but also in the fields of education, health, delinquency, defence, and elsewhere—a 'trait' approach of the kind outlined above seems more useful and more acceptable than most. We shall therefore adopt it for our present purpose. Moreover, we shall take the view that it is the prime task of the psychologist to be well informed about traits. It is his special business to advance our knowledge about them—about their nature, their identification, their measurement, their modification through training and experience, their pathology, and their use. There are, of course, other ways of formulating the scientific function of the psychologist, but it seems reasonable to outline his assignment in this fashion. Perhaps the best-thought-out trait approach is that of Allport,[1] well summarized and discussed by Hall and Lindzey.[10]

Capacities and Inclinations

Let us return for a moment to our interviewer and his search for signs of general and persisting traits. We should now note that he is probably thinking of two kinds of trait. He is looking for some which will enable him to judge what his applicant is capable of doing; and for others which will lead him to conclusions about what he wants (or would at least be willing) to do. The first of these kinds we shall call capacities; the second, inclinations. This sort of classification of traits is, in one form of words or another, both old and widely used. Some have spoken of abilities and interests, some of aptitudes and preferences, some of talents and temperaments. A current way of thinking about the split is to be found in frequent references to skills and attitudes.

In the notion of 'intelligence' we have an important example of a general and persisting capacity. This label has been given to a trait which is held to play a large part in governing what we are intellectually capable of doing in tackling problems of many kinds (and is therefore general) and which seems to be only slightly modifiable by training and experience (and is therefore persisting). Burt[4] defined intelligence as 'inborn, general intellectual capacity'; and although some psychologists nowadays would shrink—a little to the left, perhaps—from the bold use

218

of the adjective 'inborn' and would prefer the less committal word 'persisting', it is clear that the concept Burt here employs is still widely favoured.

Some progress has been made in the identification of capacities less general and less persisting than intelligence, but broad and enduring enough to warrant attention in some selection and guidance work. What is often called 'verbal facility' is one of them, and 'number facility' is another. Yet another is 'mechanical aptitude', though this does not seem to be a very good name for it, because it is now plain that what it was meant to cover (that is, facility in grasping how mechanical things work) is an even broader capacity than used to be thought, and takes in appreciation of the structure and functioning of all kinds of contrivances, mechanical and non-mechanical.

Less advanced is our knowledge about general and persisting inclinations. Burt[4] has tried to show that, as a sort of opposite number to 'general intelligence' (a better term than 'intelligence') among our capacities, we can identify 'general emotionality' among our inclinations; but few seem to have been convinced. More recently, Eysenck,[8] pursuing a similar line of attack, and starting from similar presuppositions about the importance of what used to be called cognition, conation, and affect, has sought to identify inclinations of high generality and persistence which he has labelled 'neuroticism', 'introversion', and 'psychoticism'. Burt and Eysenck have both made use of statistical techniques of factor analysis in reaching their conclusions. It is difficult to see how they could have reached them in any other way, but it is clear that this fact alone has been enough to make many psychologists look askance at them.

It should be noted in passing that Burt's quest for general and persisting capacities and inclinations has been carried out mainly with material collected in the fields of education and delinquency. Eysenck's has been carried out mainly with material from the mental health field. As their tool, factor analysis, is essentially one for classifying observations, and the end-products are inevitably derived from the particular raw material gathered in their investigations, it follows that the emergent capacities and inclinations may be distinctly coloured by their origins. Indeed, the nature of all the traits (or factors or dimensions or qualities or whatever we call them) that we use for explanatory and predictive purposes in psychology is bound to be determined to some extent by the circumstances in which, and the means by which, they are 'discovered'.

This has an important implication for us. We should not expect that psychologists who study employment problems, even when they are using the same tools as Burt and Eysenck, will reach the same conclusions about general and persisting capacities and inclinations. Indeed, there may be shocks coming to us when we wield these instruments thoughtfully—as we undoubtedly should—in the occupational field. Possibly, for example, in the world of employment, where people are freer to work or not to work than they usually are at school, inclinations may often be of far greater importance for success than capacities. Conceivably, also, the general and persisting capacity most valuable in the world of employment may be less like the 'intelligence' of educational psychologists than we have sometimes supposed.

In short, we in the occupational field have probably much to learn from our colleagues—in the educational and clinical fields particularly —in our thinking about traits, and in our ways of researching into them; but we must avoid the mistake of assuming that traits or factors or dimensions which will do for them will do for us. Ours should be derived, not from contrasts between educational successes and failures; nor yet from contrasts between neurotics, psychotics, and normals; but from contrasts between people who, in their work, prove suitable or unsuitable. Moreover, our traits should be given their proper status as 'convenient fictions' and kept under constant review. Further, because suitability and unsuitability is partly dependent on the state of the labour market, and a person who is suitable at one time or in one place may not be suitable in other circumstances, it is clear that the traits we are after in the occupational field never stand still.

Satisfactoriness and Satisfaction

We have spoken of people as being suitable or unsuitable for their work. Now we must recognize the need for yet another distinction, usefully enough expressed, perhaps, by the terms 'satisfactoriness' and 'satisfaction'.[11, 15] A satisfactory worker is one who is satisfactory to his employer. A satisfied worker is one who is satisfied with his job. Many satisfactory workers are dissatisfied, and many satisfied workers are unsatisfactory.

Here we must touch on some points of similarity and difference between personnel selection and vocational guidance. In personnel selection the task is to select, from the candidates available, those whose capacities and inclinations appear to suit them best for the employment or training for which they have applied. In vocational guidance the task is to advise an individual—commonly a school-leaver, a student, or a misfit adult—on the choice of an occupation suited to his capacities and inclinations.

Now, although these are both ways of tackling the 'round peg' problem, there are important differences between them. It is clear that personnel selection is, primarily, an employer's affair. It is the employer who is picking workers or trainees; and he is doing it with his eye on the need for having employees who will work competently. If they enjoy doing it, he may benefit; but he is not usually much concerned with their enjoyment. He wants people who will do their work well and keep out of trouble.

In a word, his primary interest is in their satisfactoriness, not in their satisfaction. In vocational guidance it is otherwise. The more satisfactory a person is in his job, the better his prospects are likely to be; but normally he is rather more anxious to be satisfied with his job than to be satisfactory to his employer.

This difference in objective is naturally reflected in the atmosphere of the selection and guidance interviews. In the first case the applicant is in competition with other applicants; in the second he is a recipient of personal advice. In the first he will tend to conceal his weaknesses and at least some of his likes and dislikes; in the second he will talk with greater candour. In addition to this difference in the attitudes of the people asking for employment on the one hand and advice on the other, there is usually a consequential difference in the attitudes of the selector and the adviser. Inquiries which would be quite inappropriate in the selector's office are sometimes considered not out of place in the adviser's consulting-room.

But despite these differences, selectors and advisers—if they are good—have much in common in the information they take into account—and in the procedures they use in gathering it together. Both aim at covering capacities and inclinations in a systematic way. In doing so, both make use—according to the circumstances—of questionnaires, tests, and interviews.

The most important difference of all is one we shall see clearly when we look at vocational guidance problems specifically. It arises from the plain fact that, ordinarily, the selector is faced with a simple problem of accepting or rejecting an applicant for a particular kind of training, while the adviser is expected to give advice. Those who have done both selection and guidance are under no illusions about the relative difficulties of the two tasks. It may be easier to select a good works manager than to give good advice to a fifteen-year-old secondary modern school leaver.

There are of course circumstances in which the line between selection and guidance is thin. For example, in the selection of management trainees the employing organization may have no very clear picture of the appointments likely to be available when the young men they select come to maturity. Again, in the guidance of the severely handicapped, the opportunities may be so restricted that the word 'allocation' would be more appropriate than either selection or guidance, because the problem is that of taking virtually all applicants and fitting them all in somewhere within an organization. Examples of this are to be found in the Borstal experiment in vocational guidance and the H.M.S. *Gosling* experiment in the selection of air mechanics and air fitters of various kinds.[19]

Fitting the Man to the Job and Fitting the Job to the Man

We have touched on some points of similarity and difference between selection and guidance. Before we consider these separately, let us look briefly at the links between both of them and some of the other problems tackled by psychologists in the occupational field. This is important, because it is becoming increasingly apparent that failure to appreciate these connexions is wasteful of time and effort. What has been thought to be a selection problem turns out to be a training problem; or what has been diagnosed as an equipment design problem turns out to be a payment problem.

It is convenient to marshal the occupational psychologist's practical problems under two complementary headings, and to make subdivisions under each, thus:

1 Fitting the man to the job
    through (a) vocational guidance
            (b) personnel selection
            (c) occupational training

2 Fitting the job to the man
    through (a) methods development
            (b) equipment design
            (c) the arrangement of working conditions and rewards.

He does not claim to be 'the' expert in any of these fields. Indeed, there are specialists in each of them—youth employment officers, personnel officers, training officers, work study officers, and others. His particular assignment, if he adopts the approach suggested at the beginning of this chapter, is to help such specialists to do their own work better, by showing them how to think more systematically and more profitably about capacities and inclinations, and how to assess these more accurately.

Of course, he must gain enough direct experience in his various fields to ensure that he is capable of talking good sense about them. He is not likely to make much impact on his users and collaborators, if he is found to be unfamiliar with their problems and the backgrounds against which they are set. He must be capable of giving advice which is technically sound, administratively convenient, and socially acceptable.

Personnel Selection and Vocational Guidance

But he must remember that in practical affairs his function is primarily advisory and collaborative. He should not settle the problems of others for them: he should help them to settle their own.

It is unfortunate that the two main fields outlined—fitting the man to the job, and fitting the job to the man—tend to attract rather different people. Not only is there little movement between them, but in both there is a good deal of ignorance about what is happening in the other. Yet, on the argument put forward here, there should be important common ground in the study of general and persisting capacities and inclinations, for this is clearly as important to the 'fjm' psychologists as it is to those on the 'fmj' side of the fence.

Personnel Selection: Problems

There is considerable diversity in the problems encountered by people concerned with personnel selection. The selection, from a group of appropriately trained and experienced people, of the one who is most suitable for appointment as a managing director presents a situation far removed from the selection, from a group of secondary modern school leavers, of half a dozen worth taking on as craft apprentices.

But in each case there is the same primary need for a job-specification. This is a term commonly used for a statement which covers the answers to three separate questions:

1. What does the worker have to do in his job?
2. How, where, with what, and with whom does he do it, and how is he rewarded?
3. What are the 'requirements' of the job?

Job-specification is often done in a highly unprofitable manner. Sometimes this happens through sketchiness, particularly evident in the 'back-of-an-envelope' approach, when little trouble has been taken to prepare thoughtfully for the specification procedure. Sometimes it happens through over-elaboration, when a formidable 'check-list' has been used by someone who does not understand how to sift what is important from what is trivial. In consequence, many job-specifications soon find their way into pigeon-holes.

To prepare a good job-specification, we must be clear what we want it for. It may be needed for personnel selection, but it may be needed for some other purpose; for example, for the drafting of a training programme, or the development of a new method of doing a job, or the modification of an equipment design or lay-out, or the devising of a new scheme of supervision, or the revision of a payment system. Good job-specifications for these and other purposes will have much in

223

common, but they will display differences in their content and their emphasis.

For most purposes, however, it is important that a job-specification should focus attention on what we shall call the 'difficulties and distastes' of the job and of the conditions under which it is done. These must be highlighted, if we are to steer clear of applicants who will prove unsatisfactory or dissatisfied; but very little else need be. Indeed it might be said that the most important things a selector should know about a job he is selecting people for are its danger-points.[9, 16, 18].

First, then, he should ask himself, 'What are the things about this job that people seem to find difficult? What are the things that we have to give special attention to in training people for it, and later in supervising them and inspecting their work? What are the mistakes people make that prod us into simplifying our methods or our equipment? What are the things that are so important that we have to be ready to pay higher wages to have them done satisfactorily? What are the things that we may, in the last resort, sack people for doing badly?' Secondly, he should ask himself, 'What are the things about the job that people seem to find distasteful? What do they try to get out of? What makes them ask for a change of work? What makes them stay away at the slightest excuse? What makes them become clock-watchers? What makes them grouse or put in claims for better amenities or more pay? What makes them keep an eye on the "Situations Vacant" column, or even decide to pack up before they have another job to go to?'

In short, the goodness of a job specification can be judged by the extent to which it provides the selectors—and, through them, the applicants—with comprehensive and accurate information about the tasks which must be done well and the conditions which must be tolerated. And this is the case at all levels. Here, for example, is an advertisement, 'distilled' from a job-specification, in which special care has been taken to convey as much information as possible to the thoughtful reader about the difficulties and distastes of the work, and, by implication, about capacities and inclinations likely to find scope for expression in it.

MANAGEMENT CONSULTANCY

XYZ LIMITED

invite applications from men, aged from 30 to 37, for appointment to the

PRODUCTION DIVISION

of their Consultant Staff, Basic requirements are a qualification in engineering or other technology or in science, from a university or professional institution, and some five years' responsible experience of production management in industry.

The work involves (i) diagnosing problems of production method, control, and organization; (ii) devising solutions; (iii) convincing the board room, management, and operatives of the soundness of the solutions; and (iv) implementing agreed proposals. Special training for this work is given at the Company's own training centre, and in operating conditions under guidance.

Reasonable mobility within the British Isles for a few years is expected. Emoluments are high, and are based on an attractive salary policy, with partnership profit-sharing and a pensions scheme. There are openings abroad for those who want them.

Applicants should send, in confidence, a short but comprehensive statement about their careers and background to the Company, at XYZ House, London, S.W.1.

Earlier in this section, in listing three questions for the writer of a job-specification, we put the word 'requirements' in quotation marks. Our purpose was to draw attention to the fact that there is a good deal of loose thinking about the capacities and inclinations to be looked for in applicants for a particular job. Its requirements are quite likely to vary from time to time and place to place, because they are dependent on the state of the labour market. A simple illustration of this fact of life is to be found in variations in the height requirement for police recruits. When or where men are hard to get, the tendency is for the minimum height requirement to fall; and when or where recruitment improves, the tendency is for it to go up. But the same phenomenon is observable in professional occupations, even when the august bodies concerned solemnly assure the public that grave shortages will be met without any relaxation of standards. Indeed, no statement about the requirements of a job can be regarded as final. Sometimes employers are able to boast about being 'choosy'. At other times they complain that they have to take anyone they can get.

Personnel Selection: Methods

For most kinds of selection, the interview is the chief instrument. Ever since Hollingworth[12] reported that one sales manager, having interviewed 57 men, put at the top of his list an applicant for a sales job who had been ranked 57th by another sales manager, interviewing has been attacked for low accuracy ('validity') and low consistency ('reliability'); but there is still no sign of any serious wane in its popularity for selection purposes. It is clearly acceptable to selectors and applicants alike.

Anyway, it is not always as useless as it is made out to be.[3, 20]. It is unfortunate that some psychologists, in their proper concern for the development of 'objective' ways of assessing people, should have been led to disparage it. It is equally unfortunate that they should be willing to accept 'evidence'[13] of the uselessness of the personnel selection interview which has been gained in a non-selection situation. Can it really be argued that interviews with 'candidates' who know they have been accepted are comparable for this important purpose with interviews with genuine candidates? And what are we to think of psychologists who sweepingly condemn interviewing and offer us in its place 'objective' devices which have been validated by reference to interview assessments made by others, usually psychiatrists? Is there any reason why psychiatrists' interview judgements should be regarded as of criterion status and those of others quite worthless?

In any event, it is not usually very profitable to argue about the efficiency of 'the' interview. We would not expect surgeons to discuss the efficiency of 'the' operation. Interviews differ; so do interviewers. Interviewers who take trouble over their job-specifications; who explore their labour market properly; who try to keep their attention on variables that are demonstrably relevant, reasonably independent of one another, conveniently few, and possible to assess in the circumstances in which the assessment has to be made; who therefore know what they want to find out; who set about their task in a systematic way; who do their best to spot their own prejudices and other defects; and who practise note-taking skill—such interviewers are likely to draw sounder inferences and make better predictions than those who do 'research' interviews from the touch-line of some field with which they have little or no familiarity. Vernon and Parry[29] have drawn attention to work on differences between interviewers which supports the conclusion that much can be achieved by the careful selection and training of interviewers.

Normally, a major function of the interview is to take account of information gathered previously by other devices, including 'objective' tests and questionnaires. Vernon has dealt with these elsewhere in this book. To his useful survey the present writer would add two comments. First, the choice of such aids to interview assessment must often be made on grounds additional to whatever data are available about their technical soundness (that is, their validity and reliability): it must frequently depend on their convenience and their acceptability. For example, potential applicants for top management positions may not take at all kindly to the idea of doing intelligence tests, or filling up 'personality inventories', or gathering round a table with their competitors for a group discussion; and the selectors may not want to take the risk of frightening good applicants away. Secondly, there can be no doubt that tests of capacity (that is, of attainment, general intelligence, and specialized aptitudes) are, broadly speaking, more useful than devices for assessing inclination (that is, interests and what is sometimes called disposition); and in practice this means that we are likely to derive more benefit from them in selecting workers for occupations of what we shall later call 'mainly office' and 'mainly practical-constructional' kinds than we shall in picking workers for 'mainly people' and 'mainly active-outdoor' occupations.

It may be noted here that the label 'group selection procedures' is usually reserved for procedures which involve the participation of several candidates in some joint activity, such as a group discussion or the group performance of a practical task (for example, the manhandling of a piece of heavy equipment over a series of obstructions). However, group selection procedures do in fact normally include individual interviews. They were first used extensively by the British Army and Navy in officer selection, and by the Civil Service Commission in the selection of entrants to the highest classes of the civil service. Their underlying aim is to let the selectors see each candidate dealing with a variety of problems, not only as an individual but also as a member of an *ad hoc* group. It has never been claimed that such methods, often called in the early days 'country house' procedures, produce results of outstanding validity: rather, it is claimed modestly that on the whole they produce better results than more conventional techniques of the boardroom interview kind. Unfortunately, the organizations best placed to offer evidence of their value, Government departments and large firms, rarely do so, partly because they wish to preserve the confidentiality of their techniques and results. However, some information is available;[26, 30] and there seems little doubt that, even when they are used inexpertly, they may serve their underlying purpose fairly well, at least to the extent of enabling the selectors to feel more confidence in their judgements. They are employed chiefly in the selection of applicants for senior appointments or traineeships, because they tend to be expensive to operate; but some use is made of them in the selection of supervisors.

Main stages (consecutive or concurrent) in the planning and execution of a typically good personnel selection routine may be outlined thus:

1. The preparation of a job-specification of the kind and scope already described.
2. The 'distillation', from the job-specification, of an advertisement which is concisely informative and is not unwisely reticent about difficulties and distastes commonly experienced by people in the job.

Alec Rodger and Peter Cavanagh

3. The publication of the advertisement through media likely to receive the attention of suitable men.

4. The preparation and dispatch of an application form (or a supplement to a standard application form) which will elicit relevant information about an inquirer's record, and which will throw some preliminary light on his chances of surmounting the common difficulties and tolerating the common distastes.

5. The preparation and dispatch, with the application form, of a note giving information which for any reason could not be given in the advertisement.

6. The scrutiny of written applications and the listing, by a 'topping and tailing' procedure, of those worth further consideration.

7. The administration of any tests (including 'situational' tests) or other devices (for example, additional questionnaires) which, because of direct or presumptive evidence of their value, are regarded as relevant.

8. The interviewing of short-listed applicants, preferably by at least two interviewers sitting separately, even if it has been decided that these (or other) interviewers should finish with a board interview of the conventional kind.

9. The notification of the decisions made about all applicants and the appropriate annotation of the application forms of unsuccessful applicants who might be worth consideration on another occasion.

The thoroughness with which these stages are tackled will of course be determined by, among other things, their cost. In the selection of trainees for relatively low-grade work from a plentiful labour market, it will not usually be regarded as defensible to do anything 'elaborate'. Heavy costs may, however, pay off in finding well-qualified candidates for a post of exceptional responsibility.

The scheme outlined above is particularly convenient for use when selection has to be done in one operation. There is a growing tendency to make use of 'progressive' selection procedures, which aim at giving a new employee or trainee a chance to show what he is best at, and likes most, before allocating him to this or that category. Such notions have long been in use in large organizations, even at the higher occupational levels (for example, in trying-out assistant principals and principals in the Civil Service and management trainees in industry and commerce). One of the authors found a good illustration recently, at a lower level, in the Nigerian oilfield. Apprentices in the trade school run by Shell-B.P. are given a month on each of five types of engineering work before allocation to one of them for the rest of the apprenticeship period. Approached in this enlightened way, personnel selection displays close links with vocational guidance, to which we shall now turn.

Personnel Selection and Vocational Guidance

Vocational Guidance: Problems

In vocational guidance, as we have remarked, we are giving advice to people about their own careers, not to employers about the relative merits of their applicants. Moreover, we are dealing with people who are often preoccupied with worries about their own satisfaction, not with employers whose chief concern is with the satisfactoriness of their employees.

Our main stumbling-block in this field is our sad but excusable ignorance about the demands likely to be faced by those we advise. It is not simply that employers of people in any given occupation are many and varied; it is also that occupations themselves are constantly changing. No vocational adviser ever has the information he would like to have about occupations or about those who ask him for advice. In the circumstances, there is much to be said for envisaging the basic vocational guidance task as a double one with both negative and positive aims. The negative aim is gently to steer people away from work likely to prove unsuited to their capacities or inclinations or both. The positive aim is to supply information about apparently suitable occupations, and to foster an attitude of 'planned procrastination'[17] in the consideration of them.

It is clear, however, that this is far removed from the primitive 'placement' view of vocational guidance still commonly held, even in H.M. Treasury. In a report of the Select Committee on Estimates (1957) the Treasury have gone on record as saying, in effect, 'If a boy knows what he wants, the Youth Employment Service should help him to find the kind of vacancy he asks for. If he seeks information about several occupations, the Service should either give it to him or tell him where to look. But he should not be encouraged to ask for advice in sorting out his problems.' The Central Youth Employment Executive, who are responsible for the Service, disagree. Without minimizing the importance of its placement and information functions, they now lay considerable stress on its guidance function.

But what does this involve? The double aim outlined above needs elucidation. We shall not be able to do much about its achievement until we have a satisfactory way of classifying occupations, because we must be in a position to handle them in batches. The vocational guidance problem, as it commonly presents itself, is this: 'John Jones seems well suited for occupation A, but for various reasons that is out of the question. What else might he do, his capacities and inclinations being what they are?' Unless we have a sound classificatory scheme, we shall find ourselves clutching at straws blown in by chance remarks of the kind, 'Somebody told me that Mr X is looking for a lad.'

In Britain and America, the tendency is for work to be classified, for

Alec Rodger and Peter Cavanagh

vocational guidance purposes, according to its 'level' and 'type or types'.[6, 22, 24] The former is largely a matter of what we have called capacity; the latter is largely, but not wholly, a matter of inclination. The scheme used by the British Youth Employment Service may be summarized thus:

LEVEL \ TYPE	office	practical-construc-tional	active-outdoor	people	artistic
Grammar School A level					
Grammar School O level					
Secondary Modern Top					
Secondary Modern Rest					

This means that advisers are being invited to consider first of all the level at which the youngsters they are interviewing will, or should, enter the employment market. A secondary modern boy may fling himself into competition with boys from grammar schools. In that event, he must be judged by grammar school standards. For this reason, the problem of his level cannot be settled merely by noting the name of his school. The issue is more complicated than that, and it is increasing in complexity all the time. It should be added that, in considering types of work, advisers recognize that few occupations fall neatly under one of the five headings used above. Many occupations do, in fact, present mixtures of three or four.

It may be objected that the 'type' categories arrayed across the top of our grid display no recognizable *fundamentum divisionis*. This is true. The list is not logical and makes no claim to be exhaustive or exclusive. Its basis is, rather, phenomenological. It draws attention to aspects of occupations that strike many people forcibly, and which in many cases influence greatly their attitudes towards them. What was said earlier about the study of occupational difficulties and distastes is highly relevant to consideration of the classification problem.[14] To be useful, a classification must derive from similarities between occupations, not only in the difficulties and distastes commonly experienced in them, but also in the capacities and inclinations needed to cope with them.

Personnel Selection and Vocational Guidance

Vocational Guidance: Methods

The contributions of psychologists to the literature of vocational guidance have been concerned largely with techniques of gathering information about people wanting advice. They tell us about tests of many kinds; about questionnaires of many kinds (including application forms, report forms, and inventories); and about interviews. There is no need for us to delve into all this here. Vernon has provided a good deal of relevant material in his chapter. Anyone who wants more should look at some of his earlier work[27, 28, 29] and at some American books.[2, 7, 25]

What is less frequently discussed is the way in which a programme involving a number of these devices is put together. Let us take, as an example, the routine followed in the Industrial Rehabilitation Service of the British Ministry of Labour, which in its seventeen Units (IRUs) deals with about 10,000 adults a year, most of whom require vocational guidance because a disability will prevent them from returning to their previous work. The IRU scheme is of interest, not only because it handles large numbers, but also because it shows what can be done conveniently and acceptably within the framework of a public service.

On admission to his IRU, probably on the recommendation of a doctor, the 'rehabilitee' is put into an entry workshop. Then he joins the rest of the week's intake (of about a dozen) for an explanation of the aims and practices of the unit. Next, he and the others are given a series of standard group tests of general intelligence (verbal and non-verbal), mechanical comprehension, arithmetic, elementary mathematics, and spatial judgement. These are supplemented by group tests of mechanical and electrical information. Individual tests, usually the Wechsler Adult Intelligence Scale, are given when they are considered by the psychologist to be desirable. Next there is an interview with the psychologist, which is concerned not only with the man's employment record, but also with his education, his leisure, and his background; and which takes account of facts and opinions gathered from others, outside the unit and inside. Then comes further consideration of his suitability for this workshop or that, and it may be decided to try him out on several kinds of work. After a few days there is a case-conference, at which the rehabilitation officer (the head of the unit) takes the chair for a discussion in which the participants are the doctor, the psychologist, the social worker, the disablement resettlement officer (concerned with placement), and the chief occupational supervisor, all of whom have by this time some knowledge of the man and those who have come into the IRU with him. The man's prospects, immediate and more remote, are discussed and the rest of his course planned. A final case-conference is held shortly before he is due for discharge.

231

Two features of this scheme are worth notice. First, the advisory process is spread out over a period and is in the hands of a team. Secondly, a systematic attempt is being made, through a well thought out punched-card plan, to discover the predictive value of information available at the entry stage, using, as criterion data, facts and opinions gathered during the man's stay in the unit and later when he has left it. There are some deviations from the scheme as we have outlined it, but most of them do not affect the general plan, which is applicable to many guidance, selection and training problems.[21] Developments are reported in *IRU Notes*, circulated privately by the Training Department of the Ministry of Labour.

Another gap in the literature is found when we consider what is done about gathering information on occupations and their 'requirements' (an explanation of the quotation marks is given in the section on Personnel Selection). This is particularly evident when we glance at the Continental output. In France, Germany, and Switzerland, especially, there has been an immense and unbalanced concentration of attention on the study of the applicant, much of it by means of apparatus tests of capacity, projective tests of inclination, and graphological tests of almost everything. But relatively little has been said about the study of occupations, despite the fact that most people, including psychologists, accept in one form or another the idea that vocational guidance involves the 'matching' of people and jobs.

It is true that in some places, not least in America, much use has been made of systematic job-specification. Investigators have been asked to record facts about the activities performed in an occupation under review, about the conditions under which they are performed, and about the rewards they offer; and they have been invited to draw inferences about its requirements. But the schemes used tend to woolliness. The fault lies, once more, in the absence of clear thinking about what is relevant and what is not.

In Britain, where we are becoming appreciative of the crucial importance of what we have called difficulties and distastes, the outlook seems more promising. What is happening in the Youth Employment Service, for example, is that collectors of information about occupations and their requirements are focusing their attention on employers' accounts of the commonest mistakes of workers, and on workers' accounts of what they tend to dislike in their work and working conditions.[5] It is maintained that, armed with knowledge of these, a youth employment officer may make very useful judgements of a boy's or girl's suitability for an occupation, even if he has no more than a sketchy acquaintance with its daily or weekly routines.

However, it is clear that even a realistic approach of this kind will not take us far scientifically unless we pin down our difficulties and

Personnel Selection and Vocational Guidance

distastes in an operational way. As we have noted, difficulties are manifested in mistakes. If mistakes are important, the employer will act—perhaps by taking more care in the selection of his workers, or by the more careful training of them, or by improving his arrangements for supervising them or inspecting their work, or by changing the method of work, or by modifying the design or layout of the equipment used, or by paying for more skill. The importance an employer attaches to mistakes is reflected in what he does about them.

Similarly, distastes are manifested in aversions. If these turn out to be important, and workers either refuse to come to the employer or soon leave him, again he will act. He may adopt one or more of the devices we have listed for use in dealing with mistakes, for distastes as well as difficulties can often be reduced by such means; but he is more likely to find a solution by attending to the working conditions of his people. He will try to find out what pushed them beyond the limits of their endurance—what made them slack, or careless, or watch the clock, or look glum, or stay away, or ask for their cards.

A conclusion we are bound to reach, in reflecting on both guidance and selection, is that for the advancement of our knowledge we must look primarily to the study of occupational misfits, of those whose capacities or inclinations prove unequal to the strain. Even if our interest in these two fields is mainly practical, and we are seeking to keep people out of jobs they will almost certainly find too hard or too unattractive, we must build on what we can learn about the nature and etiology of occupational casualties and near-casualties.

REFERENCES

1. ALLPORT, G. W. (1937) *Personality: a Psychological Interpretation* New York: Holt.
2. ANASTASI, A. (1954) *Psychological Testing.* New York: Macmillan.
3. BECHTOLDT, H. P. (1951) 'Selection', in *Handbook of Experimental Psychology,* edited by S. S. Stevens. New York: Wiley.
4. BURT, C. (1935) *The Subnormal Mind.* London: Oxford Univ. Press.
5. Central Youth Employment Executive (1955) *The Study of Occupations.* Memorandum 20. Not generally available.
6. Central Youth Employment Executive (1960) *Choosing Your Career.* Pamphlet 1 in Choice of Careers Series. London: H.M.S.O.
7. CRONBACH, L. J. (1958) *The Essentials of Psychological Testing.* 2nd ed. New York: Harper.
8. EYSENCK, H. J. (1953) *The Structure of Human Personality.* London: Methuen.
9. FLANAGAN, J. C. (1954) 'The Critical Incident Technique'. *Psychol. Bull.,* **51**, 327–58.
10. HALL, C. S., & LINDZEY, G. (1957) *Theories of Personality.* New York: Wiley.

Alec Rodger and Peter Cavanagh

11. HERON, A. (1954) 'Satisfaction and Satisfactoriness: Complementary Aspects of Occupational Adjustment'. *Occup. Psychol.*, **28**, 140–53.
12. HOLLINGWORTH, H. L. (1929) *Vocational Psychology and Character Analysis*. New York: Appleton.
13. KELLY, E. L., & FISKE, D. W. (1951) *The Prediction of Performance in Clinical Psychology*. Univ. of Michigan Press.
14. REEB, M. (1959) *An Investigation of Judgements of Similarity between Common Occupations*. Unpublished Ph.D. Thesis. University of London Library.
15. RODGER, A. (1937) *A Borstal Experiment in Vocational Guidance*. Report 78 of the Industrial Health Research Board. London: H.M.S.O.
16. RODGER, A. (1939) 'The Work of the Vocational Adviser', in *The Study of Society*, edited by F. C. Bartlett and others. London: Kegan Paul.
17. RODGER, A. (1939) 'Planning for Vocational Guidance'. *Occup. Psychol.*, **13**, 1–9.
18. RODGER, A. (1945) 'On the Selection of Business Executives'. *Labour Mgmt.*, **27**, 30–35.
19. RODGER, A. (1950) 'Industrial Psychology', in *Chambers' Encyclopedia*. London: Newnes.
20. RODGER, A. (1955) 'The Effective Use of Manpower'. *Advanc. Sci., Lond.*, **12**, 237–49.
21. RODGER, A., & CAVANAGH, P. (1959) 'Training and Professional Problems', in *Electronic Engineer's Reference Book*. London: Heywood.
22. ROE, A. (1956) *The Psychology of Occupations*. New York: Wiley.
23. Select Committee on Estimates (1957) *The Youth Employment Service and Youth Service Grants*. London: H.M.S.O.
24. SUPER, D. E. (1957) *The Psychology of Careers*. New York: Harper.
25. THORNDIKE, R. L. (1949) *Personnel Selection: Test and Measurement Techniques*. New York: Wiley.
26. VERNON, P. E. (1950) 'The Validation of Civil Service Selection Board Procedures'. *Occup. Psychol.*, **24**, 75–95.
27. VERNON, P. E. (1953) *Personality Tests and Assessments*. London: Methuen.
28. VERNON, P. E. (1956) *The Measurement of Abilities*. 2nd ed. London: Univ. of London Press.
29. VERNON, P. E., & PARRY, J. B. (1949) *Personnel Selection in the British Forces*. London: Univ. of London Press.
30. WILSON, N. A. B. (1949) 'The Work of the Civil Service Selection Board'. *Occup. Psychol.*, **21**, 204–12.

13

OPERATIONAL

RESEARCH IN INDUSTRY

M. G. Bennett

OPERATIONAL RESEARCH is akin to a movement rather than a scientific discipline, and yet no such generalization is quite true. It has its special techniques; but the subject is more than the sum of its techniques, just as the art of the doctor is more than the techniques of surgery and medicine. It is a movement in the sense that it is difficult to define, although it can be described; it is difficult to identify its origin as an idea, but easier to see when and how it grew into a thing of importance; it has not yet, and may never have, a static and delimitable content. However, for present purposes, it can, perhaps fairly be regarded as the way of attacking the problems of industry by setting aside groups of people trained in the methods of scientific research, to study freely the functional, as distinct from technical, problems that arise.

Apparently the term was invented to describe the activities of a small section of the Air Ministry at Bawdsey in 1937–39 ([11], p. 39) concerned with the best use to be made of a new invention—radar. But operational research has come to mean something much wider than the study of the use of inventions. Moreover, such studies has begun long before 1937, under other names or none. It has been claimed by Davies and Silman ([5], p. 36) that the successful modification of the phalanx by Alexander the Great was the result of a piece of operational research: and it is not fantastic to argue that the men of the early twentieth century who studied the methods of industry and applied such inventions as the spinning jenny and the steam engine to enlarge output were unconscious pioneers in operational research. Later, we find the subject developing as a more special study and widening its scope and therefore qualifying more fully under our definition—as, for instance, in production engineering (i.e. the conscious planning of the steps of production), in the work of such men as Gilbreth in America on time-and-motion study, and in the use of statistical mathematics and mathematical models in economics and political philosophy. Some of these lines of study were, or have since become, highly developed subjects in themselves, with their own titles and techniques; operational research cannot be said to include them, though it may use them all.

The Second World War brought many new problems and inventions. The scope for the scientific study of function and method was therefore naturally very great. The literature holds many fascinating examples[1, 2] from the bombing of submarines to the estimation of the war potential of enemy countries. As spectacular as any was the revolutionary effect of radar on the air defence of the United Kingdom. The movement met with much success and grew rapidly. It was natural therefore, after the war to try to see what it could do for industry. The post-war development has, however, been along rather different lines from the war work—and this change again justifies the use of the word movement. Its present value and future development must and can rest on its achievements in industry.

The range of subjects of papers in the Quarterly Journal of the Operational Research Society is very wide. It must be much wider in confidential reports. One of the earliest papers was by Tippett[10] on Operational Research at the Shirley Institute. Activity here started in about 1926 and, after the second war, grew into a substantial part of the work of the Institute. The work is of interest in itself and also because it typifies much of post-war industrial operational research as distinct from war work. Modern methods of measurement and analysis were applied to a traditional industry, largely in an exploratory fashion. In parts of the industry there was much development and redeployment, and it was a matter of great importance to discover in what ways the changes had been successful or otherwise. The problem was complex, for numerous changes had occurred simultaneously and the circumstances of no two units of the industry were quite similar. New units of efficiency had to be devised which could be analysed and synthesized like costs, and many statistical data had to be treated in new ways to yield values for the units. Technical particulars were assembled of the type of cotton in use, hank numbers of the various products in the sequence of processes, machine speeds, the weight of material on each bobbin, and the labour deployment. It must always have been true that all these factors were known to be involved in resultant efficiency; but to have their contributions and interdependence measured no doubt provided a new tool for management. It would probably be difficult to trace any particular executive decision solely to this new tool, because experience and judgement must always be ingredients of any decision, but proper measurements must be better than guesses.

A whole series of papers in the *Quarterly* deal with road accidents. Here surely is a matter—and a serious one—where guesswork, prejudice, attitudes of mind, generalization from too little evidence, and other hindrances to clear thought are all too rife, so that removal from the realm of emotion to that of measurement is an essential preliminary to effective remedy. It is often thought loosely that in a complicated matter such as road accidents, if every cause that may be operative is tackled, then, whether or not the relative incidence of all the causes is known, everything possible by way of prevention is being done; but this is not necessarily so, for a remedy of one contributing cause may act against the remedy of another. For instance, a pedestrian crossing can give either a real or a false sense of security, or, again, great accelerating power may sometimes enable an accident to be avoided, and at other times invite a driver to take a risk. In such cases the optimum course of action is a compromise between conflicting courses. Life is full of situations calling for compromise. In the papers mentioned, factual information is given on the effect of traffic flow, type of road, type and state of vehicle, parking regulations, traffic lights, one way streets, speed restrictions, segregation of cyclists, junction design, road signs, police action, pedestrian choice and judgement, driving skill, and road and vehicle lighting. It is a task for the operational research worker to sort out the effects of these various factors, to balance quantitatively the pros and cons of different lines of action, and to put forward constructive proposals which are practical and economic. This he finds stimulating and rewarding.

The way in which techniques and research experience gained in one field can serve another (which is part of the justification for setting up *units* for carrying out operational research) was well illustrated by a Symposium on Marshalling and Queueing organized by the Operational Research Club ([8], vol. 3). This symposium also shows well the approach to a problem which is commonly practised. First there is the building up of a physical concept of the nature of the problem—in this case, of persons or objects (the 'input') arriving at a 'gate' (or the gate arriving at the persons, as in a restaurant), the service time, and the marshalling arrangements to deal with the queue. Then comes the mathematical model, with the further and more exact definitions it usually entails to distinguish, for example, the random input and the general independent input, the impartial gate and the gate that gives preference to V.I.P.'s, continuous and intermittent processes. One application of this was to

M. G. Bennett

Hospital Administration. The extent of out-patients' waiting time depends on the punctuality of patients and staff, on the duration of the consulting time and on the times at which the patients were told to attend. The expression of this statement in mathematical form showed what numerical facts were needed; these were then observed in practice and the mathematical equations were solved. It may be, however, that reduction of patients' waiting time should not be the main aim, but increase in consulting time, and there may be inhibitions such as limited space or refusal to conform. Gradually, however, the problem was unravelled. Very often, the clarification of aims is not the least of the advantages of subjecting a problem to operational research.

There are many obvious industrial applications of this type of model, such as railway booking-offices, help-yourself shops, and telephone kiosks and exchanges. Other examples are of a less obvious or more complex nature such as the following:

(a) Civil Aviation has many queueing problems in regard to the control of aircraft in the air and arriving at and leaving airports, the control of vehicles attending on the aircraft, car parking, and passengers passing through Customs and Immigration, and awaiting or leaving aircraft.

(b) The discharge of ore from ships has been studied, the objective being to find the cheapest way of avoiding delay and to decide how much to spend for the purpose. The National Coal Board have a two-way queue situation, as, for instance, in dirt arriving at a service point to be loaded into tubs, where the 'input' of both dirt and tubs has to be considered.

To all of these problems a basic mathematical model is a valuable conception, but a complete model plus solution is not always feasible. Indeed, the beautiful ideal of a complete theory, including every factor, with measurements of them all, is very rare. The usual method of progress is to visualize a tentative picture, propound a simple theory, measure the most important items, test and if necessary correct the simple picture, study the disturbances and so on, until by gradual approximation a picture emerges sufficiently complete to enable control of the situation to be exercised as far as may be desired. Approximation may be enforced by inability to express the problem in mathematical form, by the impossibility of collecting the field data necessary to solve the equations, or because of the sheer time involved in working out the results. To meet the last type of difficulty the electronic computer is an invaluable tool. It is in no proper sense of the word an electronic brain, since it exhibits none of the higher faculties of the brain. It merely does sums and tries out possible solutions to order, but it does this at very high rates, so that calculations which could not be entertained before are now possible. This has become a highly involved specialism on its own, which is used by operational research workers gratefully, where it is appropriate.

Agriculture is apt to differ somewhat from industry as an area for operational research. Farmers are individualists, only very loosely organized: the production cycle may run into years: the uncontrolled and uncontrollable factors are very wide and potent, and frequently highly correlated between themselves. Boyd[4] has provided a very interesting account of a scrutiny of the British potato crop, which is one of the most important of the crops grown for human consumption and for which Britain is very largely dependent on home production. Potatoes are an inelastic commodity, so that over-production goes unrewarded, but a minor shortage tends to loom as 'famine'. The emphasis, as always, was on measurement—in this case, of crop yield from sample weight and of the practice of growers in different parts of the country. The sampling procedures, which are vitally important in this kind of study, had to take into account not only such facts as that, while most farmers grow a small acreage of potatoes for home and local consumption, there is also a smaller number of specialist growers, but also practical points such as the amount of the surveyor's time that would have to be spent in travelling from office to farm and between farms. It appeared from the results that earlier estimates had tended to underestimate good and overestimate poor crops, which fact alone is an important piece of information.

Having established that national yields were apparently higher than had been supposed, attention was turned to husbandry practices. This involved a thorough re-examination of existing information on this aspect of the problem and the bringing into the picture of the results of a number of isolated experiments. Such reassessment of existing information is usually worth doing, but it rarely obviates the need for additional field work to supply missing links in the sequence of argument. Operational research therefore can never be tied to the desk! Boyd concludes his paper with the comment that 'a good deal more experimentation is required'.

One of the most familiar procedures of Operational Research is known as linear programming. Put mathematically, this is a procedure for finding the particular solution of a set of linear equations, containing more unknown quantities than there are equations, which will satisfy some further stated conditions. The example which has probably been more frequently discussed in text-books than any other is the so-called 'transportation' example. Given a number of, say, buses or wagons located at different places, from which it is necessary to supply other places with stated numbers, how should the redistribution be made to minimize the bus or wagon miles involved, assuming certain conditions to apply? It is not difficult for a mathematical statistician to frame a set of computational rules—i.e. a procedure—for such a problem, but in practice there may be difficulties. Some success was achieved in an early application to the problem of the distribution of empty wagons on British Railways, but it is now clear that the method will have to be elaborated before it can deal with that problem in general. One important thing that has brought linear programming into prominence for this purpose is the development of electronic computers. Without these, the enormous number of calculations involved in most real problems would have made the procedure of little practical value. Interestingly enough, it has shown that the older 'trial and error' methods often came very near the mathematical ideal, when there was time available to adjust to changing circumstances. It is the rapidity of change nowadays, coupled with the speed of electronic computing, which makes linear programming a promising field of investigation.

It is of course an over-simplification to regard the problem of the distribution of empty wagons, from unloading to collecting points, and thence to loading points, as merely a matter of the movement of empty wagons in such a manner as to minimize wagon-miles. Such movement is inextricably bound up with the movement of loaded wagons and of engines: and there can be many cases where a longer route may be preferred to a shorter one for some sound operating reason; it may be less busy or it may avoid some marshalling. No programming method has yet been developed for dealing with the movement of loaded and empty wagons and engines as one problem. It is one of the principal tasks on which the Operational Research Unit of the British Transport Commission is engaged. If realizable it would constitute a major portion of the complete description of the railway operating system in mathematical form. Coupled with the use of computers, it could become a most powerful tool to show quickly how services and routes should be adapted to meet changing traffic conditions. The prizes are glittering—it remains to be seen if research can win them.

However, even if a completely general and comprehensive formula is unobtainable, experience shows that useful practical results may be obtained from more limited exercises. This may arise in a number of ways. The adjustment of train schedules to meet traffic changes is a continuous process which it is difficult to keep up to date, and one actual outstanding success for simple linear programming of empty coal wagons in a particular area was probably due to the fact that it enabled an unavoidable lag in the normal process to be overcome quickly.

The carrying out of even a limited linear programming exercise requires that the real cost of each route should be assessed, and this, as previously mentioned, includes not only mileage but all the other factors combining to form preferences, such as congestion and marshalling. Quantifying all these factors is useful because it leads to clarity of thought and also makes possible a subsequent test of the result of the exercise to see how much improvement has taken place. Such measured changes, coupled with modern costing, can make certain the path of progress.

The points have been made that modern industrial operational research is concerned as much with exploration and reappraisal in traditional industries as with problems of innovation; and that it is concerned very much with compromise, or the balancing of the complexities of situations. More often than not, it deals with situations that are active and are apt to be modified by the very process of investigation. But these are not its only characteristics. It must possess the qualities of independence and breadth, as well as the necessary skills and opportunities. It must have independence, in order to have time to think and freedom from the pressures of executive crises or 'interest' or prejudice; and yet it must be so closely knit into the organization it serves, that it can have clear insight into its problems and sympathetic consideration of its ideas: unfortunately such independence and integration are not always easy to combine. Operational research cannot work in blinkers, but must be encouraged to review *whole situations*, if its conclusions are not frequently to fail because they are not directed to quite the right point or because some repercussion has been missed. That it must have the opportunities goes without saying. Finally, the necessary skills are manifold, so that a variety of talent is required in an operational research team if it is to be fully effective. The clear tenacious thinking that can discern the basic purpose through a screen of relevant but minor detail: mathematics (and particularly statistical mathematics) both to plan experiments and analyse the results: enough knowledge of the undertaking to be studied, but not so much as to stultify imagination, together with an understanding of the principles of many things, such as economics, computers, work study psychology, market research, costing, and so-called management techniques: all these are wanted.

Blackett[3] has truly said: 'Since the (O.R.) groups must generally, and even preferably, be small, it is essential that their work is canalized into those fields where results of interest to the executives are likely. Drawing again on war experience, one of the best methods of achieving this is to put the group in close personal contact with the executives and let them watch them at work—that is, let them watch the decisions being made and give them the right to ask such questions as, "Why did you decide to do A rather than B?" or to intervene with the executives thus, "Next month you will have to decide between course of action D, E, or F. You will probably have no firm data on which to base a choice and you will, in all probability, have to guess which course is best. We think that possibly we may be able to help you by analysing quantitatively the effects of these possible actions. But we must have access to all the available facts and have authority to go and collect those that are not available,'

A remarkable event in the history of operational research was an International Conference in Oxford in September 1957. Such a conference could not have been organized by anything but a very lively movement. For four days, people active in operational research from all over the world, discussed their aims, their techniques, and their achievements. Over 30 papers were presented and many group discussions were arranged. As is usually the case, there was some intangible general discourse; there was also, very usefully, some consideration of techniques, experimental, mathematical, and statistical, expressed by specialists for specialists in their own terminologies; but there was also a refreshing and encouraging amount of information of definite practical pieces of work done. A second and even more successful International Conference was held at Aix-en-Provence in 1960, and it is planned to hold another in 1963 in Scandinavia.

Despite the record of achievement, concern has been expressed that the capabilities of operational research are not fully exploited. Such 'divine discontent' is natural and right on the part of those engaged in the work. They undoubtedly have a sense of vocation—many of them have abandoned promising careers in other directions to render service to industry in this way. Their discontent is to some extent justified. They are at pains to examine the cause and they discuss the arts and practice of exposition and training. After allowing for everything, however, it is perhaps true that peace-time industrial operational research has rarely had the opportunity to reach the heights that it did sometimes in the war. No doubt peace is more complex than war and the arts of peace are practised with greater skill than those of war, because there is more experience. Certainly, since the war, much of the time of operational research has been spent on relatively small (but always useful) matters. But this is the way, perhaps, for it to grow from secure foundations, and one hears of operational research teams working in the background at the highest levels behind governments and large industrial units. It is difficult to assess their potency because much of their work must be confidential.

What of the future of operational research? Surveys made successively by Goodeve and Ridley,[7] Gander,[6] and Rivett[9], although not statistically rigorous, support the general impression that operational research has spread widely since the war, both in Britain and America. In America there appears to have been more academic study of techniques than in Britain, judging from the sophistication of the mathematics in the *Journal* of the Operations Research Society of America. Will all this go on? Some people think that saturation may come and thereafter a decline of new problems as old ones become solved. Certainly, it is to be hoped that many of the techniques of operational research will be absorbed into the normal working of executive departments as they prove their value, and in so far as this happens the service of special groups may decline. But the present age is surely one of accelerating rate of change in many directions—in technique, in administration and economics, in government and social organization, and some would say even in morals. More than ever before, therefore, is there the need for the broad, independent, and scientific study of change, which is the aim of and perhaps the best definition of operational research.

REFERENCES

1. *Advanc. Sci. Lond.* (1948) **4.**
2. BLACKETT, P. M. S. (1948) *Advanc. Sci. Lond.,* **5.**
3. BLACKETT (1950) *Operational Research: Its Application to Peace-time Industry.* Manchester Joint Research Council. p. 13.
4. BOYD, D. A. (1957) *Operat. Res. Quart.,* **8.**
5. DAVIES, H., & SILMAN, K. E. (1958) *Operational Research in Practice.* London: Pergamon.
6. GANDER, R. S. (1957) *Proceedings of the First International Conference on Operational Research.* London: English Univ. Press.
7. GOODEVE, C. F., & RIDLEY, G. R. (1953) *Operat. Res. Quart.,* **4.**
8. *Operat. Res. Quart.* (1950–9) Vols. **1** to **9.**
9. RIVETT, B. H. P. (1959) Paper read to Operational Research Society. Unpublished.
10. TIPPETT, L. H. C. (1950) *Operat. Res. Quart.,* **1.**
11. WILLIAMS, E. C. (1954) 'Reflections on Operational Research'. *Operat. Res. Quart.,* **5** (2).

B. SOCIAL PATHOLOGY

Problems of social pathology are also discussed in Chapters 8, 21 and 31.

14

ACCIDENTS AT WORK

A. B. Cherns

AS a subject for social research accidents have many disadvantages, but one great advantage—there is no shortage of material. This grim fact, however, is no cause for congratulation. In Great Britain in 1958, the latest year for which full figures are available, 19,000 people died and 200,000 received serious injuries as a result of accidents. While attention is focused on the dramatic figures for road accidents, which accounted for 6,000 deaths, these are outnumbered by accidents in the home, which killed 8,000 and, like road accidents, increase yearly. Industrial accidents (including factories, coal mines, and farms) killed 1,200.* Here then is an area in which social science, if it can be successfuly applied, is of obvious potential benefit.

There has been much research and much speculation. Freud[20, 21] directed our attention to the destructive or self-destructive unconscious wishes underlying some kinds of accident, and these we must not neglect in our survey. With the classic statistical inquiry of Greenwood and Woods in 1919[22] the serious scientific investigation of accidents began. The concept of accident-proneness, which then seemed full of possibilities, has, as we shall see, led to rather disappointing results.

One obvious difficulty facing the investigation of accidents is the nature of an accident itself. Leaving aside those accidents which can be described as due to 'Acts of God', and also those which it is beyond our present capacity to predict (e.g. aircraft accidents due to previously unsuspected component fatigue), an accident is an *error with sad consequences*. Many similar errors have no significant consequences, and some may have a happy outcome. These 'near accidents' mostly go

* Statistics supplied by Royal Society for Prevention of Accidents, 1960.

247

A. B. Cherns

unrecorded and unexamined. Social scientists meet this kind of problem in other spheres; our knowledge of delinquency is largely confined to those delinquent acts which have been detected and brought home to their perpetrators. Any factor tending to discriminate between those errors which have bad consequences and those which do not is as inaccessible to study as the factors differentiating the delinquent who gets caught from the one who escapes detection.

Accident Proneness

Greenwood and Woods[22] made an examination of the accidents which happened to women munition workers in the process of shell manufacture. They noted that while many women had no accidents and some had one, there were others who had as many as five in a period of thirteen months. This might of course be due to chance; on the other hand individual women might differ in their 'proneness' to have accidents. There is the further possibility that the women who had one accident became unnerved and liable to commit errors leading to further accidents.

It can be shown[32] that if the distribution is due to pure chance, a Poisson series* should fit the data. It is likewise possible to construct hypothetical distributions which would follow from the assumption of different individual proneness (unequal initial liability) and from the assumption that one accident leads to another (biased hypothesis). In Greenwood and Woods' experiment the results were:

Women Working on 6-in. H. E. shells, 13 February–20 March 1918.

Number of accidents per individual in Shop A	Number of individuals having Accidents	Expected Distribution based on Hypothesis of:		
		Chance (Poisson)	Unequal Liability	Biased Hypothesis
0	447	406	442	452
1	132	189	140	117
2	42	45	45	56
3	21	7	14	18
4	3	1	5	4
5	2	0·1	2	1
Total	648	648·1	648 (p = ·39)	648 (p = ·13)

* A 'Poisson' series is given by the formula: $e^{-\lambda}(1 + \lambda + \frac{\lambda^2}{2!} + \frac{\lambda^3}{3!} + \ldots)$ where λ = n (the number of accidents) divided by N (the population at risk).

248

Both the second and third hypotheses fit the observed data reasonably well, but the 'proneness' hypothesis fits better. As the authors put it, 'In the table p $= 0 \cdot 13$ for the biased distribution means that, were the hypothesis valid, then in every 100 trials we should get no better agreement than is actually observed here thirteen times. But for the unequal liability hypothesis, the chance is better, viz. 39 in 100 times.' While in their fourteen samples the proneness hypothesis proved superior to the biased hypotheses only eight times, it failed to satisfy the data only twice against five times for the biased hypothesis, and its margin of superiority was sufficient for the authors to prefer it. Subsequent investigators have confirmed the superiority of the proneness hypothesis in fitting observed data, often applying less self-critical procedures than did Greenwood and Woods.

The value of the concept clearly depends, however, on the extent to which it can be used—in this case to detect accident-prone individuals and either to render them less prone or to remove them from hazardous situations. Here the results have been on the whole disappointing, although in some cases considerable success has been claimed.

To begin with, it must be established that the individuals who are found to be accident-prone during one period of time are the same as those found to be accident-prone in a subsequent period.

To take the extreme chance hypothesis; if all accidents occurred to individuals by chance, their incidence would not be uniform, i.e. one would not have an accident at regular intervals. Individuals might pass through a period in which accidents occurred in a bunch, followed by a period of average or below average frequency. If on the other hand we could show that the same people have more than their share of accidents in fairly widely spaced periods, we could claim that, for them, accident-proneness is an enduring characteristic.

Newbold[47] compared the incidence of accidents among members of eleven different groups over successive periods mostly of a year in length. The correlations of accidents sustained in one period with those occurring in the second period ranged from $- 0 \cdot 01$ to $+ 0 \cdot 62$, with a median value of $0 \cdot 36$. These results suggest that individuals' liability to accidents, at least in some groups, is a fairly stable function over a period of two years.

Removal of Accident Repeaters

If accident repeaters can be removed from the group studied, the rate of accidents in that group should decline to the extent that the accident repeaters consist of genuinely prone individuals.

The most thorough study of this kind comes from the field of road accidents. Forbes[19] analysed a series of studies carried out from 1931 to

249

1936 of accidents occurring to private transport drivers in Connecticut. He found that the 398 accident repeaters who were responsible in the 1931–1933 period for no fewer than 847 accidents, had only 129 accidents out of the 3,351 reported for the whole group in 1934–36. If all these accident repeaters had been removed the accident rate would have been improved by only 4 per cent from ·128 to ·124 per driver. Furthermore, the accident repeaters in the first period were not in the main the accident repeaters of the second. Their removal after the first three years would have reduced the accident repeaters in the second three years by only 7 per cent.[3] It would seem fair to conclude from these results that while individual differences in proneness to accidents may have existed, these differences were not very stable from one period to another.

Predicting Accident-Prone Individuals

So far we have been dealing only with attempts to identify accident-prone individuals within the accident situation. Should it prove possible to predict them from other indicators, we should be better able not only to understand the nature of accident-proneness but also to take prophylactic measures.

A comprehensive attempt to find test results which would predict accident-proneness was made by Farmer, Chambers and Kirk[18] in their study of dockyard apprentices. They found three groups among the apprentices in which individuals' work, and therefore exposure to risk, was similar enough to give stable accident records and provide a reliable measure for the individual.

Cognitive tests correlated only to a small degree with accident rates, the coefficients (r) ranging from -0.07 to $+0.31$ between a linguistic intelligence test and accident rates for twenty-seven engine fitters. With such a small sample, this correlation is not significantly different from zero. Tests of reaction time produced little better results. Farmer and Chambers's best results were produced by a battery of 'aesthetokinetic' tests consisting of a choice reaction test, a simple co-ordination test, and a number-setting test. This battery produced a significant but low correlation (0·20) with accident rates for the whole group of subjects.

Lahy and Korngold,[35, 36] in their study of French railway workers, achieved somewhat better results with a two-handed co-ordination test, McDougall's dotting test, and with a test of divided attention (*attention diffusée*). Using a measure of correct responses to visual and auditory stimuli, they achieved a critical ratio of the differences between the scores of workers with and without accident records of 8·84 (with one group, 10·57). The probability is 1,000 to 1 against such a result occurring by chance. The experimenters drew attention to the fact that the best result was obtained with a 'paced' task (i.e. one in which the tempo is set by the apparatus and not by the subject).

Both the studies reported and many others[4, 8, 9, 39, 45] have dealt with particular occupational groups, and any significant results may well be specific to these groups. Furthermore the method in each case has been to take as criterion the number of accidents sustained during the period up to the time of testing, and to compare with this criterion the results of the tests employed. The next step is clearly to apply these tests to a group newly entering the occupation, to record the results while not using them for selection, and to compare them with subsequent accident records. The relationship of tests to a criterion always contains an element specific to the group tested and to the situation in which the criterion was obtained. Subsequent validation of the tests yields lower correlations. We must therefore look critically at the reported results before concluding that it is possible to predict accident-proneness successfully.

For a further and more damaging criticism we may quote Arbous[3]: 'The necessary prerequisite to an adequate predicting device (viz. a stable and reliable criterion) is lacking, and no amount of subsequent statistical juggling will compensate for this deficiency.' Or, as Marbe[42] put it in 1926, 'Proneness is only a reaction to a certain situation.'

Stress

Many accidents are due to inadequate or incorrect motor responses in conditions of emotional stress. Davis[12] used a test in which the subject was required to move a pointer to coincide with a specific line in the direction indicated by a lamp. When two lamps, equally or nearly equally bright, were lit simultaneously the subject was under some stress owing to the difficulty of deciding in which direction to move his pointer. The detailed records of pointer movements produced by a subject can be rated according to the general degree of 'organization' his activity shows. Davis[14] and Whitfield[63] found a relationship between this rating of 'organization' and the accident rates of coal miners and air pilot trainees.

Biesheuvel and White[4] made a comprehensive study of 200 pilots who had been involved in flying accidents during training and, as a control group, 400 other pilots who had completed their training without an accident. Among the tests they applied was a clinical assessment of personality based on observational, biographical, and interview material. Each pilot was assessed on three temperamental variables: activity (drive and persistence in the face of obstacles), emotionality (the degree to which feeling is a determining factor in behaviour), and

A. B. Cherns

'secondary function' (tempo, variability, impulsiveness, and 'stimulability'). They found secondary function higher among the accident group with a critical ratio of 2·89. The difference between the two groups gave a critical ratio of 3·28 in the case of emotionality; the accident group being more 'emotional'. Löwenstein[38] had earlier noted that 'the movements of persons who are liable to accidents are characteristically influenced by their emotions'.

Smiley[53] made a clinical study comparing accident repeaters in the aircraft industry with an accident-free control group. His accident repeaters lost twice as much working time as his controls for reasons other than accidents, and were more liable to peptic ulcer and to psychosomatic absences. They made more frequent visits to the 'medical department' and were more liable to other 'neurotic' symptoms such as palmar and plantar sweating and albuminurea. He concluded that accident-prone workers are socially maladjusted and suggests that they may be found to have hypothalamic lesions. In interpreting the tests which tend to distinguish the accident-prone he points out that 'the mere fact of submitting a nervous subject to a test of any sort is apt to induce an emotional state (if only minor), and this would increase as the test grew more difficult'. One might add that anyone who has had one or more accidents and suspects that he is being tested on this account may well feel more nervous than a control subject.

Unconscious Motivation

We have already mentioned the importance attached by Freud to unconscious wishes in precipitating accidents. And, indeed, it is possible very often to find, in the recent history of a person who has sustained an accident, some disturbing occurrence. This may operate by distracting his attention and lowering his vigilance, but may also lead him to expose himself unnecessarily to risk. Menninger[43] wrote: 'There is a little murder and a little suicide dwelling in everybody's heart. Influence people's inhibitions or irritations or frustrations and diminish their suppressive control by alcohol or fatigue and the murder or suicide may get committed. The impulse to punish oneself is often just as strong as, or even stronger than, the wish to hurt someone else.' He found in a study of men and women reporting to a clinic as accident cases that 90 per cent had histories of provocation, frustration, or disappointment just before their accident.

Moseley[46] points to four unconscious motives leading to accidents: a sadistic-masochistic drive, tensions due to guilt, a wish to die, and the secondary gain arising from the accident itself (if I break my wrist I cannot be expected to finish writing this chapter).

While it is well to remember that an accident may occur as an episode in the working out of someone's unconscious motives it is extremely difficult to evaluate the evidence for the importance of this aspect. The unconscious motivations of people who have not just sustained an accident or shown other signs of psychological or social pathology are seldom the subjects of clinical study. Enduring unfavourable states of mind may, however, be part of the structure of the accident-prone individual. As Menninger[44] again says, 'All of us are accident-prone at one time or another for brief periods'.

Fatigue

As Thorndike[54] has pointed out, fatigue is an ambiguous and slippery concept, and has been approached from at least four different angles: (*a*) subjective feelings of tiredness; (*b*) physiological and chemical changes after continued work; (*c*) decrement in performance after continued work; and (*d*) boredom and loss of willingness to continue with a task. The relations between these are complex and elements of each may be present in the syndrome we refer to as fatigue. In particular (*c*) and (*d*) are important to the consideration of accidents. The decrement in skilled performance with time is especially apparent in the errors likely to be made in the task. This is particularly true of tasks requiring constant vigilance in which for periods of time nothing important is happening. After comparatively short spells of time subjects become more and more likely to miss informative signals.[14, 40] This effect of long exposure to a vigilance task is clearly important in road accidents where vigilance may be lowered (or reactive inhibition raised)[17] to the point at which the driver falls asleep at the wheel. The disinhibiting effect of irrelevant stimulation has led some authorities to recommend car radios as a prophylactic measure.

Just how complex is the relation between fatigue, boredom, and accidents is demonstrated by the fact that while factory accidents tend to rise to a peak about an hour before the end of the morning and afternoon periods of work, falling again towards the end of the period, accidents during night shift start at a maximum and decline steadily.[5, 56] While the peak of accidents during the daytime coincides with peak production, this does not hold for the night shift.

A safe generalization is that fatigue and boredom are factors affecting skilled performance and that any conditions which adversely affect skill lead to errors. Some errors result in accidents. Among these conditions we must number environmental conditions such as heat and cold, and health factors affecting efficiency such as colds and even menstruation.[11]

A. B. Cherns

Skill and Error

We turn now to consideration of the mechanisms responsible for the human errors which lead to accidents.

In recent years it has come to be recognized that one of the main limiting factors in skilled performance is the time taken by the central mechanisms in discriminating signals, coding them, and selecting the appropriate response. Hick[26, 27] and others have shown that the time taken is in many cases a linear function of the information coded for this process. Errors occur when insufficient information is coded.

Further, there is substantial evidence that these central mechanisms form a single information channel.[7, 15, 28, 59, 60] In all activities a very great deal of the information we receive from our sense organs is redundant. Acquiring skill is a process of reducing the amount of coding or translation to a minimum in which most of the redundant information is ignored, thereby reducing response time and absorbing less channel capacity. Thus the expert always appears to have plenty of time however deft and rapid his movements. An emergency finds him with capacity to spare. The task appears to have comparatively low information content for him. The tyro who has not yet learned to code the information effectively makes many more responses than are needed by responding to redundant information and thus has less capacity to spare for emergency signals.

Training in skill may be a process of teaching the most effective strategy for coding the information. Many existing training methods are probably poor because the strategy taught is itself far from ideal.[2]

While the central channel is occupied with processing one signal or set of signals, further incoming information must queue. For this some means of storage is needed and its capacity appears to be strictly limited.[30, 41] Moreover, it appears to be just this limited function of immediate memory that is one of the most easily disrupted factors in human performance. Familiarity with the sequence of signals enables maximum use to be made of capacity by treating a whole sequence as one 'item'.

Broadbent* describes a study in which the subject was required to carry out various simple tasks of cancelling numbers. He was also given an auditory task to perform. If this was combined with the cancellation of the same number throughout, it caused no increase in errors. Combined, however, with a task in which the number to be cancelled varied from time to time so that the subject had to remember whether he was now to cancel every 2 or every 3 and so on, it induced gross errors; the subject was likely to forget he was cancelling 3s and to start cancelling 4s, for example. There are many tasks in which forgetting one's

* Personal Communication.

254

Accidents at Work

position in a sequence of signals may have drastic consequences. Some of the apparently inexplicable gross errors of railway engine drivers may result from this cause.

Certain bad design features of equipment unnecessarily increase the information content of a task, as, for example, when the relationships between the signals for action and the action itself are complicated. Conversely when the motor response required is 'compatible' with the display in the sense that a natural or well learned 'coding' enables the subject to relate the two together simply, the information content is lowered. An example of a compatible display-response is the clockwise turn of a knob to increase gain* or the forward movement of a lever to lower height. A grabline designed so that a forward movement of the control corresponded to raising the grab gave rise to expensive accidents when the operator had to act in a hurry.[24]

Many motor cars are designed to this day with a fine-looking battery of identical knobs in one or two parallel rows operating such dissimilar functions as choke, windscreen wiper, lights, cigar lighter, etc. Even after some years' experience of driving the same model it is still possible in an emergency to intend to start the windscreen wiper but to douse one's lights instead.[16] How many accidents and near accidents have resulted from such faults of design it is impossible to say, but the number must be large.

Other Ergonomic Considerations

Davis[13] has drawn attention to three psychological mechanisms contributing to the causation of accidents. First, in the face of danger the action of the sympathetic nervous system in liberating adrenalin into the bloodstream poises the organism for the massive 'fight or flight' responses. These, while of biological value in enabling us to react rapidly and vigorously, are a disadvantage when controlled deliberate and accurate responses are required. Our clumsy reactions may increase our distress, setting up a vicious circle ending in disaster.

Secondly, when a task becomes difficult, and particularly when anxiety is aroused, we tend to concentrate on the most immediate aspect of the task, neglecting what appears to be less urgent. We may then fail to observe signals peripheral to what is engaging our attention, 'trying hard not to spill the over-full cup of tea one is carrying, one trips over the dog'![13] To overcome this difficulty among aircrew, British European Airways is to try an experiment with the captain monitoring the activities of two 'flying' pilots.[55]

* Taps however reduce flow when turned clockwise (screw action). This can lead to confusion—the author sustained a 'near accident' with a drip-feed oil heater as a result.

A. B. Cherns

Thirdly we strive after meaning in all our perceptions. Given a vague or incomplete display we form a hypothesis or expectation about what we are seeing or hearing and of what will happen next. When anxious we are less able to tolerate uncertainty and more likely to adopt a hypothesis prematurely. Once the hypothesis is formed, even contradictory evidence may be seen as confirming it: 'Ah, yes, that was a red light—Good, full speed ahead!' would be the unformulated response. Whether we see red or green or attach the wrong meaning to the colour correctly perceived, the outcome is the same. This phenomenon is most likely to occur towards the end of a long anxious task. Davis concludes that the 'unexpected' signal needs to be stronger or more insistent than the expected or confirmatory signal. This, however, will not always ensure that it is perceived correctly. The methods of imparting information to the operator so as to counteract the effects of a possible false hypothesis, where this can be foreseen, need careful consideration in each individual case.

Age and Accidents

Because ageing is a slow process it allows us to adjust to our continuously changing powers. Thus although we may continue to undertake the same work as we did when younger the way we do it is different. Because of this adjustment we may continue with a highly skilled activity which makes considerable demands on the perceptual and central mechanisms well beyond the age at which we could ever hope to acquire such a skill from scratch.

Under normal conditions of operating to which he is accustomed, then, the older worker is likely to have no more accidents than the younger. When these conditions are disturbed or make heavy demands the older man tends to have more accidents. Vernon and Bedford[57, 58] found that while coalminers over fifty had no more accidents than young men at temperatures below 70°, they were significantly more liable to accidents when the temperature rose above that figure.

Comparative figures of younger and older workers are dangerous to interpret, as older men are commonly engaged upon different work from younger, and thus are exposed to different risks.[34] Even where the work is the same to all appearances the different methods and tempo employed by the older men will tend to affect the hazards of the task. Welford[61] has argued that older people need longer to complete the process of dealing with the perception and organization of responses to an event. They may take longer to 'clear the decks' for action in an emergency. It appears that older people require information that would be redundant to their juniors. The task has thus more information content for them and channel capacity is not so readily available for emergencies.

256

To allow for slowness they have to lay down a longer strategy ahead. The consequent loss of flexibility will have been noted by anyone who has tried to direct an elderly motor car driver over an unfamiliar route.

To these causes of increased propensity to accidents on the part of older people, we must add the loss of sensori-motor control that appears to expose them to more frequent falls. Once unbalanced for any reason, they seem unable to correct quickly enough to avoid a fall, 'Once you're going you've got to go'. Sensori-motor slowness may indeed account for many of the categories of accident which show a significant rise with age.[33]

Griew[23] points out that there are many jobs which are traditionally the preserve of the young, and that when older workers are found in these jobs they tend to be regarded as particularly liable to accidents. Older men are unable to meet the demands of these jobs, which, however, could probably in many cases be modified to suit their capacities.

THE SOCIAL ASPECTS OF ACCIDENTS

We must now inquire into the relationship between the characteristics of the group or of the society and the accidents which occur within it. As with other symptoms of social pathology, the type of accident which occurs, and the social response to it when it has occurred, will tend to reflect a complex of social attitudes and values. Unlike other symptoms such as suicide rates and types and rates of delinquency, accident rates of different groups have not been systematically studied. There has, however, been some attempt to study the natural history of accidents among units of the armed services. In the following discussion we have drawn from the work of Paterson[48] illustrations whose value does not depend upon the theoretical interpretations placed upon them by their author.

One obvious difference between societies is the degree of sophistication with which they regard accidental occurrences. Complex chains of causation readily understood in some groups are beyond the comprehension of others. The degree of remoteness of the original action which can be seen as responsible for the final event depends not only on the knowledge of the linkages in the chain but also on the degree of probability for which the members of the group are accustomed to accepting responsibility. Let us take the example of the mechanic servicing an aeroplane. He may be told that a loose nut may come off in flight; the screw it retains might then fall into one of the moving parts of the engine and there cause some vital part to misfunction sufficiently to endanger the whole machine. But it hardly seems likely even to a trained man that a small thing such as a nut could imperil such a large and powerful object. Children are taught the jingle about the kingdom that was lost for the want of a horseshoe nail, but they do not believe it to be true except in the sense that they can accept fairy stories. As we shall see later, this has consequences for safety propaganda.

In some social groups sustaining an accident may be an accepted method of withdrawing from an unpleasant or unbearable situation. Hill and Trist[29] noted the very high rate of accidents in the British as compared with the American iron and steel industry. They showed that the men who stayed away from work most as a result of accidents tended to be those who were prone to other kinds of absenteeism (able-bodied absence for no accepted reason) and to be less likely than others to be absent with prior permission or with permission obtained retrospectively. They concluded that their results confirmed their hypothesis that accidents can be regarded as 'a means of withdrawal from the work situation through which the individual may take up the role of absentee in a way acceptable both to himself and to his employing organization'. On the other hand Keatinge and Box[31] examined absence sickness and accident rates in an ironworks and found that their 'low' accident group had a consistently *worse* record of absence without good reason. Their groups were small, thirty-nine in each, and different in age, the low accident group being older on average. They suggest that 'individuals do share a need to withdraw from work on occasion, but exhibit "preferred" means of doing so'. Some prefer to take a day off, some to find an excuse for a visit to the surgery. Many of the accident injuries were trivial and, as the authors point out, the accident records reflect differences in the tendency to report accidents as much as differences in tendency to sustain them. Castle[10] attempted to replicate Hill and Trist's findings in Kodak's Middlesex factory. His results also failed to substantiate their hypothesis that absence through accidents would be found to be positively related to other unsanctioned absences and negatively related to sanctioned absences. He pointed out that the social conditions of a light engineering establishment in a London suburb differed greatly from those of a heavy engineering works in the Northern Midlands and concluded that 'Accidents cannot be fruitfully studied otherwise than in their social context'. Although this sounds an austere judgement, it is notable that the findings of investigators seldom appear to hold for the groups and situations studied by other investigators. All the results reported must be (and to do their authors justice often have been) regarded as true 'for this group in this situation'.

Social groups differ not only in the probability which they assign to the likelihood of an accident resulting from their actions but also in the probability of injury or damage that they will accept. In particular the toleration of the danger of an accident will be high if taking care

Accidents at Work

conflicts with some other value strongly held. Recently concern was high over the practice by groups of American adolescents known as 'playing chicken'. Along the lines of children's 'last across', this involved driving old cars on a collision course; the 'chicken' being the first to take avoiding action. Among service pilots adherence to certain safety regulations tends to conflict with other cherished values (e.g. the pilot as a 'press-on type'). The belief that 'good' flying involved showing control of their aircraft, and therefore their ability to cut the margin of safety in landing prescribed by regulations, led even average pilots to errors in landing and sometimes to accidents.[48] To take another example; a group drinking in a pub has the convention that each member stands a round. Furthermore, the members of the group pride themselves on their ability to hold their liquor and to remain fit to drive home. This is an illustration of the common phenomenon of social facilitation of undesirable actions repugnant to the individual.

The rate at which accidents actually occur may depend upon the opinions of the group as to their inevitability. It is quite common for an aircraft newly received into service to acquire a reputation of being dangerous to operate: its initial accident rate is high compared with familiar models. As time passes the accident rate declines, partly because of mechanical modifications, partly because of accumulated experience. In time the machine is regarded as safe and fit to be flown by less experienced pilots. Aircraft differing vastly in every other characteristic share the same life history in this respect. It is likely that the most important factor accounting for the improvement in safe operation which occurs after the 'teething' period is the attitude of the group towards the chance of accident.

There is evidence that the frequency of accidents sustained in a group is related to its morale.[1, 49] Among the indicators of low morale which he found to be associated with large unit size of colliery, Revans[49] was able to include accident rates.

We may offer the hypothesis that people of low sociometric status may tend to exceed the normal rate of accidents for their group. Although the evidence for this is scanty, Paterson[48] mentions a pilot who was isolated by his group, regarded by them as 'sure to prang', and ultimately broke the group's clean accident record.

One has to live up to the expectations of one's group. It we stray too far from the role assigned to us we risk our comrades' disapprobation. 'The pilot might even find it easier to rebel against the dictates of the R.A.F. authorities than to act contrary to what his friends expected of him. What was expected of each pilot was the standard of his squadron, with a permissible latitude of behaviour according to the judgement of his particular idiosyncrasies. Jimmy indulged in aerobatics which were too low, but this was excused on the grounds "That's just like Jimmy",

259

whereas Bob did the same thing and his co-pilots, amazed, asked, "What's taken old Bob today?" Jimmy was expected to indulge occassionally in deviant behaviour, Bob was not. And both knew it!' It is not only the isolate who may be pushed by his relationships with his group over the bounds of safety.

Even where there is agreement as to what is and what is not safe, it is one thing to design safety procedures but quite another to get people to operate them. It is obvious that the safe way may not be the quickest and most immediately profitable; it may, for example, involve cumbersome or unaesthetic protective clothing or footwear. Even Draconian attempts to load the scales against the dangerous short cut by the threat of instant dismissal for anyone caught disobeying the regulations frequently fail because the penalty is not accepted as reasonable by the group, which may react to a dismissal with a strike. Even devices intended to make the unsafe method technically impossible may be frustrated by ingenious operators if they feel too constrained by them.

Quite a different problem is encounted when certain prophylactic measures are attempted. The reporting of an occurrence which might lead to an accident and its thorough investigation may place a heavy load of responsibility on the shoulders of men untrained to accept and unaccustomed to exercise it. To take another example from service life, a mechanic who mislays a tool after working on an aircraft must report the loss immediately. He knows that if he does, the aircraft will be completely stripped, if necessary, to search for it—a long and expensive procedure. If the tool is found, his carelessness in losing it is, of course, far outweighed by his caution and public spirit in reporting the loss and possibly averting a disaster. But suppose the aircraft is stripped down and no tool is found? Would he ever be able to live that down? The decision whether or not to report and have the aircraft stripped down is his, and a difficult one for him to take. In such a situation many of us would prefer prayer to action.

Maintenance staff at one refuelling depot were instructed to examine carefully aircraft tyres and report to the tyre specialist any appearing to be even slightly damaged. An unexpectedly high rate of tyre failures led to an inquiry. It appeared that, unwilling to call out the specialist time and again to no purpose, the maintenance staff were making sure of any doubtful crack by ripping it further with a penknife. By this action they were freed from both the risk of derision and the fear of failing to prevent an accident.

Safety Propaganda

Some of the considerations we have mentioned above are relevant to the conduct of safety campaigns. It is obvious that a favourable attitude to the campaign on the part of those to whom it is directed is essential for its success. If cautionary tales are used, they must have simple chains of causation. Complex chains, even if the stories are true, may be thought far-fetched and will lack conviction.

Accident or near-accident reporting drives may fail or may achieve results the reverse of what is desired. In one establishment, of which the units were proud of their safety record, the drive to obtain sufficient records for comparison led to widening the definition of accidents. To keep its own good record each unit tended to suppress reports of near-accidents. This partly undid the beneficial practice of reporting all 'special occurrences' on the basis of which it was hoped to learn the causes of accidents.

The best way to encourage safety-mindedness and the observance of safety precautions might well be to place responsibility in the hands of a respected member of the group—not an outside expert, nor a member of the group chosen for the task because he is less valuable in other ways than his colleagues. An indication in favour of this view is the finding that the buying and wearing of safety footwear by steelworkers was in response to hearsay and secondhand opinion from workmates of high prestige rather than to the urging of official propaganda.[6] A typical further indication comes once more from a service situation: to conceal from themselves their responsibility for minor accidents pilots at 'Bogfield' blamed the condition of the airfield runways;[48] the notion that some of their number were careless or poor pilots would have endangered the cohesion of their group and could not be accepted. Any attempt to tighten observance of safety measures imposed from outside the group would be bitterly resented—'chairborne' advice is scorned. In such circumstances the best hope for improvement lies in a group decision to adopt higher standards; for this the lead must come from a respected member of the group. Appointing and training a member of a working group as safety officer is likely to be more effective than recruiting or appointing a safety officer from outside the group.

The safety 'message' must not conflict with other cherished values of the group. A group which prides itself on being 'death or glory boys' is unlikely to be receptive of pleas for caution. Safe operation as the summit of skill must be inculcated. The Royal Air Force aerobatic team is accorded immense prestige by pilots who are prepared to accept their record of freedom from accidents as a model, and an increasingly sound basis for safety in flying lies in the serious professionalism of the modern pilot's outlook.

An underlying factor opposing the acceptance of 'safety first' attitudes may be the need felt by many who lead a secure sheltered life for the tonic stimulus of risk. If people, as Scott[51] suggests, go through their work subconsciously balancing economy of effort against

261

risk-taking so that their liability to accident remains constant, the removal of obvious hazards may be less effective in reducing accidents than the provision of some more exciting off-duty activity. The message of the safety poster may even be, in its ultimate effect, 'Take risks and be a gay, carefree character', and Scott instances Fougasse's 'famous last words' series as possibly having this effect.

The message should be factual rather than hortatory; instructive rather than horrifying. For example, Laner and Sell[37] have shown that posters demonstrating the correct procedure for hooking a crane sling were effective in improving practice, and concluded that the more relevant to their situation the poster was felt to be by those at whom it was aimed, the more effective it was likely to be.

Conclusion and Summary

In some respects, as the reader will have seen, accidents are an unsatisfactory subject for study. Those accidents accessible to study do not constitute a unique class of events; many occurrences that would be classified as accidents in one setting or by one set of investigators would be unrecorded in other settings or ignored by other investigators. Those occurrences which are by common consent accidents, owe this distinction to the fact that they involve damage to property, or injury to the person, of a more than trivial nature. Yet the fact that injury is sustained or damage caused is itself a function of chance: if a man on a scaffolding drops a brick unintentionally, there is an accidental error; it may fall into a patch of mud with no damage even to the brick, or through a greenhouse or on to a passer-by with greater or lesser injury to him. In the last case who has had the accident, the bricklayer or the passer-by?

With a class of phenomena so unamenable to identification and classification, any refinement of statistical analysis is likely to give disappointing or even spurious results. The discussion of accident-proneness served the purpose of demonstrating the fact that individuals differed in their liability to figure in the statistics of accidents recorded. It failed to establish that proneness to accidents was an enduring characteristic of certain individuals that would be apparent in all their activities.

Attempts to find tests predictive of individual liability to accidents are limited by the inadequacy of the criterion against which the tests have to be measured and by the instability of the factors sought. Furthermore the results achieved suggest strongly that there is present an element highly specific to the task situation in which the accidents occur. That is to say, the tests are predictive largely to the extent that they contain elements of the skill present in the task. People liable to error in the task are liable to error in the test. The exhaustive study by Häkkinen[25] of 1,000 bus and train drivers in Helsinki, using a battery of fourteen tests and producing predictive correlations with accident records as high as a 'multiple r' of 0·64 in the group studied, did not establish the advisability of their use for purposes of preselection.

It has been possible to show that heightened emotional states are associated with some accidents and that unconscious aggressive or self-destructive motives are often present. It is clear also that the attributes of the social group are important determinants of the likelihood of accidents occurring to its members and that these are particularly relevant to the effectiveness of safety measures.

What then are the further studies which we may hope will serve the social purpose of reducing accidents?

Improved Ergonomic Design

There has in recent years been no more encouraging development in applied experimental psychology than the great leap forward in the analysis of skill. The way in which the human operator functions is now much better understood, though a great deal remains to be learned. Man's abilities as a monitoring and regulating mechanism and the limits of these abilities are largely known. We can predict the kind of situation which makes demands upon the operator which are likely to lead to errors. Attention can now be paid to designing tasks in such a way as to fit in with man's known capacities and to supplement them where they are known to be weak. In particular we know that man's capacity for immediate memory is comparatively poor and liable to disruption or interference by other activities. By transferring from the operator to the machine the function of retaining information we can make the task easier and safer.[49] It is beginning to be realized that not all the mechanization and automation that has been introduced has been completely satisfactory in improving either efficiency or safe working. The choice of the functions that are to be mechanized is sometimes made on grounds which do not take into consideration the kind of task best removed from the human operator because of his limitations or best left to the exercise of human capacities. Understandably the functions which are chosen for mechanization tend to be those for which engineering developments have made mechanization possible. An increasing proportion of tasks in industry are vigilance tasks which have their own characteristic opportunities for errors. Fortunately it is often possible to build in engineering safety devices in highly mechanized plant, and careful study is required of the sources of error worth counteracting in this way.

A. B. Cherns

The Social Setting

Accidents occur in a social context, and if they are to be fully understood must be studied in their context. Comparative studies of the incidence and types of accidents occurring in different social groups will tell us much not only about the groups but also about the factors which must be manipulated if accidents are to be avoided. Safety propaganda is tricky to handle. If it appears to constitute a danger to group cohesiveness it will be rejected. Even good ergonomic design of the job may fail to yield its full return either in work done or in accidents avoided if it does not take account of the whole job situation.

The studies conducted by the British Iron and Steel Research Association[6] take as their point of departure the new entrant into industry and regard accidents not as isolated incidents but as symptoms of his social and occupational adjustment. They are concerned with the interplay between accidents and other aspects of an employee's relationships with the employing works. Safety is associated with selection, placement, induction, and training and thus is not a specialist function but a direct responsibility of management at all levels. This wider view is a welcome development.

The Interdisciplinary Approach

Within the compass of this chapter we have been able to regard accidents from a position which affords a view of the psychological and sociological aspects of the problem. But we have said nothing of the economic and legal aspects. Our social attitudes towards accidents, and industry's concern about their financial and social cost, have been affected not only by the growth of our knowledge but also by the increasing economic cost of labour and by the statutory duties laid on employers by successive Factories Acts. Nor is the law of workmen's compensation based solely on statutory provisions; the tendency of the courts to impose wider interpretations of the common law duty of care has been a product of, and a stimulus to, a growing belief that accidents can and should be prevented and that the employer has a duty to take active steps to prevent them. Investigators have naturally tended to emphasize the variables with which their own specialisms are concerned.[50] This is, however, an area of social study which ought to repay the interdisciplinary approach: the goal of fitting the whole job to the whole man cannot be attained by specialists in one discipline alone.

Accidents at Work

REFERENCES

1. Acton Society Trust (1953, 1957) *Size and Morale*, parts 1 and 2.
2. ANNETT, J., & KAY, H. (1956) 'Skilled Performance'. *Occup. Psychol.*, **30** (2), 112.
3. ARBOUS, A. G. (1951), see below, no. 32, Part I.
4. BIESHEUVEL, S., & WHITE, M. E. (1949) 'The Human Factor in Flying Accidents'. *South African Air Force Journal*, **1**, 25–31.
5. BOGARDUS, E. S. (1912) 'Relation of Fatigue to Industrial Accidents'. *Amer. J. Sociol.*, **17**, 206–22, 351–74, 512–39.
6. BOX, A. (1960) 'Accident Research in the British Iron and Steel Industry'. British Iron and Steel Research Association. Report, OR/HF/64/60, November 1960.
7. BROADBENT, D. E. (1958) *Perception and Communication*. London: Pergamon.
8. BROWN, C. W., & GHISELLI, E. E. (1947) 'Factors Related to the Proficiency of Motor Coach Operators'. *J. appl. Psychol.*, **31**, 477–9.
9. BROWN, C. W., & GHISELLI, E. E. (1948) 'Accident Proneness among Street Car Motormen and Motorcoach Operators'. *J. appl. Psychol.*, **32**, 20–23.
10. CASTLE, P. F. C. (1956) 'Accidents, Absence and Withdrawal from the Work Situation'. *Hum. Relat.*, **9** (2), 223.
11. DALTON, KATHARINE (1960) 'Menstruation and Accidents'. *Brit. med. J.*, 12 Nov. 1960, 1425.
12. DAVIS, D. R. (1948) 'Increase in Strength of a Secondary Drive as a Cause of Disorganization'. *Quart. J. exp. Psychol.*, **1**, 22–28.
13. DAVIS, D. R. (1958) 'Human Errors and Transport Accidents'. *Ergonomics*, **2** (1), 24.
14. DAVIS, D. R. (1949) 'The Disorder of Skill Responsible for Accidents'. *Quart. J. exp. Psychol.*, **1**, 136–42.
15. DAVIS, R. (1957) 'The Human Operator as a Single Channel Information System'. *Quart. J. exp. Psychol.*, **9**, 119–29.
16. DREW, G. C. (1960) 'Human Problems in Transport'. Paper read to 'Ergonomics in Industry', 29 September 1960 (D.S.I.R. Conference on Ergonomics).
17. EYSENCK, H. (1960) 'Psychology and the Prevention of Road Accidents'. *New Scientist*, 7 July 1960, 18.
18. FARMER, E.; CHAMBERS, E. G.; & KIRK, F. S. (1933) 'Tests for Accident Proneness'. *Industrial Health Research Board* Report no. 68.
19. FORBES, T. W. (1939) 'The Normal Automobile Driver as a Traffic Problem'. *J. gen. Psychol.*, **20**, 471–4.
20. FREUD, S. (1915–17) *Introductory Lectures on Psycho-Analysis.* London: Allen & Unwin, 1952, p. 48.
21. FREUD, S. (1901) *The Psychopathology of Everyday Life.* London: Benn, 1960.
22. GREENWOOD, M., & WOODS, H. M. 'The Incidence of Industrial Accidents upon Individuals with Special Reference to Multiple

A. B. Cherns

Accidents'. Industrial Fatigue Research Board Report no. 4. London: H.M.S.O.

23. GRIEW, S. (1958) 'A Study of Accidents in Relation to Occupation and Age'. *Ergonomics*, **2** (1), 17.

24. GUIGUET, S. & FDÉDA, D. (1956) 'Première étude sur les cabines de pelles mécaniques'. *Bull. Cent. étud. rech. psychotech.*, **5** (4), 407–23.

25. HÄKKINEN, S. (1958) 'Traffic Accidents and Driver Characteristics: A Statistical and Psychological Study'. Helsinki: Finland's Institute of Technology, Scientific Researches, no. 13.

26. HICK, W. E. (1952) 'On the Rate of Gain of Information'. *Quart. J. exp. Psychol.*, **4**, 11–26.

27. HICK, W. E. (1952) 'Why the Human Operator'. *Trans. Soc. Instrum. Tech.*, **4**, 66–77.

28. HICK, W. E. (1948) 'The Discontinuous Functioning of the Human Operator in Pursuit Tasks'. *Quart. J. exp. Psychol.*, **1**, 36–51.

29. HILL, J. M. M. & TRIST, E. L. (1953) 'A Consideration of Industrial Accidents as a Means of Withdrawal from the Work Situation'. *Hum. Relat.*, **6** (4), 357.

30. KAY, H. (1953) 'Experimental Studies of Adult Learning'. Cambridge University Library, Ph. D. Thesis.

31. KEATINGE, G. F. & BOX, A. (1960) 'Accident, Sickness, and Absence Records; A Comparative Study of the Matched Group'. British Iron and Steel Research Association. Report OR/HF/62/60, October 1960.

32. KERRICH, J. E. (1951) in ARBOUS, A. G. & KERRICH, J. E., 'Accident Statistics and the Concept of Accident Proneness: Part II. The Mathematical Background'. *Biometrics*, **7**, 391–432.

33. KING, H. F. (1955) 'An Age-Analysis of Some Agricultural Accidents'. *Occup. Psychol.*, **29**, 245–53.

34. KING, H. F., & SPEAKMAN, D. (1953) 'Age and Industrial Accident Rates'. *Brit. J. industr. Med.*, **10**, 51–58.

35. LAHY, J. M., & KORNGOLD, S. (1936) 'Recherches experimentales sur les causes psychologiques des accidents du travail'. *Travail hum.*, **4**, 1–64.

36. LAHY, J. M., & KORNGOLD, S. (1938) 'Stimulation à cadence rapide et motricité chez les sujets frequemment blessés.' *Année psychol.*, **38**, 86–139.

37. LANER, S., & SELL, R. G. (1960) 'Experiment on the Effect of Specially Designed Safety Posters'. *Occup. Psychol.*, **34** (3), 153–69.

38. LÖWENSTEIN, H. (1934) 'The Nature of Industrial Accident Proneness'. *Industr. Saf. Surv.*, **10** (1).

39. MCFARLAND, R. A., & MOSELEY, A. L. (1954) 'Human Factors in Highway Transport Safety'. Boston: Harvard School of Public Health.

40. MACKWORTH, N. H. (1948) 'The Breakdown of Vigilance during Prolonged Visual Search'. *Quart. J. exp. Psychol.*, **1**, 6–21.

41. MACKWORTH, N. H., & MACKWORTH, J. F. (1950) 'Remembering Advance Cues during Searching'. MRC APRU Report, 258, 1950.

42. MARBE, K. (1926) 'Prakt. Psychologie d. Unfälle und Betriebsschäden' Oldenbourg, Munich.
43. MENNINGER, KARL (1959) 'Protecting the Whole Man: Mental Health'. *Occup. Hazards*, April 1959, p. 29.
44. MENNINGER, KARL (1959) *Nat. Safety News*, May 1959, p. 25.
45. MKELE, N. (1955) 'The Two-Hand Co-ordination Test'. *J. nat. Inst. Pers. Res.*, **6**, 30–33.
46. MOSELEY, A. L. (1959) 'Motives Leading to Safe and Unsafe Acts'. *Nat. Safety News*, May 1959.
47. NEWBOLD, E. H. (1926) 'Contribution to the Study of the Human Factor in the Causation of Accidents', *Industrial Health Research Board Report* no. 34.
48. PATERSON, T. T. (1955) *Morale in War and Work*. London: Parrish.
49. REVANS, R. W. (1955) 'Scale Factors in the Management of Coalmines'. *Operat. Res. Quart.*, **6** (3).
50. SAINT-JUST, R. C. (1956) 'Evolution des idées sur les accidents du travail'. *Bull. Cent. étud. rech. psychotech.*, **6** (2). 193–204.
51. SCOTT, T. H. (1953) 'Accidents, the Unsafe Attitude'. *Brit. J. industr. Safety*, **24**, 213.
52. SHELDON, J. H. (1960) *Brit. med. J.*, 5214, 10 December 1960, p. 1685.
53. SMILEY, J. A. (1955) 'A Clinical Study of a Group of Accident-prone Workers'. *Brit. J. industr. Med.*, **12**, 263.
54. THORNDIKE, R. L. (1951) 'The Human Factor in Accidents'. USAF School of Aviation Medicine, February 1951.
55. 'Three Pilot System in Vanguard'. *The Times*, 19 December 1960, p. 3.
56. VERNON, H. M. (1919) 'Two Contributions to the Study of Accident Causation'. *Industrial Fatigue Research Board, Report no. 19.*
57. VERNON, H. M., & BEDFORD, T. (1928) 'A Study of Absenteeism in a Group of Ten Collieries'. *Industrial Fatigue Research Board, report no. 51.*
58. VERNON, H. M., & BEDFORD, T. (1931) 'The Absenteeism of Miners in Relation to Short Time and other Conditions'. *Industrial Health Research Board*, report no. 62.
59. WELFORD, A. T. (1952) 'The "Psychological Refractory Period" and the Timing of High-speed Performance; a Review and a Theory'. *Brit. J. Psychol.*, **43**, 2–19.
60. WELFORD, A. T. (1959) 'Evidence of a Single-Channel Decision Mechanism Limiting Performance in a Serial Reaction Task'. *Quart. J. exp. Psychol.*, **4**, 193–210.
61. WELFORD, A. T. (1958) *Ageing and Human Skill*. London: Oxford Univ. Press.
62. WELFORD, A. T. (1960) *Ergonomics of Automation: Problems of Progress in Industry no. 8*. Department of Scientific and Industrial Research. London: H.M.S.O.
63. WHITFIELD, J. W. (1954) 'Individual Differences in Accident Susceptibility among Coalminers'. *Brit. J. industr. Med.*, **11**, 126–39.

I5

ROAD ACCIDENTS

F. Garwood

THE PROBLEM

THE problem of road accidents can be regarded in the first place as one facing governmental and other organizations who are trying to provide for the safe and efficient use of roads. The legislature is responsible for making and amending the highway laws, while the police and the judicature enforce and administer these laws. They cannot, however, be constantly enforced on every mile of road and the authorities must continually strive to improve road usage by education and propaganda, or must make roads and vehicles more foolproof. Their problem is very often that of obtaining enough resources—parliamentary time for legislation, man-power for police work, money for road improvements and propaganda. But a major difficulty is a general apathy, on the part of most people, towards the seriousness of the problem.

The individual's point of view is another way of considering the problem. It is a serious matter to some, as for example the mother who has to keep her child out of harm's way when there is inadequate garden space. At the other end of the age-scale there are people who are ill-fitted to see, hear, and react to vehicles when they are crossing a road; they are a worry to those responsible for their welfare. There are the relatives and friends of those who are killed at the annual rate of about seven thousand, to say nothing of the others who are permanently incapacitated. For other people, however, the problem does not appear to be one which ranks with domestic and personal worries, and it is against this background that the authorities must try to provide the resources.

F. Garwood

The magnitude of the problem is further indicated in the detailed statistics of casualties to the different classes of road user in the official returns of the Ministry of Transport and of the Registrars General; it is worth noting that the number of deaths is below the pre-war level, but appears to be rising, while the total number of casualties has reached a record high level.

Another way of approaching the problem is to compare the risks of travelling by various forms of transport, which involves the computation of annual vehicle-miles on various classes of vehicle.[7] The data available for 1952–1957 show that the risks of death per 10^9 miles travelled in Great Britain were as follows:

	Risk of death per 10^9 miles
Rider of motor-cycle	246
Rider of pedal cycle	57
Driver of other vehicle	11
Passenger on railway	3·7

The magnitude of the problem has also been assessed in economic terms. Reynolds[37] estimated the cost of road accidents occurring in 1952 to be £72 millions, of which one-half resulted from the loss of output due to injury and death, one-quarter from damage to property, and the rest from medical treatment and the administration of motor insurance. The annual cost, which does not attempt to assess human suffering, is estimated for more recent years to exceed £100 millions.[20]

Causes and Factors

It should be emphasized that a policy of accident reduction cannot usefully be based entirely on a technique of collecting the statistics of causes of individual accidents and giving priority to attempts to remove the commonest ones. Most accidents may be found to be caused by certain human errors, but this does not justify concentrating all efforts on removing them; they may be very hard to remove. In addition there are the difficulties of collecting relevant facts about each accident or of interpreting the facts in relation to causes.

Although these cause statistics are of value if interpreted with caution, it is preferable to regard the frequency of all accidents as the dependent variate and to find how it is related to other variates. For instance, it is known that reductions in the accident rate occur at sites where certain changes in road layout or road surfaces are made, and a further example is the provision of good street lighting in place of bad, which reduces the proportion of accidents which occur at night. In this case the improvement occurs in spite of a slight tendency for speeds to increase. Where deliberate attempts are made to reduce speeds the indication is that accident frequencies generally fall. Several examples of this effect in the case of speed limits are described by Garwood and Duff,[18] and another notable instance occurred as part of the Slough Experiment[25] in which a length of trunk road A4 was fitted with a set of eleven linked lights designed to control the speed at about 26–28 m.p.h. The frequency of fatal and serious accidents fell by about 70 per cent after this was done.

This was one feature of an experiment in which the people of the town of Slough, Buckinghamshire, the police, and various government departments and organizations participated. The measures covered a wide field, dealing with such aspects as education, training, poster campaigns, vehicle-testing schemes, police activity, experimental warning signs, and various road engineering and traffic schemes. The experiment showed that a co-operative effort in a small town could achieve a useful reduction in accidents, estimated in the case of serious accidents at 20 per cent. It is of interest to note that after the end of the experiment a measure affecting a wide cross-section of the population was introduced, namely an order making it an offence to allow dogs to be free on any road in the borough. In the following ten months no personal-injury accident involving a dog occurred, compared with an expected number of about eight. Behaviour and attitude were observed during the experiment by the Social Survey, who have done much work on the kind of publicity which is most readily recalled, and the way in which behaviour tends to be related to opinion. Thus Willcock[44] found that pedestrians who made better use of crossings tended, when interviewed, to say that the best type of publicity was one which emphasized the importance of safety at all times; the less careful pedestrian preferred themes which were of a horrific nature, or stressed the need to look after one's own skin. The work of Belbin[4] on the effects of propaganda on recall, recognition, and behaviour may also be referred to in this connexion.

Conflicts of Interest

Had the potentialities of the internal combustion engine been foreseen, better facilities for road transport might have been provided, such as wider streets, more roads avoiding the narrow streets of small towns, and the proper segregation of pedestrians and traffic. To do this now would be expensive, and although some of the changes may be economically justified there may be opposing desires to preserve certain amenities such as old buildings of architectural interest. Conflicts of interest of other kinds may arise, for instance, between the inhabitants of a village and the highway authority; the former may press for a speed limit on a busy road running through it, while the latter may be faced with many similar claims of varying importance elsewhere. Another example is supplied by 'no loading or unloading' restrictions; these may increase the cost of delivering goods to shops, but may also be an aid to safety and free-flowing traffic which benefits perhaps a wider group of people.

Legal Restrictions on Road Users

Such conflicts of interest are inevitable in society, and no substantial progress towards a solution of the problem is likely unless road users generally accept some incursions into what they now regard as freedoms. How far, in fact, are various classes of road user now legally restricted, and how far do they observe the law and the Highway Code? Detailed answers are not possible, but a few can be given.

All that was effectively asked of the pedestrian until 1956 was that he should not loiter on a pedestrian crossing. By the Road Traffic Act of that year he was required to obey a policeman's direction to stop crossing or proceeding along the road, which most people would regard as a small additional restriction on their freedom. It is a common observation that pedestrians, like other road users, often ignore the Highway Code. For example, day-time counts showed that, where roads had no footpaths, two-thirds of pedestrians walked with their backs to traffic and so disobeyed Rule 3 of the Code. Accident statistics show that to walk in this way is one-and-a-half times more dangerous than if the traffic is faced, so that the rule is sound.[39] To obey the Code sometimes involves a prohibitive effort: if the alternative to the surface of the road is a subway, the latter will be ignored by most pedestrians unless its use takes less time. A bridge needs to be 25 per cent quicker in order to attract most pedestrians.[35] Pedestrians are rarely found liable in legal proceedings, but almost all the 2408 who died in 1958 must be regarded as having paid the supreme penalty for offences against the law or the Highway Code, whether committed by themselves or by others.

Pedal cyclists are also comparatively immune from the direct attention of the law. Recent legislation has tightened things up somewhat in respect of cycling recklessly or under the influence of drink, failing to stop after an accident (these offences previously applied to motor vehicles only), and in respect of lighting—surveys in 1950 proved that 12 per cent of cyclists were not showing a rear light at night.[38] As with pedestrians, the penalty which they pay, as a group, is a heavy one. In 1956, in those fatal accidents involving two vehicles of which one was a pedal cycle, the people killed included 514 pedal cyclists, 14 motorcyclists or their passengers, and 4 drivers or passengers of other vehicles;

136 pedal cyclists were killed in other accidents, about half of them involving pedal cycles only.

In contrast, the owners and drivers of mechanically-propelled vehicles are subject to a wide set of legal restrictions, and the number of recorded offences is correspondingly high—674,000 in England and Wales in 1958, resulting in fines totalling more than £1·7 million, excluding costs. Among the specific offences the commonest were speeding in built-up areas (88,435) and obstructions of the highway or parking offences (90,145). More than 1400 additional charges were dealt with by committal for trial, 'under the influence of drink or drugs' accounting for 639.[26]

Whether or not a motorist is committing an offence at some particular instant may be a subjective question; there can be no clear line separating dangerous from careless, or careless from safe driving. On the other hand, many offences, such as exceeding the speed limit, are factual. Speed measurements taken in the course of various studies support the very common observation that there are many places where the legal speed limit is frequently broken. This applies not only to the 30 m.p.h. limit in restricted areas for all vehicles, but also to the general 30 m.p.h. limit for goods vehicles and public service vehicles. When it was in operation the 20 m.p.h. limit for heavy lorries was exceeded in almost all the measurements; the limit was raised to 30 m.p.h. in 1957, and at three sites where comparisons were made before and after, the percentage of heavy goods vehicles exceeding 30 m.p.h. changed from 45 to 56 (Road Research Laboratory, unpublished report).

The breaking of the letter of the law can be observed quantitatively in other ways. The Road Research Laboratory[40] has observed the frequency with which vehicles pass traffic lights when at 'red' or which fail to stop at 'Halt' signs, while voluntary tests at the vehicle-testing station of the Ministry of Transport showed,[43] among other defects, that 14 per cent of cars under ten years old, and 18 per cent of older cars, had one or more of the side and rear lights not working or not showing the correct colour.

These observations do not, of course, by themselves provide evidence that dangerous conditions always occur as a result of this widespread law-breaking. Nevertheless, many people think that the state of society cannot be regarded as satisfactory if its laws are transgressed so often. There is no doubt, too, that the law is consciously broken. When the police made a radar speed check in the Slough experiment at the outskirts of a restricted area, and advertised their presence by notice boards, average speeds of all vehicles fell by about 1½ m.p.h. The presence of a policeman can also improve the general standard of behaviour at uncontrolled pedestrian crossings, and this may operate directly both for drivers and pedestrians. Police activity can have a quite rapid effect

F. Garwood

on the condition of vehicle maintenance. On the first day of a check by the Cambridge police on the brakes of cycles stopped at random only one cycle in four had both brakes efficient, but this proportion rose steadily during the first week to a level of about three out of four. In the pre-war Home Office Motor Patrol Scheme[27] the number of police on traffic duties was augmented in a number of areas; this prevented about 10 per cent of accidents, and was no doubt due in part to the actual presence of police on the road.

Distribution of Accidents among Individuals

It should be noted that the average driver rarely has an accident. The average private car, for instance, is involved in one personal-injury accident every thirty years, and appears in an insurance claim once every six years. It is possible that an accident is likely to encourage a driver to make a frank appraisal of his driving ability and perhaps to cure temporarily his more obvious errors. But the low average rate suggests that such learning from experience is not likely to occur frequently, and many drivers may be lucky and escape accidents while persisting in bad driving habits which tend to depress the generally accepted standards.

The 'average driver' is of course a statistical fiction, and the distribution of accidents per driver is wider than would occur if chance were the only factor. It is necessary to introduce a mathematical model and to postulate a more complex hypothesis, and an appropriate one is that each driver would have attached to him an 'expected rate' of λ accidents per year. This would be regarded as compounding the effects of mileage, possible physiological or psychological characteristics, including age, and the traffic and road conditions to which the driver is exposed. Evidence that the latter exist is shown by the different rates per vehicle-mile on various roads in rural areas, or by the rates per bus-mile on different routes. Of drivers with a given λ, the proportion with any number of accidents would be given by chance, i.e. by the Poisson distribution with mean λ, and the final proportion obtained by superimposing a suitable distribution of λ over the population. Students of industrial accidents have used a Pearson Type III distribution for the latter, leading to a negative binomial for the accidents. Motor insurance claim records[30] have also been fitted reasonably well in this way. However, it should be emphasized that this hypothesis is not completely satisfactory. It is the personal-injury accidents, particularly the fatal and serious ones, which make the greatest drain on the economy of the country, and no information is available about the distribution of drivers involved in this class. It is known from the regular returns of the Ministry of Transport that the statistical severity of any group of accidents tends to be higher when the associated conditions involve higher speeds. For example, on roads subject to a speed limit, the proportion which are fatal or serious is lower than the corresponding proportion on unrestricted roads, and it tends to be higher for the faster vehicle. It is therefore conceivable that the distribution of 'expected rate' for the more serious accidents is different in shape from that for all accidents; furthermore it is more likely that the original hypothesis will fail in that the occurrence of one serious accident will influence the chance of another one occurring.

One corollary of the hypothesis is that drivers who have an accident rate higher than average in their earlier years do so also in later years. This is confirmed in the insurance study referred to, but it is also observed that the drivers in this group tend to improve, whereas those who had no claim in their first year tended to remain at a uniform level from the second year onwards.

Psychological and Physiological Factors

Many attempts have been made to find characteristics which can be used to predict the drivers likely to have a high accident rate, or, from the statistical point of view, to find human characteristics correlating with the hypothetical λ. The results of these tests, which range from pencil and paper questions to elaborate psycho-physical tests, are frequently disappointing. There is conflicting evidence, for instance, on the importance of a short reaction time, and about intelligence.[6, 19, 21] Physical characteristics, such as blood pressure, vision, and hearing were found to have a very small—often non-significant—correlation with accidents. Farmer & Chambers,[16] using a battery of tests of manipulative skill, found differences which were just statistically significant. The Eno Foundation for Highway Traffic Control, Saugatuck, Connecticut[14, 15] has also published numerous reports on the subject, and has also given useful descriptions of schemes used in some states (e.g. Connecticut, Texas, and Oregon) for driver improvement and control. In some of these records are kept of traffic offences and accident involvement on a points system, leading to interviews and tests with the object of revealing possible faults, or at the other extreme, to suspension of licence. For studies of the effect of age the reader may be referred to[24, 36], and the annual reports of the Road Research Laboratory for 1955 and 1958. Häkkinen[23] in his report on the important investigation of accidents to drivers of buses and trams in Helsinki, reviews much of the previous work on the subject. He found a continuous reduction in accidents during the first 4–5 years of employment, and also a continuous decline up to the age of 45–48. He claims to have found associations of accident rate with eye-hand co-ordination, psycho-motor, personality and other tests, although it would be useful to know more about his method of allowing for age differences than can be discovered from his report.

It is sometimes held that something other than pure skill or physical fitness but rather like temperament is important.[1, 13, 42] This can be defined roughly as mental and emotional outlook. Clark,[8] in an investigation for the British War Office, found that army drivers who were involved in accidents frequently had a history of military indiscipline and in civilian lives changed jobs frequently, and reference may also be made to recent work by Davis & Coiley.[10]

It seems that information about a person's temperament and background, together with his accident record, would appear to offer the most promising means of indicating accident-proneness. In general, such information will enable an accident-prone group of individuals to be selected from a larger group of drivers. If, however, such tests are used for selection or detection of accident-prone individuals, then injustice will be done to some people. The chief usefulness of accident-proneness testing is likely to be in the field of commercial and passenger transport organizations. There is an extensive literature on accident-proneness and driver selection; further useful information and references are given, for example, in [29, 34,] and [2,] the last being a critical review of the concept of proneness, where the reader will find in particular a full mathematical treatment with references to the original work by Greenwood & Woods.[22]

There is a very extensive and useful review of the literature on the human factor by McFarland, Moore and Warren,[32] who found that the correlations between driver characteristics and accidents were low, and useless as a basis for predicting the accident tendencies of individual drivers. They thought that the study of accident repeaters and of the circumstances of their accidents was more likely to result in basic knowledge than attempts to prove differences in susceptibility, and they saw promise in the concept that 'a man drives as he lives' as a practical method of detecting the accident-repeater.

Effect of Alcohol

The official figures probably underestimate the number of accidents to which alcohol contributes. Thus in 1954, 2 per cent of the road fatalities in Great Britain were attributed to persons being under the influence of drink or drugs. On the other hand, when detailed reports of all fatal accidents in three sample areas were examined,[28] it was found that out of the total of 376 fatalities, in 18 per cent at least one of the principal parties was recorded as having recently drunk alcohol. When accidents between 10 p.m. and 4 a.m. only were considered, 50 per cent

Road Accidents

of the drivers and 62 per cent of the pedestrians had been drinking. Even more pronounced results were obtained over the Christmas of 1959.[41] A more positive way of demonstrating the effect of alcohol, carried out in Toronto, was to compare the distribution of blood alcohol of drivers involved in accidents with that of samples of four or more drivers passing the scene soon after each accident. This produced the following results:

	Accident Sample	Control
Percentage of drivers with at least 0·05 per cent blood alcohol . . .	22·5	8·7
Percentage of drivers with at least 0·15 per cent blood alcohol . . .	11	1·4

indicating the greater alcohol content of the accident group. Drew et al.,[12] using a laboratory measurement of a skill resembling driving, showed that performance deteriorates progressively from very low concentrations (0·02 per cent); Cohen et al.[9] deduced from a controlled experiment on bus drivers, involving the driving of a bus through narrow gaps, that small amounts, roughly the same as those given by Drew, adversely affected the judgement of the drivers and increased their confidence at difficult tasks. In Sweden and some American states it is an offence to drive if the blood content exceeds 0·15 per cent, and in Norway the level is 0·05 per cent. At present, however, British law does not lay down any figure for the level of blood or urine alcohol content, the exceeding of which shall constitute an offence. Further references are given in the Proceedings of the First International Conference on Alcohol and Traffic,[17] and a comprehensive survey of the whole position was made by a Special Committee of the British Medical Association,[5] which concluded, among other things, that 'relatively low concentrations of alcohol in the tissues cause a deterioration in driving performance and increase appreciably the likelihood of accident', and 'The existing legislation does not come into effective operation until a very much higher concentration of alcohol in the tissues has been reached, and is unsuccessful as a measure to prevent accidents caused by alcohol'.

Accidents to Children

Some of the factors which may be influencing the accident rate among children have been studied by Backett and Johnston.[3] By comparing the family background of 100 children concerned in non-fatal pedestrian accidents in Belfast with those of 100 control children matched in

277

F. Garwood

respect of age, sex, and living area, they showed associations of the accident group with histories of family illness, preoccupation of the mother with other young children, inadequate playing space, and similar factors. Some of the variations with social class are indicated as a by-product of the follow-up study of 5,000 children made by Douglas & Blomfield,[11] who found that the number of children of manual workers knocked down by cars exceeded the corresponding number of children of nonmanual workers, the reverse being the case for children injured in other accidents associated with cars, presumably while riding as passengers.

The time distributions of child accidents in various months of the year bring out the dangers associated with going to and from school, and in this connexion it may be noted that in the Slough Experiment children were persuaded to use safer routes to one of the schools. Other associations revealed by the statistics include the tendency for young children to be involved with goods vehicles, particularly those used for delivering purposes, which start up from rest and trap the child who may be playing too near or under them. One feature of the situation which offers slight encouragement, however, is the fact that the standardized fatality rate among child pedestrians is falling, especially as compared with rises in other age groups. Thus the standardized death rate to pedestrians under 15 in Great Britain fell by one-third from 1949 to 1958, while those in the age groups 15–60 and over 60 rose by 25 per cent and 18 per cent respectively.

From this brief survey it will be evident that there is much scope for research in tackling the road accident problem, and much of this should consist of a scientific study of our society as it functions today.

REFERENCES

1. ALEXANDER, C. (1953) *Traffic Quarterly*, Eno Foundation for Highway Traffic Control, p. 186. Saugatuck, Connecticut.
2. ARBOUS, A. G., & KERRICH, J. E. (1951) *Biometrics*, **7** (4), 379.
3. BACKETT, E. M., & JOHNSTON, A. M. (1959) *Brit. med. J.*, 14 Feb. 1959, p. 409.
4. BELBIN, E. (1956) *Brit. J. Psychol.*, **47**, 164 and 259.
5. British Medical Association (1960) *The Relation of Alcohol to Road Accidents*.
6. BRODY, L. (1941) *Personal Factors in the Safe Operation of Motor Vehicles*. New York: N.Y. University Centre for Safety Education.
7. CHANDLER, K. N., & TANNER, J. C. (1958) *J. R. statist. Soc.* (A), **121**, 420.
8. CLARK, B. (1949) *The Drivers who have Accidents*. London: War Office (unpublished).

Road Accidents

9. COHEN, J., DEARNALEY, E. J., & HANSEL, C. E. M. (1958) *Brit. med. J.*, 21 June 1958 (5085), 1438.
10. DAVIS, D. R., & COILEY, PATRICIA A. (1959) *Ergonomics*, **2**, 239.
11. DOUGLAS, J. W. B., & BLOMFIELD, J. M. (1958) *Children Under Five*. London: Allen and Unwin.
12. DREW, G. C., COLQUHOUN, W. P., & LONG, H. A. (1958) *Brit. med. J.*, 25 Oct, 1958, **2**, 993.
13. DUNBAR, FLANDERS (1944) *Med. Clin. N. Amer.*, **28**, 653.
14. Eno Foundation for Highway Traffic Control (1948) *Personal Characteristics of Traffic Accident Repeaters*.
15. Eno Foundation for Highway Traffic Control (1954) *Driver Control*.
16. FARMER, E., & CHAMBERS, E. G. (1939) *A Study of Accident Proneness among Motor Drivers*. Medical Research Council, Industrial Health Research Board, Report no. 84.
17. *First International Conference on Alcohol and Traffic*, Stockholm, 1950.
18. GARWOOD, F., & DUFF, J. T. (1960) 'Changes in Accident Frequency after Changes in Speed Limits in the United Kingdom'. Paper presented at the 5th International Study Week in Traffic Engineering, Nice, 1960. World Touring and Automobile Organization, London.
19. GHISELLI, E. E., & BROWN, C. W. (1948) *Personnel and Industrial Psychology*. New York: McGraw-Hill.
20. GLANVILLE, W. H., & SMEED, R. J. (1958) *Proc. Conf. Highway Needs Great Britain*, 1957, 17–53.
21. GREENSHIELDS, B. D. (1936) *J. appl. Psychol.*, **20**, 353.
22. GREENWOOD, M., & WOODS, H. M. (1919) 'The Incidence of Industrial Accidents upon Individuals with Special Reference to Multiple Accidents'. Industrial Health Research Board, Report no. 4.
23. HÄKKINEN, S. (1958) 'Traffic Accidents and Driver Characteristics: A Statistical and Psychological Study'. Finland's Institute of Technology, Scientific Researches, no. 13.
24. Highway Research Board (1952) *Bulletin* no 60. Washington: National Research Council.
25. HILLIER, J. A., & ARNOLD, J. M. (1958) *Surveyor*, **117** (3472), 1085.
26. Home Office (1959) *Offences Relating to Motor Vehicles in 1958*. London: H.M.S.O.
27. JEFFCOATE, G. O. (1950) *Nature*, **166** (4224), 639.
28. JEFFCOATE, G. O. (1958) *Brit. J. Addict.*, **54** (2), 81.
29. JOHNSON, H. M. (1946) *Psychol. Bull.*, **43** (6), 489.
30. JOHNSON, N. L., & GARWOOD, F. (1957) *J. Inst. Actu.*, **83**, III (365), 277.
31. LUCAS, G. H. W., KALOW, W., *et al.* (1953) *Alcohol and Road Traffic*. Proceedings of Second International Conference, Toronto.
32. MCFARLAND, R. A., MOORE, R. C., & WARREN, A. B. (1955) *Human Variables in Motor Vehicle Accidents*. Cambridge, Mass.: Harvard School of Public Health.
33. Ministry of Transport (1957) *The Slough Experiment*. London: H.M.S.O.

F. Garwood

34. MOORE, R. L. (1956) *J. Inst. Auto. Assess.*, **8** (1), 32.
35. MOORE, R. L. (1956) International Study Week in Traffic Engineering, 1–6 October, 1956, Stresa, Italy. World Touring and Automobile Organization, London.
36. *Motor Vehicle Traffic Conditions in the United States. Part 6. The Accident-Prone Driver.* (1938) Washington: U.S. Government Printing Office. p. 36.
37. REYNOLDS, D. J. (1956) *J. R. statist. Soc.* (A), **119** (4), 393.
38. Road Research Laboratory (1951) *Road Research 1950.* London: H.M.S.O.
39. Road Research Laboratory (1951) *Surveyor*, **110** (3110), 642.
40. Road Research Laboratory (1954) *Road Research 1953.* London: H.M.S.O.
41. Road Research Laboratory (1960) *Road Accidents Christmas 1959.* Department of Scientific and Industrial Research, Road Research Technical Paper no. 49. London: H.M.S.O.
42. TILLMAN, W. A., & HOBBS, G. E. (1949) *Amer. J. Psychiat.*, Nov. 1949, **106** (5), 321.
43. TOYNE, G. C. (1956) *Motor*, 12 Dec. 1956, **110** (2855), 791.
44. WILLCOCK, H. D. (1949) 'Attitudes to Road Safety and the Road Safety Campaign'. *The Social Survey.*

16

THE STUDY OF CRIME

Hermann Mannheim

THE subject of the present contribution is the study of crime and delinquency. The scientific discipline devoted to this study is called 'criminology' and is concerned with both crime and delinquency. The word 'delinquency' is often used in a narrower sense to refer only to minor acts of anti-social behaviour and in particular to those committed by juveniles. More recently, however, its scope has widened. To give only a few illustrations, the Institute for the Study and Treatment of Delinquency in London (I.S.T.D.), founded in 1932, and the *British Journal of Delinquency*, published under its auspices since 1950, do not limit their activities to delinquency in that narrower sense but try to cover the whole subject of criminology. As proof of this the name of the Journal has recently been changed to the *British Journal of Criminology*. The French word *délinquance*, too, is not confined to the misbehaviour of juveniles.

There is no universally accepted definition of criminology. While it is generally taken as being concerned with the study of crime, of its factual evolution and potential causes, its treatment and prevention, the meaning of the fundamental concept of 'crime' in this definition is controversial. Should it be limited to crime in the legal sense, as a violation of the criminal law, or should it also include the study of certain forms of anti-social behaviour regardless of whether or not they are legally crimes? The present writer favours the second, wider interpretation, since otherwise the boundaries of criminology would differ according to time and place, depending on the not always reasonable attitudes of the criminal law. Criminologists in one country would have the right to study such subjects as, say, homosexuality, adultery,

Hermann Mannheim

prostitution, attempted suicide, whereas in other countries in deference to their legal systems they would be barred from doing so. It should be the task of criminology to examine the various forms of anti-social behaviour and to collect the material which would enable the legislator to decide which of them are suitable for punishment by the criminal law.* That the adoption of this wider, non-legal, definition of the scope of criminology introduces an element of ambiguity and vagueness cannot be disputed, but it is an ambiguity more in keeping with the non-legal nature of criminology than would be an artificial attempt to attach it too closely to the band-wagon of the criminal law. Two illustrations may serve to show that it can be advantageous to free criminological research from a too rigid dependence on legal concepts: as the legal definition of murder varies widely from country to country criminologists have to find a definition which, while paying due attention to national differences, contains the psychologically and sociologically essential elements of this crime and is therefore more generally acceptable for purposes of research. Similarly, with regard to the offence of embezzlement Cressey has shown that the sociological concept of 'violation of financial trust' is more suitable for research than the many varieties of legal definitions to be found in the Penal Codes of American States.[21] To avoid confusion, the term 'crime' itself should, however, be used only with reference to behaviour which is a violation of the criminal law in the country concerned.

In another direction, too, the scope of criminology has in recent years been expanded by including the study of the victim. In the case of many offences, sexual as well as non-sexual, justice can be done to the offender only by paying due attention to the role played by the victim. While a few recent writers have gone so far as to ask for the establishment of a new discipline of 'victimology', there is no reason why the study of the role of the victim should not find its place within the already existing discipline of criminology.† On the other hand, the working out of a practical programme for legislative or administrative reforms is the task of the so-called *politique criminelle* (in German *Kriminalpolitik*) rather than of criminology, which has merely to collect the factual material on which such a programme should be based. It has to be borne in mind, however, that criminology, though not a normative but a factual discipline, can as little as any other branch of the social sciences work without a system of values, and that the latter will all too often intrude into, and dominate, its fact-finding sphere. It is a

---

* The various reasons why so many types of anti-social behaviour are unsuitable for the machinery of criminal justice have been briefly discussed by me in [56], pp. 5–6.

† This is also the conclusion arrived at in Paul Cornil's brief but valuable discussion of the subject. [20]

matter of more than mere historical interest that the reform programmes of the *politique criminelle* have frequently been formulated at
too early a stage, i.e. before even the most elementary knowledge of the
relevant facts had become available.

The scientific study of crime goes back to the first half of the nineteenth century, to the work of such pioneers as Quételet and A. M.
Guerry, Rawson and Fletcher, when it was mainly focused on the
study of crime as a 'social or collective phenomenon of which individual
behaviour is a component, rather than on the motivation of crime in
the individual' ([70] p. 42). In the second part of the nineteenth and the
beginning of the twentieth centuries this sociological-statistical approach
was more and more overshadowed by the anthropological-biological
theories of the Positivist School of Lombroso and his followers. It has
been only in more recent decades that, in particular in the United States
and Great Britain, side by side with the growth of psychological and
psycho-analytical studies, a closer relationship has been established
between criminological research and modern sociology.

In view of the nature of its subject, which branches out in so many
directions and requires for its proper study the co-operation of so many
scientific disciplines, it has been, and may well be, questioned why
there should be a need for the establishment of criminology as a
separate discipline. 'Criminologists,' it has been argued, 'are kings
without a country' (Sellin); their interests can be adequately taken care
of by psychologists and psychiatrists, social and physical anthropologists, statisticians, sociologists, and lawyers. Are there, in fact, any
criminologists forming a separate profession, or are there only psychologists, sociologists, lawyers, and so on, who are interested in the
study and treatment of crime and working in this field? Is not the recent
establishment in Britain of a few full-time senior academic teaching
posts in criminology, and of a Criminological Institute at Cambridge, a
step in the wrong direction? The answer is, briefly, this: The study of
crime, as part of the study of society and of the study of the individual,
has so far been, and will be for many years to come, largely dependent
on the willing co-operation of those other disciplines. To leave it
entirely to them, busy as they are with their many other problems, could,
however, hardly produce that well-balanced and systematically planned
study of our subject which is required. Nor would there be much
prospect of overcoming the differences in approach and in techniques
of research which still separate those other disciplines. In short, criminology should, first of all, by providing a neutral territory, try to promote
better planning and an atmosphere of better understanding between all
those actively concerned in the study of crime. More perfect team-work
is of course needed not only between members of different disciplines,
especially psychologists, psychiatrists and sociologists, statisticians and

those primarily interested in the individual case, but also within each discipline and, particularly important in criminological work, between the universities and the various correctional agencies.* The criminologist in charge of a research project should see to it that there are in it representatives of every discipline which has to make a real contribution to the research and that no single one should unduly dominate the others. The Gluecks have rightly been criticized for not including a single sociologist in the team which assisted them in that well-known investigation reported in *Unraveling Juvenile Delinquency*.[37] † It would be unrealistic, however, not to admit the very real difficulties still to be overcome before criminology can take its part alongside the other branches of social science. Criminology as a separate profession is, in many countries, still in an embryonic stage in the sense that of the large number of scholars working in this field only a few regard themselves in the first place as criminologists. With the greater part of their academic training lying elsewhere and with very limited prospects of obtaining academic positions in criminology they have to be careful to make it known that they are in fact psychologists or sociologists or lawyers, as the case may be, rather than criminologists. It is too dangerous for young men to be branded as narrow specialists in a subject which may well turn out to be a 'blind alley'. It is only in rare cases, therefore, that they are able to develop the sense of really 'belonging' to criminology —a feeling which, perhaps more than the mere quantity of the criminological work done, might be used as a criterion to enable an individual worker to call himself a criminologist. This is most unfortunate. Our discipline is still in too precarious a position to allow itself to become unduly crowded with, and dependent on, birds of passage finding temporary shelter within its territory but constantly longing for a warmer climate. If society wants crime to be tackled on scientific lines it should see to it that criminology can exist without remaining too heavily indebted to its older sister disciplines.

It might be argued that the scarcity of workers who can properly be called criminologists has its root cause not so much in lack of encouragement as in the very nature of the subject, which not only, as said before, branches out in many different directions and depends on the co-operation of so many different disciplines, but lacks the fundamental qualities of a 'science'. However, as C. Wright Mills writes, 'the word "science" has acquired great prestige and rather imprecise meaning.' ([68] p. 18, fn.2). The criteria needed to make a subject acceptable as an independent branch of scientific study are far from clear. Even the claims of sociology

---

* On the whole subject of teamwork see O. A. Oeser in [31] pp. 408 ff.; [61] esp. pp. 259ff.; [34].

† See [37] pp. xi, xii, and 24–5; and for the criticism, among others, [78] pp. 75ff.; [42]; [17] p. 121; [84] pp. 107ff., 115ff.

The Study of Crime

have sometimes been questioned. 'Is it just a hotchpotch of fragments drawn from other fields?' asked T. H. Marshall as recently as 1947.* Is it essential that a body of studies, in order to become a separate scientific discipline, should have its own subject, its own problems, its own method, or all three? Or that it should be something on which it is possible to establish causal sequences and generalizations?

No doubt, criminology possesses its own subject, either crime or anti-social behaviour, but it could be objected that crime is a subject too arbitrarily defined by the various national systems of criminal law and that anti-social behaviour is a term too vague for scientific treatment. The first of these objections can be dismissed if, as suggested above, the second definition of criminology is preferred.† Admittedly, the term 'anti-social behaviour'—even if focused on suitability for criminal legislation—is vague, but there are others, well-established scientific disciplines, including sociology,‡ with equally ill-definable frontiers. That there is no lack of problems in need of scientific study will also be conceded, and that they cannot be adequately taken care of by any other discipline has been shown above.

Some twenty years ago, when a symposium entitled *The Study of Society* was published in order to bring together contributions from the several interested disciplines, criminology and its literature had not yet attained in Britain adequate status to be represented, and criminological subjects and studies were only occasionally and very briefly referred to in some of the chapters.§ The presence of a separate chapter in the present book is therefore appreciated as a recognition of the progress made in the intervening period. The importance of the role played by crime in our society is sometimes overrated; too much attention is paid to it, and it is often sensationally exploited for purely financial or political reasons. Nevertheless, it remains true that crime occupies a focal point in society in terms of human suffering as well as of economic loss and of the injury done to the whole social fabric. For the social scientist, many of whose problems are too vast and unwieldy for constructive treatment, crime seems to provide a subject relatively more tangible and less difficult to cover; here he can hope to observe some of the phenomena which might evade him in the wider setting of society as a whole. It

---

* [64] p. 10. On this see [101] pp. 67ff.; [75] pp. 6ff., 134, *et passim*.

† Recently, Barbara Wootton has joined the thinning ranks of those who dislike the existence of criminology as 'one of the recognized academic disciplines' ([103] pp. 306-7). Her reason that such a discipline has to attach undue weight to the mere fact of 'conviction' falls to the ground once the non-legal definition of criminology is adopted.

‡ See, e.g., the definitions of sociology quoted by Ginsberg ([31] [32] vol. I, pp. 163ff., vol. II pp. 105ff.) and Lockwood ([51] pp. 141-2).

§ See, e.g. pp. 81, 433, 473.

is significant that many writers who embarked on a study of problems of social pathology wider than those covered by criminology had to give pride of place to crime.* Moreover, criminology includes, besides the study of anti-social behaviour and of those who are guilty of it, also the study of the manifold ways in which state and society react to such behaviour, in particular the study of punishment, its history, philosophy and psychology.† In a stimulating essay[46] C. R. Jeffery has recently stressed the need for criminologists to pay more attention to these latter aspects instead of too closely following the narrow individualistic interpretation of criminology initiated by nineteenth-century positivists; and there are other symptoms, too, of a revival of some of Durkheim's views on crime and punishment which stress the indispensability of the former and concentrate on the social functions of the latter rather than on its effects on the individual offender.‡

Criminology, it can hardly be disputed, possesses its own subject and problems, but has it been able to establish its own 'laws' and generalizations? Many generalizations, it is true, have been attempted by criminologists, and from Quételet to the Gluecks such generalizations have not infrequently been formulated as 'laws'. According to Quételet's 'thermic law of delinquency' crimes against the person are more frequent in warmer climates, whereas crimes against property flourish in colder ones ([77] vol. 2, pp. 266ff., 275ff.); and the Gluecks, using a number of variables which showed statistically significant differences between their delinquent and non-delinquent groups, have produced 'a tentative causal formula or law' of juvenile delinquency ([37] pp. 281–2; 36, p. 249). However, Quételet's thermic law was hardly intended to be more than a summary of a limited number of statistical associations indicating trends which might well be changed through administrative manipulation. If, for example, measures of social welfare and police protection of property should be arranged in such a way as heavily to discriminate in favour of colder regions, their volume of economic crime might well fall below that of warmer districts. The Gluecks, too, qualify their formula by adding the proviso that 'a scientific law must always be considered

---

* In particular Barbara Wootton in her survey of social pathology [103], Clinard [18], to a smaller extent Elliott and Merrill [26].

† The present writer has so far taken the view that the study of the attitudes of society to crime and punishment is the task of the sociology of law rather than that of criminology ([59], pp. 264ff.). It has to be admitted, however, that those attitudes may represent important criminogenic forces which should be the subject of criminological studies.

‡ On Durkheim's criminological theories see [52]. Critical of Durkheim's theory of punishment is Rose ([80] p. 17). The otherwise excellent special number of the *American Journal of Sociology*[1] on Durkheim and Simmel contains very little on Durkheim's criminological theories in general but concentrates on the discussion of his research techniques.

as a temporary statement of relationships' and that their 'law may have to be modified after more intensive, microscopic study of the atypical cases'. Even without such study of atypical cases, however, we can say already from our present knowledge that, for example, the finding of the Gluecks—which forms part of their 'law'—that delinquents as a group are 'physically distinguishable from the non-delinquents in being essentially mesomorphic in constitution (solid, closely knit, muscular)' has not invariably been repeated in Britain. Among the ordinary school-leavers in Glasgow examined by Ferguson after the last war conviction rates were, on the contrary, higher among boys of poor physique than among boys whose 'general level of physical assessment' was good ([27] p. 115). Neither the Massachusetts sample of the Gluecks nor the Glasgow sample of Ferguson can of course be accepted as representative of their respective countries, but the contrast between the two might at least serve as just another reminder how careful criminologists should be to avoid hasty generalizations. For their failure to establish any criminological 'laws' they will hardly be blamed. Not even the, apparently, most common criminological observations, i.e. that there is more crime among the young than among the old, and more among males than females, can be regarded as more than mere trends requiring many qualifications and in part depending on a certain socio-cultural structure.*

II

Turning to the methods of study used in criminological research there is no need for us here to embark upon a discussion of the controversy 'problem versus method' or to present a comprehensive survey of methods. While rejecting the 'primacy of method' theory—method for method's sake—we are not altogether indifferent to the 'charms of methodology'.[54] While believing that criminology requires a theory, 'not only to organize the findings of research so that they make sense, but, more basically, to determine what questions are to be asked' ([71] p. 232), we are aware of the quite exceptional difficulties which this new discipline has to face in matters of methodology and we realize its equally exceptional need for reliable techniques of research. The reasons for the dilemma in which the academic criminologist is placed are fairly obvious. It is surprising to see that they are either totally ignored or at least not fully understood in Barbara Wootton's recent strictures ([103,] esp. chaps. iii, v, x), which, in any case, add hardly anything to what

* In a subsequent book [37a] the Gluecks tried to find explanations for the considerable excess of mesomorphs in their delinquent as compared with their non-delinquent groups (60 per cent as against 30 per cent). This, however, is a question with which we are not here concerned. On the whole problem of 'laws' versus trends in the social sciences see Popper [75].

† The matter has been admirably treated in [80] chap. 14.

Hermann Mannheim

has been for many years a commonplace to workers in our field. What is the nature of this dilemma?

There is, on the one hand, the well-known fact that historically criminology, in particular its penological section, owes its existence largely to the revolt of humanitarians against the cruel, soulless and ignorant machinery of criminal justice in the eighteenth and nineteenth centuries. Ever since, the humanitarian lay element has taken an active part in penal reform, further encouraged in Great Britain by a legal system which places a very large part of the administration of criminal justice almost unreservedly in the hands of lay magistrates and lay jurors. Whether this interest of the man in the street in penal matters has in recent years been declining as a consequence of the gradual abolition of cruel methods of treatment is a moot question which cannot here be further pursued.* The point we wish to make in the present connexion is that the strength of the lay element in the administration of criminal justice—coupled as it is with the lack of interest in the scientific study of crime still prevailing among many professional lawyers—makes it particularly difficult to secure due recognition for the need to apply scientifically sound methods in the daily work of the criminal courts and in the penal system.[59] The choice between the two conflicting values, lay participation and scientific knowledge in administering criminal justice, is not easy and the solution of the conflict by no means obvious. Moreover, ignored by the universities and by private foundations alike, the study of crime had in the time before and shortly after the Second World War largely to be left to the enthusiastic amateur who could not be expected to apply scientifically sound methods.

It is, however, not only the choice between the conflicting claims of these two opposing values which has to be faced, but there is also the conflict between the basic criminological principle of individualization of treatment according to scientifically established differences in personality, on the one hand, and the traditional interpretation of justice as equal treatment for everybody with only a minimum of concessions to individual circumstances ([56] p. 228; [103] pp. 335–6; [104] p. 53). As far as the sentencing function of the criminal courts is concerned, no general formula has so far been agreed upon to enable the courts to decide which individual factors in offence and offender should be taken into consideration and in what way.[62] It is here that fairly wide discretion has inevitably to be left to individual and communal prejudices and political convictions.† From this it follows that it is not altogether

* See also the author's remarks in [33] p. 265.

† Barbara Wootton [103] is right in saying that 'the courts must function in the setting of the community which it is their business to service; and they cannot afford wholly to ignore the attitudes, or even always to override the prejudices, of that community'.

certain which of the findings of criminological research are of significance to the practical work of the courts. Criminologists cannot be
expected, however, to confine their researches exclusively to problems
whose practical usefulness can be guaranteed in advance. Some space
must be left for 'pure' research, particularly as practical utility is a
concept which may change its contents according to time and place.
Naturally, there are whole sections of criminological work whose
raison d'être is entirely dependent on the acceptance of a certain type
of penal philosophy and its underlying system of social values. Prediction studies, for example, make little sense unless we accept a philosophy
of prevention, through either deterrence or reformation, rather than
one of retribution; within the framework of a preventive system, however, these studies can be placed impartially at the disposal of deterrent
or of reformative systems without discriminating between the interests
of society and those of the individual offender.* It is not the fault of
the criminologist if the interests of the individual should fit more easily
into their prediction tables than those of society.

One final difficulty peculiar to criminological research is the existence
side by side of research based on the methods of the natural and on
those of the social sciences. Given the indisputable fact that both have
to make essential contributions to the study of crime no easy solution of
this dilemma can be expected either. Moreover, even within the social
sciences there are fundamental conflicts over methodological issues
which, though not peculiar to criminology, are nevertheless of crucial
importance in the study of crime. We have in mind in particular the so
far unresolved conflict between some clinical, especially psycho-analytic,
uncontrolled studies of individual cases, on the one hand, and the
rigidly controlled, mostly statistical, type of research preferred by most
psychologists, on the other—a conflict recently once more exposed by
Gardner Lindzey ([50] pp. 8ff.).

To make matters still worse, practically every one of the various
disciplines interested in criminological studies has shown strong tendencies to claim a monopoly of the right methods and answers in our
subject. In some countries it is the biologist who dominates the field, in
others the psychiatrist or sociologist. There are probably other than
purely personal reasons for such differences. Sometimes it has been
suggested that in countries with a low crime rate the lawbreaker is likely
to be an abnormal individual, whereas a high crime rate is an indication
that social rather than individual abnormalities are responsible. In
countries belonging to the former category criminology is, therefore,
believed to show a biological and psychiatric bias, whereas in countries

---

* Barbara Wootton's criticism of prediction studies ([103] p. 236) that 'they
concentrate attention solely upon the future convicted person himself (!) as though
no one else in the world existed' is therefore unfounded.

Hermann Mannheim

of the latter group the sociologist is more useful. This may not be the complete answer,* but at least the example of the United States, with its very high crime rates and equally strongly developed criminal sociology,† seems to support it. On the other hand, in Italy where the volume of crime is also considerable criminologists have traditionally— though with notable exceptions such as Enrico Ferri—shown more interest in the biological than in the sociological approach.

'Since the bulk of the literature in American criminology is by sociologists it goes without saying,' writes Marshall B. Clinard, 'that American criminology and sociology have developed together . . . such disagreements as exist among writers in the field of criminology are but reflections of the confusion in sociological theory and research' ([18], p. 550). True as this is of conditions in the United States, it does not to the same extent apply to conditions in other countries, where the dependence is often one on psychiatry and biology rather than sociology. Moreover, the dependence, although it undoubtedly exists, is slowly changing its character. Notwithstanding our previous remarks on its precarious position, criminology, it may be asserted, has in the course of the present century been progressing from colonial to some sort of semi-dominion status, though it is not yet accepted as a full member of the Commonwealth of the social sciences. What is still missing is the development of a real two-way traffic between criminology and those other disciplines on which it has so far been dependent. Whereas criminologists have been only too willing to acknowledge their indebtedness to them, their own contributions have usually been ignored by representatives of the older disciplines. The confusion, to which Clinard refers, exists in the field of criminological theory rather than in that of method. And, as a consequence, whatever advances have been made in recent years are mainly confined to the latter.

With regard to theory, a great deal of confused controversy exists as to the place to be allotted to problems of causation as against those of prediction and evolution. There is a growing tendency to concentrate on the more factual study of the historical development of criminal careers, of the prediction of its likely future trends and of the differential success rates of the various forms of treatment within the penal system ([63; 103] pp. 173–4). Research into the causes of crime, if not altogether abandoned, is often given second place as a subject too intractable to admit of an early solution, and therefore unlikely to produce any practical results ([97] esp. pp. 15ff., 88ff., 117ff.). It was significant that at the Third International Congress of Criminology, held in London in 1955, with 'Recidivism' as its focal theme, there were separate sections on 'the

* Sellin [88] thinks that 'deeper culturally conditioned attitudes toward behaviour determinants in general' are the explanation.
† An admirable survey of American criminal sociology up to 1950 is given in [15].

290

descriptive study of forms of recidivism and their evolution' and on 'prognosis' in addition to those on the causes of this phenomenon, its definition, statistics, and treatment. In theory, this distinction between the descriptive and the causal study of crime problems is sound enough, and it has the merit of counteracting the previously excessive preoccupation of criminologists with matters of causation without adequate observation of the facts. In practice, it has become only too clear, however, that the attraction of causal interpretations, hazardous as they may be, often proves too strong to allow the facts to speak for themselves, and many of the studies pretending to be purely descriptive are actually replete with attempts at such interpretations. With some of the various methods of descriptive study employed in criminology we shall briefly deal below.

In the theory of crime causation, controversy is still raging between the view that crime is always due to a multiplicity of factors and the various attempts to explain it in terms of one single factor. Whereas Sheldon Glueck is at present the protagonist of the multiple factor theory,[35] previously sponsored by William Healy and Cyril Burt, the opposite view ([42], p. 725), has been tenaciously defended by the late Edwin H. Sutherland and his many pupils. The single factor put forward by Sutherland and his school, often even as the one and only explanation of criminal behaviour, is 'differential association'. Many variants of this theory have been produced in the twenty years of its existence, but its simplest formulation is perhaps that 'criminality is learned in interaction with others in a process of communication';* such learning occurs mainly 'within intimate personal groups . . . the learning includes (a) techniques, (b) the specific direction of motives, drives, rationalizations, and attitudes', which direction is learned 'from definitions of legal codes as favourable and unfavourable'; and an individual becomes delinquent 'because of an excess of definitions favourable to violation of law over definitions unfavourable to violation of law' ([94] pp. 5–9). The recent posthumous publication of a few, previously only privately circulated, papers by Sutherland shows how profoundly his own belief in the soundness of his theory as the only possible explanation of the causes of crime had been undermined by his critics. The monopolistic claims of the theory of differential association—the 'most sociological of all the theories' in criminology[42]—are in fact no longer upheld by some of Sutherland's most eminent pupils. Clinard stresses that it 'entirely neglects the psychogenic trait component of personality and, in attributing all crime to a mathematical ratio of exposure to criminal norms, makes it often difficult to explain why some engage in crime while others do not' ([15; 16] pp. 308ff.). Even Cressey, the editor of Sutherland's 'Principles', regards it as 'highly doubtful whether the

* [95] p. 77. The theory was first formulated by Sutherland in [93].

differential association theory can be subjected to a crucial empirical test' ([21] pp. 147ff.).

While it is very likely that much criminal behaviour, like any other form of human action, is learned, common sense experience and knowledge of individual criminal cases shows the futility of any such attempt to force the endless variations of crime and criminals into the Procrustean bed of the theory of differential association, or indeed of any other single factor. Having said this, we have at once to admit, however, that the opposite extreme of a purely eclectic theory of crime causation, mechanically adding up all the factors which might ever have been considered as criminogenic in criminological literature, is equally unsatisfactory. Many of the 'old-fashioned' factors, from 'low intelligence' and the Lombrosian stigmata to the various types of 'broken homes' and the movies, have been either completely discarded or at least re-defined, subdivided, and presented in a slightly modernized dress,* with captions expressing cautious scepticism. Those which have survived will, in ever-changing forms, probably remain indispensable as partial explanations of limited categories of cases, but much further effort will be needed to clarify their mutual relationships; to see whether combinations of some of them will produce a useful typology; and, above all, whether the statistical associations so far established do in fact prove any causal nexus.

What is perhaps of even greater theoretical interest than the future of any of the traditional single factors in crime causation is the fate of those far more sophisticated recent theories, psychological or sociological, of crime causation which, with aspirations almost equal to those of the differential association school, have made their appearance in the past twenty or thirty years. John Bowlby's maternal separation theory has received some very rough handling on the part of R. G. Andry,[2] Siri Naess,[72] and Barbara Wootton ([103] chap. iv.). In the sociological field, the theories of culture conflict, with special reference to the American immigrant, and of social disorganization and anomie, the ecological 'delinquency area' theory of the Chicago School, Robert Merton's 'illicit means' (Albert K. Cohen) theory of the 'dissociation between culturally prescribed aspirations and socially structured avenues of realizing these aspirations' and Cohen's own criminal subculture and cultural transmission theory of juvenile delinquency have all found many supporters, but also encountered a great deal of criticism.† Space does not permit of dealing with these theories and

* For criticisms of these ill-defined concepts see [58], esp. pp. 135–6; and at greater length [103] chap. iii *et passim*.

† On these theories see, e.g. [87; 42] pp. 719ff. (on social disorganization); [66] chap. iv, esp. pp. 132ff. and 176ff. (on anomia); [19, 70, 49] (on the ecological theories); briefly also [59] pp. 8–9; [60].

The Study of Crime

their *pros* and *cons*. It might appear paradoxical, but is nevertheless true, to say that most of them are brilliantly argued and well founded, or at least plausible, even where at first sight they seem to be mutually incompatible. They are right in relation to some types of crime and criminals, but wrong in relation to others, so that each of them becomes absurd when it aspires to be 'the grand theory', a 'universal scheme' (Mills) covering the whole field of crime causation ([68] p. 46). This all the more so as most of these recent sociological theories have been formulated in the United States in terms relating to the American crime problem without being tested and validated on non-American case material and within a non-American society. In fact, some of them have not even been tested on American material either.* What is needed is a series of parallel field studies in different countries, as suggested by the present writer and Marshall B. Clinard ([60] pp. 151–2; [17]). Such parallel studies are vital to the future of criminology if it is to avoid parochialism and to become a truly international discipline instead of retaining its present narrowly national or regional character ([59] pp. 209–10).

There is still another, perhaps even greater, danger of parochialism arising from the way in which criminological studies have, until recently, been conducted, and from their former subservience to the criminal law. In accordance with the class bias which the latter has frequently shown ([56] sects. iii and iv), criminological research has, at least in the field of economic crime, too narrowly concentrated on the comparatively less significant and less harmful traditional types of property offences, ignoring the typically middle-class forms of anti-social behaviour now usually labelled 'white-collar crimes'. The face of criminology is at present undergoing a process of profound change following the pioneering work of Sutherland, Clinard, and others on this new concept, but much further fact-finding and re-thinking will be needed before the right balance between old and new theories of crime and between law and criminology will be found ([96, 16, 10] pp. 119ff.).

In many ways similar, though in others very different, is the problem of the traffic offender who, numerically at least, now takes precedence over all other offenders. Here, as in the case of white-collar crime, it is true of criminologists, criminal lawyers, and penal administrators that, as C. Wright Mills has said with regard to social scientists in general, for the first time in the history of their disciplines they 'have come into professional relations with private and public powers well above the level of the welfare agency' ([68] p. 95). This large group of motor traffic offences, too, is forcing criminologists to think afresh and to adjust their traditional image of the criminal to the demands of present-day society. It has recently been pointed out by Barbara Wootton with considerable force of conviction that, whereas statistically these offences

* See, e.g. [48] on Cohen's theory; [73].

have become far more numerous than any other category (even property offences), 'this revolution is generally ignored alike by the public and by the professional sociologist—to a degree that really queers all criminological discussion' ([103] pp. 25 ff.). While the emphasis she gives to the subject is only too welcome, her criticism of the sociologists, or rather criminologists, is not altogether justified, and it is somewhat regrettable that Lady Wootton has ignored the existing literature on the subject.* Apart from criminological literature there has been a continuous flow of discussion in periodicals and newspapers, mainly on the question of penalties. What has to be admitted is the absence in Britain of any large-scale scientific study of the whole problem—a gap which is, however, unfortunately not confined to traffic offences. It might be a worth-while task for the Home Office Research Unit to undertake or instigate such a project,† which should be carried out on comparative lines by a team on which sociologists and statisticians, psychologists and psychiatrists, lawyers, and possibly economists and technical experts, too, would have to be represented to see the subject in all its ramifications. As long as the present tendency, so conspicuous in particular in the Press discussions of recent years, prevails to concentrate on a few aspects such as inadequate penalties, no solution is likely to be found, although it may be of interest to compare, for example, the use made of prison sentences for motorists in this country and abroad.

III‡

Considering that criminology can make no claim to possess any special research techniques of its own it would be futile in a symposium such as this to give a detailed account of the way in which each of the generally known techniques has been used in our field. All we can do is to draw attention to a few recent developments which seem to be indicative of present-day trends and to a few problems and difficulties which are peculiar to criminological research.

(a) *Statistical techniques.* As in other fields, opinions on the value of statistical techniques have greatly differed. At present, the most widely accepted view seems to be to regard them as a necessary evil. As far as

* No complete bibliography can of course be here given, but the following sources may be quoted: [56] pp. 56ff.; [89] p. 497; [41] esp. pp. 925ff.; [11]; [52] pp. 283ff. Published too late to be considered by Barbara Wootton: [6] pp. 120ff.;[67] . On motor car theft, an offence closely related to traffic offences, [85]. [29] is quoted in Wootton's book.

† The list of projects published in the Home Office White Paper [45] Appendix B, contains nothing on the subject.

‡ For the following text see the more detailed methodological chapters in [59], especially chaps. 1 and 6.

the various official publications of criminal statistics, such as *Criminal Statistics for England and Wales,* are concerned, their weaknesses are only too obvious. Twenty years ago, the present writer undertook a detailed analysis of the 'Structure and Interpretation of the Criminal Statistics for England and Wales' ([55] Part I), which has now partly been brought up-to-date by Lord Pakenham and Barbara Wootton.* In brief, these are the principal weaknesses: (*i*) the 'dark numbers' of crimes remaining altogether unknown may well distort the whole picture to such an extent as to make these figures almost useless for purposes of information and research; (*ii*) the highly emotional attitude of the public may greatly affect the volume of crime brought to the knowledge of the authorities; (*iii*) before the appointment, approximately ten years ago, of a trained statistician the compilation of the various series of Home Office statistics was entirely left to laymen; (*iv*) the numbers of convictions are influenced by the legal rules of criminal procedure and evidence, which may result in the acquittal of many offenders. Finally, while the statistics of the penalties and other forms of disposal are no doubt correct, up to recently very little has been done officially to assess the effect of the various measures employed; the following up over a period of time of individual offenders is not only unpopular but also very difficult on account on the absence of police registration on Continental lines.

Outside the regular official publications statistical techniques have been extensively used in criminological research although, as indicated before, sometimes rather crudely. Only comparatively few of these researches can here be quoted, and for reasons of space we have to limit our references to British publications.† Some of them are predominantly control group studies, such as Cyril Burt's *Young Delinquent,* A. M. Carr Saunders, H. Mannheim, and E. C. Rhodes, *Young Offenders* (delinquent and non-delinquent samples are compared) or Norwood East's *The Adolescent Criminal* (a group of 4,000 Borstal boys, first offenders compared with recidivists).[9, 13, 24.] There are, moreover, several follow-up studies and assessments of the effect of treatment,[5, 30, 38, 39, 57, 79, 99] one of which is also a prediction study[8, 63, 83]; and there is a statistical investigation of sex offences.[12] It goes without saying that some of these researches, notably Burt's and a few of the follow-up studies, are by no means limited to statistics.

(*b*) *Sociological Investigations* of a not predominantly statistical nature.

---

* Lord Pakenham,[74] and Wootton. [103] Moreover, see [51a] and for international historical developments. [37b]

† For fuller, though not exhaustive, lists see the section 'Research and Methodology' of the *British Journal of Delinquency,* and for current research [45]; also [59] pp. 10ff.

As pointed out elsewhere,[59] they are usually studies of social groups such as the family, or of social institutions, or of areas; or a combination of two or three of these subjects, encouraged or even enforced by the inevitable overlapping of the problems of groups, institutions, and areas. While ecological area studies have been repeatedly undertaken in England* there is a conspicuous absence of research into the criminological implications of social institutions such as class and property ([56] sects. i and iv). Research into white-collar crime has recently been carried out, but the results are not yet available. Much more popular has been the study of social groups, in particular of family problems, with special emphasis on the problem family, although Barbara Wootton's complaint that 'thousands of pounds have been spent on problem family research' seems somewhat exaggerated.† Other social groups have also been studied, such as, for instance, delinquent boys living in a Liverpool slum area and belonging to a city youth club, institutional groups such as the boys in a Borstal institution, and—although it may be doubtful whether they can properly be regarded as 'groups'—ex-service men in a few English prisons and Borstals and habitual criminals in selected recidivist prisons. [65, 69, 82, 90]

(c) The line between the sociological and the *psychological* approaches to criminological problems is sometimes not easy to draw, especially as social psychologists and even psychiatrists are no longer disinclined to pay proper attention to the sociological problems of the individuals or groups—whether gangs, children separated from their mothers, juvenile prostitutes, car thieves, or homosexual offenders—with whom they are concerned.[92, 2, 3, 86, 29, 102, 7] In his Chapter on 'Sociology and History' Asa Briggs rightly stresses 'how artificial are most of the boundary lines between the different social studies'. Even in more specifically psychiatric researches, such as electro-encephalographic studies, the possibility that environmental factors may play some part in determining or at least modifying an individual's criminal career is not entirely excluded. However, as we are here merely surveying the methods of study used by members of the various disciplines, we can confine ourselves to the statement that many psychologists and psychiatrists engaged in criminological research are at present, at least in Britain, inclined to present their findings in statistical form rather than as elaborate case studies and that the statistical correlations shown are concerned with social factors not much less than with individual ones.[43, 91, 30, 44] Compared with this, it is rather unfortunate and can do only harm if intransigent and unbalanced statements such as 'Crime is essentially a social phenomenon and jurists and sociologists should

* Liverpool [4]; Cambridge [57]; Radby [14]; Croydon [7]; Leicester [47].
† [103] p. 60. In addition to the other studies there mentioned, there is now [100].

study it, not doctors and biologists' should have been repeated with apparent approval by a distinguished American sociologist ([42] p. 712). Crime—it should no longer be necessary to repeat this platitude—is both an individual and a social phenomenon, and it is futile to try and draw an iron curtain in front of any of the disciplines legitimately concerned with it. The criminal psychopath is one of the types where the close affinity of psychiatric and sociological factors shows itself with particular clarity (see, e.g. Partridge's 'sociopath'),* and the 'inadequate personality', a concept so prominent in the recent writings of prison psychologists, is another example.† In all this, however, we are no longer concerned with mere questions of method but with causation.

(d) *Individual Case Studies.* One of the 'Conclusions' unanimously adopted by the Third International Congress of Criminology in 1955‡ requested the Scientific Commission of the International Society of Criminology to establish a sub-committee to study the scientific and practical possibilities of international team research using uniform data in the collection of case histories. So far this recommendation has not been acted upon, although there is an obvious need for the collection of case histories which are detailed and on uniform lines. In a way, these two requirements may be incompatible, since the more detailed such histories are, the less likely will they be to follow identical lines. One might have to be content, therefore, with either the one or the other of these requirements,[3] and in fact they serve different purposes. Uniform, though not too detailed, case records are indispensable, for example, for the construction of prediction tables and other statistical purposes.§ Full histories are needed for research into causation and to improve the statistical prediction tables ([63] p. 174), also for teaching and for the information of all those who have to deal with individual offenders, notably courts, probation officers, institutional staffs, social workers, psychologists, and psychiatrists. Until recently, the uniform case material needed for prediction was not available, but improvements have been made of late. The scarcity in England of full life histories, on the model of those published in the U.S.A. by Clifford Shaw, Sutherland, Karpman, Wertham, Lindner, and others, has been due in part to the reluctance of psychiatrists and psycho-analysts to publish their case material in detail and in part to the difficulty experienced by other research workers using official material to obtain permission to do so.

---

* A survey of the literature on psychopaths for the first half of the present century is given in [40].

† For a recent discussion of this concept see [22].

‡ [97] p. 219, and the more detailed discussion with special reference to recidivism in [78] pp. 88ff.

§ On the whole subject of standardized records in criminological research see [63] chap. ix, esp. pp. 214ff., ch. iv., pp. 56ff.

Hermann Mannheim

It is here that the position of criminologists, dependent as they usually are on official case material, seems to be even more precarious than that of workers in other fields. It has to be stressed, however, that the Home Office, in particular, has recently shown considerable understanding of this problem, and a great many case histories of a type somewhere between the two extremes described above have in fact been published.* Needless to say, this material is confined to the traditional types of crimes and criminals, excluding such newcomers as the white collar criminal.

Criminological research, handicapped by the scarcity of detailed, reliable, and representative biographies and autobiographies of criminals, might possibly profit from the study of eminent non-criminals whose full life stories, scrutinized by professional biographers, have become available. Many of them had to contend with difficulties not dissimilar to those only too familiar from typical criminal careers, and it might be illuminating to speculate on the reasons why they have been able to abstain from crime.

(e) Obstacles to *experimental research* in criminology—even more formidable here than elsewhere in the social sciences—have been discussed before ([59] pp. 127, 136, 146ff., 218ff.). As the example of the United States shows, experimentation in the field of treatment is, however, not entirely impossible. The three outstanding cases are the Cambridge-Somerville Study, the Highfields Experiment, and the work of the Californian 'Special Intensive Parole Unit'.† The first of these was entirely private; the second is a combination of judicial and administrative experimentation, and the third entirely administrative. Space forbids a discussion of their respective weaknesses, but they have this in common that they come nearer than anything else in the field of penology to the idea of a controlled experiment and that their evaluation has been entrusted to outside experts unconnected with the study. It is on such lines that progress in penology is most likely to be achieved.

Operational research, as defined in this symposium by Mr Bailey, has recently been done in the fields of prediction and short-term imprisonment and is at present being carried out in English prisons on the subject of group relations in prison. Moreover, what Bailey writes about the designing of hospital buildings is equally applicable to prison architecture.

Research on the sentencing policies of criminal and juvenile courts is also of considerable interest to criminologists in as much as such

* See, e.g. the case histories published by Burt, Morris, Spencer, Mays, Terence Morris, Stott, in the books mentioned, and in [55].

† [76]. On this see [59] pp. 146ff., [98], [53] On the Californian study see the unpublished reports by the Division of Adult Paroles [23]. In Beutel [6] the term 'experimental' is used in a different sense.

The Study of Crime

policies to a considerable extent determine not only the treatment of the convicted offender but also his future attitude to society and crime. Such researches have been repeatedly undertaken in Britain in the past ten years.*

CONCLUSIONS

1. In conclusion, it can be said that during the post-war period progress has been made in the study of crime and its treatment in the following directions:

   (a) There is a greater willingness now to use more advanced techniques of research and more clearly defined terms, and to strengthen inter-disciplinary co-operation and team research; all this coupled with:

   (b) a tendency away from studies into the causes of crime and towards more specialized research of a descriptive and predictive nature and the observation of the effects of the various methods of treatment, strictly limited to specific types of offences, offenders, and methods of treatment.

   (c) This has led to better knowledge of the kind of person[1], so far mainly juveniles and adolescents, found guilty by the courts and sent to institutions or placed on probation; of the kind of area from which these offenders come; and of the nature and likely effects of the various methods of treatment.

2. These developments have been facilitated, and to a large extent even made possible, only through the assistance given by some of the large private Foundations, mostly British but occasionally American, and by the Home Office. Criminological research has thereby more and more been taken out of the hands of individual workers and has assumed the shape of a triangle or trio consisting of Home Office Research Unit, one of the Foundations, and a University or similar Department or Institute, directing or supervising the research team. To an increasing extent, research, mostly into penological problems of treatment rather than into criminological subjects proper, is also being done by the Research Unit without the assistance of outside agencies. The most appropriate policy of distribution will still have to be worked out. Another problem still to be solved is the relation between research and the work of Government Committees and Royal Commissions appointed to study specific topics. The idea that there should be an organic link between their work and research has not yet been clearly grasped and is far from being generally accepted.

---

* See the account given in my [62]. Further research, still unpublished, has been done on the variations in the use of prison sentences by Magistrates' Courts and on short-term prison sentences.

Hermann Mannheim

REFERENCES

1. *American Journal of Sociology* **63** (6), May 1958.
2. ANDRY, R. G. (1957) 'Faulty Paternal and Maternal Child-relationships, Affection and Delinquency', *Brit. J. Delinq.*, **8**, 34ff.
3. ANDRY, R. G. (1960) *Delinquency and Parental Pathology*. London: Methuen.
4. BAGOT, J. H. (1941) *Juvenile Delinquency*. London: Cape.
5. BENSON, SIR GEORGE (1959) 'Prediction Methods and Young Prisoners'. *Brit. J. Delinq.*, **9**, 192ff.
6. BEUTEL, FREDERICK K. (1956) *Some Potentialities of Experimental Jurisprudence*. Lincoln, Neb.: Univ. of Nebraska Press.
7. BOWLBY, JOHN (1946) *Forty-Four Juvenile Thieves*. London: Bailliere, Tindall and Cox.
8. *British Journal of Delinquency*, **6**, 2, Sept. 1955.
9. BURT, CYRIL (1944) *Young Delinquent*. 4th ed. London: Univ. of London Press.
10. CALDWELL, ROBERT G. (1948) *Federal Probation*, **22**, 1.
11. *California Juvenile Traffic Study* (1952) Committee Report.
12. Cambridge Department of Criminal Science (1957) *Sexual Offences, A Report*. London: Macmillan (English Studies on Criminal Science, 9).
13. CARR SAUNDERS, A. M., MANNHEIM, H., & RHODES, E. C. (1942) *Young Offenders*. London: Cambridge Univ. Press.
14. CARTER, M. P., & JEPHCOTT, P. *The Social Background of Delinquency*. Unpublished.
15. CLINARD, MARSHALL B. (1951) 'Sociologists and American Sociology'. *J. crim. Law Criminol.*, **4**, 549ff.
16. CLINARD, MARSHALL B. (1952) *The Black Market*. New York: Rinehart.
17. CLINARD, MARSHALL B. (1956) 'Research Frontiers in Criminology'. *Brit. J. Delinq.*, **7**, 110ff.
18. CLINARD, MARSHALL B. (1957) *Sociology of Deviant Behaviour*. New York: Rinehart.
19. COHEN, ALBERT K. (1955) *Delinquent Boys, The Culture of the Gang*. 2nd ed. Glencoe, Ill.: Free Press; London, Routledge.
20. CORNIL, PAUL (1959) 'Contribution de la "Victimologie" aux sciences criminologiques'. *Rev. Droit pen.*, April 1959.
21. CRESSEY, DONALD R. (1953) *Other People's Money*. Glencoe, Ill.: Free Press.
22. DE BERKER, PAUL (1960) '"State of Mind" Reports: The Inadequate Personality'. *Brit. J. Criminol.*, **1**, 6ff.
23. Division of Adult Paroles, Department of Corrections, State of California. Special Intensive Parole Unit, Reports: Phase I (November 1956); Phase II (December 1958). Unpublished.
24. EAST, NORWOOD (1942) *The Adolescent Criminal*. London: Churchill.
25. EAST, NORWOOD (1949) *Society and the Criminal*. London: H.M.S.O.

The Study of Crime

26. ELLIOTT, MABEL A., & MERRILL, FRANCIS E. (1950) *Social Disorganization*. 3rd ed. New York: Harper.
27. FERGUSON, THOMAS (1952) *The Young Delinquent in his Social Setting*. London: Oxford Univ. Press.
28. GIBBENS, T. C. N. (1957) 'Juvenile Prostitution'. *Brit. J. Delinq.*, **8**, 3ff.
29. GIBBENS, T. C. N. (1958) 'Car Thieves'. *Brit. J. Delinq.*, **8**, 257ff.
30. GIBBENS, T. C. N., POND, D. A., & STAFFORD-CLARK, D. (1956) 'Follow-Up Study of Criminal Psychopaths'. *Brit. J. Delinq.*, **6**, 126ff.
31. GINSBERG, MORRIS (1939) *In The Study of Society*. (Ed. F. C. Bartlett and others) London: Kegan Paul.
32. GINSBERG, MORRIS (1959) *Essays in Sociology and Social Philosophy*. 2 vols. London: Heinemann.
33. GINSBERG, MORRIS (ed.) (1959) *Law and Opinion in England in the Twentieth Century*. London: Stevens.
34 GLOVER, EDWARD (1954) 'Team Research in Delinquency; A Psychoanalytical Commentary' *Brit. J. Delinq.*, **4**, 173ff.
35. GLUECK, SHELDON (1956) 'Theory and Fact in Criminology'. *Brit. J. Deling.*, **7**, 103ff.
36. GLUECK, SHELDON (1959) *The Problem of Delinquency*. Boston: Houghton Mifflin.
37. GLUECK, SHELDON AND ELEANOR (1950) *Unraveling Juvenile Delinquency*. New York: Commonwealth Fund.
37a.GLUECK, SHELDON AND ELEANOR (1956) *Physique and Delinquency*. New York: Harper.
37b.GRÜNHUT, M. (1951) 'Statistics in Criminology.' *J. R. statist. Soc.*, **114**, 139ff.
38. GRÜNHUT, M. (1952) 'Probation as a Research Field.' *Brit. J. Delinq.* **2**, 287ff.
39. GRÜNHUT, M. (1955) 'Juvenile Delinquents under Punitive Detention'. *Brit. J. Delinq.*, **5**, 191ff. (1960) 'After-effects of Punitive Detention'. *Ibid.*, **10**, 178ff.
40. GURVITZ, MILTON (1951) 'Developments in the Concept of Psychopathic Personality (1900–1950).' *Brit. J. Delinq.*, **2**, 88ff.
41. *Handwörterbuch der Kriminologie* (1935) 'Verkehrspolizei', vol. 2, pp. 921ff. Berlin and Leipzig.
42. HARTUNG, FRANK E. (1958) 'A Critique of the Sociological Approach to Crime and Correction', *Law and contemp. Prob.*, **23**, 706ff.
43. HILL, DENIS & POND, D. A. (1952) 'Reflections on One Hundred Capital Cases submitted to Electroencephotography'. *J. ment. Sci.*, **98**, 23ff.
44. HODGE, R. SESSIONS, WALTER V. J., & WALTER, W. GREY (1953). 'Juvenile Delinquency: An Electrophysiological, Psychological, and Social Study'. *Brit. J. Delinq.*, **3**, 155ff.
45. Home Office (1959) *Penal Practice in a Changing Society*. (Cmd. 645). London: H.M.S.O.

46. JEFFERY, C. RAY (1959) 'The Historical Development of Criminology'. *J. crim. Law Criminol.*, **50**, 3ff.
47. JONES, HOWARD (1958) 'Approaches to an Ecological Study'. *Brit. J. Delinq.*, **8**, 277ff.
48. KITSUSE, JOHN I., & DIETRICK, DAVID C. (1959) 'Delinquent Boys: a Critique'. *Amer. Social. Rev.*, **24**, 208ff.
49. LANDER, BERNARD (1954) *Towards an Understanding of Juvenile Delinquency.* New York: Columbia Univ. Press.
50. LINDZEY, GARDNER (ed.) (1958) *Assessment of Human Motives.* New York: Rinehart.
51. LOCKWOOD, DAVID (1956) 'Some Remarks on "The Social System"'. *Brit. J. Sociol.*, **7**, 134ff.
51a. LODGE, T. S. (1953) 'Criminal Statistics.' *J. R. statist. Soc.*, **116**, 283ff.
52. LUNDEN, WALTER A. (1958) 'Pioneers in Criminology XVI—Emile Durkheim (1858–1917)'. *J. crim. Law, Criminol., and Police Sci.*, **49**, 2ff.
53. McCORKLE, LLOYD W., ELIAS, ALBERT, & BIXBY, F. LOVELL (1958) *The Highfields Story.* New York.
54. MACRAE, DONALD (1958) Review of Gunnar Myrdal, 'Value in Social Theory', *Manchester Guardian*, 21 March, 1958.
55. MANNHEIM, HERMANN (1940) *Social Aspects of Crime in England between the Wars.* London: Allen and Unwin.
56. MANNHEIM, HERMANN (1946) *Criminal Justice and Social Reconstruction.* London: Routledge.
57. MANNHEIM, HERMANN (1948) *Juvenile Delinquency in an English Middletown.* London: Routledge.
58. MANNHEIM, HERMANN (1949) 'Why Delinquency, The Limits of Present Knowledge'. In 59, pp. 128ff.
59. MANNHEIM, HERMANN (1955) *Group Problems in Crime and Punishment.* London: Routledge.
60. MANNHEIM, HERMANN (1956). 'Prison Reform I.' *Brit. J. Delinq.*, **7**, 148ff.
61. MANNHEIM, HERMANN (1957) 'The Unified Approach to the Administration of Criminal Justice'. *Proceedings of the Canadian Congress of Corrections*, pp. 241ff. Montreal.
62. MANNHEIM, HERMANN (1958) 'Some Aspects of Judicial Sentencing Policy'. *Yale Law J.*, **67**, 961ff.
63. MANNHEIM, HERMANN, & WILKINS, LESLIE T. (1955) *Prediction Methods in Relation to Borstal Training.* London: H.M.S.O.
64. MARSHALL, T. H. (1947) *Sociology at the Crossroads.* London: London School of Economics.
65. MAYS, JOHN B. (1954) *Growing Up in the City.* Liverpool: Liverpool Univ. Press.
66. MERTON, ROBERT K. (1957) *Social Theory and Social Structure.* 2nd ed. Glencoe, Ill.: Free Press.
67. MIDDENDORFF, WOLF (1959) 'Die kriminologische Bedeutung der Verkehrsdelikte'. *Recht der Jugend*, **7**, 289ff.

The Study of Crime

68. MILLS, C. WRIGHT (1959) *The Sociological Imagination.* New York: Oxford Univ. Press.
69. MORRIS, NORVAL (1951) *The Habitual Criminal.* London: Longmans.
70. MORRIS, TERENCE P. (1958) *The Criminal Area. A Study in Social Ecology.* London: Routledge.
71. MYRDAL, GUNNAR (1958) *Value in Social Theory.* London: Routledge.
72. NAESS, SIRI (1959) 'Mother-Child Separation and Delinquency.' *Brit. J. Delinq.*, **10**, 22ff.
73. NETTLER, GWYN (1959) 'Anti-Social Sentiment and Criminality'. *Amer. Sociol. Rev.*, **24**, 202ff.
74. PAKENHAM, LORD (1958) *Causes of Crime.* London: Weidenfeld & Nicolson.
75. POPPER, KARL R. (1957) *The Poverty of Historicism.* London: Routledge.
76. POWERS, EDWIN, & WITMER, HELEN (1951) *An Experiment in the Prevention of Delinquency*: The Cambridge-Somerville Youth Study. With a Foreword by Gordon W. Allport. New York: Columbia Univ. Press.
77. QUÉTELET, ADOLPHE (1869) *Physique sociale, ou Essai sur le développement des facultés de l'homme.* Brussels, Paris, St Petersburg.
78. RECKLESS, WALTER C. (1955) *The Crime Problem.* 2nd ed. New York: Appleton-Century.
79. ROSE, A. G. (1954) *Five Hundred Borstal Boys.* Oxford: Blackwell.
80. ROSE, ARNOLD M. (1954) *Theory and Method in the Social Sciences.* Minneapolis: Univ. of Minnesota Press.
81. ROSE, ARNOLD M. (ed.) (1958) *The Institutions of Advanced Societies.* Minneapolis: Univ. of Minnesota Press.
82. ROSE, A. G. (1956) 'The Sociological Analysis of Borstal Training. *Brit. J. Delinq.*, **6**, 202ff. 'Sociometric Analysis and Observation in a Borstal Institution.' *Ibid.*, 285ff. (1959) 'Status and Grouping in a Borstal Institution'. *Ibid.* **9**, 258ff.
83. ROSE, A. G. (1957) 'Follow Up and/or Prediction?' *Brit. J. Delinq.*, **7**, 309ff.
84. RUBIN, SOL, & REISS, ALBERT J. (1951) 'Unravelling Juvenile Delinquency, I and II'. *Amer. J. Sociol.*, **57**, 107ff., 115ff.
85. SAVITZ, LEONARD D. (1959) 'Automobile Theft'. *J. Crim. Law, Criminol. and Police Sci.*, **50**, 132ff.
86. SCOTT, PETER (1956) 'Gangs and Delinquent Groups in London', *Brit. J. Delinq.*, **7**, 4ff.
87. SELLIN, THORSTEN (1938) *Culture Conflict and Crime.* New York: Social Science Research Council, Bulletin 41.
88. SELLIN, THORSTEN (1950) 'The Sociological Study of Criminality'. *J. Crim. Law, Criminol. and Police Sci.*, **41**, 412.
89. SELLING, LOWELL S. (1949) 'Traffic Violator', in *Encyclopaedia of Criminology* (ed. V. C. Branham and S. B. Kutash). New York: Philosophical Library.
90. SPENCER, JOHN C. (1954) *Crime and the Services.* London: Routledge.

Hermann Mannheim

91. STAFFORD-CLARK, D. W., POND, DESMOND, & DOUST, J. W. LOVETT (1951) 'The Psychopath in Prison'. *Brit. J. Delinq.*, **2**, 117ff.
92. STOTT, D. H. (1950) *Delinquency and Human Nature.* Dunfermline: Carnegie United Kingdom Trust.
93. SUTHERLAND, EDWIN H. (1939) *Principles of Criminology.* 3rd ed. Chicago and Philadelphia: Lippincott.
94. SUTHERLAND, EDWIN H. (1947) *Principles of Criminology.* 4th ed. Reprinted in: *The Sutherland Papers.* Ed. A. Cohen, A. Lindesmith and K. Schuessler. Philadelphia: Lippincott.
95. SUTHERLAND, EDWIN H. (1955) *Principles of Criminology.* 5th ed. Revised by D. R. Cressey. Philadelphia: Lippincott.
96. SUTHERLAND, EDWIN H. (1949) *White Collar Crime.* New York: Dryden Press.
97. *Third International Congress of Criminology* (1957) *Summary of Proceedings.* London.
98. WEEKS, H. ASHLEY (1958) *Youthful Offenders at Highfields.* Ann Arbor.
99. WILKINS, LESLIE T. (1958) 'A Small Comparative Study of the Results of Probation'. *Brit. J. Delinq.*, **8**, 201ff.
100. WILSON, HARRIETT C. (1958) 'Juvenile Delinquency in Problem Families in Cardiff'. *Brit. J. Delinq.*, **9**, 94ff.
101. WINCH, PETER (1958) *The Idea of Social Science.* London: Routledge.
102. WOODWARD, MARY (1958) 'The Diagnosis and Treatment of Homosexual Offenders. *Brit. J. Delinq.*, **9**, 44ff.
103. WOOTTON, BARBARA (1959) *Social Science and Social Pathology.* London: Allen and Unwin.
104. WURTENBERGER, THOMAS (1959) 'Strafrichter und soziale Gerechtigkeit'. *Schweiz. Z. Strafrecht,* **75**

17

CRIMINOLOGY:

AN OPERATIONAL RESEARCH

APPROACH

Leslie T. Wilkins

SENIOR Common Rooms may discuss for many years to come whether criminology is or is not a science, and the outcome of the debate, if any, will not change the situation of fact in any way. None the less, since criminology is concerned with the crime problem in society it is a proper field for the application of operational research methods. The cost to society of crime runs into several millions of pounds annually, and it is reasonable and desirable that society should use research workers to assist in social defence. Such a policy was explicitly adopted in Britain when, by the Criminal Justice Act 1948, the Secretary of State was empowered to spend public funds on 'the conduct of research into the causes of delinquency and the treatment of offenders, and matters connected therewith'. The New York State Youth Commission Law (Chapter 636 of the Laws of 1956, as amended—Article 19-A of the Executive Law) is very specific. After setting up the Youth Commission (413–415), 416 reads 'The Commission shall also have the power and *it shall be the duty* of the Commission to make necessary studies and analyses and to conduct research with respect to (a) . . .' (listing twelve specific areas a-1) and '(m) such other matters as the commission deems relevant and desirable.'

In 1957 the Home Office set up a research unit to carry out research and evaluation within the machinery of government, and for some years

Leslie T. Wilkins

previously had made funds available to universities for the conduct of research in criminology. Britain was not alone in doing this. In 1957 the Financial Analyst of the State of California (who has similar functions to the British Treasury) sent back the estimates for the Department of Corrections with a requirement that a supplementary estimate be prepared to cover research. Authorized expenditure on penal research in California is now equal to nearly 2 per cent of the costs of penal administration, and other funds are available to the official research unit from external sources.

The doctrine underlying State action to support or organize criminological research may be summarized as 'Any administrative system spending large sums of public money should undertake research to *evaluate* and *improve* its functioning as an integral part of the administrative process'.

Operational research requires a clear statement of the problems to be investigated and the ends that it is desired to achieve. It is necessary to state the problems in a language which enables the concepts to be *manipulated*—not merely *communicated*. Operational research is most effective if it is a co-operative effort between the administrator and the scientist. If the administrator can state the ends desired, the work of the operational research team is to assess the likely outcome of a number of possible means towards the desired ends. Problems must be limited and specific and be oriented towards action—general solutions are not sought. A large amount of planning and logical analysis must necessarily precede the research operations.

Just as an engineer uses models to gain information about his problems, so the operational research worker is concerned with models which may represent in some way and more or less accurately the 'real' problem. In the field of behavioural science these 'models' are normally verbal or symbolic (e.g. mathematical models) and are of a form which enables inferences to be made from patterns of variation in the numbers generated. Models enable techniques worked out in one branch of inquiry to be used in others concerned with quite different subject matter.

This chapter will first briefly indicate some of the difficulties in pinning down the concept of crime by the use of a simple mathematical model. The main emphasis will, however, be upon considerations of the ends desired in the disposal of offenders and the action that might be taken by research workers to assist society to deal with the crime problem. A four-fold classification of ends will be used as a framework within which action-oriented research might be developed.

Criminology: An Operational Research Approach

How Large is the Crime Problem?

No estimate of the total cost of crime to the community has yet been made in Britain, although such a study is planned.[10] In the United States an estimate was made by the Wickersham Commission in 1931.[16] Their estimate could not include certain items which might legitimately have been regarded as expenditure due to crime, and it is on the low side. None the less they estimated the annual cost to be in the region of 1000 million dollars.

Whatever the cost to Britain in money terms, the number of 'crimes known to the police' was, in 1959, the largest ever recorded in its history. The 'cause' of the 'crime wave' is often attributed to the low moral values of contemporary society. Detailed examination of this argument may show that it is circular, but such an examination is not possible without further definition of terms. If the argument is not circular, is it a fact that today the average citizen is more likely than in previous years to become the victim of criminal attack on his property or person? It will be noted that the majority of 'crimes known to the police' do not become known to them by direct observation, but are reported by the victims. It is also well known that the legal definitions of most crimes, while clear enough, are extremely wide in scope. For example, the value of the stolen article is not relevant to the legal definition of larceny.* There must be many professors and civil servants who are (technically) guilty of fraudulent conversion or larceny by reason of using for their personal purposes stationery supplied for official use. Few children over seven years of age have not been so fortunate as to find some small coin or apparently discarded article which they have retained and in consequence are guilty of larceny by finding. A large proportion of shops regard shoplifting as a normal hazard of business and merely treat a proportion of turnover as an 'on-cost' rather than take measures to reduce the incidence of this offence. The latter course would be more expensive. Included in what is usually regarded as normal behaviour are acts which are crimes by legal definition, but at the extreme end of a distribution are crimes which all sane persons, even the offenders, regard as such. There can be no discrete break in the continuum of actions. It is convenient to envisage human acts as a continuum from the most saintly to the most depraved, as shown in FIGURE I. There are few extremely saintly acts, and few extremely depraved; the majority of our actions are 'normal'. Thus the crimes known to the police do not include a large proportion of the

---

* Damage may be done by vandals, but the offence is not indictable, and hence not within the scope of 'crimes known', unless the value exceeds £20. In this case whether an incident is a 'crime' depends upon the value of the goods and the value of the £ at the time.

Leslie T. Wilkins

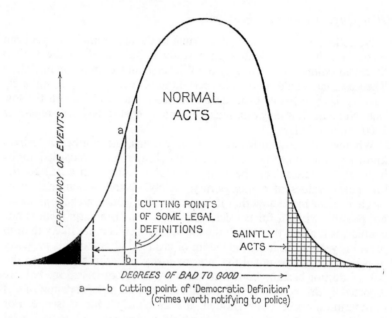

a——b Cutting point of 'Democratic Definition'
(crimes worth notifying to police)

FIGURE I.

crimes committed, and these crimes are additional to the 'dark figure' of undetected crime. The 'crimes known' represent a biased sample of crime, because reported crime has to be defined *socially* both as a crime and as being *worth notifying* to the police, usually by the victim. There is considerable scope for this social definition to vary both from place to place and from time to time without any change in the actual situation. Any such change in the definition of 'crimes worth notifying' would, in completely stable conditions, influence the bias in the sample of crimes represented by the 'crimes known' figure.

It is thus possible to argue that if our moral standards are improving (becoming more stringent in that a more conforming standard of behaviour is expected) the definition of the social concept of a crime-that-should-be-notified-to-the-police will tend more closely to agree with the strict legal definition. Without criticism of the legal definitions, which are intended to serve legal purposes, it is clear that the *social implications* of crime are not measured by figures based on *legal* definitions. This distinction is not often clearly realized in social research. The concept of 'crime' is a difficult one upon which to base research analyses.

Criminology: An Operational Research Approach

A Classification of Areas for Research

The Criminal Justice Act 1948 classified criminological research into two parts, 'the causes of delinquency and the treatment of offenders'. This subdivision is useful. Somewhere between the two aspects of 'cause' and 'treatment' comes the concept of justice. There may on occasions be a conflict between the ends of justice and the desirable treatment. In any event the evaluation of treatment can be made only if the objectives of the court in sentencing an offender to one treatment rather than to another are known. These objectives are not usually stated, but it is clear that treatment, in the reformatory sense of that term, is not always the only consideration of the courts, although it may be the main factor.* Standard textbooks in jurisprudence describe the task of the court in sentencing as selecting a balance between the factors of deterrence (to others), retribution, and reclaiming the offender. To these three concepts must be added that of protection of the public by ensuring that the potentially dangerous recidivists are placed in security (e.g. Preventive Detention). The narrow concept of retribution is perhaps better extended to mean any ethical considerations. Thus it seems that four factors appear in the judgement of the courts, treatment (maximizing the likelihood that the offender will not repeat his offence), deterrence (maximizing the likelihood that what is done in this case will stop others from offending), protection of the public, and fourthly some ethical element which may be retributive or an act of faith based on some other aspect of ethics and belief which, by definition it is not possible to measure. Research has a proper function in attempting to evaluate the best strategy in respect of the first three factors, but research is concerned with crime and not with sin.†

The concept of the protection of the public is, of course, far more significant in the role of the police than of the courts. The police are concerned also with aspects of deterrence and treatment. The action of the courts in respect of deterrence is conditional on the probability of detection, and the police (particularly juvenile liaison officers) are concerned to some degree in treatment in that an effective warning may be an appropriate treatment for a young offender. The concept of the 'causes' of crime may be integrated with crime prevention, since there is no meaning in or definition of the causes of crime except that causes

* In the case of juveniles, the courts are enjoined by law to consider the reform of the offender.
† Ethical considerations are outside the scope of the scientific method, but are in some senses superior. Ethics impinges on research but is not concerned with it. Ethics may be concerned with the ends desired but not with the processes of inference or the techniques of measurement. Ethics may discuss what is desirable but not what is valid. What is true (valid) has nothing necessarily to do with what is right. In this chapter we are concerned with inference and validity only.

309

Leslie T. Wilkins

are factors which, when modified, tend to reduce or prevent the occurrence of an event. Perhaps these four areas or concepts may form a basis for scientific study. (i) Treatment which is related to (ii) Public protection, and (iii) Deterrence which is related to (iv) Crime Prevention and the causes of crime.

Treatment Research

(a) Evaluation

The many advances in the treatment of offenders that have taken place in the last century were, in the main, stimulated by humanitarian (ethical) considerations; the heart rather than the head has been the source of innovation in penal matters. There can, of course, be no objection to this. Indeed, if a case can be made for any change on humanitarian grounds it may override scientific considerations. On the other hand it must not be assumed that humanitarian grounds are scientific. The argument that because a thing is right it must also be profitable is not sound. Whether kindness is more or less effective than a strict disciplinarian routine in achieving the reform of offenders it is possible to find out. If kindness is desirable, it may be desirable enough to be preferable even if it is less effective, but the desirability cannot reasonably be established without the scientific measurement of effectiveness. To date very few treatments have been subjected to any form of evaluative analysis. There are reasons for this; the two most important are, lack of tools to do this work and lack of funds to develop the tools. Many people still regard the treatment of offenders as a field of human activity which should not, in principle, be subjected to scientific analysis, because crime and its treatment are regarded as essentially a matter for religious or ethical determination. The courts, by some authorities, are seen to be acting on behalf of God in the punishment of evil.*

Treatment research cannot make use of the most usual tools of the scientific method; experimental designs are almost impossible to fit into the legal structure. Two or more different treatments cannot be allocated at random to a 'control' and 'experimental' group, because to do so would not be seen as justice. There are notable exceptions to this in some other countries where the philosophy of treatment differs from that in England. In some American states, for example, public disapprobation is strongly expressed if treatment fails (the offender recidivates) but not if the sentence (by British standards) is regarded as either too lenient or too severe. Where there is emphasis on treatment

* This view was expressed in a B.B.C. Third Programme discussion and underlies some of the argument on the Wolfenden Report. It is a view which is seldom made explicit today.

310

Criminology: An Operational Research Approach

to the exclusion of almost all other considerations it seems to become evident to the public that the authorities must experiment if they are to find the best treatments; experiment is not seen to conflict with the demands of justice. In California several experiments have been made where offenders have been allocated at random to different treatments, both in institutions and on parole.*

In Britain it is necessary to use systems for evaluating different treatments which do not require experimental variation of the action taken by the courts in disposing of the offender, but which take account of the differences in the types of offenders selected for each treatment. The classical method for such problems is the 'matching' technique. There are occasions in criminology where the method may be used, but it is usually unsatisfactory. The disadvantages of the matching method are lack of power and wasteful use of data. There are problems too in what may be the nature of legitimate inference from studies based on this system. The number of factors which might be matched is usually large, but it is necessary to select one or two, whose validity is often assumed rather than tested.

Recently a system of regression matching or matching by prediction methods has been evolved and applied to treatment evaluation problems. Two such applications are those of Ashley Weekes[15] in evaluating the Highfields experiment, and Mannheim and Wilkins'[7] borstal training study.

An illustration of the 'prediction' approach may be given by reference to the borstal training problem. FIGURE II shows the pattern of decisions that are made after a crime is committed. In respect of borstal training, about which rather more information is available than for other forms of treatment, the 'flow' diagram indicates the results of treatment. Roughly one in three of the offenders dealt with in 'open' institutions committed further crimes within three years from release, whereas approximately two out of every three of those trained in 'closed' institutions were similarly reconvicted. But every borstal lad was first sent to a reception centre, where, after a period of observation, he was allocated to the training institution considered most suitable. Clearly the allocation procedure will tend to ensure that 'better' material is sent to 'open' conditions. The problem in evaluating 'open' as against 'closed' treatment is mainly concerned with finding out *how much* of the difference in subsequent success rates between the two broad categories of treatment is due to the different classes of lads received. Prediction methods enable measurements of the nature of the 'input material' to be made and compared with the results of the 'output'. This is done by setting up a theoretical model relating to the stage immediately following the sentence of the court, that is, before the

* See p. 316 for details.

311

Leslie T. Wilkins

offender is received into the Reception Centre. At this stage a quantity of information is available which does not, of course, include any reference to the type of treatment to be received. This information may be used to estimate the probability of failure after treatment. Although this approach has commonly been termed 'prediction' it is more appropriate to think of it as providing an estimate of the 'pre-sentence probability' of success or failure, since only information available before sentence is used as a basis for the calculation. A short description of this procedure and some examples may indicate the utility of the method.

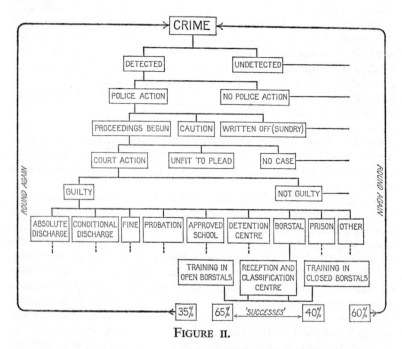

FIGURE II.

As Mannheim and Wilkins[7] pointed out, statistical prediction tables, like any other forms of prognosis, are based on experience. In their study, in order to obtain the necessary 'experience', they selected one in every three of the boys committed to (not released from) borstal training between mid-1946 and mid-1947. About these lads were assembled as many facts and opinions as possible which were known and recorded in the official case history files, covering the period before sentence. This provided the material for the 'pre-sentence probability' estimates. Other information known only during training or subsequently was also noted. Using information available before committal, it was desired to 'predict' the likelihood that the lad would or would not be reconvicted. It was easier to define failure of treatment than success. There seemed to be only one clear simple and direct criterion, namely, that a further offence was committed by the lad after release, the residual (success) group might contain some cases successful only in avoiding further detection. The problem of definition of criteria did not seem to Mannheim and Wilkins to provide grounds for serious objection to their method. They found that a number of possible criteria were highly correlated. They report, 'Whether criteria of success or failure are taken as the simple fact of further conviction or no further conviction, or whether some attempt is made to assess degree of failure, the same system of prognosis seems to hold equally well. This seems to suggest a general tendency to crime as measured by the experience tables. An analogy is seen with the concept of "general health", which when low, predisposes individuals to attack by a variety of risks of infection; when the general resistance to crime is low, the likelihood of serious failure is greater and the greater is the risk of more failures' (⁷, p. 203).

In all practical research to evaluate treatment it is necessary to specify a time limit to apparent 'success'. Fortunately for statisticians, if a person is going to return to crime he is likely to be reconvicted within a short period from release. For borstal training it was shown that convictions within three years from release accounted for at least 80 per cent of those who would ever be reconvicted.

Using the information collected in respect of lads committed to borstal in 1946/47, it was possible by 1952 to divide the sample into two distinct halves—those who had failed within three years from release, and those who had not. There was a category for 'sheep' and a category for 'goats', but no completely satisfactory criterion for degrees of 'sheepishness' or 'goatishness'.[17] The methods used in this study were ruled by four principles:

    (i) Repeatability (reproduceability)
    (ii) Validity (power)
    (iii) Efficiency
    (iv) Simplicity.

It is perhaps necessary only to illustrate the point of efficiency. Efficiency requires that the smallest number of items of information are used, and that no item is added unless it contributes something of significance to the estimation of the probability of failure—that is, to the 'prediction'.* This point may be seen by reference to the pioneering

---

* The term 'prediction' has a wider meaning than the 'pre-sentence probability', the latter term is restricted to a prediction based on limited information related to a specific criterion.

work of the Gluecks,[4] who used a large number of items of information (which they call factors) and added together those items which, singly, were most prognostic of failure. By the use of six items of information they derived a prediction represented by a coefficient of 0·45, whereas using only one of the six items they could have obtained a prediction coefficient of 0·42. The gain, using six items instead of one, of 0·03, was of course, insignificant. This was due to a problem they subsequently recognized and termed 'overlapping'. Mannheim and Wilkins examined over sixty items of information but attempted to reduce these to a *minimum* which *maximized* the specification of failure. For this purpose they used the statistical technique of *discriminant analysis*. Some modifications were necessary because they had to use information of various types—attributes, classification, and variables. These different types of data had to be combined. Using these methods they derived a result which is shown in Table I below.

TABLE I

Items used, and results of the first-stage classification into group according to risk of failure

ITEMS USED

	Maximum possible weight
Previous convictions	45·0
Longest period in any one job	11·7
Living in industrial area (Industrialization index) . . .	8·0
Living with parents	7·5

RESULTS

Risk class	Raw score (range)	Results of Training success	failure	No. of cases	Success rate %
A	0 – 9·9	47	7	54 ⎫ 126	87 ⎫ 75
B	10·0–14·9	48	24	72 ⎭	67 ⎭
X	15·0–23·9	96	65	161	59
C	24·0–39·9	28	54	82 ⎫ 98	34 ⎫ 30
D	40 or more	2	14	16 ⎭	13 ⎭
ALL CASES		221	164	385	57

The four items which proved useful are given above the table. It is worth noting some of the original items which were among the sixty studied which do *not* appear amongst the predictors. These include such factors as: broken homes, overcrowding, religion, and indeed many others which are known to distinguish between delinquents and non-delinquents. From this it seemed that items which distinguished between delinquents and non-delinquents did not necessarily discriminate the relatively good from the relatively bad risks among delinquents themselves, at least as found in the borstal population. This may explain why subjective judgements did not provide very satisfactory information for discriminating types of risk.

From Table I it will be seen that the top two groups combined had a success rate of 75 per cent, while the last two groups were successful in 30 per cent of the cases. Taking every case entering one of the two Reception Centres during the latter part of 1948 it was possible to check this result. Using only the items at the top of Table I, and using *the same* weights as shown there, the results shown in Table II were obtained.

TABLE II

Comparison of the predicted success rate and that actually achieved with a further group of cases when classified into risk groups by pre-sentence probability

Risk Category and success rate %	1948 *intake at a Reception Centre* subsequent successes	subsequent *failures*	*Actual success rate* %
AB 75%	90	30	75%
CD 30%	27	65	29%

As the diagram of FIGURE II shows, 'open' treatment seems to be more successful than 'closed'. By use of the prediction equations it was possible to examine this outcome more closely. It was found that the belief that 'open' institutions obtained better material than closed was justified. In fact, 74 per cent of the A.B. group and only 39 per cent of the C.D. group went into open treatment. It was thus only to be expected that there should be better results from open institutions, and the prediction tables (i.e. the estimates of pre-sentence probability of failure) could assist in evaluating *how much* better results should be expected, because they indicate *how much* better was the material. In other words it is possible to use the pre-sentence probability prediction equation to partial out the difference expected owing to the nature of the material. The results of calculating the success rates for the different types of treatment within each risk group are shown in Table III.

Although the overall difference between the open and closed treatments, after making allowance for the type of material received, dropped from 22 per cent to 8 per cent, the difference remained significant. It cannot, of course, be claimed that this is a rigorous proof that open treatment (as such) is better. It does not mean that open treatment is

TABLE III

Comparison of success rates for open and closed treatment using (prediction) tables.

| Risk category | Success rate (%) | | Excess success |
	Open	Closed	in open Borstals
AB	78	67	11%
X	61	56	5%
CD	38	28	10%
ALL CASES	58	36	22%

desirable for all cases; that all borstals should be open institutions. It is possible to explain the differences in favour of open treatment in terms of an interaction factor which may be of various forms, and which, owing to the design of the study, is confounded with error. As Martin remarks in his review[8] of Mannheim and Wilkins' work, 'with all types of lad open borstals were significantly more successful than closed borstals. This is demonstrated at some length and appears to be an unshakable conclusion. It is possible, however, as no doubt the authors would agree, that the difference may not be entirely due to the general merits of open as opposed to closed borstals; the method of the study precluded consideration of the point, but may it not have been that when a "bad" risk went to an open borstal one of the factors that influenced him was the high proportion of "good" lads to be found there? In other words, the explanation of the better success rates of open borstals may lie partly in the composition of the social groups within them rather than solely in the methods of treatment adopted.' This is one hypothesis, and there are a number of others which may be put forward to explain the difference in outcome other than the simple direct conclusion that open treatment was better.

The finding that one form of treatment was better than another, after making an allowance for the type of material fed into the treatment system, has not been supported by other studies. Wilkins,[18] using the well-known matching technique to compare probation with other forms of treatment, found no significant differences between them. This is the more usual finding.

Whether prediction or matching methods are used, any methods which rely upon mathematical models cannot be as convincing as direct experimentation. In California[13] offenders have been released on parole in accordance with a rigorous experimental design. Parolees were allocated *at random* to officers having case loads of fifteen, thirty, sixty, and ninety men, and whether an offender was released three months early or not was also randomly determined. A follow-up over two years

Criminology: An Operational Research Approach

failed to reveal any difference in outcome due either to time of release or case-load size.

It is fair to summarize treatment research to date as showing that there is no generally good treatment—no treatment is suited to all types of cases. But which type of treatment is suited to which type of case is unknown. It seems that it is necessary, however, to examine the interplay between offender and treatment rather than to consider treatment as a single variable. The treatment indicated for different types of offenders may be contra-indicated for others. The problem becomes, who should do what, with what, and to whom?

Treatment Development

Research, evaluation, and development are closely allied fields. Evaluation is a fairly specific procedure limited to problems involving on-going treatment systems. Research methods useful for the study of evaluation problems are receiving considerable attention. But evaluation of what exists does not *necessarily* indicate new ways to develop treatment. Hypothesis testing is a different procedure from that of setting up hypotheses. One way towards treatment development involves a study of the results of testing hypotheses.

Usually such testing results in the destruction of hypotheses, and, from the wreckage of previous theories some phoenix may arise in the mind. Although it cannot be said to have been proved that all existing treatments are equally effective or ineffective, the time is ripe to set up and study hypotheses which are consistent with that *assumption*. Such a study made in the light of the previous negative research results already mentioned could indicate in what way experimental treatment might be set up and how treatment might be developed.

First, however, it is necessary to consider whether prediction or matching systems of evaluation do not have important limitations. This is necessary even though experimental work lends support to the conclusions derived from mathematical models, since there may be a fallacy common to both. If a fallacy exists or gaps can be found in the logical network, this could be valuable in that it might suggest areas for investigation. There are in fact, important gaps in most cases in the methods mentioned.

The prediction, matching, and the experimental techniques so far discussed have used designs which evaluate the system of treatment studied *as a whole process for all* offenders concerned. The methods do not indicate what may be good or bad features within any treatment, and if the differences within treatments cancel out differences between treatments, no differences between the treatments would appear. Certain features of one treatment might be good for some types of cases and bad

317

for others, and if the interaction between types of persons and types of treatments were due to features not covered by the experimental methods or the 'model', again no differences will appear; indeed all techniques could have similar limitations. Prediction provides criminological research workers with *one* instrument that, appropriately used, will help with *some* of their tasks, but every instrument of research is limited. The microscope is not a substitute for the thermometer; a stopwatch will not measure blood pressure. Prediction methods are like thermometers, they tell us better than a hand-on-brow technique which offenders are 'hot'. The pressing need is for more and better instruments in criminology and the behavioural sciences generally. Particularly there is a need for an appreciation of the scope and limitations of existing instruments and some hard thinking regarding the types of measurement that could be developed. Thus in the given example, the better outcome from 'open' treatment in borstal may be explained in a number of ways which the research design did not and could not test. The design tested only whether *overall* one treatment was better, there was no way of testing more refined hypotheses until the simpler hypotheses had been examined. In addition to the theory put forward by Martin the work of Grant may be relevant.

Grant and others[5] have recently adapted some of the theoretical concepts of perceptual processes to the theory of treatment. This approach is a new development in treatment research. Before discussing the results obtained, it may be desirable to say something about the theoretical concepts of perceptual processes, and particularly to define briefly the concept of 'social perception'. It is assumed that all knowledge is derived indirectly; that man constructs his knowledge by orderly translation of coded signals, and this process is called cognition. What appear to be intuitive direct responses in perceiving or thinking result from practice and predisposition, but are achieved by inferential processes, no matter how short-cut they may become through learning and experience. The development of an idea, the communication of an idea in words, the recognition of symbols, objects, or persons, and all other activity involves selecting or constructing a means appropriate to some end. Perception is conditioned by experience. Social perception refers to the way in which the social world is perceived. It relates to the processes of observing, recording (coding), and organizing the experience with people, groups, and social organizations. The same term is used also to refer to the ways in which social factors influence observations of the social world; how people 'understand' other people, and how they relate this 'understanding' of other people to modifications of their own behaviour. Attempts have been made to measure and describe the differences in the ways in which people observe, describe, and judge other persons and themselves.[1, 3]

Criminology: An Operational Research Approach

It was work in this general area of social perception which influenced Grant et al.[14] to describe 'social maturity' and to postulate that differences between offenders in the ways in which they tried to 'make sense of the social world' might interact with the nature of the treatment they received and thus help to explain differences in outcome. This led to an experiment which, so far as is known, is the only one that has been able to suggest ways of differentiating offenders according to the type of treatment indicated or contra-indicated. It was a project carried out by the Office of Naval Research in the United States of America.[5] Offenders were intensively studied and classified in many ways, but in particular according to measurable personality characteristics related to the ways in which they perceived the world—their reaction to problems of social interaction. Some were classified as 'socially mature', others as 'socially immature', after an intensive standardized interview. A rigorous experimental design was used to place the classified offenders into three treatments, where two (T1 and T2) were intensive 'living group therapy', the third (S) was the more normal training of a Naval Correctional Establishment. The results were tested by follow-up. The percentage successes in the three treatments revealed no differences between treatments *overall*; it was only when treatments were broken down by the type of offender *as classified by the 'social maturity' scale* that differences were observed. The results were as shown in Table IV.

TABLE IV

Result of experiment allocating at random to different treatments offenders of high and low levels of social maturity.

Personality type (Offender)	% successful Treatment type		
	T1	T2	S
Socially mature	70	72	61
Socially immature	41	55	60
All	59	65	61

It will be noted that the 'S' type treatment did not interact with the social-maturity rating of the offenders, whereas the intensive case work methods showed a marked interaction. Some cases were far more likely to recidivate after receiving the 'progressive' and intensive treatment. Optimum results would have been obtained by reserving the intensive group therapy for the 'socially mature', and subjecting the 'socially immature' to the simpler (and perhaps emotionally less threatening) retraining routines. It should, perhaps, be stressed that the offenders in the experiment were classified in several other ways—by intelligence and personality typologies, including the Minnesota Multiphasic Personality Inventory (M.M.P.I.)—but it was only the classification based

319

Leslie T. Wilkins

on the conceptual framework of 'social perception' that proved significant. Grant's experiments were too costly to form a basis for normal treatment practice. Moreover, all three treatments were highly standardized. Research is at present going on to try to find simpler instruments which can be substituted for the intensive standard interview while serving equally well as a basis for classification.

In current treatment practice the precise process is not constant for all institutions, and different offenders may receive different treatments within any one treatment type. Probation under one probation officer is likely to be different from probation under another. No matter how intensive the training the officers receive, they are different personalities. At the present time it is generally believed to be the personal contact between the officer and the offender that has a therapeutic effect, but very little is known of exactly what elements make up this or any other treatment system. Features such as group counselling can be isolated, but beyond this the treatment process has not been subjected to analysis.

Offenders are highly variable, the treatment processes are complex, and even the criteria of successful treatment are not firmly based, so that there is plenty of room for operational research into treatment. Even the studies by Grant, which seem to make possible a big step forward, did not indicate exactly what factors *within* the T1 and T2 treatments resulted in their being good for some and bad for others. In this case, as in the Borstal study, it is not completely demonstrated that the differences found were due to 'treatment' rather than to other things which 'just happen' to different individuals undergoing different treatments. Although this is better than the earlier findings of no differences, still very little is known about the treatment of offenders. The nature of our ignorance is, however, beginning to be revealed, and this is encouraging.

Public Protection

It has been remarked that the concepts of treatment and of public protection are related. For example in the sentence of preventive detention the emphasis is on the protection of the public from the dangerous criminal, but when the offender has passed into the penal system it is the duty of those who are charged with retaining such offenders in security conditions to keep in mind also the task of reformation, no matter how small the probability that attempts at this will be effective. In some other countries the two concepts of treatment and public protection are more closely linked in the penal philosophy and sentencing practices. The indeterminate sentence relies on a philosophy which requires the correctional establishments to retain the

Criminology: An Operational Research Approach

offender until such time as the treatment is regarded as completed and the offender is no longer likely to be a danger to society.

It has also been believed, although without much evidence, that the majority of serious crimes are the work of the hardened offender, and that the best way to minimize the damage from crime is to reform offenders before they are committed to a life of crime. In Britain it is not true that the bulk of crime is due to habitual offenders; roughly one-third of crime is juvenile delinquency, one-third is committed by first offenders, and the remaining third is due to persons who have had one or more previous convictions. What is 'serious' crime is subject to many forms of definition. It is not by any means certain that the crimes which the law regards as most serious are those which attract the greatest amount of public disapprobation. Murder and sexual crimes are certainly committed in the majority of cases by first offenders, and the rates of recidivism are low in comparison with offences against property. Treatment has an important contribution to make to the protection of the public, since if it is successful it reduces recidivism, but no treatment can protect the public from the first offender unless he can be treated before he has actually committed an offence—while, in fact, he has shown no more than a predisposition to do so. Except in cases of certain mental disorders, treatment of potential offenders is not regarded as ethical, nor are there satisfactory methods for isolating the crime-prone. A contribution to public protection is made both by deterrence (which will be examined in the next section) and treatment, but over and above these contributions there is a further small contribution from custodial care, such that *even if it were known* that treatment would not be effective, the offender should be retained in security conditions. The nature of these conditions is a matter for ethical consideration, and regard should also be paid to the cost of maintaining the offender in security compared with the cost (which could be actuarially assessed) to society of his being allowed to move more or less freely. In this, as in other matters, it is possible to 'over-insure', and part of the premium is the restriction of liberty paid by the offender.

Deterrence

In recent years the concept of deterrence has not received its quota of attention. It is likely to be found necessary to devote much more research effort in the near future to this difficult area. No scientific policy for dealing with the crime problem is possible without taking this aspect of criminology into account. It is not now satisfactory to discuss the idea of deterrence from the approach of the historian.[11] Neither history, which merely argues from the fact that the severe penalties of the past did not deter, nor statistical time series analysis provide proofs

321

Leslie T. Wilkins

of the efficiency of deterrent measures. The death penalty for stealing a sheep may not deter a hungry and demented thief, while the stocks will not deter a mentally deranged sex offender. But today there is no hunger to drive the body to prefer the probability of death to its certainty, and mental illness is no longer treated by whipping or confinement to the snake pit. Deterrence cannot now be dismissed lightly. Deterrence is a concept with many facets which need consideration before the subject can be thought about in more detail.

Advocates of corporal punishment and other severe forms of disposal quite frequently claim that such punishments are more likely than humanitarian methods to deter the offender and through fear, rather than treatment, to make it less likely that he will repeat that type of offence for which such punishment was given. In so far as it has been possible to test these two hypotheses by means of available data, they have been proved untrue; in particular, those flogged were equally or more likely to be recidivist than those otherwise dealt with.[2] Although 'pre-sentence probabilities' were not calculated, some matching was used to make some allowance for differences in 'input'.

There are, however, honest people who cannot believe the figures which are generally assumed to confirm that flogging does not deter. The majority who at the present time advocate severe punishments place their faith in the deterrent effect *upon others* who might commit such offences rather than on the reformative or deterrent effect on the offender himself. This is a more difficult hypothesis to test without actual experiment. The problem of deterrence in this form is the problem of normal behaviour—why people do not commit crimes. It is difficult for the social scientist to obtain access to, or to create, situations which could measure normal behaviour and the nature of the restraints which keep most persons on the right side of the courts if not on the right side of the law. In the main the difficulty in studying deterrence is due to the wide definition; it is necessary to ask exactly what deterrence means in terms of the practical consequences in actual day-to-day events.

The word 'deterrence' itself suggests a pressure in the direction towards crime which is to be offset—deterrence can be considered only as a counter-force effecting some sort of balance: there must be an incentive towards crime in order for there to be any meaning in the concept of a deterrence to crime. Can it then be argued that deterrence has no substance or meaning if there is no need to deter? The average normal housewife does not need to be deterred from poisoning her husband, but possibly does need a deterrent from shoplifting. Where then does deterrence begin to have a meaning? Are there some crimes or some persons that always have need of a deterrent? How do the attitudes and controls of normal people balance their position? Clearly no thing or action may be regarded as a deterrent in its own right and in

322

all circumstances; it is necessary to postulate that it will deter in respect of some persons and some actions. That is to say, before any action may be termed a deterrent it is necessary to *predict* its effect. Before it is possible to predict an effect upon people it must be assumed that people behave in a consistent manner, even if their behaviour is otherwise irrational. If the behaviour of criminals or would-be criminals is unpredictable, then no action may logically be termed a deterrent.

Prison officers in the olden days used to say that the criminals they handled were not capable of being dealt with as ordinary human beings —they could not be reasoned with or controlled by the techniques of normal human relationships. This view is in conflict with the humanist view of treatment today, but there may be still some measure of truth in the statement in so far as it summarizes experience. It is possible that people who have never felt pressure towards crime and who need no deterrent, may not be able to visualize the mental 'set' of those who face such pressures. The projected views of persons who have never known hunger on the ways hungry men might behave are unlikely to be very sound. Is there any reason to suppose that the views of those of us who have never needed a deterrent are sound when we postulate what actions are or are not likely to deter those who are subjected to heavy pressure towards crime? It seems, and there is a large body of psychiatric evidence to support this view, that some persons commit crimes because they *want* to be punished. It is difficult to conceive of a deterrent in such cases except that of withholding punishment! The number of persons to whom this applies may be small, but if there is any truth in the statement at all it serves to show that a deterrent cannot be general, and, once the argument of limitation is accepted, the whole question of deterrence appears in a different light from that in which it is usually discussed.

It might be considered a satisfactory limitation to suppose that deterrence is meaningful in respect of those persons and actions which can be predicted. Prediction relies on consistent patterns, and it is not far from consistent behaviour to the concept of rational behaviour.*

It is convenient to follow the line suggested by the concept of rational behaviour. 'Rational behaviour' in relation to the actions of a criminal is a difficult concept, and it is no easier to apply to those of the would-be criminal. It seems to follow that the more rational the criminal the more 'normal' his behaviour. Severe (deterrent) penalties are usually desired by the public for crimes of violence and sexual assault which few people would regard as 'normal' or rational. The public must, of course, be protected from these offences, but it does not seem that reliance on

---

* Whether it is possible to have consistent irrational behaviour is not in question; but whether consistent but irrational behaviour could reasonably be expected to be predicted by normal rational persons.

Leslie T. Wilkins

the deterrent aspects of social action is the ideal method of protection. On the other hand attempts to get money, even if by illegal means, are more in keeping with the behaviour of rational men. An action (deterrent) must result in a predictable reaction (at least to a high degree of probability) on the part of the would-be offender before it can be a deterrent. What then is rational behaviour for criminals? Is it the same as rational behaviour for non-criminals?

It may be suggested that a rational criminal follows the pattern of behaviour described in the theory of strategy which nations use in warfare. He must weigh the probability of gain against the probability of loss for his contemplated crime. If he sees the risk to be small and the gain probably large, he may be inhibited by moral considerations, but if not, he may attempt the crime. A deterrent may thus be seen as something which changes *either* the value of the likely gain or the probability or size of the loss, thus changing the 'pay-off' of the criminal strategy. A deterrent which changes the *size or the probability of the gain*, that is, reduces the opportunity structure for the would-be offender, is not commonly regarded as a *deterrent*. Usually only the other half of the 'pay-off' matrix is considered, namely the increase in the likelihood of penalty and the size of the penalty; and it is expected to change would-be offenders' assessment of the pay-off by action on *other* offenders. This is, perhaps, the most unsatisfactory point in the doctrine of deterrence.

If the action taken in respect of *other* persons and *other* crimes is to influence the strategy of would-be offenders, an essential requirement is the *communication* of such action to those whom it is desired to deter.*
It seems probable that in most serious offences the offender is not aware of the true probabilities of being caught, nor is he aware of the likely penalty should he be caught. If he knew these facts, would his behaviour be different? The doctrine of deterrence states that it would. But, and this is an important point, he may be deterred only because his beliefs about what might happen to him are *not* correct; he may have *over*estimated the risk and the likely penalty, or *under*estimated the gain.

It is certain that people's actions are determined by what they believe to be true rather than what is in fact true, and there may be little association between facts and belief.†

* In some cases this is formally done by society, for example, the penalty for pulling the communication cord in a train, or depositing litter. But such formal communication is associated with trivial offences or regulations.
† This was shown to be the case in respect of the effect of P.A.Y.E. on overtime and production bonus earnings. Persons who were reluctant to work either faster or for longer hours and to earn more money occasionally did not do so because they thought that by earning more they might receive less pay owing to a higher tax rate. [12] There was very little association between the facts regarding P.A.Y.E. and beliefs about its effect.

Criminology: An Operational Research Approach

If there were absolute justice, exactly similar crimes would presumably receive exactly similar punishment, and a would-be offender could know fairly precisely the risk factor in so far as, if he were caught, the 'standard' penalty would be imposed. The whole picture of deterrence would be changed in such circumstances from the current position where there are often wide differences in the actions of the courts.* But it might perhaps be argued that a measure of *uncertainty* is necessary to maximize the effect of deterrence to crime. In terms of the theory of strategy, this means that an element of randomness may be necessary to achieve the maximum social controls of deterrence. If so, deterrence could require the replacement of the scales of Justice by the throw of dice!

The concept of deterrence is clearly a very difficult one, and represents an area where different aims and means in dealing with crime are mutually inconsistent, in any event, as seen in their present setting in society.

Although very little work has been done in this problem area in criminology, it is interesting to note that a deterrent may be regarded as a negative incentive. A fair amount of research work has been carried out into problems of incentives in industry, and it may be that some of the research findings might apply to deterrents. It has been shown that what is an incentive to persons of high intelligence is not likely to be a very strong one to persons of low intelligence. May this result not be true of deterrents? It has been shown that some persons seek long-term incentives whereas others prefer short-term. May it not be that deterrents that are seen as remote may apply to some people and not to others? In this connection it is interesting to consider the attraction of football pools for the majority of the population. Investment in such pools holds out the chance of a large gain with an extremely low probability, yet the very remote chance of winning attracts millions of persons and pounds. On the other hand the certainty of small interest in savings bonds is not attractive to the persons most attracted to the pools. Football pool behaviour in terms of gain and the probability of gain is not rational behaviour in the usual economic sense. No chairman of a board of directors could satisfy his shareholders with an explanation of the company's investments in the same economic terms as apply to pools investors. That is to say, the subjective evaluation of the 'pay-off' (probability × prize) is different for the two economic situations, and, perhaps for the two classes of persons. A different set of 'utilities' characterizes these different behaviours. It may, for example, be suggested that the thrill of the remote chance of winning a large prize from the pools has *itself* an economic value. Perhaps both the 'kicks'

* An appeal case recently had a sentence of ten years' preventive detention reduced to probation.

325

and the possibility of a large haul together influence criminal strategies. But criminology has not yet broken down the concept of criminal motivation into elements. Many concepts in criminology, and the concept of deterrence in particular, are not developed beyond the impressionistic stage. Impressionistic concepts cannot be used in scientific analysis. Nor are they really effective for communication, because they have a tendency to change meaning with context and with the personality of the user. Such concepts are fertile ground for argument but not for research progress. Until quite recently 'intelligence' was also an impressionistic concept. Even today, 'intelligence' is still argued about, but operational definitions and systems of measurement have made it possible to harness this concept to various problems in education and employment as well as in connexion with disorders of the mind. It seems probable that the theory of strategy may suggest an approach to the problem of deterrence so that it may be broken down into useful operational definitions.

Deterrence is only one facet of the social, economic, and personal control mechanisms which man has developed. A number of control mechanisms which were effective in the small tribal communities have been continued into the present time, but are no longer effective because they depended upon features of the smaller society which have now vanished. It is not surprising to find vestigial features from earlier times in social organizations, but it is difficult to recognize them because social systems have been subject to so little scientific study. It is possible to consider deterrence from the scientific viewpoint by regarding it in its setting of social, personal, and economic control mechanisms. Perhaps such study may show that at least part of the concept was useful in small societies, but that today the setting is very different, and a restructuring of the concept may be necessary if it is to carry out a useful function.

The Causes of Crime—Crime Prevention

Some sociologists consider it most unlikely that crime will ever cease to occur, because society has a need of crime and criminals if it is to function as a society. If actions which are currently defined as crimes were to cease to attract some persons, or were no longer defined as crimes, some other actions would be found and defined as crimes in order to focus public disapprobation upon something and some people. Whether or not this is so is not particularly relevant. The behavioural scientist in common with all other human beings is a product of his time and age.* Thus in considering crime from the point

---

* If he is too far ahead of his time he is defined as mentally ill (or, previously—"possessed"), and if he is too far behind he cannot be a scientist!

of view of research, the behavioural scientist is concerned with the modification of the current social structure, and particularly of sub-structures, in a way that society believes desirable. Stripped of value judgements, crime problems become the problems of minority groups in society. There are some crimes which even a society of criminals (as normal society defines them) would have to punish or deal with in some way, and other crimes of a still more disintegrating effect. It is interesting to note that in New York the writer was asked about the nature of juvenile gangs (the 'teddy boy' phenomenon) in London, and, after describing their behaviour, was told that if that was the size and extent of the juvenile crime problem in New York, they would regard the problem as solved. In one week in New York there were four juvenile gang murders. Yet public concern in London was not noticeably less than in New York. Would New York in fact regard the problem as solved if their problem were the same as in London, or define more acts as crimes or otherwise 'equate' the position as suggested by the theory noted above?

It is clear that certain crimes enable society to simplify or avoid social problems by making it possible to blame an individual instead of dealing with the more intractable social problem. If for example, it is possible to blame a particularly disastrous fire on a fire-raiser, the problem is simplified if not solved; if it is possible to blame all cheque frauds on swindlers, the need for change in the credit system can be avoided. In other words, if it is possible to bring in ethical factors, it is considered to be unnecessary to try to deal with the more difficult problem of social control mechanisms. Moreover, if a society were to acknowledge that their social control systems were inadequate, that society would be accepting collectively some measure of guilt, whereas by invoking extra-social factors in criminal acts, society divests itself of guilt by laying it on 'the offender'. Even social responsibility is not much sought after. These are interesting problems which should not be avoided in thinking about the 'causes' of crime; but they cannot now be developed.

These considerations reflect on the nature of the problem of the causes of crime. Crime, if thought of in this way, is not of a fixed meaning. The concept of causation involves the concept of prediction, and as has been noted earlier, the concept of prediction involves the concept of stability. Hence if the definition of 'crime' is unstable, the concept is not very satisfactory for scientific manipulation. If a form of social pathology could be defined such that all criminal acts were defined in terms other than the law itself, it might be found that a cybernetic model could reinstate the concept of causes in the field of criminology in a meaningful way. The idea of causes is, at present, useful only in so far as it helps in the setting up of hypotheses.

The definition of 'cause' which has obtained most support in the

Leslie T. Wilkins

philosophy of science is due to Tsarky, and states: if there exists a 'universal law' and according to this law, two events, x and y, are related to each other so that y is the *logical consequence* of x *and* this law, then x may be said to be the cause of y. But universal laws are summaries of observations. Universal laws are not found until a science has reached a stage of some development. Social science has not, at least so far as criminology is concerned, reached this stage. Criminology has not yet obtained enough observations to make successful summaries. There is, perhaps, a more fundamental reason why it is necessary to be very careful about the concept of cause. Experiments in the physical sciences can separate the effects of, say, x from x' and x'' — that is, the input information can be uncorrelated. Experimental methods in the physical sciences can therefore isolate the variance due to x, x' and x'' in y. In the social sciences, it is unknown for x, x', x'' to be uncorrelated, so that we can talk only of joint effects. To some extent this argument is similar to that advanced by those criminologists who put forward the 'multiple causation' theory. But in the strict language of science, the phrase 'multiple causation' is meaningless: a cause cannot be multiple. At present we may seek *efficient solutions*, but not *unique* solutions. Models in *decision theory* are more appropriate than the particular methods of the physical sciences.

The problem of the causes of crime, therefore, has to be reduced to the operational problem of: what *action*, taken in the light of what *information*, leads to a reduction of those acts of which *our* society disapproves? The social scientist is a member of society,[3] and it is not necessary for him in his role *of scientist* to consider whether society is right in approving or disapproving of certain acts. He may concern himself with identifying those acts which tend towards the breakdown of the social structure, and these acts may be defined, from the sociological viewpoint, as 'crimes'. Whether other acts are 'crimes' is debatable, and whether it is right (desirable) for any society to seek to preserve itself by these means is an ethical question.*

If crime may be seen as a social malfunction, then it becomes clear that the end result (crime) may be changed by modification of any one of the many processes in the whole functional system.

---

* In Western democratic societies it is usually considered that society should be an evolving process which continues to increase individual freedoms through social co-operation between individuals. If this sort of society is *given* as an *ethic*, scientific methods and principles may be evolved within it. Scientific methods could also be worked out in a society based on a different ethic. It does not seem possible to apply scientific methods to the concept of sin. In most respects the scientific method is independent of ethics—requiring only that its methodological structure is consistent. None the less it must be recognized that it is possible to conceive of a society based on an ethic such that it would be impossible to apply scientific methods as we know them. [9]

Criminology: An Operational Research Approach

As was noted earlier, the concept of deterrence can be applied to two independent functions in the behaviour of the postulated rational criminal—a change in the estimated 'utilities' of a crime might be obtained by changing *either* the function related to the risk (e.g. more police) or the function related to the opportunity (e.g. ease of access to valuables). These two functions are operationally independent until they are resolved into 'utilities' in the mind of the would-be criminal. It is possible to examine all the other areas of criminological thinking from a similar research viewpoint. It then becomes possible to consider the attack upon the problem of crime from a large number of independent angles. If we are faced with a problem of 'multiple causation' it seems that we can consider ourselves fortunate, because the multiple factors offer us a wide choice for operational modifications which the scientist and administrator may test with a view to effecting an end result which is socially desirable. This is because multiple causation of a social malfunction can be related to multiple social control mechanisms in the structure of society. If this is so it is surprising that the approach to the control of crime has been so very limited. Perhaps it has been so because crime has *not* been considered as a failure of social controls but has been simplified to the wrongdoing of single persons or gangs. It is easy to say 'He did it—deal with him!', but difficult to inquire further into a multiplicity of social control mechanisms. It should now be clear that 'dealing with him' has not solved the problem of crime and seems unlikely to do so.

This is, of course, not an argument that the offender should not be dealt with, but is stated in this forthright form to emphasize that there are social as well as personal control mechanisms, and that to operate on only half the problem may not solve even half of it, let alone the whole. There are macroscopic control mechanisms which are used in national economic planning—the budget, the rate of interest, and the like—which lead the members of our society to behave in a way which society desires, at least in respect of certain forms of economic behaviour. Motor insurance companies grant a no-claim bonus to encourage a behaviour that they desire. And there are other examples. But consider the crime problem in this light. Nearly all controls are 'negative' mechanisms—presumably because the offender has done wrong and it is natural to think of punishment for wrong rather than reward for what is right. But which is preferable—better locks on car doors or better locks on prison doors? Which procedure is preferable merely in terms of the cost to society? Or again, if a householder spends a sum of money on making his house more secure (reducing the opportunity structure for would-be criminals) he is doing something which is socially desirable, but he has no incentive so to do in any direct form—he pays the same insurance premium as other householders who do not take such precautions. There is a large body of knowledge regarding ways of making crime less attractive by making it more difficult, and since every offender is at some time a first offender, the argument that the professional criminal will not be defeated does not carry much weight. Yet these methods are not widely known, and very few indeed are related to any direct incentive to the potential victim to apply them. In addition to ways of making crime less economically attractive, there are doubtless ways of making it less attractive psychologically and sociologically, but these are not yet explored. In the United States a very large number of taxi drivers are held up and robbed, yet in London such robberies are extremely rare. It is interesting to ask whether if New York used the London design of taxi the rate would be reduced. The sliding glass partition in the London cab may be little more than a psychological barrier, but it might be just that and still be effective. In Britain homosexuality between females is not an offence, but it is regarded as a serious crime between males, whether consenting and adult or not. Homosexuality between females is not a social problem, but between males it is rated as a serious one. In Denmark and other countries consenting males and females are treated equally and homosexuality is not a problem for either sex. It seems that there may be macroscopic psychological control mechanisms as well as microscopic or individual control mechanisms, but our present thinking in this area is no more than unsystematic flounderings in uncoordinated n-sphere space.

Conclusions

Everything was so very much simpler in the days when society merely punished offenders and did not consider treating them, deterring them, or others; when there was thought to be a simple relationship between cause and effect, and when devils could be blamed for things that could not be conceived within this straightforward structure. The problems to be faced now, before operational research can safely get very far, before we can be sure that the feed-back from the applications of effective research does not leave us in a worse situation at some later time, are problems of ends rather than means. Objectives as seen today are often conflicting.

The analysis of ends in most criminological writings suggests that most people would wish to force all types of persons and classes into a middle-class norm of conforming behaviour—preventing crime perhaps, but inhibiting also those other aspects of nonconformity by which society progresses. Some would see all become consuming 'organization men', some have other ideas. Perhaps it is a good thing that man is an organism highly resistant to treatments of any kind, and that the ends— any ends—that we may seek are likely always to be somewhat out of

Criminology: An Operational Research Approach

step with our methodology! None the less, if we believe in progress, we must continue with the tremendous task which lies ahead, even although we may only hope that the direction which we believe to be 'ahead' is not in fact astern or to port or starboard. We shall only be able to know if we continually check our position according to some standard other than our own personal intuitive impressions of progress.

REFERENCES

1. BASS, J., *et al.* (1960) Technical Reports, nos. 8 and 9. Urbana: University of Illinois, Centre for Research in Social Psychology.
2. *Corporal Punishment.* (1960) Cmd. 1213. London: H.M.S.O.
3. FIEDLER, F., *et al.* (1960) Technical Report no. 3. Urbana: University of Illinois, Centre for Research in Social Psychology.
4. GLUECK, S., & GLUECK, E. (1930) *500 Criminal Careers.* New York: Knopf.
5. GRANT, D. (1959) 'The Treatment of Non-Conformists in the Navy'. *Annals* (322), March, 1959.
6. JOHNSON ABERCROMBIE, M. L. (1960) *Anatomy of Judgement.* London: Hutchinson.
7. MANNHEIM, H., & WILKINS, L. T. (1954) *Prediction Methods in Relation to Borstal Training.* London: H.M.S.O., 1955.
8. MARTIN, J. P. (1955) Review in Case Conference.
9. MERTON, R. K. (1957) 'Priorities in Scientific Discovery'. *Amer. Sociol. Rev.*, **22**, 6.
10. *Penal Practice in a Changing Society.* (1959) Cmd. 465. London: H.M.S.O.
11. POPPER, K. (1957) *The Poverty of Historicism.* London: Routledge.
12. Royal Commission on Taxation. Second Report. (1954) Cmd. 9105. London: H.M.S.O.
13. Special Intensive Parole Organization. Annual Reports of Department of Corrections, California.
14. SULLIVAN, C. E., GRANT, M. W., & GRANT, J. D. (1957) 'The Development of Interpersonal Maturity: Applications to Delinquency'. *Psychiatry*, **20**, 373.
15. WEEKES, ASHLEY (1958) *Youthful Offenders at Highfields.* Ann Arbor: University of Michigan Press.
16. Wickersham Commission (1931) *The Cost of Crime.* Washington: U.S. Government Printer.
17. WILKINS, L. T. (1955) 'Some Developments in Prediction Methodology in Applied Social Research'. *Brit. J. Sociol.*, **6**, 348.
18. WILKINS, L. T. (1958) 'A Small Comparative Study of Probation'. *Brit. J. Delinq.*, **8**, 3.

18

THE INHERITANCE OF
PERSONALITY DISORDERS

Valerie A. Cowie

Valerie A. Cowie

SOCIOLOGICAL CONSIDERATIONS

BEFORE discussing current genetical and psychiatric views on hereditary factors in disorders of personality, it will be helpful to consider the close relationship between psychopathological and social concepts.

Personality itself is to a great extent a sociological phenomenon, in that it manifests itself by the interaction of individuals and the society in which they live. Cultural norms are, ideally, essential criteria in deciding whether or not certain behaviour indicates personality disorder. They are also involved in the complex problems of the degree of temperamental deviation that can be regarded as compatible with mental health, and the vexed question of criminal responsibility in the case of psychiatrically abnormal personalities. Cultural norms can be reduced, although admittedly only in a limited way, to statistical variables which differ according to the characteristics of the society in which they operate. There are, therefore, no absolute or constant standards against which a deviant personality can be measured. The best that can be done is to regard the individual as a member of the society in which he lives and to assess his personality traits in terms of the current modes of that society. Thus, for example, male homosexuality was accepted as normal in ancient Greece, whereas in Britain today it is commonly regarded as a gross sexual deviation for which psychiatric treatment is frequently recommended.

333

Valerie A. Cowie

The limitations on the reduction of cultural norms to statistical variables are due mainly to the lack of objective measures. Wootton[53] in her lucid exposition of problems concerning social pathology and the concept of mental health sets out in a very clear way the difficulties of defining mental health and mental ill-health in objective scientific terms free from subjective moral judgements. Without such terms, she points out, there can be no reliable criterion to distinguish the sick from the healthy mind.

Great efforts towards establishing an approach to the problems of abnormality of human personality by means of objective measures have been made in the field of psychometry. The work of Eysenck[8, 9, 10] is notable in this connexion. By measuring human reactions in test situations he has amassed a large amount of evidence supporting the view that human neurosis and psychosis, rather than being disease entities qualitatively different from the normal, are points on various continua which range, each as an axis, through normality between poles of abnormality. Psychological studies of behaviour in test situations are by definition contrived, and therefore must contain elements of artificiality. They can be compared to experiments *in vitro*. On the other hand, the attempts of the sociologist and the psychiatrist to observe human individuals in the natural setting of the society in which they live are comparable to experiments *in vivo* which, though the opportunity for objective assessment is reduced, provide much more adequate information from a biological point of view.

The psychiatrist's attempt to view his patient against the background of his social setting has been fostered by the influence of the psycho-biological school, founded by Adolf Meyer.[30] This school has had an important effect upon modern British psychiatry: according to its precepts, the patient is regarded as a unique individual whose illness is a psychological reaction to stress. To understand the patient and the nature of his breakdown, Meyer emphasized the importance of studying in detail the personalities and past histories of psychiatric patients, paying special attention to social, psychological, and other environmental factors. In this way, the relationship between the individual and society can be seen, on the one hand, in terms of qualitative and quantitative discrepancy between features of the personality and the corresponding cultural norms, and on the other, in terms of the pressures exerted by society on the patient which have caused him to break down.

The psychiatric formulation, however, is not complete without considering the extent to which genetical causes play a part. Furthermore, the dualistic view that heredity and environment play entirely separate and independent roles is now outdated, and the importance of the interplay between them is becoming increasingly recognized amongst practising psychiatrists.

The Inheritance of Personality Disorders

It is helpful to keep this approach in mind in discussing the inheritance of disorders of personality. A predisposition to certain kinds of breakdown may be regarded as being laid down by heredity, but whether breakdown occurs and the form which it takes when it does occur are largely dependent on the kinds of stress imposed by the environment.

The Classification of Personality Disorders

It is not within the scope of this chapter to discuss systems of classification within psychiatry, but it is necessary to preface genetical considerations of personality disorder by mentioning some difficulties of definition. In broad terms it can be said that a disorder of personality may show itself primarily in one of two ways. It may cause conflict and suffering chiefly within the individual himself, who may then be said to be suffering from a neurosis. Eysenck[11] defines neuroticism as a person's general emotional lability and his liability to neurotic breakdown under stress. This definition may beg the question, but at least it contains the concept that both constitutional and environmental factors play a part. On the other hand, the main effect may be seen not so much as the conflict and suffering within the individual himself, but in his behaviour towards others. The emphasis laid by British and American psychiatrists upon this last effect as a cardinal sign of psychopathy emerges from the many definitions of the psychopath that have been made from time to time.* Curran and Mallison[6] in reviewing the relevant literature point out that 'the salient feature of the psychopathic personality is stressed as essentially consisting in persistent or repeated disorder of *conduct* of an anti-social type'. The German psychiatrist Kurt Schneider,[42] however, defines psychopathic personalities as 'those abnormal personalities who suffer from their abnormality or cause society to suffer'. In this way he introduces the two classes of effect which have come to be regarded as characteristic of the neurotic and the psychopath respectively in British and American psychiatry. From clinical observation, however, even if a distinction is made on these lines between the neurotic and the psychopath, it is usual to find elements of one in the other. Accordingly a sharp division between the two is artificial. Clearly a broad basis for classification to comprise the relationship between these aspects of disorder of personality is desirable. Another criticism that can be made of Schneider's concept is that it restricts the class of psychopaths in a rigid way to persons whose abnormality is inborn, to the exclusion of those in whom a personality change has been brought

---

* Notable amongst these are definitions by Cheyney[4], Henderson[17], North[32], Levine[26, 27], and Bullard[3].

Valerie A. Cowie

about by injury, disease, or other environmental factors. Such a narrow concept is untenable if an unrestricted biological and sociological view is to be taken.

The concept of neurotic constitution formulated by Slater[47] was a great advance towards providing a comprehensive basis for a classification to embrace both psychopathy and neurotic reaction. It is a biological concept which rests upon considerations of aetiology, taking into account hereditary factors. It allows classification to be made in a natural way on the basis of the incidence of symptoms in connexion with underlying features of personality. In addition, it has the great advantage of bringing neurotic personality into relationship with psychopathic personality on common ground. It overcomes the difficulties that arise when articifial and arbitrary distinctions are made which do not fit the facts.

According to Slater's concept, the constitutional predisposition to neurosis depends upon the deviation from an average value to one or other extreme along a number of different lines representing distinct qualities of personality. On this basis can be explained not only individual variation to susceptibility to neurotic breakdown in a quantitative sense, but the great range of qualitative differences in symptomatology. Thus according to this idea certain individuals are prone to break down under specific types of stress which would be harmless to others. The degree of stress required before breakdown occurs also varies from individual to individual, and the symptoms of the breakdown bear a close relationship to the basic personality traits of the individual in question. Moreover, the common observation that neurotic reactions of 'pure type' are rarely if ever seen, falls readily into place. The appreciation of the relationship between the individual and his environment is essential to this concept, in the practical application of which sociological considerations may be of primary importance.

Evidence of the Constitutional Basis of Personality

The evidence of a genetical basis of personality and, in consequence, of personality disorders, is strongly supported by the existence of innate constitutional physical factors related to personality type. It is therefore relevant to consider these when reviewing the part played by heredity.

Theories associating types of temperament with bodily characteristics have existed from antiquity. Hippocrates propounded the idea that there were four main temperaments corresponding to the four humours of the body. This notion persisted for a very long time, and the adjectives 'sanguine' and 'phlegmatic' in present-day usage have their roots in this ancient theory.

The Inheritance of Personality Disorders

In recent times, attempts to relate types of body-build to different kinds of temperament were pioneered by the German psychiatrist Kretschmer.[22] He described three 'pure' types of body build: the leptosomatic or asthenic type, the athletic type, and the pyknic type. The leptosomatic or asthenic build is characterized by leanness, narrowness, long thin bones and poor musculature. The athletic type possesses the features of good firm musculature, strong bone development, and in the male wide shoulders and a trunk tapering to a narrow pelvis. Characteristics of the pyknic build include large body cavities of thorax and abdomen, a rounded face and figure and a tendency to be well padded with fat. Besides these 'pure' types Kretschmer described mixed types. This addition is of special interest in the present context since it embodies a notion on the same lines as that inherent in Slater's concept of neurotic constitution. This idea is that the body-build types do not represent clear-cut types of individual, but rather correspond to basic constitutional factors capable of quantitative and qualitative variation from one individual to another. Kretschmer suggested that leptosomatic or asthenic physique was associated with schizothymic temperament, characterized by such traits as reticence, quietness, eccentricity, timidity, sensitivity, seriousness, restraint, detachment and coldness. He also noted a tendency for pyknic body-build to be associated with the cyclothymic temperament, features of which include friendliness, sociability, abundance of energy and drive, emotional warmth, generosity, open-heartedness, capacity for feeling for others, and lability of mood.

A major criticism of Kretschmer's theory has been its insufficiency to cover the facts. In practice, his 'mixed' types outnumber his 'pure' types in such vast proportions that the correlations he suggested between temperament and feature of physique become tenuous to the point of extinction if extended on a wide basis in the general population. This is, however, to be expected when one considers the infinite variety of physical and psychological features possible in man. Moreover, if it is remembered that his 'pure' types of body-build are representative of very small and limited groups, his correlations of attributes of temperament and physique can be taken as showing a common constitutional basis in relatively rare individuals providing clear-cut and recognizable 'markers' in these respects.

Notable amongst subsequent work along similar lines is that of Sheldon and his co-workers[43, 44, 45]. By means of measurement from photographs and living subjects they defined three primary components of physique for which they used the terms endomorphy, mesomorphy, and ectomorphy, corresponding to the basic embryonic layers. Endomorphy corresponds closely with Kretschmer's pyknic type, and Sheldon found it to be correlated with a dimension of

337

Valerie A. Cowie

temperament which he called 'viscerotonia' and which incorporated many of the cyclothymic qualities already described, together with love of comfort and relaxation. Mesomorphy resembles the athletic type of Kretschmer, and is correlated with 'somatotonia', characterized by vigour and assertiveness, and love of action and power. Ectomorphy closely corresponds to the asthenic or leptosomatic type of Kretschmer, and is correlated with the temperamental dimension of 'cerebrotonia' which closely corresponds to the schizothymic temperament.

The work of Sheldon provided great impetus for work along similar lines, but on the whole positive correlations between attributes of physique and temperament, though frequently observed, have been small and usually of the order of only $+0 \cdot 2$ or $+0 \cdot 3$. Sheldon's correlations between such factors were of a high order, as follows: endomorphy and viscerotonia $+ 0 \cdot 79$; mesomorphy and somatotonia $+ 0 \cdot 82$; ectomorphy and cerebrotonia $+ 0 \cdot 83$. Such high correlations have not been repeated, and it has been suggested that they may have been influenced by 'halo' effect, ratings of physique and temperament having been made by the same observer. Tanner,[52] in an appraisal of the evidence available, points out that such studies as have been made offer only mild support to Sheldon's original claims, and lead generally to a lower degree of association than would be expected from his work.

A substantial contribution to study along these lines has been made by Parnell,[36] who proposed modifications of Sheldon's system with ratings of fat (F), muscularity (M), and linearity (L) to supplant those of endomorphy, mesomorphy, and ectomorphy. He views Sheldon's system as 'an abstract concept describing the genetically determined path through life that is expected for a healthy individual of a particular build'.[38] The evidence he has obtained of positive correlation between features of physique on the one hand and psychological attributes and performance in various fields of human activity on the other are indicative of underlying inborn common factors.[7, 34, 35, 37]

Using an approach by factorial analysis of human body-build, Rees and Eysenck[40] found that in terms of a factor involving stature and transverse chest diameter (i.e. a factor of body breadth), patients suffering from anxiety, depression, and obsessional states tended to be characterized by leptomorphy, whilst hysterics were more frequently eurymorphic (thick-set and of broad body build). The author stressed, however, that these categories of physique are not intended to suggest in any way that they are disparate types. They represent ranges of body-build which are based upon objective measurements and are demarcated by statistical criteria. The concept that they lie on a continuum is in line with the genetical concept of continuous variation, or infinitesimal gradation between individuals in the population, for common

338

The Inheritance of Personality Disorders

human characteristics amongst which features of physique can be included. Kretschmer's findings would at once become more meaningful if his 'pure' types could be conceived thus as points on a continuum.

Rees[39] in a short but excellent review of constitution and neurosis sums up by saying that two main hypotheses may be postulated: first, that the associations are an outcome of the individual's life experiences which give rise to conditioning processes linking certain psychological attributes to particular physical traits; secondly, that they are 'integrated biological relations between different constitutional aspects, and that the association may prove to be genetical with the genes responsible for body-build exerting a modifying influence on the manifestation of inherited aspects of personality and the genetically determined psychiatric illnesses'.

Rees himself considers this last hypothesis to be a more probable explanation. Both hypotheses, however, have their supporters, and it would seem unbalanced and unrealistic to hold exclusively to one or the other in the face of the scientific evidence available and of common experience.

Reference has already been made to the contribution of those working along the lines of experimental study into human behaviour. This work and similar studies of animal behaviour have contributed greatly to the knowledge of patterns of innate responses. Classical work in this field is that of the Russian physiologist Pavlov, who should be mentioned here in connexion with the attempts that have been made to differentiate types in relation to basic factors of constitution. Pavlov found that some of the dogs in his laboratory were capable of acquiring positive conditioned reflexes quickly, and, once acquired, these remained stable. Other dogs, however, were slow to acquire positive-conditioned reflexes, and these were rapidly and easily lost, although inhibitory-conditioned reflexes were easily learned and retained by these animals. On this basis, Pavlov classified the dogs as of 'excitatory' and 'inhibitory' types respectively, believing their behaviour to be directly dependent upon constitutionally determined organization of brain-function. This idea has found further support in the field of human experimental psychology from Eysenck,[10] who has made observations to confirm his prediction that in human subjects introverts are more conditionable whilst extraverts, including neurotic extraverts (hysterics), are more difficult to condition.

Along physiological lines, the study of the electroencephalogram (EEG), which is the record of electrical discharges from the brain, has provided some evidence in support of the constitutional basis of personality. Studies in this field have the advantage over those concerned with the investigation of mental disorder in that they provide direct information about the function of the brain itself. Electrophysiology

Valerie A. Cowie

is now so well established that a great deal is known about the normal and abnormal patterns of brainwaves seen on the EEG under different conditions. The constancy of this pattern for the individual has been confirmed, besides the subtle differences between individuals to be expected in the case of a constitutional variable.

Special studies have been carried out to investigate the possible relationship of the EEG and personality deviations. From these it appears that some association exists, although it does not seem likely that changes in EEG pattern bear any specific relationship to types of personality disorder. Thus Gallagher, Gibbs and Gibbs[15] found in a sample of two hundred boys that, while no fixed relationship existed between the EEG and personality, there was a marked tendency for a wide departure from the normal in the EEG to be related to abnormal personality. Hill and Watterson[18] found that among temperamental traits showing some association with abnormality in the EEG, aggressiveness was the most consistent. These workers demonstrated similarities between the EEGs of psychopaths liable to crimes of violence and those of young children, and postulate a 'cortical immaturity' in the brain of the aggressive psychopath. Such a finding is strong evidence of a fundamental constitutional factor.

As regards EEG investigations of groups of subjects whose behaviour has brought them into conflict with society, Stafford-Clark and Taylor[50] stress that the type of EEG abnormalities found in various groups by different investigators is by no means specific, and that the incidence of abnormalities reported covers a wide range. In their own study of sixty-four prisoners charged with murder, a non-specific abnormality was found in over 70 per cent of prisoners whose crimes appeared motiveless and who were considered to be otherwise clinically sane and normal. In a subsequent study by Stafford Clark and his co-workers,[49] 83 per cent of a sample of prisoners displaying clinical evidence of aggressiveness had an abnormal EEG as compared with less than 50 per cent of those without overt aggressiveness. These findings are in line with those of Hill and Watterson[18] in whose sample 82 per cent of subjects showed abnormality in the EEG. A much lower incidence was found by Gibbs et al.[16] These workers found the incidence of abnormal EEG records to be 34 per cent in a random sample of one hundred prisoners as compared with 15 per cent in a control series of one thousand adults. In a larger group of prisoners selected for type of crime, they found only a 19 per cent incidence of abnormal EEG records among men whose crimes were characterized by unnecessary violence.

A certain degree of variation in the incidence of EEG abnormalities assessed in different clinical groups is inevitable on the grounds of the arbitrary nature of the criteria and the subjectivity of interpretation.

340

The Inheritance of Personality Disorders

Furthermore this effect is enhanced in groups of subjects where the EEG abnormality is not specific in character and where no particular type of abnormality is being specially looked for. Generally it may be said that in a marked proportion of cases studied where antisocial behaviour has led to transgression of the law, an underlying constitutional factor associated with disorders of the central nervous system has been indicated by abnormalities in the EEG.

To sum up briefly, attempts have been made using physiological, anthropometric, psychological, and psychiatric methods to distinguish and correlate physical and temperamental factors, correlations between the two kinds of factor being strongly indicative of their innate and inherited nature. Although constellations of factors are found to be correlated, no clear-cut distinction of discrete and separate physical or psychological 'types' of individual has emerged. Instead there is evidence of continuous variation between individuals, and the findings fit well into the concept of underlying constitutional factors genetically determined by multifactorial inheritance. The significance of this will be discussed later on in this chapter when specific modes of inheritance are considered.

The Relationship between Basic Personality Features and Specific Neurotic Reactions

The necessity for the psychiatrist to consider his patient's present state as the product of many factors, both hereditary and environmental, has already been discussed. The past history of the patient contains many clues to the meaning of his present symptoms. Especially significant may be the characteristics of his personality before he became ill. Thus, for example, in the case of the patient who is suffering from severe obsessional symptoms such as hand-washing or other compulsive rituals that may occupy the greater part of his day, the previous personality is often marked by obsessional traits. A psychiatric history in a case of this kind frequently reveals features such as excessive regard for tidiness, orderliness, cleanliness, and punctuality, together with rigid adherence to customary habits that may acquire the semblance of rituals, having to be performed in a certain order. These characteristics might almost be regarded in retrospect as having foreshadowed the symptoms of the obsessional illness, but it should be made clear that many well-integrated personalities who never break down, even under stress, possess obsessional features. The connexion, nevertheless, is often seen to exist between the qualitative features of a nervous breakdown and of the personality in which they occur. This is understandable in view of the evidence of relationships between constitutional and

341

Valerie A. Cowie

temperamental variables: temperamental traits and their quantitative or qualitative changes under stress in a nervous breakdown can be regarded as sharing the same constitutional basis.

The existence of a relationship between previous personality and type of neurotic breakdown, though very frequently observed, cannot be regarded as an invariable rule. Thus Foulds and Caine[14] drew attention to a distinction between 'symptom clusters' (or syndromes) and 'trait clusters' (or personality types), and quote Curran and Guttmann[5] and Lewis and Mapother[28] who remark that a specific type of previous personality is not always found in a patient displaying symptoms corresponding to that basic type. Foulds and Caine, using psychological tests and psychiatric ratings of personality type, suggested an independence of 'symptom clusters' and 'trait clusters' in the group of patients tested. These findings were later confirmed on a second sample.[13]

The relationship between previous personality and qualitative manifestations in neurotic breakdown is taken into account in Slater's concept of the neurotic constitution. The form of the breakdown, according to this concept, is determined by the same genetical factors that determine the basic qualities of the personality previous to the breakdown. The existence of this relationship is strongly supported by the work of Eysenck[8, 9, 10] who has provided abundant evidence to indicate that patients who have had neurotic and other forms of psychiatric illness provide characteristic values when certain psychological responses are measured in test situations. These facts indicate the presence of constant inborn components of temperament, peculiar to the individual, which are of value for predicting the kind of breakdown an individual is likely to suffer under stress.

This basic biological concept of the relationship of basic features of personality to specific neurotic reactions provides a basis for the interpretation of findings made in special genetical investigations.

Genetical Studies of Personality Disorder

Numerous twin studies and family studies have been carried out in connexion with specific forms of personality disorder, and within the scope of this chapter it is possible only to outline briefly the various fields that have been covered and to give some indication as to how the results may be evaluated.

In a classical study by Eysenck and Prell[12] series of uniovular and binovular twins together with a criterion group of neurotic children were tested with a battery of objective personality tests. By means of factorial analysis, a 'neuroticism' factor was extracted. Intra-class correlations with respect to this factor were found to be high for the

The Inheritance of Personality Disorders

uniovular twins ($+0.851$) and lower for the binovular twins ($+0.217$). It was considered that the findings showed some 80 per cent of individual differences in the neuroticism factor to be due to heredity and only about 20 per cent to environment, demonstrating that neurotic predisposition was to a large extent genetically determined.

Much attention was paid by genetical investigators in pre-war Germany to the criminal and psychopathic social offender. Lange[24] carried out a study of same-sexed twins with known criminal records and found a very high incidence of concordance for criminal record (ten pairs out of thirteen) amongst the uniovular twins in his groups, and a low concordance rate (two pairs out of seventeen) amongst the binovular pairs. This strongly supports the view that a genetical factor is operating since in theory uniovular twins share the same genetical endowment, while binovular twins should be no more alike than ordinary brothers and sisters.

Objections to twin study methods have been raised from time to time on the grounds of cytological and embryological theory ([48] pp. 3–6). It has been said, nevertheless, that Nature has provided her own genetical experiment in twins, and despite theoretical objections and the limited information afforded by twin study, this method of research has been put to good use in human genetics from which experimental procedures are to a great extent precluded.

Stumpfl[51] studied sixty-five twin pairs from the point of view of criminal record. His findings are much in the same direction as those of Lange, in that of same-sexed twins 39 per cent of uniovular pairs and 63 per cent of binovular pairs were discordant. However, he found that there was much less concordance with respect to crimes committed late in life or in conflict situations than with respect to criminality that had begun early or was often repeated. This is in line with the view that social circumstances are the main factors responsible for a large amount of criminal behaviour.

Kranz[21] studied 125 twin pairs, and found concordance in respect of criminal record between the twins of 66 per cent of the uniovular pairs, 54 per cent of the same-sexed binovular pairs, and 14 per cent of the opposite-sexed binovular pairs. In reviewing Krantz's work, Slater and Shields[48] point out that whilst the high concordance rate in binovular pairs can be interpreted as partly due to similarities of environment, and, 'though a criminal act is often a product of fortuitous circumstances, the personality that is so endangered is itself moulded to a very remarkable degree by biological factors'.

Rosanoff et al.[41] in the U.S.A. studied twins from the point of view of psychiatric disorder of various kinds, including that distinguished by delinquency and criminality. Their material included adult criminals and juvenile delinquents, as well as children with behaviour disorders

343

in whose case no legal action had been taken. High concordance rates for uniovular twins of both sexes were found in all three of these categories. The concordance rates dropped with respect to the binovular pairs, especially amongst the adults. Rosanoff and his co-workers distinguished between the less inured involvement in crime and a 'strong and persistent constitutional tendency which manifests itself under various conditions of no special difficulty or strain'. Concordance between twins was found to be more marked for this deep-seated 'criminalism' than for the more casual involvement in crime. This supports the view that though environment undoubtedly may play an important part in the causation of a criminal act, the predisposition to repeated criminal behaviour is constitutionally determined.

In connexion with sexual deviations which may or may not bring individuals into conflict with the law, Kallmann[19, 20] in the U.S.A. studied male homosexual twins. His material consisted of forty uniovular and forty-five binovular pairs. There was 100 per cent concordance between the uniovular pairs. Moreover there were marked similarities in the type of homosexual behaviour between members of the uniovular twin pairs. The concordance rate for homosexuality dropped in the case of the binovular twin pairs, and amongst the same-sexed binovular twin-partners of male homosexuals he found very little more than the incidence of homosexuality expected in a random sample of the population. These findings are strong evidence in favour of a genetical influence in the predisposition towards homosexuality.

The theory put forward by Lang[23] that homosexuality is a form of genetically determined intersexuality found upholders for many years. Lang suggested that if male homosexuality were dependent upon a state of genetical intersex, then an excess of males would be expected amongst their siblings on the basis that the sex ratio in the general population shows only a very slight excess of males. In support of his theory he was able to demonstrate an excess of brothers amongst the siblings of a group of male homosexuals. In recent years, however, it has been discovered that the sexes differ by the presence or absence of a small nodule of chromatin at the periphery of cell nuclei. This nodule, which is said to consist of sex-chromatin, indicates the presence of the XX chromosome complex characteristic of the female: the nodule is rarely seen in the nuclei of males, who carry only one X chromosome. Pare[33] and Levij *et al.*[25] found that among male homosexuals they studied the proportion of cells with sex chromatin nodules showed no shift from typical male values. On these grounds Lang's theory is refuted. A study of transvestists by Barr and Hobbs[1] also failed to show a discrepancy. These findings indicate that aberrations of sexual behaviour are unlikely to be associated with anomalies involving the sex chromosomes, but this does not by any means discount the part that may be played by genetical influences in the predisposition towards homosexual attitudes.

Noteworthy Scandinavian studies bearing on the causes of personality disorder include those of Skoog,[46] who made a clinical study of the anancastic or obsessional syndrome and its relation to personality attitudes. Although this is not a genetical investigation it provides evidence of constellations of features strongly indicative of underlying constitutional factors. The careful study of Ljunberg[29] on hysteria again shows the diversity of manifestation within a clinical group and the relationship of neurotic symptomatology to personality traits of the patient and of his relatives.

A classical study in British psychiatry of the incidence of neurosis of different types amongst the relatives of neurotic patients is that of Brown,[2] who classified patients into main diagnostic groups of anxiety neurosis, obsessional neurosis, and hysteria. Examining neurotic symptoms among the relatives of his patients, he found that anxiety symptoms were most frequent in the relatives of patients with anxiety neurosis, obsessional symptoms in the relatives of obsessionals, and hysterical symptoms in the relatives of hysterics. The correspondence of type of symptom between patient and relative was not, however, exclusive, and an excess of neurotic symptoms of all types were found amongst the relatives of the patients. These findings are compatible with the concept of neurotic constitution which was later formulated by Slater,[47] and with the idea that genetical influences may determine a constitutional predisposition to neurotic breakdown, and that the form the breakdown takes is shaped by various factors, both hereditary and environmental. If a part is played by multifactorial inheritance, where many genes of small effect exert their action, some similarity of symptomatology is to be expected between relatives. Where such a mode of inheritance is assumed, however, even when no allowance is made for environmental effect, some variation of neurotic manifestation amongst relatives is to be expected.

Amongst genetical investigations into neurotic illness without special reference to particular symptomatology, the twin studies of Newman, Freeman and Holzinger[31] and of Slater and Shields[48] deserve special mention. Newman and his co-workers in the U.S.A. studied uniovular twins who were brought up separately in different environments. They found that these twins were remarkably concordant for qualities of temperament, and that similarities between them were even more marked with respect to personality traits than with respect to level of intelligence. However, the British investigation of Slater and Shields[48] into psychotic and neurotic illnesses in twins yielded different results. The decisive role played by *environmental* factors in determining neurosis and psychopathy was indicated by a *low* concordance rate

Valerie A. Cowie

between uniovular twins, and by the development of very similar child-hood behaviour disorders in three binovular pairs despite marked differences in personality. This study confirmed the frequently made observation that, on the whole, neurotic symptoms appear as exaggerations of traits present in the personality at other times, and that the form of the symptom is more closely related to the basic personality than it is to the form of stress precipitating the breakdown. Moreover, there were indications that the main traits of personality among the relatives of neurotic and psychopathic twins showed rather little tendency towards family resemblance, which runs counter to the findings of Brown.[2]

What, one may ask, emerges from the evaluation of the mass of genetical data that have been collected? In the first place, many of the studies have been twin investigations. Twin studies only provide genetical information of limited kind: they give an indication of the extent to which a trait investigated may be due to hereditary or environmental influences. They give no direct information as to the mode of inheritance. The twin studies described above give strong support to the view that factors of inheritance play a decisive role in determining certain specific qualities of personality, such as the predisposition to crime and to homosexuality. On the other hand, when specific traits were not singled out for special study the results were less unanimous as to the relative extent to which genetical and environmental factors were operative. Thus Newman and his co-workers in the United States found strong evidence in favour of a genetical basis for neurotic illness without special reference to neurotic symptomatology, whilst Slater and Shields in Britain found evidence of the greater influence of environmental factors, although the action of genetical factors was not excluded.

As to the mode of inheritance, it seems most likely that genetical factors of a multifactorial kind play a part in determining personality and its predisposition to disorders. Multifactorial inheritance, according to genetical theory, is the kind of hereditary transmission responsible for biological characteristics which show variation between one individual and another in infinitesimal degree, It is thought to be mediated by the additive effect of many genes, each exerting a small influence, in contrast to the action of single genes of large effect which are said to operate in dominant and recessive modes of inheritance.

Finally it must be said that although the evidence points to the existence of such genetical factors, it would be taking an extremely unbalanced view to underestimate the probably far greater part that is played by environmental influences, amongst which social factors are of major importance. Environmental factors clearly play an extremely important part in the production of personality disorders, and in this

346

The Inheritance of Personality Disorders

field of psychiatry the interplay of 'nature and nurture' is especially critical in its effects.

REFERENCES

1. BARR, M. L., & HOBBS, G. E. (1954) *Lancet,* **i,** 1109.
2. BROWN, F. W. (1942) *Proc. R. Soc. Med.,* **35,** 785.
3. BULLARD, D. M. (1941) *Psychiatry,* **4,** 231.
4. CHEYNEY, C. O. (1934) *Outline for Psychiatric Examinations.* Utica, N.Y.: State Hospitals Press.
5. CURRAN, D., & GUTTMANN, E. (1949) *Psychological Medicine.* Edinburgh: Livingstone.
6. CURRAN, D. & MALLISON, P. (1944) *Recent Progress in Psychiatry* (Ed. G. W. T. H. Fleming). London: Churchill.
7. DAVIDSON, M. A., McINNIS, R. G., & PARNELL, R. W. (1957) 'The Distribution of Personality Traits in Seven-Year-Old Children'. *Brit. J. educ. Psychol.,* **27,** 48–61.
8. EYSENCK, H. J. (1947) *Dimensions of Personality.* London: Kegan Paul.
9. EYSENCK, H. J. (1952) *The Scientific Study of Personality.* London: Routledge.
10. EYSENCK, H. J. (1957) *The Dynamics of Anxiety and Hysteria.* London: Routledge.
11. EYSENCK, H. J. (1959) *Manual of the Maudsley Personality Inventory.* London: Univ. of London Press.
12. EYSENCK, H. J., & PRELL, D. B. (1951) 'The Inheritance of Neuroticism: an Experimental Study'. *J. ment. Sci.,* **97,** 441–65.
13. FOULDS, G. A. (1959) 'The Relative Stability of Personality Measures Compared with Diagnostic Measures'. *J. ment. Sci.,* **105,** 783–7.
14. FOULDS, G. A. & CAINE, T. M. (1958) 'Psychoneurotic Symptom Clusters, Trait Clusters and Psychological Tests'. *J. ment. Sci.,* **104,** 722–31.
15. GALLAGHER, J. R., GIBBS, E. L., & GIBBS, F. A. (1942) *Psychosom. Med.* **4,** 134.
16. GIBBS, F. A., BLOOMBERG, W., & BAGCHI, B. K. (1942) 'An electroencephalographic study on adult criminals'. *Trans. Amer. neurol. Ass.* **68,** 87–90.
17. HENDERSON, D. K. (1939) *Psychopathic States.* New York: Norton.
18. HILL, D. & WATTERSON, D. (1942) *J. Neurol. Psychiat.* **5,** 47.
19. KALLMANN, F. J. (1952) *J. nerv. ment. Dis.,* **115,** 283.
20. KALLMANN, F. J. (1952) *Amer. J. hum. Genet.* **4,** 136.
21. KRANZ, H. (1936) *Lebensschicksale krimineller Zwillinge.* Berlin: Springer.
22. KRETSCHMER, E. (1936) *Physique and Character.* 2nd ed. London: Miller.
23. LANG, T. (1940) *J. nerv. ment. Dis.* **92,** 55.
24. LANGE, J. (1931) *Crime as Destiny.* London: Allen and Unwin.

Valerie A. Cowie

25. LEVIJ, I. S., VAN SCHAIK, C. T. & TOLSMA (1956) *Ned. Tijdschr. Geneesk.* **100**, 2121.
26. LEVINE, M. (1940) *Ohio St. med. J.*, **36**, 848.
27. LEVINE, M. (1942) *Psychotherapy in Medical Practice.* New York: Macmillan.
28. LEWIS, A. J. & MAPOTHER, E. (1941) *Price's Textbook of the Practice of Medicine.* London: Oxford Univ. Press.
29. LJUNBERG, L. (1957) *Acta Psychiat.*, *Kbh.*, Suppl. 112, Vol. 32.
30. MAYER-GROSS, W., SLATER, E., & ROTH, M. (1960) *Clinical Psychiatry.* London.
31. NEWMAN, H. H., FREEMAN, F. N., & HOLZINGER, K. J. (1937) *Twins: a Study of Heredity and Environment.* Chicago: Univ. of Chicago Press.
32. NORTH, E. A. (1940) *Dis. nerv. Syst.*, **1**, 136.
33. PARE, C. M. B. (1956) *J. Psychosom. Res.*, **1**, 247.
34. PARNELL, R. W. (1951) 'Some Notes on Physique and Athletic Training. *Brit. med. J.* **i**, 1292.
35. PARNELL, R. W. (1953) 'Physique and Choice of Faculty'. *Brit. med. J.* **ii**, 473.
36. PARNELL, R. W. (1954) 'Somatotyping by Physical Anthropometry'. *Amer. J. phys. Anthrop.* **12**, 209.
37. PARNELL, R. W. (1954) 'The Relationship of Masculine and Feminine Traits . . . to Academic and Athletic Performance'. *Brit. J. med. Psychol.* **28**, 247.
38. PARNELL, R. W. (1959) 'Physique and Family Structure'. *Eugen. Rev.* **51**, 75.
39. REES, L. (1960) 'Constitution and Neurosis'. Advances in Psychosomatic Medicine. Symposium of 4th European Conference on Psychosomatic Research. p. 106.
40. REES, W. L. & EYSENCK, H. J. (1945) *J. ment. Sci.*, **91**, 8.
41. ROSANOFF, A. J., HANDY, L. M. & ROSANOFF, I. A. (1934) *J. Crim. Law Criminol.*, **24**, 923.
42. SCHNEIDER, K. (1923) *Die Psychopathischen Personlichkeiten.* 9th ed. (1950) Vienna: Deuticke.
43. SHELDON, W. H. (1949) *Varieties of Delinquent Youth.* New York: Harper.
44. SHELDON, W. H., STEVENS, S. S., & TUCKER, W. B. (1940) *The Varieties of Human Physique.* New York: Harper.
45. SHELDON, W. H., STEVENS, S. S., & TUCKER, W. B. (1942) *The Varieties of Temperament.* New York: Harper.
46. SKOOG, G. (1959) *Acta psychiat. Kbh.* Suppl. **134**, Vol. 34.
47. SLATER, E. T. O. (1943) *J. Neurol. Psychiat.* **6**, 1.
48. SLATER, E. T. O. & SHIELDS, J. (1953) *Neurotic and Psychotic Illnesses in Twins*: M. R. C. Special Report Series, No. 278. London: H.M.S.O.
49. STAFFORD-CLARK, D.; POND, D. A.; & LOVETT-DOUST, J. W. (1951) 'The Psychopath in Prison'. *Brit. J. Delinq.* **2**, 1–3.

The Inheritance of Personality Disorders

50. STAFFORD-CLARK, D., & TAYLOR, F. H. (1949) 'Clinical and EEG Studies of Prisoners Charged with Murder'. *J. Neurol. Psychiat.* **12,** 325.
51. STUMPFL, F. (1936) *Die Ursprünge des Verbrechens dargestellt am Lebenslauf von Zwillingen.* Leipzig: Thieme.
52. TANNER, J. M. (1956) *Physique, Character and Disease. Lancet* **ii,** 635.
53. WOOTTON, B. (1959) *Social Science and Social Pathology.* London: Allen and Unwin.

19

SOCIAL FACTORS IN THE
MAJOR FUNCTIONAL PSYCHOSES*

Christopher J. Wardle

INTRODUCTION

LUNACY, insanity, madness, or as we now prefer to say mental disorder, are all social concepts, not medical ones. They define a class of people who cannot fit into the norms of behaviour expected by the society in which they live. Their impact upon society and the way society has reacted to them have been and always will be important social problems. That mental illness is a likely cause of irrational and aberrant behaviour has not always been and is still not always recognized. This has led to curious and cruel treatment of the mentally ill when the behaviour was disapproved and to society's being led a strange dance when the behaviour was accepted. Social scientists have a valuable part to play in the study of the impact of society on the mentally disordered in the community.

The chains began to be struck from the lunatics' wrists at the turn of the 18th century, when they were for the first time regarded as patients. In the middle of the 19th century the bars and locks began to be taken away from their doors. Attempts at rational treatment of mental illness began at the turn of the 20th century, although sometimes sedation was a mere substitute for chains. In the middle of the present century the accent was on active treatment rather than custodial care. The trend in

* This chapter makes use of material contained in the author's Thesis approved by the University of London for the degree of Doctor of Medicine. [81]

351

its second half is to try to treat and rehabilitate the patient in the community. This will bring the community face to face with the problem which it has hitherto avoided by hiding its mentally ill in large closed barracks in the remote country. Constant watch and education is necessary to prevent a return to one of the earlier stages, if not actually to the gas chamber or chains. That such a reaction is possible is illustrated by the treatment of the mentally ill in Germany under Hitler. A premature attempt at community treatment without most careful planning and education of the community might lead to such a reaction. The psychiatrist is concerned with helping his patient; the sociologist can offer valuable assistance in ensuring that he does so to the maximum benefit of both patient and community.

This chapter reviews some of the past work in the field of social psychiatry, which has concentrated on epidemiology and ecology and has consisted mainly of a search for social causes of mental illness. It is our thesis that there is little evidence of any social cause for the major functional psychoses, and that while these studies provide valuable social data, the work of social psychiatry in the future may be more usefully concentrated on problems of educating the community and rehabilitating patients into it.

Diagnosis and Classification

Psychosis is defined as the more severe type of mental disorder in which the patient's contact with reality is so impaired that he talks, behaves, or perceives irrationally, and does not recognize this irrationality even when it is pointed out to him. All cultures and societies have some measure of irrationality in their beliefs and behaviour; delusions (irrational false beliefs held in the face of irrefutable contrary evidence) and hallucinations are in certain settings socially acceptable or even expected: it is therefore necessary to add to our definition of psychosis that the irrationality is inappropriate both for the social milieu in which the individual is found and for those which he has experienced. Because they are inappropriate and fail to follow the conventions, psychotic delusions and hallucinations can be distinguished even in a culture where delusions and hallucinations are in certain circumstances acceptable.[75]

We are not in this chapter concerned with those psychoses where some organic alteration in the brain structure or function has been established as the cause, though in some cases genetic factors appear to predispose individuals in certain families to a particular type of mental disorder[74] and subtle abnormalities in brain biochemistry may be proved responsible for the changed mental state. We have used the term 'major psychoses' as a distinction from the minor irrationalities or eccen-

Social Factors in the Major Functional Psychoses

tricities which do not interfere with the individual's social life as a whole, and the milder and more restricted mental disorders—the neuroses and personality disorders—where social reason is not seriously impaired, and the disorder of function does not extend to all fields of the individual's life, so that, though disabled, he continues to live in contact with social reality.

Within the major functional psychoses two main classes of mental disorder have been distinguished: the schizophrenias (Dementia Praecox) and the affective disorders (Manic-depressive psychoses). The distinction of the polar cases showing extreme and unmixed manifestations of these two classes is relatively simple. Although there is alleged to be no pathognomonic symptom or sign of schizophrenia,[52] examination of the literature suggests that there is general agreement about those symptoms which are most typical and characteristic. In brief, these appear to be as follows:

(i) There is a diminution in, or incongruity of, the patient's affective reactions to his experiences, real or delusional.

(ii) The patient experiences a subjective feeling of being changed or controlled by some intangible external influence, and may feel that his thoughts are being read or broadcast.

(iii) Thought, perception, and speech are disarticulated, with the intrusion of bizarre, dream-like mental content and an inability to exclude the irrelevant.

(iv) The patient appears to lack the ability to adapt his talk and behaviour appropriately to the social context; instead they appear fickle and inconsequential fragments, little related to previous fragments or to the outside world ('schizo– is meant to imply fragmentation rather than a splitting into two consistent halves; it does *not* mean dual personality).[40, 52]

Various authors have emphasized one or other of these classes of symptoms as being the more important, but whatever their theoretical orientation, few psychiatrists would disagree about the diagnoses when a patient manifests any of them in a setting of clear consciousness and in the absence of affective symptoms.

The symptoms of the *affective disorders* are less diffuse and more easily recognized. Essential to the diagnosis is a persistent alteration in mood (affect), so that the patient is either excessively and irrationally depressed or (much less often) elated. Disorders of behaviour, perception, and mental content are closely related to and consistent with the mood. If the mood is sad, thought and action are likely to be slowed, the mental content will be gloomy, the outside world will be perceived as dismal, while any delusions will be of being evil or useless or guilty of

353

imagined crimes; death will be an attractive alternative to this misery. This close relationship between mood, perception, mental content and behaviour contrasts with the disarticulation between the mental functions in schizophrenia.

The distinction of typical and severe cases is readily made and will be readily agreed; unfortunately in a fairly large number of cases symptoms of affected disorder and schizophrenia are mixed. Of one group of 288 psychotic patients, 105 were found to have mixed affective and schizophrenic features, yet only 18 were diagnosed 'schizoaffective disorder' (a subcategory of schizophrenia for cases with affective features).[81] It should be noted that even if so diagnosed, these mixed cases would be included under the diagnosis schizophrenia in research, using the International or American Classifications.[77]

The boundaries of mental disorders are not clearly defined, and the diagnosis of schizophrenia is not restricted to those persons who manifest the clear-cut symptoms outlined above. American psychiatrists tend to use a much wider concept of schizophrenia, and there is evidence of great disunity among the diagnostic concepts of French, German, and Swiss psychiatrists.[5] The remarkably varied systems of classification in use tend to defeat comparisons of research undertaken in different countries or even in different centres of the same country.[77] An example of the effect of this is quoted by Gruenberg:[27] of 1,177 cases who were admitted to both Boston Psychopathic Hospital and also a neighbouring state mental hospital 383 were diagnosed either 'manic depression' or 'dementia praecox' in both hospitals. In a further 316 cases the diagnosis of manic depression or dementia praecox was made in one but not in the other hospital, in 70 cases the patient was diagnosed dementia praecox in one hospital and manic depression in the other. This is not an isolated example.[43]

Variation in classification, lack of agreed definition of the limits of the diagnostic categories yet agreed distinction of the two polar categories schizophrenia and affective disorder, may well account for the paradox of great variation in incidence[43, 55] and diagnostic practice,[5, 27, 77] yet consistent correlations between schizophrenia and other variables. It would also account for failures of attempts to repeat results of work on schizophrenia when only small numbers of cases are used. Where diagnosis must be either 'yes' or 'no' it is inevitable that different workers will classify borderline and mixed cases in an arbitrary and variable way, and their decision may be influenced by extraneous factors, possibly even by those being investigated (see Page 361).

The foregoing must lead us to be very circumspect in considering research using psychiatric diagnosis as one variable, particularly as it is very rare to find an operational definition of these diagnoses written

Social Factors in the Major Functional Psychoses

into the research design. Usually the authors appear satisfied with the terms 'patients diagnosed schizophrenia' or even 'schizophrenics' and 'patients diagnosed manic depression' or 'manic depressives', as if these were established entities. That any results emerge suggests that within these heterogeneous and arbitrary groups there are extreme cases with extreme social and other characteristics which account for the characteristics ascribed to the groups as a whole.

Work described later[81] demonstrates that differences in social classes between the two diagnostic groups are the result of extreme differences between the cases most typical of the diagnoses. Use of the current pigeon-hole type of classification will obscure these relationships unless mixed cases are excluded and the 'pigeon-holes' clearly defined, with the unsatisfactory result that at least half the cases have to be excluded from consideration, since those completely typical of the current diagnostic groupings are not typical of the population of mental hospitals. The possibility of relating social parameters to the degree of presence or absence of different dimensions of abnormal behaviour has not been fully explored.

The Social Characteristics

The following characteristics have been found, in a variety of populations, to be associated consistently with a relatively high incidence of diagnosed schizophrenia :*

  (i) Being aged between twenty and thirty-five.
 (ii) Being of low socio-economic status.
(iii) Dwelling in disorganized central areas of large cities.
 (iv) Being a migrant.
  (v) Being unmarried.
 (vi) Being of seclusive introverted personality.

On the other hand, both *middle age* and *social extraverted personality* are found to be associated with a relatively high incidence of diagnosed manic-depressive psychosis. No consistent association is found between the incidence of manic-depressive psychosis and *marital state, socio-economic status, migration status* and *domicile*. Patients so diagnosed tend to resemble the general population in these characteristics.

Social Class

The concept and classification of social class presents difficulties similar to those of the concept of psychosis and the classification of

* For a useful summary of the literature see Rose [69].

Christopher J. Wardle

mental illness. The classes are arbitrarily defined; the different systems define differing numbers of classes and the classes so defined have no clear borders; only members of extremely different classes can be distinguished reliably.

The reason for dividing society into social classes lies in the observation that certain social characteristics, such as type of occupation, level of income, education, and the situation and quality of dwelling, appear to be highly correlated. These characteristics can be used to indicate the approximate status of an individual in relation to others. This observation would have little value to the student of human behaviour except for the implication that individuals occupying a specific position in a social hierarchy are likely to possess certain attributes in common which differ from those of individuals in other positions in the hierarchy. These attributes include particular aspirations, attitudes, patterns of socially approved and disapproved behaviour, and a particular way of life at least some aspects of which are peculiar to a particular class position. In addition, a social class structure carries the implication of various putative ecological differences between the classes. These include differences in child-rearing practice, life experience, physical and psychological stresses to which the individual is exposed and patterns of behaviour learnt by him to deal with his environment. Social class position may limit and define the roles which an individual takes in relationship with other people and which other people take in relationship with him. It is these implications which link the work of sociology to work in the field of biology[7, 15, 26, 42, 47].

Because of the high correlations between the various social characteristics and because of the implications outlined above, social class, as indicated by occupation or other indices, has been used as a parameter in research in medicine and psychiatry. The aim has been to discover whether any specific ecological differences in different social classes are pathogenic, or predispose the members to illness, or militate against recovery. Social class differences in incidence or morbidity rates are invaluable as crude indicators of areas for more refined investigation of the associations between specific aspects of social class and specific aspects of disease. The complicated intercorrelations of social characteristics and the wide implications of an individual's social class mean that many diverse factors may lie behind an association between social class and incidence rate for a particular condition. The social class of an individual may indicate at one and the same time (i) his opportunities, (ii) the kind of environment to which he is or has been exposed, (iii) the patterns of reaction to the environment which the individual has learned, and (iv) his achievement.

It would seem obvious that there can be no evidence in an observed association between social class and the incidence of a particular disease for any particular interpretation of the association. The association merely raises the following possibilities:

(a) that some factor associated with the disease (disability or pre-morbid personality) results in the patient's being in that class.

(b) that some factor associated with the patient's social class position plays a part in the genesis of his condition.

(c) that the association is the result of a concomitant association between some factor associated with social class and some factor associated with the disease.

(d) that the association is an artefact resulting from the construction of the classifications of either social class or diagnosis.

Only if an association is demonstrated between a clinical characteristic and an index of social class which is independent of the achievement of an individual could one consider a hypothesis that socio-economic factors play a part in the aetiology of mental illness.

Most studies have used the patient's occupation as the index of his social class; others have used a multiple index.[34] The latter is likely to obscure any relationship there might be between a single component of the combination and other variables being studied, so that there is *loss* of information.[7, 44]

A few studies ascribe socio-economic status to a neighbourhood and stratify the patients according to where they were living (e.g. [34, 36, 41]). In considering such data it must be recalled that ecological correlations cannot be assumed to reflect individual correlations. A positive ecological correlation can occur in the presence of a negative individual correlation.[68] For example, areas in the United States with high mental deficiency rates were those with high foreign-born populations—leading to the ecological conclusion: foreigners tend to be less intelligent than natives—yet investigation of individuals showed that the foreign-born population had a higher average intelligence than that for the general population. Despite this salutary warning some sociologists continue to draw ecological conclusions.[22, 37] This is not to decry epidemiological studies, which are of great value in indicating areas for individiual investigation.[54]

It has been suggested that the low social status of many patients diagnosed schizophrenia is the result of the patient being born into a socially disadvantageous situation. It has been the fashion to contrast this point of view with the 'drift hypothesis';[56] it was thought that if the drift hypothesis could be discounted then these sociogenic theories were tenable. The drift hypothesis originally stated that the observed differences in rates of schizophrenia for different social classes are the result of these patients' drifting into occupations of low status or into deteriorated ecological areas after the onset of the illness. This is a limited concept. In a social hierarchy there will be a constant two-way traffic of individuals rising or falling in status. An accumulation of patients in situations of lower status could also be the result of a failure on the part of these patients to rise as high as healthy individuals starting with the same opportunity. If this occurred, there would be an accumulation of patients in occupations of low status as a result of the illness, yet with no downward drift. It is likely that both drift and failure to rise play their part in the accumulation of schizophrenics in the lower social classes. Evidence outlined later suggests that the drift or disadvantageous mobility may occur before any obvious onset of mental illness.

Hollingshead and Redlich[34] present results of their own and other authors which they consider refute the drift hypothesis. They found that in New Haven, Connecticut, 91 per cent of patients diagnosed schizophrenia were in the same social class as their 'family of orientation'. The absence of social mobility among these patients is remarkable when compared with the 36 per cent of the general population of U.S.A. who were in the same class as their fathers.[15] In the latter study, occupation was the index of social class, whereas Hollingshead and Redlich used a multiple index combining such factors as education and place of residence which are highly correlated with the father's social status. Since there was no other group for comparison one must either conclude that the index used was unsuitable for investigating social mobility, or that their patients were unusually immobile.

They quote a further study by La Pouse *et al.*[41] who found that a disproportionate number of 587 patients diagnosed schizophrenia were concentrated in the lower socio-economic area of Buffalo. The investigators were able to trace the addresses of 89 cases back to 1925 and to match them with controls living as nearly as possible next door at the time. Between 1925 and the date of the investigation there was certainly no more downward drift among the schizophrenics than among the controls, but fewer of the schizophrenics had improved their lot. The result of this disadvantageous net mobility among the schizophrenics was the accumulation of schizophrenics in the lower social areas without any drift downwards. Unfortunately the sample on whom mobility was investigated was a small one and the method of its selection is dubious (apart from anything else, it was not randomly selected from the original 587), so that no conclusion can be drawn.

In studies[31, 48, 81] which compare the patient's occupational status immediately before admission with that of his father, the patients diagnosed schizophrenia showed significantly more downward inter-generation social mobility than a control group. The results can only be taken as suggestive, as the groups were small and not a random sample of patients.

Social Factors in the Major Functional Psychoses

Perhaps the most conclusive result yet to be reported is that of Morrison,[55] who investigated patients diagnosed schizophrenia in mental hospitals. Morrison uses an index of social status which must be independent of the patients' achievements, namely the occupation of the father recorded on the patient's birth certificate. If social origins play a part in the genesis of schizophrenia, then the distribution of these occupations should not be a random one. Morrison found that the occupations were distributed through the five social classes of the Registrar General in the same way as expected for the general population of the same age.* The finding fulfils the requirements for confirming the hypothesis that adverse net inter-generation mobility accounts for the association between incidence of schizophrenia and socio-economic status.

This adverse net mobility is probably in part the result of a fall in status during the patient's work history, which occurs significantly more frequently before first admission among patients diagnosed schizophrenia than among other mentally ill patients.[81] A greater frequency of job changing and unemployment among these patients is additional evidence of something marring their success in the labour market[73, 81]. This disability in the occupational field cannot be attributed entirely to the effect of overt symptoms since when the best status ever achieved is considered patients diagnosed schizophrenia have a lower average net inter-generation social mobility than do patients diagnosed affective disorder. This difference was found to be due to an extreme difference between patients with symptoms completely typical of the two diagnoses. The patients with atypical symptoms were intermediate in mobility, and among them there was little difference in average mobility between the two diagnostic groups.[8] This finding was based on patients aged over twenty-five, the majority of whom had at least five working years with no obvious mental disability to prevent similar success in the two extreme clinical groups.

The disability in work does not, apparently, affect success in the educational field. The proportions of patients receiving different types of education were almost identical in the diagnostic groups schizophrenia and affective disorder. The proportions with grammar school education who completed a professional training were also very similar (as shown in Table I from ref. [81]). It should be noted that opportunity in the two groups was similar since they were matched for the social class of the patient's father.

* Morrison's findings are puzzling if schizophrenia is genetically determined. If schizophrenia is associated with poor work record in one generation one might expect the same association to apply to the previous generation, since at least some of the fathers must either have suffered from schizophrenia or carried the disadvantagous gene.

359

Christopher J. Wardle

Education received by two diagnostic groups matched for age and for father's occupational class

Education received	Diagnostic category	
	Schizophrenia	Affective disorder
Elementary only	42	39
Apprenticeship or Vocational training	17	18
Grammar School	33	33
University	16	18
Total cases	108	108

TABLE IB

Education achieved by patients who attended Grammar School

	Diagnostic category	
	Schizophrenia	Affective Disorder
Completed training for a profession	22	26
No training, or not completed	27	25
Total cases	49	51

It must be concluded that adverse net inter-generation mobility explains the apparent prevalence of schizophrenia in the lower socio-economic classes. This in turn is the result of some disability often operating long before the onset of illness. Since the disability does not impair academic success, it seems likely to be in the field of personal relationships.

Other hypotheses about the relationship of social class and schizophrenia will be considered briefly.

The hypothetical ways in which social status may play a part in the genesis of schizophrenia have been reviewed by Schneider,[71] but in the

Social Factors in the Major Functional Psychoses

absence of clear evidence that patients so diagnosed start at a social disadvantage these hypotheses might appear somewhat superfluous. However, even if the differential status is the result of differential achievement it is possible that the social situation so achieved is disadvantageous to the patient and may contribute to the onset, relapse, or continuation of mental illness, or to its content or form.

It is likely that the social origins of the patient determine the care he receives from his relatives. The fewer letters and visits a patient gets the longer he is likely to stay in hospital.[8] The treatment a patient received has been shown to be related to his social class;[34] in the United States the well-to-do are more likely to get psycho-analytic treatment, the unskilled workers more likely to get physical treatments.

A patient's socio-economic status might influence the physician in making his diagnosis. This may occur in two ways. First, it is possible that the more closely a patient approaches his physician in socio-cultural characteristics, the more loath would be the physician to diagnose schizophrenia and the more painstaking he might be in assessin the symptoms and in noting those weighing against the diagnosis. Secondly, the further the patient is from the physician in socio-cultural characteristics, the more difficult would be communication between them. This parataxis might result in such patients being diagnosed schizophrenia more frequently. In addition, personality factors associated with the patient's lower socio-economic status might cause his symptoms to resemble schizophrenia more often: for example, difficulty in self-expression, suspiciousness, uninhibited aggression, a tendency to concrete thinking and inability to interpret proverbs. Such factors would tend to swell the proportions of those diagnosed schizophrenia in lower classes.

It has been suggested[63] that there is a social class differential in the reporting of cases because people's ideas of what is 'crazy' and their tolerance of crazy behaviour varies with educational and social class backgrounds. Owen suggested that psychotic behaviour in a socially isolated person in the central area of a large city is more likely to lead to early admission than similar behaviour in a well-to-do home. The opposite view has been expressed, that eccentricities and solitary habit will be less noticeable in impersonal lodgings in a busy urban area.

Occupation

It has been found that among occupations of the same social class some have a higher rate for schizophrenia than others. Examination of the occupations with high rates suggest that they are those which require less initiative, less social contact with other people, less ability to get on with other people, and less responsibility: in short, less social aptitude.

Christopher J. Wardle

As early as 1912 Ludwig von Stern reported differences between occupational groups in the ratio of numbers diagnosed schizophrenia to the number diagnosed manic depressive disorder among patients admitted to the Psychiatric Clinic in Freiburg.[72] The ratio of schizophrenia to manic-depressive psychosis was found to be highest for unskilled and manual workers and lowest for professional workers, business proprietors, managers and employers.

Carstairs and others[12] also reported differences, within the five social classes, in the rates of schizophrenia for specific occupations. The Registrar General has investigated the rates for specific occupations in considerable detail.[66] The findings are striking and will be quoted at some length.

In Class I the categories of occupations with the highest rate of schizophrenia are engineers, surveyors, architects, scientists, doctors, and chemists, while those with the lowest rates are 'Financial, Administrative' and 'Service Officers'.

In Class II the categories of occupations with the highest rates of schizophrenia are teachers, draughtsmen, and 'miscellaneous professional and technical workers'. Those with low rates are 'Civil Service executives and Local Authority officials', proprietors and managers.

In Class III two occupational categories have very low rates for schizophrenia, namely building foremen and 'Foremen, engineering and metals'. Low rates were found for drivers of all kinds, commercial travellers, insurance brokers and agents, policemen, firemen, roundsmen, and van salesmen. Specific occupations with high rates include hewers and getters of coal, erectors, fitters, clerks, cooks, and waiters.

In Class IV and V the specific jobs with low rates were watchmen, caretakers, office keepers, and costermongers. The labouring and casual occupations all had very high rates.

In all the occupations quoted above, the rates for manic-depressive and other mental disorders do not follow the same pattern as for schizophrenia, suggesting that there were real differences in incidence for these occupations.

Further examination of the Registrar General's tables reveals that in classes II to V the rate of schizophrenia was highest among the less clearly defined categories (e.g. categories described as 'other', 'miscellaneous', etc.). This may be an artefact of the classification rather than an indication of a property of those occupations, since the rates for *all* mental disorders are found to follow the same pattern. This suggests that the data on occupation collected at the census are more accurate than those provided by mental hospitals about patients, which limits the value of comparisons based on specific morbidity rates for occupations.

In his classifications of occupations E. C. Hughes[35] divided occupa-

362

Social Factors in the Major Functional Psychoses

tions according to the characteristics of personality he considered they demanded, as follows:

(i) Missions—demanding a vocation or calling.
(ii) Professions—demanding a lengthy training.
(iii) Enterprises—demanding practical ability and aptitude in relationships with people and ability to 'shift' and adapt.
(iv) Arts—demanding special talents.
(v) Trades—demanding an acquired special skill.
(vi) Jobs—which are entered without training or special attributes of personality according to demand in the labour market.

Some occupations once entered are seldom left, particularly those classified as professions: other occupations are associated with varying frequency of change of occupation and employer. Occupations Hughes classified as 'jobs' are associated with a very high frequency of such changes. Thomas[78] and Jeffreys[38] have shown that the frequency of job changing increases as occupational status falls, and is highest for unskilled and labouring occupations.

Many of the occupations found by the Registrar General to have a low rate of schizophrenia and a relatively high rate of manic-depressive psychosis are those which could be classified as enterprises, while the occupations with the highest rate of schizophrenia—labourer, kitchen hand, and the like—would be classified as jobs.

The kind of occupation which has a low rate of schizophrenia seems to be one which would bring the employee into contact with many people, would require him to be in close contact with the social milieu, to be good at getting on with people and at taking initiative and responsibility. The majority of occupations with a high rate of schizophrenia seem to be those which can be followed by an individual quite cut off from social contact with his fellow men. If this interpretation is correct, a possible explanation of the finding becomes clear. The schizophrenic's 'premorbid' life has been found to be characterized by a tendency to isolate himself from his fellow men and to be gauche and inadequate in dealing with other people. The early symptoms of schizophrenia are also such as would disable an individual in a managerial position, but would not be so disabling in an unskilled or solitary occupation where contact with other people did not matter.

Two sociologists rated the occupations of 302 patients on two scales indicating the responsibility and the contact with other people involved in their occupations. Their ratings agreed in 70 per cent of cases and the remainder were agreed on discussion. Both the responsibility and contact scales were found to be highly correlated with the social status of the occupations, but when a correction for this was applied, the patients diagnosed schizophrenia still had a significantly lower mean score for responsibility and contact-with-people than had those diagnosed affective disorder. This difference was found to be due to an extreme difference between patients presenting only symptoms typical of the diagnosis. Those presenting atypical symptoms did not differ significantly (Table II).[81]

TABLE II

Occupational responsibility and contact with others in four clinical groups.[81]

Diagnosis	Symptoms	N.	Responsibility Index †		Index of contact with people †	
			Mean	S.D.	Mean	S.D.
Schizophrenia	Typical	64	4·2	1·8	4·3*	1·0
	Atypical	93	4·7	1·5	4·7	1·4
Affective Disorder	Typical	118	5·0	1·8	4·9*	1·4
	Atypical	27	5·0	1·8	4·6	1·5

It was thought that the occupational differences in contact-with-other-people would be the result of differences in premorbid sociability between the two diagnostic groups. Table III demonstrates that this is not so; the difference in contact persists among both the sociable and the unsociable.[81]

Ecological Area

Farris and Dunham[22] were the first to report schizophrenia to be more prevalent among those living in the central parts of great cities with a shifting population of isolated younger people mainly domiciled in single person households. This finding has been made also in a number of American cities[72] and in Bristol.[29] The rate for all mental illness is higher in urban areas than in rural; the ratio is usually about 1·6:1. This may be partly due to a greater tendency in urban areas to hospitalize cases whose symptoms could be tolerated in the community (urban and rural rates for psychosis were identical in an investigation in South

---

* Difference significant at 1 per cent level C.R. + 3·38.

† These refer to the patient's best ever achievement and are corrected for the association between social class and score for responsibility or contact.

Social Factors in the Major Functional Psychoses

TABLE III

Diagnosis	Symptoms	Premorbid Personality					
		Sociable			Unsociable		
		N.	Mean Contact	S.D.	N.	Mean Contact	S.D.
Schizophrenia	typical	21	4·3	1·3	39	4·4	1·4
	Atypical	42	4·6	1·4	48	4·7	1·4
Affective Disorder	Typical	87	4·9	1·5	29	4·8	1·2
	Atypical	12	5·1	1·4	15	4·3	1·4

(In 9 cases data on sociability were not available).

Wales) the more sophisticated urban dweller may be more ready to seek psychiatric advice, and this may be more readily available in large cities.[12] These explanations do *not*, however, account for differences in relations between urban and rural rates for different psychiatric syndromes.

Hollingshead and Redlich thought that the areas with high rates of schizophrenia in Newhaven Connecticut were characterized not so much by a shifting migratory population as by low socio-economic status; they found very little geographical mobility among their patients, nor did Lystad.[48]

Stein[76] investigated four London boroughs; two West boroughs characterized by an unusually high proportion of individuals with occupations of higher status, and two East End boroughs with an unusually high proportion of individuals with lower status. Surprisingly the rate of schizophrenia was found to be higher for the West boroughs. It was found that the schizophrenia rates per 10,000 males in each social group were higher for certain classes in the West boroughs than in the East boroughs (Table IV).

The West boroughs had a higher incidence of single persons and people living alone and suicide rates were high,[64] whereas the East boroughs had a preponderance of family dwellings and a stable, well-knit community.[83]

Despite the protests of a number of authors[22, 34, 41] it seems likely

Christopher J. Wardle

TABLE IV

Schizophrenia rates per 10,000 males in certain London Boroughs.[76]

Social Class	I + II	III	IV + V
East Boroughs	2·73	2·21	3·04
West Boroughs	2·32	3·07	5·38

that the excess of schizophrenia in the central areas of cities is due to a minority of single young persons who have moved away from their families to live there alone. The addresses of the 70 per cent of patients still living with their families before admission are randomly distributed throughout their cities.[25, 30]

The observation that areas with a high incidence of schizophrenia are also areas with many features of social isolation has led to the ecological conclusion that social isolation plays a part in the genesis of schizophrenia.[22, 37, 71] However, while the findings might suggest an association between living alone and developing schizophrenia, this cannot be concluded unless a higher incidence of schizophrenia can be demonstrated in those actually living alone compared with those actually living with their families in the same area. When considering ecological or social causes of schizophrenia we must inquire why all the individuals in the putative disadvantageous situation do not fall ill. It is worth noting that Dunham[19] found that the premorbid personalities of patients in a slum area, who later developed catatonic schizophrenia, were quite different from those of the local boys who did not fall ill; they did not present an exaggeration of the local personality traits.

Migration and Acculturation

Schizophrenia is more prevalent among people who have recently migrated from one community to another than among established members both of the community to which they have migrated and of that from which they came.[50, 58]

Ødegaard found that the relative rates for schizophrenia among Norwegians living in Minnesota and Norwegians living at home were 100 to 50; the corresponding figures for manic-depressive psychosis were 100 to 110. Malzberg found the relative rates of schizophrenia for Foreign-born, Native-born and Native-born of native parents were 100 : 68 : 51 respectively (Leacock[43]). Ødegaard points out that whether or not migration is associated with a high rate of schizophrenia will depend on the nature of the migration. He found that the rate for migrants within Norway was lower than for the population in general but that rates both for migrants to the big seaport of Oslo and for those migrating out of the country were higher. He suggests that migration within the country is 'a logical step upwards for the capable and well-trained'. In contrast, the restless, isolated individual, lacking in personal ties and contacts, is more likely to drift to the seaport and to foreign parts. His individual case studies confirmed that frequently a schizoid personality or incipient schizophrenia was the cause of the migration. Hollingshead and Redlich,[34] on the other hand, found no significant association between nativity and the presence or absence of schizophrenia in New Haven, but an unusually high proportion of immigrants were in Class V in this study (though the authors conclude there is no evidence of 'drift' among the schizophrenic patients).

Studies of the incidence of schizophrenia in different cultures and types of community appear to demonstrate a higher incidence among people undergoing a process of acculturation (e.g.[17, 82]) while schizophrenia is rare in small highly structured societies. For instance manic depressive psychosis was found to be more prevalent and schizophrenia less prevalent among the closely-knit and highly structured religious community of the Hutterites.[21] Studies of different cultures and communities are, however, seldom exactly comparable, partly because the observed incidence of mental disorders is likely to increase with the care and closeness of the observations (e.g.,[46]), and partly because some of the observations are by psychiatrists while others have been made by interested but not psychiatrically qualified observers.

In general, ecological studies suggest the possibility that schizophrenia is more prevalent in socially disorganized situations where anomie[20] is high. The studies are, however, inconclusive, and the possibilities remain that the findings are spurious or are the result of either movement of schizophrenics or potential schizophrenics to such areas or of a failure of such people to move away.

Marital state and heterosexual activity

First admission rates of schizophrenia are approximately eight times higher for single persons than for those ever married (Table V) in all occupational groups[66] in England,[57] Norway,[61, 62] and the United States.[49] It is curious that this, the most clearly established relation with schizophrenia, should have received very little attention and that little attempt has been made to investigate its significance.

Three explanations can be advanced:[45]

(1) *Marriage protects the individual against psychotic breakdown.* This is not confirmed for types of mental disorder other than that diagnosed schizophrenia; the rate of first admission with manic-depressive disorder is almost identical for married and single.[65]

367

Christopher J. Wardle

TABLE V

5-yearly first admission rates per 10,000 of the 1951 census population.
(Men aged twenty and over).[66]

Marital	Social Class				
Status	I	II	III	IV	V
Single	16·4	25·4	30·8	32·1	68·0
Ever Married	2·3	2·3	3·9	4·0	8·0

(ii) *Married people have someone to care for them and protect them from the community's reaction to abnormality, and so are less likely to be sent into hospital.* Patients who had been discharged from hospital with a diagnosis of schizophrenia were least likely to be readmitted if they went to live in lodgings or with distant kin on discharge and most likely to be readmitted if they went to parents or wives. The failure of those with relatives could not be attributed to more severe cases being sent home to relatives; more of those mild cases who were relatively well on discharge relapsed if they were with relatives. It seems likely that, far from being protective, a close relative is more likely to spark off emotional disturbances and possibly to fan the flames, whereas patients in less intimate lodgings may pass unscathed because of the smaller chance of friction from close contact.[9, 10] Freeman and Simmons found that patients diagnosed schizophrenia who returned to a conjugal home were more successful than those returning to a parental home.[23]

(iii) *Some factor, connected with schizophrenia or with the premorbid constitution peculiar to those who develop schizophrenia, militates against achievement of the married state.* Hypogonadism, testicular atrophy, and histological degenerative changes in the testes have been found more frequently among patients diagnosed schizophrenia than among other mental patients.[5] The atrophy of the testis seems to antedate the mental change and may reach a severe stage before the psychosis is well developed.[32, 33] These findings were not confirmed in a smaller series,[6] so they cannot be regarded as conclusively established. However, if they are true, they suggest that hypofunction of the gonads among schizophrenics may decrease their libido and hence lower their sexual interest and activity. Other causes of failure to marry may be as follows:

(*i*) Physical or mental handicap of a severely disabling kind.
(*ii*) Faulty psychosexual development or psychological conflict

368

Social Factors in the Major Functional Psychoses

centring on the sexual object or act, resulting in deviation of, or inhibition of, normal sexual drives.

(*iii*) Personality traits resulting in inability to make adequate contact with other people, particularly seclusiveness and inadequate empathy.

(*iv*) Lack of communication and contact with society so that the individual is unaware of or insensitive to the social pressure to marry.

(*v*) Protection from the social pressure by other pressures operating in the opposite direction, such as approval of his single status by persons significant to the individual, or disapproval of any attempt to alter this status.

Any or all of these causes can be seen as likely to occur in people who develop or are predisposed to develop schizophrenia.

Not only are patients diagnosed schizophrenia seldom drawn from the ranks of the married, but the sex life of the single is much more limited and superficial than that of single patients diagnosed affective disorder. This difference is found to be due to a remarkable lack of any heterosexual interest or activity among patients presenting an absolutely typical clinical picture of schizophrenia.[64, 81] Although those who were sociable before their illness were more likely to be married or heterosexually active, the relationship appears to be independent of this (Table VI). Note that all these patients were over 25; in age group 25–29, 65 per cent of the general population are married, and in age group 30–34, 81 per cent. Comparative figures for psychotic patients were 24 per cent and 40 per cent.[81]

It would appear that patients who develop a psychosis whose clinical features are typical of schizophrenia differ in constitution from other patients in a way which prevents them from having any active interest in the opposite sex and hence militates against marriage. One effect of this will be to lower the fertility rate among those patients so that if a predisposition to schizophrenia is genetically determined it must be mainly transmitted by gene carriers who do not manifest the disease or the constitutional heterosexual disability themselves.

Since marriage is very rare among patients with typical schizophrenic symptoms but more common among patients diagnosed schizophrenia with atypical symptoms, and since typical symptoms are associated with a very gloomy prognosis, the interpretation of any success of patients discharged to conjugal homes may be the result of a greater proportion of such patients having atypical symptoms carrying a better prognosis. The evidence for the protective value of marriage is therefore rendered doubtful.

369

Christopher J. Wardle

TABLE VI

Marital state and Heterosexual activity in four clinical groups: Sociable compared with Unsociable. (Active = had one or more girl friends or intercourse at least once. Inactive = only superficial brushes with opposite sex and never had intercourse). (From [81])

	Married (1)	Single but active (2)	Inactive (3)	Total (4)	(3) as % of Total
Sociable before illness					
Typical Schizophrenia	4	6	11	21	53%
Atypical Schizophrenia	15	14	10	39	26%
Typical Affective Disorder	53	24	10	87	12%
Atypical Affective Disorder	6	3	3	12	25%
Unsociable before illness					
Typical Schizophrenia	2	7	34	43	80%
Atypical Schizophrenia	4	11	26	52	50%
Typical Affective Disorder	13	7	9	29	31%
Atypical Affective Disorder	3	2	10	15	67%

Sociability and Contact with Other People

Schizophrenia and manic-depressive psychosis are alleged to arise in two opposite kinds of personality. The type of person who develops schizophrenia tends to be retiring, solitary, and unsociable before his illness and has very little contact with people outside his family; he tends to be rather gauche and inept socially and to be out of contact with his social surroundings. This premorbid personality has been variously termed 'shut in', 'schizoid', or 'introverted'. In contrast the type of person who develops a manic-depressive psychosis tends to be sociable, outgoing, 'hail-fellow-well-met', 'the life and soul of the party'. This premorbid personality has been termed extravert. It might be thought this relationship was well established, but the relationship claimed varies from 100 per cent[47] to 0 per cent.[5]

The significance of the association is in debate. It is possible that the premorbid personality may in fact be the surreptitious beginnings of the disease itself; certainly Dunham's[19] detailed description of the social personality of the catatonic schizophrenic has features in common with descriptions by various authors of features to be regarded as warning signals of schizophrenia.[51] Other authors have suggested that the premorbid personality predisposes the individual to develop schizophrenia, or alternatively that this type of personality determines the form of the psychosis if an individual falls ill. It has been suggested that a person with less contact with his fellows and with the material and social realities of life would tend to have less support from companions, and that, having formed a faulty habit of withdrawal from reality, such a person might be more prone to retreat into unreality under stress. It has been suggested that the premorbid personality traits associated with schizophrenia are the result of social experiences.

Two theories have been advanced: (*i*) that child-rearing practices and early sociocultural experiences lead to a personality more vulnerable to certain life situations, and (*ii*) that the isolation and lack of communication experienced by persons in certain strata of society result in a seclusive personal habit and 'indifference to communication' which culminates in schizophrenia.[17] The second theory is difficult to support in face of evidence that schizophrenia occurs in people from social situations which are not isolated and that people admitted with schizophrenia from socially isolated situations appeared to have moved there fairly recently, possibly as a result of their illness[25, 30].

The objective indices of the extravert personality are the amount of social activity and interest he shows; these appear to decline with occupational and socio-economic status. Though many manual workers and people in lower income groups and living in poor areas belong to clubs, go to pubs, and take part in sport and entertainment and some play an active part in the social life of the community,[3, 14] they tend to do so to a relatively small extent. People in manual occupations and in the lower income groups belong to fewer clubs and organizations and play less part in those to which they do belong; they read less and go to fewer social and religious activities and entertainments outside the home. In short, they have less communication with their fellow men[14, 67]. People living in areas of lower socio-economic status and with high rates of schizophrenia have been noted to be more likely to be isolated from friends and neighbours and again to belong to fewer clubs and organizations.[4, 37] In contrast, those in professional and administrative jobs tend to be more active in all social fields and take an active part in organizing social amenities as well as enjoying them. The social

Christopher J. Wardle

factors which seem to influence the individual's communication are the status of his family of origin and his education rather than his own occupational status, although even when educational differences are controlled, the status difference in communication persists.

When, however, personality tests are applied to individuals in various socio-economic groups only small differences are found.[1] The responses to the tests by members of lower socio-economic groups suggested slightly more introversion, seclusiveness, and social passiveness. The differences are slight, and tests such as the Minnesota Multiphasic Personality Index showed no significant differences in the mean responses of the members of different classes.

We must conclude that social factors are unlikely to have much influence on the basic personality dimension extraversion/introversion, although they undoubtedly influence form and content of behaviour, for example anomie is inversely related to income.[2]

It seems more likely that personality influences the individual's achievement and choice of occupation or domicile, hence his social situation is to some extent a function of his personality. It may be that a measure of social disengagement is salutary for schizophrenics in the community.[10] The possible importance of premorbid personality in determining the type of occupation and marital status of patients diagnosed schizophrenia or manic-depressive psychosis has already been discussed.

We can summarize by saying that patients diagnosed schizophrenia

TABLE VII

Premorbid Contact with other people in two diagnostic groups—those with atypical symptoms separated. Male first admissions aged 25–44.

Clinical Category	Mean Score*	Standard Deviation	N.
Typical Schizophrenia	5·8	1·6	64
Atypical Schizophrenia	6·8	2·0	87
Typical Affective Disorder	8·6	2·0	117
Atypical Affective Disorder	6·6	2·3	26

* Summarizing index combining ratings of contact with people socially, heterosexually, and in occupation. A higher score indicates more contact—maximum 12, minimum 3.

Social Factors in the Major Functional Psychoses

and patients diagnosed affective disorder differ significantly in their amount of premorbid contact-with-other-people in their occupation, and in their social and sex life. The more typical the symptoms of the illness, the more extreme are the differences between the diagnostic groups (Table VII). These differences are not the result of disability resulting from the overt manifestations of the patients' illnesses, since acute schizophrenics also had little contact. There is no evidence that the amount of premorbid contact with other people is related to social origins (Table VIII).[81]

TABLE VIII

Premorbid contact in two diagnostic groups by father's occupational class (Hall-Jones Classification).

	Diagnosis			
	Schizophrenia		Affective Disorder	
Father's Occupational Status	Patients' Mean Contact Score	Number of Patients	Patients' Mean Contact Score	Number of Patients
1	6·4	16	7·8	19
2	6·5	21	8·6	8
3	6·7	7	9·1	11
4	6·3	20	7·3	11
5	5·9	20	8·7	15
6	6·5	25	8·3	42
7	7·1	14	8·1	14
8	6·1	22	7·8	18
Total		145*		138*

* Data on father's occupation not available in 5 affectives and 6 schizophrenics; hence difference in totals from Table VII.

Conclusion

This review of the literature suggests that three criteria must be fulfilled before considering an aetiological interpretation of a relationship observed between a social factor and incidence of a mental disorder.

373

(*i*) Correlations between the factors at issue must be demonstrated in individuals (ecological correlations are only indicative of a field for exploration).

(*ii*) The index of the social factor (socio-economic status, residence, etc.) must be independent of the patient's achievements. If the social factor could be influenced by the patient's behaviour yet is still thought to play an aetiological role in the genesis of that behaviour, then evidence must be provided to demonstrate this.

(*iii*) The social factor must be demonstrated to be related to actual symptoms or to a specific type of behaviour (diagnostic categories are ill defined, so that an association with diagnosis can only be regarded as an indication for more detailed exploration).

When an attempt is made to meet these criteria no evidence is found that a patient's socio-economic status plays a part in the aetiology of schizophrenia or the affective disorders. Though patients with typical schizophrenia were much more isolated from their fellow-men than other patients before their illness, this is not the result of any difference in socio-economic origins, and seems to be a way of life chosen by these people because of some constitutional factor. It is not clear whether this constitutional difference from 'normality' is genetically determined or acquired, but if it is acquired there is certainly no evidence that socio-economic or ecological factors play any part in determining it.

Where an index of socio-economic status is used which is dependent on the patient's achievements, all studies find that patients diagnosed schizophrenia achieve less and an excess is found in the lower classes. When an index independent of achievement (such as father's occupation) is used, patients diagnosed schizophrenia do not differ from those diagnosed affective disorders or from the general population in their socio-economic class distribution.

The tendency of patients diagnosed schizophrenia to be unsociable, single migrants, of unskilled occupation of low status, living in disorganized central areas, can all be accounted for by peculiarities in premorbid constitution which evoke such situations.

We therefore suggest that sociological theories of the aetiology of the major psychoses are premature, until unequivocal evidence is produced for an association, in individuals, between social factors and the development of a specific symptom pattern.

Much progress has been made over the centuries in achieving a more humanitarian and less superstitious and fearful attitude towards the mentally ill. As treatment and nursing becomes more enlightened the characteristics of the mentally ill appear to be changing; the symptoms are less florid and patients are less often regarded as, or found to be, aggressive or dangerous.[18]

It would have seemed impossible two hundred years ago that there

Social Factors in the Major Functional Psychoses

would be a time when lunatics did not have to be chained behind barred doors. Is it possible that in two hundred years from now the mentally ill will not have to be 'insane' and will be treated in the community? Hasty and ill-conceived attempts at educating the public may lead to anxiety and reaction,[16] but education is badly needed and is being attempted.[13] The future value of sociology in this field lies not in discovering causes but in investigating the impact of the mentally ill and society upon one another. Such investigations may indicate how society and the mentally ill may be modified so that the mutually harmful effects of this impact may be reduced to a minimum.

REFERENCES

1. AULD, F. (1952) *Psychol. Bull.*, **49**, 318–32.
2. BELL, W. (1957) *Sociometry*, **20**, 105ff.
3. BELL, W., & BOAT, M. D. (1956) *Amer. J. Sociol.*, **62**, 391–8.
4. BELL, W., & FORCE, M. T. (1956) *Social Forces*, **34**, 345–50.
5. BELLACK, L. (1948) *Dementia Praecox*. New York: Grune and Stratton.
6. BLAIR, J. H., SNIFFEN, R. C., CRANSWICK, E. H., JAFFE, W., & KLINE, N.S. (1952) *J. ment. Sci.*, **98**, 464–5.
7. BROWN, G. W. (1959) *Prestige Ranking Studies of Populations*. Unpublished.
8. BROWN, G. W. (1959) *Brit. Med. J.*, ii, 1300–02.
9. BROWN, G. W., CARSTAIRS, G. M., & TOPPING, G. (1958) *Lancet*, ii, 685–689.
10. CARSTAIRS, G. M. (1959) *Proc. R. Soc. Med.*, **52**, 279–81.
11. CARSTAIRS, G. M., & BROWN, G. W. (1958) *J. ment. Sci.*, **104**, 72–81.
12. CARSTAIRS, G. M., TONGE, W. L., O'CONNOR, N., & BARBER, L. E. D. (1955) *Brit. J. prev. soc. Med.*, **9**, 187–90.
13. CARSTAIRS, G. M., & WING, J. K. (1958) *Brit. med. J.*, ii, 594–7.
14. CAUTER, T., & DOWNHAM, J. S. (1954) *The Communication of Ideas*. London: Chatto and Windus (Readers Digest Association).
15. CENTERS, R. (1948) *Amer. Sociol. Rev.*, **13**, 197ff.
16. CUMMINGS, J. & E. 'Mental Health Education' in *Health Culture and Community*. (Ed. Paul), New York: Russell Sage Foundation.
17. DEMERATH, N. J. (1942) *Amer. J. Psychiat.*, **99**.
18. DIETHELM, O. (1953) *Amer. J. Psychiat.*, **111**, 421ff.
19. DUNHAM, H. W. (1944) *Amer. J. Sociol.*, **49**, 508–18.
20. DURKHEIM, E. (1893) *De la division du travail social*. Paris: Alcan. Also *Suicide: A Study in Sociology* Trans. Spaulding, J. A., and Simpson, G., London: Routledge, 1952.
21. EATON, J. W., & WEIL, R. H. (1955) *Culture and Mental Disorder*. Glencoe, Ill.: Free Press.
22. FARRIS, R. E. L., & DUNHAM, H. W. (1939) *Mental Disorders in Urban Areas*. Chicago: Univ. of Chicago Press.
23. FREEMAN, H. E., & SIMMONS, O. G. (1959) *Amer. Sociol. Rev.*, **24**, 345ff.
24. FRUMKIN, R. M. (1955) 'Occupation and Major Mental Disorders'. In Rose (Ed.) *Mental Health and Mental Disorder*. New York: Norton.

Christopher J. Wardle

25. GERARD. D., & HOUSTON, L. G. (1953) *Psychiat. Quart.*, **27**, 90–101.
26. GLASS, D. V. (Ed.) (1954) *Social Mobility in Great Britain.* London: Routledge.
27. GRUENBERG, E. M. (1955) In: *Epidemiology of Mental Disorders.* New York: Milbank Memorial Fund.
28. HARE, E. H. (1955) *Brit. J. prev. soc. Med.*, **9**, 191–5.
29. HARE, E. H. (1955) *J. ment. Sci.*, **102**, 349–57.
30. HARE, E. H. (1956) *J. ment. Sci.*, **102**, 753–7.
31. HARRIS, A., LINKER, I., NORRIS, V., & SHEPHERD, M. (1956) *Brit. J. prev. soc. Med.*, **10**, 107–14.
32. HEMPHILL, R. E. (1944) *J. ment. Sci.*, **90**, 676–709.
33. HEMPHILL, R. E., REES, M., & TAYLOR, A. L. (1944) *J. ment. Sci.*, **90**, 681–95.
34. HOLLINGSHEAD, A. B., & REDLICH, F. C. (1958) *Social Class and Mental Illness.* New York: Wylie.
35. HUGHES, E. C. (1928) *Amer. J. Sociol.*, **33**, 754–68.
36. HYDE, MAJOR R. W., & KINGSLEY, SGT. L. V. (1944) *New Engl. J. Med.* **231**, 543–48 and 571–7.
37. JACO, E. G. (1954) *Amer. Sociol. Rev.*, **19**, 5–57.
38. JEFFREYS, M. (1954) *Mobility in the Labour Market.* London: Routledge.
39. JOHNSON, EVA (1958) 'Schizophrenia in the Male'. *Acta psychiat.*, *Kbh.*, Suppl., 125.
40. KASANIN, J. S. (ed.) (1946) *Language and Thought in Schizophrenia.* Los Angeles: Univ. of California Press.
41. LA POUSE, R., MONK, M. A., & TERRIS, M. (1956) *Amer. J. publ. Hlth.*, **46**, 978–86.
42. LASTRUCCI, C. L. (1946) *Amer. Sociol. Rev.*, **11**, 78–84.
43. LEIGHTON, A. H. ,CLAUSEN, J. A., & WILSON, R. N. (1957) *Explorations in Social Psychiatry.* London: Tavistock.
44. LENSKI, G. E. (1956) *Amer. Sociol. Rev.*, **21**, 458–64.
45. LEWIS, A. (1957) *Eugen. Rev.*, **50**, 91–105.
46. LIN, T. Y. (1953) *Psychiatry*, **16**, 313.
47. LOGAN, W. P. D. (1954) *Brit. J. prev. soc. Med.*, **8**, 128ff.
48. LYSTAD, M. H. (1957) *Amer. Sociol. Rev.*, **22**, 288–92.
49. MALZBERG. B. (1936) *Psychiat. Quart.*, **10**, 245–61.
50. MALZBERG, B., & LEE, E. S. (1956) *Migration and Mental Disease.* New York: Social Science Research Council.
51. MAYER-GROSS, W. (1938) *Brit. med. J.*, **ii**, 936–9.
52. MAYER-GROSS, W., SLATER, R., & ROTH, M. (1954) *Clinical Psychiatry.* London: Cassell.
53. MEARES, W. (1959) *Lancet*, **i**, 55–58.
54. MORRIS, J. N. (1957) *Uses of Epidemiology.* Edinburgh: Livingstone.
55. MORRISON, S. L. (1959) *Lancet* **i**, 304 (Quoted by Morris, J. N.).
56. MYERSON, A. (1938) *Amer. J. Psychiat.*, **96**, 996.
57. NORRIS, V. (1956) *J. ment. Sci.*, **103**, 467–86.
58. ØDEGAARD, Ø. (1932) *Acta psychiat. Kbh.*, Supple. 4.
59. ØDEGAARD, Ø. (1946) *Ment. Hyg., Lond.*, **20**.

Social Factors in the Major Functional Psychoses

60. ØDEGAARD, Ø. (1945) *Acta Psychiat. Kbh.*, **20**.
61. ØDEGAARD, Ø. (1946) *Psychiat. Quart.*, **20**, 381–99.
62. ØDEGAARD, Ø. (1953) *J. ment. Sci.*, **99**, 778.
63. OWEN, M. B. (1942) *Amer. J. Sociol.*, **47**–48.
64. PHILLIPS, L. (1953) *J. nerv. ment. Dis.*, **117**, 515–25.
65. Registrar-General (1955) *Statistical Review of England and Wales for the Years* 1950–51. Supplement on General Morbidity, Cancer and Mental Health, London: H.M.S.O.
66. Registrar-General (1958) *Statistical Review of England and Wales for the two years* 1952–53. Supplement on Mental Health. London: H.M.S.O.
67. REICHMANN, L. (1954) *Amer. Sociol. Rev.*, **19**, 76–84.
68. ROBINSON, W. S. (1954) *Amer. Sociol. Rev.*, **15**, 351–7.
69. ROSE, A., & STUB, H. R. (1955) In: (Rose, Ed.) *Mental Health and Mental Disorder*. New York: Norton.
70. SAINSBURY, P. (1955) *Suicide in London*. Maudsley Monograph, I. London: Chapman & Hall.
71. SCHNEIDER, E. V. (1953) In: *Interrelations Between Social Environment and Psychiatric Disorders*. New York: Milbank Memorial Fund.
72. SCHROEDER, C. W. (1942) *Amer. J. Sociol.*, **48**, 40–47.
73. SCHWARTZ, M. (1951) Unpublished M.A. dissertation. Univ. of Chicago, Department of Sociology.
74. SLATER, E., & COWIE, V. (1959) 'Psychiatric Genetics'. In *Recent Progress in Psychiatry* Vol. 3 (Ed. G.W.T.H. Fleming & A. Walk). London: Churchill.
75. STAINBROOK, E. (1952) *Amer. J. Psychiat.*, **109**, 330–5.
76. STEIN, L. (1957) *Brit. J. prev. soc. Med.*, **11**, 181–95.
77. STENGEL, E. (1959) 'Classification of Mental Disorders' (Bulletin of the World Health Organization, **21**, 601–63.
78. THOMAS, G. (1950) *The Social Survey: Labour Mobility in Great Britain*, 1945–49. Inquiry for the Ministry of Labour and National Service.
79. TIETZE, C., LEMKAU, P. V. & COOPER, M. M. (1941) *Amer. J. Sociol.*, **47**, 167–75.
80. TIETZE, C., LEMKAU, P. V. & COOPER, M. M. (1942) *Amer. J. Sociol.*, **48**, 29–39.
81. WARDLE, C. J. (1960) Social Achievement and the Functional Psychoses (Unpublished M.D. Thesis, University of London). This Thesis reviews the literature extensively and describes two investigations. (1) An investigation of the occupational histories and social mobility of 313 male first admissions. (2) An investigation of the 'premorbid' achievements of 336 male patients in the fields of occupation, heterosexual activity, and social activities. The patients were from the Maudsley and Bethlem Royal Hospitals, age range 25–44.
82. WEDGE, B. M. (1952) *Amer. J. Psychiat.*, **109**, 255.
83. YOUNG, M., & WILLMOTT, P. (1957) *Family and Kinship in East London*. London: Routledge.

20

FAMILY ENVIRONMENT AND
MENTAL ILLNESS

D. Russell Davis

INTRODUCTION

THE first part of this chapter reviews some recent investigations into
the effects upon mental health of disturbances in the family environment of early childhood. The latter sections give some examples of
researches that have been guided by the viewpoint, advocated by
Sullivan[54] amongst others, and in the tradition of psycho-analysis, that
the essence of mental illness lies in disturbances in inter-personal
relationships, and that acute illness arises out of a crisis in such relationships.

One of the most important assumptions of psycho-analytic theory is
that nervous and mental disorders originate in disturbances in relationships with parents and sibs during early childhood. The patterns of
behaviour to which these disturbances give rise recur, it is supposed, in
relationships outside the family in childhood, adolescence, and adult
life. Consisting mainly of memories revived under special conditions,
the evidence adduced in psycho-analytic investigations has not, however,
been regarded as a satisfactory basis for a scientific theory, and attempts
have been made to develop better research methods.

Several difficulties beset investigations with human subjects. The
psychopathologist is not permitted deliberately to create disturbances
in the family environment in order to observe their effects. He has,
therefore, to make use of natural experiments, i.e. experiments of

opportunity, and has often then to rely on accounts given by patients, relatives, or other informants after the significant events have taken place, despite the many sources of error in retrospective accounts. Follow-up investigations, in which children brought up in disturbed environments are reviewed in adult life, would provide more reliable data in some respects, but have obvious practical disadvantages, not least the length of time required to complete them, and the literature contains few examples worth noting. In these few, children seen in child-guidance clinics or special schools during their school years have been followed up one or more decades later;[13, 45] the results hitherto have been of practical rather than theoretical interest.

Retrospective investigations can hardly be dispensed with, but their results have to be interpreted with caution. In most of the important investigations of recent years, patients have been observed during or soon after a significant change in the family environment has taken place, and have then been followed up, usually for a relatively short period.

To nominate the first modern publication would be arbitrary, since methods have improved gradually, but were one to do so, Bowlby's[6] paper on 'The Influence of Early Environment in the Development of Neurosis and Neurotic Character' would be a candidate. Stern's paper[53] in which he concluded that the roots of schizophrenia lie in 'prolonged mental stresses in early life, followed by later exciting factors', received less attention than it deserved. Much more influential was Bowlby's paper,[7] in which he reported that a large proportion of juvenile thieves of 'affectionless character'—twelve out of fourteen cases—had suffered separation from their mothers for a period of six months or more during the first five years of life. Barry[2] was one of the first to report on the incidence of parental loss during childhood in the histories of adult patients. He found that a significantly high proportion of patients admitted to mental hospitals for the first time under the age of forty years had lost their mothers through death, desertion, or illness in their infancy or early childhood, the critical age appearing to be less than eight years. Interest in the family disturbances responsible for schizophrenia, in particular, was aroused by the papers of Lidz and Lidz,[35] Tietze,[55] and Gerard and Siegel.[22] All these were retrospective investigations.

Bowlby's monograph, *Maternal Care and Mental Health*,[8] which achieved an enormous circulation and gave impetus to research in this field, drew attention to direct observations of the effects upon intellectual development and personality of separation from the mother during the first five years. Its thesis, that the essential condition for the healthy mental development of the child is 'a warm, intimate and continuous relationship with his mother in which both find satisfaction and enjoy-

Family Environment and Mental Illness

ment', has been generally accepted, although the evidence it cites in support has been criticized (e.g.,[42]). Although Bowlby supposes that any disturbance in the mother-child relationship may be the cause of ill-health or retardation, he has laid stress on physical separation, partly because this is a relatively easy variable to work with. From the study of its effects he has gone on to consider the nature of the child's tie to his mother,[9] and has recently published a new review of this and other theoretical issues.[10]

The shortcomings of investigations with human subjects, and the desire to develop an experimentally based theory, have turned attention more and more to studies of animal behaviour. Many investigations into the effects of removing young mammals from their mothers are now in progress, and views are likely to change rapidly during the next few years. A few animal experiments will be discussed briefly in the next section in order to indicate some of the psychological mechanisms that at present appear important. A review of the animal experiments having a bearing on the thesis that behaviour in maturity is determined by early experiences[4] led to the conclusion that much of the evidence is equivocal, but the recent evidence obtained a few years ago would justify a more positive conclusion.

SOME ANIMAL EXPERIMENTS

Great interest has been taken in the experiments of Hebb and his colleagues,[14] who have shown that rats brought up with a free run of a varied environment show greater learning and problem-solving capacity in maturity, i.e. are more intelligent, than animals of the same strain reared in the restricted environment of a cage; the lower the age at which the more varied experience is gained, the greater the effect. These and other similar experiments have given weight to the idea, readily accepted in the North American culture, that a stimulating environment in early childhood favours mental development.

Liddell's experiments[34] show how attachment to the mother affects the young animal's behaviour in a stimulating environment. Goat kids removed from the mother for a period immediately after birth do not subsequently make a normal attachment to her, and remain detached from the social group throughout their lives, which tend to be shortened; also, they are inactive sexually after they have reached maturity. In particular, they are unduly prone to develop experimental neurosis, i.e. their behaviour readily becomes disordered under stress. They then show marked reduction in exploratory behaviour, tending also to show 'freezing' and immobility, even in the mother's presence. Conditioning is more difficult and produces more disturbance. These observations suggest that, when a normal attachment has been made, the mother

381

D. Russell Davis

serves as a 'conditioned security signal' and reduces the vulnerability of the young to stress. Her function is, in this sense, protective.

Rather similar effects of the failure of 'primary socialization' have been demonstrated by Pfaffenberger and Scott.[47] Puppies form a social attachment soon after weaning, usually to litter mates, but occasionally to a human being, who becomes the master.[51] There is a critical period for this process, lasting from three to ten, or perhaps thirteen weeks, after which age the capacity to form an attachment is greatly reduced. The highest proportion of failures in a school for guide dogs for the blind occurred amongst the dogs kept alone in kennels until after they were thirteen weeks old, and not removed before then to foster homes, where they would have had opportunities to form an attachment to a human being. Thus, dogs did not get full benefit from training in the school if primary socialization had not taken a normal course.

These and other similar experiments have shown that the formation of a social attachment in infancy is of great importance in determining, not only the social habits and patterns of mating behaviour in the mature mammal, but also its capacity to adapt its behaviour and physiological responses to new situations. They have also shown that there is a relatively short critical period, during which the attachment is normally made. These findings give point to the question: What is the nature of the social attachment made by the infant mammal?

Bowlby argues that the attachment made by the human infant is mediated by a number of instinctual response systems, such as crying, smiling, sucking, clinging, and following, and attaches less importance to the mother's functions in satisfying hunger, or relieving fear, or meeting other needs, whether primary or secondary. Thus he sets store by Harlow's[25] demonstration that infant monkeys reared in isolation prefer dummy mothers giving 'contact comfort' to those giving milk. He supposes also that the child's tendency to follow his mother depends upon mechanisms like those responsible for the 'following' responses established in certain species of birds during the first few hours after hatching, i.e. 'imprinting'. In the researches to which he refers, these mechanisms have been regarded as instinctual, but other more recent researches[40] suggest that 'following' responses serve to relieve fear and are acquired through the ordinary processes of learning (see also[27]). Giving greater weight to the instinctual than to the learned components of the attachment, however, and recognizing that instinctual responses tend to be directed towards a particular individual, or group of individuals, and not promiscuously towards many, he argues that the child shows 'monotropy', i.e. attachment to a single person. Monotropy is an interesting concept, and if it proves valid an important one.

Final conclusions are not yet possible. It would be as well to suppose for the present, however, that the bonds which attach the child to his mother and the members of a family to each other have several strands, some instinctual and some learned, and especially that members of social groups hold together because doing so relieves fear and anxiety and gives protection. A striking example of the protective function of social grouping is seen in the aggregation of fish in schools whenever they are frightened.[31] Sexual and aggressive motives have also to be taken into account in any attempt to understand the organization of social groups (e.g. [61]). At any rate, much more is involved than sexual attraction between members of opposite sexes and 'identification' of members of the same sex, to which early versions of psycho-analysis gave almost exclusive attention.[20]

THE HUMAN FAMILY

A new family is formed when a man and woman set up a home together. In the cultural pattern prevailing in Britain the man tends to detach himself from his parents and to go to live in the neighbourhood of the woman's family—matrilocal residence.[60] The woman is given away in marriage to the man by her father, her attachment to her father then changing in character and weakening. Her attachment to her mother tends to weaken less, and she serves with her an apprenticeship as housewife and mother.

The degree to which husband and wife have detached themselves from their parents is of some importance in deciding the character of the relationship between them as well as affecting the conditions in which the children of the marriage grow up. Cultural and class differences are large. For instance, the conditions for the children are very different in the wide organization of three or more generations which composes the family typical of the Italian ethnic group from those in the isolated conjugal unit typical of the Anglo-Saxon managerial classes.

In some cases the nuclear family is not properly formed at all, because either husband or wife, or both, remains primarily attached to a parent or sib. Failure of this kind is a common characteristic of the nuclear families of schizophrenic patients.[19]

The Relationship between the Parents

The birth of a child requires the reorganization of the relationship each parent has with the other. The relationship is strengthened if each identifies with the child and accepts the diversion on to the child of some of the attentions and affections of the other, for in the care of the child they have a new basis for co-operation. Either or both may show symptoms of illness while the reorganization is taking place, especially in the first six weeks after the birth. Lomas[38] has remarked that puerperal

D. Russell Davis

illness occurs more often when the links between parents and grand-parents are weak, but it is uncertain how far his observations on this point can be generalized.

In general, the reorganization makes greater demands on the mother than on the father. Her attachment to the child is strengthened during the puerperium and thereafter, as a result of the satisfactions which caring for him brings her, but conflicts in her attitudes towards him may be lit up. His birth may revive the anxieties experienced in her relationships with her parents, and especially her mother. The child may be unwanted or inconvenient, or require her to give up her career or make considerable changes in her way of life, or she may feel guilt because conception occurred before or outside marriage. She may entertain doubts about her capacity to retain her husband's affections, or to care properly for the child, or to reconcile her husband's and her child's demands upon her. The new-born child may have blemishes or be damaged. Or she may be unduly anxious because the child has been born after a long period of sterility, or after a miscarriage or stillbirth. All these factors are relatively common and may affect adversely the way in which she cares for the child.

Sometimes the relationship between the parents is weakened by the birth of a child, and reintegration as a triad does not take place. The commonest pattern of disturbance is then the displacement of the husband by the child in the mother's affections. Sexual intercourse is sometimes not resumed, or if it is resumed, the wife may for a while be less responsive than before. The alienation may be progressive; if so, open rivalry to gain control over the child sooner or later occurs.

Adverse features of this kind are often well to the fore in the families of schizophrenic patients, and contribute to what Lidz and his colleagues[36] call schism and skew in the family. Usually the mother forms a close, although anxiety-ridden, relationship with the child, while the father is excluded; the reverse occurs occasionally when the patient is a daughter. The parents have usually become alienated from each other soon after the birth of the patient, and have ceased to have sexual intercourse with each other for several years before the patient has become ill.[16] Discord between the parents is of course a relatively common finding in the histories of all classes of psychiatric patient.

The Attachment of the Child to the Mother

Taken altogether, the evidence at present available suggests that the child normally attaches himself to the mother in the second half of the first year, and that, if he does not do so before he is eighteen months old, he remains more or less permanently detached. The year from six to eighteen months old appears to be crucial. The most decisive evidence comes from studies of children admitted to hospital, which show that separation from the mother produces no definite effects when it takes place before the child is seven months old.[49, 50] Similarly, the effects of removal before this age from one mother to another, as in adoption, are thought to be minimal. When separation takes place after seven months old, the adverse effects are clear-cut. A definite sequence of reactions can be made out in children aged from fifteen to thirty months, which Bowlby[10] has summarized as protest, despair, and detachment. Recovery takes place gradually when the young child rejoins his mother.

The Father's Role

The father's role, which Bowlby[8] describes as giving emotional and economic support to the mother, is certainly of less importance than the mother's during the first few years. Whether it is of a different order of importance, as the concept of monotropy would suggest, is debatable. At any rate, the father makes a contribution to the protection of the young child. The degree to which the first child is disturbed by the birth of a second child, for instance, appears to depend inversely upon the degree to which the father participates in the family life. Also, he makes a positive contribution to the upbringing of the children, perhaps particularly to that of the boys. As Andry[1] has pointed out, the manner in which he plays his part is of significance in the aetiology of delinquency. On the other hand, whereas loss of the mother before the age of five years is relatively common in the histories of psycho-neurotic patients, loss of the father is not.[3]

The Effects of Disturbances in the Family Environment during Infancy

Animal studies suggest that the capacity to form a social attachment declines steeply at the end of a critical period in infancy, if an attachment has not been made for one reason or another. Whether it does so similarly in man is uncertain. The outcome in cases of 'early infantile autism', of which the cardinal symptom is detachment and the onset typically in the second year, might give some indication, although it is doubtful whether the failure to form an attachment is primary. Eisenberg[18] reports that the outcome depends on whether the child has acquired 'useful' speech at the age of five years; of thirty-one cases without useful speech, it was 'fair' in one case only, and 'poor' in thirty; on the other hand, sixteen of the thirty-two with useful speech had made, at a mean age of fifteen years, adjustments which included some meaningful contacts with other people. The disability in social relationships in some cases of psychopathic personality appears to have begun in early childhood, because of lack of opportunity to form an attachment to a mother-figure, and this fact suggests that failure to form an attachment then *may not be* retrieved; it does not of course show that it *is never*, or even not usually, retrieved.

In other cases of psychopathic personality, the history suggests that the causes of the disability in social relationships lie in maternal deprivation, after an attachment has been made, as a result of separation, for a substantial period in the first five years of life. However, it is not known in what proportion of such cases of maternal deprivation this disability occurs and is permanent: Bowlby[11] has concluded that, although it is not common, it occurs in 'a far from negligible proportion'. In Barry and Lindemann's[3] large series of cases of neurosis and psychosomatic disorders, the peak in the incidence of maternal loss in the female patients was in the third year; a disproportionate number of male patients had lost their mothers during childhood, but there was no peak at this age. It is not known what proportion of children losing their mothers in the third year suffer subsequently from psychiatric illness.

In many cases of psychopathic personality, however, the history is one not of separation from the mother during early childhood, but of disturbed relationships in a family of normal structure, one aspect of the disturbances sometimes being lack of maternal affection; or ill-health springs from being with parents rather than away from them.[28] The disturbances in the family environment are then much more difficult to define, but are not less important than separation. In some cases the child's behaviour disorder begins in the fifth year as an 'oppositional syndrome',[33] in the genesis of which over-strict discipline by the father probably plays an important part. Wilkins[59] has recently shown, from an analysis of the observed crime rates for the years 1946–57 in England and Wales, that the greatest crime proneness was associated with that birth group who passed through their fifth year during World War II, and suggests the hypothesis that disturbed social conditions have their greatest impact on children between the ages of four and five years. Children born during the years 1939–42 have also shown high death rates from road accidents.[29]

MENTAL RETARDATION

The feeble-minded, the border-line defective, and the educationally subnormal without organic defect tend to come from poor homes and to have parents of defective or inferior intelligence,[23, 46, 52] although some come from good material circumstances and have parents of normal intelligence. These well-known facts are customarily explained by reference to the theory of multifactorial inheritance, which supposes that the children have inherited unfavourable combinations of genes from their parents and are accordingly of inferior constitution. They can also be explained, however, by an environmental theory. The two theories are complementary to and compatible with one another.

In the context of an environmental theory, retardation in mental development during early childhood is regarded as the result of inadequate stimulation or inadequate protection from stress, because of the incapacity of the mother, mother-substitute, or other parent-figure, or perhaps because of especially unfavourable circumstances. Inadequate protection from stress appears to be the most important factor in the majority of cases. Too little protected, the young child succumbs under stress to a disorder akin to the experimental neurosis observed in Liddell's experiments.

Little can be said about the nature of the disorder in the young child. The mechanisms may be assumed to be similar to those concerned in experimental neurosis, although the term 'neurosis' is misleading in this context. 'Psychosis' might be preferable, although this term too is confusing because of the several senses in which it has been used in discussions of the aetiology of mental defect.[44] Bourne,[5] who has shown that relatively severe mental defect without organic cause is associated with 'grossly perverted rearing', proposes the term 'protophrenia' to describe 'abortive failure in organization and integration of ego functions' and 'psychosis' for the disintegration of ego functions already organized; any such distinction is necessarily arbitrary.

Incapacity of the mother is probably the commonest cause of inadequate protection. The 'disorder' theory does not specify the reasons for her incapacity and allows that they may be several and various.[15] Adherents of the theory of multifactorial inheritance also admit the incapacity of the mothers, which they attribute to lack of intelligence, but deny that the incapacity is causal. The practical implications of the two theories are different. On the theory of multifactorial inheritance, the incapacity of the mother is held to be constitutional and not amenable to treatment, and improvement in the care given to the child is not expected to do more than mitigate some of the effects of the child's constitutional inferiority. On the disorder theory, on the other hand, the incapacity of the mother is potentially amenable to treatment, and she can be helped to play her protective role more effectively. Any improvement in the care she gives to the young child is expected to be reflected in the rate and course of his mental development.

That children in poor homes are given inadequate care by their parents is not controversial, for they tend also to suffer more often in early childhood from bronchitis, pneumonia, infective diarrhoea, and vomiting, and to sustain more accidents, than children in good homes.[39] Maternal incapacity has long been regarded as an important factor in educational backwardness ([12], p. 133). However, it is much more difficult to say in what sense the mothers of retarded children coming from socio-economically good homes are incapable. The writer has unpublished data to show that mothers of this kind, but not the fathers, tend to have experienced disturbances in their relationships with their parents during adolescence and to have entered into marriage and motherhood with relatively unfavourable attitudes. Their children tend to have a weak attachment to them. When the result is mental retardation, the adverse effects of maternal incapacity are probably produced during the first two or three years of life. The prognosis in these cases is better than in cases of retardation with organic causes; the I.Q.s of the former tend to rise during the school years, whereas the I.Q.s of the latter tend to remain steady or to fall.

MENTAL ILLNESS IN ADULT LIFE

Disturbances in the family environment in early childhood, amongst other things, have to be taken into account in any explanation of pre-disposition to mental illness in adult life, but, since they are remote in time, information about them is likely to be scrappy and unreliable. The most that can usually be done in practice is to piece together a description in broad outline of the main features of the family during the first few years of the patient's life: the presence or absence of mother and father and sibs, and the age at which any major changes in the composition of the family, or illness in any member of the family, occurred.

During the years of adolescence after puberty, the young person's relationships with parents and sibs and others outside the family undergo reorganization, the course and outcome of which is in part determined by experiences in early childhood. Detailed information about adolescence is much more readily obtained than is that about early childhood, and studies of disturbances during these years help towards the understanding of mental illness in adult life. Several examples of such studies will be briefly discussed below.

If the family environment has been harmonious, and sympathetic relationships have been established with each parent, the young person has adopted the attitudes of, and has modelled his behaviour on, that of the parent of the same sex. He is then prepared to play the social, sexual, and occupational roles appropriate to his sex. Shortly after puberty the relationship with the parent of opposite sex tends to deepen and take on a more definitely sexual character, but the affection displayed in this relationship is soon transferred to a young person of opposite sex outside the family. The choice of person to be courted is determined in a complex manner. Studies of animal behaviour suggest that the love object tends to be similar to that to whom the attachment

Family Environment and Mental Illness

was made in early childhood. Thus a jungle cock reared by a human being and isolated for the first month from members of its own species courted, when mature, human beings only and not females of its own species.[26] Whatever their relevance, these observations serve as a reminder that the direction taken by adult sexual behaviour is not fully decided by the circumstances prevailing during adolescence.

Homosexuality in the Male

Transient homosexual interests are relatively frequent during adolescence. Much less often do they persist into adult life. This result is not explained by any bodily abnormality, except possibly in very few cases, and has to be attributed to disturbances in the family during adolescence or earlier. Studies of patients attending psychiatric clinics have shown[58] that male homosexuality is associated with a characteristic pattern of relationships in the family. There has usually been a more than normally close relationship with the mother, who has been possessive and over-protective, whereas the relationship with the father has been shallow or antipathetic. Various explanations of these associations have been suggested. Similar investigations into female homosexuality have not been reported.

Maternal Over-protection

A pattern of relationships within the family similar to that found to be associated with male homosexuality has been discussed by Levy[32] under the rubric 'maternal over-protection', for which his criteria are excessive contact, prolongation of infantile care, prevention of independent behaviour, and lack or excess of maternal control. He followed up into adult life a carefully selected group which included nineteen males, but found no evidence of male homosexuality, as would be expected, or impotence; on the contrary, several boys who had also been indulged by their mothers had developed heterosexual behaviour at a relatively early age. The reasons for the contradiction are uncertain. Presumably they lie in differences in the patterns of relationships which are not as yet defined. Certain other features of the families studied by Levy deserve mention. In most cases, the relationship between the mother and father was disturbed, the two parents being sexually and socially incompatible with each other. The mother tended to monopolize the child, the father to be submissive and to play a minor role in his son's life.

389

D. Russell Davis

Schizophrenia

In the last few years a number of pieces of information have been fitted together, and a fairly clear picture of the family environment of the schizophrenic patient during childhood and adolescence is beginning to emerge. Admittedly there are still large gaps, not all the pieces fit properly, and much of the evidence is controversial. The main findings, some of which have been mentioned already, are summarized in the following paragraphs. References are given only if the point has not been made explicitly by Fleck[19] in a recent review.

The incidence of schizophrenia in patients' relatives is raised. This fact, usually cited in support of an inheritance theory (e.g. [30]), also belongs to a description of the family environment. Many other relatives are eccentric or more or less seriously disturbed. In a quarter or more cases, the family structure has been 'broken' before the patient is fifteen years old by the loss of a parent by death, divorce, or separation; loss of a parent before five years old, especially, is relatively common[57] as is death of a younger sib before six years old.[48]

There is schism due to strife between the parents and lack of reciprocity in the roles each plays in the life of the family. The parents tend also to be estranged sexually. One or both parents is still primarily attached to one of his parents or sibs. There is 'skew', in that one relationship between two members dominates the family. The normal distinctions in roles between the parental and child generations are blurred. In their behaviour and attitudes the parents have provided inconsistent and confusing models for 'identification'; for the children, sexual identity and sexual roles are therefore uncertain. The family tends to be isolated from the community and is pervaded by irrational and usually paranoid ideas.

The patient has not gained independence during childhood, and has not become emancipated from his parents during adolescence. Development of sexual behaviour after puberty has been disturbed. Homosexual interests have been relatively common, but most patients have remained sexually inactive and have not made sexual partnerships.[16] Relatively few marry.[41, 43] During adolescence the patient has become more closely attached to the parent of opposite sex, in a more definitely sexual way, and has not transferred affections to a person of similar age; the closer attachment has been given some encouragement by the parent.

The acute illness probably begins in reaction to a change in the relationship with the parent of opposite sex, of a kind likely to increase the anxiety arising out of this relationship; in some cases, incestuous desires contribute to this anxiety.[16] Thus in a series of fifteen young male patients, the crucial event was in four cases the appearance of a rival for the affections of the mother, in two cases the father's illness,

390

and in two cases the mother's illness. The disturbance in the relationship of parent and patient may make the parent ill too. When his illness begins in such circumstances, the patient sometimes takes flight and moves away from his home into a socially disorganized area, whence he is admitted to hospital. This is one of the reasons for the relatively high incidence of schizophrenia in such areas, when incidence is judged on hospital admission rates.[21, 24]

Bereavement

The stresses which bring on the acute illness in schizophrenia are complex, the pre-morbid personality abnormal, and the onset of the illness indefinite. For these and other reasons, correlation of symptoms and circumstances is difficult. Much easier is the investigation of the effects of a definite event, such as a bereavement, upon a person of normal personality in good health, and several studies of this kind have recently been reported.[37] By bereavement is meant the loss of a loved one, or, in the jargon, the cessation of interaction with an emotionally relevant person, as a result of death, a quarrel, house-moving, etc. Events like these are commonly reported as having occurred shortly before the onset of a depression, for instance, or an acute psychosomatic illness, such as a gastric ulcer. Almost all severely bereaved persons are impaired in their functioning, Lindemann asserts, for a period often lasting several weeks.

The anxiety caused by bereavement, it is supposed, is similar to and derived from that experienced by the young child when separated from the mother. It is dealt with by a variety of psychological mechanisms, such as denial and depression, sometimes with identification with the deceased. The bereavement constitutes a change in social environment to which the patient has to adapt, and recovery involves reorganization in the pattern of social interactions and some degree of modification of social role ('role transition').

CONCLUSION

The arguments of this chapter are governed by the views that the essence of mental illness lies in disturbance in inter-personal relationships, that the main consequence of illness is alienation, and that recovery comes through reintegration into a social group. These views have roots deep in psycho-analysis, but they draw also from other areas of knowledge. If honour is paid to Freud, it should also be paid to his contemporaries: Trotter,[56] who pointed out again the protective function of social groups, and, in particular, Durkheim[17], who attributed certain types of suicide to failure of integration of the individual into society, and assembled a wealth of factual data in support of his thesis.

D. Russell Davis

REFERENCES

1. ANDRY, R. G. (1960) *Delinquency and Parental Pathology.* London: Methuen.
2. BARRY, H. (1949) 'Significance of Maternal Bereavement before Age of Eight in Psychiatric Patients'. *Arch. Neurol. Psychiat.*, **62**, 630–7.
3. BARRY, H., & LINDEMANN, E. (1960) 'Critical Ages for Maternal Bereavement in Psychoneurosis'. *Psychosom. Med.*, **22**, 166–81.
4. BEACH, F. A., & JAYNES, J. (1954) 'Effects of Early Experience upon the Behaviour of Animals'. *Psychol. Bull.*, **51**, 239–63.
5. BOURNE, H. (1955) 'Protophrenia: A Study of Perverted Rearing and Mental Dwarfism'. *Lancet*, **269**, 1156–63.
6. BOWLBY, J. (1940) 'The Influence of Early Environment in the Development of Neurosis and Neurotic Character'. *Int. J. Psycho-Anal.*, **21**, 154–78.
7. BOWLBY, J. (1944) 'Forty-four Juvenile Thieves: Their Character and Home Life'. *Int. J. Psycho-Anal.*, **25**, 19–53.
8. BOWLBY, J. (1952) *Maternal Care and Mental Health.* W.H.O. Monograph, No. 2. London: H.M.S.O.
9. BOWLBY, J. (1958) 'The Nature of the Child's Tie to his Mother'. *Int. J. Psycho-Anal.*, **39**, 1–24.
10. BOWLBY, J. (1960) 'Separation Anxiety'. *Int. J. Psycho-Anal.*, **41**, 89–113.
11. BOWLBY, J., AINSWORTH, M., BOSTON, M., & ROSENBLUTH, D. (1956) 'The Effects of Mother-Child Separation: A Follow-up Study'. *Brit. J. med. Psychol.*, **29**, 211–47.
12. BURT, C. (1937) *The Backward Child.* London: University of London Press.
13. CHARLES, D. C. (1953) 'Ability and Achievement of Persons Earlier Judged Mentally Deficient'. *Genet. Psychol. Monogr.*, **47**, 3–71.
14. COOPER, R., & ZUBEK, J. (1958) 'Effects of Enriched and Restricted Environments on the Learning Ability of Bright and Dull Rats'. *Canad. J. Psychol.*, **12**, 159–64.
15. DAVIS, D. R. (1961) 'A Disorder Theory of Mental Retardation'. *J. ment. Subnormal.* **1**, 13–21.
16. DAVIS, D. R. (1961) 'The Family Triangle in Schizophrenia'. *Brit. J. med. Psychol.*, **34**, 53–63.
17. DURKHEIM, E. (1897) *Suicide: A Study in Sociology.* London: Routledge, 1952.
18. EISENBERG, L. (1956) 'The Autistic Child in Adolescence'. *Amer. J. Psychiat.*, **112**, 607–12.
19. FLECK, S. (1960) 'Family Dynamics and Origin of Schizophrenia. *Psychosom. Med.*, **22**, 333–44.
20. FREUD, S. (1913) *Totem and Taboo.* Std. Edn. Vol. XIII. London: Hogarth, 1955.
21. GERARD, D. L., & HOUSTON, L. G. (1953) 'Family Setting and the Social Ecology of Schizophrenia'. *Psychiat. Quart.*, **27**, 90–101.
22. GERARD, D. L., & SIEGEL, J. (1950) 'The Family Background of Schizophrenia'. *Psychiat. Quart.*, **27**, 90–101.

392

23. HALPERIN, S. L. (1946) 'Human Heredity and Mental Deficiency'. *Amer. J. ment. Defic.*, **51**, 153–73.
24. HARE, E. H. (1956) 'Family Setting and the Urban Distribution of Schizophrenia'. *J. ment. Sci.*, **102**, 753–60.
25. HARLOW, H. F. (1959) 'Affectional Responses in the Infant Monkey'. *Science*, **130**, 421–32.
26. HESS, E. H. (1959) 'Two Conditions Limiting the Critical Age for Imprinting'. *J. comp. physiol. Psychol.*, **52**, 515–18.
27. HINDE, R. A. (1961) 'The Establishment of the Parent-Offspring Relation in Birds, with some Mammalian Analogies'. In: *Current Problems in Animal Behaviour.* Ed. Thorpe, W. H., and Zangwill, O. L. London: Cambridge University Press.
28. HOWELLS, J. G., & LAYNG, J. (1955) 'Separation Experiences and Mental Health'. *Lancet*, **ii**, **269**, 285–8.
29. JEFFCOATE, G. O. (1954) 'The Chance of Being Killed in a Road Accident for People Born during Periods of National Disturbance'. Unpublished report of the Road Research Laboratory.
30. KALLMANN, F. J. (1946) 'The Genetic Theory of Schizophrenia'. *Amer. J. Psychiat.*, **103**, 309–22.
31. KENLEYSIDE, M. H. A. (1955) 'Some Aspects of the Schooling Behaviour of Fish'. *Behaviour*, **8**, 183–248.
32. LEVY, D. M. (1943) *Maternal Overprotection.* New York: Columbia University Press.
33. LEVY, D. M. (1955) 'Oppositional Syndromes and Oppositional Behaviour'. In: *Psychopathology of Childhood.* Ed. Hoch, P. H. and Zubin, J. New York: Grune & Stratton.
34. LIDDELL, H. S. (1961) 'Contributions of Conditioning in the Sheep and Goat, to an Understanding of Stress, Anxiety and Illness'. In: *Lectures on Experimental Psychiatry.* Ed.: Brosch, H. W. Pittsburgh: Univ. Press.
35. LIDZ, R. W., & LIDZ, T. (1949) 'The Family Environment of Schizophrenic Patients'. *Amer. J. Psychiat.*, **106**, 332–45.
36. LIDZ, T., CORNELISON, A. R., FLECK, S., & TERRY, D. (1957). 'The Intrafamilial Environment of Schizophrenic Patients. II. Marital Schism and Marital Skew'. *Amer. J. Psychiat.*, **114**, 241–8.
37. LINDEMANN, E. (1960) 'Psycho-Social Factors as Stress Agents'. In: *Stress and Psychiatric Disorder.* Ed. Tanner, J. M. Oxford: Blackwell.
38. LOMAS, P. (1959) 'The Husband-Wife Relationship in Cases of Puerperal Breakdown'. *Brit. J. med. Psychol.*, **32**, 117–23.
39. MILLER, F. J. W., COURT, S. D. M., WALTON, W. S. & KNOX, E. G. (1960) *Growing Up in Newcastle-upon-Tyne.* Nuffield Foundation. London: Oxford University Press.
40. MOLTZ, H. (1960) 'Imprinting: Empirical Basis and Theoretical Significance'. *Psychol. Rev.*, **57**, 291–314.
41. NORRIS, V. (1956) 'A Statistical Study of the Influence of Marriage on the Hospital Care of the Mentally Sick'. *J. ment. Sci.*, **102**, 467–86.

D. Russell Davis

42. O'CONNOR, N. (1956) 'The Evidence for the Permanently Disturbing Effects of Mother-Child Separation'. *Acta Psychol. Hague*, **19**, 174–91.

43. ØDEGARD, Ø. (1960) 'Marriage Rate and Fertility in Psychotic Patients before Hospital Admission and after Discharge'. *Int. J. soc. Psychiat.*, **6**, 25–33.

44. O'GORMAN, G. (1954) 'Psychosis as a Cause of Mental Defect'. *J. ment. Sci.*, **100**, 934–43.

45. O'NEAL, P. & ROBINS, L. N. (1958) 'Childhood Patterns Predictive of Adult Schizophrenia: A 30-year Follow-up Study'. *Amer. J. Psychiat.*, **115**, 385–91.

46. PENROSE, L. S. (1949) *The Biology of Mental Defect*. 2nd Edn. London: Sidgwick & Jackson, 1954.

47. PFAFFENBERGER, C. J., & SCOTT, J. P. (1959) 'The Relationship between Delayed Socialization and Trainabilty in Guide Dogs'. *J. genet. Psychol.*, **95**, 145–56.

48. ROSENZWEIG, S., & BRAY, D. (1943) 'Sibling Death in the Anamneses of Schizophrenic Patients'. *Arch. Neurol. Psychiat.*, **49**, 71–92.

49. SCHAFFER, H. R. (1958) 'Objective Observations of Personality Development in Early Infancy'. *Brit. J. med. Psychol.*, **31**, 174–83.

50. SCHAFFER, H. R., CALLENDER, W. M. (1959) 'Psychological Effects of Hospitalization in Infancy'. *Pediatrics*, **24**, 528–39.

51. SCOTT, J. P. (1958) 'Critical Periods in the Development of Social Behaviour in Puppies'. *Psychosom. Med.*, **20**, 42–54.

52. STEIN, Z., & SUSSER, M. (1960) 'Families of Dull Children. Part II. Identifying Family Types and Subcultures'. *J. ment. Sci.*, **106**, 1296–1303.

53. STERN, E. S. (1941) 'The Aetiology and Mechanisms of Dementia Praecox'. *Brit. J. med. Psychol.*, **19**, 112–23.

54. SULLIVAN, H. S. (1953) *The Interpersonal Theory of Psychiatry*. London: Tavistock Publications.

55. TIETZE, T. (1949) 'A Study of the Mothers of Schizophrenic Patients'. *Psychiatry*, **12**, 55–65.

56. TROTTER, W. (1916) *Instincts of the Herd in Peace and War*. London: Unwin.

57. WAHL, C. W. (1956) 'Some Antecedent Factors in the Family Histories of 568 Male Schizophrenics in the United States Navy'. *Amer. J. Psychiat.*, **113**, 201–11.

58. WEST, D. J. (1959) 'Parental Figures in the Genesis of Male Homosexuality'. *Int. J. soc. Psychiat.*, **5**, 85–97.

59. WILKINS, L. T. (1960) *Delinqent Generations*. Home Office Research Unit Report, No. 3. London: H.M.S.O.

60. YOUNG, M., & WILLMOTT, P. (1957) *Family and Kinship in East London*. London: Routledge.

61. ZUCKERMAN, S. (1932) *The Social Life of Monkeys and Apes*. London: Kegan Paul.

C. POPULATION STUDIES AND PROBLEMS

2 1

THE FAMILY*

O. R. McGregor and Griselda Rowntree

THE family is a primary unit in all societies and has thus received sustained attention from anthropologists, sociologists, and demographers. Since it provides the environment in which the young grow up, it is of vital concern for all who teach or in any way seek to inculcate standards of opinion and behaviour. Over the past century censuses and surveys have provided measurements of the formation, the structure, the resources, the environment, and the breakdown of the family. Such measurements have charted fundamental changes in family life in England in the twentieth century. This chapter reviews these changes and indicates their impact on those parts of the law which regulate family life.

Family Formation

In his census and civil registration statistics the Registrar General provides regular measurements of the reservoir of unmarried people in England and Wales. The total of bachelors and spinsters of fifteen to fifty-four years (an age-span to which the data are conveniently reduced and in which 99 per cent of all first marriages occur) shows, at each twentieth century census, the numbers and changing sex-ratio of those who can become founders of new families.

The twentieth century has so far been a period of outstanding changes in the sex-ratio. The shortage of bachelors, produced in its early years by their more frequent emigration, became much more pronounced after 1918 as a result of the heavy toll of casualties among young men in

* This chapter was written in the summer of 1959.

O. R. McGregor and Griselda Rowntree

TABLE I

Numbers and Sex-ratios among single persons aged 15–54 years at
successive censuses

Year of Census	No. of persons 15–54 years old Bachelors	Spinsters	Bachelors per 1000 spinsters
1901	4,172,000	4,338,600	962
1911	4,630,800	4,820,300	961
1921	4,436,400	4,962,300	894
1931	4,811,400	5,135,100	937
1951	3,933,000	3,611,000	1,089

Source: 1951 Census of England and Wales: General Tables. Tables 21A and 22A.

the Kaiser's War. The toll of young life during the Second World War was lighter and, by 1951, when the generations who lived through the first war were all over fifty years of age, the bachelors within the fifteen to fifty-four age-span became more numerous than the spinsters.

The sex-ratio is not the only determinant of the numbers of new families which are created, since some of those for whom spouses exist (at least in the national aggregate) remain single. One of the most significant features of recent times has been the increasing popularity of marriage. The annual total of first marriages has risen with the growth in population from about 225,000 each year in the 1900s to nearly 300,000 in the 1950s,* but some part of this increase reflects also a growing propensity to marry. Among women born in various nineteenth-century quinquennia, a steady proportion amounting to 860–880 per thousand had married by the ages of fifty to fifty-four years ([63], Table XIII). By contrast, a rather more sophisticated nuptiality calculation, based on the marriage registrations of 1951–55, showed that as many as 945 women per thousand (i.e. some seventy-five per thousand more than in the Victorian period) would be likely to marry before they were fifty.†

These figures illustrating marriage or family formation relate to all persons in England and Wales, whatever their social status. Biographical

* The annual totals of marriages between bachelors and spinsters will be found in successive issues of the *Reports of the Registrar General* [56] up to 1920 and of his *Statistical Review* [57] *Part II* since 1921.

† [57] (1956), Part III, Table XXXI. A detailed account of the methods used in compiling this nuptiality table will be found in [14] Appendix 2 to Chapter 4.

and impressionist studies suggest, however, that the opportunities and incentives to marry may differ from one social or occupational group to another. Regrettably, the available information does not permit a quantitative assessment of such differences. Although the General Register Office obtains much of the data essential for an inquiry into the trends in marriage-incidence at the various social levels, the technical difficulties of isolating one group from another when there is some movement between them, especially at marriageable ages, have so far prevented the publication of a regular series of tabulations on this subject.[3]*

The analysis of social class variations in family formation is further complicated by the age-at-marriage differential. During the last hundred years the overall age at marriage rose until about 1911; then began a steady fall, halted only in the trough of the inter-war depression. Over the past two decades of relative prosperity the age has dropped to low levels which are without precedent.† Nevertheless, the brides of pro-

Year of Marriage	Persons per 1000 first marriages	
	Bachelor grooms	Spinster brides
1901–05	441	591
1911–15	393	548
1921–25	403	566
1931–35	368	563
1941–45	490	684
1951–55	509	723

fessional and managerial status have been estimated to be on an average about $1\frac{1}{2}$–2 years older than their working class contemporaries.‡ This continuing difference can be further illustrated from the 1951 census material relating to married women under fifty years of age. Tables compiled for those married once only and enumerated with their

* One table does exist showing the proportions of all men in successive age-groups in each social class who were returned as married in the 1911 Census ([13], Part II, Table XXXIV.) Its value as an indicator of marriage-incidence was however limited because it failed to allow for such class-linked variables as age at marriage and early widowerhood.

† The above figures extracted from the Registrar General's *Statistical Review* [57], Part II, Table K, show for selected quinquennia since 1900 the proportions (per 1000) of bachelor grooms and spinster brides marrying under 25 years of age.

‡ [31], Table 8. The marriage-ages of women in the different social classes have been investigated in greater detail than those of men because of their relevance to class-differentials in fertility. The various official fertility studies determine wives' social status by their husbands' current occupations at the time of the inquiry, and not by that at the date of the marriage. In this way they avoid, at least for those who have been married for some time, the problem of classifying the wives of men who continue to shift up or down the occupational ladder during the early years of their married lives.

O. R. McGregor and Griselda Rowntree

husbands showed early marriage to be much less common among the wives of men in professional, managerial, and semi-professional occupations than among the wives of manual workers ([14] Tables 3.1 and 3.2).

Family Building and Family Limitation

There has been a striking fall in the size of family in all social classes since mid-Victorian days. In the course of this reproductive revolution the average number of live births per woman fell from six for those married in the 1870s, to three in the 1900s and to two in the 1920s. The detailed history can be traced in the Fertility Census in 1911 and in the Family Census, commissioned by the Royal Commission on Population in 1946.* The latter spliced the results of both inquiries in order to present a continuous series of comparable figures covering the complete fertility experience of women married in the crucial years between the 1870s and the 1920s. These studies measured the disappearance of the quiverful of ten or more children and the growing preference for small families. This is summarized in Table II†

TABLE II

Distribution of women marrying in 1870–79, 1900–1909, and 1925, with varying numbers of live births

No. of live births	Proportion of women (per 1000) with specified no. of births who were first married in:		
	1870–79	1900–09	1925
0	83	113	161
1 or 2	125	335	506
3 or 4	181	277	221
5 to 9	434	246	106
10 or more	177	29	6
ALL	1,000	1,000	1,000

Source: Papers of the Royal Commission on Population, Vol. 6, Table 2.

* The full analysis of this *ad hoc* sample inquiry is published in [31].

† This table refers to women in Great Britain who were married before the age of 45. It is adjusted to allow for differential mortality among women marrying in the earlier years under review in the two fertility studies.

The Family

Although the steady decline in family size occurred in each class, the professional, employer and white collar stratum pioneered the small family system in the latter nineteenth century,* and continued in the twentieth to produce fewer children on average than manual workers. Table III shows the differences in fertility according to husband's occupation among two groups of women married in 1900–09 and in 1920–24.

TABLE III†

Average family size, by occupational status, of women married in
1900–09 and in 1920–24

Occupational Status of Husband	No. of live births per woman first married in:	
	1900–09	1920–24
Non-manual:		
Professional . . .	2·33 ⎫	1·75 ⎫
Employers	2·64 ⎪	1·84 ⎪
Working on own account .	2·96 ⎬ 2·81	1·95 ⎬ 1·90
Farmers & farm managers .	3·50 ⎪	2·31 ⎪
Salaried employees .	2·37 ⎪	1·65 ⎪
Non-manual wage-earners .	2·89 ⎭	1·97 ⎭
Manual:		
Manual wage-earners . .	3·96 ⎫	2·70 ⎫
Agricultrual workers . .	3·88 ⎬ 3·96	2·71 ⎬ 2·72
Labourers	4·45 ⎭	3·35 ⎭
All Categories:	3·53	2·42

Source: Papers of the Royal Commission on Population Vol 6, Tables 5 and 6.

New data for women marrying since the 1920s, available under the Population (Statistics) Act of 1938‡ and in the 1951 Census ([14], p. xlix), show that, while the fall in family size has been halted, some class-differences in fertility remain even though professional couples are now producing more children than in the recent past.

* Middle-class motives for family limitation at this time are examined in detail in Banks.[2]

† See footnote to Table II.

‡ The use to which this information can be put in measuring current class-differences is illustrated in a special report prepared for the Royal Commission on Population by Hopkin and Hajnal ([37]).

O. R. McGregor and Griselda Rowntree

These persisting differences do not to any great extent result from the age-at-marriage differential, although the older brides in the higher social classes risk pregnancy for a shorter period than women who have married at younger ages. They are to be explained largely by the earlier, more extensive and more effective use of contraception by middle and white collar class couples than by their working class contemporaries. There has so far been only one national investigation which covers class variations during the interesting transition period from largely uncontrolled to extensively planned fertility. This was carried out in 1946–47 by Dr Lewis-Faning for the Royal College of Obstetricians and Gynaecologists, who had been approached for information by the Population Commission.[43] The group of married women selected for investigation, all patients in hospital for non-obstetric reasons, were not fully representative of all wives sharing in decisions on family building in Britain; nevertheless, the detailed analysis of their experiences by class and marriage-date set out in Table IV gives a consistent picture of the trends in contraceptive practice.

TABLE IV

Percentage of married women in different occupational groups using any form of birth control, by date of marriage

Year of Marriage	Percentage of wives of men in the following groups who had used birth control			
	All non-manual workers	Skilled manual workers	Other manual workers	All Classes
Before 1910	26	18	4	15
1910–1919	60	39	33	40
1920–1924	56	60	54	58
1925–1929	58	60	63	61
1930–1934	64	62	63	63
1935–1939	73	68	54	66
1940–1947	67	53	47	55

Source: Papers of the Royal Commission on Population, Vol. 1, Table 37.

Before 1920 wives in the non-manual group led their contemporaries in the use of birth control. Between 1920 and 1935 prevailing economic uncertainties seem to have persuaded working class couples marrying in the depression years to limit their families as frequently as did their financial betters; thereafter the earlier class differences reappear. For the most recently married (i.e. in 1940–47), this is explained by the fact that young working class couples, many of whom were in any case separated for long periods during the War, tended to adopt contraceptive techniques later in their married lives than the better off and probably by 1946–47 had not yet started to use them ([43], Table 76).

Parental limitation of the number of children has resulted in striking improvements in the quality of family life. Among other things it has involved what Professor Titmuss has called 'the revolutionary enlargement of freedom for women'. ([69], pp. 88–103). They now live much longer, and the span of years spent in pregnancy and in caring for small children has been so reduced that they can give more attention to their smaller families. Moreover, they now complete their maternal duties while still young and vigorous enough to extend their interests beyond the home and, at least in times of full employment, choose whether or not they will resume work in middle age.

Married women's freedom from the debilitating burdens of too frequent pregnancies was gained by securing control over their own fertility in the teeth of established disapproval and sectarian hostility. Although a growing understanding of sexual physiology, together with the development of contraceptive appliances and chemical spermicides, have multiplied the techniques available for controlling fertility,* their effective utilization under medical supervision is still today obstructed by bodies which use political means to secure theological ends. There is a continuous history of the advocacy of birth control since the early nineteenth century. But the pioneers were on occasion prosecuted, notably in 1877, when Charles Bradlaugh and Annie Besant were brought to court for re-publishing Knowlton's forty-year-old pamphlet, *The Fruits of Philosophy*. The unintended effect of this and other trials was gratuitous publicity for the possibility of family limitation.† From 1877 onwards the spread of information by pamphlet and through the industrial 'grapevine', probably the factory workers' main channel of information, was supplemented by the propaganda of Bradlaugh's Malthusian League and by the publication of discreet advertisements for contraceptives (alongside those for abortifacients) in the radical press. Organizations established to give advice to individuals and to fit and to supply appliances under medical supervision did not exist before the 1920s, when Dr Marie Stopes and the Malthusian League pioneered clinics.‡ The Family Planning Association, a voluntary body, was

* The chief authority on the world-wide history of birth control practices is N. Himes. [35]

† J. A. and O. Banks [3] have reviewed press comment on the Bradlaugh-Besant trial and its impact on public opinion.

‡ The first chapter in Glass [30] is the authoritative account of the spread of information on birth control in Britain.

founded in 1930 and, twenty years later, its enterprise had created ninety-one clinics annually attended by 40,000 new patients who could obtain advice on birth control or sub-fertility. The provision of such facilities as part of the statutory services has been less enterprising. In 1931 local authorities were permitted to give contraceptive advice in their clinics, but only to those 'women for whom further pregnancy would be detrimental to health'.[47] This ruling still stands, despite the 1949 Population Commission's recommendation that 'public policy should assume, and seek to encourage, the spread of voluntary parenthood' ([63], pars. 657, 667) through a more comprehensive service.

Parents' desire to restrict the size of their families has been sufficiently potent during the last ninety years to overcome both the initial hostility of the medical profession and the long-sustained antagonism of the churches. Within their own family circles doctors were subject to the same social pressures as other middle-class folk. They had also to respond to the insistent demands of their fee-paying patients as well as to protect them from harmful contraceptives peddled by the unscrupulous and the unqualified.* The reaction of the churches provides an instructive illustration of the process by which theological principles have been adapted to rapidly changing social situations. Until 1930, the resolutions of the Lambeth Conference denounced contraception outright, that of 1930 was grudgingly permissive, and that of 1958 was positively welcoming. The attitudes of the other main Protestant communions have changed similarly, although there have been differences of timing and emphasis. The Church of Rome, on the other hand, has resolutely maintained its condemnation of contraceptives while following, since 1930, the example set by the Church of England in the early years of this century by permitting its members to regulate, in certain circumstances, their domestic intimacies in accordance with the rhythm of the alleged 'safe period'. None of the main Christian churches today condemns the control of fertility, but there is continuing controversy between Protestant and Roman Catholics concerning the morality of different means to this end.† For the Christian couple entering marriage few decisions are more important than those concerning the limitation and spacing of their family. Nevertheless, the experience of the last hundred years has demonstrated the inability of the churches to influence behaviour in this area of life. Contrariwise, the power of behaviour to

* The change in medical opinion on birth control is briefly reviewed in Banks [2], pp. 146–7 and 155–59.

† The ethical and theological issues are lucidly disentangled in the admirable book of Fletcher, [24], pp. 65–99. The range of views within the Church of England is set out in the report of a group convened by the Archbishop of Canterbury [17], esp. pp. 129–154. The dogma of the Church of Rome is interpreted in the authoritative manual of Bonnar,[7] pp. 63–80.

influence the churches has been striking. It is now promoting what a Church of England committee has recently described as 'the mental effort . . . needed to grasp the nature of new situations and to ensure that the theological principles brought to bear are not contaminated with out-of-date sociological assumptions ([17], p. 120).

Marriage Breakdown—Fact and Opinion

Such mental effort has largely been restricted to the theological issues raised by the extension of contraception. But the gloomy interpretation which the churches read into the rapid rise in the number of divorce petitions in England and Wales, from an average of 808 in the years 1906–10 to one of 30,177 between 1952 and 1956, also gives wide scope for the work of decontamination. Four main influences explain this great increase. First, the disruption of family life by two world wars. Secondly, an extension of the grounds of divorce in 1937. Before that date, adultery was the only offence that legally warranted the dissolution of marriage. Of the new grounds, only three are statistically significant today. Adultery and desertion each account for some 40 per cent of all divorces, and all but an insignificant fraction of the remainder result from cruelty. Thirdly, in 1923 women were for the first time given equal advantages with men in respect of the grounds on which they could petition for divorce. The figures for recent years suggest that the rates of petitioning by husbands and wives are likely to remain roughly equal. Finally, there has been a radical change in the accessibility of the divorce court. Between the establishment of the Divorce Division of the High Court in 1857 and the beginning of Hitler's War there were, in effect, two systems of matrimonial relief in England. The wealthier classes could go to the High Court and there obtain a divorce which enabled them to marry again. Many poor people could not afford to petition and were ill served by the mean inadequacies of the poor persons' procedure. They had to make do with the remedies first provided in magistrates' courts in 1878 which preserved their marriage bonds intact whilst enabling them to live apart. The combined effects of reduced unemployment, the legal aid system set up in 1950, and the penetration of knowledge about divorce through all social strata have now given the whole population near equality of access to divorce facilities. The social consequences of this new situation are indicated in Table V.

This table shows a remarkable similarity in the occupational structure of the divorcing and still-married populations. It must be interpreted with caution, because the number of manual workers' petitions must have been inflated by the backlog of legal-aid cases coming to court in the first full year of the new scheme. It nevertheless permits the

O. R. McGregor and Griselda Rowntree

TABLE V*

Occupational structure of the divorcing and the continuing married
populations in England and Wales in 1951

Couples	Husband's Present Occupation			
	Professional & Managerial	Farmers and Shopkeepers	Black-coated Workers	Manual Workers
	%	%	%	%
Divorcing	13·5	8·0	9·0	69·5
Continuing married	13·9	8·4	8·1	69·6

* ([61], p. 223.) This study also provides, *inter alia*, a quantitative assessment of
the contribution of the various factors promoting increased divorce since 1871.

inference that a manual worker (or his wife) may soon be as likely to
seek a remedy for his matrimonial difficulties by divorce as his employer
(or his wife).

The sharp rise in the number of petitions during the immediate post-
war years has led to persistent exaggeration of the amount and social
significance of divorce. The marriages contracted in the early years of
Hitler's War can now be seen to have been at exceptional risk, and it
may well be that as many as 10 per cent of such couples who survive to
old age will have been divorced. But post-war marriages are significantly
more stable. The proportion already dissolved suggests that only 5 per
cent (or less) will eventually terminate in the divorce court. Moreover,
in the recent past some two-thirds to three-quarters of divorced people
have married new partners, so that the net loss to the married population
is small. Thus the present incidence of divorce is not spectacular,
although it represents a considerable increase since the period before
the Kaiser's War when less than 1 per cent of marriages were dissolved in
the High Court. In some important respects the characteristics of the
divorcing population have changed very little during the last sixty years,
despite the achievement of equality of access to the court. 55 per cent
of the divorces between 1899 and 1903 and 59 per cent of those between
1951 and 1954 occurred amongst marriages which had lasted for more
than ten years. In the same two periods, about one-third of dissolved
marriages were childless and, in some two-thirds, there was only one
child or none.

This increase in divorce has caused acute anxiety to religious and lay
opinion, expecially since 1945. Historically, all the Christian churches

The Family

(with the one exception of the Latter-Day Saints) have held marriage to be a divine institution ordained as an inviolable contract between one woman and one man to the exclusion of all others and terminable by death only. Although they agree about the interpretation of divine law, they differ irreconcilably concerning its application. The Church of Rome asserts that lifelong monogamy is an invariable rule to be observed in all cases, and therefore prohibits divorce absolutely. The Protestant churches insist that Christian marriage defines the ideal standard to which all spouses should attempt to conform, but permit divorce as the lesser of two evils when certain obligations of marriage have been violated. Despite this doctrinal disagreement, Protestants and Roman Catholics share a common detestation of divorce and a like assessment of its social consequences.* They have interpreted the divorce rate as an index of broken homes and as a measure of 'the flight from stability in marriage' ([51], p. 59). Such conclusions, shared by many other lay witnesses before the Morton Commission on Marriage and Divorce, were reflected in its *Report*, which diagnosed 'a tendency to take the duties and responsibilities of marriage less seriously than formerly' with the result that 'marriages are now breaking up which in the past would have held together' ([62], pp. 8–9). These—and similar— widely held beliefs result both from historical forgetfulness and from a failure to discriminate between the *a priori* deductions of theology and the conclusions reached by a sociological analysis of empirical evidence. In so far as marriage is held to be a divine institution dissoluble only by death, a fortyfold increase over fifty years in the number of temporally severed marriage bonds is indisputable evidence of a flight from stability in marriage. But the formal truth of this proposition is independent of, and conveys no information about, the actual number of marriage breakdowns in the real world. There is no evidence that a significantly higher proportion of marriages break up today than fifty years ago; the significant development has been a massive increase in *de jure* dissolutions of marriages already broken *de facto*. The above-quoted statement of the Morton Commission is thus unproven and unprovable guesswork. There is very little firm knowledge concerning prevalent attitudes to marriage or divorce, and none to suggest a causal connexion between the difficulty or ease with which a divorce may be obtained and the rate at which marriages break down. The assertion that the twentieth century has witnessed a decline in respect for the sanctity of marriage is true only in the sense that fewer people today than in the past regard God as a partner in their marriages. The increasing quantity of marriage, the trend towards earlier marriage, and the high proportion

* The useful source is the evidence presented to the Morton Royal Commission on Marriage and Divorce appointed in 1951, e.g. the Church of England, *Evidence* 6th Day, and the Catholic Union of Great Britain, 16th–17th Days.

O. R. McGregor and Griselda Rowntree

of divorced persons who marry again are indications of considerable enthusiasm, if not of respect, for a secular institution.*

Prevalent sexual habits reveal the conflict between actual and traditionally approved behaviour at its sharpest. All moralists, from the clergy to the writers of advice columns in women's magazines, agree in their teaching that sexual activity must be restricted to the married and in their condemnation of pre-marital intercourse. Table VI provides a minimum measure of the general failure to observe this prohibition.

TABLE VI

Illegitimate maternities and pre-maritally conceived legitimate maternities, 1938 to 1956, England & Wales

Year	Illegitimate maternities	Pre-maritally conceived legitimate maternities†	Total maternities conceived extra-maritally		% of extra-maritally conceived maternities legitimated by marriage of parents before birth of child
			Numbers	% of all maternitites	
1938	27,440	64,530	91,970	14·4	70·2
1942	32,597	40,705	78,302	11·8	52·0
1946	55,138	43,488	98,626	11·8	44·1
1950	35,816	54,188	90,004	12·8	60·2
1954	32,128	50,901	83,029	12·2	61·3
1956	34,113	54,895	89,008	12·6	61·7

Source: The Registrar General's Statistical Review of England and Wales, 1956, Part III, Commentary, Table XI, p. 16.

This table may be interpreted as measuring the consequences of either immorality or unreliable contraceptives. From the latter point of view it underlines the importance of the current search for a simple, harmless, and wholly reliable contraceptive. The certainty of ultimate success in this research points the urgency of clarifying the basis and rules of sexual ethics in modern society. Christian doctrine no longer commands universal acceptance, and therefore no code which relies upon super-natural sanctions is likely to command general respect or to become a

* There is a general discussion of the history and social significance of divorce in McGregor. [45]

† From 1952 onwards the figures relate to women married once only.

408

The Family

main determinant of conduct. Inherited rules are customarily justified by two social considerations: first, the risk and consequences of unwanted pregnancies, and second, the dangers to the happiness and stability of marriages established by partners who have indulged, whether with their future spouses or with others, in pre-marital relations. Future developments in contraceptive technique will destroy the cogency of the first consideration; the second invites empirical investigation by the social sciences. At present there is insufficient knowledge to determine the desirable basis for sexual relationships. Until the social sciences contribute fuller understanding, the existing divergence between adult conduct and the precepts enjoined upon children must widen.*

Family Environment

The study of the modern family has suffered from excessive preoccupation with the morbid. Indeed, the family is in danger of being regarded simply as a nursery for potential deviants. This distortion has in part resulted from the past and necessary concentration of the social sciences on the pathological; in part, too, from the similar concern of theology and law with what is customarily described as abnormal behaviour. Attention has been lavished upon such topics as homosexuality, prostitution, and artificial insemination by donor, and the habits of ordinary folk have been neglected. Little is known about the norms of sexual, marital, and familial behaviour at different social levels.

For this among other reasons, it is hardly an exaggeration to suggest that working-class family life has been described and interpreted as a deviation from the norm set by middle class ideals. This norm derives from the comfortable mid-Victorian family, or rather, as a critic of the modern family revealingly remarks, from 'the real Victorian family . . . portrayed in the novels of, for example, Trollope, and not the nightmare of Butler's *The Way of All Flesh*' ([50], p. 16). Such selectivity is representative, though rarely so explicitly stated. The family of Trollope's or Butler's description was an authoritarian unit in which the members owed duties to a male head. The functions of the family—the provision of a clean and decent home, the moral training and education of children, the protection of dependents, for example, could be discharged by the self-helpful provision of private houses, private schools, and personal thrift. In the squalid environment of Victorian industrial-

---

* These issues are clarified in Comfort [19]. The investigation of Chesser [16], was a pioneer study in this country. Unhappily for the sociologist, its primary emphasis is psychological and its authors' intention was to demonstrate the evil consequences for marriage resulting from a decline in church-going. The assembled data give little support to this hypothesis. There are interesting chapters on attitudes to love, sex, and marriage in Gorer. [32]

ism few working-class families could afford to be self-helpful. The stark contrast between middle class family life and the imperfect performance of working people's families was a recurring theme in the literature of social protest and investigation. In part, the social legislation of the early twentieth century was directed towards the collective provision of some of the means by which alone the industrial working class could build family units appropriate to industrialism.

Although material standards have improved, environmental and functional differences persist and help to perpetuate varying codes of behaviour. Income and housing are the main indices of the quality of family environment, especially when there are young children. The reduction in working class families' poverty and the improvement in their housing during the twentieth century indicate the growing capacity of working class people to aspire to and to command some of the material comforts long enjoyed by their financial betters.*

The many local studies of household resources carried out between the 1880s and 1930s all demonstrated the inadequacy of working class incomes for bringing up families.† In many areas it had become the established habit for a family with young children to rely when possible on the earnings of the male breadwinner. These earnings, low for the unskilled, were in no way related to increasing familial needs and were always interrupted by spells of unemployment and sickness. Such insecurity could be mitigated only by friendly society benefit, the poor law, or charity. After 1911, national insurance provided for compulsorily insured workers a minimal benefit which, from the 1920s onwards, was supplemented by a small allowance for each dependant. Even when the breadwinner had a steady wage throughout the years of family building and growth, this inflexible income had to be stretched to support additional children. In these circumstances it was inevitable that the surveys of Crawford, Boyd Orr, and the British Medical Association in the 1930s should disclose that poor families endured grossly inadequate diets.‡ As Hajnal and Henderson aptly remark in commenting

---

* Income and housing have been subjects for intermittent inquiry over most of the period of industrial urbanization. Most of the early studies concentrated on working-class conditions alone, but, since the 1930s, the middle classes have been increasingly included within the scope of investigation. Unfortunately, some of the all-embracing studies, notably the Ministry of Labour's recent *Enquiry into Household Expenditure in 1953–54* [48], have used class or occupational status as just one of a number of variables, and not as a fundamental category; the data are broken down first by class, then, for instance, by family size, then by religion, then by type of dwelling occupied, etc., and we are not given a comprehensive analysis of the interrelations of these secondary variables for each class by itself.

† These include [8, 9, 10, 25, 26, 38, 39, 52, 59, 60, 66, 68, 70] The findings of the interway studies concerning poverty in families of different sizes have been conveniently summarized by Hajnal and Henderson in [34].

‡ The results of these studies are usefully summarized in le Gros Clark and Titmuss [18], pp. 145–154.

The Family

upon the table reproduced below: 'Having a large family was in the 1930s, in the working class at any rate, almost enough to guarantee poverty'.*

TABLE VII

Percentage of working-class families in poverty by number of children

Survey	Numbers of Children					
	1	2	3	4	5	6 or more
London (1929)	5·4	8·4	11·6	17·6	25·0	37·0
York (1936)	28·8	36·6	46·7	59·3	69·5†	
Bristol (1937)	6·5	11·1	24·9	51·3‡		
Birmingham (1939)	3·0	11·0	27·0	55·0	60·0	82·0

Source: Papers of the Royal Commission on Population, Vol. 5. p. 7.

The experience of total war from 1939 to 1945 required a scientific and functional assessment of the community's needs and consumption, and forced the adoption of planned distribution policies as part of the siege economy. Some of these developments were carried over into the post-war period when full employment, income-tax allowances,[12] and social benefits such as family allowances, school meals, and milk and food subsidies have helped to relieve growing families of some of their financial burdens. Nevertheless, the Ministry of Labour *Household Expenditure Enquiry*[48] of 1953–54 and the Ministry of Food reports on *Domestic Food Consumption and Expenditure*[46] for the years since 1940 show that not only in working class but also in middle class homes a large family still involves relative if not absolute deprivation, and may mean that family members go short of essential nutrients in the crucial

---

* Varying definitions of poverty (as well as varying phases of the trade cycle) account for the considerable difference in its incidence in the studies included in the table. The usual procedure was for the investigator first to calculate the income he believed to be necessary to provide for the minimum needs of households of each size, and then to obtain from a representative group of working-class households sufficient data on their composition and incomes for him to place each of them on a scale above and below his pre-determined poverty line. This procedure has been rightly criticized (by P. E. P.[53] and Townsend[71]) for ignoring the households' own spending patterns, but it has the merit of providing some objective measurement of the relative shortage of income in families of different sizes, even though this may not coincide with their own assessment of their circumstances.

† 5 or more children.
‡ 4 or more children.

years of the children's development.* According to a post-war National Survey of Child Health, the material disadvantages of childhood in the larger working-class families were reflected in the lesser average height of the children and in the greater incidence of lower respiratory infections ([22], pp. 55–62, 68–74).

In their attempt to avoid the relative financial hardship associated with children, an increasing number of mothers in the twentieth century have not only limited their fertility but have also gone out to work in order to supplement their husbands' earnings. Leser, in a comparative analysis of the data available in the 1911 and 1951 censuses, has shown the essential contribution which married women make to the female labour force.[42] While many of those in employment do not have young or large families, the National Survey of Child Health showed that more than one quarter of the mothers of pre-school children in each occupational group, except the professional and salaried, had been either in full or in part-time employment at some period during the first five years of their children's lives.† This would suggest that, at least in the favourable employment situation of the late 1940s and early 1950s, a substantial number of mothers were trying to make some contribution to the family income even when the children were still young. The traditional pattern in which fathers normally acted as sole breadwinners for their households is changing.

The twentieth-century improvement in housing has largely come about by families moving from old dwellings, rented from private landlords and frequently deficient in repair and amenity, into better equipped dwellings which they either rent from local authorities or purchase from speculative builders or private owners. Local authorities first catered mostly for the average or well-paid wage earners, since even when they operated rebate schemes, their rents were sometimes too high for the poorest families.‡ Among those able to afford a Council rent, priority in housing allocation has usually been given to large

* The Ministry of Food reported ([46], 1955): 'There was the usual reduction of all nutrients with the addition of each child to the household' (p. 57), and 'households with three or more children and those with adolescents as well as children were obtaining less than 95 per cent of the estimated requirements of protein and calcium' (p. 60). 'Differences in family composition have a greater effect on the household diet' than any other factor (p. 40).

† [22], p. 120. A helpful analysis of the contribution which married women of varying occupational status and family responsibilities now make to the labour force has been published by Kelsall and Mitchell. [40]

‡ In the depressed areas of the inter-war years some families compulsorily rehoused under slum clearance schemes were found to be more seriously impoverished after removal to Council houses than before because their increased housing expenses compelled them to economize on food, thus restricting still further an already inadequate diet ([44], pp. 108–129).

The Family

families, though in the chronic shortage of good working-class housing which has persisted since the early nineteenth century, even these priority cases have sometimes had to wait for several years. The alternative is to purchase a modern house on mortgage. This common middle class practice has usually been beyond the means of most working class families in the lower wage-brackets.*

Some of the results of these alternative means of selecting up-to-date houses were shown in a study undertaken by the Government Social Survey among a random sample of all households in 1947, when the average earnings of men over twenty-one years in industry, transport, and service trades was £6. 8. 0d. ([49], April 1948). The information on tenure or dwelling-ownership which is given in Table VIII was tabulated not by class but by the related factor of economic group as determined by the wage rate or other income level of the household head.

TABLE VIII

Tenure of household by their economic group

Tenure of household	Proportions of households with different tenures in each of the following economic groups in 1947				
	£3–£4 %	£4–£5. 10s. %	£5. 10–£10 %	Over £10 %	All groups† %
Tenancy a part of wages	7	4	3	3	4
Tenancy from private landlord	59	64	48	30	57
Tenancy from Council	14	17	10	1	13
Dwelling being purchased	2	2	9	3	4
Dwelling fully owned	18	13	30	63	22
Total %	100	100	100	100	100
No.	476	2619	1757	478	5997†

Source: Gray, P. G., Social Survey, *The British Household* (1947) (mimeographed material), p. 18.

* The official budget studies among working class households in 1937–38, ([49] December 1940) and among all households in 1953–54 ([48], pp. 202–220), both show how the incidence of house purchase increases as economic resources grow.

† The total also includes 667 cases with incomes of less than £3. Since these are mostly the households of old age pensioners who are no longer earning they are not shown separately in the body of the table.

413

O. R. McGregor and Griselda Rowntree

Since 1947 further building by local authorities and private firms, together with the resumption of slum clearance, has reduced the proportion of all households renting obsolete private properties and has increased that in council dwellings and in owner-occupation. Nevertheless, the Ministry of Labour Inquiry of 1953–54 suggests that economic-group gradients persist: the poorest still most frequently rent privately owned dwellings and the better off, including the middle and professional classes, are most often owner-occupiers.

Even within the same class, smaller families have more often than large been able to take advantage of better housing provision. The typical old working-class dwelling in England and Wales has no more than four or five rooms, so that family growth, if uncontrolled, sooner or later entails overcrowding. This has been approximately assessed in successive censuses since 1891, and has been more elaborately measured by the statutory *Overcrowding Survey* of 1936.* The favourable position of small families has persisted in the post-war period. According to the National Survey of Child Health already mentioned, completed families living in cramped conditions in 1946 were better able to alleviate their overcrowding if they had only one or two children than if they had more ([22], p. 40). The same survey showed that large families with four or more children also suffered more often, at least in 1948, from other deficiencies of accommodation: many more of their houses were in bad repair, and rather more of them had no bathrooms and no running hot water than was the case in families with only one or two children.†

Relationships within the Family

Life in frequently overcrowded and often squalid homes, maintained on low and uncertain incomes, conditioned behaviour in many working class families in the past. On the evidence of recent local investigations, these continued to be significant factors in the 1950s.‡ As Lady Bell pointed out in her study of steel-workers' households in Middlesbrough

---

* For a review of this and other evidence on the subject see [63], paras. 370–380.

† [22], p. 41. *The 1951 Census of England and Wales:* Housing Report [15], pp. xcviii–cx) showed that many households lacked the full range of modern conveniences: 37 per cent had no fixed bath, 9 per cent no water closet, and 6 per cent no piped water supply. Deficiencies increased with density (i.e. number of persons per room), but were not fully tabulated by social class or family size.

‡ The studies of patterns of family behaviour include [4, 20, 32, 41, 55, 58, 64, 65, 67, 72, 74]. Since there is now considerable interest in the type of personality produced by particular environments, some of these studies [41, 65, 67] use psychological as well as sociological and anthropological techniques. The studies vary in method from the completely impressionistic to the primarily statistical, but the latter also use a great deal of impressionistic material to support and elaborate their findings concerning intangible relationships.

The Family

at the turn of the century, the working class family has attached paramount importance to maintaining their chief breadwinner's capacity and willingness to earn for the support of his family. He has been entitled to eat the best food, to be waited on by his female dependants and to keep a portion of his earnings for his own pleasures: chiefly drinking, betting, smoking, and watching football. On his wife, companion of his bed but customarily partner in few of his leisure-time activities, there lay the responsibility for rearing the children and for 'figuring out' the disbursement for the increasing family of the housekeeping money, often a fixed sum handed to her on pay day each week. This clear and complete division of function between husband and wife was disrupted under the stress of inter-war unemployment in the depressed areas and elsewhere,* but has revived, according to Dennis, Henriques, and Slaughter, in the single-industry coal-mining village of today. In some textile towns and in the larger urban centres where employment is more diversified, the husband of a woman who goes out to work does not, according to Zweig, play the same dominant role, and is expected to share some domestic and child-minding tasks with his wife. In their studies in London, Slater and Woodside and Young and Willmott have also noted the growth over the past twenty years of a greater degree of companionship between husbands and wives, with more joint discussion of problems of household management, familybuilding, and child-rearing. In certain slum studies such as that conducted in Liverpool by Madeline Kerr, 'Mum' emerges as the dominant figure within the extended family circle, not by virtue of her being the regular breadwinner, but because she is more stable than her male partner, or series of partners, who are periodically prevented by casual, migrant, or sea-going employment from fulfilling the role of steady family supporter. Some elements of a matriarchal system, or at least of a matrilocal distribution of the kinship group, are found in many of the long-settled working class communities studied, probably because the mother evokes a warmer and more loyal response from her young children than the father, teaches her daughter essential domestic skills, and is valued after the daughter's marriage as an adviser on household matters and as a grandchild minder.

Some of these documented patterns, shaped in the relatively impoverished and deprived past, are now being modified in the more prosperous modern environment. Not only has the broadening of the educational ladder enabled more working class children to climb into the professional classes where other codes prevail, but the means adopted for satisfying the demand for better housing has led to the geographical dispersal of formerly close-knit, localized kinship groups.

---

* Some of the domestic repercussions of unemployment were examined by E. Wight Bakke in his Greenwich study [1] and by the Pilgrim Trust [54].

O. R. McGregor and Griselda Rowntree

New houses with gardens have chiefly been built on suburban estates or in the new towns, and the responsible authorities have accepted and attracted as tenants mostly young couples with growing families.* As Young and Willmott show in their comparison of settled Bethnal Green residents with Bethnal Green migrants to 'Greenleigh', London County Council estate in Essex, removal to such areas involves young families in many more than financial adjustments. For instance, the absence of relatives forces these couples into a closer partnership in the interests of the children for whose sakes they have usually made the move.

Some of the recent studies of family behaviour have concentrated on the traditional kinship patterns of old-established working class communities. There has been less interest in the development of new modes of living, particularly in the more child-centred households of the new estates and towns. The Institute of Community Studies which conducted the Bethnal Green and 'Greenleigh' inquiry has so far devoted its resources to the problems and kinship relations of adults, widows, and old people, but has not yet investigated changing habits in child-rearing. The kinship group emerges from this and other inquiries as the provider of aid and support in times of family crisis, and the extent to which the collectively provided school, health, and welfare services have reduced the compelling need for kinship ties has not yet been adequately investigated. There is a danger that a sentimentalized picture of working class family life may emerge from such studies and may come to be accepted as representative. The corrective of further studies is urgently necessary.

The Legal Results of Social Change

The approach of women to equality of citizenship, the transformation of personal relationships within the family, and the rising standard of child care which has accompanied the steady reduction in family size have been responsible for momentous legal changes of great interest to sociologists.†

* Full accounts of the household composition, employment problems, administrative developments, and shortcomings in community services on London County Council inter-war estates will be found [23] and [73]. The *Annual Reports* of the Development Corporations of the individual New Towns are also informative on post-war problems.

† Only within very recent years has family law become a respectable legal specialism. There are only a few text-books, such as Bromley [11], which treat the subject as a whole. Fortunately for sociologists, Mr Bromley's study possesses a clarity and readability unusual in legal manuals. The history of family law is summarized in [33]. Friedmann's symposium [29] contains a sociologically illuminating account of English developments by Prof. O. Kahn-Freund. It is significant that the important work of Friedmann [27] now contains in its new, enlarged and re-written form [28] an illuminating chapter (pp. 205–260) on family law.

The Family

Marriage is a contract which creates a status. English law insists that marriage must be a voluntary, monogamous union which the parties intend to be lifelong. Unlike other contracts, it requires the strict observance of statutory formalities,* it is restricted to those outside the prohibited degrees of kindred and affinity,† it cannot be terminated by agreement,‡ and the partners are not free to negotiate their own terms. The married status not only imposes reciprocal rights and duties upon the parties, but may also affect their nationality, and is likely to affect their property as well as altering other people's rights. The status can be acquired by anyone over the age of sixteen who is not a lunatic, or acting under duress, or in error as to identity or the nature of the ceremony. The parents or guardian of a minor under twenty-one may withhold their consent, but they may be overruled by the courts. In recent years, the proportion of brides and grooms under twenty-one has risen sharply. For men it has risen from 3·4 per cent in 1938 to 8·7 per cent in 1956, and for women from 16·4 to 32·2 per cent in the same period. (⁵⁷, 1956, Part III, Commentary, p. 51).

'By marriage,' wrote Blackstone in a famous passage, 'the husband and wife are one person in law; that is, the very being or legal existence of the woman is suspended during the marriage, or at least is incorporated and consolidated into that of the husband; under whose wing, protection, and *cover*, she performs everything . . . Upon this principle of a union of person in husband and wife, depend almost all the legal rights, duties, and disabilities, that either of them acquire by the marriage' (⁶, Bk. I, ch. xv). The modern law regulating familial relations is a jumble of unsystematic expedients elaborated through the *ad hoc* adaptation of this common law doctrine to changing social circumstances by the interventions of equity and statute. A century ago, wives were subservient and inferior members of their families; today they have become co-equal heads. The nature of this beneficently democratic revolution can be seen in the growth of wives' capacity to own and to control property and to exercise parental rights.

* Set out in the Marriage Act, 1949.

† *Ibid.* First Schedule. This Act maintained antiquated and socially harmful survivals of canon law. Thus, a man might marry his dead wife's sister (or aunt or niece) but not his divorced wife's sister (or aunt or niece) or vice versa.

‡ A validly contracted, consummated marriage can be terminated only by the death of a spouse or by divorce. The use of contraceptives has caused difficulties for the courts in their definition of 'non-consummation'. In 1947, the House of Lords held that a husband's insistence on using a sheath did not amount to wilful refusal to consummate. This makes possible a situation, as Bromley (¹¹, p. 73), points out, in which a marriage may never be consummated because the husband refuses to use a contraceptive and the wife refuses intercourse unless he does. In this case neither spouse could be held to have wilfully refused to consummate as both were willing for intercourse in circumstances approved by the courts.

417

O. R. McGregor and Griselda Rowntree

Property and earnings in most people's families yesterday and today must be devoted to the common needs of their members for whom, in industrial societies, the family is the unit of consumption. The poorer the family, the larger must be the proportion of its members' resources that will go into the general purse. No matter what the system of matrimonial property law,* in everyday life the practice will be to pool resources and to distribute according to need. In earlier days, the common law had stripped a married woman of practically all rights over earnings and property, except freehold land, brought into or acquired during her marriage. Few were thereby affected, for, in this respect, the common law served only the common people whose poverty preserved them from all anxieties concerning rights in matrimonial property. Had the common law rules applied to the wealthy, the property of a married woman and thus, through her, of her kin group, would always have been at the mercy of her husband and his kin. Since the end of the sixteenth century, equity had therefore devised the safeguards of trust and marriage settlement which enabled a married woman to own and to control a 'separate estate' conveyed to her separate use. By the early nineteenth century, equity had evolved the further device of 'restraint on anticipation' which could be used to prevent a married woman assigning her separate estate to a masterful husband. In these cumbrous ways, of use only to the rich, equity mitigated the harshness of the common law not for the benefit of the married woman but in order to protect the property of her kinfolk. By the middle of the nineteenth century there had come to be well established 'not in theory but in fact one law for the rich and another for the poor' ([21], p. 395).

After 1850, middle-class demands for cheap law and for equality before laws which favoured the landed interest merged with some aims of the 'women's rights' movement and the attempts of upper-middle-class women to reduce their social and legal inferiorities. One result was a series of statutes which generalized the provisions of equity relating to matrimonial property. Just as the Matrimonial Causes Act, 1857, extended to middle-class people the divorce facilities previously accessible only to those who could command a private act of parliament, so the seminal Married Women's Property Act, 1882, gave all women who married and who possessed or acquired property after that date a separate estate in it. Equity had tempered the wind to the well fleeced: this statute gave the same protection to the whole flock. For the next half-century married women continued to own and to enjoy their property as separate property. This anomaly was removed in 1935, when it was enacted that 'a married woman shall be capable of acquiring, holding, and disposing of, any property . . . in all respects as if she

* This theme is brilliantly developed in the contribution of O. Kahn-Freund to [29], pp. 267–314.

The Family

were a *feme-sole*.'* The restraint upon anticipation disappeared in 1949.†

Professor Kahn-Freund has shown how, as a result of the 'connexion at common law between inequality of status and the combination of both spouses' property in the hands of the husband, the idea of separation of property became in the minds of people, lawyers and laymen, interwoven with that of equality with which intrinsically it has very little to do' ([29], p. 278). As long as equality had not spread much beyond the ballot box and the grounds of divorce, and the majority of married women were, in fact or in prospect, financially dependent on their husbands, this connexion between separation of property and personal equality caused little difficulty. But, with the great extension of married women's employments during and after Hitler's War and with the great potential reduction in wives' dependence on male breadwinners, the unintended consequences of this legislation have been formidable. In theory, marriage does not affect the spouses' property rights in earnings or in nest eggs brought into it. In practice, such eggs get well scrambled in the process of living together. Mercifully, questions of ownership rarely arise unless a marriage breaks down, and normal people do not legislate in advance for this contingency. The courts have therefore been forced to exercise much ingenuity in adapting the principle of spouses' separate property, inherited from the 1882 Act, to the social reality of the common matrimonial purse. The present position both as regards earnings and property appears to be that stated by Lord Denning in a judgement quoted at length because it clarifies the attitude of mind in which the judges now approach this aspect of family life:

'If it is clear that the property, when it was acquired, was intended to belong to one or other absolutely, as in the case of investments, or that they intended to hold it in definite shares, as sometimes happens when they run a business, then effect must be given to their intention; and in that case the title so ascertained is not to be altered by subsequent events unless there has been an agreement to vary it. In many cases, however, the intention of the parties is not clear, for the simple reason that they have never formed an intention; so the court has to attribute an intention to them. This is particularly the case with the family assets, by which I mean the things intended to be a continuing provision for them during their joint lives, such as the matrimonial home and the furniture in it. When these are acquired by their joint efforts during the marriage, the parties do not give a thought to future separation. They do not contemplate divorce. They contemplate living in the house and using the furniture together for the rest of their lives. They buy the house and furniture out

---

* By *The Law Reform* (*Married Women and Tortfeasors*) *Act*, Section 1 (i).
† By *The Married Women* (*Restraint upon Anticipation*) *Act*.

419

of their available resources without worrying too much as to whom it belongs. The reason is plain. So long as they are living together, it does not matter which of them does the saving and which does the paying, or which of them goes out to work or which looks after the home, so long as the things they buy are used for their joint benefit. In the present case it so happened that the wife went out to work and used her earnings to help run the household and buy the children's clothes, whilst the husband saved. It might very well have been the other way round. The husband might have allotted to the wife enough money to cover all the house-keeping and the children's clothes, and the wife might have saved her earnings. The title to the family assets does not depend on the mere chance of which way round it was. It does not depend on how they happened to allocate their earnings and their expenditure. The whole of their resources were expended for their joint benefit—either in food and clothes and living expenses for which there was nothing to see or in the house and furniture which are family assets—and the product should belong to them jointly. It belongs to them in equal shares.*

In such ways since 1945 'the courts have begun to recognize that (wives) have equal rights with respect to the matrimonial home' ([11], p. 148).

The transformation in wives' property rights has been paralleled by equally sweeping changes which gave them a settled right to personal liberty in 1891, and equal rights as parents in 1925. Marriage confers on spouses the legal rights and reciprocal duty to share bed and board, but the duty is no longer legally enforceable. In a case decided in 1840, authority was found for the proposition that 'for the happiness and honour of *both* parties (the law) places the wife under the guardianship of the husband, and entitles him, for the sake of both, to protect her from unrestrained intercourse with the world, by enforcing cohabitation and a common residence.'† Some fifty years later, public and legal opinion had so far shifted that it was held, in the rightly celebrated *R. v. Jackson* in 1891, that a husband had no right under English law to beat or to imprison his wife. This adjustment of the common law to new conceptions of the dignity of women followed logically from a clause in the Matrimonial Causes Act, 1884, which removed the court's power to imprison wives who refused to comply with orders for the restitution of conjugal rights. Thereafter such refusal ranked simply as desertion. But wives' capacity to exercise personal freedom depended as much on their financial situation as upon formal law. The wife who brought a success-ful action for separation or divorce had been able to obtain protection

---

* *Fribrance v. Fribrance* (1957) 1, All E. R. 357, 359–60, C.A., quoted [11], p. 391. Lord Denning has been the leading figure in the post-war process of drawing out the legal consequences of the equality of men and women.

† From the judgment of Coleridge J. *in re Cochrane* (1840), 8 Dowl. 633, per Coleridge J.; quoted D. Mendes da Costa in [33], p. 179.

The Family

for her earnings as well as maintenance since 1857. But few men and fewer women could afford to litigate their marital disputes in the High Court. It was not until the Matrimonial Causes Act, 1878, that poor women obtained the means in the magistrates' courts to be separated and to receive maintenance from husbands found guilty of aggravated assault upon them. Before this date the common law doctrine of henosis imposed upon husbands the duty to provide their wives with necessaries. As a wife could not sue her own flesh, the common law generously gave her power to pledge her husband's credit with any tradesman philanthropic enough to accumulate bad debts. The vital principle first established in 1878 was extended in a series of Acts which are the basis of the present matrimonial jurisdiction of summary courts and of their power to award maintenance of up to £7 10s. a week to a wife and fifty shillings each for her children.* The old practice in the High Court was to award permanent alimony of such a sum as would bring the wife's income up to one-third of the joint income. This rough rule has now been qualified by taking into consideration the income and earning power, as well as the conduct, of the parties.

The statutory provision of maintenance for separated and divorced wives and the great expansion of professional and white-blouse occupations are together in the twentieth century making a reality of the personal rights secured by married women in the nineteenth. Maintenance raises two important difficulties precipitated by the recent extension of divorce to all social strata. Firstly, there is the acutely difficult practical problem of securing justice and equity between husbands and wives whose marriages are to be dissolved. A small minority of wives are not financially dependent, the majority are; and the degree of dependence varies greatly over the span of married life. The moral requirements of equality have to be reconciled with the facts of the labour market, and both have to be fitted into the framework of the one important branch of family law which has made no concessions to half a century of social change. The principle underlying divorce law is that a 'guilty' spouse must have committed a carefully defined offence (in practice, adultery, cruelty, or desertion) against an 'innocent' spouse who is either untainted by, or able to persuade the court to condone, any such offence. Divorce is thus a remedy optionally available to the 'innocent' and a penalty to be suffered by the 'guilty'. This doctrine does not accord with the reality of mid-twentieth-century marriage. What little evidence there is indicates that most spouses do not

* There were 24,655 such applications in England and Wales in 1958 of which 13,795 were granted. [36] The statistics supplied by the Home Office concerning the matrimonial work of magistrates' courts are so inadequate that nobody knows the ages of the applicants, the duration of their marriages at the time of application, the ages or number of their children, or even the average amounts of maintenance awarded.

seek divorces because their partners commit offences, but because they cannot make their marriages work. What matters to them is the fact of breakdown, of which only they can be the judges. What matters to the court is to establish the commission of a statutory offence in the absence of collusion, connivance, or condonation. Provision for dependent members of broken families cannot be rationally determined under such a system.

In the second place, there is the equally difficult problem of ensuring security for the casualties of broken homes. The community has never been able to force unwilling spouses to live together; it now permits divorce, and places no obstacles in the way of remarriage. A man may thus lawfully acquire a legal obligation to maintain two families. For those at the top and bottom of the income scale, public funds will carry much of the burden of supporting the deserted family, although the administrative procedures differ markedly according to income level. The income-tax payer is able to obtain support for his ex-wife and her children from the Exchequer by deducting the amount of their maintenance from his taxable income. Most men whose incomes are too small to attract direct taxation cannot discharge their legal obligations to support their two families because there is not enough money to go round. Many must default on their maintenance payments, and the magistrates' courts make some 14,000 orders annually. Nobody knows how many past orders are still current, how many other legally enforceable claims on husbands or ex-husbands are in existence, or the extent to which such obligations are honoured. But in 1956, some 5,000 defaulters were in prison and the National Assistance Board had some 79,000 clients living apart from their husbands. Many such women suffer grinding poverty and endure humiliation, nagging insecurity and the distasteful necessity of pursuing defaulting husbands through the courts.* As marriage creates dependences, so its dissolution must create casualties. These are ill cared for by social policy which has altogether failed to recognize their special and often temporary needs.

The old common law doctrine of the unity of husband and wife gave fathers rights over the custody of their children so absolute that they could deny access to their mothers during their lifetime and even, by appointing testamentary guardians, after their death. *Re Besant* in 1878 showed how little these autocratic powers had been curbed by the first two Custody of Infants Acts of 1839 and 1873. Mrs. Besant lost the custody of her young daughter, awarded under a separation agreement, on the ground that the infant would be 'helpless for good in this world' and 'hopeless for good hereafter' if entrusted to an atheistical mother

---

* The Maintenance Orders (Attachment of Wages) Act, 1958, offers no solution. It is designed to protect women whose husbands or ex-husbands will not pay. They are a tiny minority. The real problem is that the majority cannot pay.

who propagated information about birth control. Mrs. Besant's comment on her experience is a substantially accurate account of a mother's position at that time. '. . . The law says to every woman: "Choose which of these two positions you will have: if you are legally your husband's wife you can have no legal claim to your children; if legally your husband's mistress, then your rights as mother are secure"' ([5], p. 168). A series of statutes from 1886 onwards gradually assimilated the rights of fathers and mothers until equality was established by the Guardianship of Infants Act, 1925, which provided that:

> 'Where in any proceeding before any court . . . the custody or up-bringing of an infant, or the administration of any property belonging to or held on trust for an infant, or the application of the income thereof, is in question, the court, in deciding that question, shall regard the welfare of the infant as the first and paramount consideration, and shall not take into consideration whether from any other point of view the claim of the father, or any right at common law possessed by the father, in respect of such custody, upbringing, administration or application is superior to that of the mother or the claim of the mother is superior to that of the father.'*

This act not only gave full legal status to mothers but also emphasized the trend of modern legislation which has equipped children with enforceable rights against their parents or guardians.

Illegitimacy is, perhaps, the greatest disadvantage a child can suffer. A legitimate child is one born, though not necessarily conceived, in lawful wedlock.† Monogamous marriage can be maintained only if the status of legitimacy is restricted to children born within it. The modern treatment of illegitimacy is therefore the product of a conflict between the desire to preserve the greater good of monogamy and, at the same time, to relieve the harsh position of blameless children. English law does not maintain a fiction that can transform an illegitimate into a lawful child, but it has accepted the concept of legitimation under which two categories of children born out of wedlock can enjoy some, but not all, of the advantages of legitimacy. The Legitimacy Act, 1926, provided for the legitimation of children whose parents married after their birth but were not married to other persons at the time. This act brought into English law for the first time the *legitimum per subsequens matrimonium* of Roman law which the canon lawyers had proposed when the Statute of Merton was debated in 1236. Then the Barons of England retorted with the celebrated and, as events proved, remarkably influential dictum: *nolumus leges Angliae mutare*. The Legitimacy Act, 1959,‡

* Section 1.
† There is an unimportant exception to this general statement (see [11], p. 258).
‡ This act makes one significant change by conferring on the putative father, for the first time in English history, rights of custody over and access to his illegitimate children.

O. R. McGregor and Griselda Rowntree

extended legitimation to the children of parents who marry after their birth but who were not free to marry at that time. This act simply extends to the children of adulterers what the 1926 act had conceded to the progeny of fornicators. Any legislation seeking to mitigate the hardships suffered by bastards is always opposed by those who fear the removal of 'powerful deterrents to illicit relationships'. Such arguments invariably rest on unexamined assumptions concerning the relation between law and conduct. The recent Act, for example, could be held to have removed a deterrent to immorality only if potential adulterers were better informed about the law of legitimacy than about techniques of contraception. But if they were assumed to know enough law to be deterred from their courses before 1959, they must also be presumed to have known that they could already achieve fewer disadvantages for their unlawful children by adoption than by legitimation. The Adoption Act of 1958 enables the married parents of illegitimate children to secure greater advantages under its provisions than can be obtained under the legitimacy acts. No further change can improve the legal position of the illegitimate child of unmarried parents without completely undermining the principle of monogamous marriage. The improvement of the lot of such children must now await new social attitudes and policies.

CONCLUSIONS

Democratic advance has altered the environment of the family as it has transformed the legal relations of its members. A century ago, middle and working class families shared little in common save their high fertilities. If early industrialism floated some families to affluence or modest security and enabled them to perform their functions self-helpfully and thus to serve as an exemplar, it also destroyed the capacity of humbler folk to discharge the familial duties prescribed for them by moralists. Their family history is a story of the painfully slow recognition that only through public enterprise and collective provision of houses and schools and care for dependents could the middle class ideal become a general reality. In the twentieth century, the reduction in family size and the extensions of social policy have together given working people the means to adopt some habits of middle class life. Today, the performance of all families is conditioned and improved by the social services.*

Victorian pioneers of democratic and egalitarian habits within the family enjoyed material security and the leisure to explore the delicate problems of personal relationships. There is abundant testimony to their success in breaking up the authoritarian character of the middle

* Titmuss [69] has provided a measure of the great and increasing extent to which upper-income groups have come to rely on social provision in recent years.

class, mid-Victorian family. Of the changing character of personal relations within the less articulate families lower down the social scale, there is insufficient evidence to support generalizations. Research has still much to contribute before a reliable assessment of the quality of present-day family life can be made. There is little empirical knowledge of the attitude to marriage in different social strata or of people's expectations of this most popular state. Such research is a pressing need, for, in the absence of knowledge, confident but baseless assertions proliferate. The National Marriage Guidance Council did not hesitate to tell the Morton Commission of a 'modern tendency to regard marriage as nothing but a legalized physical relationship,'* Similarly other lay and ecclesiastical bodies have diagnosed a sick community slipping unthinkingly and irresponsibly into and out of too easily contracted marriages with the result that the family is disintegrating and social stability imperilled. These anxieties have become established themes in the anxieties for the family now fashionable amongst those well-meaning persons and organizations dedicated to saving other people from the consequences of their assumed irresponsibilities. The widespread pessimism about the family is difficult to sustain in the face of the material assembled in this chapter. Although much of the life of the family can be seen only through a glass darkly, there is enough clear evidence to warrant its description as one of the twentieth century's great success stories.

REFERENCES

1. BAKKE, E. WIGHT (1933) *The Unemployed Man.* London: Nisbet.
2. BANKS, J. A. (1954) *Prosperity and Parenthood.* London: Routledge.
3. BANKS, J. A. & O. (1954) *Popul. Stud.* **8,** 22–34.
4. BELL, FLORENCE (LADY) *At the Works.* London: Arnold.
5. BESANT, ANNIE (1885) *Autobiographical Sketches.* London: Free-thought Publishing Co.
6. BLACKSTONE, WILLIAM (1765–9) *Commentaries on the Laws of England.* Oxford: Clarendon Press.
7. BONNAR, ALPHONSUS (1952) *The Catholic Doctor.* 6th edn. London: Burns Oates.
8. BOOTH, CHARLES (ed.) (1897) *Life and Labour of the People in London.* Industry Series, vol. 5. London: Macmillan.
9. BOWLEY, A. L., & BURNETT HURST, A. R. (1915) *Livelihood and Poverty.* London: London School of Economics.
10. BOWLEY, A. L., & HOGG, M. H. (1925) *Has Poverty Diminished?* London: King.
11. BROMLEY, P. M. (1957) *Family Law.* London: Butterworth.
12. CARTTER, A. M. (1953) *Popul. Stud.* **6,** 218–32.

* *Evidence,* 5th Day, p. 109.

13. *Census of England and Wales*, 1911, Vol. 12: 'Fertility of Marriage'.
14. *Census of England and Wales*, 1951, Fertility Report.
15. *Census of England and Wales*, 1951, Housing Report,
16. CHESSER, EUSTACE (ed.) (1956) *The Sexual, Marital and Family Relationships of the English Woman*. London: Hutchinson.
17. Church of England Moral Welfare Council (1958) *The Family in Contemporary Society*.
18. CLARK, F. LE GROS, & TITMUSS, R. M. (1939) *Our Food Problem*. Harmondsworth: Penguin Books.
19. COMFORT, ALEX (1950) *Sexual Behaviour in Society*. London: Duckworth.
20. DENNIS, N., HENRIQUES, F., & SLAUGHTER, C. (1956) *Coal Is our Life*. London: Eyre and Spottiswoode.
21. DICEY, A. V. (1914) *Lectures on the Relation between Law and Public Opinion during the Nineteenth Century*. 2nd edn. London: Macmillan.
22. DOUGLAS, J. W. B., & BLOMFIELD, J. M. (1958) *Children under Five*. London: Allen and Unwin.
23. DURANT, RUTH (1939) *Watling*. London: King.
24. FLETCHER, JOSEPH (1955) *Morals and Medicine*. London:
25. FLORENCE, P. SARGENT; SOUTAR, M. S., & WILKINS, E. H. (1942) *Nutrition and Size of Family*. London: Allen and Unwin.
26. FORD, P. (1934) *Work and Wealth of a Modern Port*. London: Allen and Unwin.
27. FRIEDMANN, W. (1951) *Law and Social Change in Contemporary Britain*. London: Stevens.
28. FRIEDMANN, W. (1959) *Law in a Changing Society*. London: Stevens.
29. FRIEDMANN, W. (ed.) *Matrimonial Property Law*. London: Stevens.
30. GLASS, D. V. (1940) *Population Policies and Movements in Europe*. Oxford: Clarendon Press.
31. GLASS, D. V., & GREBENIK, E. (1954) *The Trend and Pattern of Fertility in Great Britain*. Papers of the Royal Commission on Population, 6. London: H.M.S.O.
32. GORER, GEOFFREY (1955) *Exploring English Character*. London: Cresset.
33. GRAVESON, R. H., & CRANE, F. R. (eds.) (1957) *A Century of Family Law*. London: Sweet and Maxwell.
34. HAJNAL, J., & HENDERSON, A. M. (1950) *The Economic Position of the Family*. Papers of the Royal Commission on Population, 5.
35. HIMES, N. (1936) *Medical History of Contraception*. London: Allen and Unwin.
36. Home Office. *Criminal Statistics* 1959. (Cmd. 803) London: H.M.S.O.
37. HOPKIN, W. A. B., & HAJNAL, J. *Occupational Fertility 1931 and 1939*, Registrar General's Decennial Supplement for 1931, part IIb. London: H.M.S.O.
38. INMAN, J. (1934) *Poverty and Housing Conditions in a Manchester Ward*. University of Manchester Economics Research Section, Pamphlet 3. Manchester: Manchester University Press.

The Family

39. JONES, D. CARADOG (1934) *Social Survey of Merseyside*. 3 vols. London: Hodder and Stoughton.
40. KELSALL, R. K., & MITCHELL, SHEILA (1959) *Popul. Stud.*, 13, 19–33.
41. KERR, M. (1958) *The People of Ship Street*. London: Routledge.
42. LESER, C. E. V. (1955) *Popul. Stud.* 9, 142–7.
43. LEWIS-FANING, E. (1949) *Family Limitation and its Influence on Human Fertility during the Last Fifty Years*. Papers of the Royal Commission on Population, 1.
44. M'GONIGLE, G. C. M. & KIRBY, J. (1936) *Poverty and Public Health* London: Gollancz.
45. MCGREGOR, O. R. (1957) *Divorce in England*. London: Heinemann
46. Ministry of Food. *Domestic Food Consumption and Expenditure*.
47. Ministry of Health (1931, 1934) Memorandum 153/M.C.W.; Circular 1208; Circular 1408.
48. Ministry of Labour. 1957 *Enquiry into Household Expenditure in 1953–4: Report*.
49. *Ministry of Labour Gazette.*
50. NEILL, STEPHEN (1949) *The Breakdown of the Family*. London: Oxford University Press.
51. O'MAHONY, P. J. (ed.) (1959) *Catholics and Divorce*. London: Nelson.
52. OWEN, A. D. K. (1933) *A Survey of the Standard of Living in Sheffield*. (Sheffield Social Survey Committee, Survey Pamphlet no. 9).
53. P.E.P. (1952) *Planning*, 19, 344.
54. Pilgrim Trust (1938) *Men Without Work*. London: Cambridge Univ. Press.
55. REEVES, MRS PEMBER (1913) *Round About a Pound a Week*. London: Bell.
56. Registrar General of England and Wales. *Reports*. London: H.M.S.O.
57. Registrar General of England and Wales. *Statistical Reviews*. London: H.M.S.O.
58. RICE, M. SPRING (1939) *Working-class Wives*. Harmondsworth: Penguin Books.
59. ROWNTREE, B. S. (1912) *Poverty: A Study of Town Life*. London: Macmillan.
60. ROWNTREE, B. S. (1941) *Poverty and Progress*. London: Longmans.
61. ROWNTREE, GRISELDA, & CARRIER, NORMAN H. (1958) 'The Resort to Divorce in England and Wales, 1858–1957.' *Popul. Stud.*, 11, 188–234.
62. Royal Commission on Marriage and Divorce (Morton Commission) (1956) *Report* (Cmd. 9678). London: H.M.S.O.
63. Royal Commission on Population (1949) *Report* (Cmd. 7695). London H.M.S.O.
64. SHAW, L. A. (1954) 'Impressions of Family Life in a London Suburb.' *Sociolog. Rev.*, N.S., 2, 179–94.
65. SLATER, E., & WOODSIDE, M. (1951) *Patterns of Marriage*. London: Cassell.
66. SMITH, H. LLEWELLYN (ed.) *New Survey of London Life and Labour*. London: King.

O. R. McGregor and Griselda Rowntree

67. SPINLEY, B. M. (1953) *The Deprived and the Privileged.* London: Routledge.
68. TAYLOR, R. M. (1935, 1938) *A Social Survey of Plymouth.* London: King.
69. TITMUSS, R. M. (1958) *Essays on the 'Welfare State'.* London: Allen and Unwin.
70. TOUT, H. (1939) *The Standard of Living in Bristol.* Bristol: Arrowsmith.
71. TOWNSEND, PETER (1954) *Brit. J. Sociol.,* 5, 130–7.
72. YOUNG, M., & WILLMOTT, P. (1957) *Family and Kinship in East London.* London: Routledge.
73. YOUNG, T. (1934) *Becontree and Dagenham.* (Report made for the Pilgrim Trust.) London: Sidders.
74. ZWEIG, FERDYNAND. (1952) *Women's Life and Labour.* London: Gollancz.

22

REPRODUCTIVE LOSS

J. W. B. Douglas

THIS chapter discusses illegal abortion in Great Britain and also attempts to identify the factors that have led to the recent decline in the rates of maternal deaths, stillbirths, and first-week deaths. These topics were chosen because they raise interesting social and medical problems. In concentrating on death rather than illness I do not wish to imply that the levels of death rates give a satisfactory indication of the state of the maternity services or of the health of mothers and children, but in the absence of suitable information on maternal and infant health, there is no alternative to using them.

Maternal deaths, stillbirths, and first-week deaths have all declined in recent years. But whereas the maternal mortality rate today is only one-eighth of what it was twenty-five years ago, the stillbirth and first-week death rates have been reduced by only one-half and have been virtually stationary for the last ten years. The fall in maternal deaths is looked on by many as the greatest achievement of the maternal and child welfare services, and the stability of perinatal deaths as their greatest failure. Very little is known about either the level or the trend of abortions.

Abortions

There are two types of abortion,* 'spontaneous' and 'induced'. Spontaneous abortions are mainly a problem of obstetrics and need not

---

* An abortion is defined as 'the expulsion of the products of conception from the uterus at any period up to the twenty-eighth week of pregnancy'.

concern us here. Induced abortions, on the other hand, raise social problems that should be a major concern of the maternity and child welfare services.

In Great Britain, any action taken to procure a miscarriage is a criminal offence unless done in good faith for the purpose of preserving the life of the mother. Since there is a natural reluctance to admit criminal actions, we can only guess at the number of illegal abortions successfully performed in this country, and there is even less information on the number of unsuccessful attempts. It is evident, however, that the law is freely disregarded by women of all types and classes, and that illegal abortions are responsible for a large but undefined amount of maternal ill health and impaired fertility.

In the Family Limitation Survey[17] 1 per cent of all pregnancies were terminated illegally and a further 0·5 per cent survived attempts at abortion. These are minimal figures. The Interdepartmental Committee on Abortion[15] concluded that 6–8 per cent of all pregnancies ended in illegal abortion, and the Biological and Medical Committee of the Royal Commission on Population[23] put the figure at 2–5 per cent. It is a reasonable guess that there are 20–30,000 illegal abortions a year in Great Britain, and that they occur mainly among married women. Some would put the number at twice as high as this.

Information on the type of woman who seeks abortion, though lacking in Great Britain, is available for Denmark and Sweden. Since 1939 these countries have had laws that allow abortion to be induced for a wide variety of reasons; e.g. serious risk to life and health if the pregnancy goes to term, poor living conditions, or hereditary disease. The aim of these laws is to bring the whole problem of abortion into the open and to attack the causes that make a woman risk her life and health rather than carry an unwanted child to term.

Since the introduction of these laws legal abortions have increased from less than 1 per cent of all conceptions in 1939 to a peak of 6 per cent in 1953. Some, worried by this increase, wish to revise the law; others believe that the reduction in illegal abortions has more than compensated for the increase in legal ones.

An early observation was that 42 per cent of those asking for abortion were not pregnant.[11] There is no reason to believe that women in Great Britain differ from Scandinavian women in this respect, and since the illegal abortionist is unlikely to confirm the fact of pregnancy before taking action, a confidential pregnancy diagnosis service might save many women in this country from criminal interference.

In Scandinavia it is mainly married women who seek abortion, in particular those over forty-five and with other children. There appears to be a group of tired, worn out, or physically sick women who cannot face the disturbance and change of routine that having a child involves.

They are a resistant group in the attempts made in Scandinavia to reduce the frequency of abortion.

One must be careful in applying Scandinavian figures to Britain, and we ourselves should try to find out whether similar groups exist in this country. It would be a serious reflection on the achievements of the maternity services, and a challenge to them, if women who had raised families with their help, sought abortion when faced with the problem of later and unintended pregnancies.

The Royal Commission on Population stated: 'Abortion is a form of family limitation, resorted to, for the most part, because of failure, through ignorance or other cause, to prevent conception' ([24], par. 534), and for this and other reasons they recommended that 'the giving of advice on contraception to married persons who want it should be accepted as a duty of the National Health Service and the existing restrictions on the giving of such advice by public authority clinics should be removed'. This recommendation has not been implemented.

The relation of the maternity and child welfare services to the family planning movement has always been ambiguous. In theory, but not always in practice, women are referred by local authority clinics to family planning clinics only if they are suffering from conditions such as tuberculosis or heart disease which are likely to be affected adversely by a further pregnancy. The maternity and child welfare services, however, cannot so easily dissociate themselves from the family planning movement. By raising the status of motherhood and emphasizing the need for a high standard of maternal care and a close relationship between mother and child, they have increased the need for planning family size and spacing children. The accepted standards of child care today are designed for the small family, and with few exceptions women can match up to them only if they limit the number of their children. Thus, the success of the maternity services is founded on the acceptance of the small family pattern, and those who use them achieve this pattern, if not by medically efficient methods of birth control, then by less desirable ones.

It is by no means certain that more widely diffused and effective knowledge of birth control would be followed by a fall in the incidence of criminal abortions. Indeed, a high rate of abortion has been reported among women who use sophisticated birth control techniques.[2] But apart from this, the widespread use of effective birth-control methods would be likely to reduce the incidence of stillbirths and infant deaths, since both these mortalities are high when births are closely spaced. It might also improve marital relations; 'the use of relatively unreliable methods of contraception (e.g. *coitus interruptus*) is the cause of other distress that does not find expression in this extreme form (i.e. abortion); the harm arises not only from the failure but also from the fear of

431

failure; and the evidence submitted to us suggests that much marital disharmony can be traced to the anxiety that accompanies the practice of *coitus interruptus*.'[24]

More research is needed both into the social background of illegal abortion and into the practice of birth control at different stages of married life. This type of research bristles with problems, but the family-limitation study and recent American surveys have shown that women will talk readily about these matters if approached in the right way.

Maternal Deaths

Maternal mortality is measured by the number of deaths from pregnancy or childbirth occurring per thousand registered births. Before 1928 only live births were registered and maternal deaths were related to them. Since 1928 stillbirths as well as live births have been used in calculating the rate, and this has led to an apparent reduction of about 4 per cent in mortality. Even this method of calculation, however, exaggerates the risks of maternity, since these deaths should be related to the number of abortions (which is unknown) as well as to still and live births.

Maternal deaths have been a matter of long-standing concern. Since 1881 the Registrar General has sent out letters of inquiry about all deaths that appear to be associated with parturition. At the end of the last century there was a fall in maternal mortality in England and Wales, but from 1906 to 1934 the rate was virtually stable at a level of four deaths for every thousand births. This level is high by present-day standards, but even so deaths from pregnancy and childbirth were only one in eight of all deaths among women of child-bearing age. People were concerned not so much about the level of the rate, which was exceeded in many Western countries, but by its stability, which contrasted with the falling general mortality and with the dramatic fall in the infant death rate. Moreover, it was felt that 'the knowledge of these disasters is apt to produce in many women and their husbands a fear of maternity, with a deterrent effect on the birth rate'.[4]

In 1928 Neville Chamberlain appointed a Departmental Committee of the Ministry of Health to advise upon the application of available medical and surgical knowledge to maternal mortality and morbidity and to inquire into the need and direction of further research. The two reports of this committee suggested that at least half of all maternal deaths were preventable and showed that in certain hospitals they were being prevented; for example, in the British Hospital for Mothers and Babies, Woolwich, maternal deaths over four years were only three out of 4221 deliveries. While the committee laid emphasis on the need for an all-round tightening up and strengthening of each unit of obstetric

Reproductive Loss

care, they also realized that the problem involved was no ordinary medical one, '. . . it is an issue of civilization in origin and in solution'.

The reports of the Departmental Committee were followed by departmental investigations into maternal mortality in England, Wales, and Scotland.[7] These showed large and constant regional differences. The areas with the highest rates lay to the north of a line running from the Bristol Channel to the Humber, and in these all causes of maternal death were high, although it might have been expected that some would show an excess of one cause (say sepsis) and others an excess of another (say toxaemia).

Many of the worst areas had also high infant and general mortality rates; but this was by no means a rule, and a high risk of death in childbirth in an otherwise healthy area was not infrequently noted. Nor were the worst areas always those with bad maternity services or the best areas those with good ones. The widespread employment of married women, particularly in the textile industries, was generally associated with high risks of maternal death, and many of the worst areas had an unfortunate social history which suggested that under-nutrition in early life might have been a root cause.

The social pattern of maternal deaths was obscure. They were as frequent in years of plenty as in years of unemployment, and they were not related to overcrowding or economic circumstances. Death rates were, moreover, higher in Social Classes I and II than in Classes III, IV, and V, and the same relationship between the classes was found for each individual cause of death—except death following abortion, which was equally common in all classes.

In 1934, three years before the publication of the report of the Departmental Committee, the maternal mortality rate rose to a peak of 4·6 deaths per 1000 live and stillbirths; thereafter it fell each year and in 1955 reached the low level of 0·6.* Until 1940 the fall was gradual and was mainly accounted for by a reduction in deaths from sepsis. Since 1943 there has been an extremely rapid reduction in maternal deaths from all causes. The relevant figures are set out in Table I.

The Registrar General described the fall in maternal mortality as 'a notable example of what can be achieved by the concentration of medical specialists, biochemists, and public-health workers when the public conscience has at last been aroused by the persistent presentation of unpleasant statistical facts'([21], p. 231). It is, however, difficult to say what part of this fall may be ascribed to improvements in medical and obstetrical care and what to less tangible factors. In the case of puerperal sepsis, both a diminished incidence and more effective treatment seem to have combined to reduce mortality. The early decline in maternal mortality may be ascribed to the use of sulphonamides to

* Figures for England and Wales only.

433

J. W. B. Douglas

TABLE I
(Source: *R. G. Stat. Rev.* 1955, Commentary, Page 100)
MATERNAL DEATHS PER 1,000 LIVE AND STILLBIRTHS

Year	Sepsis (excluding Abortions)	Abortions	Other Causes	Total
1931	1·41	0·68	2·02	4·11
1932	1·33	0·73	2·13	4·19
1933	1·49	0·80	2·23	4·52
1934	1·58	0·82	2·22	4·62
1935	1·35	0·74	2·06	4·15
1936	1·18	0·67	2·01	3·86
1937	0·79	0·58	2·00	3·37
1938	0·71	0·55	1·98	3·24
1939	0·63	0·55	1·95	3·13
1940	0·54	0·44	1·70	2·68
1941	0·46	0·54	1·80	2·80
1942	0·41	0·46	1·61	2·48
1943	0·38	0·46	1·46	2·30
1944	0·28	0·41	1·24	1·93
1945	0·24	0·33	1·23	1·80
1946	0·18	0·19	1·06	1·43
1947	0·16	0·16	0·85	1·17
1948	0·12	0·15	0·75	1·02
1949	0·11	0·15	0·71	0·97
1950	0·13	0·14	0·60	0·87
1951	0·10	0·15	0·57	0·82
1952	0·09	0·13	0·50	0·72
1953	0·10	0·11	0·54	0·75
1954	0·10	0·11	0·49	0·70
1955	0·11	0·10	0·43	0·64

control puerperal sepsis rather than to advances in obstetric technique or preventive medicine. Prontosil, discovered in 1935 by Domagk in Germany, was being used effectively for the treatment of puerperal sepsis in Queen Charlotte's Hospital early in 1936. As more effective antibacterial therapy was introduced, both the notifications of puerperal sepsis and the deaths per hundred notified cases fell dramatically.[8]

It is of interest that the fall in maternal deaths from sepsis occurred at a time when there was a rapid increase in the proportion of confinements taking place in hospital. In other circumstances such an increase might have been accompanied by an increase in maternal mortality. In Aberdeen, for example, in 1918–1927 the maternal death rate was 2·8 per 1000 deliveries in midwifery practice, 6·9 in the practice of doctors, and 14·9 in in-patient institutional practice, the excess mortality in hospital being partly explained by a high incidence of sepsis there.[16]

Reduction in maternal mortality from causes other than sepsis has coincided with advances in obstetric technique, but 'with only mortality rates available it is difficult to *prove* that more effective handling of patients is a major part of the explanation rather than that the frequency of the condition has altered'.[8] That there is still scope for improving obstetric care is shown by a confidential inquiry into the causes of 861 maternal deaths occurring in England and Wales in the years 1955–57.[20] 41 per cent of these deaths were regarded as 'avoidable'. A substantial number could have been avoided by better and more intelligent ante-natal care and by a proper selection of patients for hospital confinement, but in some the patient herself was wholly responsible.

The full explanation for the great reduction in the maternal mortality rate since 1935 will probably never be known. If we had greater knowledge of the incidence of the non-fatal complications of pregnancy, we would be a great deal nearer to understanding what happened; but in spite of recommendations in the Reports on Maternal Mortality no serious attempt has been made to obtain this information. It is to be hoped that the Ministry of Health will pay more attention to determining levels of morbidity during pregnancy and early childhood, since without these we cannot assess the achievements of the service and may again be faced with changes in mortality—either favourable or unfavourable—that cannot be explained.

Perinatal Deaths (*Stillbirths and first week deaths*)

In Great Britain a child is said to be stillborn if he issues from his mother after the twenty-eighth week of pregnancy and does not breathe or show any sign of life. Stillbirths, therefore, include both babies that have died before the onset of labour (or for that matter before the twenty-eighth week of pregnancy if they are not expelled from the uterus until after that date) and those dying during it. On the other hand, deaths immediately after birth, many of which are due to essentially similar causes, are excluded. It is becoming increasingly popular to use the perinatal death rate, that is to say the number of stillbirths plus the number of first week deaths expressed per 1000 births, both live and still, and in international comparisons this rate has the clear advantage that it avoids problems arising from differences in national definitions of a 'stillbirth'. Too great an emphasis, however, should not be placed on perinatal deaths as a 'clinical entity', since stillbirths and first-week deaths do not always show the same trends; with maternal age and parity, for example, very different patterns emerge.[12]

435

J. W. B. Douglas

Stillbirths have been registered only since 1928 in England and Wales* and 1939 in Scotland. This is unfortunate, for it means that reliable figures are available for only a few years before the sudden decline in perinatal deaths that started during the Second World War.

Even in the earliest days of birth and death registration it was realized that the registration of stillbirths was an essential step towards the accurate registration of infant deaths as well as a protection against infanticide.[25]† In the early part of this century both the Interdepartmental Committee on Physical Deterioration and the Royal Commission on Venereal Disease strongly recommended it.

An attempt was made in the Births and Deaths Registration Act of 1874 to ensure that no stillborn child was buried without a certificate signed by a doctor or midwife or other qualified person ([10], p. 107), but this was never successfully enforced. Some local authorities required the notification of stillbirths from 1907, and after the Notification of Births (Extension) Act 1915 they were generally notifiable. But although all births had to be notified there was no compulsion to say whether the child was live or still-born,[18] and the stillbirth rates obtained from these notifications were considerably lower than those found when registration was introduced.

The failure to register stillbirths before 1928 was not owing to any inherent difficulty in setting up a register; in Denmark, where the definition of a stillbirth is the same as in Britain, one has been in existence since 1800. The late registration of stillbirths in Great Britain deprived us of the opportunity to see how the stillbirth rate responded to the environmental changes in the early part of this century and to the attack on venereal disease after the first world war. The figures for the years 1929–58 are shown in Table II.

The great importance of stillbirths and first-week deaths is shown by the fact that the *16,309* stillbirths and *1,013* first-week deaths occurring in 1958 exceeded in number all deaths between the end of the first week of life and the end of the thirty-ninth year.

Since stillbirths were first registered the perinatal mortality rate has declined by *27.5* per 1000 total births, that is to say, if the rates of 1928 were effective today there would have been *47,000* perinatal deaths instead of the *26,522* actually registered. The greater part of this fall occurred during a period of approximately ten years. A gradual decline in the late nineteen-thirties was accelerated during the war years and then levelled out, so that since 1949 the perinatal death rate has been relatively stable, though there has been a slight decline since 1955.

---

* Or more exactly, mid-1927.

† See minutes of evidence by Farr (5036) and 'Observations', p. 58. The Registrar General, however, considered that registration of stillbirths would be indelicate and useless (6434).

Reproductive Loss

TABLE II

THE COURSE OF THE PERINATAL DEATH RATE

Year	Perinatal death rate per 1000 total births	Year	Perinatal death rate per 1000 total births
1929	61·40	1944	44·79
1930	61·90	1945	45·06
1931	62·08	1946	44·34
1932	62·84	1947	40·22
1933	63·39	1948	38·49
1934	62·19	1949	37·96
1935	61·87	1950	37·67
1936	60·76	1951	38·12
1937	60·20	1952	37·51
1938	58·57	1953	37·00
1939	58·07	1954	38·11
1940	56·12	1955	37·55
1941	54·03	1956	36·82
1942	51·80	1957	36·22
1943	47·98	1958	35·15

The greatest fall in perinatal mortality occurred at a time when the obstetric services were scantily staffed and often located in makeshift premises, when bombing and evacuation were leading to deteriorating living conditions, and when many women were employed in factories during pregnancy.

In contrast, the perinatal mortality rate remained stable during a period when the obstetric services were improving, when there was a growing interest in neonatal paediatrics, when hospital confinements were on the increase, and when premature baby units were being set up in many parts of the country. Moreover, more and better houses were becoming available and an increasing proportion of women of child-bearing age had passed their childhood in the relatively prosperous times of the middle and late nineteen-thirties and had benefited, during their growing years, from war-time rationing. This formidable array of favourable events should have led to a fall in perinatal mortality. That it did not do so makes us wonder whether further reductions are possible without new advances in medical knowledge. The geographical and social inequalities in death rates described in the following paragraphs strongly support the view that perinatal mortality could still be substantially reduced by applying more effectively the knowledge we already have.

Several other countries have lower perinatal mortality rates than England and Wales. Holland, for example, had a rate of 28.0 in 1956 as compared with 36·8 in this country. This is a remarkable achievement in a country where 75 per cent of babies are delivered at home.[3] In Sweden and Norway too, with very different patterns of institutional confinement, similarly low rates are recorded, and on this showing it should be possible to reduce the mortality rates in Great Britain by some eight per thousand total births with a saving of six thousand infant lives.

Regional variations in perinatal mortality within Great Britain are still considerable, though in general smaller than when stillbirths were first registered. In 1928, for example, the perinatal mortality rate was *75·7* in Wales as compared with *48·5* in London (a Welsh excess over London of 56 per cent) whereas in 1956 the corresponding rates were *43·5* and *33·3* (a Welsh excess over London of 31 per cent).* In general the areas with high rates have been bad areas for many years and are the same as those which in 1935 were outstanding in maternal deaths.

Although the perinatal mortality rate has not shown itself to be sensitive to a general improvement in social conditions, it is markedly lower in the most prosperous classes. Rietz[21] in 1930 showed that stillbirths were twice as frequent among the poorest classes in Stockholm as among the wealthiest, and the Registrar General's analysis of stillbirths in 1939 by social class (prepared for the Royal Commission on Population) showed that Class V stillbirth rates were 63 per cent higher than Class I rates. Even after allowances were made for social class differences in mother's age and parity the social class differences in stillbirth rates were practically unchanged. Similar social class differences were found in an analysis of stillbirths in England and Wales in 1949 when it was again shown that standardization by mother's age and parity did not materially alter them.[23] The considerable fall in the stillbirth rate during these ten years affected all social classes proportionately, so that the gap between Social Class I and Social Class V was not diminished. Moreover, the same proportional improvement was found for mothers of each age and for each order of birth.

Stillbirth rates are high among women over thirty-five who are having their first baby and among mothers of six to ten previous children. These women also have an excess of first-week deaths, as also do young mothers who have already borne several children.[12] Approximately 60 per cent of children dying in the perinatal period are prematurely born (i.e. weigh 5½ lb. or less at birth), and it is relevant to note that these light-weight births are common among women who have had a rapid succession of births. Here it appears that birth spacing rather than age and parity is the important factor.[5] It has been calculated that better family planning would reduce the incidence of premature second and higher order births by 21 per cent. If so, this is a weighty argument

* Owing to boundary changes in London this comparison is not exactly equivalent in the two periods.

Reproductive Loss

for the closer association of family planning with the maternity and child welfare services.

The regional and social variations suggest that perinatal mortality could be greatly reduced, but they give no indication of how this could be done. Unfortunately there is no reliable information on the causes of stillbirth to help us. Causes are registered in Scotland, but in the absence of a post-mortem—which is rarely obtained for stillbirths occurring at home—the causes given are often of doubtful value.* The figures, such as they are, suggest that there has been no preferential decline in any single cause—for example, hazards of birth.[13]

To summarize: the fall in the perinatal death rate affected similarly all parts of the country, all social classes,† all ages of mother, all birth orders, and both sexes. Moreover, this fall was not limited to any one cause. A fall so general must be attributed to general rather than specific factors,[26] and the most probable are improvements in nutrition, changes in the age of marriage and childbearing, improvements in obstetric or ante-natal care, and changes in the attitude of women to maternity.

The uniform fall in the stillbirth rate in all social classes speaks against an explanation in terms of nutrition either during pregnancy or in early life. If improved feeding during the growing period were the cause of the downward trend in stillbirths, one would expect to find the greatest improvement in the poorest classes and in the youngest age groups; but this is not so. Moreover, the downward trend should have continued to the present day, since each year an even larger proportion of the women bearing children have grown up during the years of plenty. Baird's observation[1] that short women run high risks of stillbirth and premature birth has been taken as an indication of the importance of early nutrition in reproductive performance. But even in the social classes where malnutrition at any age can be largely excluded, short women have a similar excess of premature births,[9, 19] and some now feel that the association of short stature with poor reproductive efficiency is more likely to be explained in terms of heredity than malnutrition.[27]

There have been great changes in the age at marriage in recent years, but they explain only a small part of the fall in the perinatal death rate. Moreover similar improvements in the rate are found for births to mothers of all ages and all parities.

The main decline in perinatal mortality occurred at a time when, owing to war conditions, obstetricians and midwives were scarce. It seems unlikely, therefore, that rising standards of obstetric care can explain this trend, which, moreover, was not limited to, or even

* The perinatal survey of 1958 supplies unique post-mortem data on stillbirths from all parts of Great Britain.

† My information here refers to stillbirths only, but it is extremely probable that first-week deaths show a similar trend with social class.

439

J. W. B. Douglas

predominantly due to, a fall in the proportion of deaths attributed to hazards of birth. On the other hand, in spite of the shortage of trained civilian personnel during the war, the emergency maternity services provided in many areas more continuous and thorough ante-natal provision than had been previously available. During the war years also the attitude of the expectant mothers may have changed—when human lives are at their cheapest the desire to preserve life and health is at its highest[28]—and if so, this may well have helped to lower mortality by increasing the use of the available maternity services and in other less easily defined ways. Unfortunately, we know little about the attitudes of women to child-bearing, either today or before the war, and although we may suspect there have been profound changes we can neither define their nature nor measure their extent.

Although the reasons for the fall in perinatal mortality and for its recent stability are largely unknown we can reasonably hope to take action that will reduce these deaths, at any rate to the levels now found in Scandinavia. In Public Health, when causes are obscure results have often been obtained by focusing care on the groups that most obviously need it. If we could define relatively small groups of women whose children run excessive risks of being stillborn or dying in early infancy, we might gain some clue to the reasons for this high wastage and, by increased care, help to avoid it. We might, for example, describe these women in terms of the occupation of their husbands or even of their own fathers. But such occupational descriptions suffer from the fact that, today at any rate, job changes are frequent. In the National Survey of Child Health, for example, nearly half the husbands changed their occupational group on one or more occasions during a period of eleven years.* The rate of change, moreover, was particularly high in just those groups, the semi-skilled and unskilled, that would be expected to provide the 'vulnerable population'. In these circumstances the husband's occupation gives only a rough indication of the social background of the family, and when[14] we extend the process backwards and relate the occupation of the mother's father, which may well have had the same quality of impermanence, to that of her husband, we are on very shaky ground indeed.

Many factors are associated with high perinatal mortality and so might help to define 'vulnerable groups':—for example pre-marital conception, illegitimacy, a history of previous reproductive loss, poor maternal care, and low-measured intelligence. Maternal age and parity are also important.

Although many factors are associated with perinatal mortality, one characteristic is common to most of them, namely, the mother's failure to make full use of the available ante-natal services. Women who are

* Unpublished data.

unsatisfactory in their ante-natal clinic attendances suffer heavy reproductive loss both in the perinatal period and after it. They also neglect the child welfare services, and there is suggestive evidence that the high mortality of their children results from their failure to secure timely and adequate medical care.[6] Here we have a simple method of isolating a 'vulnerable group' by which women who come late for ante-natal care and attend irregularly may be brought into hospital before term. After the lying-in period every effort should be made, through the Health Visiting Services, to see that medical care is available when needed, even if the mother herself has not recognized the need.

The general theme of this chapter has been the need for more information about many aspects of reproduction. In particular, we need to know more about the extent of illegal abortion, the use of birth-control methods, and the attitudes of women to the maternity and child welfare services. We have been content to judge the achievements of these services by changes in mortality rates, and have never faced the problem of how to measure the incidence of non-fatal complications of pregnancy and childbirth or of illness in early infancy. Without this information we can neither understand the changes in mortality that have already occurred nor see what steps should be taken to reduce the present high incidence of perinatal death.

REFERENCES

1. BAIRD, D. (1945) *J. Obstet, Gynaec. Brit. Emp.*, **52,** 339.
2. CALDERONE, M. S. (1958) 'Abortion in the United States'. Hoeber Harper.
3. DE HAAS, J. H. (1958) *Acta paediat. Stockh.*, **47,** 446.
4. Departmental Committee on Maternal Mortality and Morbidity (1930) *Interim Report*. London: H.M.S.O.
5. DOUGLAS, J. W. B. (1950) *J. Obstet. Gynaec. Brit. Emp.*, **57,** 143.
6. DOUGLAS, J. W. B., & BLOMFIELD, J. M. (1958) *Children under Five*. London: Allen and Unwin.
7. DOUGLAS, C. A., & McKINLAY, P. L. (1937) *Report on Maternal Morbidity in Scotland*. (Cd. 5422 and 5432). London: H.M.S.O.
8. DOUGLAS, C. A., & McKINLAY, P. L. (1959) *Health Bulletin*, **17,** 18.
9. DOUGLAS, J. W. B., & MOGFORD, C. (1953) *Arch. Dis. Childh.*, **28,** 436.
10. FARR, WILLIAM (1885) *Vital Statistics*. London: Royal Society for the Promotion of Health.
11. GILLE, H. (1948) *Popul. Stud.*, **2,** 3.
12. HEADY, J. A., & MORRIS, J. N. (1959) *J. Obstet. Gynaec. Brit. Emp.*, **66,** 577.
13. HEADY, J. H., STEVENS, C. F., DALY, C., & MORRIS, J. N. (1955) *Lancet*, **i** 499.
14. ILLSLEY, R. (1955) *Brit. med. J.*, **i,** 1520.

J. W. B. Douglas

15. Interdepartmental Committee on Abortion (1939) *Report*. London: H.M.S.O.
16. KINLOCH, J. P., SMITH, J., & STEPHEN, J. A. (1928) *Maternal Mortality in Aberdeen*. Edinburgh: Scottish Board of Health.
17. LEWIS-FANING, E. (1949) *Report of an Inquiry into Family Limitation and its Influence on Human Fertility during the last Fifty Years*. London: H.M.S.O.
18. Local Government Board (1918–19) *Report*, p. 112. (Also earlier reports of the Board.)
19. MARTIN, F. M. (1954) *Med. Offr.*, **92**, 263.
20. Ministry of Health (1960) *Reports on Public Health and Medical Subjects*, no. 103. London: H.M.S.O.
21. *Registrar General* (1955) *Statistical Review*. London: H.M.S.O.
22. RIETZ, E. (1930). *Acta. paediat. Stockh.*, **9**, Suppl. 3.
23. Royal Commission on Population (1950) *Papers*, vol. 4. London: H.M.S.O.
24. Royal Commission on Population (1949) *Report*. London: H.M.S.O.
25. Royal Sanitary Commission (1869). *Second Report*.
26. SUTHERLAND, IAN (1949) *Stillbirths*. London: Oxford Univ. Press.
27. THOMSON, A. M. (1959) *Eugen. Rev.*, **51**, 157.
28. TITMUSS, R. M. (1950) *Problems of Social Policy*. London: Longmans.

23

NATIONAL INTELLIGENCE

James Maxwell

DURING the present century an impressive mass of information has been accumulated about the physical and social well-being of the nation. Nearly all the evidence points to an improving standard of living, better housing, better conditions of work, better health, and longer life. It is natural to ask whether a corresponding development has been taking place in the intellectual level of the population. The simplicity of the question is deceptive. For one thing the amount of evidence available in comparison with that for, say, health and longevity is meagre. Also both the terms *national* and *intelligence* need careful definition.

The term *national* can be accepted in its conventional political sense, as meaning e.g. Swedes, French, Scots, Canadians, and so on. But it is not possible in practice to assess the intelligence of a whole nation, or even of a random sample of it. There is no measure of intelligence available which would be equally applicable at six months, six years, sixteen years, and sixty years of age. Tests such as the revisions of the Binet Scale, which apparently cover an age range from about three years to adulthood, are in fact a series of different tests, and the Intelligence Quotient of a six-year-old is derived from a different set of tests from those administered to a sixteen-year-old. Thus any assessment of national intelligence is in fact based on the assessment of a fairly homogeneous group of the population, not representative of the population as a whole. In practice, nearly all reasonably comprehensive assessments of national intelligence are based on samples of children of school age, male recruits for the armed forces, or university and college students. Any findings from such surveys are as much a function of the method of selecting the sample tested as of the level of national intelligence as such. Statements about national intelligence therefore are particular rather than general. They refer to the specific group of the population tested, and not to the population as a whole. The various implications of this are fairly obvious and need not be developed here.

The other term, *intelligence*, requires even more careful consideration. Current psychological thinking on this topic tends to make a very sharp distinction between intelligence, in the sense of intellectual capacity, regarded as innate and constant for any individual, and what will here be called I.Q. (Intelligence Quotient), which is the measure derived from an assessment of observed behaviour, usually in the form of answers to an intelligence test. 'Intelligence', as here used, is a capacity and is not measurable. The capacity to acquire intelligent forms of behaviour may be present in an individual, but if the opportunity to acquire these is not given or made, then the individual's behaviour is not observed to be intelligent, and the I.Q. is low. Put crudely and briefly, a high I.Q. implies both intelligence and opportunity, a low I.Q. implies either lack of intelligence, or of opportunity, or most commonly of both. It follows that any discussion of national intelligence can only be in terms of I.Q. and, as I.Q. is an assessment of behaviour, it becomes necessary to keep in mind the conventions on which the measurement of I.Q. depends.

There is no identifiable psychological entity called intelligence. But there is a substantial amount of agreement about the characteristics of intelligent behaviour, and as a result of this common agreement most tests of intelligence bear a strong family resemblance to each other, and all assume a body of cultural knowledge and skills common to the community for which the test is used. Differences in performance between individuals are conventionally expressed in terms of Intelligence Quotient; a performance which is average for the population assessed is given the value of 100. There is no uniformly accepted convention expressing the distribution of I.Q.s among the population, but in general most distributions of I.Q. in a population are assigned a standard deviation of about 15 points. This means that about 2·5 per cent of the population have I.Q.s higher than 130, and 2·5 per cent lower than 70. The I.Q.s are distributed according to the mathematical properties of a 'normal' distribution. This is done for convenience in interpretation; there is no evidence that intelligence is 'normally' distributed, and I.Q.s can be distributed as the test maker sees fit. The 'normal' distribution of I.Q. is a convention, but one which does not offend common observation.

It follows that direct comparison between the intelligence of different nations is not possible. If the Ruritanians and Laputans were to dispute about which were more intelligent, and each constructed and administered an intelligence test to the same representative sample of their population, the average I.Q. of both would be 100, and if they adopted the same convention for distribution of I.Q., the two populations would be identical in respect of Intelligence Quotient. Were it decided to use a test equally appropriate for both populations, it would be found in practice that such a test, having eliminated the items involving cultural knowledge and skills, such as language, which differentiate the two nations, ceases to be an adequate assessment of what either nation would regard as intelligent behaviour. Alternatively, where the same test is appropriate to both groups, as with Scottish and English children, the distinction between the groups is political only.

Attempts to Measure Changes of National Intelligence

It is, however, possible to assess the development of intellectual level within any national group, provided that too great cultural changes have not taken place in the intervals between successive assessments. The most systematic and thorough investigation of the trend of national intelligence was made in Scotland, where the two Scottish Mental Surveys, one in 1932 and the other in 1947, enable a direct comparison to be made. In 1932 all eleven-year-old Scottish children were given a group verbal intelligence test, and a sample of one thousand were given an individual intelligence test. In 1947 the procedure was repeated. The same group test was used, but a different version of the individual test was given to a more carefully selected sample of about twelve hundred children. On the group test, the 1947 children scored significantly higher than the 1932 children. On the individual tests, however, the average I.Q.s of the 1932 and 1947 samples were not significantly different after adjustment had been made for the difference in the two tests. On balance, the evidence suggests some rise in I.Q. over the fifteen-year interval, and establishes that no decline in average I.Q. had occurred. This finding is in general agreement with observations elsewhere. In England, where group verbal intelligence tests are extensively used for the 'eleven plus' examinations, it has been found that the standard of children's performance has risen. A score that would, ten years ago, have given an I.Q. of 100, now gives an I.Q. of slightly less than 100. An extensive, but less precise, investigation in the U.S.A. showed that the standards used in the testing of intelligence for army recruits in World War I were not applicable when the same tests were used in World War II. The standards had become too low. Apart from the Scottish Surveys the evidence is indirect, but it all points in the same direction.

James Maxwell

Explanations of Observed Changes

This increase in average I.Q. is not easy to interpret. The Scottish Survey in 1947 was specifically designed to test the hypothesis that average intelligence was diminishing, as a result of differential fertility for intelligence. It had been frequently observed that the average I.Q. in children in large families was lower than that of children in small families, from which it was argued that, as the large families contributed more to the next generation, the intellectual level of the population would steadily decline.

This feature of differential fertility for I.Q. has been observed in countries other than Scotland, and seems to be a feature of societies of the European and American types. Whether this feature is also characteristic of, say, Asian and African societies is not known; in any case so little is known about I.Q. levels in these societies that fruitful discussion is limited to European and American observations. For the Scottish data, there was a clear relationship between socio-economic class as measured by the fathers' occupation, the number of children in the family, and the average I.Q. of the children. For instance, on a test with a mean of 37 points of score and standard deviation of 16 points, and in a population with a mean family size of 3·8 children, the children of parents in the professional and employer class obtained an average score of 52 points on the test, and their average family size was 2·6 children. At the other end of the socio-economic scale, the children of unskilled workers obtained a mean score of 31 points, the average family size being 4·6 children.

This differential fertility for I.Q. cannot, however, be attributed wholly, or mainly, to socio-economic differences. Within each of the socio-economic grades used in the Scottish Survey there is clearly evident a corresponding pattern of differential fertility for I.Q., not greatly different from that prevailing in the population as a whole. For instance within the professional and employer group, the average test score runs from 53 points for children in families of one child to 42 points for children in families of five children. Socio-economic differences still exist, of course, within these grades, but are very much smaller than those between grades.

Further evidence comes from more recent data on the follow-up of a representative group of Scottish children. These children, eleven years old in 1947, are now young men and women, many of them married with children of their own. The children are still too young to be tested, but the I.Q.s of the parents, as recorded when they were eleven years old, are available. Of the eleven hundred or so Survey children followed up, 201 boys and 367 girls are now married. When the I.Q.s of these 568 married members of the Survey follow-up group are

446

related to the present number of their children, the following table is the result:

Average I.Q. (at 11 years) by number of children

Number of Children

	0	1	2	3	4 or more
Boys	104	100	99	94	–
Girls	104	98	95	95	85

These data are as yet incomplete, but the differential fertility for I.Q. is clearly evident, this time by I.Q. of parent. Also, these young men and women are in their early twenties, and have not yet segregated themselves to any great degree into socio-economic grades; indeed the married members tend to be a fairly homogeneous group socially, as the majority of those training for the professions or more highly skilled occupations have not yet married.

When the implications of differential fertility for I.Q. are being considered, two aspects should be kept separate. One of these, to be discussed later, is the relation of I.Q. to educational opportunity and social mobility; the other is the effect of differential fertility on the level of national intelligence. The Scottish data indicate that differential fertility for I.Q. is not incompatible with a stable, or even a rising, level of national intelligence. One possible explanation for the small rise in the average I.Q. in Scottish children is that it is a function of an accelerated rate of growth in children. This, however, would not also explain the similar rise of I.Q. in American Army recruits. It may also be that increased familiarity with tests has contributed, though on this point positive evidence is rather thin. Another factor to be taken into account in any explanation is that, in the Scottish Survey, the greater part of the increase in the group-test score was contributed by the girls—a feature which renders it unlikely that differential fertility, or any other factor operating equally for both sexes, is the main cause of the changing level of national I.Q. This same feature of an increased average score of girls is also found in the English 'eleven plus' results already mentioned.

GENETIC VERSUS SOCIAL FACTORS IN THE DETERMINATION OF I.Q.

All the evidence available, and there is not much of it, on changing levels of national intelligence is based on short-term observations. An interval of half a generation, such as separated the two Scottish Surveys, is far from adequate for any genetic changes, unless very drastic, to manifest themselves. It is not unlikely that genetic trends do exist, but they are not at present susceptible to observation. Genetic factors

James Maxwell

underlie observed differences of intellectual ability in a population, but it is not easy to distinguish genetic from social and culturally determined differences. The techniques for doing so are limited. The most satisfactory is that based on the comparison of identical twins reared apart and with different cultural and social opportunities. Being genetically identical, the intelligence of the twins is the same: any difference between them in I.Q. is therefore an index of the effect of differing social opportunity. The degree of concordance of I.Q. is an index of the extent of genetic determination of I.Q., plus the effects of common elements in social conditions. Similar investigations can be made with foster children, where it has been shown that such children tend to approach the intellectual level of their foster parents, whatever their original genetic endowment may have been.

The 'nature versus nurture' controversy has in recent years lost much of its interest and significance, not because it has been solved, but because it is now apparent that the genetics of human intelligence is a much more complex topic than was originally believed, and because it is also becoming apparent that the issue of nature and nurture was stated in far too simple terms. It is not possible, for instance, to consider intelligence and I.Q. separately, and compare the one with the other. Cultural and social opportunities, though physically the same, are not the same for a highly intelligent and a dull child.

Of more significance and interest is the question of how the fund of intelligence in a population can be most fully developed; in other words, even if the intelligence of a population were static, how far can the I.Q. of that population be increased. Interest in this topic has tended to concentrate on three main points: firstly, in U.S.A., on the question of the intelligence of various ethnic groups, particularly Negroes; secondly, in many countries with a tradition of Western European civilization, on the relation between I.Q. and social class, or urban versus rural up-bringing; and thirdly, on the relation between education and I.Q.

The question of racial differences in intelligence is one which is bedevilled by social and political factors; but a substantial body of remarkably consistent evidence has demonstrated a lower average I.Q. in Negroes than in whites in the U.S.A. There is, of course, overlap; Negroes of high I.Q. have been reported, but less frequently than whites, and correspondingly there are whites of low I.Q., but again fewer proportionately than Negroes. The I.Q. of Negroes in the Southern States is lower than that of Negroes in the Northern States; but in both, the Negro average I.Q. is lower than that of whites: the general trend of evidence is that the average I.Q. of Northern Negroes is a little below the average of Southern whites, though sampling difficulties make exact comparison impossible. The most reasonable interpretation of the higher I.Q. of Northern Negroes is that it may be attributed to a combination of selective migration and better cultural environment and opportunities.

Nearly all investigations also show an increasing divergence between white and Negro I.Q. with increasing age. The interpretation of this is not easy, though it almost certainly involves both the greater unreliability of tests of young children and the increasing complexity of educational and social demands on the adult and older child.

Even Negro college students are of lower average I.Q. than their white counterparts, although the former are probably more highly selected. A higher urban than rural I.Q. seems to occur both for Negroes and for whites.

The apparently well established differences in I.Q. level between American whites and Negroes raises a number of questions pertinent to any discussion of national intelligence. If the term national is defined *ethnically*, the question is whether the observed differences of average I.Q. are of degree only, or whether there are differences in the quality or pattern of abilities between races. In relation to the first question, it may be noted that the lower average I.Q. of Negroes and some other coloured peoples is not found among Chinese and Japanese. Performances in verbal and non-verbal tests among Negroes are of much the same order, even where the low level of school education would imply a relatively greater verbal-educational disadvantage. As regards the second question, there is, however, some suggestion that the difference between white and Negro I.Q. may be partly qualititative. In the various intelligence tests used, the type involving abstract design proves to be especially difficult for Negroes. Poor performances on tests like Koh's Block Design (a test involving the arrangement of differently coloured wooden blocks into such designs as a diamond or chevron) have been reported both from the U.S.A. and from Southern and Central Africa. Also suggestive of qualitative differences is the difficulty being experienced in Africa of developing any tests of intelligence similar to those which are successfully used in Britain to select children for different levels and types of formal education. Despite many attempts, no satisfactory test of this kind has been constructed. Tests of this type do tend to become more applicable, however, after children have received some formal education of a European type.

The evidence about qualitative differences in intelligence between racial groups is at present far from conclusive, but the proposition is not inherently absurd. Consistent racial differences can be established by physical measures, such as those of skin colour, skeletal structure, hair texture, and the like, and it is not impossible that psychological measures may reveal differences of a similar order. At present, the data are derived from measuring instruments, such as intelligence tests, which are adapted to white norms. It may be that the white is, in sporting terms, playing on his home ground, while the Negro is playing away, and is at some disadvantage for this reason. Fresh light on the question may come from future social and political developments in Africa and in Israel, though it does not appear likely that adequately controlled scientific observations will be made. The gaining of independence and the spread of education in Africa are likely to reveal whether any qualitative difference in intellectual ability will emerge, reflected in a pattern of Negro culture and intellectual achievement different from the European pattern. Similarly in Israel, the pattern of culture is largely being set by Jews of European origin, who despite many years of racial discrimination against them, have not been seriously charged with a low average I.Q.; into this pattern are being absorbed Eastern Jews, of basically the same racial strain, but whose cultural and probably intellectual level is at present considerably lower: it remains to be seen whether in this mixture the European pattern will prevail.

If, on the other hand, the term national is defined *politically*, certain consequences appear to follow from the available evidence. On the American evidence, it would be expected that the average level of I.Q. of a nation of mixed European and Negro constituents would be lower than that of a parallel wholly European nation, and that this difference of level of I.Q. would not appear to apply between a European population and a mixed European and Chinese-Japanese population. Here again it must be pointed out that the evidence is by no means conclusive; the degree to which emigration from China and Japan has been selective is unknown. Another feature which has been suggested as possibly operating in a mixed population is 'heterosis', or 'hybrid vigour', according to which the first generation, at least, of hybrids is biologically fitter than either of its parent strains. This feature would lead us to expect that a nation or group in which substantial intermarriage is occurring would be superior. This expectation does not seem to be fulfilled in the U.S.A., where comparatively few American 'Negroes' are racially pure Negro; rather, there is a positive correlation between I.Q. and lightness of skin colour. It may be, however, that a half-caste does not qualify biologically as a hybrid, or it may be that heterosis does not operate for intelligence.

In the field of intelligence there is little support for an egalitarian philosophy. The evidence all demonstrates considerable differences among individuals within national groups, and points to differences between social groups within the larger national groups. The evidence for differences between national groups is rather scanty, but difference between nations is more in keeping with the general pattern of evidence than is equality.

National Intelligence

The Relationships of Social and Educational Factors to I.Q.

The positive relation between social class and I.Q., particularly in children, has been observed for many years. About a year after the 1911 Binet Intelligence Scale was produced, W. Stern noted that the average I.Q. of children was higher in the upper social classes than in the lower. Whether this feature is due to the better cultural and educational environment of upper class children, or whether it is mainly due to the more intelligent parents securing for themselves a better social standing, is uncertain. Most likely it is a combination of both factors: indeed it is difficult to imagine it otherwise.

More recent investigations have suggested that changes in socio-economic conditions are accompanied by changes in I.Q.; it is, however, not yet known to which components in the socio-economic complex I.Q. is most sensitive. It is also very probable that a raising of the general social and cultural level tends to be accompanied by a rise in I.Q.; but the effects of various aspects of the cultural environment have not yet been adequately analysed. There is fairly clear evidence that familiarity with group-intelligence tests can raise children's I.Q.s by about five points: there is, however, a definite limit to the amount of improvement that can be attained by coaching in test technique. Length of education appears also to be related to increase of I.Q.: in Sweden, the I.Q.s of a group of young adults were compared with the I.Q.s of the same group as children; those whose education was of greater duration showed increased I.Q.s: those with the shorter period of school education showed no such increment.

It is an extreme, and almost certainly wrong-headed, argument to maintain that differences between individual I.Q.s in a community are solely, or indeed mainly, the outcome of differences in social and educational opportunity. Virtually all the findings on this point are based on the testing of school children, or young adults; and those nations where such surveys have taken place tend to be those whose educational facilities are well developed and uniform. The extensive Scottish and French surveys were conducted on primary school children, whose educational opportunities were remarkably uniform, as in neither case had they entered upon the differential types of education provided in secondary schools. With older children, and with adults, differences in educational opportunity would have been a more relevant factor. In so far, therefore, as the educational and social conditions are relatively uniform, differences in I.Q. may reasonably be attributed to genetic constitution, i.e. differences in I.Q. are to a considerable extent determined by differences in intelligence. Consistent with this is the fact that within any family there may be a fairly wide range of variation in the I.Q.s of brothers and sisters. The correspondence between the I.Q.s of the younger brothers and sisters of the children of the Scottish Survey follow-up group ($r = + 0 \cdot 5$) is at a level which implies quite a wide possible range of difference between children of the same family.

The members of the population in the higher I.Q. levels are apparently not numerically reproducing themselves; on the whole they marry later, have fewer children, and not all those children are of high I.Q. If the proportion of the nation above a given level of I.Q. remains constant over a period of years, it must be in virtue of recruitment of its numbers from the upper reaches of the I.Q. distribution of children whose family average I.Q. is centred at a lower level. In so far as differences of I.Q. in the population are linked to social class, there is thus evidence for a change of persons within the various social and educational strata. In those nations where the hereditary principle has become replaced by an educational selection based ultimately on competitive examination, academic achievement, which is closely linked with I.Q., is one of the main avenues of social advancement.

It is of some interest to consider whether it is possible to increase the numbers of the high I.Q. group by manipulation of the social and educational system. During the last few years, most of the 'developed' nations have been suffering from a shortage of able and educated men and women, particularly in the technical and professional fields. In nearly all these nations the opportunities for higher education are greater than the number of persons taking advantage of them. In the United Kingdom, for instance, early school-leavers include a number of children whose I.Q. is consistent with a higher educational and vocational level than they actually reach: estimates vary, but centre on a figure of about one-third as the possible increase over the present number reaching University entrance level. It is also known that the probability of a pupil of given I.Q. reaching this educational standard is greater if the pupil comes from the 'middle' social classes than from the 'lower'. The other major factor, not always distinguishable from social class in a predominantly middle-class educational system, is best described in terms of personality and character. Higher education implies hard work, and not all pupils can meet this demand.

Social mobility implies social distinctions, and in the present structure of Western European society these distinctions appear to operate in such a way as to restrict an increase of the proportion of highly intelligent persons in the population. Those who move, by virtue of intellectual abilities and conformable personal qualities, into a high social stratum, enter a social group whose attitudes and way of living appear, on the face of it, to develop high I.Q.s in their children; but at the same time they have fewer than the average number of children. To this social factor must be added the, probably genetic, factor of differential fertility for intelligence, which operates in the same direction. Broadly speaking, it seems as if the most that the development of educational and social opportunities for gifted children can do is to increase the rate of circulation within the structure of national intelligence. It is unlikely to change the structure itself to any significant extent.

The situation with the trend of *average* national I.Q. is not the same. In the United Kingdom, for example, there has been a conspicuous extension of educational opportunity during the present century. The best education today is probably not greatly superior to the best a century ago, but the poorest education, and not even that was available to all, was certainly worse than the poorest today, when all children attend reasonably efficient schools for at least ten years. Housing, literacy, communications have all improved, with consequent effects on I.Q. There is little doubt that, had a survey of national intelligence been made a century ago, the average I.Q. found would have been perceptibly lower than that obtained today.

The fact that socially desirable types of education depend to some extent on tested intelligence is in itself a factor making for a higher level of average I.Q. in three ways: firstly, interest in and preparation for intelligence tests does raise I.Q. to some extent. Secondly, social mobility is partly dependent on intellectual level, and those who have achieved a higher social level tend to try to establish their children, by education among other means, in the same niche as they themselves have reached. Thirdly, it is also probable that methods and attitudes in child-rearing have to some extent been influenced by the prevalent use of intelligence tests. Such factors could, even over a relatively short period of ten or fifteen years, especially when concerning children, influence the average level of I.Q., and are likely to be one explanation for the higher average I.Q. of the children observed in the 1947 Scottish Survey.

The social and political significance of a small rise in average I.Q. of the nation's children is not great. It is possible that any increase in average I.Q. represents an increase in the rate of development, adult intellectual maturity being reached at an earlier age, but not necessarily at a higher standard. Also, a small increase in average I.Q. does not necessarily imply a higher level of national intelligence, even among children; it probably means that existing intelligence is being more adequately developed—a desirable process, but one which has limits set by genetic intellectual endowment.

Factors Affecting the Distribution of Intelligence and I.Q.

What is of greater social significance, but has been largely neglected in the few investigations that have been made, is a possible change in the *distribution* of intelligence. Is the proportion of mental defectives and 'geniuses' in the population increasing or not? The Scottish Surveys

James Maxwell

showed a small increase in the standard deviation of I.Q. in 1947, but the interpretation is not clear. It seems fair to remark, however, that though the number of mental defectives is not precisely known, it is probable that they are increasing—not as the result of genetic changes, but with advances in medical science, which have increased the expectation of life for such persons. Predictions of increased incidence of mental defect as a consequence of differential fertility for intelligence are unlikely to be fulfilled. Less is known of the incidence of persons highly gifted intellectually. Very possibly there is an increase in the number of high I.Q.s in the population due to factors such as increased educational opportunity, and as regards high *intelligence* there is doubt whether the pattern of differential fertility for intelligence applies at the extremes of the distribution.

The Need for more Information

It is trite to say that intellectual ability is an important national asset· Yet an inquiry into the state and trends of national intelligence reveals a distressing paucity of information, which becomes more evident in contrast to the accumulated data on other aspects of the nation's life and resources. Is the level of national intelligence rising, falling, or remaining static? Is adequate use being made of the intellectual resources of the nation? Are there more or fewer 'geniuses' and defectives? And where do we look for them? Is the difference between the very bright and very dull intellectually becoming greater or less? The present answer is that we do not really know.

A survey or surveys intended to answer these questions would have to be made over an extended period of years, in order to reveal any significant changes not only in average I.Q. but also in the distribution and *pattern* of intelligence-test scores. The prerequisites of such a survey are more precise means of assessing I.Q. The type of general purpose intelligence test used to ascertain general intellectual trends is not sufficiently reliable at the extreme ends of the I.Q. distribution to provide sound data on changes in distribution of I.Q. To investigate further the relation between I.Q. and various socio-economic conditions, a series of more limited inquiries seems to be indicated. These, however, depend on the development of effective means of assessing those socio-economic differences which may be related to differences of I.Q. If this were done it would be possible to investigate more fully such questions as the connexion between parental attitudes to education and I.Q.; the effect of improved housing conditions on I.Q.; whether there is a continuous relation between I.Q. and social conditions, or whether there is a critical level of such conditions above which there was no further rise of I.Q.

National Intelligence

Such a programme of investigation would be extensive and necessarily spread over a number of years. But there is no other way of extending our knowledge in this area, and though such a programme of inquiry may appear formidable, it is without question inherently possible.

BIBLIOGRAPHY

ANASTASI, A. (1958) *Differential Psychology*. 3rd edn. London: Macmillan.
BURT, CYRIL (1946) *Intelligence and Fertility*. Eugenics Society: Occasional Paper no. 2. London: Hamish Hamilton.
FLOUD, J. E., HALSEY, A. M., & MARTIN, F. M. (1956) *Social Class and Educational Opportunity*. London: Heinemann.
GLASS, DAVID V. (ed.) (1954) *Social Mobility in Britain*. London: Routledge.
HUSEN, T. (1951) 'The Influence of Schooling upon I.Q.' *Theoria*, **17**.
Institut national d'études démographiques. Cahier 13. *Le Niveau intellectuel des enfants d'âge scolaire*. Paris: Presses Univ. de France. 1950.
KALMUS, H. (1957) *Variation and Heredity*. London: Routledge.
McINTOSH, D. M. (1959) *Educational Guidance and the Pool of Ability*. London: Univ. of London Press.
MAXWELL, J. (ed.) (1950) 'The Psychological Quality of the Population'. *Advanc. Sci. Lond.*, **6**, 24.
NEWMAN, H. H., FREEMAN, F. N., & HOLZINGER, K. J. (1937) *Twins: A Study of Heredity and Environment*. Chicago: Chicago Univ. Press.
PENROSE, L. S. (1949) *The Biology of Mental Defect*. London: Sidgwick and Jackson.
Scottish Council for Research in Education. V: *The Intelligence of Scottish Children* (1933); XXX: *The Trend of Scottish Intelligence* (1949); XXXV: *Social Implications of the 1947 Scottish Mental Survey* (1953); XII: *Educational and Other Aspects of the 1947 Scottish Mental Survey* (1958). London: Univ. of London Press.
SHUEY, A. M. (1958) *The Testing of Negro Intelligence*. Lynchburg: J. P. Bell.
'Symposium on the Effects of Coaching and Practice on Intelligence Tests.' *Brit. J. educ. Psychol.*, **23–24**. (1953–4)
THOMSON, G. H. (1947) *The Trend of National Intelligence*. Eugenics Society: Occasional Paper no. 3. London: Hamish Hamilton.
TUDDENHAM, R. D. (1948) 'Soldier Intelligence in World Wars I and II'. *Amer. Psychol.*, **3**.

455

24

DEMOGRAPHIC ASPECTS OF THE AGEING OF THE POPULATION

N. H. Carrier

INTRODUCTION

'AGEING' of human populations is important, not in the main because of the demographic consequences, such as its effect on death, marriage and birth rates, but for its implications on such questions as the proportion of the population which has to be kept by the workers, the housing of old people, and pensions. The other important facet of ageing is that there is a popular misconception that the process is a simple consequence of the extension of human life by medical discoveries. This is, in fact, not so, and in this chapter the demographic process of ageing will be examined.

The nature of demographic data (i.e., census populations by age, birth and death rates, etc.) implies that frequently a more incisive study can be made of chronological age than of a particular age-associated characteristic in which major interest may lie. In such a case, study of the characteristic may be greatly assisted by a parallel study of chronological age, tailored to suit the particular age-associated characteristic involved. This tailoring will have regard especially to the nature of the relationship between the characteristic and chronological age. If economy of effort was of primary concern, and retirement from the labour force was being studied, a parallel study restricted to males over age 45 in five-year groups to 60, by single years to 65, and again in five-year groups, might be deemed appropriate, because the operation

457

of various pension schemes makes the relationship between age and retirement between ages 60 and 65 rather complicated. In the present study we have not in mind any specific age-associated characteristic, and so the appropriate analyses of chronological age are those with the widest application.

Although, for an individual, chronological age obviously progresses steadily throughout life, for a population, or group of individuals, the situation is different. In a year's time an individual will be just one year older. This will be true also of all individuals of the group who survive the year and remain in the group, but some individuals will die, at ages varying from extreme youth to senility, and their places will be taken by an equal number, more or less, of babies. In the general case, the rejuvenation brought about by the replacement of the old by the young may or may not exceed the ageing of the survivors. Thus, whereas an individual either dies or ages, a wide range of possibilities may happen to a group. Further possibilities still are added by changes due to migrations.

The form of this discussion, contrasting only youth and the aged, is in general unsuitable as a parallel to the study of an age-associated characteristic, since most characteristics do not, even approximately, progress steadily from the cradle to the grave. Many, such as physical, mental and reproductive powers, are at a minimum at the extremes of life and rise to a maximum at some intermediate age. In general, then, the very simplest study of age structure that can be of any relevance to the study of age-associated characteristics must examine the content of at least three age groups; a young and an old group, where the characteristics are deemed to be at a minimum; and an intermediate group where powers are at a maximum. The expedient of splitting the intermediate group will add considerable refinement, since it will enable allowance to be made for the important fact that ages of maximum power vary considerably as between different characteristics.

Some characteristics, such as requirements for food and education, change rapidly through the early years of life, and their proper study requires the distinction of small age groups. In a broad study such as this, only a single age group can be allocated to childhood. Considerations of school leaving and entry to the labour force, the beginning of reproduction, and the minimum age at marriage, suggest somewhere between 15 and 20 as the end of childhood, and 15 is conventionally chosen. In Britain, 16 might be a better choice on social and economic grounds, but 15 is convenient as a boundary between conventional five-year age groups.

At the other end of life, the provisions of the National Insurance Acts suggest 65 for men and 60 for women as appropriate boundaries between the labour force and the retired. This choice would, however,

Demographic Aspects of the Ageing of the Population

have disadvantages for a general study: selection of different age-groups for men and women prevents observation of the natural sex-ratio, and there are advantages in splitting life into broad age-groups of equal length; 60 readily fits into such a scheme (with groups conveniently of length 15 years), but 65 does not. It seems preferable, therefore, to choose 60 and over as the old-age group, divided, where finer division is required, into 60–74 and 75 and over.

As part of the same scheme, the main working-age group, 15–59, may on occasions be split with advantage into 15–29, 30–44, and 45–59. For instance, only the 15–29 group experiences high fertility, whilst virtually all women aged 45–59 are past childbearing; the roles of these age groups in the labour force differ; their housing requirements are influenced by the age of their children, and so forth.

This study then will comprise an examination of past trends in age structure, in terms of three main groups and their subdivisions, identification of the causes of these trends, and an attempt to foresee future trends.

Past Trends in the Age Structure of Great Britain

Table I shows the proportion of the whole population in 15-year age groups for each sex and a summary consolidating into the three main groups (persons under 15, 15–59, and 60 and over) at fifteen-year intervals from 1861 to 1951.

In terms of the three broad age groups of the summary, the trend in age structure may be seen to show three features: (i) A relatively constant structure from 1861 to 1876; (ii) From 1876 to 1931, a steady decrease in the proportion of children, with complementary increases in the proportions at working ages and of the aged; and (iii) From 1936 to 1951, a stabilizing of the proportion of children, a reversal of the trend for the proportion of working ages, and a continuing increase in the proportion of aged. The most consistent feature, then, has been the tendency for the proportion of aged to increase, a trend which was slow until 1906, but which has led to the proportion more than doubling in the first fifty years of the present century.

Examination of the narrower 15-year age groups for each sex shows new features, in addition to those already observed for the broad age groups. The proportions in the separate groups of boys and girls under 15 each broadly follow the trend seen already for the combined group. A minor feature is that, whereas boys and girls were previously equally numerous (in 1876, the proportions of boys and girls in the population were 182·6 and 182·0 respectively), since 1906 the boys have built up a slight numerical superiority (in 1951, boys constituted 114·3 per 1000 of the population, girls 109·5). This is due to a decline in pregnancy

N. H. Carrier

TABLE I

Per thousand distribution of the population in 15-year age groups by
sex: Great Britain, 1861–1951.*

Sex-Age Group	1861	1876	1891	1906	1921	1936	1951
Males							
0–14	179·4	182·6	175·8	158·7	140·5	112·4	114·3
15–29	126·8	128·1	131·8	132·6	120·0	123·4	102·7
30–44	88·5	85·8	88·7	99·0	98·9	105·4	110·0
45–59	56·5	55·4	55·1	60·1	76·5	81·6	89·9
60–74	28·2	28·3	27·5	28·2	35·0	48·2	52·2
75 & over	6·0	5·8	5·6	5·6	6·6	9·0	13·6
All Ages	485·4	486·0	484·5	484·2	477·5	480·0	482·7
Females							
0–14	177·4	182·0	175·6	158·5	138·6	109·9	109·5
15–29	139·2	136·2	141·9	142·6	134·9	126·2	103·3
30–44	96·8	93·8	95·1	106·4	114·3	117·3	112·6
45–59	60·5	61·2	61·5	65·5	82·1	94·7	100·8
60–74	32·7	33·1	33·5	34·5	42·0	57·3	69·5
75 & over	8·0	7·7	7·9	8·3	10·6	14·6	21·6
All Ages	514·6	514·0	515·5	515·8	522·5	520·0	517·3
Persons							
0–14	356·8	364·6	351·4	317·2	279·1	222·3	223·8
15–59	568·3	560·5	574·1	606·2	626·7	648·6	619·3
60 & over	74·9	74·9	74·5	76·6	94·2	129·1	156·9
All Ages	1000	1000	1000	1000	1000	1000	1000

wastage and infantile mortality from which boys previously suffered far
more than girls.

The proportion in the broad working-age group, 15–59, rose from
1876 to 1936, and then fell back slightly, finishing in 1951 some 10
per cent higher than it had been in 1876. Had it not been for the losses
inflicted on the men in World War I, the age groups 15–29 and 30–44
of men as well as of women would have reflected this trend to the extent

* Age proportions in non-census years obtained by 4-point interpolation.

460

Demographic Aspects of the Ageing of the Population

of showing a rise and subsequent decline. The magnitudes of rise and fall involved are different from those of the working-age group as a whole, however, because the proportion in the age group 45–59 has persistently increased from 1876 to 1951. If the proportions in each of the three age groups in 1951 are compared with the proportions in 1876, there is, for each sex, a decline in the age group 15–29, a modest rise in the age group 30–44, and a steeper rise in the age group 45–59. This pattern of changes implies that the ageing which was found in the population as a whole is present also within the population of working age. These figures also show the move towards numerical superiority of men, already observed for the age group under 15. In no group are the men yet as numerous as the women, but in the age groups 15–29 and 30–44 they have narrowed the gap which existed in 1876. The age group 45–59 in 1951 is exceptional, since World War I losses came partly from this group.

The pattern of changes in the groups of working age is even stronger in the old-age groups. The proportion of population in the age group 60–74 about doubled from 1876 to 1951, whilst the proportion in the age group 75 and over nearly trebled. Neither group reflects the narrowing of the gap between the sexes seen in younger groups. The 60–74 age group will have suffered from World War I losses, whilst the number of males in the 75 and over group recorded in 1876 may well have been inflated owing to overstatement of age.

There are, then, three outstanding features in the trend of the British population age-structure shown in Table 1. Firstly, *ageing* has occurred in the population as a whole so that, for instance, the ratio of those retired to workers has risen; and has also taken place within broad age groups so that an increasing proportion of the retired are very old, and the average age of the labour force has risen. Secondly, a long decline in the proportion of children has been checked since 1936. Thirdly, except for the older age groups in 1951, who suffered the World War I losses, there has been a move towards numerical superiority of males, though in most groups this is as yet seen only as a decrease in the former female numerical superiority.

The Causes of Change in Age Structure

It is a common fallacy to attribute the ageing of the population to the contemporaneous decline in mortality, which certainly will result in an increase in the proportion *of each generation* which will survive to old age. A clear demonstration will be given later that the ageing of the population as a whole is not due to mortality decline, but first the mechanism of age structure must be considered.

Age-structure depends essentially upon the relative numbers of the

461

N. H. Carrier

population in different age groups. Since, if migration can be neglected,* absolute numbers derive from the original numbers born less the losses due to deaths occurring between birth and the present age of each generation, age structure depends upon the relative number born in the various generations comprising the present population, and the relative mortality through which each generation has passed. Thus *a priori*, fertility as well as mortality changes can be expected to influence age structure. In the last hundred years, both fertility (the extent to which women of child-bearing ages have in fact borne children) and mortality, have changed substantially. Mortality has declined during the whole period, though the decline has been more rapid in the present century. Fertility declined from the 1870s to the 1930s, partially recovered, and now appears almost constant at a level somewhat above its lowest point. The influence of fertility on age structure may be separated from that of mortality by calculating the hypothetical populations that would have been produced (*i*) if fertility had remained constant whilst mortality followed its actual course, and (*ii*) if mortality had remained constant whilst fertility followed its actual course.†

The resulting age-structures are shown in Table II. A comparison of the proportions shown with those in the same age groups in Table I indicates clearly that the changes in age-structure, already noted, are attributable to the changes of fertility that have occurred, not to the decline in mortality.

Considering first the proportion of children: the actual proportion (Table I) declined from 364·6 in 1876 to 222·3 in 1936, virtually the same proportion being shown in 1951 (223·8). The lower half of Table II shows that much the same trend would have been recorded had fertility alone changed, the decline being to 212·6 in 1936 and a similar proportion, 208·7, in 1951. The upper half of Table II shows that, in contrast, a decline in mortality alone would have led to a small *rise* in the proportion of children, to 390·7 in 1951.

The proportion aged 15–29 was shown in Table I to have risen from 560·5 in 1876 to 648·6 in 1936, subsequently declining by 29·3 to

* That migration on the scale encountered does not significantly influence the age structure of the British population is demonstrated in *External Migration*, by Carrier and Jeffery, H.M.S.O. 1953, Appendix 3.

† A comparison of the age-structure of high- and low-mortality life table populations does not demonstrate the influence of mortality change on age-structure, since these life table populations require, not only different mortality, but also different fertility (so that the net reproduction rate remains unity). Such a comparison does not even show the influence of the appropriate joint change of fertility and mortality, since, after the change, it takes many years before the structure settles down to its new form. This question is discussed in *The Ageing of Populations and its Economic and Social Implications*. United Nations' ST/SOA/A. 26, Chapter 2.

Demographic Aspects of the Ageing of the Population

TABLE II

Per thousand distribution of the population in broad age groups:
Hypothetical populations* of Great Britain. 1861 to 1951.

Age Group	1861	1876	1891	1906	1921	1936	1951
	Constant fertility, actual mortality						
0–14	356·8	364·6	365·0	366·1	377·7	380·9	390·7
15–59	568·3	560·5	562·0	564·6	549·4	542·0	537·1
60 & over	74·9	74·9	73·0	69·3	72·9	77·1	72·2
All Ages	1000	1000	1000	1000	1000	1000	1000
	Constant mortality, actual fertility						
0–14	356·8	364·6	349·7	316·3	269·1	212·6	208·7
15–59	568·3	560·5	573·9	603·4	638·5	667·3	638·5
60 & over	74·9	74·9	76·4	80·3	92·4	120·1	152·8
All Ages	1000	1000	1000	1000	1000	1000	1000

619·3 in 1951. The lower half of Table II shows that a not very dissimilar trend would have resulted from the fertility changes alone, the
rise in the proportion being a little steeper, to 667·3 in 1936, with a
similar decline of 28·8 to 638·5 in 1951. The upper half of Table II
shows that, again, the mortality decline alone produces a quite different
trend, a slight rise in the proportion, to 564·6 in 1906, followed by a
slight fall to 537·1 in 1951.

Finally, the trend in the actual proportion of the aged, which Table I
showed to be a rise from 74·9 in 1876 to 156·9 in 1951, is shown in the
lower half of Table II to be paralleled by a similar trend that would have

* (i) The index of fertility employed was the ratio of births (for each sex
separately) to the sum of the number of women aged 15–29 and one-half
the number of women aged 30–44.
(ii) Mortality was measured by 15-year survivorship ratios: from 15-year
births to age group 0–14, from 60 and over to 75 and over, and from one
15-year age group to the next at intermediate ages.
(iii) Where 'constant' fertility or mortality was assumed, it was that of 1861–76.
The 1861 and 1876 proportions are thus actual, as shown in Table I.
(iv) Features of this treatment which are theoretically unsatisfactory, but are
thought to have introduced no significant error, are, first, that migration
gains or losses have been absorbed into the 'survivorship factors', and
secondly, sex-ratio at birth has been associated with fertility, i.e. kept at
the 1861–76 level or changed as it actually did, according to whether fertility
was assumed 'constant' or 'actual'.

been experienced as a result of the fertility changes alone—a rise to 152·8. The upper half of Table II, however, shows that the mortality decline alone would hardly have altered the proportion of aged at all; the figures indeed show a slight decline (to 72·2).

It is seen then that, had the mortality decline of the last seventy-five years been experienced without any change of fertility, such changes in age-structure as there were would in general have been in the opposite direction to those that actually occurred. The effect of a mortality decline alone is, however, better described as no change at all, since such changes as there were were relatively slight. In contrast, the fertility decline from the 1870s to the 1930s and the subsequent recovery, if experienced without any change of mortality, would have led to a trend in age-structure following somewhat closely that which actually occurred.

Having recognized that mortality changes have little influence on age-structure, and that the trend in fertility is its major determinant, the relative timing of fertility and age-structure changes may be examined.

The decline in fertility ran from the 1870s to the 1930s, the timing corresponding almost exactly with the decline in the proportion of children in the population. Common sense suggests that the latter will lag a few years after the former, and indeed the decline is not steep until after 1891. The rise in the proportion of population in the working-age groups also appears directly after 1876, and again the rise becomes faster after 1891. The proportion in the old-age group, however, shows no significant rise until after 1906, many years after the onset of the fertility decline.

The above evidence suggests that the recent halting of the fertility decline should be paralleled by checks in the decline of the proportion of children and rise of the proportion at working ages and, after some years, in the rise of the proportion of the aged. The first two checks are already visible from Table I; the third is to be expected in the future. The erroneous assumption that the ageing of the population was attributable to mortality decline would lead to the expectation that the rise in the proportion of the aged would continue without check, at least in the foreseeable future.

This last qualification is necessary because we have confined our examination to the specific mortality decline which has recently been experienced in Great Britain. Mortality declines so far experienced in other countries have, broadly speaking, the same properties. All, however, derive in the main from control of infectious diseases and thus consist of sharp declines in death rates at early ages with relatively little improvement at old ages. An epoch-making discovery, such as a cure for cancer, would invalidate the assumption that past factors in determining age-structure will continue to operate in the future and

Demographic Aspects of the Ageing of the Population

would thus upset present predictions. It must, however, be stressed that really revolutionary changes would be required to do this.

The Future Age-Structure

Clearly no useful prophecy can be made as to what medical discoveries will be made in the coming decades. It is however useful to trace the future and reveal the ultimate consequences of past events on

TABLE III

Per thousand distribution of the population in 15-year age groups by sex: Great Britain, 1954, 1964, and 1979

Sex-Age Group	1954	1964	1979
Males			
0–14	114·9	108·2	103·4
15–29	100·5	104·6	103·8
30–44	108·2	103·0	100·3
45–59	94·1	96·5	94·4
60–74	52·0	59·2	68·7
75 & over	14·3	14·9	19·7
All Ages	484·0	486·4	490·3
Females			
0–14	110·0	102·8	97·8
15–29	99·5	102·1	99·2
30–44	110·0	102·6	98·4
45–59	102·6	101·3	96·1
60–74	70·3	77·3	83·3
75 & over	23·6	27·5	34·9
All Ages	516·0	513·6	509·7
Persons			
0–14	224·9	211·0	201·2
15–59	614·9	610·1	592·2
60 & over	160·2	178·9	206·6
All Ages	1000	1000	1000

the assumption that nothing revolutionary will happen. The populations of Great Britain in 1964 and 1979 on such assumptions, constructed from the 1954 population, have been calculated by the Government Actuary.* The age-structure of these populations is shown in Table III.

Even on the assumption of no major calamities and no major medical discoveries, there is latitude for varying assumptions, notably in fertiliy, which may have significant effects on the resulting age-structures. In 1954, when the Government Actuary prepared his projections, fertility was still declining from the post-war peak of 1947, and it is evident from the declining proportion of children shown in Table III that he saw no grounds for making optimistic fertility assumptions. The proportions of the aged in his projections therefore continue to rise. Since 1954, however, the fertility rates actually recorded have been higher than was expected, so that slightly higher proportions of children and lower proportions of the aged than those shown in Table III may be expected.

It is, however, evident that the general ageing of the population and ageing within the broad age groups previously examined will continue to some extent in the immediate future, although modified by the check in the decline of fertility during the 1930s.

Table III also shows that, on the Government Actuary's assumptions, numerical superiority of males will reach up to age 45 by 1964. The next age group, 45–59, has not gained superiority by 1979, but as the gap between the sexes continues to narrow between 1964 and 1979, it is clearly a possibility that males may ultimately exceed females in this group too. The situation at the oldest age groups, even in 1979, is distorted by the male losses of World War I. An eventual narrowing, although not a closing, of the gap between the sexes may be expected in these age groups.

CONCLUSION

These substantial changes in the sex and age structure of the British population which have already occurred, or may confidently be expected in the near future, have had, or will have, far-reaching effects on the life of the country through the many characteristics associated with age. An understanding of the underlying demographic factors concerned demonstrates that, to some extent, ageing of the population in the immediate future is inevitable, and all that is possible at this time is to prepare for it by the necessary social and economic measures. Amelioration of the ill-effects of the ageing of the population in the more distant future is possible through the adoption of appropriate population-policies to mould, primarily, the birth-rate. In this connexion, however,

* *National Insurance Act, 1946. Report by the Government Actuary on the First Quinquennial Review.* H.M.S.O. 1954.

Demographic Aspects of the Ageing of the Population

it must be stressed that it is not only through age-structure that demo-graphic factors influence economic prosperity: both the absolute size and the growth-rate of population are also important. It is beyond the scope of this study to consider the optimum balance between the conflicting demands of various requirements some of which demand a high birth rate, some a low.

The ill-effects being reaped today were sown many decades ago. In some respects demographic forces are slow to act, but the corrective action for any unbalance acts equally slowly, so that the penalties for past mistakes can scarcely be avoided. Population structure must be planned for the future if it is planned at all, and, if it has not been in the past, we must, in the present, put up with the consequences.

25

THE SOCIAL MEDICINE OF
OLD AGE

C. A. Boucher

THOSE countries with a high standard of living and with well developed medical and social services inevitably, in the course of time, tend to reveal an ageing population, and thus to some extent the existence of a large and growing number of old people indicates the healthiness of a nation. In Biblical times old age was regarded with high esteem and old people were revered for their knowledge and wisdom, but later in history attitudes appeared more contradictory; the Greeks despised the physical imperfections of old age, and in ancient Rome old age was regarded as a disease, yet senescence has always commanded respect in China, where the strong family ties included the elderly.

The welfare of the elderly in Britain reflects a record of voluntary effort, legislation, and philanthropy. In the Middle Ages responsibility for their care devolved mainly on the Church and on the Merchant or Craft Guilds, who discharged it by the provision either of housing, such as almshouses for destitute old people, or of allowances in money or kind. The dissolution of the monasteries and convents in the sixteenth century caused much poverty and a rapid increase in the number of beggars; the resulting Poor Law Statute of 1601 ruled that the welfare of the aged was a civil as well as a religious responsibility, and the parishes responded mainly by erecting 'houses of habitation and dwelling'. At the close of that century, in 1697, Bristol became the first town to build a 'workhouse', and this pattern of development was slowly followed throughout the country; the Poor Law (Amendment)

Act of 1834, which followed the report of a Royal Commission appointed two years earlier, required the general establishment of workhouses. During the remainder of the nineteenth century there was increasing concern about the provisions of the Poor Law, and another Royal Commission in 1909 reported grave defects in the system. Under the Local Government Act of 1929 the Boards of Guardians were replaced by Public Assistance Committees of County and County Borough Councils, which became responsible for the appointment of relieving officers and for the administration of the workhouses, which were now called 'institutions'. Meanwhile the first Old Age Pensions Act was passed in 1908, followed by various amending Acts in subsequent years, and in 1940 the Assistance Board was made responsible for granting supplementary pensions to those in need. Finally, in 1948, the National Assistance Act abolished the Poor Law, and County and County Borough Councils were made responsible for providing residential accommodation for those in need of care and attention.

The estimated mid-1958 population of England and Wales was 45,244,000,[8] including 5,311,000 persons (11·8 per cent) aged 65 or over. As many as 1,887,000 persons (4·2 per cent), including 1,211,000 women and 676,000 men, were aged 75 years or more. At the beginning of this century 1 in every 21 of the population was aged 65 or over; now the proportion is 1 in 9, and it has been estimated that after another two decades an additional two million old people will raise this proportion to one in seven.[7] This pattern of age has resulted primarily from a gradual fall in the birth rate since the end of the last century; in addition the expectation of life has now risen to 69 years for males and 73 years for females, but although more people, including the less robust, are reaching retirement age they can expect, having attained that point, to live little longer than did their forefathers a hundred years ago. These trends are appearing in all civilized countries, but the pattern in Britain shows two special features: the rate of increase in the number of old people is faster than in most other countries, and the elderly women far outnumber the men.

The existence in the community of a large and growing number of old people creates strains and tensions which can appear formidable. These may be aggravated by such factors as smaller families, dispersal of families so that ties of kinship become weakened, increasing employment opportunities for women so that fewer remain available to care for their older relatives, and an attitude of mind which maintains that the State should accept responsibility for all dependants. There is no substantial evidence of a weakening of individual responsibility, but rather a desire that this burden should be shared by the State. It is generally accepted that old people should not be isolated as a special group but should be integrated with the rest of the population, but it is recognized that some will require assistance given with the object of helping them to help themselves to maintain their independence. They need, and want, to remain useful members of the community for as long as possible—as contributors rather than consumers.

Ageing must be regarded as a continuous process which starts perceptibly in early adult life. Physical prowess, and possibly intelligence, are considered to reach their peak in the middle twenties; deterioration in visual perception may be noticed in the middle forties, followed perhaps in the next decade by some loss in hearing acuity; some people in middle age begin to exhibit some slowing of movement and a prolongation of reaction time. The conception of old age as beginning at 65 years for men and 60 for women arises from the selection of these ages for eligibility for retirement pension, but chronological age is in itself of little significance; an individual's capabilities may be masked by his physical limitations, while those endowed with considerable intellect may show relatively little sign of ageing. It would seem reasonable to suggest that old age begins at a point where, without evidence of disease, there is such mental and physical deterioration that independence cannot be maintained without assistance. This point is often reached in the middle seventies.

More housing accommodation specially designed for old people is being built, 20,132 one-bedroom dwellings were erected by local housing authorities during 1958, although it is not known how many of these are occupied by the aged. This is the equivalent of 17·8 per cent of all local authority dwellings completed during that year.[3] Many housing authorities and housing associations have also converted suitable buildings to provide bed-sitting-room accommodation. It has been estimated that 50,000 old people reside in almshouses, on which considerable sums of money have been spent in recent years. Many old people feel the strain of maintaining homes which have become too large for their personal needs, and, understandably, bungalows and flats have become increasingly popular. In addition to the contribution made by private building enterprise 70,000 to 80,000 bungalows have been built by local authorities since the end of World War II. In an attempt to mingle all age groups local authorities have usually erected these bungalows, or flats, on the larger housing estates on the periphery of the towns. The dwellings give no cause for criticism, but complaints are sometimes heard of high rents, remoteness of shops, cost of public transport, and loneliness; Droller[1] found that many old people were being moved to a new environment without an adequate preliminary assessment of their mental and physical fitness, and that some who were not fully ambulant experienced many difficulties after transfer. There is no doubt, however, that if old people are suitably housed they are usually more contented and are able to maintain their independence for longer than would otherwise be the case; their health improves as the strain on their physical resources diminishes.

About 96 per cent of old people live at home, and the great majority are well and active, but the Census of 1951 revealed that nearly one million, mainly elderly women, were living entirely alone. A substantial proportion of old people have no children on whom they can call for assistance; Titmuss[5] has stated that one quarter of the elderly are childless or unmarried. Some local surveys have suggested that perhaps 10 per cent of the elderly are so infirm as to be housebound, including some who are bedfast; many are living without any effective human contacts, and some married couples continue just to maintain their independence only by their united efforts. While loneliness is a common complaint it is probable that the greatest cause of unhappiness is ill-health or a feeling of being no longer wanted; fear of illness or accident also contributes to a feeling of insecurity. With the passage of time more of the expanding local authority domiciliary services are being devoted to old people. Perhaps one tenth of the time of the health visitors, whose duties in this respect are becoming more akin to social work, is concerned with old people, to whom they paid more than a million visits during 1958; some local authorities have appointed 'special health visitors' for this purpose. Again, during 1958, 61 per cent of the visits paid by home nurses were to the elderly, and 70 per cent of the cases assisted by home helps, who play a vital part in the supporting domiciliary services, were in this age group. Some local authorities have also organized a service of night attendants who are usually directed to old people who may be dying alone, or those who are ill and awaiting admission to hospital, or in order to give temporary relief to relatives. General practitioners find that the demand for their services increases with the age of their patients.

Some local authorities recognize that a few old people find considerable difficulty in washing their soiled clothes and bedding, and have accordingly organized a special laundry service, either directly or through the agency of the voluntary services. Many local authorities are in the process of organizing a chiropody service, priority being given in the first place to the elderly, the physically handicapped, and expectant mothers; many elderly people show foot defects, and this service is expected not only to lessen their suffering but to enable them to maintain their independence longer. Some elderly patients are admitted to hospital with signs of malnutrition, which may arise from an inability to purchase food with discrimination or an unwillingness to prepare adequate meals; many voluntary organizations have therefore developed, with the help of the local authorities, a 'mobile meals service', which distributes nutritious midday meals in heated containers to selected persons at least once a week. More than thirteen hundred local Old People's Welfare Committees have been formed under the guidance of the National Old People's Welfare Council; these committees, widely representative of local voluntary organizations, make a substantial contribution to the well-being of the aged by such means as day clubs, visiting services, holiday schemes, and assistance with transport and shopping.

The old person may reach a stage when he is no longer able to maintain his independence at home even with the assistance of these domiciliary services. He may be able to make private arrangements for his own care, but otherwise he is likely to seek admission to a welfare home administered by the local authority. Local welfare authorities are required by the National Assistance Act, 1948, to provide residential accommodation for those in need of care and attention; until recent times this was available mainly in large institutions, formerly the 'workhouses', but the tendency now is to establish smaller homes for 30–60 residents. Since the end of World War II 1,053 such small homes have been opened, including 133 new homes built for the purpose.[4] At the end of 1958 there were 79,877 persons, including 69,340 aged persons, living in residential accommodation provided directly by the local welfare authorities or through the agency of voluntary organizations; although the newer small homes accommodate 33,000 residents, the demand has so greatly increased that most large institutions remain fully occupied. The age and infirmity of the applicants for admission and of the residents is steadily rising, which may be an indication of the strength of the domiciliary services, and design of the modern welfare homes has to take account of the increasing frailty of the residents. Stairs present the greatest difficulty, and lifts have to be installed; more staff, including sometimes night staff, have to be employed and those with nursing experience are often in demand. Welfare authorities expect to give the sort of nursing care that would normally be given at home by relatives or friends, with the advice of home nurses, to those suffering from minor temporary illness, and all the residents register with a local general practitioner. There is a persistent waiting list for such accommodation, particularly on the ground floor, and careful preliminary assessment of applicants is needed. Welfare authorities and voluntary organizations have sometimes been criticized in the past for appearing to accept or retain those for whom other arrangements seemed equally suitable. Return to independent life rarely follows admission, and Ruck[9] describes three classes of resident who should not need admission if there were adequate housing. It is probably true to say that most old people would prefer to remain at home and be cared for by their relatives provided temporary admission to welfare homes could be arranged at regular intervals in order to relieve the pressure at home. A few local authorities and voluntary organizations have experimented with 'boarding out' schemes which enable old people, no longer able to live independently, to reside in the house of another person willing to accept them and to give the necessary attention. Such schemes, even though numerically small, have proved their worth.

The pattern of the hospital population is changing, for more of the general hospital beds, as well as the out-patient clinics, are being occupied by elderly patients; there are also 58,000 chronic sick beds, equivalent to 1·3 per thousand population or 10·9 per thousand population aged 65 or more. Out of these chronic sick beds, which are sited mainly in the former municipal hospitals, have developed geriatric units which exist to ensure that the patient receives expert diagnosis, the best medical and nursing attention, and effective rehabilitation; ninety such units exist in Britain, including two within the curtilage of teaching hospitals. Although the average period of occupancy of a bed is six months, it is reduced to about forty days if the long-term cases are excluded; these, perhaps 10 per cent of the admissions to geriatric units, do not respond to treatment but require long-term nursing care and medical supervision. There is no doubt that the geriatric unit with its emphasis on accurate diagnosis and energetic rehabilitation makes effective use of hospital beds and gives hope and encouragement to the elderly patients. Some units favour geriatric out-patient clinics primarily for the initiation of treatment of those patients awaiting admission and for the continued supervision of those recently discharged; a few units have established 'day hospitals' within their curtilage which aim to prevent or retard mental and physical deterioration and thus diminish the pressure on hospital beds; they tend to select patients with signs of mental confusion, for whom they usually provide a midday meal, supervision, physiotherapy and occupational therapy. The physician in charge of the geriatric unit is concerned with the diagnosis and treatment of his patients, and he develops considerable knowledge and experience of the sociological factors influencing disease in the elderly and of the contributions to be made by the other services outside the hospital. There is often a waiting list for chronic sick beds, and the physician usually finds that domiciliary visits to the patients are justified in order to assess priorities, to exclude those who would benefit from other arrangements, and to acquaint himself with the patient's own home conditions; perhaps half of such patients are found not to require hospital admission. The effectiveness of a geriatric unit is assisted by having access to all diagnostic facilities and to the ready availability of physiotherapy and occupational therapy. There is no doubt that many units suffer by their isolation from general hospital beds, and particularly the teaching hospitals; the medical student has only a vague concept of chronic sickness, and McKeown's[6] plea for a balanced hospital community is very timely. In the last ten years the King Edward's Hospital Fund has established twelve 'Homes for the Aged Sick' in the London area; each of these is connected with a geriatric unit, and accepts patients discharged from the unit for the purpose of continuing their rehabilitation before their return to independent life at home.

A similar picture can be found in the mental hospitals. About 20 per cent of the admissions are elderly patients, and about a third of the in-patients are in that age group, mostly women. It is generally believed that, although there is no evidence of wrongful certification, many of these patients could equally well be treated in the general hospitals. The Society of Medical Officers of Health, in their evidence to the Royal Commission on Mental Health, stated that only about 20 per cent of elderly patients to whom local authority mental health officers are called are sufficiently disturbed to need treatment in a mental hospital. In the mental hospitals of one hospital region it has been estimated that 20 per cent of their elderly patients, mostly female, were fit to live elsewhere, either at home or in welfare accommodation. The popular opinion that the admission of an elderly patient to a mental hospital allows of no return is fallacious; only one-fifth of such admissions remain in hospital at the end of a year, while two-fifths will have been discharged. Ideally, except for those who need urgent and immediate treatment in a mental hospital or who require admission for their own protection or for the protection of others, the aged disturbed patient should first be admitted to a general hospital or to a geriatric unit, where his mental condition can be assessed, before his final destination is decided.

The Government Actuary in consultation with the Registrar General forecasts a considerable increase in the number of old people during the next two decades; their number and proportion may then remain static, but further unforeseen advances in medicine could easily alter the picture. It might be assumed, therefore, that the demands for institutional treatment or care would become more urgent, but this may prove an over-simplification. The general improvement in health may reduce the institutional needs of younger people and thus release more beds for the elderly; and at the same time the elderly of the future may themselves prove healthier and more robust. An analysis of hospital patients on the night of the Census of 1951 has encouraged Abel Smith and Titmuss[7] to suggest that the higher marriage rates in recent decades and the fall in the proportion of marriages broken by death could influence the picture; their analysis showed that the proportion of married men and women patients was small, and that most of the hospital beds occupied by elderly patients, including those in mental hospitals, were filled by the single, the widowed, and the divorced—and the Government Actuary's estimate of the number of single people in

C. A. Boucher

the population during the next quarter-century shows no significant increase.

While many people in their sixties and seventies still make a substantial contribution to the wealth of the country which is of benefit to their physical and mental health, some become very frail, and ill health and social breakdown must be regarded as a risk and challenge; much of this breakdown could be prevented if the signs and symptoms were detected at an earlier stage, and appropriate action taken. More thought needs to be given to the preservation of health in middle age, and more advice on adaptation to change and on preparation for retirement, for a sudden break in routine at an advanced age can rapidly, particularly in men, precipitate physical and social breakdown. Most local authorities and general practitioners recognize the importance of preservation of health and prevention of disease, and some local authorities have taken the practical step of establishing advisory health clinics for old people; although these clinics deal only in small numbers, it is hoped that they will begin to attract younger people of middle age. The developing strength of the social services is an indication of the demands made by the dependent sections of the population. The contention that old people should be able to live in their own homes for as long as possible, even with considerable assistance from general practitioners, local authority services, and voluntary organizations, must be regarded as right, for there is no doubt that in most cases the health and the happiness and stability of the old person depends on the maintenance of his independence; but this contention can only prove acceptable if it is appreciated that it will probably mean the provision of sufficient housing suitable for the aged, an effective system of supporting domiciliary services, and, perhaps, substitute occupations for those who have retired.

REFERENCES

1. Droller, H. (1959) *Med. Pr.*, **241**, 162.
2. Her Majesty's Stationery Office (1956) Cmd. 9663.
3. H.M.S.O. (1959) Cmd. 737.
4. H.M.S.O. (1959) Cmd. 806.
5. *Old Age in the Modern World.* International Association of Gerontology: Third Congress. London, 1954. London: Livingstone.
6. McKeown, T. (1958) *Lancet*, **i**, 701.
7. Registrar General (1955) *Quarterly Return for England and Wales*, no. 428, Fourth Quarter, 1955, Appendix B.
8. Registrar General (1958) *Statistical Review of England and Wales for 1958.* Part II.
9. Ruck, S. K. (1959) *The Times*, 9 June, 1959, p. 11.

The Social Medicine of Old Age

SUGGESTIONS FOR FURTHER READING

AMULREE, LORD (1951) *Adding Life to Years.* London: National Council of Social Service.

Committee on the Economic and Financial Problems of the Provision for Old Age (1954) *Report.* London: H.M.S.O., Cmd. 9333.

HOBSON, W. (1956) *Modern Trends in Geriatrics.* London: Butterworth.

HOWELL, T. H. (1953) *Our Advancing Years.* London: Phoenix.

SHELDON, J. H. (1948) *Social Medicine of Old Age.* London: Oxford Univ. Press.

SHENFIELD, B. E. (1957) *Social Policies for Old Age.* London: Routledge.

Survey of Services Available to the Chronic Sick and Elderly, 1954–55. London: H.M.S.O., Reports on Public Health and Medical Subjects no. 98 (1957).

TOWNSEND, PETER (1957) *Family Life of Old People.* London: Routledge.

WALKER, KENNETH (1952) *Commentary on Age.* London: Cape.

WELFORD, A. T. (1958) *Ageing and Human Skill.* London: Oxford Univ. Press.

D. ASPECTS OF SOCIOLOGY

Sociological questions are also discussed in Chapters 5, 6 and 11.

26

URBAN SOCIOLOGY

Ruth Glass

I

TO the traveller into the area of the social sciences a prospectus of sociology may well look rather like the large noticeboard of Departures at Waterloo Station. He will find a long list—from A, the sociology of Aachen beer cellars, to Z, the sociology of Zen Buddhism. He will be given directions, as perhaps under F: 'For Family, sociology of, see Storchentreu and Mischpotch, Vol. IX; change at Kinship.' And below, under H: 'For Humour, sociology of, see O'Tenterhook and Greulich; stop at Satire.' But the traveller will usually not be told that the destinations to the many different sociologies thus indicated are fictitiously precise; and that, in any case, the journeys to them often run on parallel tracks.

It is worth while, however, to remind ourselves from time to time that a catalogue of disparate 'sociologies' does not make much sense. Sociology in the plural is a contradiction in terms. While some distinctions between various branches of social inquiry are technically useful or convenient, so long as they are used just for the sake of convenience, a rigid segmentation in the study of society is antisociological.

This reminder, though a truism, is unavoidable, especially in an introduction to the subject of 'urban sociology'. For in fact there is no such subject with a distinct identity of its own. The term 'urban sociology' is merely a verbal umbrella, conventionally held over a heterogeneous range of studies, dealing in different ways and in different places with different aspects, individual or general, of urban

481

structure and development. Such studies can be regarded as being loosely interrelated. But they also increasingly diverge from one another as separate, specialized types of investigation.

In a conventional primer of sociology, we should, to begin with, include under the heading of 'urban sociology' all sorts of studies in an urban setting, dealing with social phenomena, which typically appear, or which are particularly noticeable, in that setting; or which may be conditioned, influenced, or modified by that setting. In other words, the investigation of anything that exists in towns—be it a social group, institution, organization, or problem, a social structure or any of its parts—can be included in that list, irrespective of whether such investigation is extensive or intensive, local or comparative. Accordingly the list ranges from the classic large-scale urban surveys of poverty (in which quantitative and descriptive methods are combined) to minute intensive inquiries into the shopping habits, kinship patterns, or neighbourly relations of a few families.

While in theory such a list is an endless one, in practice several classifiable sub-branches of study have developed, in the wake of practical problems, brought about or revealed by urbanization; and also in response to shifting foci of academic interest in the social sciences.

Thus primarily in terms of their approach, which also largely determines their scale, we can roughly distinguish a few categories of inquiry, though the divisions between them are by no means hard and fast.

First, there is the policy-oriented type of urban survey, focused on needs for social reform within or throughout the urban scene—on matters such as employment; standards of living; housing; nutrition; social services; delinquency; and other aspects of social disorganization. Such surveys are concerned with the incidence, configuration, and distribution of specific problems, for the explicit purpose of contributing to the formulation of social policies, and for the incidental purpose of advancing concepts and methods of social investigation. Their range is usually that of a large city or metropolitan area (though some comparative studies of this kind are also available). Consequently, their main media of presentation are statistical and cartographic.

The early pioneering surveys of this kind (from the late 19th century until the 1930s) were generally far-reaching both in terms of geographical area and subject matter, looking at the panorama of urban groups and institutions with the object of identifying those aspects which urgently required practical reform.* More recently, a second

* The major surveys of this type were carried out in this country. These are: Charles Booth (*ed.*), *Life and Labour of the People in London* (17 vols, and maps), 1892–1903. (An earlier version of the first of these three series was published under the title *Life and Labour of the People*, 2 vols, and maps, 1889–91.) Smith,

Urban Sociology

category of urban inquiry (though still closely akin to the first) has developed. Surveys of the policy-oriented type have become increasingly specialized, in keeping with the growing ramification both of social services and research techniques. Thus there is now a number of sub-branches, dealing with particular aspects of education, town planning, public health, and social pathology. While the parentage of such studies is quite clear, and their theatre of investigation is usually an urban one, they are establishing separate families of their own, and could, therefore, be labelled either as 'urban sociology', or in terms of their diverse specializations (such as criminology or sociology of education).

A similar, though equally unimportant, border dispute might also be carried on with reference to the classification of studies of minority groups and race relations. These subjects—like those of internal migration, social disorganization and poverty, to which they are related—have conventionally been included under the heading of urban sociology since they have become prominent in the course of urbanization, and have been investigated largely in the urban environment. And studies of minority groups and race relations are also generally motivated by a positive interest in social policy—the policy of *status quo* or social change—even if their interest is not as unequivocal as that of the general or specialized social surveys mentioned. However, while social research on racial and ethnic groups usually has an urban address and close colleagues in other urban fields, it is also associated with other branches of sociology (in particular, with those of social stratification and group behaviour) as well as with other disciplines of the social sciences—with social psychology, anthropology, and history.

A further branch, conventionally included under the heading of urban sociology, is that of community studies, which has quite a number of sub-branches, including those concerned with neighbourhoods and primary groups in particular urban localities. Though this

---

H. L. (*ed.*), *The New Survey of London Life and Labour*, 9 vols., 1930–5. Rowntree, B. S., *Poverty—a Study of Town Life*, 1901. (This survey of York has two sequels, published in 1942 and 1951.) Jones, D. C., *The Social Survey of Merseyside*, 3 vols., 1934. In addition, there are a number of similar, though less voluminous, surveys of British towns—of Middlesbrough (1907); West Ham (1907); Tyneside (1928); Southampton (1931 and 1934); Sheffield (1931–3); Brynmawr (1934); Plymouth (1935); Edinburgh (1936); Bristol (1938) Oxford (1938–40). The example of the classic British surveys has also been followed in the twenties and thirties in other countries—as shown, for example, by the survey of Pittsburgh in the United States and by a massive, and in many respects exceptional, study of the Prague region (Ulrich, Z., *Sociologische Studien zur Verstädterung der Prager-umgebung*, 1938). Since the end of the inter-war period the comprehensive urban surveys in Great Britain have been focused on problems of housing, town planning, and local administration rather than on those of poverty and employment.

branch, like others, is heterogeneous, it has a common denominator, in so far as it represents the application of the anthropological approach to small segments of contemporary urban society. Thus studies of this kind are generally focused on questions of face-to-face relationships within a small circle; their range is a narrow one; their methods are intensive and descriptive rather than quantitative. (And whenever quantification is attempted, this is bound to be a hazardous enterprise, in view of the restriction of scale.) In all these respects, and not least by virtue of its usual detachment from significant issues of social policy, this section of urban sociology differs from the policy-oriented or policy-interested types of urban social survey and research.*

There is one, rather rare, variant of community studies, however, which is only very superficially related to the rest. In a few exceptional cases, the investigation of communities has been broad in scope and intention: a particular city or town has been explored as a microcosm of society, of culture and of social transformation, actual and potential.†

There is yet another quite distinct group of urban sociology (though it does have affinity to the branch of policy-oriented surveys). This group of studies does not deal only with social phenomena in the urban setting, but also, and indeed primarily, with the setting itself. It is its object to investigate the structure and types of urbanism and urbanization—in particular places or comparatively; or, again by particular and general analysis combined. In a sense this is the most important group of urban sociology; and yet it takes up very little space in the literature; indeed its influence has been declining. Although, in principle, this group might have many branches, in practice it consists of a few individual exponents, following diverse ways, though with similar intentions. Their products include historical, statistical, and socio-ecological studies, ranging in type from Max Weber's *The City* to the work of the Chicago urban sociologists in the twenties.‡

* The accent is on 'significant' issues of policy. Quite often, some interest is expressed in practical issues though these appear to be rather peripheral ones, especially as they seem to be selected at random, without a stated framework of priorities.

† The classic examples of this type, which have few successors, are, first of all, that of Friedrich Engels, *The Condition of the Working Class in England* (1892). And then again, in quite a different vein, that of the two Middletown books by Robert and Helen Lynd: *Middletown—A study in American culture* (1929); and *Middletown in Transition—A study in cultural conflicts* (1937).

‡ So far there has been no single distinguished contribution to the structural analysis of urbanism in this country, though there is incidental material of this kind in the *avant-garde* of British urban social surveys; and these have also been a stimulus to the studies in social ecology of the Chicago group. However, a statistical study of urban typology is now available: C. A. Moser and Wolf Scott, *British Towns—A statistical study of their social and economic differences*, 1961. This

Urban Sociology

While so brief a tour into the territory of urban sociology is by no means an exhaustive one, it does indicate that in this field the demarcation between historical, statistical, anthropological, geographical, and sociological contributions is usually very blurred. In fact, there is not much sense in bothering with such borderlines: it is not only, inevitably, difficult to define the division of labour between different disciplines of the social sciences, but also to distinguish clearly between urban sociology as such and its source materials—which include data of scholarly and administrative origin, as well as novels and social reportage. Is social pastiche, for example, a part of sociological literature, or does it only deserve that status when it is dressed up with anthropological jargon and a few footnotes? How should the work of writers of the British 19th-century social protest group, that of Henry Mayhew and of some contemporary American journalists, be classified, as compared with that of academic (though less vigorous and less widely travelled) tourists in urban byways?

II

What then is 'sociology'? And what is—or rather what is not—urban? We shall probably find it even more difficult to answer the second question than the first. And indeed it is obvious at once that although the term 'urban sociology' has its uses, as a shorthand device, in an index of sociological literature, it cannot possibly denote a clearly delimited category of social study. Matters urban are so characterized by contrast with matters rural: both are parts of the same continuum.* Consequently, urban and rural sociology also belong to one continuum and should be merged: the distinction between these two sections is an artificial and usually an unhelpful one. It is, therefore, occasionally discarded in professional discussion; a single subject, 'urban-rural sociology', is considered, not a pair, made up of two 'sociologies'.

But even this sort of notional combination is no longer adequate when societies, for various reasons and in their various ways, become highly urbanized. In the course of this development cities spread out;

---

provides the necessary basis for further sociological inquiry. The best introduction to the work of the Chicago group is a collection of essays: Robert E. Park, E. W. Burgess, R. D. McKenzie, *The City*, 1925. The outstanding products of this school are: E. W. Burgess (*ed.*), *The Urban Community*, 1926 (which includes a famous essay by Robert E. Park on 'The urban community as a spatial pattern and a social order'); Louis Wirth, *The Ghetto*, 1929; H. W. Zorbaugh, *The Gold Coast and the Slum*, 1929; Franklin Frazier, *The Negro Family in Chicago*, 1932.

* It is true that we could imagine a science fiction world which is wholly urban, but then this characterization could only be maintained so long as memories of rural physical and social conditions survive.

towns and countryside merge; traditional differences between their physical, social, and cultural features become blurred. And it may also be found that assumptions about the historical or actual existence of such differences were erroneous. In such circumstances, when urbanism itself expands, rapidly and dramatically, it is hardly feasible any longer to demarcate the specific area of urban sociology (or that of urban-rural sociology). It would then be quite unrealistic to attempt to do so.

Thus in a highly urbanized country such as Great Britain, the label 'urban' can be applied to almost any branch of current sociological study. In the circumstances, it is rather pointless to apply it at all.

The process of urban diffusion occurred in Britain throughout the 19th century and has been steadily accelerated in the 20th.* Already in 1911, almost 80 per cent of the British population lived in areas classified as urban; since then this proportion has remained almost constant.† Moreover, in occupational terms Britain has been for long even more thoroughly urbanized: in 1901 only just under 8 per cent of the occupied population were working in agriculture, forestry, and fishery; by 1951, this proportion had dropped to just under 5 per cent. And urban diffusion has been as striking in the cultural sphere as in the territorial and occupational sphere.

It would not be appropriate to speak of a homogeneous national culture of Britain. But neither is it appropriate any longer to speak, in general, of a rural, as distinct from an urban, culture. The cities draw workers from suburbs, from exurbia, and from even more remote hinterlands. Holidays with pay and the greatly increased speed and provision of public and private transport have resulted in a frequent exchange of visits between town and country. The same media of communication reach everywhere; the same films, the same national and regional newspapers, radio and television programmes are received everywhere. The same chain stores which serve urban customers have become accessible to rural customers; the same branded goods displayed in city supermarkets are also bought in village stores. The National Health Service is ubiquitous. Differences between the educational opportunities of urban and rural populations—though not those of the various social classes among those populations—have narrowed considerably. And all this has, of course, also brought about a good deal of similarity in urban and rural modes of thought, expression, and

* Urban diffusion may be defined as the spread of urban characteristics and the consequent blurring of differences between urban and rural features. The spread of the various kinds of urban characteristics—physical, occupational, and cultural —does not, however, necessarily occur evenly and jointly.

† The proportions of the population of Great Britain living in urban areas at different periods were as follows: 50 per cent in 1851; 72 per cent in 1891; 78 per cent in 1911; 80 per cent in 1931, 1951 and 1961.

behaviour. In most cases, and in many respects, distinctions between urban and rural characteristics have become rather faint: it is the regional distinctions which are clearly noticeable at first acquaintance; it is the class distinctions which are paramount.

Similar symptoms of urban diffusion are visible in many industrialized countries of the world, East and West, though there is, apparently, no other country as yet in which this development has been so dominant, and is already so far advanced, as it is in Britain. It is only in Britain, by virtue of her geography, history, and socio-political structure, that urban diffusion is, in a sense, so 'single-minded'. For it is only here that the various factors in such diffusion—urbanization in physical, occupational, and in cultural terms—converge, reinforce one another, and thus operate simultaneously almost everywhere in the British Isles. In most other industrialized countries—in the United States, for example—one or more of these factors operate, but not to the same degree and in the same combinations throughout the nation. And in such countries, these factors may also have to compete with other forces in the national situation, as with conflicts of interest between regions, resulting from their unequal development, especially in a federal system of government. Thus while in those countries, too, the trend towards urban diffusion is unmistakable, it is there more qualified than it is in Britain.

However, despite the variations in the contemporary processes of urban diffusion in the prosperous, industrialized areas of the world, there is one characteristic feature which is visible in all such areas. The same paradox is apparent: the attempt to contain urbanism, or even to escape from it, leads to the spread of urbanism. It is not that the cities themselves reproduce themselves, multiplying in their own city-like forms; it is not that landscapes are transformed into townscapes. Instead, large numbers of the population who previously lived, and who continue to work, in cities are dispersed; and so are many urban functions. The countryside is overrun and festooned with ribbons of pseudo-rural habitations. New towns, or new parts of towns, are made in the same fashion: they, too, have neo-rustic neighbourhood units.

Thus in fact a new configuration of settlements is emerging: most strikingly in the metropolitan regions of Tokyo, of London, of Los Angeles, and along the Eastern seaboard of the United States. Such a metropolitan region is a sprawling expanse, neither town nor country, and here and there submerging the remnants of both. It is so vast and undifferentiated that traces of nucleation are obscured; it appears to be featureless; monotonous; without contours. To anyone not yet used to it, it looks like the chaos of a new order.

It is clear that such conurbations do not reflect a rural revival, despite all their anxious attempts to achieve a semi-rural look. They are the

Ruth Glass

habitat of populations with urban occupations, within the spheres of influence of urban media of communication. Thus the phenomenon which these conurbations represent is undoubtedly that of urban diffusion.

All sorts of names have been invented to characterize the new ranges of suburbia and exurbia, which become whole regions in their own right, dwarfing their parent cities and extinguishing the individual identities of previous settlements along their path. For they cannot be described simply as combinations of urban and rural settlements, or just as an intermediate type. They are a new species; they show that we have to find new terms of reference. Indeed, it has been one of their main effects to obliterate distinctions between specific 'urban' and 'rural' characteristics, the existence of which had been taken for granted.

Elsewhere in the world, in the 'underdeveloped' countries, the blurring of such distinctions is visible also, though for different reasons. In any case, in such countries, Western classification in terms of a simple dichotomy—urban versus rural—is clearly out of place. (That this has probably for long been inadequate in the West, too, is being discovered only slowly in retrospect.)

Every single aspect of life in most of the expanding cities of Asia, Africa, and Latin America—their physical structure, their economy and culture—has dual characteristics, both urban and rural (quite apart from the fact that such characteristics are anyhow highly complex and diverse). There are genuine villages within these cities, whose people raise cattle and poultry, and sell milk and dairy products in the nearby markets. In other parts of the city, too, families keep livestock, just as they would in the countryside. Cows, buffaloes, donkeys, goats, and, occasionally, camels wander through the streets of workshops and bazaars. Cottage crafts and industries are at home in towns and villages. Any one quarter and any one family may carry out both agricultural and non-agricultural kinds of work in close proximity. Any one man may have both types of occupation, either simultaneously or successively. Most important, a substantial proportion of the population of such cities is in origin a rural population, with dual allegiance to town and country, and sometimes even with dual roots.

There are not only daily journeys to work in the city as in the industrialized countries of the West. There are also seasonal and occasional migrations. Men come to work in the cities for varying periods, often leaving their families behind. And even those who settle in or near urban areas retain their rural ties. Inevitably, these rapidly growing cities are peopled, to a considerable extent, by first generation immigrants from the countryside.

There is thus interaction, and even fusion, of urban and rural influences. Just because the cities are, so to speak, bi-cultural, presenting both urban and rural characteristics, the villages are drawn into the urban catchment area. A good deal of rural expenditure is dependent upon urban earnings, however scant. When the villagers listen to the tales of returning migrants or urban settlers—to first-hand, second-hand or third-hand tales—they get a share, if only vicariously, of new experiences and images. And the same happens when rural people vote in state and national elections; and also when they become acquainted —directly or indirectly, favourably or unfavourably—with a new network of social services and economic planning policies.

Thus as the industries of Asian and African countries expand, and as their cities grow in number, in area and population, both as permanent settlements and as camping grounds, the urban frontier is pushed far beyond municipal boundaries. Industrial and urban growth generates a trend towards urban diffusion. This has, of course, happened before elsewhere. But in the now advancing countries, urban diffusion is bound to be accelerated because it happens at this particular period of history.

The people in the cities and villages of such countries are not only within the spheres of influence of their own regions and nations; nor are they confined to a particular stage in their domestic calendar of development. They are also, though not all of them are aware of it as yet, citizens of the latter part of the 20th century. They may never have had piped water and electric light; they may use primitive tools and trade by barter. But they also belong to the period of the beginnings of space travel. Their horizon is not restricted to that of their own streets and fields.

The coexistence of different stages of history in their lives is perhaps most strikingly demonstrated by their spectacular population increase— the product of a far more rapid decrease of mortality than of fertility. It is the apparatus of the 20th century that is lengthening their life expectation. Many of these people themselves may never acquire sufficient knowledge to comprehend even the rudiments in the advance of modern science and technology. But they are caught up in that advance in many different ways. Before long they will learn that such knowledge is available and that progress can be made. Indeed, their own political and scientific élites are entirely at home in the nineteen-sixties, often more so than their counterparts in the 'developed' countries.*

When Britain was industrialized in the 19th century, time travel forward was an impossible expedition. At that period, the differences between the economic and technological conditions of major areas of

* Although (or perhaps because) it has become a cliché to speak of the startling coexistence of different stages of history in underdeveloped countries, this point is one which not only can bear repetition, but which needs to be repeated, whenever any aspect of their development is discussed. For it is doubtful whether the significance and implications of this coexistence are as yet fully realized.

the world were neither as large nor as dramatic as they are now.* There
was then no Soviet Union or United States of the mid 20th-century type
to serve as demonstrations of potential divergent routes. China, India,
Ghana, Nigeria, and the other now advancing countries are not so
handicapped. They have external data for comparisons and anticipa-
tions: there is a new dimension in their development.

It is this new dimension above all which distinguishes the current
movements towards industrialization and urbanization in the ex-colonial,
poor territories from those which occurred earlier in the now prosperous
territories. In a sense, the whole world has become a metropolitan area:
more obviously interdependent than ever before; governed by urban
influences in the spheres of international trade and politics, in technology and culture. The process of urban diffusion is indeed a global
one, though varied in its pace and pattern.†

III

Any sketch, however oversimplified, of types of urbanization in the
world today is an indispensable opening for a discussion of urban
sociology. For even such a sketch indicates that the subject is wide
open, without limits; and that, therefore, the adjective 'urban' is an ana-
chronistic one when applied to the noun 'sociology'. No doubt, the conventional division of labour in the study of societies needs to be revised.

More important, in practical terms, is the great variety of themes for
sociological inquiry, which are suggested by the diverse manifestations
of urban diffusion. So far these have only been sporadically investigated.
If they were pursued systematically, urban sociology, as a textbook
category, would presumably vanish. Instead, most of the branches of
inquiry grouped under that name might merge with a much wider field
—that of the 'sociology of development' (to use another current, but
more promising, label). Thus investigations of the manifold aspects of
urbanism and urbanization would have a better chance of being comparative, and would also become more closely linked than hitherto with
the examination of the levers of social change and their cumulative

* In the past this was true also when other countries, with the exception of
Japan, became industrialized. At no time previously has there been so obvious
and so wide a development gap between different areas of the world.

† There are, of course, many more variants of that process than have been
indicated here; for example, that of planned urban diffusion, the deliberate
decentralization of urban population, industry, and commerce. Urbanization in
cultural terms can, moreover, also be brought about, paradoxically, through
planned rural diffusion when (as in Israel) urban people establish rural communities and take up agricultural occupations. And again in some parts of the
world (as in Turkey, for instance) the first stage of urban diffusion may be that of
'articial urbanization', when communities with predominantly rural characteristics become towns in name by being given the status of urban administrative units.

effects—that is, with studies of social institutions; of social stratification; of communications; with political sociology; with demography; and, generally, with social history. All these branches now overlap and, in fact, have common themes. But they could collaborate more productively if such themes, which are indeed inter-disciplinary and international, were made more explicit.

Of course, the actual social developments, and especially the attempts to control such developments, demonstrate the need for integration in the study of social change. But there are also counteracting tendencies; and there is always a time lag in recognition.

Thus so far the conventional boundaries between the various 'sociologies' have been maintained or even accentuated. New boundaries have been drawn. Urban sociology, in particular, has on the whole become more parochial, both in terms of the aspects and the territory covered, than it was at an earlier period when German philosophical and historical sociologists, as well as French sociological historians (Marx and Engels, Max Weber, Sombart, and Pirenne) were direct or indirect contributors to the subject. Hence the current bibliographies of sociology *per se* (on both sides of the Atlantic as well as in other parts of the world) do not as yet reveal a widespread, systematic concern with manifestations of urban diffusion, and with their causes and consequences, on an international scale.*

This gap can be attributed to a number of reasons, several of which are particularly relevant in the present context.

First, urbanization has brought about a chain of practical problems —of poverty, of employment, of housing, of social pathology. These problems have called for urgent attention; and they have been chiefly investigated on the local scale, though they would be also subject to international comparisons within a wider framework of development experience. A considerable part of the literature of urban sociology in all countries which have such a literature is, therefore, devoted to practical local inquiries: to local social surveys, originating from the description of the panorama of urban poverty; and to inquiries into special aspects, such as crime, race relations, public health, and nutrition, in an urban setting. As Britain was the first country in recent history to feel the pangs of urbanization, it was here that a great deal of the pioneer work of this branch of social investigation, focused on particular aspects of social policy, was done. And although, in sociology generally, direct concern with social policy has everywhere been rather pushed aside by a pseudo-scientific, pseudo-sophisticated search for

---

* It is in the field of sociology, especially, that the lack of concern with processes and consequences of urban diffusion is so marked. In several other fields—those of town planning, public administration, and journalism—such matters are very much discussed, though not comparatively, on the international scale.

scholarly purity, the practical, policy-committed investigators have also found new recruits. Comprehensive local social surveys or studies of urban social ecology are nowadays rarely attempted (at least in Britain and the United States).* But the catalogue of investigations into special aspects of direct interest to local policy and administration has become longer and more diversified. (For example, inquiries relevant to town planning have been added to the list.) In some respects, interests have thus been widened, though at the expense of increasing specialization, and also of local 'fixation' in the scope of social inquiry.

The second reason for the lack of systematic, comparative study of urban diffusion is related to the first. This reason, or rather complex of reasons, is an obvious one: there has been a reluctance to study modern urbanism fully because there has been a reluctance to come to terms with it. In Britain, anti-urbanism was already a traditional attitude before the new industrial towns of the 19th century grew up. Since then this attitude has snowballed and has also become influential abroad, notably in the United States.†

The troubles of 19th and 20th century urbanization as experienced on the local and national levels have been, and still very largely are, uppermost in many people's minds. The early formative stages of large-scale urbanization during that period have been invariably the by-product of uncontrolled (or only partly controlled) industrialization within a capitalist economy. And *laissez-faire* urban growth is ugly and painful; conducive to social disorganization, but also, with its 'massed millions', a stage setting for potential organized social transformation. This latter image, in particular, used to be predominant among all those devoted to the maintenance of the established social order: large cities were disliked and feared because they were regarded as the training centres of social rebellion. And often they were indeed just that. Although the acute fear has evaporated, the dislike has persisted and percolated into many social strata, especially in Britain and in the United States. Moreover, when dislike of industrial cities has led to their neglect, they have become self-fulfilling prophecies of gloom, thus setting off a new chain reaction of resentment. It is this cumulative anti-urbanism which has been to a considerable extent responsible for the formidable conurbations, dressed up in fake rusticity, which are still growing around the national and provincial capitals of the prosperous industrial countries. And of course their growth brings about new troubles and new animosity.

* In several other countries, however, such studies are being developed. This is so in some places in Europe, notably in France, and also in India, where there is a growing literature of urban social surveys.

† But recently, especially in Britain, there have been definite signs of reactions against anti-urbanism, though it is still too early to say how effective these are likely to be.

Urban Sociology

All this—quite apart from lingering ancient memories of oppressive urban systems—adds up to a long sequence of emotional and ideological resistance against urbanization. And while such resistance has not prevented urban expansion, but on the contrary has helped to promote expansion, it has had a share in preventing a comprehensive, comparative analysis of the unpalatable subject.

The social sciences have not been immune to anti-urbanism. In their case, this attitude is reflected in various ways. There is not only a reluctance to give up the strait-jacket of conventional, dichotomous categorization—rural versus urban—although this never was, and is certainly no longer, adequate in disentangling the complex permutations of social phenomena. There is also, associated with this kind of rigidity, a persistent, though not necessarily explicit, preference for the small-scale (*alias* rural) versus the large-scale (*alias* urban) type of settlement, social group, institution, and organization. It is a preference both for the small-scale object and for the small-scale study of small objects. The only thing which is not small in this department of studies is its output.

Thus a considerable branch of urban sociology, a fashionable and a fertile one, has developed in which various tendencies, associated with anti-urbanism, are combined. This branch is that of community studies (including microscopic investigations of primary groups) which has already been mentioned. The main theme of such studies is usually that of the social ritual, and of social roles, within small groups.

No doubt there is a legitimate interest in such inquiries (quite apart from the fact that they are popular because they provide the reader with vicarious 'neighbouring'). The interest would be enhanced if such inquiries belonged to broader schemes of research, and thus could achieve at least some measure of comparability. Usually, despite the similarity of their subject matter and its treatment, inquiries of this kind are conducted sporadically, each within its own little principality, so that their findings are neither subject to generalizations, nor illuminate generalization derived from other, more extensive data.

But in the present context, it is less relevant to pursue the question how the results of such inquiries can be interpreted than to ask the reason why. How can their purpose be interpreted?

This particular branch of urban sociology is preoccupied with certain defects, or alleged defects, of urbanism—with the concept of anomie; with problems of personal relationships in an urban setting. Attention is focused on such problems, apparently on the assumption (though quite often a tacit one) that these are crucial social problems; and also that it is the 'urban way of life' which is responsible for them; it is that which is believed to have caused depersonalization and anomie.

But is urbanism really the culprit or the scapegoat? Is it not the social system that has created cities in its own image to which problems of

493

Ruth Glass

face-to-face relationships must be ascribed? And how serious are such problems in fact? To what extent do they really exist?

Such questions are neither asked, nor could they be answered, by the 'sociability' section of urban sociology. For sporadic, detailed evidence about personal relationships within individual small communities or primary groups does not, by itself, suffice to evaluate such relationships, nor is it of much help in identifying the impersonal divisive or unifying forces to which such groups are subjected.

Nevertheless, parochialism has remained fashionable for sociological studies within the urban scene; indeed it is the current vogue. And it is this tendency which indicates the third, and most important, reason for the lack of systematic concern with the world-wide phenomena of urban diffusion. Perhaps the social sciences in one part of the world are still preoccupied with the bric-à-brac of their own parlours because urban diffusion has not yet gone far enough to compel them to give their attention to more important problems on the global scale?

This is a very much oversimplified question (although it is intended to be a rhetorical one). For undoubtedly the opposite can be argued: it can be said that parochialism in many spheres has been, and still is, a reaction against, and thus a by-product of, urbanization, nationally and internationally. Of course, it is the inescapable fact of global inter-dependence, with the threats to domestic security which it implies, which makes it so comforting to take refuge, personally and pro-fessionally, in the trivia of introspection. And it is the very fact of global intercommunication which makes Western sociology into a profitable export commodity; and which explains why its fashions (in subjects and methods of study) are copied in countries for which these are hardly suitable without major modifications. Even so, it can also be said that urban diffusion on the global scale is still too limited to have the capacity of counteracting the introverted tendencies effectively: the processes of global interdependence and intercommunication have so far been, and certainly have so far been seen as, one-sided ones, with far more traffic going from the 'developed' to the 'underdeveloped' areas than in the opposite direction, especially in the social sciences.

At some stages, this kind of one-sided traffic—of technical assistance, of sociological tourism, and of occasional slumming in some corner of Asia, Africa, and Latin America—might have been inevitable. The traveller can return from such visits with renewed self-satisfaction, though not necessarily with that sense of participation in the human condition from which the drive towards the understanding of its diverse developments springs. We, from the prosperous countries, have been engaged in advising the poor countries to solve their problems in our terms; we have hardly attempted as yet to understand ours in their terms. (Midtown New York instructs Calcutta on how to arrest her

494

blight. If such instruction were reciprocal, Calcutta might remind New York of the continued growth of blight in uptown Harlem next door.) The time has certainly come when the lack of a genuine dialogue between the West Ends and the East Ends of the world seriously impairs the vision, and the progress in the understanding, of both.

IV

In every respect—those of approach and object, theme and scale, methods and sources—urban sociology is beset by boundary problems. Although most of these are general, perennial problems of the social sciences, they do occur in this branch of sociology in an accentuated form.

There is always a difficulty in demarcating the area of study—the territory both in terms of subject matter and geography. Any line drawn around an object of investigation, or again around, and within, a town, is an arbitrary one. Moreover, arbitrariness tends to be cumulative, as the definition of 'urban' usually is (or at least has to begin and end with) an administrative definition, which is a discretionary one.* The administrative limits of a town are not necessarily its 'natural' limits. Moreover, there are no unequivocal objective criteria for the definition of such 'natural' urban limits. (There will be always many Londons and many Birminghams, irrespective of precise borders drawn by Royal Commissions or socio-geographic surveys.)

All this means that urban sociology finds it even harder to obtain cumulative knowledge than several other branches of sociology: it deals largely with objects that are, or that may well be, only nominally alike. (Canterbury and Merthyr Tydfil, Dover, Durgapur and Port-of-Spain, Durham in England and Durham in North Carolina are all called towns; and there, in many respects, their resemblance ends.) Thus urban sociology is concerned very largely with objects that are not, in fact, comparable, or the comparability of which is very much in doubt.† Even within any one culture, the distinction between an urban

* We have to adhere to the municipal map, however empirical we are in the handling of data for municipal areas, and however much we subdivide and re-arrange municipal data. For such re-grouping can be made understandable only if it is translated in terms of existing administrative divisions. (For example, as a result of an empirical re-definition of London areas, it might be said that Wimbledon, or a section of Wimbledon, is regarded as a part of London.)

† This is so also because the comparability of source materials for urban studies is often more apparent than real, quite apart from the fact that changes in standards of living and similar matters require consequent changes in criteria of assessment (for example, in the definition of a 'poverty line'). In any one country, census definitions, coverage, and accuracy vary over time. In cross-national comparisons, there is the additional complication that like definitions neither mean the same things, nor are recorded with like accuracy, at the same intervals.

Ruth Glass

and a rural area is certainly far vaguer, more variable and more spurious than, for example, the distinction between males and females; or the definitions of social institutions, such as the school, the family, and the law.

Moreover, as it is so difficult to achieve, or to recognize, comparability in urban social studies, it is equally difficult to make the transition from the particular to the general, from an aggregate of concrete, specific findings to the level of their abstract significance. In the nature of things, towns (or slices of urban structure) are studied, and can usually only be studied, in small numbers. And they are also almost invariably, and often inevitably, investigated *ad hoc*: both place and time of inquiry are chosen casually, not systematically; both place and time are out of context; there is neither physical nor historical continuity.* In the circumstances, the social investigator may well be so preoccupied with the baffling, fascinating individuality of the phenomena which he observes, that he will hardly attempt to draw more than obvious, or utterly trivial, general inferences from his material.

Thus altogether in most sections of inquiry now categorized as urban sociology, it is often barely possible to see the wood for the trees; to piece together from a considerable, but amorphous literature of urban studies in particular places at particular moments a coherent account of processes and characteristics, causes and consequences of urbanization. Of course, we are not entirely ignorant about these matters: there are signposts. But in the recent period, especially, these have been contributed more by associated disciplines, by history and demography (and also by plain common sense) than by urban sociology as such.

This is hardly surprising. Just because urban sociology is potentially so vast and inchoate, especially in a period of rapid urban diffusion, it is rather tempting to remain within the local boundary of its interests. It is always possible to retreat behind a domestic hedge or a particular municipal border, and to adhere to a limited sense of kinship and neighbourliness. Indeed, urban sociology can maintain an identity, if rather a vague one, so long as it also maintains a parochial, or even an anti-urban, tendency.

It is this tendency which has been increasingly noticeable in sociological literature. Undoubtedly, it will always be an absorbing pastime to put slices of urban culture under a microscope. It will certainly always be necessary to study cities *per se*; and to investigate specific problems of urbanization for the purpose of making specific proposals for local

* There are hardly any repetitive or longitudinal studies of cities, or parts of cities, or of particular urban phenomena within them. The follow-up of Charles Booth's survey, *Life and Labour of the People in London* (1889–97) by Sir Hubert Llewellyn Smith (1930–35); Rowntree's three surveys of York (1902, 1942, and 1951); and the Lynds' two studies of *Middletown* (1929 and 1937) are exceptions. And even these lack further continuity.

reform. But it is also necessary, though more exacting, to move on from the discrete investigation of particular places and phenomena; to see them in the context of the social systems within which they are located; and, therefore, to study cities both as instances of, and as contributors to, social change. That kind of approach is not committed to the *status quo*; it goes beyond the local periphery in all respects, not least in the formulation of criteria of social development which it requires.

Moreover, if the horizon were thus broadened, attention would be paid equally to the positive as to the negative features of urbanism. The city is both divisive and unifying; it brings about both separation and *rapprochement*. Urbanism is more than a symbol of social interdependence; it can hardly be maintained without a high level of social organization, based on the recognition, implicit or explicit, of mutual social responsibility.

It is the affirmation of such interdependence and mutual responsibility which has been rather lacking in the literature of urban sociology so far. There will have to be a new image of urbanity before the study of urbanism can advance.

BIBLIOGRAPHY

There are several bibliographies which provide useful references to the existing literature of urban sociology, at least in Western countries, though none of these are cross-national and quite up-to-date.

For American material see:

PAUL K. HATT, & ALBERT T. REISS, JR., *Cities and Society: the revised Reader in Urban Sociology*, Glencoe, Ill. 1957. (Bibliography, pp. 827–57.)

For the French, British and Scandinavian literature, see:

Current Sociology, UNESCO, Vol. IV, nos. 1 and 4, 1955. These contain trend reports and annotated bibliographies on urban sociology in France, by P. Chombart de Lauwe (Vol. IV, No. 1); in Great Britain, by Ruth Glass; and in the Scandinavian countries, by John Westergaard (Vol. IV, No. 4).

It is worth while also to consult an earlier 'bibliography of the urban community' by Louis Wirth. This is included in:

ROBERT E. PARK, E. W. BURGESS, & R. D. McKENZIE, *The City*, Chicago, 1925 (pp. 161–228).

For a concise general account of contemporary problems of urbanization in economically underdeveloped areas, see Part II of: UNITED NATIONS, *Report on the World Social Situation*, New York, 1957.

27

RURAL SOCIOLOGY

V. G. Pons

THE broadly distinctive features of farm and village life in the modern
world are so striking that we often tend to think of rural sociology as a
special branch of contemporary empirical sociology. Any attempt to
define the scope and limits of rural sociology in general terms, however,
is fraught with immediate difficulties. The term 'rural', like the term
'urban', has a highly relative and subjective connotation. We can of
course draw up a list of objective physical and demographic criteria on
the basis of which the rural sector of any country or region can be
delimited for practical purposes, but any such definition inevitably
involves drawing a line of division which is to some extent arbitrary.
Moreover, there is no *a priori* reason to expect a definition of 'rural' in
physical and demographic terms to correlate at all closely with 'rural'
as either a social or a cultural type. Nor, for that matter, is there any
justification for thinking of 'rural' as a general type that can be readily
defined in strictly sociological terms.* Most rural sociologists implicitly
recognize these difficulties, and current definitions of the subject are
usually tautologies of the kind 'rural sociology is the sociology of
rural life'.†

* There is, of course, a large theoretical literature on 'types' of societies which
is directly relevant to the theory of rural-urban sociology. The concepts developed
by Maine, Tonnies, Durkheim, and Redfield—to mention only a few of the outstanding figures in this field—have had a far-reaching influence on exploratory
definitions of 'rural' as an ideal-type. But 'rural' none the less remains a broad
descriptive term which cannot readily be translated into a set of definable analytical
concepts.

† Thus, for example, Lynn Smith [23] defines rural sociology as 'the systema-
tized body of knowledge which has resulted from the application of the scientific
method in the study of rural society, its organization and structure, and its
processes'. Similar examples could be quoted from practically every general text
on the subject.

V. G. Pons

To outline the scope and limits of rural sociology, we have, therefore, to do so in terms of the topics which the subject is, by use and wont, considered to cover. In practice, however, this procedure carries its own difficulties, for the recognition accorded to rural sociology as a subject varies between different countries. The main contrast here is between the U.S.A. on the one hand, and Britain, France, and most other European countries on the other. In the U.S.A. there is a long tradition of research on the rural community as an entity, and rural sociology has become firmly established as a major subdivision of empirical sociology. This is reflected in the numerous general texts on rural society, in the regular publication of the journal *Rural Sociology*, in the long-standing practice of giving courses in rural sociology to undergraduate students, and in the existence since 1937 of the Rural Sociological Society. In sharp contrast, in Europe there has up to the present been little systematic investigation into the rural community as such, and we have today no general body of rural sociologists and little literature that would readily pass as rural sociology.

If, then, rural sociology is neither a distinctive discipline capable of definition in abstract terms nor a subject with a conventional individuality even within the urban-industrial countries of the West, there can be little point in attempting a concise general statement on it. Instead, I propose, in the first part of this chapter, to refer briefly to the development of rural sociology in the U.S.A. and to indicate its scope as reflected in general texts in common use in universities and colleges, and then, in the second part, to turn my attention to Britain, reviewing the relevant literature and attempting a brief assessment of the tasks confronting rural sociologists here.

THE DEVELOPMENT AND SCOPE OF RURAL SOCIOLOGY IN THE U.S.A.

The early growth of rural sociology in the U.S.A. was directly fostered by widespread public concern over practical social and economic problems in the countryside.* Both state and church authorities clamoured for systematic studies of rural society, and rural sociology, even as handled in the universities, was inextricably bound up with a general movement of rural reform and betterment. Thus we find that up to the 1920s most of the literature consisted either of factual reports on the conditions of life in rural areas or general dissertations on topics such as 'the decline of the influence of the country church', 'the crisis of the countryside', and 'rural welfare'.

The first general text designed for use in universities and colleges

* For two general accounts of the history of the development of rural sociology in the United States, see [11, 23].

500

appeared in 1913. This book, significantly entitled *Constructive Rural Sociology*,[9] stated categorically that the tasks of the subject were 'to take a full inventory of the conditions of life in rural communities . . . (to) discover their tendencies and deficiencies, map out special problems, and *indicate ways of betterment according to the best ideals of social life*' (my italics).

From the 1920s onwards the literature on rural society became increasingly 'scientific', and in 1929 we find Sorokin and Zimmerman[24] stressing, in the preface to one of the most influential texts yet published on rural sociology, that their 'book does not try to preach and does not bother itself with any evaluation of what is good and bad in rural life'. Following on Sorokin's and Zimmerman's study, however, American rural sociologists by no means abandoned their utilitarian outlook, and practical interests continued to be the mainspring of much social research in the countryside.* Thus we find a number of more recent texts devoting whole sections to methods of effecting change in rural society, and in one well-known symposium, published as recently as 1949, a plea for 'accurate description' and 'scientific analysis' of the rural scene is immediately followed by a strong reminder that 'the primary aim of rural sociology is the improvement of the social conditions of the people on the land'.[26] Since the days of Sorokin's and Zimmerman's self-conscious denial of interest in the good and the bad in country life, however, a growing sophistication has led to an ever-clearer recognition of the distinction between what Sanderson terms 'Rural Sociology as a science' and 'Rural Social Organization as a technology'.[19]

In view of this history of close association between 'academic' and 'practical' interests, between 'research' and 'action', it is not surprising that rural sociology as understood in the U.S.A. has a broad and highly varied content. Here, perhaps more than in any other field, the American sociologist has developed in the image of Robert Park's early conception of what a sociologist should be: . . . 'a kind of super-reporter . . . (reporting) a little more accurately, and in a manner a little more detached than the average . . . (recording) what is actually going on rather than what, on the surface of things, merely seems to be going on'.[17]

To illustrate the broad coverage of American rural sociology, the major topics receiving detailed attention in one or more of five standard textbooks are listed below: [12, 16, 19, 24, 26]

(i) The ecology of the countryside, including the study of types of farming areas, patterns of settlement, and trade and service areas.

* See, for example, [22].

 (ii) The changing social and demographic composition of the rural population.
 (iii) The nature, causes and consequences of rural-urban migration.
 (iv) Rural-urban differentials in demographic composition, in vital processes, and in intelligence, attitudes, and opinions.
 (v) Levels and standards of living in different socio-economic strata.
 (vi) Social relations within locality and associational groups of various kinds.
 (vii) The institutional structure of politics, education, and religion.
 (viii) Marriage, the family, and kinship.
 (ix) Occupational differentiation and social stratification.
 (x) Rural-urban relations and the impact of increasing urbanization on rural society.

This list may well be influenced by the present writer's own biases, for each of the five texts consulted covers such a wide range of topics that any attempt to enumerate their main points of focus is likely to be somewhat subjective. Even allowing for this, however, the list adequately illustrates how rural sociology in the U.S.A. is thought of as the comprehensive description of the rural community.

Those who would work to a narrow conception of sociology as consisting only of the analysis of social relations and social facts *sui generis* may quite understandably protest that much American rural sociology is not sociology at all. Moreover, by far the greater part of the field data gathered and presented as rural sociology in the U.S.A. is not distinctively 'rural'; to write of 'rural sociological theory' or to refer to rural sociology as a 'distinctive discipline', as a number of writers do, is pretentious and misleading. The main achievement of American rural sociologists has been the practical one of presenting a detailed and comprehensive description of rural society within their own country.

THE LITERATURE ON RURAL SOCIETY IN BRITAIN

If the genesis and development of rural sociology in the U.S.A. have been largely influenced by the concern of a nation over the welfare of its rural inhabitants, the absence of any significant literature of rural sociology in Britain can be partly attributed to the failure of a people to recognize the existence of a general problem in the changing but old-established social order of the countryside. In Britain the rural way of life has invariably been extolled as morally and spiritually superior to the urban. Since the earliest days of the Industrial Revolution towns have been viewed as the centres of social disintegration, whereas farm, village, and country house were regarded as the fountain-heads of the nation's moral stamina. Social problems set by the new urban environment roused the public conscience and indirectly gave rise to a large

Rural Sociology

literature of empirical urban sociology,* while the changing rural scene prompted mainly nostalgic and idealistic comment.

The tendency to idealize the countryside is, however, only one of the factors underlying the undeveloped state of rural sociology in Britain. It must be remembered that while public concern over the evils of town life and, later, public recognition of the need to plan urban development, stimulated a great deal of painstaking fact-finding in towns, the absence of a systematic body of urban sociology is an equally characteristic feature of present-day British sociology. The plain fact is that in Britain the existing knowledge of both rural and urban society was built up in an intellectual atmosphere in which little encouragement was accorded to sociology even as a general academic discipline. Thus, in contrast to the situation in the U.S.A., neither rural nor urban sociology flourished. But whereas our factual knowledge of urban social conditions is on the whole concrete and objective, our knowledge of rural life is largely impressionistic and surrounded by a haze of myth and sentiment. As noted by Carrington, 'one can almost speak of a Religion of the Countryside'.[6]

With this brief apology for British rural sociology, let us take stock of what sober literature there is. This literature is so scattered and so varied that it defies any neat and rigid classification, but for working purposes we may usefully distinguish a few very broad categories.

First, there is a substantial body of popular writing clamouring for serious attention to be devoted to the country-side, aiming to debunk the townsman's lingering view of Merrie England, and attempting everyday common-sense characterizations of the changing countryman and the changing village. This is by far the broadest of the categories being distinguished here, and it would be difficult to define precisely; most typically, it consists of realistic commentaries on rural society by laymen with first-hand experience of village life and long records of public service at the level of the local community. Most studies falling in this category date from the pre-war period. As examples we may cite Robertson Scott's outspoken essays on village life in the 1920s,[21] Bourne's attempts to dispel the sentimental view of cottage life in Surrey,[4] and Thomas's assessments of trends of change in 'rural civilization' in Devonshire in the 1930's.[27] In studies of this kind we frequently encounter open value judgements of the 'new' and the 'old' in rural society, and in most cases the authors clearly have an axe to grind. Yet such studies are valuable not only as a general corrective to the mass of nostalgic writing on village life, but also more positively, on account of the inside knowledge they provide on changing attitudes and values in rural society.

* For a discussion of the present state of urban sociology in Britain, see Glass,[10]; also chapter 26 in this volume.

V. G. Pons

Secondly, there are the studies of the demographic composition of the rural population and of rural-urban migration. Since 1801 successive censuses have provided us with adequate data for precise demographic analyses, and there has been considerable comment on the contrasts between the characteristics of the rural and the urban sectors of the population. As the drift to the towns reached its peak in the second half of the nineteenth century, both national and local studies of rural depopulation multiplied, and the whole problem of rural-urban migration has continued to hold the attention of specialists in several fields up to our own day. As a result, this is the one aspect of the changing rural scene on which we have relatively precise and systematic information.*

Thirdly, there are social surveys and community studies conducted with some measure of professional competence. Up to the present time, such studies have been few, and they have varied considerably in their emphases. Early in the century, we had the occasional village study devoted primarily to measuring the poverty of agricultural labourers in the Booth tradition of urban surveys (e.g., [7, 13]). Then we had a number of surveys designed mainly to gather information on the general conditions of life and on the distribution of amenities and services in particular villages or wider rural areas (e.g., [1, 5, 25]). Finally, during the past ten years we have received a few community studies of a more sociological character.[8, 18, 28]

To these three broad categories, we have to add the contributions of the occasional sociologist writing all too briefly on one or other particular aspect of rural social structure (e.g., [14, 15]), as well as the incidental but usually well-informed comments on rural society of a few agricultural economists (e.g., [2, 3]).

If the literature referred to above were our only source of information, knowledge of Britain's rural community would indeed be meagre and haphazard. As is always the case, however, in regard to contemporary society, we know a great deal more than can be acknowledged by referring to particular studies and particular categories of literature. Although the nature of the changing rural scene is largely unanalysed, it is not unobserved or undocumented. Even if we choose to discount fiction, we have a vast amount of information on rural society in newspapers, periodicals, and journals, in various attempts to take stock of the work and the growth of voluntary associations such as Women's Institutes and Young Farmers' Clubs, in county development plans, and in a wide variety of official and unofficial reports on education, the Church, agriculture, local government, and the like. Our understanding of rural society is inadequate not because we have no knowledge of it, but because our knowledge is unsystematic and uncoordinated, and

* For a systematic review of the literature on rural depopulation, see [20].

504

because so few attempts have been made to bring any sociological insight to bear on the explanation of facts which are in themselves commonplace.

THE TASKS OF RURAL SOCIOLOGY IN BRITAIN

What, in the circumstances outlined above, are the appropriate tasks facing rural sociologists in Britain? What, in practical terms, are the kinds of research projects required at the present time? A general answer to these questions may be given by referring to two recent studies.

In his review of the literature on rural depopulation over the past hundred years, Saville[20] has given us a good example of one kind of study which is sorely needed. Beginning with a broad discussion on the historical background to the rural exodus, Saville gives us a detailed summary of the evidence on changing patterns of migration at different periods over the past century and an extremely useful assessment of the main features of the contemporary problem. His study is thus an attempt to co-ordinate a mass of existing knowledge.

We may think of this kind of work as 'stock-taking' research; it does not answer specific sociological problems, but it pinpoints questions that require detailed investigation, it corrects and refines aspects of a total configuration which is generally known, and it places existing knowledge in a perspective which encourages fruitful discussion. Thus, for example, Saville brings much-needed stimulus and direction to the discussion of the decreasing rural-urban differentials in social and demographic composition and to the even wider problem of defining the rural and urban sectors of England and Wales.

As far as the writer is aware, Saville's study is the only one of its kind on rural society in Britain. It is probably no accident that it focuses on demographic data for, as was pointed out above, the characteristics and movements of the rural population have up to the present been the subject of more objective study than other aspects of the changing rural scene. Yet other aspects of rural society, such as the position of the Church in village life and the growth of educational facilities in rural areas, could with equal profit be subjected to systematic reviews of this 'stock-taking' kind even if the basic data are either less plentiful or less satisfactory. We do ourselves a disservice when we refrain from bringing seemingly commonplace knowledge into the kind of systematic order which would allow some measure of sociological interpretation.

A study which gives us a quite different lead is Frankenberg's[8] analysis of the way in which internal feuds and disputes affect the political, associational, and religious life of a small village in North Wales. Unlike either Rees[18] in his study of another Welsh parish or

505

Williams[28] in his account of a village in West Cumberland, Frankenberg is not concerned to present a comprehensive description of the small community where he conducted his researches. Instead, he focuses on a single aspect of the community and attempts to develop a rigorous sociological thesis to explain his observations.

Studies such as those of Rees and Williams are of course useful, and we must recognize that if we had a larger number of straightforward descriptive accounts of this kind we would be in a much better position to generalize about rural social structure in Britain. But Frankenberg's study has a greater potential value. It sets up a thesis capable of being confirmed, refuted, or modified in the future, and such theses are essential if sociologists are to do more than repeat the descriptions of daily life found in fiction. It is for this reason that Frankenberg's study is here singled out as a promising model for future work.

In some respects Frankenberg's and Saville's studies are polar extremes. The one is a minute analysis of field data gathered by an observer participating in small-group situations, the other a close examination of a mass of information accumulated over a century on a nation-wide basis; the one develops a definite thesis, the other seeks to clarify through systematic review. My contention is that both these broad types of studies are urgently required if we are to develop a significant literature of rural sociology in Britain. It is futile to argue for one type against the other. The two are not alternative approaches, and both are equally necessary to give new meaning to the everyday knowledge we already have.

REFERENCES

1. Agricultural Economics Research Institute (1944) *Country Planning: A Study of Rural Problems.* London: Oxford Univ. Press.
2. ASHBY, A. W. (1935) *The Sociological Background of Adult Education in Rural Districts.* London: British Institute of Adult Education.
3. ASHBY, A. W. (1939) 'The Effects of Urban Growth on the Countryside'. *Sociolog. Rev.* **31.**
4. BOURNE, C. (1912) *Change in the Village.* New ed. London: Duckworth, 1955.
5. BRACEY, H. E. (1952) *Social Provision in Rural Wiltshire.* London: Methuen.
6. CARRINGTON, NOEL (1949) Introductory Essay to Bawden, Edward, *Life in an English Village.* London: Penguin.
7. DAVIES, M. (1909) *Life in an English Village: An Economic and Social Survey of the Parish of Corsley in Wiltshire.* London: Unwin.
8. FRANKENBERG, R. (1957) *Village on the Border: A Social Study of Religion, Politics and Football in a North Wales Community.* London: Cohen and West.

Rural Sociology

9. GILLETTE, J. M. (1913) *Constructive Rural Sociology*. New York: Macmillan.
10. GLASS, RUTH (1955) 'Urban Sociology in Great Britain: A Trend Report'. *Curr. Sociol.*, **4** (4).
11. LIVELY, C. E., *et al.* (1938) *The Field of Research in Rural Sociology*. Washington: U.S. Dept. of Agriculture.
12. LOOMIS, C. P., & BEEGLE, J. A. (1950) *Rural Social Systems: A Textbook in Rural Sociology and Anthropology*. New York: Prentice-Hall.
13. MANN, H. H. (1904) 'Life in an Agricultural Village in England'. *Sociological Papers*, vol. 1.
14. MITCHELL, G. D. (1950) 'Social Disintegration in a Rural Community'. *Hum. Relat.*, **3** (3), 1950.
15. MITCHELL, G. D. (1951) 'The Parish Council in the Rural Community'. *Public Administration*, **29**, Winter, 1951.
16. NELSON, L. (1955) *Rural Sociology*. Cincinnati: American Book Co.
17. PARK, R. E. (1950) 'An Autobiographical Note'. In *Race and Culture*. Glencoe, Ill.: Free Press.
18. REES, A. D. (1950) *Life in a Welsh Countryside*. Univ. of Wales Press.
19. SANDERSON, D. (1942) *Rural Sociology and Rural Social Organization*. New York: Wiley.
20. SAVILLE, J. (1957) *Rural Depopulation in Engand and Wales*, 1851–1951. London: Routledge.
21. SCOTT, J. W. ROBERTSON (1925) *England's Green and Pleasant Land*. London: Cape. New ed., Harmondsworth: Penguin, 1949.
22. SIMS, N. C. (1946) *Elements of Rural Sociology*. New York: Crowell.
23. SMITH, T. LYNN (1957) 'Rural Sociology in the United States and Canada: a Trend Report and Bibliography'. *Curr. Sociol.*, **6** (1).
24. SOROKIN, P., & ZIMMERMAN, C. C. (1929) *Principles of Rural-Urban Sociology*. New York: Holt.
25. STEWART, C. (1948) *The Village Surveyed*. London: Arnold.
26. TAYLOR, C. C., *et al.* (1949) *Rural Life in the United States*. New York: Knopf.
27. THOMAS, F. G. (1939) *The Changing Village: An Essay on Rural Reconstruction*. London: Nelson.
28. WILLIAMS, W. M. (1956) *The Sociology of an English Village: Gosforth*. London: Routledge.

28

SOCIAL MOBILITY

D. Lockwood

THE study of social mobility may be defined as the investigation of the causes and consequences of individual or familial movement within a hierarchy of social strata differentiated in terms of social status or social prestige. Changes in the relative positions of whole strata, and geographical mobility, while relevant to the study of social mobility, are not as such central problems of this branch of sociology. In general, the field is relatively unexplored, and most research has concentrated on the measurement of actual rates of mobility within the national community and specific occupational categories. Of the various factors affecting social mobility, most attention has been devoted to the process of educational selection, which, in modern industrial communities, assumes an ever more crucial role in the allocation of individuals to occupations. The social and psychological consequences of social movement constitute another important problem area, but one in which only the most tentative results have been obtained.

Any empirical study of social mobility presupposes a measure of social status, and most studies have in fact been based on some kind of occupational index. The choice of occupation is supported by three considerations. First, that it is closely correlated with those various factors which enter into the determination of social status: income, education, consumption patterns, style of life, and typical social and cultural predispositions of various kinds. Secondly, it has been shown that there is a fairly widespread consensus about the ranking of occupations in a hierarchy of relative social prestige. Thirdly, for purposes of large-scale research, occupation is a convenient, more or less objective, and easily obtainable datum. The use of such an index is not, of course, without its drawbacks, especially for the study of the more subtle aspects of social status and social mobility. Occupational prestige hierarchies do not, for instance, take into account the degree of 'social distance' between types of occupations (such as the pronounced jump between manual 'working class' and non-manual 'middle class' occupations) which is so important for the demarcation of social classes. Nor does occupational mobility necessarily imply social mobility in the sense of social acceptance of the newly arrived, although the degree to which this is so is likely to be important for the social and psychological effects of mobility. But in a field which is still largely uncultivated, a hierarchy of occupational strata, provided that it is differentiated in such a way as to allow for subsequent analysis which takes into account the subtler aspects of social mobility, is a useful initial classificatory device.

Causes of Social Mobility

The problem of who moves where, when, and how, is in principle reducible to the operation of the following sets of factors. Some of these factors are interrelated with one another, and the nature of their combined working cannot be set down in any exact way. However, each may be briefly mentioned in its bearing on social mobility before the discussion turns to the more detailed relationships which research has illuminated. (i) The *occupational structure* affects mobility in two main ways. First, in that the ratio of 'higher' or 'lower' positions sets objective limits to the amount of social movement that could conceivably occur. Secondly, by the degree to which occupations call for highly specific skills or for the application of more diffuse criteria of ability; that is, in so far as the nature of the occupation itself allows for the intrusion of considerations of 'social origins' in the selection of personnel, certain types of jobs are inherently more open to mobile individuals than others. (ii) Given the structure of occupations, and its change over time, the *differential fertility* of the various occupational strata will determine the extent to which these groups are potentially self-replacing in a biological sense; and, therefore, the extent to which, especially at the higher levels where fertility tends to be generally lower, there exists a 'social vacuum' which must be filled by external recruitment. These two factors—occupational structure and occupational fertility—taken together determine the total number of vacancies, and may, through their change, create possibilities of social mobility independently of changes in the means by which such movement is regulated. The index of association[16] between the occupational status of father and son, which compares the actual amount of occupational 'inheritance' with that which would be expected if there were equal probabilities of movement for sons of all social origins, conveniently eliminates the inter-generational effect of changes in the factors just mentioned, and thus indicates the combined influence of those next on the list in making for a stronger or weaker parental-filial tie. (iii) The *structure of educational institutions* increases in importance the more entry into higher occupations demands formal certification, and the more chances of mobility are determined by educational opportunities and performances at an early age. The degree to which access to education is determined by scholastic ability or ability to pay, the way in which different types of educational institutions feed into the occupational system, and the effect of the 'social climate' of the school on the educational performance of pupils from different social origins, are all problems which bear heavily upon the possibility of social movement. (iv) The *distribution of innate abilities* among the different occupational strata of the population, in so far as these abilities are isolable from the effects of varying social environments, determines the supply of talent that is available to the society; and, in so far as careers are open to talent, sets limits to the amount of social mobility that takes place. But since neither of these two assumptions is tenable, the view of social mobility as a process of 'natural selection' is only a very crude approximation to reality. Of the abilities in question, that of general intelligence is of paramount importance; particularly so, since there is a widespread use of tests of intelligence in educational selection. But the exact degree to which such tests measure innate or learned ability is problematic, and raises difficult problems which lie at the frontiers of genetics, psychology, and sociology. For this reason, but also because of the concentration of social research on the distribution of educational opportunity, sociologists have usually taken measured intelligence as a given datum.[4, 18, 28, 30] (v) The *distribution of opportunities* of educational and occupational advancement available to individuals in the various social strata is determined by differences in family income and property and the fairly obvious advantages that result therefrom; but also by such factors as differential knowledge about schools and jobs, and personal influence. (vi) Closely connected, but analytically and empirically separable, is the *distribution of the motivation* to achieve, which is as much a function of the social and psychological environment of the individual as of his material advantages in a narrower sense. Levels of aspiration vary not only between, but within, social strata, and it is one of the tasks of sociology to discover the social roots of such striving and to see whether it is matched by actual social mobility.

Given the objective structure of occupational positions, and given also the increasingly close bond between educational level and occupational opportunity, the study of the causes of social mobility has tended to concentrate on the relationship between parental social status and the

D. Lockwood

educational opportunity and performance of the child, taking into account, so far as is possible, differences in measured intelligence. The results of such studies may be discussed in relation to the conclusions which can be drawn from the empirical investigation of social movement.

The Patterns of Mobility: Britain

The facts about social movement in this country are to be obtained largely from one major national study of inter-generational mobility,[16] a series of studies of the social origins of persons in professional, business and white collar employment,[5, 6, 7, 8, 21, 24, 29] a national study of intra-generational job mobility[32] and a few studies of the first occupations of business men.[1, 6, 7] Without attempting to give anything like a systematic summary of this material, the following general relationships appear to be fairly clearly established.

There is a considerable amount of short-range movement between adjacent occupational levels. In the study by Glass (Table I) it was found that in none of the seven occupational status groups was the majority of sons to be found in the same position as that held by their fathers; and that, in the sample as a whole, the proportion of sons with the same status as their fathers was roughly one-third. As far as longer-range movement is concerned one-fifth of the sons of the highest group, professional and high administrative workers, was downwardly mobile into manual or routine non-manual jobs; and a similar proportion of the sons in the latter category rose to positions in the non-manual grades proper, mostly into positions of middle and subordinate status.

The greatest opportunities for movement on the part of sons of manual workers are of necessity within the range of manual skills. This pattern is confirmed by Thomas's study of labour mobility (Table II), and by the other more specific studies, which show clearly also that lower white collar employment is the main avenue of upward mobility out of the manual working class and that the sons of clerical workers (and those who start in clerical work) have markedly higher chances of upward mobility than the sons of manual workers (and those who start in manual work). The greatest amount of interchange, therefore, takes place within the grades of manual employment and between this level and the lower white collar group. This would, indeed, be expected, given the shape of the occupational hierarchy in which these categories of employment form by far the greater proportion of all jobs.

The extent to which sons inherit the occupational status of their fathers has therefore to be seen in terms of the proportion of all jobs which different occupational strata represent. From this point of view,

TABLE I

Sons' Occupations in Relation to Fathers' Occupations (Men, aged 21 and over, England and Wales, 1949)

Father's Occupation	Son's Present Occupation						
	Professional, High Administrative %	Managerial and Executive %	Higher Inspectional & Supervisory %	Lower Inspectional & Supervisory %	Skilled Manual & Routine Non-Manual %	Semi-Skilled Manual %	Unskilled Manual %
Professional and High Administrative	**38·8**	14·6	20·2	6·2	14·0	4·7	1·5	(100)
Managerial and Executive	10·7	**26·7**	22·7	12·0	20·6	5·3	2·0	(100)
Higher Inspectional and Supervisory	3·5	10·1	**18·8**	19·1	35·7	6·7	6·1	(100)
Lower Inspectional and Supervisory	2·1	3·9	11·2	**21·2**	43·0	12·4	6·2	(100)
Skilled Manual and Routine Non-Manual	0·9	2·4	7·5	12·3	**47·3**	17·1	12·5	(100)
Semi-Skilled Manual	0·0	1·3	4·1	8·8	39·1	**31·2**	15·5	(100)
Unskilled Manual	0·0	0·8	3·6	8·3	36·4	23·5	**27·4**	(100)

NOTE: The underlined figures show the proportions of sons of fathers in given occupational groups who had the same kind of occupation as their fathers.

D. Lockwood

TABLE II

Present Occupation in Relation to First Occupation (Men, aged 21 and over, Gt. Britain, 1945–7).

First Occupation	Present Occupation						
	Profes- sional %	Mana- gerial %	Clerical %	Skilled %	Semi- Skilled %	Un- skilled %	
Professional	80	11	2	2	4	1	(100)
Managerial	—	—	—	—	—	—	
Clerical	6	32	34	11	15	2	(100)
Skilled	3	20	2	53	17	5	(100)
Semi-skilled	2	20	2	9	51	16	(100)
Unskilled	1	14	2	15	42	26	(100)

NOTE: 'Managerial' includes jobs such as chief clerks and foremen.

the actual chances of a son inheriting the status of his father are very much greater in the highest occupational strata than they would be on the assumption of 'random' mobility (i.e. assuming equal probabilities of movement for persons of all social categories). Thus in Glass's study, although over 60 per cent of the sons of professional and high administrative workers were employed in lower status occupations, their chances of following in their fathers' footsteps were in fact thirteen times greater than would have been expected if mobility had been 'random' or 'perfect'. Whereas, for those sons of skilled manual and routine non-manual workers, almost half of whom were in the same occupational group, the association between parental and filial status was only slightly larger in fact than what it would have been on a random basis of job distribution. This greater degree of relative self-recruitment in the higher strata is also clearly confirmed by several studies of the social origins of elite groups.

Such differences in chances of occupational inheritance reflect the combined influence of 'innate' ability, differential opportunity and motivation. In the mobility studies themselves, there is no possibility of disentangling the relative influence of these various factors, but what is abundantly clear is that the chances of different types of education vary greatly according to the social status of the subject measured by father's occupation. The higher the status of the father, the greater the chances of the son having had a grammar- or public-school education. For example, with respect to grammar-school education alone, for those born between 1910 and 1919, the sons of professional, administrative, and managerial workers were eight times more likely to receive such an education than were the sons of semi- and unskilled workers. Thus, given the importance of selective secondary education in increasing the chances of upward mobility for low status sons and decreasing the likelihood of downward mobility for high status sons, the class differential in educational chances was a decisive factor in maintaining the high degree of relative self-recruitment of the upper occupational strata. In this process, the outstanding importance of the independent 'public' school education (which was enjoyed by less than 2 per cent of the men in Glass's survey) is attested to by the noticeable 'over-representation' of men with this type of educational background in all studies of high-ranking occupations.

Ability, Educational Opportunity, and Social Mobility

The studies of social mobility mentioned above all deal with populations unaffected by the educational reforms of the Act of 1944, an act which, so far as social stratification is concerned, has been described by Glass as 'probably the most important measure of the last half-century'. Nor do they take account of the role of ability in the process of educational and occupational selection. Nevertheless, it is clear that throughout this period the chances of upward mobility for persons from lowly social origins were heavily circumscribed by the fact that, despite increased opportunities for secondary education, ability to pay for such education was a condition of entry not only to public schools but also to a large extent to secondary grammar schools as well. The economic circumstances and social outlook of many working-class parents also prevented able children from taking up educational opportunities which were available to them. The degree to which able children from different social origins had unequal access to grammar-school education is revealed in a study carried out in 1933, which showed that while nearly all the children from the professional and well-to-do business classes who possessed high ability (as measured by intelligence tests) enjoyed secondary education, the corresponding figure for clerical and commercial employees was 50 per cent, for skilled manual workers 30 per cent, and for unskilled workers only 20 per cent. On the other hand, 50 per cent of the children from the homes of the highest status group, whose measured ability was less than the standard used in the study, did have an opportunity for secondary education.[19] Thus, even if measured intelligence at the point of entry to grammar school is taken as an index of 'innate' ability, it can be seen how much the structure of educational institutions and the economic advantages and disadvantages of social position limited the free flow of this ability within the occupational system. In Glass's words: 'I.Q. as such is by no means a sufficient explanation of educational differences within the 1949 adult population.

D. Lockwood

Crude economic, together with more subtle social and cultural, factors account for the major differences.'

The effects on mobility of the full application of the merit principle to grammar-school selection after 1945 may perhaps be tentatively inferred from the findings of recent studies in this field. The main results seem to be as follows. First, that children who attain a certain level of ability on the basis of educational tests do in fact secure grammar-school places, irrespective of the social status of their parents, although the proportions of children in the various social strata who reach the specified levels of attainment in the tests are still markedly different. Thus, although the proportion of working-class children in the grammar-school population has increased, the chances of a working-class child obtaining a grammar-school education are not very much greater than they were before the war. Secondly, that, while the material environment of the home distinguishes the successful from the unsuccessful working-class children, among working-class families at the same level of material comfort, the children who have the greater chances of getting into a grammar school are those who come from homes with social characteristics more like those of the 'middle class'.[13] Thirdly, that the economic and social obstacles which previously stood in the way of the able child from the working class at the point of entry to grammar school are now more evident in their effects on the performance of these children within the grammar school. Within the grammar school, class differences in achievement show up in a pronounced fashion, and demonstrate how much the performance of the child is determined, not solely by his measured ability, but by the influence of parents and friends, and possibly also by the social climate of the school itself. A recent inquiry by the Ministry of Education showed, for instance, that a considerable proportion of the working-class children who are placed in the top group of ability at grammar-school entry end up by doing badly in their examinations at the end of the course or leave before completion of their studies, whilst an equally considerable proportion of children from middle-class homes who are placed in the lower groups of ability at point of entry improve during their stay at grammar school and do well in the terminal examinations.[27] This wastage of ability among children from lowly social origins, which is naturally even more pronounced at the point of admission to university, means that, despite 'equality of opportunity' in secondary state education, the higher one goes up the educational ladder, the more the social and economic effects of parental status and attitude outweigh the factor of sheer individual ability in determining the chances of further education, and hence, to a very great extent, occupational attainment (Table III). Finally, the fact that the independent public schools are not equally open to able children from all social origins (whether or not this would lead to desirable

516

consequences) means that all the advantages of this type of schooling—in quality of teaching, chances of university entrance, and in subsequent careers—are almost entirely enjoyed by the children of higher social strata and thus operate to reinforce the tie between parental and filial status at this level of the social system.

TABLE III

Performance at Grammar School Selection, during Grammar School, and Admissions to University, by Occupation of Father (Boys, England and Wales 1955–6)

Occupation of Father	Top group at entry to Grammar school %	Grammar school record of two passes at 'A' level %	Students admitted to University from Grammar schools %	Students admitted to University from all (including public) schools %
Professional, Managerial and Clerical	33·5	52·6	63·5	74·0
Skilled Manual	45·3	38·8	30·3	21·7
Semi-Skilled Manual	16·3	7·1	4·9	3·4
Unskilled Manual	4·9	1·6	1·3	0·9
	(100)	(100)	(100)	(100)

Source: Kelsall[22]

There can be little doubt that the educational system now affords greater chances of upward mobility for the children of low social status than before. At the same time, the nature of the stratification system itself functions so as to curtail the possibility of substantial and long-range mobility. The higher professional and administrative occupations are not only still few in number, but also remain relatively much more closed to potential candidates from the manual working class than are the middle ranks of non-manual 'white collar' occupations, which appear to be growing at a relatively faster rate than most other jobs. The exact degree to which educational opportunities are facilitating upward social movement, and modifying the relative chances of occupational inheritance at different levels of the stratification system, must await further inquiries for which those mentioned above provide a systematic base.

Such inquiries are likely to probe more deeply into the complex interplay between social stratification, the family, and the educational milieu; and to provide an opportunity for close collaboration between psychologists and sociologists. More needs to be known, in particular, about the way in which different types of family environment are related to intra-class variations in the 'mobility-proneness' of individuals at all levels of the social system. These differences, while less tractable from the point of view of social policy, are nevertheless of undoubted importance in the process of social mobility. And they will become even more decisive, the more the obvious barriers to social movement are reduced, and the more efficient become the means of educational selection.

The Consequences of Social Mobility

More than half a century ago the French sociologist Émile Durkheim argued that in modern industrial societies the main pre-condition of social solidarity was the greatest possible degree of social fluidity, so that each individual could perform the function best suited to his talents. At the same time, he was not unaware of the psychic costs to the individual that such movement could produce. The various facets of this problem have only just begun to be treated systematically by contemporary sociologists. The major lines of inquiry, few of which have been pursued in Britain, can only be indicated; the answers to them are as yet too tentative to permit of generalization.[23]

The social and psychological effects of mobility and immobility raise a whole range of fascinating questions that are central to the structure and dynamics of modern societies. What, for instance, is the relationship between social selection and economic efficiency?[12] Is the net effect of upward and downward mobility a greater political conservatism? Are societies with a more 'open' system of stratification characterized by less class conflict? To what extent does the process of educational selection foster new lines of social differentiation?[25] Do mobile persons experience greater social isolation,[20] and does their mobility make them more prejudiced, and more liable to mental illness? How does a society which puts a premium on individual achievement handle those whose aspirations are thwarted? How damaging to the self-respect of the unsuccessful are the implications of an almost comprehensive system of selection that is based on 'objective' criteria of merit? Do they contract out of the competition by lowering their sights; do they reject the official definition of merit altogether and adopt alternative definitions of social worth; or do some turn more readily to crime and delinquency?[26]

Social Mobility

These are the kinds of questions to which current research on social mobility is increasingly addressing itself now that the major quantitative relationships have been clearly mapped out.

REFERENCES

1. Acton Society Trust. *Management Succession*. London, 1952.
2. BENJAMIN, B. (1958) 'Inter-Generation Differences in Occupation'. *Popul. Stud.*, **11** (3).
3. BERENT, J. (1952) 'Fertility and Social Mobility'. *Popul. Stud.*, **5**.
4. BURT, C. (1959) 'Class Differences in General Intelligence'. *Brit. J. stat. Psychol.*, **12** (1).
5. CHAPMAN, S. J. & MARQUIS, F. J. (1912) 'The Recruiting of the Employing Class from the Ranks of the Wage Earners in the Cotton Industry'. *J. R. statist. Soc.*, **75**.
6. CLEMENTS, R. V. *Managers: A Study of their Careers in Industry*. London: Allen & Unwin, 1958.
7. COPEMAN, G. H. *Leaders of British Industry*. London: Gee, 1955.
8. ERICKSON, C. *British Industrialists: Steel and Hosiery 1850-1950*. London: Cambridge Univ. Press, 1960 (Chaps. 2, 4, 8).
9. *Fifteen to Eighteen*. Report of the Central Advisory Council for Education, Vol. II. London: H.M.S.O., 1960.
10. FLOUD, J. E. 'Educational Opportunity and Social Mobility'. *Yearbook of Education*, London, 1950.
11. FLOUD, J. E. 'Education and Social Class in the Welfare State'. In: Judges, A. V. (ed.), *Looking Forward in Education*. London: Faber & Faber, 1955.
12. FLOUD, J. E., & HALSEY, A. H. 'Education and Occupation: English Secondary Schools and the Supply of Labour'. *Yearbook of Education*, London, 1956.
13. FLOUD, J. E., HALSEY, A. H., & MARTIN, F. M. *Social Class and Educational Opportunity*, London: Heinemann, 1957.
14. FURNEAUX, W. D. *The Chosen Few*. London: Oxford Univ. Press, 1961.
15. GINSBERG, M. 'Interchange between Social Classes'. In: *Studies in Sociology*. London: Methuen, 1932.
16. GLASS, D. V. (ed.) *Social Mobility in Britain*. London: Routledge, 1954.
17. GUTTSMAN, W. L. (1951) 'The Changing Social Structure of the British Political Elite'. *Brit. J. Sociol.*, **9**, 15-28.
18. HALSEY, A. H. (1958) Genetics, Social Structure and Intelligence'. *Brit. J. Sociol.*, **9** (1).
19. HOGBEN, L. (ed.) *Political Arithmetic*. London: Allen & Unwin, 1938.
20. HOGGART, RICHARD *The Uses of Literacy*. London: Chatto & Windus, 1957 (chap. 10).
21. KELSALL, R. K. *Higher Civil Servants in Britain from 1870 to the Present Day*. London: Routledge, 1955.

D. Lockwood

22. KELSALL, R. K. *Report on an Inquiry into Applications for Admission to Universities.* London, 1957.
23. LIPSET, S. M., & BENDIX, R. *Social Mobility in Industrial Society.* London: Heinemann, 1959.
24. LOCKWOOD, D. *The Blackcoated Worker.* London: Allen & Unwin, 1958 (chap. 4).
25. MARSHALL, T. H. (1953) 'Social Selection in the Welfare State'. *Eugen. Rev.*, **43.**
26. MERTON, R. K. 'Social Structure and Anomie', in *Social Theory and Social Structure.* Glencoe, Ill.: Free Press, 1958.
27. Ministry of Education. *Early Leaving: A Report of the Central Advisory Council for Education* (England). London: H.M.S.O., 1954.
28. NISBET, J. D. (1952) 'Level of National Intelligence'. *Nature*, **15,** (Nov.)
29. SCOTT, W. (1958) 'Fertility and Social Mobility among Teachers'. *Popul. Stud.*, **11** (3).
30. *Social Implications of the 1947 Scottish Mental Survey, The.* London, 1953.
31. SOROKIN, P. *Social Mobility.* New York: Harper, 1927.
32. THOMAS, G. *Labour Mobility in Great Britain 1945–49.* An inquiry carried out for the Ministry of Labour and National Service, Government Social Survey. London, n.d.
33. YOUNG, M., & WILLMOTT, P. *Family and Kinship in East London.* London: Routledge, 1957 (chap. 11).

29

THE SOCIOLOGY OF
EDUCATION*

Jean Floud

EDUCATION AND INDUSTRIAL SOCIETY

THE problems that give rise to, or at least justify, the sociology of education as a specialized field of study are created by industrialism, which affects education in two main ways; firstly by disturbing and attenuating the relations between individuals and the wider society, thus complicating the problems of consensus and integration, and secondly by giving formal education an unprecedented economic importance. Both these trends of development involve new and conflicting pressures on schools, colleges, and universities. The disruption of social consensus and integration consequent on rapid social change, urbanization, increased social mobility, the multiplication of secondary groups and associations, and the generally enhanced scale and rationalization of social and economic life, leads to the demand that schools and universities should undertake broad educative functions for the mass of

* In writing this chapter, the author has drawn heavily on 'The Sociology of Education. A Trend Report and Bibliography', prepared in collaboration with A. H. Halsey for *Current Sociology*, (3), (Basil Blackwell, 1958), where students will find a much fuller discussion of the scope and problems of this field of study and a review of work in each of its principal parts. They are also referred to A. H. Halsey, Jean Floud, and C. Arnold Anderson, *Education, Economy and Society: a Reader in the Sociology of Education* (New York: Free Press, 1961). A. K. C. Ottaway, *Education and Society* (London: Routledge, 1953), and R. J. Havighurst and B. L. Neugarten, *Society and Education* (Boston: Allyn and Bacon, 1957) are both good examples of current text-books, English and American respectively.

the people which were formerly fulfilled by the now weakened 'primary groups' of family, neighbourhood and church.[38] At the same time, the growing economic significance of educated manpower, the continually rising educational threshold of employment, and the public thirst for formal educational qualifications, bring about the bureaucratization of education and its conversion into an increasingly rationalized system of mass instruction in the service of a modern labour force.

The new purposes of the economy of an advanced industrial society must eventually involve a radical break with the educational traditions of the past. Technical changes, especially in the thirties and after World War II, have altered the economic and social situation in such a way as to make education an important determinant of the economic, political, social, and cultural character of society.* The essence of this technical revolution is the introduction of mass-production methods in industry, involving a growth in the scale of enterprise both technically and financially, a still more intricate division than heretofore of the work-process, and its increased subordination to the machine. Two important consequences follow from these changes.

In the first place, since it becomes technically very difficult to manipulate output in response to fluctuations in demand, a premium is placed on the enlargement of the market as an alternative to a policy of restricting output to maintain prices when faced with a fall in demand. An expansionist drive of this kind involves heavy investment in research and innovation, which in turn involves the search for and promotion of scientific, technological, and organizing talent. The educational system is called upon to undertake this huge task of recruiting and training on which the national economy hinges and the fate of a social order may depend.

In the second place, the new techniques radically alter the position of labour in production, and the educational needs of the mass of the population. Labour is integrated into a unified process of machine production. On the one hand, this creates the problem of educating people, whose working lives are in danger of being denuded of constructive and creative qualities, to cultivate these qualities in their leisure time; on the other hand, it also gives man, at least potentially, a new status in the productive process; 'man as technician increasingly stands in opposition to labour power as a commodity'.[15] The changed status of labour makes it essential to 'improve its quality', that is to say, to educate the population at large to the mastery of new knowledge, new obligations, and new responsibilities.

* For a somewhat overstated, but vivid, account of these developments see [16].

The Sociology of Education

The demand for professional and managerial workers, and the creation of the new middle class of white collar workers, necessitate and foster occupational and social mobility, mainly through education. The secondary schools and universities have had and are still having to expand both numerically and in their scope, to embrace preparation for new technical, scientific, and administrative professions. Social selection is added to their traditional task of social differentiation: they must promote new as well as maintain old élites, and the pressure of numbers and the broadened social basis of recruitment increase the task of social assimilation. Their traditional aims and organization are strained by the attempt to turn them to the new purposes of an economy with which they are increasingly involved, and which, moreover, undermines as it develops the structure of class and status in which they have their roots and a large part of their being.

It is not surprising that British sociologists should be interested in the effects upon the educational system of these movements in the wider society, and that the relations of education to the class-structure and of both to the national economy should be the most systematically and fruitfully cultivated part of the sociology of education in Britain.

A desire for equality and justice together with economic efficiency has sustained a tradition of social investigation into the distribution of educational opportunity in relation to that of ability, its bearing on social mobility or interchange between the classes, and its demographic and economic consequences. The problems of measurement involved in the study of the waste of human resources due to inadequate distribution of educational opportunities were thoroughly considered in the thirties. The need in this work to relate the social and intellectual composition of the entry to secondary schools and universities to that of the population from which it was recruited was established; and the limitations of available measures of ability ('Intelligence Tests') were carefully explored.[25],[26],[27] This was important and cumulative work which has been closely followed up in the post-war period.

At the same time as these matters were under investigation, the social role of education was being discussed in relation to the then falling birth-rate.[35] The facts of reduced and differential fertility were linked with the increasing costs, in money and real terms, of education, and with the desire for social mobility in face of greatly extended opportunities afforded by the growing demand for white collar workers at all occupational levels, from professional and managerial to routine clerical. The changes in the occupational structure responsible for this demand, in particular the trend towards professionalization and bureaucratization, and the closing of avenues of mobility other than education, were analysed. Although the subsequent rise in the birth-rate deflected interest in the costs of education, the ground had been prepared for the post-war preoccupation with social mobility and the part played in it by education.[17, 39, 40, 41]

Earlier work on this topic leant heavily on studies of the educational antecedents of *élite* groups, of the recruitment of the nation's leaders and of the part played by the independent public schools in providing people to fill positions of power and influence in public life.[34, 40, 48] Only after the war was the question raised of the general fluidity of the social structure, and the possibility considered of assessing more precisely the contribution of education to the extent and processes of mobility, taking into account not only the independent schools but also the much larger system of grant-earning secondary schools.

Two major enterprises launched in the late forties, and two others in the middle fifties, have between them opened up the question of social selection and mobility through education, and supplied the elementary data needed for further investigation: in 1947 the Scottish Council for Research in Education undertook a mental and social survey of a large national sample of eleven-year-old children in Scotland, and subsequently followed their educational progress until all had left school.[44, 45] Then, in 1949, an investigation on a national scale was undertaken from the London School of Economics into the movement between the social classes, with particular reference to the part played by education.[21] This was followed in 1952 and 1953 by local surveys designed to build on the national investigation by examining in detail the extent and processes of mobility through education in areas of contrasting social character under post-war conditions of social and educational reform.[18] In 1954 the Committee of Principals and Vice-Chancellors of the universities of the United Kingdom commissioned an inquiry into the supply of and demand for university places, in the course of which information, hitherto unavailable, was obtained on the social and educational antecedents of entrants to universities in 1955.[33] Arrangements have since been made to follow the subjects of this inquiry through their university careers and into the labour market, thus doing for university education what the earlier inquiries had done mainly for secondary education. Finally, we have the three substantial surveys undertaken at the request of the 'Crowther Committee', which together provide the most up-to-date account available of the social distribution of educational opportunity for boys in Britain, and a valuable analysis of some of the major social influences on educability.[30]

As a result of these investigations we are, for the time being, reasonably well-informed about the social distribution of educational opportunity both before and after 1939, and its relation to the social

The Sociology of Education

TABLE I

THE SOCIAL ORIGINS OF BOYS ENTERING SECONDARY GRAMMAR SCHOOLS BEFORE AND AFTER 1944

Occupations of Fathers	Before 1944	After 1944
	%	%
South-West Hertfordshire	(1934–1938)	(1950–1953)
Professional and managerial	19	21
Clerical and other non-manual	62	35
Manual	16	42
Middlesbrough	(1934–1938)	(1948–1951)
Professional and managerial	16	23
Clerical and other non-manual	34	32
Manual	46	44
London	(1933–1944)	(1945–9 Islington and St. Pancras)
Professional and managerial	35	3
Clerical and other non-manual	31	22
Manual	25	66
England & Wales	(1930–1941)	(1946–1951)
Professional and managerial	40	26
Clerical and other non-manual	20	18
Manual	40	56

N.B. The figures for the Educational Division of South-west Hertford-shire and for Middlesbrough are derived from [18], Tables 1 & 2, pp. 29–30; those for London from Hogben, L. (ed.) *Political Arithmetic*, London, Allen & Unwin, 1938, Table VI, 404, and [9], pp. 48–49; those for England & Wales from [21], Table VII, p. 129, and [30], Table X, p. 130. Unclassified occupations have been omitted so that percentages do not always add up to 100.

The figures for the different years and areas are not strictly comparable, but the general picture will not be affected.

distribution of ability; and about the nature, in gross terms, and the incidence of social factors which influence selection for secondary and higher education, and affect educational progress at given levels of measured intelligence. That is to say, we have a foundation of elementary information on which we can build an understanding of the way in which the educational system functions as an agency of social selection and differentiation. Secondary schools and universities and the opportunities of attending them have greatly changed since the turn of the century ([29], chap. 1). Table I indicates the post-war change in the social composition of the secondary-grammar schools, and illustrates the wide local variations which underlie the national figures.

Information of this kind is not available for the universities, but the changes there have not been so substantial. Despite the increase since 1937–8 in the number of full-time students by nearly 80 per cent and the percentage of students assisted from public funds from 38·5 to 76·8, there were in 1955–6 no more than 26 per cent of the men admitted to

TABLE II

CHANGES IN THE SOCIAL DISTRIBUTION OF
EDUCATIONAL OPPORTUNITY

*Secondary and University Education of Boys reaching the Age of
11 at Various Periods**

	WORKING CLASS†		OTHER†		ALL	
	PERCENTAGE ATTENDING					
Boys reaching the age of 11	*Independent Efficient or Grammar School*	*University*	*Independent Efficient or Grammar School*	*University*	*Independent Efficient or Grammar School*	*University*
Before 1931	4·0	0·9	27·0	4·4	7·0	2·0
1931–1940	9·8	1·7	38·9	8·5	14·7	3·7
1946–1951	14·5	1·6	48·5	7·3	23·0	2·4

* Figures for national samples of boys reaching the age of eleven before 1931 and 1931–1940 derived from[21], Tables 1 and 2, pp. 118–19; those for boys in the 1946–1951 group from[30], Tables 3a and 9, pp. 122 and 130 respectively (percentages attending universities arbitrarily corrected to reduce error deriving from differences in practice as between independent and other schools with regard to deferment of military service).

† i.e. Boys of fathers following manual (skilled, semi-skilled and unskilled) and non-manual (professional and managerial, clerical and other white collar) occupations.

English universities whose fathers followed manual occupations; and this proportion varied widely as between the different universities (Cambridge, 9 per cent; Oxford, 13 per cent; London, 21 per cent; others, 31 per cent).

However, although the percentage of grammar school pupils and of university students coming from working-class homes has grown considerably, the percentage of all children at this social level who pass into the grammar schools and universities remains small, as can be seen from Table II.

Changes in the relative 'class chances' of admission to grammar schools and universities have been much less striking than might appear from the changes which have taken place in their social composition. This must be accounted for in part by the pressure of population in the post-war years, after a sustained fall in the 1930s and early 1940s in the numbers of children coming forward into the schools; in part by the wide local variations in grammar-school provision associated with variations in the social composition of the population ([11], Table K, p. 18) and in part with the more fundamental fact of the social differences, already mentioned, in ability as measured by intelligence tests. That this last factor is by no means alone responsible for the persisting social-class inequalities of educational opportunity is convincingly demonstrated in that section of the Crowther Report which deals with the distribution of 'latent ability'. A valuable series of tables is presented, analysing the educational levels achieved by boys entering the Army as recruits in six so-called 'ability groups' (the highest group 1 accounting for 10 per cent of the sample, groups 2 to 5 each for a further 20 per cent, and group 6 for a final 10 per cent).[30]

Of the entire group of recruits studied, only 2 per cent were graduates, or had achieved a comparable educational qualification. This select minority accounted for less than one in five (18 per cent) of the young men in the top ability group, and for a minute proportion (1 per cent) of those in the second. Underlying these figures, moreover, are marked social differences. Thus, in ability group 1 the son of a non-manual (professional, managerial, or clerical) father is shown as at least twice as likely to have graduated as the son of a manual worker. In ability group 2, the sons of professional and managerial fathers are three times as likely as the sons of skilled workers to have graduated, three times as likely to have got a 'good' A level G.C.E. (two or more passes), and twice as likely to have got a 'good' O level G.C.E. (four or more passes).

That these facts reflect the social distribution of educational opportunity can see from Table III. In the second ability group 58·6 per cent of recruits whose fathers were of the professional and managerial class had attended grammar or independent schools while only 22 per cent of the sons of skilled workers had done so—and it is not the case, as might be

Table III

SOCIAL CLASS DIFFERENCES IN THE SCHOOLING OF ARMY RECRUITS (1956–8) AT TWO LEVELS OF ABILITY*

FATHERS' OCCUPATION

SECONDARY SCHOOLING	Professional and Managerial		Clerical and other non-Manual		Skilled Manual		Semi-Skilled Manual		Unskilled Manual	
	Group 1	Group 2	Group 1	Group 2	Group 1	Group 2	Group 1	Group 2	Group 1	Group 2
	%	%	%	%	%	%	%	%	%	%
INDEPENDENT OR GRAMMAR	89·4	58·6	86·8	32·4	76·0	22·1	77·0	18·0	55·0	14·0
TECHNICAL	6·8	10·5	7·5	14·2	10·8	11·0	9·0	11·3	22·2	12·3
ALL SELECTIVE	96·2	69·3	94·3	46·6	86·8	53·1	86·0	29·3	77·2	26·3

* Compiled from [30], Table 2a, p. 120.

hoped, that more of these had attended technical schools instead. Even in the first ability group the social differences in schooling are marked. Elsewhere, the Report emphasizes the similarity of the maintained and independent schools in the ability of their pupils. Yet, as is well known, there is a tremendous difference in the proportion staying on for advanced work in the two types of school; of recruits in the Crowther sample who attended independent efficient schools 60 per cent had stayed on to 18 + as against 24 per cent of those from maintained schools; the corresponding figures for 17-year-old leavers were 23 per cent and 16 per cent respectively. This contrast reflects the difference in the social composition of the two types of school. Only 6 per cent of recruits from independent efficient schools were sons of manual workers, as compared with 56 per cent of those from the maintained schools, of whom 70 per cent had left before they were 17.

It seems unlikely that the post-war movement of educational reform can as yet have brought about any marked increase in the degree of social interchange between the classes established by Professor Glass and his colleagues for the pre-war period and summarized in Table IV.

TABLE IV

STATUS CATEGORY* OF FATHERS AND SONS

Status Category of Fathers	Status Category of Sons			'Same' as percentage of 'Total'
	Same	Different	Total	
1	50	79	129	38·8
2	40	110	150	26·7
3	65	280	345	18·8
4	110	408	518	21·2
5	714	796	1,510	47·3
6	143	315	458	31·2
7	106	281	387	27·4
Total	1,228	2,269	3,497	35·1

Source: [21], p. 184.

* (1) Professional and high administrative; (2) Managerial and executive; (3) Inspectional, supervisory and other non-manual higher grade; (4) Inspectional, supervisory and other non-manual lower grade; (5) Skilled manual and routine grades of non-manual; (6) semi-skilled manual; (7) unskilled manual.

Jean Floud

The abler sons of skilled workers have been drawn in to the grammar and technical schools; but ability and opportunity are still in imperfect relationship, and there is considerable wastage from the schools. We are a long way from the 'meritocracy' forecast by Michael Young[49] as the outcome of the perfect equalization of educational opportunity.

These investigations will need to be repeated. The structure of educational opportunity is changing with the modification of the tripartite system of secondary education, the expansion of the universities, and the changing status of technical schools and colleges. Family environments are changing, demographically, economically, and culturally, and so is the structure of opportunities in the labour market. The public image, as well as the official definition, of educational opportunity is changing accordingly, and so too, undoubtedly, are the social factors influencing educational selection and performance. Accurate and reasonably up-to-date information on all these matters is not only indispensable to policy-making both in education and economics, but also to the understanding of much of what goes on in schools, colleges, and universities even at the classroom level.

Social Determinants of Educability

Thus, British sociologists have been drawn to study education through their interest in problems of social stratification and mobility, and have made their contribution mainly at the structural level, elucidating the increasingly important role of education in the dynamics of stratification, and the stress felt by schools and universities as they adapt their aims and organization to new social tasks. However, in investigating social selection and mobility through education they could not long evade the fundamental problem of the educability of children from different kinds of background in different kinds of school. Their work on this problem has been somewhat bedevilled, however, by their preoccupation with the fundamental issue of heredity and environment in relation to education, and with questions such as: How far does the social distribution of measured intelligence accurately reflect the social distribution of innate capacities? How can innate intelligence be measured? There are, of course, sociological aspects of both these questions; social structure can exercise a powerful influence on the genetic composition of populations and hence on their innate educability; and the rationale and practice of intelligence testing can be criticized as being unfair to some social classes and ethnic subcultures.

Since the measuring of innate intelligence apart from the effects of social factors appears to be impossible at the present time and likely to remain so in the foreseeable future, the question of genetic limits to educability has to be by-passed. Instead effort is concentrated on analysing environmental influences on educational performance, as measured by standardized tests of 'intelligence', aptitude, or attainment, or by other criteria such as teachers' assessments, number of years spent at school, or performance in public examinations. The crucial question then becomes: what are we to understand by 'environment'?

The answer to this question has, so far, been given in terms of 'home background', that is, in terms of features of the family and neighbourhood environment including peer-groups of children and adolescents. Many investigations have been undertaken, by psychologists as well as sociologists, into the influence on educational performance of a variety of features of the social environment of children *outside school*. Thus, Sir Cyril Burt carried out some of the earliest and best work on the general influence of neighbourhood;[8] and a considerable quantity of relevant information has accumulated in the reports of the many social surveys which have shown the association of poverty, malnutrition, and squalid housing with restricted educational facilities, backwardness and poor scholastic level generally (e.g., [24], [31]). The influence on scholastic achievement of the size and socio-economic status of the family has been repeatedly and conclusively demonstrated. There is a positive relationship between socio-economic status, as judged by father's occupation, and intelligence-test scores; but there is a significantly closer relationship between father's occupation and school success. Thus, in a

TABLE V

HOME BACKGROUND AND SCHOOL PERFORMANCE*

Mean Standard Score for I.Q. and Criterion by Occupational Groups

	Professional and semi-professional	Clerical	Managerial	Highly-skilled
I.Q.	+1·59	+·87	+·57	+·75
Criterion	+1·60	+1·07	+·66	+1·09
N	11	20	36	26

	Skilled	Semi-Skilled	Unskilled	Labouring
I.Q.	+·14	−·27	−·36	−·65
Criterion	+·15	−·34	−·42	−·66
N	94	80	70	63

* Source: [20], p. 52.

recent investigation[20] into the relationship of home environment to the school attainment of some four hundred children grouped according to the occupations followed by their fathers, the mean intelligence test scores and scaled school marks ('criterion') were calculated for each group. In Table V, these mean scores are expressed in standard deviation units from the general mean of the whole group, and the closer dependence of school attainment than intelligence test score on father's occupation is clearly revealed in the fact that the scores for the former were wider spread than those for the latter—the plus scores were more positive and the minus scores were more negative for 'criterion' than for test score.

Ability is clearly no guarantee of attainment; but the relation between the two has not yet been fully investigated by psychologists, although a linear association is frequently taken for granted. McClelland remarks pertinently: 'Let us admit that morons cannot do good school-work. But what evidence is there that intelligence is not a threshold type of variable; that once a person has a certain minimal level of intelligence, his performance beyond that point is uncorrelated with his ability?'[36] And he urges thorough investigation of the relations between intelligence, socio-economic status, and attainment throughout the whole range of all three variables.

A clear and consistent relation between size of family and intelligence-test scores has also frequently been demonstrated. The decline in test scores as family size increases is not merely a reflection of the fact that, on average, the families of unskilled workers are larger than those of professional workers. The decline is visible within every occupational group and, moreover, is surprisingly regular in each. The investigation already cited makes it clear that 'the presence of a large number of siblings (or some factor related to it) is an adverse element as far as educational attainment is concerned, quite apart from the low intelligence usually associated with large families'.[20] The correlations for family size defined as the number of living children, whether resident at home or not, were:

Family Size and I.Q.: $r = \cdot404$
Family Size and Scaled School Marks: $r = \cdot458$

In attempting to unravel the relevant differences of environment which underlie these relationships, investigators understandably concentrated for a long time on gross material factors, such as poverty; but since the war, under the influence of conditions of general prosperity, the emphasis has shifted to less tangible features of background, such as parents' attitudes towards their children's education and future prospects, their educational level, or the mother's occupation before marriage; and to more subtle differences in the educative impact on the child in matters such as linguistic development, of life in large and small families.[6, 42]

Of course, the influence of crude material handicaps can still be traced; in many parts of the country the traditional association between poor schools and poor homes persists, and purely material conditions at home have been shown still to differentiate successful from unsuccessful children in the eleven plus examination, even when they are drawn from families at the same social level. But in a prosperous area, in which nearly everyone enjoys an adequate basic income and good housing, the influence of the home is more subtle. It has been shown that at a given social level in such an area, the children securing admission to grammar school are not those whose parents earn the highest income or enjoy superior standards of housing, but those whose parents are relatively better educated, more interested in and ambitious for their educational future, more familiar with the procedure of secondary selection, readier to visit the primary school to discuss the child's future with his teachers.[18] So far as income is concerned, there is some indication that it is in the nature of a threshold variable. Real economic hardship or chronic economic insecurity inhibits attainment at any level of ability; but the social survey carried out for the Crowther Committee reveals that, taking length of school life as a criterion of performance, differences are small until an income of over £16 per week is reached, which was a figure attained by only 14 per cent of the fathers of boys in the grammar and technical school sample under investigation.[30]

The educational significance of the various features of home background has not been fully explored, largely because there exists no sociology of the school to which they can be related. The social determinants of educability have been conceived in too one-sided fashion. The *interaction* of homes and schools is the key to educability, if we ignore, or hold constant, differences of personal endowment and life-history. But the social features of the school have barely been examined.

There are, in fact, two main sources of social influence on the educational process; on the one hand, family environment and general background of teachers and pupils (and, in the case of teachers, also from their professional needs and habits); and on the other the social organization, formal and informal, of schools, colleges, and universities. The child may come to school ill-equipped for, or hostile to, learning under any educational regime; but for the most part his educability depends as much on the assumptions, values, and aims personified in the teacher and embodied in the school organization into which he is supposed to assimilate himself, as on those he brings with him from his home.

Jean Floud

The Sociology of the School

This is nowhere clearer than in the case of the so-called 'early leavers' from grammar schools. The social, as distinct from the academic, character of this process of educational selection, which culminates at the threshold of the sixth form, is well established.[11] The proportion of children whose performance falls in the top one-third and who are drawn from working-class homes falls steadily, from some two-thirds at the beginning to around one-third at the end, of the seven-year school course. But although in the grammar school, the selected population and rather specific educational aims make this process of social selection very readily identifiable, it is something which, in fact, goes on to varying degrees in all types of school. The problem is not merely to document its existence but to understand its workings. This involves us in a study not merely of the 'home background' of pupils, but of the school itself as a relatively self-contained social system, purposeful in a formal sense, having its own conflicts, exerting its own pressures, and making its own demands, formal and informal, tacit and explicit.

No such sociology of the school has been attempted in Britain. There are, of course, investigations by social psychologists into the informal social life of children in school, in which sociometric techniques play a large part,[7] although these techniques have a way of stealing attention from the very issues on which they might be expected to throw light. The fundamental objection to focusing attention exclusively on the informal aspects of the school culture is that these are only secondary or contributory to the understanding of an institution such as a school. In many cases, the informal social life of pupils or students is interstitial, in the sense that it derives from and feeds on deficiencies and stresses in the formal organization of the institution. It may be possible in some instances to show that it is more than this; that a semi-autonomous adolescent sub-culture is a feature of the wider society; and that it cuts across, and is at least as generally influential as, the other sub-cultures of social class or race, of which the ramifications have been shown to extend deep into educational institutions. In either case, however, the investigation of this informal social life cannot be regarded as exhausting the sociology of the school. Indeed it does not even make a contribution to it unless it is set in the context of the formal purposes and organization of the institution, along with all the other elements in the complex interplay of forces of which its day-to-day existence is the outcome.

The first concern of a sociology of the school, as of any comparable social system such as a factory or hospital, must be with its formal constitution—the organizational set-up and the definition and distribution of roles within it, the pattern of stratification and the distribution of

534

power and authority, disciplinary arrangements, and the organization and content of the teaching. This is less a matter of simple description than might appear at first sight. These formal purposes and dispositions are the deposit of the past and must be examined in historical perspective as a preliminary to the study of the organization as an ongoing concern. In relation to schools, sociologists have done some sound preliminary work of this kind, such as the analysis of the close relationship of English secondary education to the social class and occupational structure;[2, 9] of the role of headmaster as it has evolved over the past century,[3, 4] of the professional evolution of the assistant teacher;[46] and of the prevailing concept of what a school in general, or a particular type of school, should be and do.[5, 32] But much more remains to be done, and we still await the definitive account in sociological terms of the organizational structure of the principal types of English school.

Once more it is necessary to stress the importance of the interaction of school and outside influences. The formal purposes and internal distribution of rights and obligations, as distilled from the past and continously re-interpreted, imbue the motives and inform the day-to-day activities of contemporary participants in the organization. But their definitions of the situation and of its demands on them will differ according to their social experience outside. The family and neighbourhood environment of pupils sends them into school with a variety of interpretations of, and attitudes towards, the situation inside its walls; similarly, the general background of teachers and administrators, and their professional habits and needs as well, equip them with attitudes, assumptions, and values which underlie their behaviour at work and must be analysed if the internal life of the school and its relative success or failure in its formal objectives is to be understood.

The School-Teachers

In Britain, no direct approach has so far been made to the problem of understanding the teacher's role in the classroom and his characteristic social attitudes and values. Studies in the sociology of the teaching profession have developed, in the main not out of concern with the sociology of the school, or with the social ingredients of the learning situation, but with problems of social structure, stratification, social mobility, and the professionalization of occupations. Teachers have been studied as an occupational group playing a part in general social structure, rather than as the personnel of schools; in their capacity as representatives of the new middle class, rather than in their role as professional teachers. Some interest has been evinced, mainly by psychologists, in motives for entering the profession, and the characteristics of the successful teacher;[47] and sociologists have begun to work on the internal structure of the profession—career patterns, wastage, turnover and mobility. But the emphasis has been predominantly on the social history of teaching as a profession; on teaching as an avenue of mobility (the social origins of teachers in different types of school, and the changing social basis of recruitment); on factors affecting the social status of the profession; and on its demographic characteristics (patterns of marriage and fertility, self-recruitment, morbidity, etc.).[10, 19, 46] Little attempt has been made to draw out the implications of these findings for the sociology of teaching. Yet they are very relevant in a situation in which problems of recruitment to a rapidly expanding profession become increasingly severe, and as the secondary schools and universities in a mass education service confront unprecedented tasks of social assimilation.

The difficulty is to know how many of the established professional characteristics of teachers are attributable to social factors and how many to their work. If school-teaching has traditionally been an avenue of upward social mobility; if teachers marry late, or not at all, and as a group are infertile even by white collar standards; if they suffer from 'status-anxiety' and 'social isolation'; if the profession is chronically stratified; then it is important to know how far these traits are historically determined and similar to those found in other comparable occupational and social groups, and how far they reflect stresses and strains endemic to the teacher's role.

Higher Education

The predominant interest in social stratification which has produced investigations into the social and professional characteristics of school-teachers has not done the same for university teachers, the study of which, as can be seen particularly from the considerable German literature, offers perhaps the best approach to a sociology of the university.

There exists no sociological analysis of developments in British universities analogous to the classics of the turn of the century by Weber and Veblen; nor is there relevant source material comparable in quantity or quality with that on which sociologists in Germany, and also in America, can draw in seeking to study the changing structure and functioning of the university.

Work on a limited scale has been undertaken on the social aspects of selection for higher education—less full, but on the same lines as that already mentioned relating to secondary schooling,[14, 33, 43] and a little has been done to study the process of selection within the universities.[13, 37]

But very little headway has been made in the task of identifying and studying systematically the trends of development responsible for the emerging structure of higher education in Britain: for example, the impact of technology on the social function and internal life of the universities; the relation between the older and newer foundations; the growth of alternative institutions of higher learning and of the independent institute and research unit; and the relations of both to industry and to industrial sources of patronage.[1, 22, 28] Broadly speaking, it is true to say that the sociology of British universities is a virgin field urgently needing cultivation.

CONCLUSION

Educational institutions have interested English sociologists less for their own sake than as bastions and outworks of the class-structure, and as agencies of social selection and differentiation. The movement towards a more rounded study of the educational system is, however, in its beginnings, and will no doubt receive a powerful impetus from a growing consciousness of the enhanced economic and social role of education under conditions of advanced industrialism. As the educational system moves into a strategic position as a central determinant of the economic, political, social, and cultural character of contemporary society, sociologists are being driven to develop fully a sociology of educational institutions. They need to understand the social origins of educational policies and practices, their social implications and the forces which shape their development, the structure and functioning of educational institutions as semi-autonomous social systems, the manner in which political and pedagogical purposes can be overlaid and distorted by the social pressures and expectations to which educational institutions are subjected, and the transformations which take place in the social functions these institutions serve as they are progressively involved with the wider social structure, and in particular with the economy.

The logic of investigation, ideally speaking, proceeds from the macrocosmic to the microcosmic, and the broad heads of inquiry illustrated by characteristic problems may be set out as follows:

(i) The relation of educational institutions, or of the educational system, to the wider social structure—e.g. to its demography (size and quality of the population); to the economy (supply and quality of man-power); to the political system (recruitment of the nation's leaders); to the system of social stratification (social selection and differentiation, and social mobility).

(ii) The structure and functioning of educational institutions—e.g. the school community, as a social system; the school and neighbourhood; the corporate life of universities; the transmission and inculcation of social values.

Jean Floud

(iii) The social relations inherent in, or arising out of, educational activities—e.g. social psychology and sociometry of classroom and school (social distance, modes of authority, discipline, etc.); 'sociology of teaching'.

Admittedly, to focus attention on the formal institutions of education in this way is to abstract from the total educational process; and it may be argued that the fundamental similarity of this process in all societies is thereby obscured. Margaret Mead and Karl Mannheim, each in their different ways, have insisted on the need for sociologists to take account of the educative implications of all our social arrangements in order to gain a complete picture of the process of assimilation of each individual to a cultural tradition.

But in a society in which there is elaborate provision for formal education, the informal educational influences of the social environment must be looked at as interacting with it, and promoting or hindering response to schooling or higher education. That is to say, they are part of the problem of *educability*, the joint province of geneticist, psychologist, and sociologist. The sociologist's contribution is to study the material and cultural factors promoting or hindering response to formal education—e.g. socio-economic situation, size and other characteristics of family environment; attitudes and values of social class, ethnic, religious, age-group, or other sub-cultures. To do this effectively, he must understand education as a formal institution, just as he understands the legal or economic institutions of a differentiated society. A 'sociology of childhood' is no substitute in modern society for the sociology of education.

REFERENCES

1. ASHBY, E. (1958) *Technology and the Academics: An Essay on the Universities and the Scientific Revolution*. London: Macmillan.
2. BANKS, O. (1954) *Parity and Prestige in English Secondary Education*. London: Routledge.
3. BARON, GEORGE (1952) 'The Secondary Schoolmaster, 1895–1914'. Ph.D. (London) Thesis.
4. BARON, GEORGE (1956) 'Some Aspects of the Headmaster Tradition'. *Researches and Studies*, no. 14.
5. BARON, GEORGE (1959) 'The English Concept of the School'. *Transactions of the 4th World Congress of Sociology*.
6. BERNSTEIN, B. (1961) 'Social Structure, Language and Learning'. *Educ. Res.* 3 (3).
7. BLYTH, W. A. L. (1960) 'The Sociometric Study of Children's Groups in English Schools'. *Brit. J. educ. Stud.*, **7** (2).
8. BURT, CYRIL (1937) *The Backward Child*. London: Univ. of London Press.

The Sociology of Education

9. CAMPBELL, F. (1956) *Eleven Plus and All That*. London: Watts.
10. CARR-SAUNDERS, A. M., JONES, D. C., & MOSER, C. *A Survey of Social Conditions in England and Wales*. Oxford: Clarendon Press.
11. Central Advisory Council for Education (England) (1954) *Early Leaving*. London: H.M.S.O.
12. CLARKE, E. L. (1936) 'The Recruitment of the Nation's Leaders'. *Sociolog. Rev.*, **28**.
13. DALE, R. (1952) 'Some Non-Academic Factors Influencing University Studies'. *Brit. J. Sociol.*, 3 (1).
14. DALE, R. (1954) *From School to University: A Study*. London: Routledge.
15. DOBB, MAURICE (1946) *Studies in the Development of Capitalism*. London: Routledge.
16. DRUCKER, PETER F. (1959) *The Landmarks of Tomorrow*. London: Heinemann.
17. FLOUD, J. (1950) 'Educational Opportunity and Social Mobility'. *The Yearbook of Education*. London.
18. FLOUD, J., HALSEY, A. H., & MARTIN, F. M. (1956) *Social Class and Educational Opportunity*. London: Heinemann.
19. FLOUD, J., & SCOTT, W. (1956) 'The Social Origins of Teachers in England and Wales'. *Transactions of the 3rd World Congress of Sociology*, 8. London.
20. FRASER, ELISABETH (1959) *Home Environment and the School*. London: Univ. of London Press.
21. GLASS, DAVID V. (ed.) (1954) *Social Mobility in Britain*. London: Routledge.
22. GLASS, DAVID V., (1959) 'Education', in M. Ginsberg (ed.) *Law and Opinion in the 20th Century*. London: Stevens.
23. GLASS, DAVID V., & GRAY, J. L. (1938) 'Opportunity and the Older Universities', in L. Hogben (ed.), *Political Arithmetic*.
24. GLASS, RUTH (1948) *The Social Background of a Plan: A Study of Middlesbrough*. London: Routledge.
25. GRAY, J. L. (1936) *The Nation's Intelligence*. London: Watts.
26. GRAY, J. L., & MOSHINSKY, P. (1934) 'Ability and Opportunity in English Education', in Hogben, L. (ed.), *Political Arithmetic*. London: Allen and Unwin.
27. GRAY, J. L., (1935) 'The Measurement of Educational Opportunity'. *Adult Educ.*, **18** (1).
28. HALSEY, A. H. (1958) 'The Universities and Intellectual Life'. *Univ. Quart.*, **16**.
29. H.M.S.O. (1959) 15–18 ('The Crowther Report'), vol. 1.
30. H.M.S.O. (1960) 15–18 ('The Crowther Report'), vol. 2.
31. JONES, D. C. (1934) 'Social Factors in Secondary Education', in *The Social Survey of Merseyside*, vol. 3, pp. 158–200. London: Hodder and Stoughton.
32. JUDGES, A. V. (1953) 'Tradition and the Comprehensive School'. *British J. educ. Stud.*, **2**, 1.
33. KELSALL, R. K. (1957) *Report on an Inquiry into Applications for*

Jean Floud

Admission to Universities. London: Association of Universities for the British Commonwealth.

34. KRAMER, R. (1942) 'The Reform of the Foreign Service'. *Adult Educ.*, **14**, 15.

35. LEYBOURNE-WHITE, G. (1940) *Education and the Birth-Rate: A Social Dilemma*. London: Cape.

36. McCLELLAND, D. C., *et al.* (1958) *Talent and Society*. New York: Van Nostrand.

37. MALLESON, N. (1958) 'Some Non-Intellectual Correlates of Academic Success and Failure'. *Brit. J. educ. Psychol.*, **28** (1).

38. MANNHEIM, KARL (1951) *Freedom, Power and Democratic Planning*. London, 1951.

39. MARSHALL, T. H. (ed.) (1938) *Class Conflict and Social Stratification*. London: Le Play House.

40. MARSHALL, T. H. (1950) *Citizenship and Social Class*. London: Cambridge Univ. Press.

41. MARSHALL, T. H. (1953) 'Social Selection in the Welfare State'. *Eugen. Rev. 45*.

42. NISBET, J. D. (1953) *Family Environment*. Eugenics Society, Occasional Papers, no. 8. London: Cassell.

43. P.E.P. (Political and Economic Planning). (1954) 'Background of the University Student'. *Planning*, 20 (Nov.).

44. SCOTTISH COUNCIL FOR RESEARCH IN EDUCATION (1953) *Social Implications of the 1947 Scottish Mental Survey*. London: Univ. of London Press.

45. SCOTTISH COUNCIL FOR RESEARCH IN EDUCATION (1958) *Eleven-Year-Olds Grow Up*. London: Univ. of London Press.

46. TROPP, A. (1956) *The Schoolteachers*. London: Heinemann.

47. VERNON, P. E. (1956) 'Psychological Traits of Teachers'. *Yearbook of Education*.

48. WORKERS' EDUCATIONAL ASSOCIATION (1943) *The Public Schools*. London.

49. YOUNG, M. (1958) *The Rise of Meritocracy, 1870–2033*. London: Thames and Hudson.

30

POLITICAL PARTIES AND

ELECTIONS

Richard H. Pear

POLITICAL parties and elections interest political scientists for two main reasons: firstly, because it is part of our present re-examination of the democratic process to inquire more closely into how opinion becomes transformed into political authority—and the party seems to be an obvious transformer. Second, because both parties and elections are relatively 'open' fields for study; Official Secrets Acts and other constitutional devices for restricting access to political knowledge that might embarrass statesmen do not operate within political parties, while election results are public property.

The Nature and Origins of Political Parties

Given the democratic assumptions: (i) that people do have differing opinions on matters of political importance; (ii) that the people should be involved in the business of governing; and (iii) that the only effective way for a people to govern themselves is through a system of political representation, the organ that can best relate these three factors into a continuous institutionalized mode of activity is the political party.

Until comparatively recently in the history of political science, parties were often thought of as distorting an otherwise balanced and reasonable 'public opinion'. Leaders in a legislative assembly would have different political views, but attempts to gain extra-parliamentary support to advance their parliamentary views were to be regarded as dangerous and vulgar. This conception of party was but a step from an older view that 'faction' undermined the stability of the body politic and from Hobbes' view that unofficial private associations in the state are 'like worms in the entrails of a natural man'.[14] Political parties became respectable in the nineteenth century and, perhaps because of the rationalist assumptions of many nineteenth-century political thinkers, the exact manner in which political party leaders came to (or claimed to) speak for their party followers was not often discussed. Those who did inquire into the nature of parties were often under the influence of Aristotle, Locke, or Marx, and took the robust view that parties were nothing more than vehicles for protecting and advancing the property interests of their supporters. Parties were seen as being the creatures of low-tariff enthusiasts, manufacturers, agrarian interests and industrial employees, and party pronouncements were minutely dissected for clues to material interest. In contrast, and in accord with the plain fact that some parties appeared to possess a distinct ideology, some writers took the view that a party was a vehicle for implementing philosophical ideas and primarily an embodiment of ideas rather than an association of material interests. In fact many histories of political parties were written entirely in terms of ideas and electoral appeals for support of those ideas. There was, too, the proposition that all party political struggles were really between those politicians who were in office and who profited from office and those who were out of office and envied the spoils of their opponents. Bryce's *American Commonwealth*[8] did much to popularize this view of American politics, especially in America where the spoils of office were such that they could be seen as a real cause for political rivalry. But it is difficult to see what spoils there were for British politicians in the Disestablishment of the Welsh Church, the Licensing Acts, or the pro-Boer agitation of some of Bryce's Liberal contemporaries at home. (Here one must note the possibly misleading themes often transported to England from the political culture of our American friends. The title of a famous modern American work, *Politics: Who Gets What, When and How*,[16] is not very appropriate as an outline theme for British politics where, apart from a handful of those who get Cabinet posts, very few other politicians obtain anything in the nature of substantial material reward.

The American theme of material interest in the spoils of office had a profound effect on American thoughts about parties. If politics provided openings to material reward (either directly by election or appointment to paid office, or indirectly through one's connexion with the ruling party which allocated contracts for works), it was clear that those who ran the party could, and often did, raid the public exchequer to reward the politically faithful. This corruption of the representative element in politics and degradation of the democratic dogma led, at the beginning of the present century, to demands for the right of the *ordinary voter* to participate in the *selection* of the party's candidates for office. Democracy, which had long allowed the voter to choose a Democrat or a Republican, must be extended to give him the right to choose which Republican or which Democrat was to be allowed, later on, to ask for his support. Democracy had become degraded because both parties had put up corrupt machine politicians. It had to be purified by a further injection of democratic ideology: 'primary' elections, and the devices of the initiative, referendum, and recall would result in 'returning the government of the people to the People'. Some progress toward cleaner politics was made in America by these devices, but initially it was not very impressive in amount.

For our present purpose the important thing is to note how in the course of their 'muckraking' of the political scandals of late-nineteenth-century America, American political writers set out on a course of realistic and detailed examination of political parties and pressure groups which they have never abandoned. Most writers soon abandoned the idea that a national 'Public Opinion' did, or indeed could, find expression in party political policy.[17, 18] It became apparent to the academic writers that American political parties are coalitions of political leadership groups in states and cities, and that what emerges as the national party programme for Presidential elections is a very vague and broad consensus of the preferences of the regional, local, ethnic, and religious groups which the party is hoping to attract to its cause. Thus the climate of politics in the U.S.A. has been favourable to the study of the techniques of forming and organizing political opinion in defined groups, and unfavourable to exercises in the drafting of coherent ideological and economic programmes for a unified national party. As the national party has no very important meaning in terms of nation-wide organizational coherence, the study and criticism of such organization as it has, has remained the concern of a few zealous reformers. Where the national structure is weak and national policy means, in fact, the views of the party's Leader (and the party out of the Presidency has no undisputed leader), and where state and local organization is of primary importance, attention has been concentrated on those groups which are influential in the affairs of the party at those levels.

The tendency in recent years therefore has been to seek out and analyse the workings of those groups which exert pressures on the party, at all levels. Instead of positing a party united on principles, American scholars see as a more relevant field for research the workings of 'pressure groups', each group having a parcel of demands upon which the legislators are urged to act. The pressure groups are defined as groups of persons organized and active for the purpose of putting pressure on politicians to carry out the important, if limited, aims of the group. A 'pressure group' differs from a political party mainly by the fact that though it uses political methods, it does not wish to govern the country. It must have access to legislators, but it does not wish to run its own officers or members for elections to public office if the politicians who do run for office can in other ways be persuaded of the group's political importance.

As American parties show no signs of reforming themselves and becoming more 'responsible' and nationally unified, many writers argue that pressure groups are justified, and even welcome because they express, in a way which the parties cannot, the 'real' needs of real people. Parties exist to act as brokers between such 'real' demands, and as long as they remain mere brokers, eschewing creative thought and consistent agitation, for so long will the American two-party system remain secure. Should a party become irrevocably committed to one major interest or ideology, then the body politic would become tragically split; bitter intransigence and civil strife would be the outcome. In this view attempts to strengthen the national party, to provide it with overriding national goals and to equip it with means of disciplining its members, are to be deplored. There is a complex sociological background to such views which it is not possible to explore here. But the fear seems to be that if a nationally united and disciplined party were to succeed electorally and proceed to its announced goals, the defeated party's supporters would not accept their defeat. Respect for the law is, outside the text books on citizenship, not a dominant characteristic of American society. The political health of the nation thus depends upon the abatement of serious principled political agitation—and upon the apathy of the voters: the voters fail to check the selfish interests of politicians, but the multitude of pressure groups, by urging their own selfish interests, put a desirable curb on the acquisitive instincts of the paid politician.

As Bryce started a line of criticism and investigation for American students, so did Ostrogorski for the study of British political parties. Early in the twentieth century his two great volumes on *Democracy and the Organisation of Political Parties*[27] were published. Volume I is the greatest work yet written on the evolution of British political parties and is of an unparalleled richness in its detail of nineteenth-century developments. Ostrogorski, a Lithuanian Jew who lived most of his life in France and wrote in French, became an ardent defender of a relationship between parliamentary politicians and their supporters outside parliament which was, it seemed, fast disappearing because of the increase in the suffrage. Ostrogorski, like Bryce, was a liberal, but he viewed with apprehension the control which was being claimed by extraparliamentary party organization over the acts and votes of M.P.s. Joseph Chamberlain—then a Radical—had boasted that his newly

Political Parties and Elections

created National Liberal Federation would become a Liberal 'Parliament' blowing its trumpets so loudly outside the Palace of Westminster that all Liberal M.P.s inside would defer to its true popular tones. Liberal M.P.s would be called to account by the Federation—the organization of the active rank and file. M.P.s who ignored the Federation's demands would be deprived of nomination for the next election by Federation zealots in the constituency parties. The National Liberal Federation, if noisy, was also high-minded and screechingly devoted, to the principles of that very principled man, Mr Gladstone.

These developments were to be deplored. In Ostrogorski's view uninstructed political opinion which bore none of the burdens of deliberation upon and administration of the State's affairs should not be allowed to influence the actions of M.P.s. Parliament was the proper forum for political debate; and if not Parliament, then the nation or at least the constituency. An M.P. should be required to risk the danger of defeat by his constituents whose representative he was. He should not be required to trim his sails to the gusts of passion which emanated from a few local zealots. (Moreover the National Liberal Federation leadership was adept at turning the storms on or off according to the wishes of the Chamberlainites in the party.)

Types of Party Organization

While Ostrogorski described in wonderful detail the evolution of British parties and the rise of their rank and file to a position of influence, it is not quite clear just what role he thought the rank and file should play. As a democrat and a liberal he did not wish for oligarchical parties. As a lawyer and historian he could not regard organized extra-parliamentary influence upon M.P.s as compatible with the British parliamentary system which he admired.

Until R. T. McKenzie returned to this theme in his important book[22] the study of party organization had been almost entirely neglected, particularly of that important part which had concerned Ostrogorski. McKenzie's book is the only successor to Ostrogorski's.

McKenzie's thesis is that while British parties do, and should, consist of an active organized rank and file in some sort of relationship to the parliamentary party, the extent to which the extra-parliamentary organization is effective in policy-making is much less than has been claimed by some modern democratic thinkers (notably by Clement Attlee[3] and in his latest revision of his book). Moreover whatever claims to make policy are heard from the rank and file organization, these cannot be allowed to influence important governmental policy. What for Ostrogorski is the shrill and unrepresentative voice of the local constituency zealot trying to intimidate the M.P., is for McKenzie the

545

Richard H. Pear

absurdity and constitutional impropriety of an annual conference trying to legislate for the nation: *mutatis mutandis*, both writers exhibit a high regard for the Cabinet system of British government. McKenzie's book is a masterly analysis of where political policy power lies in the Conservative and Labour Parties. In the Conservative party it lies, without any party *constitutional* doubt, with the party leader—but leaders can be, and are, overthrown in a special Tory way if they fail to heed the voices of the organized rank and file. In the Labour Party, where policy is constitutionally created by the annual conferences, the parliamentary leader as the actual or potential Prime Minister has been able to find ways of getting the conference to pronounce favourably on things he agrees with, and has usually managed to avoid conference defeats on important issues. McKenzie sums up by saying that the idea of a 'democratically' organized political party is incompatible with the British system of Cabinet government; which is a way of saying that the Conservative party, which does not claim to be 'democratically' organized, has more understanding of our constitutional ways than the Labour Party, which does make that claim. Or, lest this seem to impute bias on McKenzie's part (which is not a valid criticism of this most scholarly work) one could say that when a Labour government is in power it must drop its ideological attachment to the policy sovereignty of the annual conference—which is what in large measure it did from 1945 to 1951. The fact remains, however, that British constitutional traditions embarrass one party more than the other—which is not surprising when we consider that the British constitution is the product of political practices developed throughout history by non-Labour, 'non-democratically' organized parties.

It is hoped that this account of some important contributions to the discussion of political parties makes it clear to the reader that rather more interest is now being shown by academic political scientists in problems of party structure than in analysis of party programmes or ideologies. Current comment is, however, not devoid of value references. Party organization is being examined to discover how far *within* that organization the practice of democratic values of free discussion, free election, and free competition between individuals is actually allowed—or indeed possible: political parties in democracies ought, we feel, to incorporate the political values of democracy. But at once it becomes apparent that, within any organization, specialization by function becomes a means whereby a bureaucratic structure and outlook may develop. Political leaders and specialized political functionaries are only possible today where a large rank and file gives its financial support to a party headquarters in which leaders and specialists function. Rank and file rumblings against headquarters' bureaucracy invariably come to naught because the rank and file cannot perform the leadership or specialized functions themselves—and they often admit this, and call for other leaders or other organization functionaries. Robert Michels[23] devised an 'iron law of oligarchy' upon the basis of much research which demonstrated that organization *per se* brings in its train specialized function and a bureaucratic outlook, and that this is true of any large organization, however anti-oligarchical its ultimate faith may be.

While we have more facts about parties than ever before we are not yet within striking distance of any 'general theory' of parties which would provide us with a method of classifying different types of parties and would advance generalizations about the causes of different types of party organization. Such a theory would also direct our thoughts upon certain agreed lines of investigation when studying new political parties; it would tell us what questions should be asked about forms of organization; and it might theoretically permit us to predict the type of party (and politics) that would arise from certain social and political circumstances.

Duverger[13] has argued ably for the need for a 'general theory', and has outlined many factors and described many situations which seem to give rise to different types of parties. His main theme is that some are 'cadre' parties which see themselves as being the sources of supply of leaders in national politics, while others are characterized by a mass membership and have the features of mass social movements as well as those of political parties proper. Mass parties are usually of more recent origin than 'cadre' parties, and their various parts (the parliamentary party, the annual conference, the local units and regional federations) are well articulated. The doctrines of the party and the central machinery weld together a large mass of members who are available to carry out the political and educational duties directed by the central executive committee—on which the rank and file have representation. This committee also seeks to control the actions of the party's parliamentary representatives. The best examples of mass parties are large Communist parties in non-Communist countries. Social-Democratic and Labour parties also usually have most of the characteristics of mass parties. For this type of party the parliamentary struggle is only one aspect of the battle they are conducting to change men's minds and to reform society.

A 'cadre' party is marked by its preoccupation with the parliamentary struggle; by its small dues-paying membership and by its acceptance of the leadership of the parliamentary leaders. Its field of endeavour is less wide than that of the mass party, its aims are more limited and its history often points to its origins inside a legislative assembly before the time when mass participation in politics was thought normal. The British Labour Party is a good example of a mass party, while the British

547

Conservative party before 1950 was a fair example of a 'cadre' party. Since that date the British Conservatives have upset M. Duverger's neat division to some extent, for with the Woolton reforms the party has become a 'cadre' party *with* a mass membership. But Duverger's insight is still substantially correct. The present large Tory rank and file does not try to control the party or dictate its policy, because it does not want to. Its endeavours are more restricted than those of the Labour Party and its 'crusading' spirit less pronounced. (It is just as unthinkable that the Conservatives could have called for national mass-meeting approvals of the Suez invasion, with demonstrators in Trafalgar Square and Whitehall, as that the Labour Party could have refrained from such traditional mass party manifestations.)

What makes for these differences in party organization and organizational theory? In Duverger's view an ideological party must seek and maintain a mass membership, while a party weak in ideology will be content to operate from day to day with a less elaborate organization for stimulating its followers; and will rely for its finances not on masses of small regular subscriptions, but on large donations from a few important adherents. It will rely in its politics on the weight of influence of local and national personalities, and its contacts with the non-parliamentary world will be informal. This is in contrast to mass parties which will formally affiliate with other large popular organizations for the purposes of finance, manpower, and extra-parliamentary advice.

Another, and a very complex, set of factors analysed at length by Duverger is the effect of different electoral systems upon the number and structure of parties. Do minor parties proliferate under systems of Proportional Representation? It is very tempting to suggest that the number of parties asking for votes is related to the manner in which the electoral law splits the total vote between the major and minor parties, thereby encouraging small parties to enter the struggle where the law gives them a chance of some parliamentary success. On a detailed analysis it is rather less than obvious that P. R. always tends towards the proliferation of parties and that single member, single ballot constituencies result in fewer parties. What is clearer is that if any electoral system normally results in more than two parties gaining respectable strength in the legislature, coalition governments become usual, and *that* fact does affect the way in which parties are organized and regard their own members and the electorate. A party in a permanent state of opposition can remain organizationally and ideologically pure. A coalition-oriented party would find such purity an embarrassment.

While we are far from having achieved a 'general theory' of parties, there are enough similarities to be found amongst parties throughout the world for the attempt to be undertaken—indeed M. Duverger has already made substantial progress in his own work. National constitutional structure, electoral law, ideology, politically organized religious interest, all provide possible heads for a classification of types of party and for an eventual general theory.

With the study of elections we enter a field in which quantification has been profitably employed to test many of the insights of historians and practical politicians, and where much valuable descriptive work has been completed. As in no other political situation, elections give apparent proof of the citizens' wishes and the politician's endeavours. Public opinion may be elusive and fickle, but the political popularity test conducted at the polls brings some of the uncertainty of politics periodically to an end. Before the days of opinion polling bye-elections could be said to show approval or disapproval of a government's record—provided they occurred in the right places and that the voters could be assumed to have thought about the government's record. One great advantage of opinion polling is that we can at any time discover what is in the public's mind—or what they say is in their mind—without first putting an 'issue' to them and then asking them to decide for or against it. Electoral results too become far more interesting, and our knowledge of society far richer, when we can find out what sort of people voted as they did; and this the polling experts undoubtedly can find out. But the opinion poll gives only limited information: to be told by a man that 'I voted Tory this time because of the failure of nationalization', even if a true statement, is still only the beginning of the search for fuller reasons which would disclose what he thought was wrong with nationalization and why he believed that voting Tory would help to correct those faults. Without other types of effort the opinion poll would not tell us very much of what the election was about. If we wish archeologists of the future to understand our political culture we should bury in the foundations of some new Piccadilly site the Gallup polls *and* the Nuffield College studies of General Elections since 1945.[9, 10, 11, 11a, 21, 26] These studies have treated General Elections as current history upon which as much fact and opinion as possible have been assembled, and judgements rendered. The antecedent events are recorded and the occasion for calling the election carefully examined. Party machinery is described, candidates classified, and editorials digested. 'Stunts' and other amusing incidents are chronicled and party programmes dissected. In addition to the national campaign some local campaigns are covered, and the national result is studied in comparison with previous elections, with facts about the percentage 'swing' (nationally and locally) from one party to the other. These outward and visible signs of political activity must be recorded in detail if we are to try to understand our political behaviour. Public opinion surveys during elections have one main aim—to predict the result—though many facts of deeper significance may be collected *en route*. With an opinion poll the intention is to find out how individual voters intend to vote, and prediction (in England) has been remarkably accurate.

On a local scale, studies have been carried out in selected constituencies to discover how the various social classes do vote, to discover the extent of deviant voting, to test hypotheses about religion and voting, to discover how much the voter is influenced by general election propaganda, and to what extent he is interested in politics and how this affects voting. Two studies have been made of voting at the 1951 and 1955 elections in a Bristol constituency;[24, 25] one of voting in Greenwich in the General Election of 1950,[4] and less extensive studies have been made in Droylesden,[12] Stretford,[6] and Glossop.[5] None of these studies shows significant deviation from the pattern that social class apparently determines voting preference. We know therefore a good deal about how the various social classes vote, but do we know very much about *why* classes vote as they do?

Voting

Common sense suggests that many factors influence the decision of the voter in the privacy of the polling booth. Some will seem more obvious than others. Is the voter a man or a woman; rich or poor; a farmer or a factory worker; a keen citizen or a slack one; a Protestant, Catholic, Jew, or atheist? All these factors, and many more, in a voter's 'make-up' can be recorded in his answers to questions, and it will be found that some of them apparently weigh more heavily with him than others. But although it is as an individual that we question him, he lives amongst others, many of whom have political views which they may have urged upon him from time to time. In addition, therefore, to the process of weighing up the factors (which we assume he undertakes) he has to weigh up himself in the light of the opinions of his fellows. 'Pressures' from his social environment may be important in his voting decision. If the social pressures act in a direction opposite to that of the decision he would take if 'left to himself', they are known as 'cross pressures'. Too many 'cross pressures' have been found in some cases to lead to indecision and non-voting.[15]

Having considered, for a number of voters, an array of factors and pressures which may have influenced voting (and having asked his interviewees what they consider to be the 'most important' issues of the day), the political sociologist will be able to present a picture of those things which apparently determine the way people vote. For instance, if Catholics (as in England) vote heavily for a party which is not Catholic (and makes no *special* appeal to them) one may wonder if the specifically religious views of Catholic voters influence their vote. If, as in France, there is a Catholic party but large numbers of Catholics ignore it, it becomes clear that to many Catholics non-religious issues take precedence in their minds over religion. In this way, religious, regional, or ethnic factors may be relegated to a position of minor influence upon voters. However, a characteristic shared by the great majority of voters for one party will appear as a major reason why that party is supported by those people. Thus the probable reason why a majority of Catholics in England support the Labour Party is that most of them are not well-off, and the Labour Party appeals to the less well-off elements in our society.

To say, therefore, in such a case, that religion is not an important determinant of voting is to say that it does not *appear* as important as certain other factors. Political sociologists present the results of sample surveys and draw conclusions from statistical data. While in no way deprecating the importance of this work, it must not be forgotten that such conclusions do not purport to tell us with any logical precision *why* in an *individual* case an elector voted as he did. It would be fascinating to know why, in 1951, 8 per cent of top business executives in Britain voted Labour[7]—and who they were. Work can be done in this field, but it is extremely expensive, involving long personal interviews, with 'open-ended' questions; and the classification of types of answer to these 'open' questions is a laborious task.

Surveys of political opinion are based on statistical samples of the electorate. A random sample, taking, for instance, every 100th voter on an electoral roll, can be expected to give a representation of the views of the constituency as a whole which is reasonably accurate. When, however, it is desired to split up the sample by age, sex, occupation, religion, etc., the size of a sub-sample, for instance, 'single, Catholic, males, under thirty, may be too small for great significance to be attached to it. The remedy is to take not every 100th, but every 50th or 25th voter on the roll—in practical terms to spend more money on the survey. Another type of sample is the 'quota' sample; that is, to interview a certain quota of persons from different occupational groups on the basis of the known distribution of occupations in the community. For certain technical reasons a random sample is considered preferable in many instances to a quota sample.

Common to both methods are the assumptions of regularity and of the relative stability of the material. The first is a statistical assumption. The second assumes that interviewees tell the truth, and what they say they believe and how they say they will vote will not be falsified in their actual voting. Allowing a small margin for human perversity, the second assumption is well enough founded. Voting studies are also founded on the view that political beliefs reflect the personal hopes of individuals, *and* the ideas of the social class to which they belong. In the case of many voters it is clear that they think of themselves not only as individuals but as individuals of a certain type, and that what is good for that *type* of person is good for them.

When the results of political surveys (the percentages voting for different parties) are set against the actual percentage results of the election, the surveys, taken before the event, are seen to be extraordinarily accurate forecasts of the actual result. The longer the opinion polling continues the more accurate the result is likely to be. The Gallup Poll in America which, with much subsequent embarrassment, predicted a win for Governor Dewey in 1948 when President Truman was victorious had been too confident and had stopped polling some time before election day.

Having made the assumption (adequately supported now by innumerable surveys) that social class is the most important single determinant of voting choice, attention may be concentrated on segments of the population which deviate from the general pattern. Thus in pre-Hitler Vienna (and present-day America) the Jewish middle-class vote is more radical than that of the middle classes in general. One may assume that this is a reflection of the social position of middle-class Jews, who, because they are less than completely acceptable in gentile middle-class circles, see no reason to support those middle-class values with their vote. Negro voters in the U.S.A. used to vote heavily for the 'capitalist' party—the Republicans—though they were the most ill-paid and exploited of American workers. The Republican party was, of course, the party of their liberator, Abraham Lincoln, and they continued to pay their debt to his memory until the 1930s, when Franklin Roosevelt's 'New Deal' relief measures, by insisting on no discrimination between the white and coloured unemployed, captured the Negro vote for the Democratic party. They still support that party though its not unimportant Southern wing embodies all the racial prejudices they hate.

In recent years the U.S. Catholic vote has greatly interested both politicians and political sociologists. Originally an overwhelmingly Democratic vote—for the Democrats were the party of the underprivileged, the underpaid, the immigrants, and the 'minorities'—in the elections of 1952 and 1956 very many Catholics deserted the party and voted for General Eisenhower. This has been interpreted as a 'status shift'. Many Catholics in the post-war years having become affluent and socially more self-confident, raised their social status by leaving the party of the under-dogs. With a Catholic candidate for the White House in 1960, it was a matter of great importance to guess how these recent Republican converts would act. They acted quite unmistakably, practically all of them voting Democratic again. This was seen not as a reversion to their 'under-dog' psychology, but rather as an attempt to improve the position of Catholics in America by proving that a Roman Catholic *could* be elected to the White House.

Professor Lipset,[19] on the basis of extensive researches, has listed categories of people who vote 'high' or 'low'—that is, those who are generally keen to cast a vote and those who are usually apathetic. These categories are important for our knowledge of voting, for it is basic to our understanding of how people vote to know what kinds of people bother to vote at all. Lipset's lists must be used with some caution, for they include American voters, and while America is a 'Western' democracy, some of its political habits are very different from those of Europe—including the comparative political inactivity of the American population at large.

'High' voters include those with high incomes, high educational attainments, business men, white collar workers, government employees, commercial crop farmers, miners, Jews, whites, and men. 'Low' voters include people of low income, poor education, unskilled workers, domestic servants, subsistence farmers, and women. On each category (and Lipset gives more than those mentioned above) it would be possible to write an interpretive essay, but all it is possible to do here is to suggest certain common reasons for high voting. Two must suffice. Those with high income and high education may be disposed to regular voting because they can understand the issues, and with taxation and the regulation of business as constant features of their lives, they are not willing to let governmental policy develop in these fields without having attempted to influence it. With government employees and commercial crop farmers, government policy—on employment or agricultural programmes—is of direct and vital importance. Subsistence farming is different: Governments are interested (if at all) only from a humanitarian point of view. The prosperity of commercial crop farming is a big item in a government's foreign and domestic economic policies, and governmental concern about it gives commercial crop farmers a political interest and a bargaining position.

'High' voters are also good citizens in other respects. They belong to far more associations, clubs, and unions than do 'low' voters. Social solidarity can, even with low income, produce high voting. The best example of this sort is the mining community, where the common focus and common problem of employment in the pits, plus its normally one-class character—which means that 'ordinary' people are put into positions of social leadership—produces an enhanced sense of solidarity.

Men are better voters than women in all social groups. When women vote they vote more conservatively than men.[11] Working-class housewives are the least promising political material, in spite of what some strong feminists have said about the way in which the world would be improved if the women took over. However, in Finland, where the wives

553

of the Swedish élite are highly educated, they are better voters than Finnish men, and in America certain middle-class leisured women are very active in politics.[28] Continental radicals feared that giving women the vote would put them under the political domination of the churches and for this reason female suffrage was long postponed in certain European countries.* Many observers have considered (not altogether correctly) the long dominance of Dr Adenauer as stemming from the large female religious vote in Western Germany.

We can attempt some generalizations about where 'high left' voting occurs. Leaving aside strict class reasons, left voting is more prevalent in large cities, large industrial units, in areas of high unemployment, amongst minority groups in the U.S.A., among European workers, miners, commercial farmers, fishermen, sailors, dockers, lumbermen—and men generally. If we consider some of these categories, it becomes apparent that the 'objective' economic condition of some groups 'ought' not to lead to 'left' or radical voting. Many miners, and commercial farmers, are affluent when compared with subsistence farmers or white collar workers—and at times are well-off even by urban middle-class standards. The clues to their leftward inclinations are probably to be found in their vulnerability to economic winds of change which make them more political than others, their social solidarity which has grown out of co-operative efforts to maintain their living standards, and the memories of past battles to achieve, through collective action, their present standards. Moreover, in Western contemporary politics, a 'left government' is by tradition considered less reluctant to interfere with the 'free enterprise' economy for the purpose of righting economic misfortunes—even if those misfortunes still leave their victims with a standard of life well above the subsistence level.

We can summarize the differences between 'left' and non-left voting by saying that in general a 'left' vote indicates dissatisfaction with the *status quo*: that frequently this dissatisfaction has to do with economic problems and aspirations: that it usually looks to governmental action for improvement: and that occasionally 'left' voting indicates unease about social discriminations and inequalities amongst voters whose standard of living and economic prospects are good. One of the problems for political leaders and political theorists is, of course, whether 'left' voting or 'left' parties should be considered more 'progressive' than non-left parties or persons. The ideas of the left are now very old and some of its slogans and myths may be quite inappropriate to the solution of contemporary economic and social problems. This does not concern us here. We need only to record that the ideas of the 'left'—more government assistance to the underprivileged, more state economic activity, more economic security, a

* Swiss women still have no vote in national elections.

Political Parties and Elections

continual attack on the real or apparent power of the rich or privileged, and a sustained effort to achieve greater social equality—all of these are still very much in evidence in the politics of Western democracies.

Class

'Class' is the most important single determinant of political behaviour, and sociology (and society) is much the healthier for recognizing this. In the past only snobs and Marxists talked about class; others kept it out of polite conversation lest the recognition of its importance encouraged the lower orders to hate their betters. The lower orders were no doubt envious of the upper classes, but in the vast majority of cases they wished to join or emulate them, not eradicate them. Now that the ordinary people are, in many Western countries, reasonably affluent, they more and more take on the habits, clothes, and fads of the middle or even upper-middle classes of a generation ago. Then, of course, as 'class' is a very important psychological insurance, those whose class habits are being imitated by the upwardly mobile must put themselves out of their reach by devising new marks of 'upper classness'.

The important feature of class for politics is that when a worker, for instance, feels that he is no longer 'working-class', he does not always feel lost or 'classless'; he may put himself in a higher class and may being to think and act as a member of that class. The confusing thing for the political leader is that a voter may describe himself as non-working-class (when objectively he is) and yet continue to vote for the party which he has described as working class. For instance, Mark Abrams[1] reports that one-third of the Labour Party's working-class (skilled and non-skilled) supporters do not consider themselves part of the working class. Amongst working-class Conservative supporters, 46 per cent consider themselves working-class, 47 per cent think of themselves as middle-class and 3 per cent consider themselves 'upper-middle class'. Thus if the Labour Party is seen as losing support because of its identification with the 'working class', this is not because the country is becoming classless, but rather because those who are objectively working class prefer to see themselves as middle class.

What therefore is class? It is objectively the income and occupation group to which a person belongs. These groups (socio-economic groups) ascend from the lowest paid, lowest prestige occupations to the highest prestige, highest earning occupations and professions, and in any one society there is likely to be little difficulty in arriving at agreement on their rating. How many groups the social analyst needs is largely a matter to be determined by the purposes he has in mind. Reference to the national census of occupations will tell him what is the national distribution of the groups, so that in making certain types of survey in which it is desirable to have a sample which is the nation in microcosm, his sample can be proportioned accordingly. We know from our own experience that different groups have different ideas and aspirations, and we know too that most people know what the word 'class' suggests. Thus in voting studies 'class' is in continual use as a predictor and clarifier, and 'self-assessed class' is the most revealing predictor of political behaviour.

The 'Klassenkampf' of classical Marxism has, in Western Europe and the U.S.A., been domesticated and tamed. 'Class' is just the most useful single device with which to describe the actual social position of a man, and from which to understand his aspirations, education, associations, probable style of life, reaction to public events, and probable vote. His particular consciousness of society arises from his class position, as Karl Marx believed. While it is not true that 'lower-class' consciousness will necessarily make a revolutionary, it is quite likely to make a trade unionist, and possibly a leftist.

The most obvious fact about political party support in industrial countries is that lower income groups vote mainly for parties of the left, while higher income groups support the right. Elections have become, in the appropriate words of two American scholars, the expression of the 'democratic class struggle'.[2] The fact that in France and Italy large numbers of poorly paid workers vote Communist does not mean (because the Communist Party is undemocratic in its philosophy) that they are not part of the *democratic* class struggle. They may 'believe' in Communism, or they may vote Communist merely because the Communist Party is the most powerful and well organized left party. In France in 1956, 39 per cent of industrial workers, 37 per cent of agricultural workers, 16 per cent of white collar workers, but only 7 per cent of merchants and 5 per cent of farm owners voted Communist. Amongst poor French industrial workers 45 per cent voted Communist, while only 18 per cent of above average workers gave the party their votes. On the right, 59 per cent of farm owners gave their vote to M.R.P. or Independents, as did 38 per cent of merchants. In Italy (1953) 58 per cent of farm labourers and 33 per cent of share-cropping tenants voted Communist, as did 53 per cent of the lower paid industrial workers. The best paid workers voted 24 per cent Communist and 36 per cent Christian Democrat. 63 per cent of employers and professional people voted Christian Democrat or Liberal (Anglice, 'conservative'), while 72 per cent of large landowners voted Christian Democrat, Liberal or Monarchist.[20]

Even in the United States, where class appeals and class programmes are not part of the American tradition, class voting is clear. In the 1948 election 80 per cent of the workers voted Democrat—a figure higher than has ever been achieved in Britain, France, Italy, or Germany where 'workers' parties' are strong and well established. In that election only 23 per cent of business and professional men voted Democrat. Never since 1940 in Presidential and congressional elections have less than 61 per cent of business and professional people voted Republican, or less than 50 per cent of workers Democratic. American parties are not described as class parties, but with the Democrats' success in appealing to the less well-off since the early days of the nineteenth century, and with Republicans espousing (for most of the time since the end of the Civil War) the values of business enterprise, the American voter will use the words 'wealthy' or 'better class' to describe the Republican, and 'middle class', 'ordinary people', and 'works for wages' to describe Democratic supporters.

'Class' has a great deal to do with politics, but class is not politics *tout court*. Social class position tells a man who he is, where he is socially, and where he is likely to go, in relation to his fellow citizens. 'Class' is his occupation, his economic position, and the respect which is paid to him by others, and by him to them. It tells him a great deal about politics—but he may dislike what he learns and decide to get into a class where he will have different associates and different values. In the 1930s many young middle-class sons of Tory fathers made the change from Conservative to Labour. They became middle-class Socialists. Today working-class sons are becoming middle-class Tories, or new middle-class Socialists, or the equivalent in the future.

Perhaps the most striking example of the pulling power of social class comes from France. There, with a Catholic party by no means priest-ridden or reactionary (the M.R.P.) and a Communist party appealing openly to the class interests of the workers, in 1956 almost half the voters for Communist party candidates described themselves as Catholics.[20]

REFERENCES

1. ABRAMS, MARK, & ROSE, RICHARD (1960) *Must Labour Lose?* Harmondsworth: Penquin Books.
2. ANDERSON, D., & DAVIDSON, P. (1943) *Ballots and the Democratic Class Struggle*. Stanford, Calif.: Stanford Univ. Press.
3. ATTLEE, CLEMENT [EARL] (1937) *The Labour Party in Perspective*. London: Gollancz. Also Revised edn., 1949. London: Gollancz.
4. BENNEY, MARK, GRAY, A. P., & PEAR, R. H. (1956) *How People Vote*. London: Routledge.
5. BIRCH, A. H. (1959) *Small-Town Politics*. Oxford: Clarendon Press.
6. BIRCH, A. H., & CAMPBELL, P. (1950) 'Voting Behaviour in a Lancashire Constituency'. *Brit. J. Sociol.*, **1**, 202.
7. BONHAM, J. (1954) *The Middle Class Vote*. London: Faber.
8. BRYCE, JAMES (1888) *The American Commonwealth*. London: Macmillan.

Richard H. Pear

9. BUTLER, D. E. (1951) In: H. G. Nicholas (26 below).
10. BUTLER, D. E. (1952) *The British General Election of 1951*. London: Macmillan.
11. BUTLER, D. E. (1955) *The British General Election of 1955*. London: Macmillan.
11a.BUTLER, D. E., and ROSE, R. (1960) *The British General Election of 1959*. London: Macmillan.
12. CAMPBELL, P., DONNISON, D., & POTTER, A. (1952) 'Voting Behaviour in Droylesden'. *Manchester School*, **20**, 61.
13. DUVERGER, M. (1951) *Les Partis politiques* (Paris) (Eng. trans.; *Political Parties*. tr. B. & R. North). London: Methuen, 1954.
14. FRIEDMANN, W. (1944) *Legal Theory*. 2nd edn. London: Stevens, 1949. chap. 26.
15. JANOWITZ, M., & MARVICK, D. (1956) *Competitive Pressure and Democratic Consent*. Ann Arbor: Univ. of Michigan Press.
16. LASSWELL,HAROLD (1936) *Politics: Who Get What, When and How*. New York: McGraw-Hill.
17. LIPPMANN, WALTER (1922) *Public Opinion*. London: Allen & Unwin.
18. LIPPMANN, WALTER (1930) *The Phantom Public*. New York: Macmillan.
19. LIPSET, S. M. (1954) 'Psychology of Voting'. In: Lindzey, G., *Handbook of Social Psychology*, vol. 2. Cambridge, Mass: Addison-Wesley.
20. LIPSET, S. M. (1960) *Political Man*. London: Heinemann, pp. 225–7.
21. McCALLUM, R. B., & READMAN, A. (1947) *The British General Election of 1945*. London: Oxford Univ. Press.
22. McKENZIE, R. T. (1955) *British Political Parties*. London: Heinemann.
23. MICHELS, R. *Political Parties*. Trans. Eden and Cedar Paul. London: Hutchinson, 1916.
24. MILNE, R. S., & MACKENZIE, H. C. (1958) *Marginal Seat*. London: Hansard Society.
25. MILNE, R. S., & MACKENZIE, H. C. (1954) *Straight Fight*. London: Hansard Society.
26. NICHOLAS, H. G. (1951) *The British General Election of 1950*. London: Macmillan.
27. OSTROGORSKI, M. (1902) *Democracy and the Organisation of Political Parties*. trans. F. Clarke. London: Macmillan.
28. WARNER, W. L., & LUNT, PAUL S. (1941) *The Social Life of a Modern Community*. London: Oxford Univ. Press.

31

HOSPITAL SOCIOLOGY

T. F. Main and R. N. Rapoport

THE field of hospital sociology is peripheral both to hospital administration and to sociology. To sociologists its principal character, until recently, has been as an applied field in which there has been a tendency to consider the contributions of the parent academic discipline as far outweighing the theoretical returns from the practical application. To hospital administrators the self-conscious interest in sociological matters has tended at best to be seen as 'embroidery' and at worst as a distraction full of 'woolly-headedness' and impracticality. The interstices in which hospital sociology has lately flourished have contained individuals of both callings who have been unconvinced of the weight of these prejudices. On the medical side, psychiatry in particular has shown an early and mounting interest in sociological research. On the social science side, interest has grown mainly in the inter-disciplinary fields where sociology, anthropology, and psychology contribute perspectives in response to the requirements of pressing human problems rather than formulating and working with problems posed by the cultivation of a particular discipline's conventional domain.

While research in general hospitals has also contributed much to the development of the contemporary field of hospital sociology,[2] the greatest efflorescence of ideas seems to have occurred in the context of psychiatric hospitals. We therefore concentrate our attention in the present chapter on psychiatric hospital sociology, as a prototype and generator of developments not only in hospital sociology, but also in the study of organizational behaviour generally.

We shall consider here the most salient ideas in the field that have grown up as part of a shared development on both sides of the Atlantic.

There are, however, some interesting differences between the British and the American trends. In Great Britain work has been of a more practical kind, usually involving radical action programmes by practising hospital administrators with social science orientation. Comparatively few members of the academic disciplines have actually been involved. In these situations the literature of hospital sociology has been more helpful than its professional representatives. In America, by contrast, there has been a comparatively great research involvement of professional workers from the academic disciplines and, paradoxically, a comparatively modest programme of radical innovation.

In both the United States and in England national study commissions have been set up to report to their respective legislative bodies recommending changes in the laws and other conditions governing psychiatric hospitals.[19, 20] The composition and orientation of these two commissions reflect the differences noted. The British was composed of public-spirited individuals whose practical judgements would be respected but who claimed no professional expertise or research experience in the field. The American was composed predominantly of professional research workers. The effects of these commissions' recommendations and the ways in which they are implemented in the two countries will be interesting to observe. Pending these developments, we shall draw on what we know of the action programmes, research findings, and informed discussion in both countries in so far as they help us to understand contemporary problems of hospital sociology. Our emphasis will thus be on ideas rather than a simple accounting of people and projects.

RECENT PSYCHIATRIC HOSPITAL REFORMS

As a result of the powerful stimuli to change afforded in wartime a number of advances in 'social psychiatry' as well as in physical treatments in psychiatry have occurred in the past two decades. There had been a growing agreement among the psychiatrists that the old-fashioned mental hospital system was 'bad' in that it purchased a degree of social tranquillity outside the hospital by sacrificing offending individuals to a régime that largely 'dehumanized' them. The symptomatology that this system induces was kept in control and out of the ordinary citizen's field of awareness. The principal rationalization for maintaining the *status quo* centred on the lack of methods for handling numerous, severe disorders with available staff.

With wartime psychiatric study of group behaviour for therapeutic purposes,[7] personnel selection,[11] and ward sociatry,[1] the point was reached when medical men began to conceive of a hospital not only as an aggregate of medical skills grouped for the convenience of treatment but as a community with its own possible therapeutic or antitherapeutic effects.[14] Evidence accumulated that the social environment could play an important part in the treatment and rehabilitation as well as the destruction or malformation of personality. 'Transitional communities', were constructed by social scientists and psychiatrists to 'bridge the gap' between the social environment of war (e.g. prison camps) and that of peace, and these 'therapeutic communities' repaired much of the psychic damage that wartime experiences had brought.[6, 13]

In these developments the sociologist and the psychiatrist were each able to make his own contribution, and the traditional psychiatric hospital was quickly seen as containing problems stemming from the roles allotted to its staff by society. While the overt definition of these roles was to restore patients to mental health, covertly there were expectations that the staff should maintain the hospital as a repository for distasteful frightening misfits which the larger society was unable to tolerate. Consequently hospital staffs became aware that in their organization and procedure there were hidden reactions to carrying the burden of society's guilt, suspicion, and distaste resulting from the strong feelings aroused by their human cargoes. Against this background certain psychiatrists actively collaborated with sociologists to investigate hospital sociology.[22]

CONTRIBUTIONS OF SOCIOLOGY

The trends accelerated during the war continued in the years which followed. So radical and far-reaching have the changes been, that they have been termed by some the 'third revolution' in psychiatry. Their central feature has been the addition of a sociological dimension to the earlier frameworks that successively incorporated bio-physiological (medical) and psycho-dynamic dimensions to the conceptions of mental disorder and its treatment.

The active involvement of professional sociologists in the study of psychiatric hospitals has had many aspects. Much of the early work consisted of a joint stocktaking, with the medical men, of the past and present developments, and it led to the awareness of hospitals not only as technical but social organizations. Where the old hospital system was organized as a 'total institution' with 'custodial' goals and a 'care culture', the newer, more 'therapeutic' hospitals are organized with a 'cure culture' and an emphasis on the social relations of patients and staff and the position of the hospital in society.[9, 10] In the older system, the 'legend of chronicity' grew up to rationalize the staff's inability to achieve therapeutic and rehabilitative goals, and styles of belief and types of personality were selected and bred into the systems.[8, 23]

The challenge faced by innovating clinicians was how the appropriate social environments could now be created to counteract the undesired

561

effects of patients' earlier environments. The behavioural syndromes of patients were seen not merely as the results of 'disease' but of the social roles offered them in society and in the hospital. In its largest sense, the latter aspect of social psychiatry is often referred to as *milieu therapy*. The particular forms this takes are 'administrative psychiatry' and the 'therapeutic community'.

Milieu therapy is self-consciously practised in a variety of forms, varying with types of hospital, patient, practitioner, and local circumstances. In some cases it is a focal element of treatment; in others it is ancillary. In its emphasis on repudiating the undesirable aspects of the custodial hospital system, and 'humanizing' the treatment of patients, it resembles the 'moral' treatments of a century ago. It differs from them principally in the extent to which it is currently practised in a self-critical, analytical way—adopting attitudes and practices less on grounds of moral dogma than of therapeutic rationality, to which sociologists are expected to make a contribution. Milieu-therapy practitioners vary in the way they seek to implement their goals, some focusing on particular attitudes to be taken by staff in relation to patients, some on creating a therapeutic 'atmosphere' (ethos, morale), some on constructing an overall social structure that will have therapeutic properties.

Milieu therapists generally seem to value the kind of social system that allows for 'humanizing' patient care. Permissiveness is a frequent prescription, with the aim of allowing patients to express themselves and to learn more of their internal difficulties. By so doing, it is hoped that they can try out new solutions for their problems. Another aspect that is generally valued is 'democratization'. This implies an increase in participation of lower echelon staff and patients in decisions affecting life in the hospital. A third emphasis in the 'humanitarian' approach is on increasing the personal, face-to-face quality of relationships, as against the depersonalized, mechanized, bureaucratic forms of organization in which patients were customarily dealt with as 'things' or as infra-human creatures.

Minimally these social changes aim at making the hospital a more pleasant place in which to live and work. Maximally they are seen as effective therapeutic instruments for restoring patients to useful lives in ordinary society. Social psychiatrists advocate the blending of rehabilitation with treatment, so that the two might work simultaneously toward the same goal of returning the patient to ordinary life. The mental hospital, or some part of it, in this context becomes another sort of 'transitional community', in which even the chronically hospitalized 'backward' patients might find pathways back to a world that has left them behind.

Sociologists' studies have contributed to an understanding of hospitals by giving explicit and systematic conceptual status to several of

Hospital Sociology

their important social aspects. First, a hospital is conceptualized as a federation of status groups organized in semi-autonomous hierarchical systems with different characteristics and blocked inter-system mobility. Thus a nurse belonging to one hierarchy cannot become a doctor, who belongs to another, without leaving the system and re-entering after having acquired specialized training.[21] Furthermore these hierarchies, federated in a pyramidal structure, are seen as giving rise to 'multiple subordination' in the sense that individuals in the lower hierarchical levels are subject to directives from diverse quarters. Thus a nurse on the ward may receive orders from people higher up in several hierarchies —medical and administrative, as well as nursing.[12]

At the bottom of all these hierarchies, in terms of authority and responsibility in the system, is the patient. When physical medical care is needed the relatively passive and powerless status of the patient may be useful and not necessarily harmful to him psychologically. Psychiatric patients, however, offer special problems partly because of the apparent interrelationship between their illness and psychic regression. To the extent that the hospital fosters the latter, it works toward the confirmation of the former. Where a patient is subject to multiple subordination, as when he sees one physician for psychotherapy, developing a transference relationship with him, and another physician for practical matters of ward administration, he may become subject to an emotionally 'split field' if the two individuals disagree with one another over a matter important to him. Often these disagreements are 'covert' either as a result of lack of communication, or because the two physicians leave their disagreement unspoken in order to avoid conflict. In either case the effects on the patient have been demonstrated to be extremely adverse,[23] presumably much in the same way that a child becomes disturbed when such significant figures as his parents are in basic disagreement. Many of the psychiatric patients who have been shown empirically to become disturbed in such split social fields may have possessed personalities which were formed in discordant parental environments. The classical examples of Stanton and Schwartz showed that psychiatric patients participate covertly in social processes, including staff tensions, by manifesting behaviour such as catatonic excitement or enuresis which had hitherto been regarded as determined solely by factors within the individual. The inability of the established system of communication to cure such behaviour forced the conclusion that the social system surrounding the patient must be examined if only for his disturbance to be understood. The same workers have shown that the patient's behaviour dramatically ceases once the staff tension is resolved, even when the resolution is not overtly communicated to the patient. A further study of staff behaviour around such events has shown that disturbances between patients and staff are two-way; and that the covert staff tensions and 'rational' procedures and status systems built to hide and minimize these tensions in the nursing of difficult patients are often defensive in function and do not tend to minimize the primitive feelings that such patients arouse.[15]

The interplay between psychological disturbance and social structure is only a part of the potential field of research in psychiatric hospitals. Increasingly the hospital is seen as a place where one can study the ways in which the biological, psychological, and sociological systems, conventionally kept apart in the different academic disciplines, interact as 'linked, open systems'. If repressive action is taken or organization temporarily breaks down, individuals may attempt to handle the resulting stress on any of the three levels. If the individual is in a position of power or influence, he may be able to change the social field. If not, he may be able to handle the situation psychologically, for example, through resignation, without further troublesome consequences. On the other hand if his psychological resources are also meagre, he may have recourse to somatization, and the ultimate reaction may be seen in physiological symptoms.[5]

The social environment of the hospital provides a great variety of 'personal communities', in which individuals derive experience unique to themselves because of the network of social relationships they build up and the meanings with which they endow its constituent parts. The individual, however, is not always able to make a social network that is 'best' for him in any particular hospital environment. Aside from the differences among individuals in their capacities for using the social system for their own benefit, some social systems offer better opportunities than others for choice of relationships. In some mental hospitals the relationships are geared primarily to social control, placing the most uncontrolled patients in the most controlled environment and offering them the most restricted range of choice of relationship. Allowing social functions of a more 'normal' kind, including freedom, mixing between the sexes, occupation, etc., has been found in hospitals of this type to bear connotations of reward and punishment rather than of therapy: the individuals who were allowed to participate in the most 'ordinary' social environments in the hospital were those whose behaviour was most acceptable to the staff. This emphasis on conformity means that many patients are inevitably forced more and more towards chronic institutionalization.[9, 24]

Where psychiatrists have met the challenge of inequities in mental hospitals with the development of therapeutic milieux, sociologists have often been involved as analysts of the work of social reconstruction. It is now clear that systems of milieu therapy, however enlightened and inspired, pose problems of their own. In the face of relatively undefined prescriptions for a new system, certain of the guiding beliefs that emerge among practitioners seem to have the quality of ideology. Action of moral significance without sound empirical basis often gives rise to systems of belief held with great tenacity and emotional commitment. The ensuring sense of certainty, enthusiasm, and optimism contributes directly to the formation of a 'therapeutic atmosphere', but is sometimes in danger of denying the limits of knowledge, and thus of hampering the search for improved methods of treatment. For example, in hospitals seeking to eliminate the rigidities of the autocratic, custodial mental hospital system, reformist slogans like 'active treatment', 'democratization', 'permissiveness', 'freeing communications', etc., may be taken up as ideological tenets which become ends in themselves rather than policies aimed at therapy for individual patients. Where this happens and such attitudes and practices become crystallized in the social structure, new forms of rigidity emerge. Paradoxically, in such a setting, even the doctrine of flexibility can emerge as an ideological rigidity.

While analyses by social scientists have already helped to clarify some of the intricacies of such problems as these, they are able to offer only limited solutions,[16] and difficulties of collaboration have sometimes arisen owing to the divergent orientations of clinician and research worker.[4, 17] These pitfalls are better understood now, and even if they continue to some extent may, perhaps, stimulate further work.

NEW DIRECTIONS

Elements of milieu therapy have been assembled from a variety of sources—politicial reformist ideals, psycho-analytic theory, social science, and so on. While each of the new principles can be rationalized and demonstrated to be of therapeutic value in some circumstances, their synthesis into a system of theory and practice lacks integration and logical articulation. This means that there tends to be an inadequate development of subsidiary principles for resolving dilemmas arising, for example, when two valued principles come into conflict. An illustration of this would be if in a 'democratic' therapeutic community the patients, outnumbering the staff, decided collectively to go for long walks in the country instead of participating in the hospital régime. Here the principle of democracy would come into conflict with the principle of active rehabilitative therapy. The new values of milieu therapy do not, as part of their integral beliefs, provide formulas for the resolution of dilemmas of this kind which arise very frequently in practice. The clinicians thus face problems of defining limits as well as of articulating potentially conflicting elements in their systems of belief.

For the sociologist, accustomed to *post hoc* analysis of socio-cultural systems, the challenge is to find ways of conceptualizing the properties of highly fluid and complex social systems, like those of psychiatric hospitals which are introducing new methods, in such a way that they can be forged almost *de novo* into functioning wholes. For this purpose, critiques based on static structural 'models' are becoming increasingly outmoded and being replaced by studies of the *processes* of social change.[22]

Even while the 'therapeutic communities' have been building their own new cultural forms, they have been gearing themselves explicitly to the break-up, and so far as possible, the 'emptying' of the large hospitals. Emphasis on group interaction implies smaller units. Rehabilitation implies interaction with people in 'ordinary' circumstances, and preferably with ordinary people. In order to achieve this last the patients may be treated largely as out-patients or day-patients or may go into the community for rehearsals of ordinary social relationships; alternatively 'ordinary' people may be invited into hospital as volunteers, the hospitals employing industrial instructors so as to make conditions resemble, as far as possible, the industrial situation of the world outside.[3, 13]

This 'breaking down of the barriers' between hospital and community not only implies a new kind of hospital and a new kind of psychiatry, but new foci of research and practice extending outside the hospital. Family research becomes inextricably a part of hospital research, for the patient's social environment is shifted in the direction of a network of outside relationships with family, foster-home, or a less structured 'home' in the community. While sociology has had an interest in families as well as in hospitals, the new emphasis may call increasingly for the development of research theories and methods that will conceive of them as interlocking open systems rather than as relatively closed systems.[18]

Another implication this trend holds for the hospital sociologist is an 'action' orientation. The newness of the activities and their sociological emphasis make the practitioner tend to press the sociologist to participate actively in the experiment. An increasingly high premium in this field of research is likely to be placed on the 'clinical sociologist' who, regardless of the degree of involvement he chooses to adopt, understands the phenomena he observes from the psychological and therapeutic as well as from the purely theoretical and sociological point of view.

Because the psychiatric hospital deals with primitive disorders of behaviour and feeling, its social systems are, as we said earlier, liable to serve defensive as well as overtly therapeutic functions, and the very nakedness of these makes it a fruitful area for action-research by the sociologist. Certain hospital staffs have already formed a tradition of searching in their own social matrix for the covert motivations which may explain a patient's behaviour. In many cases they are prepared to investigate the rationale of their own behaviour and to recognize that it,

Hospital Sociology

and the social systems they erect, contain defences against anxiety which need further examination and call for experiments with other ways of ordering their social environment. In one staff study it was shown for example that certain 'medical' procedures were institutionalized responses to staff anxieties: for instance the giving of a sedative to a patient was found to occur when the nursing staff could no longer tolerate the patient's disturbance. Once this was realized other methods of dealing with disturbances were able to develop. In some psychiatric hospitals the need to solve anxieties at all levels has given rise to continuous scrutiny of social events, actions, and structure, so that conferences of patients, staff, or both, regularly meet to discover, in the furtherance of community therapy, hidden motivations and defensive needs.[23, 25] It is understandable that psychiatrists working in this field and concerned with depth psychology should seek the skills of the sociologist; and that the sociologist should welcome the ready point of entry he may find in such hospitals.

These new fields, with new horizons for research worker and practitioner, are challenging and difficult but potentially rewarding. They have the advantage of providing a great variety of structural conditions in a state of flux, so that something perhaps more approaching the experimental situation so sorely lacking in much psychiatric and sociological research is a real possibility. They also have the advantage of access to intimate materials in the personal and family life of the subjects of study through the privileged channels of psychiatric communication and participation in crisis states of emotional upset. The difficulties of collaboration between disciplines and of work with emotionally disturbed subjects, however, mean that hospital sociology is a study with unusually trying as well as unusually rewarding elements. A sociologist working in this field is put on his mettle, for in many ways the ingenuity required to make theories that 'work' is more pressing and exacting than in the academic setting. The field is in ferment; its potentialities very rich, its pitfalls trying; but its ultimate yields will almost certainly benefit practitioners of conventional psychiatry and sociology as well as the emergent discipline of clinical social science.

REFERENCES

1. BION, W. R. & RICKMAN, JOHN (1943) Intra-Group Tensions in Therapy, *Lancet*, 27 Nov. 1943, p. 678.
2. BURLING, TEMPLE; LENTZ, EDITH & WILSON, ROBERT (1956) *The Give and Take in Hospitals*, New York: Putnam.
3. CARSTAIRS, G. MORRIS (1956) The Organization of a Hospital Workshop for Chronic Psychotic Patients, *Brit. J. prev. soc. Med.*, **10**, 136.

T. F. Main and R. N. Rapoport

4. CAUDILL, WILLIAM A. & ROBERTS, BERTRAM (1951) Pitfalls in the Organization of Interdisciplinary Research, *Hum. Organiz.*, **10**, 12–15.
5. CAUDILL, WILLIAM A. (1958) *The Psychiatric Hospital as a Small Society*, Cambridge, Mass. Harvard Univ. Press.
6. CURLE, ADAM, & TRIST, ERIC, Transitional Communities and Social Reconstruction: A Study of the Civil Re-settlement of British Prisoners of War, in *Readings in Social Psychology* (revised edition), New York: Henry Holt, 1952.
7. FOULKES, S. H. (1946) Group Analysis in a Military Neurosis Centre, *Lancet*, 2 March, 1946, 303.
8. GILBERT, DORIS, & LEVINSON, DANIEL (1956) Ideology, Personality and Institutional Policy in the Mental Hospital. *J. abnorm. soc. Psychol.*, **53**, 263–271.
9. GOFFMAN, ERVING (1957) The Characteristics of Total Institutions in *Symposium on Preventive and Social Psychiatry*, Walter Reed Army Medical Center, Washington, D.C.
10. GREENBLATT, MILTON; YORK, RICHARD & BROWN, ESTHER LUCILLE (1955) *From Custodial to Therapeutic Care in Mental Hospitals*, New York; Russell Sage Foundation.
11. HARRIS, H. (1949) *The Group Approach to Leadership Testing*, London: Routledge.
12. HENRY, JULES (1954) Types of Institutional Structure, in Greenblatt, M. Levinson, Daniel, & Williams, Richard (eds.) *The Patient and the Mental Hospital*, Glencoe, Ill., Free Press.
13. JONES, MAXWELL (1953) *The Therapeutic Community*. New York: Basic Books. Published originally in England under the title, *Social Psychiatry*, London: Tavistock, 1952.
14. MAIN, T. (1946) The Hospital as a Therapeutic Institution. *Bull. Menninger Clin.*, **10**, pp. 66–70.
15. MAIN, T. (1957) The Ailment, *Brit. J. med. Psychol.*, **30**, 129–145.
16. RAPOPORT, RHONA (1960) The Family and Psychiatric Treatment: A Conceptual Approach, *Psychiatry*, **23**, 53–62.
17. RAPOPORT, ROBERT (1957) Notes on the Disparagement of Sociologizing in Collaborative Research, *Hum. Organiz.*, **16.**
18. RAPOPORT, ROBERT (1960) *Community as Doctor: New Perspectives on a Therapeutic Community*, London; Tavistock; Springfield, Ill.: C. C. Thomas.
19. *Report of the Royal Commission on the Law Relating to Mental Illness and Mental Deficiency*, London: H.M.S.O., 1957.
20. SCHWARTZ, MORRIS, *et al.*, *New Perspectives on Patient Care*. Report of the Task Force on Patient Care of the Joint Commission for the Study of Mental Illness and Mental Health in the United States, New York: Basic Books (in press).
21. SMITH, HARVEY (1958) Two Lines of Authority: The Hospital's Dilemma in Gartly Jaco (ed.), *Patients, Physicians and Illness*, Glencoe, Ill.: Free Press.

Hospital Sociology

22. SOFER, CYRIL (1955) Reactions to Administrative Change: A Study of Staff Relations in Three British Hospitals, *Hum. Relat.*, **8**, 291–316.
23. STANTON, ALFRED & SCHWARTZ, MORRIS (1954) *The Mental Hospital*, New York: Basic Books; London: Tavistock.
24. VON MERING, OTTO, & KING, STANLEY (1957) *Remotivating the Mental Patient*, New York: Russell Sage Foundation.
25. WILMER, HARRY (1958) *Social Psychiatry in Action*, Springfield, Ill.: C. C. Thomas.

ABBREVIATIONS, ETC., USED IN

LISTS OF REFERENCES

Acta chirur. scand. Acta chirurgica Scandinavica (Stockholm).
Acta paediat. Stockh. Acta Paediatrica (Stockholm).
Acta psychiat., Kbh. Acta Psychiatrica et Neurologica (Copenhagen).
Acta psychol., Hague. Acta Psychologica (The Hague).
Admin. Sci. Quart. Administrative Science Quarterly (Ithaca, N.Y.).
Adult Educ. Adult Education (London).
Advanc. Sci. Lond. Advancement of Science (London),
Amer. J. hum. Genet. American Journal of Human Genetics (Baltimore).
Amer. J. Hyg. American Journal of Hygiene (Baltimore).
Amer. J. ment. Defic. American Journal of Mental Deficiency (Albany, N.Y.).
Amer. J. phys. Anthrop. American Journal of Physical Anthropology (Washington).
Amer. J. Psychiat. American Journal of Psychiatry (Baltimore).
Amer. J. Psychol. American Journal of Psychology (Worcester, Mass.).
Amer. J. publ. Hlth. American Journal of Public Health (New York)
Amer. J. Sociol. American Journal of Sociology (Chicago).
Amer. Psychol. American Psychologist (Lancaster, Pa.).
Amer. Sociol. Rev. American Sociological Review (Manasha, Wis.).
Année psychol. Année psychologique (Paris).
Arch. Dis. Childh. Archives of Disease of Childhood (London).
Arch. int. Med. exp. Archives internationales de Médecine expérimentale (Liège).
Arch. Neurol. Psychiat. Archives of Neurology and Psychiatry (Chicago).
Behaviour. Behaviour (Leiden).
Biometrics. Biometrics (Washington).
Brit. J. Addict. British Journal of Addiction (London).
Brit. J. Criminol. British Journal of Criminology (London).
Brit. J. Deling. British Journal of Delinquency (London).
Brit. J. educ. Psychol. British Journal of Educational Psychology (London).
Brit. J, educ. Stud. British Journal of Educational Studies (London).
Brit. J. industr. Med. British Journal of Industrial Medicine (London).
Brit. J. industr. Safety. British Journal of Industrial Safety (London).
Brit. J. med. Psychol. British Journal of Medical Psychology (London).

Abbreviations

Brit. J. prev. soc. Med. British Journal of Preventive and Social Medicine (London).

Brit. J. Psychol. British Journal of Psychology (London).

Brit. J. Sociol. British Journal of Sociology (London).

Brit. J. stat. Psychol. British Journal of Statistical Psychology (London).

Brit. J. soc. Med. British Journal of Social Medicine (London).

Brit. med. J. British Medical Journal (London).

Bull. cent. étud. rech. psychotech. Bulletin du Centre d'études et recherches psychotechniques (Paris).

Bull. Menninger Clin. Bulletin of the Menninger Clinic (Topeka, Kansas).

Cahiers int. de sociologie. Cahiers internationaux de sociologie (Paris).

Canad. J. Econ. Polit. Sci. Canadian Journal of Economic and Political Science (Ottawa).

Canad. J. Psychol. Canadian Journal of Psychology (Toronto).

Circulation. Circulation (New York).

Curr. Sociol. Current Sociology.

Dis. nerv. Syst. Diseases of the Nervous System (Chicago).

Educ. Res. Educational Research.

Ergonomics. Ergonomics (London).

Eugen. Rev. Eugenics Review (London).

Federal Probation. Federal Probation (Washington).

Genet. Psychol. Monogr. Genetic Psychology Monographs (Worcester, Mass.).

Health Bulletin. Health Bulletin (Edinburgh).

Hum. Organiz. Human Organization (New York).

Hum. Relat. Human Relations (London).

Industr. Saf. Surv. Industrial Safety Survey (Geneva and Montreal).

Int. J. Psycho-Anal. International Journal of Psycho-Analysis (London).

Int. J. soc. Psychiat. International Journal of Social Psychiatry.

J. abnorm. soc. Psychol. Journal of Abnormal and Social Psychology (Boston).

J. Amer. med. Ass. Journal of the American Medical Association (Chicago).

J. Amer. statist. Assoc. Journal of the American Statistical Association (Boston).

J. appl. Psychol. Journal of Applied Psychology (Worcester, Mass.).

J. comp. physiol. psychol. Journal of Comparative and Physiological Psychology (Baltimore).

J. crim. Law. Criminol. [and Police Sci.] Journal of Criminal Law, [and] Criminology [and Police Science] (Chicago).

J. gen. Psychol. Journal of General Psychology (Worcester, Mass.).

J. genet. Psychol. Journal of Genetic Psychology (Worcester, Mass.).

J. Hyg. Camb. Journal of Hygiene (Cambridge).

J. Inst. Actu. Journal of the Institute of Actuaries (London).

J. Inst. Auto. Assess. Journal of the Institute of Automobile Assessors (London).

J. Inst. civ. Engrs. Journal of the Institution of Civil Engineers (London).

Abbreviations

J. Ment. Defic. Res. Journal of Mental Deficiency Research (Sevenoaks).

J. ment. Sci. Journal of Mental Science (London).

J. Ment. Subnormal. Journal of Mental Subnormality.

J. nat. Inst. Per. Res. Journal of the National Institute of Personnel Research.

J. nerv. ment. Dis. Journal of Nervous and Mental Diseases (New York).

J. Neurol. Psychiat. Journal of Neurology, (Neurosurgery) and Psychiatry (London).

J. Obstet. Gynaec. Brit. Emp. Journal of Obstetrics and Gynaecology of the British Empire (London).

J. Pol. Econ. Journal of Political Economy.

J. Psychosom. Res. Journal of Psychosomatic Research (London).

J. R. Inst. Publ. Hlth. Journal of the Royal Institute of Public Health (London).

J. R. statist. Soc. Journal of the Royal Statistical Society (London).

J. soc. Issues. Journal of Social Issues (New York).

Labour Mgmt. Labour Management (London).

Lancet. Lancet (London).

Law and contemp. Prob. Law and Contemporary Problems (Durham, N.C.)

Manager. Manager, The (London)

Manchester School. Manchester School (Manchester).

Med. Clin. N. Amer. Medical Clinic of North America (Philadelphia).

Med. Offr. Medical Officer (London).

Med. Pr. Medical Press.

Ment. Hyg., Lond. Mental Hygiene (London).

Motor. Motor, The (London).

Nat. Safety News. National Safety News (Chicago).

Nature. Nature (London).

Ned. Tijdschr. Geneesk. Nederlandsch tijdschrift voor geneeskunde (Amsterdam).

New Engl. J. Med. New England Journal of Medicine (Boston).

New Scientist. New Scientist (London).

Occup. Hazards. Occupational Hazards (Cleveland, O.).

Occup. Psychol. Occupational Psychology (London).

Ohio St. med. J. Ohio State Medical Journal (Columbus, O.).

Operat. Res. Quart. Operational Research Quarterly (London).

Pediatrics, Springfield. Pediatrics (Springfield, Ill.).

Popul. Stud. Population Studies (Cambridge).

Practitioner. The Practitioner (London).

Proc. R. Soc. Med. Proceedings of the Royal Society of Medicine (London).

Psychiat. Quart. Psychiatric Quarterly (Albany, N.Y.).

Psychiatry. Psychiatry (Baltimore).

Psychol. Bull. Psychological Bulletin (Lancaster, Pa.).

Psychol. Rev. Psychological Reviews (Lancaster, Pa.).

Psychosom. Med. Psychosomatic Medicine (London).

Publ. Admin. Public Administration (London).

Publ. Hlth, London. Public Health (London).

Quart. J. exp. Psychol. Quarterly Journal of Experimental Psychology (Cambridge).

Abbreviations

Researches and Studies. Researches and Studies (University of Leeds, Institute of Education).

Rev. Droit pen. Revue de droit pénal et de criminologie (Brussels).

Road Research. Road Research (London).

Schweiz. Z. Strafrecht. Schweizerische Zeitschrift für Strafrecht (Bern).

Science. Science (New York).

Social Forces. Social Forces (Chapel Hill).

Sociolog. Rev. Sociological Review (London).

Sociologie du Travail.

Sociometry. Sociometry (New York).

Surveyor. Surveyor (London).

Trans. Amer. neurol. Ass. Transactions of the American Neurological Association (New York).

Trans. Soc. Instrum. Tech. Transactions of the Society of Instrument Technology (London).

Travail hum. Travail humain (Paris).

Univ. Quart. Universities Quarterly (London).

Univ. Ia. Stud. Child Welf. University of Iowa Studies in Child Welfare (Iowa City).

Yale Law Jl. Yale Law Journal (New Haven, Conn.).

INDEX

575

Index

Argyle, M., 83
  et al., 81
Argyris, P., 207
Arkwright, Richard, 187
Army Alpha and Beta tests, 66
Army recruits, educational level, 527–8
"aspirant" and "demotic" families, 143
association(s):
  demonstration of, 8
  differential, 291–2
asthenic type, 337
athletic type, 337
attachments, social, in infants, 382
attainment tests, 68–9
authority, nature of, 102
autism, early infantile, 385

Babcock scale, 68
Backett, E. M., and Johnston, A. M., 277 f.
Baird, D., 439
Bales, R. F., 84, 87
Banks, J. A., 96
Barnard, Chester I., 188, 199 n.
Barr, M. L., and Hobbs, G. E., 344
Barraclough, Geoffrey, 95
Barry, H., 380
  and Lindemann, E., 386
Bavelas, A., 199 n.
  group experiment, 80
behaviour, rational, and crime, 324
Belbin, E., 271
Belbin, R. M., 156
belief and fact, lack of association, 324
Bell, Lady, 414
Bendix, R., 187, 188
bereavement, effects of, 391
Bertalanffy, L. von, 199 n.
Besant, Annie, 403, 422 n.
Biesheuvel, S., and White, M. E., 251
Binet-Simon scale, 64, 443
birth control, *see* contraception
Blackett, P. M. S., 241
Blackstone, W., 417
Bloch, Marc, 95, 97
body-build, *see* physique
Bonner, H., 87
Booth, Charles, 5, 6, 21, 482 n.
boredom, and accidents, 253
borstal training, results of, 312 ff.
boundaries, urban, 495
Bourne, C., 503
Bourne, H., 387
Bowlby, John, 292, 380–81, 382, 385, 386
Bowley, A. L., 6, 12
Boyd, D. A., 239
Bradlaugh, Charles, 403
Bradney, P., 211

Briggs, Asa, 296
British Boot, Shoe and Allied Trades Research Association, 179
British Iron and Steel Research Association, 264
Broadbent, D. E., 254
Bromley, P. M., 416 n.
Brown, F. W., 345, 346
Bryce, James, 542, 544
Buchsbaum Case, 193 n.
bureaucracy:
  growth of, 189
  "ideal", 190
  and industrialism, 189 ff.
Burns, T., 83, 178
  and Stalker, G. M., 205
Burt, Cyril, 68, 218–19, 291, 295, 531

California, penal research, 306
capacity and inclination, 218, 227
Carlson, Sune, 205
Carr Saunders, A. M., *et al.*, 295
Carstairs, G. M., 362
case studies:
  criminological, 297–8
  and social surveys, 15
Castle, P. F. C., 258
Catholics:
  and family limitation, 404
  and political parties, 550–51, 552–3, 557
Cattell, R. B., 70, 72
causation:
  direction of, on group experiments, 81–82
  multiple, 291, 328, 329
census:
  analyses of results, 34 ff.
  analyses, structure, 52
  definition, 25
  errors in data, 56–57
  history, in Great Britain, 29–31
  international recommendations, 32–34
  legal basis, 26–27
  questions asked, 26, 27–29
  reports, England and Wales, analysis, 58–59
  timing of, 53–54
  of 1951, questions, 31–32
  of 1961, 32
central nervous system, and motivation, 164
cerebrotonia, 338
Chapple, E. D., 84
checks, of survey results, 18–19
Cherry, Colin, 199 n.
Chesser, E., 409 n.
Chicago group, of urban sociologists, 484

576

Index

chicken, playing, 259
child development, environment and, 8
Child Health, National Survey of, 21, 412, 414
children:
   custody of, 422 f.
   and road accidents, 277–8
cholesterol, 138
Churches:
   and divorce, 407
   and family limitation, 404–5
Churchman, C. W., *et al.*, 128
Clark, B., 275
class(es):
   occupational, 47
   and political party, 555–7
   social, and disease, 129 ff.
   and health services, 130
   and I.Q., 451 f.
   and intelligence tests, 67
   and mental illness, 355 ff.
   Registrar General's scale, 129
classification, social, difficulties of, 141
Clinard, Marshall B., 290, 291, 293
clinic, organization of, 119–21
clusters, symptom and trait, 342
Cohen, Albert K., 292
Cohen, J., *et al.*, 277
Collingwood, H. G., 93
Colquhoun, Patrick, 5
communication, and status differences, 371–2
communities:
   therapeutic, 562
   transitional, 561
community studies, 483–4
complexity, 159 ff.
computers:
   effect on research, 107
   use in operational research, 238, 240
conception, pre-marital, 408
confidence interval, 13
constitution, neurotic, 342, 345
contraception, 402 f., 408
   and abortion, 431 f.
   and consummation of marriage, 417 n.
conurbations, 487, 492
coronary heart disease, 137–9
corporal punishment, 322
Coser, Rose Laub, 100
Cressey, D. R., 282, 291
crime:
   causes of, meaning, 309–10
   cost of, 307
   legal definitions, 307
   necessity to society, 326
   psychological studies, 296–7
   single and multiple factor theories, 291

social and legal conceptions, 307–8
   and social problems, 327
   sociological studies, 295–6
   theories of causation, 291 ff., 327 ff.
   use of word, 281–2
   white-collar, 293
"crimes known", 307–8
criminal justice, lay element in, 288
criminology:
   definition and scope, 281–4
   experimental research, 298
   justification of, 283
   methods of, 287 ff.
   national character of, 293
   and other disciplines, 289–90
   techniques of, 294 ff.
Cronbach, L. J., 70
Crowther Committee/Report, 524, 527, 529, 533
Crozier, M., 205, 208
Crutchfield, R. S., 80, 82
Curran, D., and Guttmann, E., 342
Curran, D., and Mallison, P., 335
cyclists, pedal, and road accidents, 272
cyclothymic type, 337

Dalton, M., 200, 201
Davies, H., and Silman, K. E., 235
Davis, D. R., 251, 255, 256
decision time, shortening, 158
delegation, effective, 158
delinquency, meaning, 281, *see also* crime
"delinquency area" theory, 292
"demotic" and "aspirant" families, 143
Denning, Lord, 419 f.
depopulation, rural, 504, 505
design faults, and accidents, 255
deterrence, 321 ff.
Deutsch, M., 79
development:
   industrial, 191
   sociology of, 490
development gaps, inter-national, 489–90
diffusion, urban, 486 ff.
disease, and social class, 129 ff.
divorce, 405 ff., 421–2
documents, as survey sources, 14–15
dogs, and road accidents, 271
Doll, R., 8
Douglas, J. W. B., and Blomfield, J. M., 8, 278
drift hypothesis, 357–8
drug prescriptions, 122
Dumazedier, J., 194
Dunham, H. W., 366, 371
Durkheim, E., 99, 286, 391, 518
Duverger, M., 547–8

577

Index

East, Norwood, 295
economic activity, and census, 43–44
ectomorphy, 337–8
education:
  bureaucratization of, 522
  higher, sociology of, 536 ff.
  and industrialism, 521
  length of, and I.Q., 451
  and mental disorder, 360
  and parental status, 514–15
  and population census, 32, 52
  social class and, 527
Education Act (1944), 515
educational attainments, tests of, 68–69
educational institutions, and social mobility, 511, 515–16
Educational Needs of Clothing Industry, Survey of, 180
educational preferences, and fathers' occupation, 517
EEG, abnormalities in, 339 ff.
Eisenberg, L., 385
Eisenstadt, S. N., 204
elections, 549–50
electoral systems, and parties, 548
electroencephalography, 339–41
Eliade, Mircea, 97
emotionality, general, 219
employment status, classification by, 45; see also occupations
endomorphy, 337–8
Engelhardt, H. N., 210
Engels, F., 484 n.
Eno Foundation for Highway Traffic Control, 275
environment:
  meaning, in relation to education, 531
  and retarded mental development, 387
  see also heredity
epidemiology, 128
equilibrium process, in groups, 87
ergonomics, 181, 198
errors:
  and accidents, 254–5
  in census data, 56–57
  in survey data, 18 ff.
estimation, from samples, 13
ethics:
  of group experimentation, 86–87
  relation to research, 309 n.
  and scientific method, 328 n.
eurymorphy, 338
Eversley, D. E. C., 96, 98
expectation of life, 470
expectations, group, and accidents, 259
experiment:
  group, ethics of, 86–87
  evaluation of results, 87

laboratory and field, 78 ff.
  measurement of results, 83 f.
  natural, 81
  small group, design of, 78 ff.
extraversion/introversion, 339
Eysenck, H. J., 72, 219, 334, 335, 339, 342
  and Prell, D. B., 342

factor analysis, in psychometrics, 63
factory:
  organization, early, 187
  system, 187–8
family(-ies):
  analysis of, 39
  as consumption unit, 418
  'demotic' and 'aspirant', 143
  division of function in, 415
  formation, 383
    class variations, 399
  property holding in, 418 ff.
  in relation to census, 36 ff.
  in relation to education, 531 ff.
  relationships within, 414 ff.
  Victorian, 409
  working- and middle-class, 409
family limitation, Churches and, 404–5
  see also contraception
family nucleus, 37 ff.
Family Planning Association, 403
family resources, working class, 410 f.
family size:
  decline in, 400–1
  and education, 531 ff.
  and intelligence, 532
  and occupation, 401
Farmer, E., et al., 250, 275
Farris, R. E. L., and Dunham, H. W., 364
fashion, in diagnosis, 136
father:
  occupation of, and education, 532
  role in relation to child, 385
fatigue, and accidents, 253
Feldman, H., 81
Ferguson, T., 287
Ferri, Enrico, 290
fertility:
  and age structure, 461 ff.
  census enquiries, 30–32, 35
  differential, and education, 523–4
    for I.Q., 446–7
  and social mobility, 510–11
  future prospects in Britain, 464
  and social class, 131
  survey of (Indianapolis), 7, 8
Festinger, L., et al., 81, 87
Fleck, S., 390
flogging, 322
Florence, Sargent, 177

578

Index

Index

Index

581

Index

Morton Commission on Marriage and Divorce, 407
Moseley, A. L., 252
mother(s):
  effects of early separation from, 380–81, 385
  employment of, 412
  tie of human child to, 384–5
  tie of young animal to, 381–2
motivation:
  and achievement, 165
  and central nervous system, 164
  distribution of, and social mobility, 511
  non-biological, 165
  principles of, 163–4
motoring offences, statistics, 273
motorists, and road accidents, 273
Myers, Dr, 173
Myrdal, Gunnar, 93

Naess, Siri, 292
Namier, Sir Lewis, 96
National Health Service, organization of, 121 f.
National Institute of Industrial Psychology, 173, 174, 181, 197
Naville, P., 194
Negroes, American, I.Q. level, 448–9
neuroticism:
  constitutional predisposition to, 336
  definition, 335
  and previous personality, 341 f.
Newbold, E. H., 249
Newman, H. H., et al., 345, 346
New York State Youth Commission, 305
'nomothetic' v. 'idiographic', 93
Nuffield Unit for Research into Problems of Ageing, 174
null hypothesis, 12
number facility, 219

observational tests, 73
obsessionals, 341
occupation:
  censal errors regarding, 57
  census analysis of, 45–47
  and social mobility, 509–10, 512–15
occupations:
  classification by personality characteristics, 363
  present in relation to first, 514
  sons' in relation to fathers', 513
occupational psychologist, problems of, 222
Ødegaard, Ø, 366
offenders, treatment of, see treatment
old age, see aged, the

Old People's Welfare Council, National, 473
oligarchy, iron law of, 547
operational research, 235 ff.
  composition of team, 123
  and criminology, 305 ff.
  literature, 123–4
  organization of, 122–3
Operational Research Conferences, 242
opportunity:
  distribution of, and social mobility, 511
  educational, class and, 7–8
organization, formal and informal, 203, 206
organization theory, 204
Ostrogorski, M., 544–5
overcrowding, 414
over-protection, maternal, 389
Owen, M. B., 361
ownership and management, divorce of, 189

Pakenham, Lord, 295
Pare, C. M. B., 344
parents:
  marriage, and detachment from, 383
  relationship between, 383–4
Park, Robert, 501
Parkinson, C. Northcote, 206 n.
Parnell, R. W., 338
parties, political:
  American, 543–4
  'mass' and 'cadre', 547–8
  nature of, 541 ff.
  organizational types, 545 ff.
  proliferation of small, 548
Paterson, T. T., 174, 257, 259
Pavlov, I. P., 339
pedestrians, and road accidents, 272
perception, social, 318
performance, unit of, 166
personality:
  disorders, classification, 335 f.
  genetic factors and, 336, 346
  inadequate, 297
  ratings, 71–72
  as sociological phenomenon, 333, 336
  tests, 70 ff.
  types, 337 ff.
personnel, relation to institutions, 105
personnel selection:
  progressive, 228
  routine of, 227–8
  and vocational guidance, differences, 220 ff.
    problems encountered, 223 ff.
  see also interview

582

Index

Petty, Sir William, 5
Pfaffenberger, C. J., 382
physical type, *see* physique
physique:
  and delinquency, 287
  and personality rating, 72
  and temperament, 336–7
play, motivation of, 163
police patrols, and road accidents, 274
policy declarations, 104
politique criminelle, 282, 283
Poor Law, 469–70
Popper, P., 287 n.
population:
  active and inactive, 43 f.
  census and estimated, compared, 56
  de facto and *de jure*, 54–55
  urban, proportion, 486 n.
Porteus Maze test, 65, 73
poverty:
  and disease, 130
  and number of children, 411
poverty surveys, 6
power, seat of, in political parties, 546
prediction:
  in criminology, 289, 312 ff.
  and deterrence, 323
pressure groups, 543
probability theory, 113–14
'processing' in industrial society, 186
programming, linear, 239 f.
prontosil, 434
property, married women and, 418 f.
prophylaxis, accident, resistance to, 260
protection, public, 309, 320 ff.
protophrenia, 387
psychiatric hospitals:
  reforms in, 560 ff.
  sociology of, 559 ff.
psychiatrists, and selection interviews, 226
psychiatry, administrative, 562
psycho-analysis, and causation of mental illness, 379
psychological attitudes, classification of, 61
psychology:
  and accident causation, 255
  and criminology, 296–7
  and physiology, 153–4
  and sociology, 154
psychometry, and abnormality, 334
psychopath, definition, 335
psychopathic personality, and maternal deprivation, 385
psychosis(-es):
  definition, 352

and ecological area, 364 ff.
and marital state, 367 ff.
and migration, 366 f.
and occupation, 361 ff.
and sociability, 370 ff.
and social class, 355 ff.
public relations, 104–5
pyknic type, 337

questionnaires:
  design of, 17–18
  mail, and surveys, 15–16
  as personality tests, 71
Quételet, A., 283, 286
queueing, 237–8

race, and I.Q., 448 ff.
  relations, studies of, 483
Radcliffe-Brown, 199
radio transmitter, locating, 115–16
randomness, in sampling, 9–10
recruitment techniques, of institutions, 106
Rees, A. D., 505, 506
Rees, W. L., 338–9
Rees, W. L., and Eysenck, H. J., 338
reliability, of interview results, 17
religion, and political parties, 551
research:
  operational, *see* operational research
  pure, and applied, 111
response, rapidity of, and accidents, 254
response rates, questionnaire, 15
responses, instinctual, 382
responsibility, principles of shedding, 158
Revans, R. W., 259
reward, material, and party politics, 542–3
Reynolds, D. J., 270
Rice, A. K., 199 n., 202 n.
Riesman, David, 95
risk, as stimulus, 261–2
Rivett, B. H. P., 243
road accidents, 269 ff.
  and age, 275–6
  and alcohol, 273, 276–7
  causes, 270 f.
  children and, 277–8
  cost of, 270
  death risk from, 270
  distribution of, 274–5
  operational research on, 237
  per capita distribution, 274
  prediction of, 275
  proneness and, 249–50
  and social class, 131
  see also accidents
road users, restrictions on, 272–3
Rorschach test, 73

583

Index

Rosanoff, A. J., 343–4
Rowntree, B. Seebohm, 6, 173
Rowntree (Joseph), Social Service Trust, 176
Rudé, George, 96
Rural Sociological Society, 500

safety officers, choice of, 261
safety propaganda, 260 ff.
salaried employees, increase in, 188
sampling, 9 ff.
  and census-taking, 27 f.
  inferences from, 12–13
  method, 6
  multi-phase, 11, 16
  non-response, 11
  quota, 10 n.
satisfactoriness and satisfaction, 220 ff.
Saville, J., 505
scales:
  attitude, 71
  interval, 62
  ordinal, 61
Schachter, S., et al., 82, 84
schizophrenia, 353 ff.
  and ecological area, 364 ff.
  and family environment, 390–1
  and marriage, 367 ff.
  and migration, 366–7
  and occupation, 361–4
  and parental relationship, 384
  and social isolation, 366
  and sociability, 370 ff.
  social characteristics, 355
  and social class, 132, 355 ff.
  and social status, 357 ff.
  symptoms, 353
  see also psychosis
schizothymic type, 337
Schneider, E. V., 360
Schneider, K., 335
school(s):
  'early leavers', 452, 534
  grammar, 105
    social origin of entrants, 525
  social standing, and backwardness of pupils, 144
  sociology of, 534–5
Schuster, Sir George, 182
Schuster, Paul, 174, 175, 177
Schutz, W. C., 82
Scientific and Industrial Research, Department of, 177, 179, 180
Scott, J. W. Robertson, 503
Scott, T. H., 261–2
Scottish Council for Research in Education, 524
Scottish Mental Surveys, 21, 445, 452, 524
Sellin, T., 283, 290 n.

Selznick, P., 100, 104, 207
sensori-motor slowness, and accidents, 257
sentencing:
  discretionary elements in, 288
  objectives of, 309
  research in, 298–9
  see also treatment of offenders
sepsis, puerperal, 433–4
sex ratio, changes in, 397–8
sexual deviation, and heredity, 344–5
sexual relationships, extra-marital, 408–9
Sheldon, W. H., 72, 337–8
Shirley Institute, 236
signals, strength of, and accidents, 256
significance testing, 12–13
Simey, T. S., 6, 177
Simon, H. A., 205, 207
Simon, John, 129
skill:
  acquirement of, 254
  analysis of, 263
Sklare, Marshall, 101
Skoog, G., 345
Slater, E. T. O., 336, 345
  and Shields, J., 342, 345, 346
Slough, road traffic experiment, 271, 278
small group experiments, design of, 78 ff.
Smiley, J. A., 252
Smith, Adam, 187
smoking, and lung cancer, 8
Soboul, Albert, 96
socialization, primary, 382
socio-economic classification, 47 ff.
sociology:
  dangers of segmentation in, 481
  historical, 92
  rural, coverage, 501–2
    definition, 499–500
    tasks of, 505–6
  of the school, 534 ff.
  segmentation in, 481–2
sociometry, 85–86
  and accident rate, 259
somatotonia, 338
Sorokin, P., and Zimmerman, C. C., 501
specificity, historic, 95
speeds, and road accidents, 271, 273, 275
spiralists, 142
Stafford Clark, D., and Taylor, S. H., 340
staffs, hospital, relation to patients, 563–4
Stanford-Binet scale, 64
statistical societies, 6

584

Index

585

Index